Alma Plew

D1624687

A volume of a series in education, edited by ERNEST W. TIEGS, Ph.D., DEAN OF UNIVERSITY COLLEGE AND PROFESSOR OF EDUCATION, THE UNIVERSITY OF SOUTHERN CALIFORNIA, *and* LOUIS P. THORPE, Ph.D., PROFESSOR OF EDUCATION AND PSYCHOLOGY, THE UNIVERSITY OF SOUTHERN CALIFORNIA

CHILD PSYCHOLOGY
· AND
DEVELOPMENT

By

LOUIS P. THORPE, Ph.D.

PROFESSOR OF EDUCATION AND PSYCHOLOGY, THE UNIVERSITY OF
SOUTHERN CALIFORNIA

THE RONALD PRESS COMPANY ⸴ NEW YORK

7

PREFACE

The twentieth century has to a considerable extent been the century of the child, and psychology has thus focused much of its effort recently on the derivation of more complete and objective knowledge concerning child growth and development. Whereas such knowledge was for a time impressionistic and speculative, it has now come to be based to a gratifying extent upon research studies and experimental methods.

This volume has been designed as a textbook which will present the essential concepts, findings, and interpretations upon which an objectively derived child psychology must inevitably be based. Student use of research and clinical studies is facilitated by a careful selection of widely scattered materials from the scientific literature. Easy access is thus made possible to many important psychological investigations which would otherwise be difficult to locate one by one, but with which some acquaintance is necessary for perspective and for breadth of understanding of child growth and development.

The text is suitable for use in courses in departments of psychology and in schools and departments of education where applications are frequently made to formal schooling. Both selected quantitative materials and theoretical concepts dealing with such topics as emotions, intelligence, so-called instincts, dynamic needs, personality traits, and the like are included to provide review and a background conducive to a thorough knowledge of the subject.

The point of view of "Child Psychology and Development" is one of broad organismic development which accepts the contributions of more than one school of psychology. This position might well be called *patterned eclecticism*. It is upon such a broad base that this comprehensive text, which utilizes a wealth of observational and experimental material from many sources, has been developed. In addition to a consideration of physical and mental development, much attention is directed toward the child's fundamental psychological needs, and the school and community conditions under which they may be realized. A thorough study of child growth and adjustment must also take account of the effects on the child's mental health and personality development of parental handling and other crucial home influences. Throughout this volume it is taken for granted that the personal and social adjustment of the child at increasingly higher levels of development is to a considerable extent the central problem of child psychology.

In addition to its formal classroom use, this book should be useful to psychologists and teachers-in-service, school administrators and supervisors, nurses, and social workers who are concerned with the problems of children in and out of school. It may also be used as a practical guide for parents who desire to rear their children in the light of modern knowledge, and as a handbook for parent-teacher associations and other child study groups.

Acknowledgment of indebtedness is made to the host of investigators in child psychology and related fields whose researches and interpretations have made possible the writing of the present volume. Wherever appropriate, this obligation has been indicated by reference to their published contributions. The author is also appreciative of the many permissions to quote extended by publishers and by editors of periodicals. In addition, he is grateful to those who read the manuscript critically and offered helpful suggestions. Appreciation is expressed as well to Mrs. Ruth Watson Alberts, head of the education library of the University of Southern California, who participated in the gathering of material, and to Miss Bertha Marie Webster, who typed most of the manuscript and otherwise assisted in preparing it for publication.

Louis P. Thorpe

Los Angeles, California
February, 1946

CONTENTS

ix

ILLUSTRATIONS

TABLES

CHILD PSYCHOLOGY AND DEVELOPMENT

CHAPTER 1

HOW TO STUDY CHILDREN

SOCIETY'S ATTITUDE TOWARD CHILDREN has not always been humane or benevolent. Many of its members have believed that the child's nature calls for severe suppression and discipline. Only the last half century has witnessed an understanding of and widespread interest in child welfare. The twentieth century probably marks the beginning of concern for the child as the "center of gravity" in education and social improvement.

The Objectives of Child Study

Traditional Ways of Dealing With Children.—Although there have always been parents who loved their children and who were solicitous of their welfare, a surprising number of others have apparently been almost totally indifferent to their happiness and development. During the Industrial Revolution in England small children were required to work long hours in dingy mines and unsanitary factories. Undeveloped boys were forced to drag coal trucks (on their hands and knees) through mine openings that men could not manage because of their size. Both boys and girls were required to work twelve to fifteen hours a day in foul-smelling factories where the work was monotonous and the machinery unsafe. Some foundries demanded that young apprentices stoke the fires in great blast furnaces from six o'clock in the morning until eleven at night. Even eighteenth- and nineteenth-century America was guilty of forcing tiny hands and young shoulders to carry burdens far too heavy for them to bear. Some unhappy children were actually required to do home chores and attend evening classes after laboring in a factory from sunrise to sunset. Ministers, even, condoned such practices on the ground that "An idle mind is the Devil's workshop." Society evidently feared that unemployed children would fall victims to vice and crime. When some of them did so succumb, they were thrown into filthy cells with diseased and hardened criminals. Such was the morbid belief concerning child nature.

The early New England schools were no exception to this rule of tyranny. They exacted instant obedience and administered severe punishment for even trivial offenses. The use of a profane word or an apparently flippant attitude toward a girl acquaintance might net an erring boy several hours astride a narrow cross-bar in the rear of the schoolroom. Most school houses were also equipped with a stout whipping post in the front yard where all might witness the flogging of "evil doers." It is a matter of record that the average successful Boston schoolmaster administered approximately 2,000 whippings per school year. Minor misdemeanors were rewarded with the dunce cap, the ruler, a birch switch, or a verbal "trimming." These fervent educators based their pedagogy on the ruling maxim of the day, "Spare the rod and spoil the child." They also rationalized by a suitable (to them) interpretation of the Biblical declaration that "Whom the Lord loveth He chasteneth."

Reasons for Present Interest in Children.—Writers are wont to call the present age the "Century of the Child." Everywhere interest is being expressed in the nature and development of wholesome child personality. Methods for guiding children along lines advantageous to them and acceptable to society are being sought by both research workers and the laity. Information based on controlled observation and careful scientific investigation is displacing uncritical belief and naive acceptance of unfounded doctrines of child nature. Books and non-technical journals devoted to the care and education of children are enjoying widespread distribution. Teachers, students, parents, and society in general seem eager to become better acquainted with developments in the field of child behavior.

It is difficult to locate the beginning of the present interest in child welfare in America. It probably followed in the wake of national social and industrial reforms.[1] These, it will be recalled, took place largely during the latter half of the nineteenth century. An initial move for the conservation of child health was the establishment of a supervised public playground in Boston in 1868. In 1887 the first settlement house was begun in New York City. Juvenile courts were placed in operation in such large cities as New York, Chicago, and Boston in approximately 1900. Since the turn of the century there have been established an increasing number of journals, institutions, and clinics devoted to the study and well-being of children and youth. Since the publication in 1904 of G. Stanley Hall's two-volume *Adolescence,* and other genetic studies of child development, public attention has been increasingly focused upon the facts and problems of childhood. Freud's epoch-making declarations concerning the causes and symptoms of personality maladjustment also did much to call attention to early childhood as the most critical period of human development.

Today, practically all professions requiring intimate contact with children are seeking more knowledge concerning their nature and their needs. Teachers, social workers, psychologists, pediatricians, nurses, and child specialists in dentistry are coming to realize that the success of their careers is to a considerable extent contingent upon their ability to understand and work with children. This need for deeper insight into the processes of child nature is one of the outstanding reasons for the increasing interest in child psychology.

More and more parents are displaying an interest in the techniques of child rearing. They are beginning to realize that infinitely more desirable results may be secured if sound psychological principles are utilized in guiding infant and child development. Many parents are eager to provide their children with more wholesome living conditions than they encountered in their younger days. Others are determined to compensate for their own unhappy childhood by making things "easier" for their children. Thousands of prospective parents and mature college students are also endeavoring to prepare themselves

[1] Francis J. Brown, *The Sociology of Childhood,* New York, Prentice-Hall, Inc., 1939, pp. 3–7.

for intelligent parenthood by studying the principles that child psychology has been able to establish. In short, society as a whole is becoming child conscious. It is recognizing that its future welfare depends upon the intelligent rearing of its children.

The New Significance of Childhood.—Psychologists are agreed that the first few years of life are the most crucial for ultimate personal and social adjustment. It is in early childhood that enduring attitudes and temperamental patterns have their origin. Not only motor and language skills, but emotional dispositions, grow out of conditions obtaining in the child's home and community. Later character and personality traits are also believed to be the inevitable results of early parental handling. His ultimate social adjustment is greatly influenced by the child's early training and the extent to which he is accorded reasonable fulfillment of his fundamental physical and psychological needs. Whether an individual is fearful, antisocial, egocentric, or well-balanced socially is apparently largely the result of the manner in which he was treated in the inner circle of his home. It is clear, thus, that childhood is a significant period in life, and that knowledge of its nature is imperative to successful child rearing.

The Immediate Aims of Child Psychology.—The accentuated interest in child development displayed by modern society has led psychologists to study more objectively the facts and processes of child nature. They feel that accurate observations and tangible data will make possible more satisfactory techniques of child rearing. Believing as they do that cause and effect operate in the development of human characteristics and conduct dispositions, psychologists are endeavoring to determine the environmental conditions most conducive to adequate growth and socialization. Thus it can be seen that child psychology aims to control and predict the behavior of children in favor of socially desirable development.

There are many aspects of child behavior which are not at present well understood and which cannot, therefore, be regulated satisfactorily. Nevertheless, enough knowledge is already available to make possible far more intelligent child-rearing methods than we see about us. Child psychology proposes to disseminate this information and to assist parents, teachers, and all others concerned with the welfare of children in creating environmental situations conducive to desirable results. Young children often exhibit unfortunate behavior trends when more wholesome ones could readily be stimulated by appropriate adult action. It is one of the objectives of child psychology to make possible such control of development.

The more specific objectives of child psychology are many. Beginning with the mechanisms of inheritance, the dynamics of infant reactions, and methods of modifying behavior in the course of development, it studies various aspects of child growth. Physical growth, health problems, early home influences, and emotional development receive considerable attention. The genetic development of motor abilities, intelligence, powers of understanding, language usage, and capacity for reasoning are studied in the light of the child's best interests. The child's social, moral, and religious growth also loom large as psychological problems. The crucial issues of mental health, social adjustment, and personality development occupy a central place in modern child study. These are the problems with which child psychology occupies itself, and concerning which it deals in the control and guidance of child growth and development.

Pre-scientific Views of Child Nature

Man has always been prone to believe unverified theories affecting his own welfare and that of his children. Only in recent times have even scholars made much of an effort to verify the doctrines handed down to them by their social group. Throughout the annals of history one finds examples of credulity in tenacious adherence to creeds, superstitions, cults, and indoctrinations. The story of man's conquest of his world is replete with exhibitions of his inability to discriminate between truth and error. He has believed that the earth is flat, that insane people are possessed of devils, that earthquakes are caused by the ill-will of gods, and that spirits make the grass grow (animism). Man has always confused fact and fancy, especially where the principle of cause and effect was concerned. Until recent times, at least, adults and children alike have displayed little tendency to doubt the many popular beliefs concerning the nature of man and his universe.

The Nature of Naive Belief.[2]—Because of his interest in children, man early developed a number of theories concerning the psychological nature of childhood. These views were evidently designed to unify and organize his experiences in the child-rearing realm. As might be expected, most, if not all, of the pre-scientific theories in question were unsound and unverified. In harmony with the loose thinking of the day, assumptions were made on the basis of superficial observations and the dogmatic teachings of uncritical leaders. Many of these assumptions were totally devoid of foundation as far as objective evidence is concerned.

Another practice common in the child field was that of deducing theories from philosophical speculation. Early thinkers often endeavored to fit the behavior of children into their own ideas of the nature and destiny of man. With little or no regard for actual observations, they ascribed motives and functions to child reactions which have since been shown to be decidedly far-fetched. Concern with the development of a coherent theory caused these so-called *rational* thinkers to neglect unfavorable facts and to be blind to negative evidence concerning their view of child nature.

Uncritical acceptance of unverified beliefs is, unfortunately, still much in vogue. Many present-day fallacies concerning child nature are based on theories long since discredited by careful students of the subject. This situation would not be so disturbing if some of the positions taken by parents and teachers did not lie at the very base of human welfare. Erroneous notions of childhood have resulted in widespread practices of a nature calculated to hinder the personal and social development of children and youth. It is important, thus, that the student of modern child psychology understand the fallacies inherent in

2 Cf. Louis P. Thorpe, "Education and Naive Belief," *Phi Delta Kappan,* 18 : 79-82 (1935).

the various pre-scientific views of child nature. It is only through an objective approach unhampered by naive, unverified preconceptions that an adequate understanding of the child can be secured.

Children as Miniature Adults.—A theory prominent until well into the nineteenth century held that the child is merely an adult in miniature, with interests and physical, mental, and moral characteristics similar to those of adults. History shows that children of this period were dressed in adult clothes and were required to adopt mature manners and activities even before arriving at school age. The widespread twentieth-century emphasis upon education as *preparation* for adult life rather than as a period of child growth and development indicates the deep impression made on modern society by the miniature adult theory.

Some early biologists believed that in the process of mating the male transmitted to the female a completely formed but very minute human being. The mother's function was that of housing and feeding the miniature individual until it was sufficiently developed to survive the birth event. It was supposed that after birth the child merely continued to grow larger and stronger until his full physical development had been reached. Modern researches dealing with growth have shown conclusively, however, that the physical proportions of children are very different from those of adults. If a one- or two-year-old child were to grow only in weight and height, at maturity he would be so out of proportion as to be a monstrosity.[3] Such an individual would have an enormous head, a long, thick trunk, and extremely short arms and legs. The process of growing up physically involves a readjustment among the many structures comprising the complete integrated mature organism. The child is not a miniature adult physically. Neither are his physical structures sufficiently mature to function as they will when growth and activity have completed their work.

Another aspect of the miniature adult concept was the belief that children are born with an innate moral sense. According

[3] Winifred Rand, M. E. Sweeny, and E. L. Vincent, *Growth and Development of the Young Child*, Philadelphia, W. B. Saunders Co., 1940, p. 28.

to this view, knowledge concerning what is right and wrong is intuitive, and a child needs only a certain degree of maturity to make possible its expression. On this basis there would be no necessity for learning to distinguish between right and wrong; moral principles, such as those embodied in the Ten Commandments, were said to be written in the "moral faculty" of the child's mind. This conception denies the more modern finding that all knowledge comes from outside sources, and insists that a child should be held "accountable" for his actions as soon as his innate moral sense is developed. The age of accountability was said to begin at the appearance of the child's ability to speak and to be completed at puberty (adolescence). The child's "soul" or moral faculty could express itself only through speech and was thus dependent for its manifestation on verbal ability. Thus the growing child was held responsible for his actions to the extent that his moral intuition, as expressed through speech, had developed. Many parents and teachers still hold to this doctrine in modified form.

The tendency to interpret child behavior in terms of such adult standards is, fortunately, declining among intelligent people. With the coming of knowledge concerning the all-important processes of learning and environmental stimulation, modern psychology is turning to a study of the influence on adulthood of experiences encountered in childhood. Science now endeavors to understand the adult in terms of the child.

The Doctrine of Innate Depravity.—A corollary of the belief that the child is a miniature adult has been the notion that his moral nature is essentially sinful. Ever since the days of St. Augustine, in the fifth century, the main body of the church has held that every child inherits the evil nature allegedly transmitted to Adam when he sinned against God in the Garden of Eden. It is believed that every infant comes into the world possessed of tendencies toward ungodliness. It is further insisted that his moral nature would become progressively more sinful unless suppressed through rigid discipline by his more mature elders. The process of education becomes one of making over the child's nature to the end that he be prepared to

live in a more righteous world to come. Thus was inaugurated
a thoroughgoing regime of suppression with its excessive restraints and taboos. The objective of child rearing was training
designed to counteract original sinful tendencies.

The belief that child nature is essentially evil has survived
the dogmatism of the Middle Ages and still dominates much
educational and parental practice. Adherence to this view explains much of the rigidity and formality in both elementary and
secondary education. It also explains the harsh attitude of
many teachers and parents toward the problems of children and
youths. Like many other *a priori* beliefs, the doctrine of innate
depravity places its adherents in the unscientific and often in-
humane position of dealing with helpless children in ways designed to serve a theory without regard to its effects upon
personality development and socialization. The facts that children are influenced by the conditions under which they live and
that the tendency to perpetrate evil deeds could not logically be
biologically inherited are apparently not considered by believers
in the doctrine of original sinfulness.

The following passage from an eighteenth-century church
publication is illustrative of the attitude described: ". . . we
prohibit *play* in the strongest terms. The students should rise
at five o'clock summer and winter. . . . Their recreation shall
be gardening, walking, riding and bathing without doors, and
the carpenter's, joiner's, and cabinet maker's or turner's business within doors. . . . A master shall always be present at
the time of bathing. Only one shall bathe at a time, and no
one shall remain in the water above a minute. No student
shall be allowed to bathe in the river. . . . The students shall be
indulged with nothing which the world calls *play*. Let this rule
be observed with the strictest nicety, for those who play when
they are young will play when they are old." [4]

The Influence of Rousseau's Teachings.—The first serious
attack on the innate sinfulness conception of child nature was
made by Rousseau in the middle of the eighteenth century.
Rousseau was so impressed by what he regarded as the for-

[4] Quoted in Clarence E. Ragsdale, *Modern Psychologies and Education*, New
York, The Macmillan Co., 1932, pp. 5-6. By permission.

mality and superficiality of his age that he set out to correct
its evils through the publication of critiques of education, religion, and government. In his brilliant but radical treatise on
education, *Emile,* he promoted the view that, instead of being
evil by nature, children are originally and naturally good. He
insisted that children remain righteous and innocent until contaminated by the customs and conventions of adults. The educational and adult superficialities of the day, not nature, directed
the child toward such evil tendencies as he manifested.

According to Rousseau, the child has within him the resources for symmetrical, socialized growth. If left to his own
resources with a minimum of interference he will develop a
personality compatible with his own welfare and that of society.
The less parents and teachers interfere, the more adequate will
be the child's character and temperament. Above all, the growing child must not be thwarted in his development by the im-
position of adult restraints and conventions. He must be free
to discover and interpret his world spontaneously and without
suppression.

Rousseau's innate goodness view of child nature has led to
the adoption of much freedom in education. Both in Europe
and America schools have been organized to promote initiative
and creative expression in children. Those who believe in the
natural goodness of the child have hoped in this way to capitalize
on his supposedly innate desirable qualities. Freedom of expression, spontaneous activity, and inventiveness have been
made the watchwords of child development. Formality and
restraint have been abandoned as relics of a misguided age. The
child must be free to learn from nature and not from books.
He must be guided by unspoiled forces and not by conven-
tionalized teachers.

This point of view obviously has something to commend it,
but like most extreme doctrines it rests upon unverified assumptions. No one has ever demonstrated the innate goodness of
human nature. Rousseau no doubt performed a useful service
in reacting against the morbid doctrine of inherited sin, but in
so doing he introduced an equally extreme and unscientific view
of child nature. Those who follow the educational implica-

tions of Rousseau's teachings should realize that they, too, are proceeding on the basis of an *a priori* doctrine the truthfulness of which has in no sense been proved, and the results of which may be detrimental to child growth and development.

G. Stanley Hall's Recapitulation Theory.——Another theory concerned with the child's nature and development is the doctrine of *recapitulation*. This theory was evidently an outgrowth of Darwin's nineteenth-century declaration that human life had evolved from lower to higher animal forms over a period of millions of years. With the coming of the belief that man is a product of evolution, it was natural that a theory of child development based upon its tenets should spring up. As a matter of fact, two theories dealing with this problem became widespread and are accepted by some to this day.

The word "recapitulation," as used by Hall [5] and his followers, means essentially that a child reenacts the evolution of the race from barbarism to civilization in his own growth and development. The theory also taught that the human embryo passes through the same stages of development as those experienced by man in the process of his evolution from lower forms of animal life. It is claimed that the presence in the human embryo of gill-slits is a recapitulation of the period in racial development when man was supposedly a water-dwelling animal. Modern embryologists have questioned the validity of this comparison, claiming that the facts indicate little basis for such a theory, and that the human embryo possesses a characteristic structure throughout its development.

As Hall saw it, the child goes through various clearly defined stages (culture epochs) of development comparable to those experiences by his more primitive ancestors. As an example, when the child crawls about he is reenacting or recapitulating the period of evolution when his forefathers were still getting around on four legs. When the small boy plays "Indian" he is exemplifying the period when man spent most of his time hunting and fighting. Even the child's tendency to play with pets is said to reflect an earlier period of animalistic existence. The

[5] G. Stanley Hall, *Adolescence,* New York, D. Appleton-Century Co., Inc., 1904, Vol. 1, Chs. 1-2.

fact that children do not follow closely such culture epochs and that their development is largely a function of maturational factors and active experience was not understood by the promoters of the recapitulation theory. They had accepted a supposedly scientific view and were thus inclined to utilize it as a point of departure in child psychology.

It is now realized that no substantial understanding of child development can rest on the overenthusiastic declarations of theorists. Knowledge concerning growth is best obtained by accurate quantitative observations of the spontaneous behavior of real children—not by speculative theories and parallels. The theory of recapitulation did much to encourage study of child life, but it harbored beliefs that were not based on precise methods of observation. Hall was a noteworthy pioneer in the child development field, but his bias for the recapitulation and culture epoch theories has led to many erroneous applications in education and home training. Students of the subject have come to realize that knowledge concerning children and youths must be obtained through a meticulous study of their interests, activities, and characteristic reactions to given situations.

The Notion of Unfolding Instincts.

The Notion of Unfolding Instincts.—It was believed for decades that the child comes into the world equipped with a number of strong innate tendencies called *instincts*. These tendencies were thought to be inner drives transmitted from parents to children as racial characteristics. Instinctive tendencies were said to be present at birth but functionally inactive until the child became mature. Each child possesses all the instincts characteristic of his species. His behavior is motivated by his instincts, all of which constantly press for expression. Thus the child is supposed to perform many involved functions, such as eating, drinking, and avoiding danger, without having learned them. Later he will mate, hoard, collect, and seek companions as a matter of inherited tendency. Such is the doctrine of unfolding instincts.

Many of the difficulties inherent in the instinct interpretation of human nature will be brought out in a later chapter, but a few may well be mentioned here. In the first place, the instinct idea does not explain child behavior, it merely describes it. Secondly, much child activity formerly thought to be instinctive has been shown to have been learned. As examples, children learn to avoid danger and to be afraid of animals. In the third place, child behavior is not nearly as fixed and stereotyped as it would have to be if inborn instincts determined responses to stimuli. Careful observation has shown that the reactions of human infants are highly modifiable. They perform few acts of an inflexible nature determined by inheritance, but exhibit marked capacity for learning new modes of response. Psychologists have amassed considerable evidence indicating that child behavior is largely determined by the kind of experiences encountered in the social environment. Children display some characteristic patterns of response, but in the main their behavior is marked by plasticity rather than fixity.

The Scientific Attitude Toward Child Nature

The soundness of theories and techniques in child psychology is obviously contingent upon the methods used in gathering fundamental data relating to child responses. Like other sciences, child psychology has progressed from naive, subjective, and unverifiable approaches to more precise and objective methods of observation. As the pre-scientific views already reviewed indicated, there has been a pronounced tendency in the child development field to continue study techniques already outmoded in the biological and physical sciences. As a result, many fallacies concerning the nature of childhood are still widely held. Fortunately, however, the scientific attitude has begun to make itself felt to a gratifying extent in this important field. In this and succeeding sections an endeavor will be made to portray the development of scientific methods in the solution of problems of child nature and growth. Following the earlier pioneer approaches, a presentation will be made of present-day techniques of child study.

Inadequacy of the Early Study Methods.—The principal pioneer approaches to child study, which involved many apparent weaknesses, but which made useful contributions, may be listed as the *biographical* method and the *questionnaire* method.

THE BIOGRAPHICAL METHOD. The beginning of the scientific method in child psychology can be discerned historically as early as the latter part of the eighteenth century. Scholars of that day showed unmistakable signs of interest in what was called "psychogenesis" or child study. In fact, the first record of early mental development was written by a German physician, Tiedemann, in 1787. His book was neglected for a time but reappeared in an English translation about the middle of the nineteenth century under the title *Consideration of the Development of Psychic Qualities in Children.*[6] At approximately the same period Bronson Alcott kept a diary of his famous daughter, Louisa, author of *Little Women,* which he called *Observations on the Vital Phenomena of My Second Child.*[7] In this diary Alcott recorded a "psychological history" or "progressive stages of earthly experience" which he hoped was destined to portray the nature of human development.

A number of other baby biographies appeared, but the most famous one of the day was published by a German physician, Wilhelm Preyer, in 1882. In his *Die Seele des Kindes* (*The Mind of the Child*), Preyer told of systematic daily observations made on his own son from birth through his third year. From this careful record of notes taken as the child developed, the facts of first reaction to light, reflex equipment at birth, early crawling reactions, development of the senses, and the like were presented.[8] This was apparently the first systematic observation of genetic development in history, and one that profoundly stimulated the study of infancy. Preyer's techniques were not those of modern psychology, but they have proved useful to this day as a source of ideas and methodology.

Since Preyer's day a number of other baby biographies have made their appearance.[9] Notable among these is Miss

---

[6] Carl Murchison and Suzanne Langer, "Tiedemann's Observations on the Development of the Mental Faculties of Children," *Pedagogical Seminary and Journal of Genetic Psychology,* 34 : 205-230 (1927).

[7] J. Bonstelle and M. de Forest, *Little Women Letters from the House of Alcott,* Boston, Little, Brown & Co., 1916, Ch. 4.

[8] Wilhelm Preyer, *The Mind of the Child* (trans. by H. W. Brown), New York, D. Appleton-Century Co., Inc., 1890.

[9] See Margaret W. Curti, *Child Psychology,* New York, Longmans, Green & Co., 1938, p. 6.

Shinn's [10] *Biography of a Baby* and Mrs. Fenton's [11] *A Practical Psychology of Babyhood*. Miss Shinn's book contains an accurate and interesting account of the development of her niece from birth through her first year. Although written in 1900 this biography is still considered useful. Mrs. Fenton's careful and attractive record of the development of her infant son during his first two years of life marked the culmination of the publication of such works. It is considered an outstanding example of the biographical method.

The biographical method proved to be useful as a pioneer technique but it possesses a number of limitations. Many of the observations made are likely to be superficial and to involve interpretations not warranted by the facts noted. Furthermore, parents and relatives are prone to be biased in the responses selected for recording. It is difficult for a father or mother to avoid emphasizing a child's superior qualities, and to make purely objective appraisals of his reactions. There is also danger of following the unsound practice of generalizing about infant behavior on the basis of one or more cases of an unusual nature. It should be recognized as well that no standard procedure for such observation has been developed that can be checked and verified by unbiased parties.

When carefully followed by competent individuals the biographical method can be very useful. It may be utilized to disclose important factors in early growth. Significant data pertaining to physical, intellectual, and social development have been obtained by this method. The concrete nature of integrated personality development may also be studied through baby biographies. Preyer's suggestion of continuous controlled observation of young children has proved as well to be a stimulus to further research in child development. Nevertheless, the inadequacies of the method have caused it to be classed as a pioneer technique, and one which might well be superseded by more modern procedures.

THE QUESTIONNAIRE METHOD. During the early days of the child study movement, psychologists and others were

[10] Millicent W. Shinn, *Biography of a Baby*, Boston, Houghton Mifflin Co., 1900.

[11] J. C. Fenton, *A Practical Psychology of Babyhood*, Boston, Houghton Mifflin Co., 1925.

anxious to secure as objective data as possible concerning the nature of children's intellectual life. Again G. Stanley Hall, father of the child study movement, came to the rescue with a proposed technique which, incidentally, had been experimented with some years before in Germany. With the assistance of four experienced Boston kindergarten teachers, Hall [12] formulated 134 simple questions designed to determine young children's knowledge of the world about them. Something over 200 children were asked singly or in groups of three such questions as "Have you ever seen a cow?" "Have you ever seen grapes on vines?" "Where does milk come from?" "Can you name three things it is right to do?" If the child reported that he had seen one of the items mentioned or that he knew where it came from, he was questioned further concerning its size, shape, or color. All the responses were recorded and subsequently published as examples of the contents of children's minds. In spite of the apparent inaccuracies of young children's ideas concerning nature, religion, and morals, the investigation was well received and proved a stimulus to further child study.

Not content with direct questioning, Hall also developed printed questionnaires in which blank spaces were left for the recording of answers. Data concerning a wide variety of subjects relating to childhood interests were gathered by this method. When the questions were too difficult for young children to comprehend, their teachers were requested to interpret them sufficiently to secure the desired responses. It was possible in this way to obtain a great deal of material pertaining to childhood in a relatively short time. The scope of the method was greatly enlarged by the construction of questionnaires suitable for adults. On these blanks men and women of maturity were asked to record many of the feelings, ideas, observations, problems, and other experiences encountered in childhood. By this addition to his questionnaire technique Hall was able to secure data from wide geographical areas with a minimum of effort and expenditure.

[12] G. Stanley Hall, "The Contents of Children's Minds on Entering School," *Pedagogical Seminary and Journal of Genetic Psychology*, 1: 139-173 (1891).

The questionnaire method is, however, fraught with many errors and unreliabilities. Unless the questions are clear and unambiguous, the answers obtained are likely to be misleading and invalid. Furthermore, children are likely to give careless and irrelevant replies to questions involving their status. Hall recognized this point when he admitted that many children are inclined to imitate others without stopping to think, and that they are likely to give answers designed to make themselves appear wise or interesting. He further acknowledged that the brusqueness of some questioners made it difficult for timid or careless children to respond adequately. Another difficulty was that of securing data from a sufficiently varied group of children or adults to insure a representation typical of the population at large. When this is not done, erroneous interpretations based, for example, on the more intelligent and cultured fraction of society, are likely to be made. It is also clear that the reminiscences of adults concerning childhood experiences are decidedly questionable. With advancing age pleasant childhood memories tend to eclipse those of a more unpleasant nature.

The difficulties listed should make it apparent that too much reliance cannot be placed on the questionnaire method of studying child development. Sound conclusions cannot be obtained from such a technique merely by multiplying the number of individuals studied and by presenting an array of tables and graphs. Nevertheless, the questionnaire served a useful purpose as a pioneer instrument for child study. It stimulated interest in the movement and raised many questions for further inquiry. It should also be recognized that the questionnaire was in many respects the forerunner of modern tests of personal and social adjustment. Refinements in technique and standardization, as well as the use of more elaborate statistical procedures, have made questionnaires and inventories useful measures of child development.

Child Study and the Scientific Movement.—With the advent of the scientific method of studying natural phenomena, child psychology received a new and powerful impetus. Whereas the earlier studies had depended upon loose observations, doubtful theories of child nature, and questionnaire techniques, the scientific method proposed to approach child study objectively and accurately. The new approach was designed to discard subjective, prejudiced methods in favor of an open-minded search for the facts of child nature and development. It was recognized that anyone who studied childhood with a bias favorable to a given theory would interpret any evidence secured in a prejudiced manner. In short, the unscientific investigator tends to accept only the facts that corroborate his views. Contrary evidence is frequently neglected. It has been the function of scientific study, in child psychology as in the natural sciences, to overcome the handicaps of loose thinking and *a priori* conclusions.

In its effort to minimize the dangers of prejudiced procedures, science has adopted certain controls designed to insure the validity of its findings.[13] First of all, scientific study endeavors to be *free from personal bias,* whether it be based on early training, authoritative writings, or cherished wishes. The scientist does not plead for a cause; neither does he defend a view that fails to take account of all known facts. Secondly, scientific study is *precise* and exacting. It uses accurate instruments of research, quantitative methods of measurement, and controlled experimental techniques. Every detail is handled with the utmost care. In the third place, scientific facts are always gathered in a thoroughly *systematic* manner and in accordance with a prearranged plan of attack. All data are studied in relation to each other and to the entire study being made. The facts of an experiment are viewed as a systematic, organic whole. Fourthly, scientific knowledge is always *verifiable*. That is to say, a scientific experiment is so carried out and described that any competent individual may repeat it under similar conditions, record his findings, and compare them with the original results. Science deals with principles of natural causation, which operate uniformly at any time.

In harmony with these principles, psychologists do not accept unverified theories of the moral nature of children. Pend-

---

[13] For a brief statement of the scientific method, see W. C. Trow, *Scientific Method in Education*, Boston, Houghton Mifflin Co., 1925.

ing the accumulation of precise observations of child behavior, the carrying out of systematic experimentation insofar as it can be accomplished, and the pooling of results by many investigators, these workers prefer to suspend their judgment. Scientists do not declare that one theory is right and that another is wrong; they search for the truth in objective, impersonal ways and follow wherever the facts lead them. Being less impassioned and more "open-minded" (ideally) than the average individual, psychologists regard the newborn child as an organism characterized by a variety of physical and psychological needs, but originally neutral so far as moral attitudes are concerned. It is recognized that the infant is not necessarily either wholly good or wholly bad, and that his ultimate character will depend upon the type of experiences he encounters. Both good and evil tendencies will be expected to appear as conditions stimulate their rise. *Personal bias should be avoided*

The Scientific Movement and Child Nature.—It should be evident that the scientific movement has brought about a new and thoroughly objective point of view concerning the nature and development of children. Infants and young children are no longer regarded as miniature adults or as possessing inborn dispositions toward either good or evil behavior. They have come to be regarded as unique individuals with dynamic needs that must be reasonably well met if they (the children) are to grow and develop symmetrically. Children are thought of as immature organisms who will ultimately become men and women, but who in the meantime should live a life commensurate with their childish natures.

The modern view of child development has been concretely portrayed by Ragsdale.[14] He writes, "This attitude can be understood if we think of children as being the raw material out of which adults are being made in much the same sense that wood and iron are the raw materials out of which automobiles are made. We may compare the school (and home) to a factory. Just as in the automobile factory, it is the business of the workers to take the raw materials, which are wood and iron,

[14] Clarence E. Ragsdale, *Modern Psychologies and Education,* New York, The Macmillan Co., 1932, p. 17. By permission.

and by using certain tools and certain methods of manufacture turn out finished automobiles, so in our school and other educational agencies it is the business of teachers, parents, and others to take the raw material, in the form of children, and make adult men and women of them by using any available tools and materials." As this author recognizes, the most useful tools and materials for such an enterprise include the home, the school, and such community agencies as playgrounds, churches, motion picture theaters, and companions.

When the view is adopted that children are raw material out of which well-adjusted adults may be made if proper conditions for development are brought to bear upon them, the way is open for careful observation and controlled experimentation. Dogmatic beliefs concerning the value of strict regulations and punishment on the one hand and excessive freedom on the other become meaningless. These and other forms of child rearing become experimental means to an end—not ends in themselves —and are only utilized when experience proves their value as determiners of desirable development. In short, scientific psychology dispenses with unfounded beliefs concerning the value of various devices and endeavors to discover the true nature of the human material with which it is working. If a given form of punishment, a regulation concerning play, or a work requirement is found useful in promoting desirable child adjustment, its use is encouraged. If these or other devices work out to the child's disadvantage, they are discarded in favor of more productive procedures. Science's quest is for the most intelligent and effective methods of fashioning children into finished products—mature adults of whom society can be proud.

The Developmental Concept in Child Psychology.—The upshot of scientific study to date is that growth is a gradual process in which the environment enters actively into the child's development. According to the older view, inner forces, over which the environment had little or no control, needed only to unfold to make a mature adult of a child. Today most students of the subject believe that the child is powerfully influenced by the experiences he encounters and that his development is to a considerable extent a function of the culture in which he is reared.

The development concept of child growth has done much to dispel the former belief in innate evil tendencies. It has made society conscious of the fact that a child's ultimate character and personality are dependent upon the manner in which he is treated by the members of his home, school, and community. As one writer [15] has aptly said, "Instead, then, of the fatalistic belief that human nature is fixed and unchangeable . . . we may find in this viewpoint (development) the basis for a new hope and renewed faith. If we adopt this newer conception of human nature as essentially plastic, capable of being directed and patterned into the configurations and expressions that are favored and sanctioned by our culture, and if we recognize that culture itself is man's own effort to order events and regulate human affairs, to give meaning and purpose to life, then indeed we are faced with a new prospect." This is the attitude that holds out hope for a better society made possible by the intelligent rearing of children. It is one of the dominant notes in child psychology today.

Techniques Used in Modern Child Study

Students of child psychology and development have long been dissatisfied with older subjective methods of research. They have thus developed a number of modern techniques that are in harmony with the attitude and methods of scientific study. Not all of these are completely objective, yet they go far toward insuring the validity that should characterize the results of investigations. The methods utilized include observations of spontaneous child activity, controlled experiments, objective tests and measurements, psycho-physiological research, case study investigations, and other less well-developed methods.

Observation of Child Behavior.—Being aware of the previously mentioned limitations of observations of infants made by parents and relatives, modern psychologists have devised

[15] Lawrence K. Frank, "The Family as Cultural Agent," *Living,* Feb. 1940, p. 18.

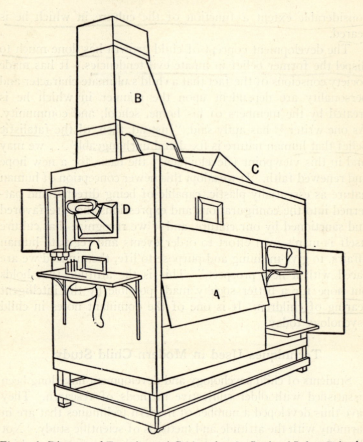

Figure 1. Diagram of Experimental Cabinet for the Study of Infant Behavior
The stabilimeter is located within the cabinet. *A* is a horizontal hinged drop door. *B* and *C* are supports for the camera and lamp for taking moving pictures. *D* is a window with a head piece through which the recorder observes the infant. (Modified from diagram in K. C. Pratt, A. K. Nelson, and K. Sun, *The Behavior of the Newborn Infant,* Columbus, Ohio State Univ. Press, 1930, p. 11.)

much more objective means of recording child behavior. Personal biases have been eliminated by use of elaborate scientific apparatus for observing and recording spontaneous activity.

At the Ohio State University, for example, the late Professor Weiss [16] and his assistants devised an isolation cabinet in which

[16] A. P. Weiss, "The Measurement of Infant Behavior," *The Psychological Review,* 36 : 453-471 (1929). See also K. C. Pratt, A. K. Nelson, and K. Sun,

Figure 2. The Yale Photographic Observatory

The operators and observers station themselves outside the dome. The infant
is placed inside. The cameras are mounted on two quadrants.

(Used by courtesy of Dr. Arnold Gesell.)

infants could be observed for prolonged periods of time. The
infant is placed in a soundproof cabinet in which heat, light,
and humidity can be regulated. He lies upon a stabilimeter
which automatically records all gross movements. Head to
foot movements and movements from right to left are also recorded mechanically on a strip of paper. In addition, carefully
trained but unseen observers indicate by code all other movements that throw light on the child's total pattern of response.
All reactions, including those made during sleep, are thus recorded by relays of observers. This is both an extensive and

The Behavior of the Newborn Infant, Columbus, Ohio State Univ. Press, 1930,
and F. C. Dockeray and W. L. Valentine, "A New Isolation Cabinet for Infant
Research," *Journal of Experimental Psychology,* 24 : 211-214 (1939).

expensive type of research, but it is designed to provide valuable data concerning spontaneous activity in infants.

Child specialist Gesell,[17] of Yale University, has constructed a dome-shaped compartment, equipped with cameras, which enables him to secure photographs of a child from several angles simultaneously. The walls of the dome are made of white enameled mesh wire screen that permits free circulation of air and a transparent view to observers outside. The infant, who is inside, is free from the distraction of observers, who are unseen because of the visual barrier provided by the painted surface of the interior of the compartment. Silent cameras, designed to move up and down on two grooved tracks at right angles to each other, may be utilized either independently or simultaneously by releasing electric switches. Pictures from a variety of angles can thus be taken of a child as he lies or moves about in an experimental crib in the dome. Play materials can be arranged in such a way as to secure indisputable records of the child's responses to them. In this way both still and motion pictures may be obtained in form suitable for objective analysis later.

Gesell [18] and his assistants have also developed a one-way screen for observing the behavior of older children. The child is unaware of his presence, but the observer can watch the child's actions with ease even when he is seated several feet from the screen. By this arrangement as many observers as desired can note the child's behavior without hindering his spontaneity. The child has the feeling of being entirely alone.

In some of the more elaborate studies,[19] young children are observed and filmed under a variety of more natural home conditions. Movable walls and other equipment make possible the setting up of rooms for sleeping, feeding, bathing, playing, and other child activities. Arrangements are made with families to

[17] Arnold Gesell, *Infancy and Human Growth*, New York, The Macmillan Co., 1928, Ch. 3.
[18] *Ibid.*, pp. 30-36.
[19] Arnold Gesell, H. Thompson, and C. S. Amatruda, *An Atlas of Infant Behavior*, Vols. I and II, New Haven, Yale Univ. Press, 1934. See also Arnold Gesell, C. S. Amatruda, B. M. Castner, and H. Thompson, *Biographies of Child Development*, New York, Paul B. Hoeber, 1939.

Figure 3. Arrangement of the Yale Guidance Nursery Showing the One-Way Vision Screen
(From Arnold Gesell, *Infancy and Human Growth*, New York, The Macmillan Co., 1928, p. 33. By permission.)

live in these quarters while their children are scientifically observed and filmed.

As a result of his elaborate objective techniques, Gesell has been able to determine the development of *adaptive, social,* and *motor* behavior in infants and young children. By the use of scientific methods he has shown the nature and rate of such growth. By finding the constant differences in the behavior of children of different ages (in months), he has obtained a developmental schedule of growth by which the degree of normality of any given child may be determined by comparison with the average performances for his age. Through the use of motion pictures, accompanied by verbal explanations and interpretations, this modern scientist has presented a picture of human development relatively unhampered by subjective judgments and loose observations.

The Experimental Method.—As previously mentioned, an experiment is a scientific method of obtaining answers to questions involving natural phenomena, and is characterized by precision of procedure, accurate measurement, the control of significant factors, and opportunity for verification. Experimentation is a refined type of observation made under controlled conditions. This careful method has only recently been used in the study of child behavior. The results secured from its utilization have, however, been gratifying.

It is not easy to experiment with infants and immature children. Yet a number of hypotheses relating to child nature and behavior have been put to experimental tests. Watson,[20] for example, demonstrated experimentally that fear of animals is not native in infants. By presenting live animals to young children who had had no opportunity of seeing them previously, he showed experimentally that no fear responses result from such stimuli. Other experiments by the same investigator suggested that fear in infants is produced by loud sounds and the experience of being dropped. Hartshorne and May[21] have

---

[20] John B. Watson and R. Rayner, "Conditioned Emotional Reactions," *Journal of Experimental Psychology,* 3:1-14 (1920).
[21] Hugh Hartshorne and M. A. May, *Studies in Deceit,* New York, The Macmillan Co., 1928.

shown experimentally that children have no honesty trait and that they cheat in certain situations when their security seems threatened.

Matched experiments have been carried out in which one group, the experimental, was subjected to experiences that were withheld from the other (control) group. Thus one group of sixth-grade children was provided with drama periods twice a week in connection with reading while a similar group studied reading without the benefit of drama periods. As in all such experiments, the objective is to measure quantitatively the influence on learning or behavior of the procedure (variable) being investigated. Such studies have been made in connection with motor performances, problem solving, social behavior, character development, verbal learning, and other tangible aspects of child development. In spite of its limitations, the experimental method bids fair to improve techniques of handling children and to uncover some of the more fundamental laws of human behavior.

Objective Tests and Measurements.—Measurement in modern child psychology involves the utilization of quantitative observations relating to both physical and psychological development. It is one of the most widely used methods in child study and education. Physical measurements have been used for many years to determine growth in height, weight, muscular strength, athletic ability, and other aspects of physical maturity. Such simple responses as reaction time, rate of finger tapping, weight discrimination, and acuity of hearing have also been measured with considerable precision. Practically all observational and experimental child investigations have utilized testing instruments and techniques.

Of great importance to child study have been tests of mental ability. After much experimentation with simple sensory and neuromuscular tests, psychologists have developed dependable measures of the higher mental processes. Since the publication in 1905 of the famous Simon-Binet mental test a number of Americans, notably Goddard, Kuhlmann, Terman, and Yerkes, have constructed instruments of increasing reliability and validity in the mental measurement field. Other psychologists have devised useful group examinations, such as the Otis Test of Mental Ability and the California Test of Mental Maturity, for use in schools where individual tests are too costly and time consuming. These instruments include both mental tests and tests of school achievement. Diagnostic achievement tests, such as the Progressive Achievement Test and the Stanford Achievement Test have enabled teachers to make far more refined determinations of pupil progress than they otherwise could.

More recently psychologists have developed objective tests and inventories for the measurement of personality and social adjustment. Development in the measurement of these more intangible factors represents one of the important goals toward which modern education is working. Thus a number of tests for the measurement of traits, of adjustment to the needs of human nature, and of social growth have made their appearance. On the child level, the best known tests or inventories include the Woodworth-Mathews Personal Data Sheet, the Marston Introversion-Extroversion Test, the California Test of Personality (Primary and Elementary Series), the Rogers Adjustment Inventory, and the Jöel Behavior Maturity Blank. These and other tests have contributed much to an understanding of the personality development of children.

The Psycho-physiological Method.—As its name suggests, this method involves a study of the relationships between various aspects of physical and mental development. Investigations based on this method have traced, for example, the relation between growth in height and degree of mental maturity. They have also been concerned with the relation between school achievement and carpal development or growth of bony structure.

The psycho-physiological approach has also emphasized the relation between mental development and such physical factors as general health, exercise, nutrition, and childhood diseases. Many modern practices relating to nutrition (dietetics) are based on the testimony of objective studies. The combined investigations of psychologists and physiologists are generally

given credit for improving the condition of thousands of malnourished and deformed children who might otherwise not have
survived or attained satisfactory adjustment.

Studies have shown, as well, that in some cases feeblemindedness, which has conventionally been attributed to defects in the
germ plasm, may be the result of prenatal infections, glandular
deficiencies, birth injuries, or malnutrition. Postnatal diseases
such, for example, as encephalitis, may also affect the mental
and personality status of the developing child. Investigations
of this kind are throwing a great deal of light on the relationship
between physical and psychological factors and are providing
data valuable for understanding the growth process in infants
and children.

The Clinical Case Study Approach.—The case study
method involves a detailed investigation of factors having a
bearing on a child's adjustment. It includes an account of his
past experiences, environmental conditions, family background,
and similar data influential in determining personality development. Normal children may be studied in this thorough manner, but the case study approach is usually utilized with children
who are experiencing marked learning or behavior difficulties.
In more involved cases information may be gathered concerning
such factors as present and past physical condition, developmental history during prenatal and childhood days, mental and
emotional growth, school history, relationships with members
of the family, and personal habits and interests.[22]

Case studies are usually carried out by psychologists or
trained social and educational personnel who understand the
techniques involved and who are in a position to secure the data
needed. Teachers familiar with mental hygiene principles and
who have the time and inclination can do much to assist and
further case study methods with maladjusted children. The
information needed may be gathered from the subject himself,
and from parents, friends, relatives, associates, teachers, court
records, the family physician, school records, and such tests as
may have been administered in the school. The goal sought is a

22 For a sample case study see E. W. Tiegs and Barney Katz. *Mental Hygiene*
in Education, New York. The Ronald Press Co., 1941, pp. 193-199.

comprehensive clinical picture of the child's personality and the conditions under which he has developed. Such a broad perspective often enables the teacher or clinician to plan a promising program of therapy for the child's personality reconstruction.

Although the case history method has proved its value as a technique in child study, it is not strictly scientific or quantitative in nature. Because of the subjective information and personal biases involved, it is necessary to accept the results secured with caution. Memory errors and superficial interpretations of developmental data may also invalidate the conclusions drawn. In spite of these weaknesses the case study method has provided invaluable material touching the needs and processes of child nature. Important cause and effect relationships have grown out of the composite findings of case studies.

Other useful methods in modern child study include psychoanalysis, responses to test situations, community surveys, rating scales, and picture and ink blot tests. These methods, too, have their limitations. The capable investigator should be able to utilize the best in all useful methods. Through careful analysis of the situation confronting a child, he should choose the method or combination of methods best suited to the requirements of the case.

The Genetic Approach to Child Development

Until approximately the beginning of the twentieth century, psychology had been concerned largely with the nature and behavior of adults. The introspective and laboratory techniques of earlier days did not lend themselves to a study of the growth and development of children. Besides, it was widely believed that the experiences of infancy and childhood were of no particular significance in the determination of mature characteristics and personality traits. Childhood experiences, no matter how frightening or frustrating, were thought to leave only temporary impressions so far as emotional adjustment was concerned. Psychologists had not yet sensed the causal connection between early experiences and the personality pattern of the subsequently mature man or woman.

The Meaning of Infancy for Adult Adjustment.—With the realization of the relatively permanent effects of early emotional conflicts and other disturbances, it became evident that childhood was the most crucial period in life for the shaping of personality and character. Psychologists and other scientists came to realize that the ultimate social adjustment of every individual is dependent upon the extent to which he was enabled to satisfy the needs of his nature in childhood. It became increasingly apparent that mental disorders, as well as lesser maladjustments, often have their roots in infancy and childhood. Society also came to see that delinquency and crime are frequently symptoms of feelings of inadequacy and other stresses acquired during the early years of development.

Much credit is due the Freudians and other psychoanalysts for pointing out the effects in later life of excessive childhood repression and feelings of inferiority. Such experiences may result in the development of a neurotic personality which, although modifiable, is likely to be marked by a variety of handicaps to social living. Investigators who have studied the origin of disturbing fears, biases, attitudes, and feelings of guilt are as a rule agreed that they, too, are often acquired in the early years It is recognized, thus, that the problem of insuring mental health is one of preventing the appearance in childhood of excessive emotional disturbances. This is the essence of the *genetic* method—it studies the facts of child development from before birth, through the years to adolescence and maturity. The genetic approach to child psychology endeavors not only to observe sequences of growth over a period of years, but to determine as far as possible cause and effect relationships between environmental conditions and mental, physical, and social development.[23]

Examples of the Genetic Method.—Prominent among those who have made a success of the genetic or growth and development approach to child study is Dr. Arnold Gesell of the Yale University Child Clinic. As already indicated, this psychologist has for years been making carefully controlled observations of

[23] W. H. Burnham, *The Wholesome Personality,* New York, D. Appleton-Century Co., Inc., 1932, p. 609.

various aspects of infant and child growth. He has discovered, among other findings, that all infants develop in accordance with an orderly sequence of events. Gesell observed, for example, that no child ever adjusted a square block in a square hole before managing a circular block-hole situation and that infants always pick up blocks with the whole hand before doing so with the thumb and one or two fingers. He concluded accordingly that it is a law of nature that one performance, such as drawing a circle, should come before another, such as drawing a square, at a given stage of growth. He believes that the laws of development have made infants of one age more or less alike and injected order into predictions of child development.[24]

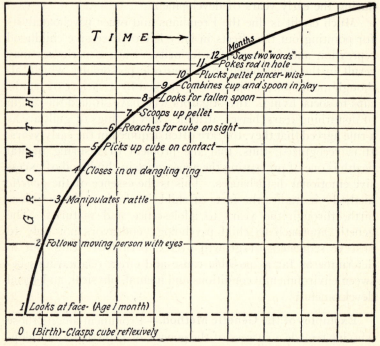

Figure 4. A Simplified Chart of Symptoms of Development, Arranged Progressively from Birth to the First Birthday

(From Arnold Gesell, *Infancy and Human Growth,* New York, The Macmillan Co., 1928, p. 382. By permission.)

[24] Arnold Gesell, *Infancy and Human Growth,* New York, The Macmillan Co., 1928, pp. 124-125.

After observing the growth of many infants, Gesell constructed a simplified schedule of behavior for the first year of life. This developmental scale, which has since been extended to include the first five years, is shown in Figure 4. The scale is not a standard mental test for infants, but it does provide a good illustration of the genetic method of child study. The chart shows the regular sequence of behavior development as Gesell found it in his genetic researches. It suggests also that infants who are not as well developed as the status given in the scale are likely later to be below average in other respects. It has been possible to use this scale in the prediction of infant and child intelligence to an extent formerly thought impossible at such a tender age.

Other scientists have contributed to child psychology through the use of the genetic method. Bridges,[25] for example, studied the development of emotions in children. She found that, except for delight and distress, originally undifferentiated (vague) patterns of emotion become increasingly differentiated (classifiable by the observer) with bodily growth and increase in experience. Emotions, like other forms of behavior, develop progressively and in accordance with genetic principles.

Fundamental Principles of Development.—Careful examination by the genetic method in child study has disclosed the existence of a few fundamental principles associated with the growth process. Since several of these are essential to an understanding of child psychology, they are presented here.

DEVELOPMENT IS CHARACTERIZED BY CONTINUITY. Growth is commonly spoken of as proceeding in stages, such, for example, as "infancy," "childhood," "pre-adolescence," and "adolescence." It is, however, a genetic fact that the developmental process is in the main continuous and gradual. There are no sharp dividing lines between so-called "epochs" of growth. Except for some instances of growth in height, development does not exhibit abrupt breaks or sudden spurts.

---

25 K. M. B. Bridges, "A Genetic Theory of the Emotions," *Pedagogical Seminary.* 37 : 514-527 (1930).

Development Is Marked by Orderly Sequences. As Gesell's scale of development shows, the order in which specific behavior forms appear is apparently the same for all children. Law and order govern the appearance of functional abilities in human development. The infant follows a moving person with his eyes before he manipulates a rattle and is able to perform the latter function before grasping a dangling ring. These laws of growth make it possible to compare a given child's development with that of children in general.

Abilities Develop from the General to the Specific. It is now evident that in infants and children, crude, gross movements and responses precede those of a more adaptive, skilled nature. The child always struggles with vague, indistinct words before he speaks clearly and understandably. He also makes large, crude marks and unintelligible "drawings" before he writes recognizable words and draws real objects. To a young child all furry animals may mean "kitty." Development and experience bring in their wake detailed skills and refined knowledge.

Correlation Rather Than Compensation Is the Rule. It was formerly believed that a child who exhibited superior qualities in one respect was almost certain to be defective or inferior in some other realm. It was popularly thought, for instance, that a child who was well developed and superior intellectually was necessarily frail or undeveloped physically. Investigations have shown that beliefs in such negative (compensatory) relationships are not borne out by the facts. Good qualities tend to be found together in the same child. A similar situation obtains in the case of inferior characteristics. Such expressions as "beautiful but dumb" and "a strong back but a weak mind" are popular misconceptions harking back to pre-scientific days. Scientific evidence shows a positive (but low) correlation among abilities and qualities.

Summary and Implications

The science of child psychology has developed to the extent that it recognizes the futility of naive, unfounded views of human nature. As they scrutinize the various pre-scientific conceptions of child nature, psychologists see why so many mistakes in child rearing have been made. Thousands of well-meaning parents and others have proceeded with the important business of human engineering on the assumption that the new-born infant is by inheritance either essentially bad or wholly good in his inclinations. Such beliefs have led to false notions of biological inheritance and to methods of child rearing calculated to produce undesirable attitudes and maladjusted personalities.

In the wake of the scientific method there has developed a demand for controlled observation and objective evidence in the field of child study. The child has come to be regarded as the raw material out of which develop the characteristics of mature men and women. Thus experimental methods, exact observations, quantitative measurements, and clinical case techniques have been utilized in an effort to predict and control child development. It is one of the avowed goals of child psychology to understand the effects of parental and other treatment on the character and personality of children.

The genetic or developmental approach to child study has grown out of the realization that both desirable and undesirable adult characteristics have their origin in infancy and childhood. It is now fairly clear that men and women are the end products of all the experiences they have encountered in the process of growing up. Informed individuals no longer believe that prolonged frustration and other emotional experiences pass from the child's life without leaving harmful attitudes and behavior trends. Thus psychology is concerned with the total span of child development from conception to maturity. Its goal is the safeguarding of development in such a way that no damaging episodes, deprivations, or emotional conflicts are permitted to mar the child's physical, intellectual, and social growth.

It can thus be said that science—certainly the science of child study—is by its very nature humane. Parents, teachers, social workers, pediatricians, and society itself are deeply interested in the welfare of children. Any contributions that scientific psychology can make to child growth and development will be welcomed by these and other groups. All of them recognize that the factual findings of science are ushering in a regime of sympathy and understanding in the rearing of children that bids fair to bring about the development of better adjusted citizens and thus a more equitable social order.

QUESTIONS FOR DISCUSSION

1. On what basis did public spirited citizens and even professional men condone the hard labor often required of children in early America? What position did their views apparently reflect concerning the psychological nature of the child?

2. What concrete evidence did believers in the doctrine of *inborn* evil tendency have for their dogma? Through what influences did such a doctrine concerning the nature of children probably originate? What has caused it to lose its former hold on the majority of parents?

3. Why does the scientific psychologist dispense with practically all assumptions concerning the inherent nature of moral proclivities? How does such a psychologist proceed in studying children's behavior tendencies? Why is he so uncertain about what the child inherits?

4. What is meant by the developmental concept of child nature? Why is such a view of more value to parents than assumptions concerning innate tendencies and the inheritance of character traits? What are your views on this question? Support them with evidence.

5. Why do some teachers believe in suppressing children's apparently natural interests, whereas others feel that they (the children) should be given unhampered opportunities to express themselves? What factual basis is there for either of these positions? What do you believe about it? Why?

6. Discuss the effects that Rousseau's doctrine of the nature of man has had upon educational practices. What educational movements and teachings appear to be based largely on Rousseauan assumptions? Mention both desirable and undesirable results of this point of view.

7. List the weaknesses of early biographical and other methods of child study. What contributions do you think infant biographies and questionnaire inquiries made to modern child psychology? Why are these methods no longer used extensively?

8. Discuss the principal differences between the experimental

and the clinical approaches to child study. Why cannot the more scientific experimental method be more widely used? To what extent can objective tests and measurements be utilized in the clinical method?

9. Explain the genetic approach to child development just as you would before members of a parent-teacher association. What are the implications here of the principle of natural causation? Distinguish between the genetic method of study and the science of genetics as an explanation of biological heredity.

10. In what sense can Gesell's work be said to constitute an example of the genetic method? What are the practical advantages to parents, teachers, and others of viewing personality status from such a developmental angle?

RECOMMENDED READINGS

Anderson, John E. "The Methods of Child Psychology," in *Handbook of Child Psychology*. (Edited by Carl Murchison.) Worcester, Mass.: Clark Univ. Press, 1933, Ch. 1.

Anderson, John E., and Goodenough, Florence L. *The Modern Baby Book*. New York: W. W. Norton & Co., Inc., 1931.

Boynton, Paul L. *Psychology of Child Development*. Minneapolis: Educational Publishers, Inc., 1938, Ch. 1.

Bridges, K. M. B. *The Social and Emotional Development of the Pre-school Child*. London: Kegan Paul & Traubner, 1931.

Brown, Francis J. *The Sociology of Childhood*. New York: Prentice-Hall, Inc., 1939, Ch. 1.

Gesell, Arnold. *The Mental Growth of the Pre-School Child*. New York: The Macmillan Co., 1925, Chs. 1-6.

Jensen, Arne S. *Psychology of Child Behavior*. New York: Prentice-Hall Inc., 1938, Ch. 3.

Merry, Frieda K., and Merry, Ralph V. *From Infancy to Adolescence*. New York: Harper & Bros., 1940, Ch. 1.

Ragsdale, Clarence E. *Modern Psychologies and Education*. New York: The Macmillan Co., 1932, Ch. 1.

Stoddard, George D., and Wellman, Beth L. *Child Psychology*. New York: The Macmillan Co., 1934, Chs. 1, 2.

Watson, John B. *Psychological Care of Infant and Child*. New York: W. W. Norton & Co., Inc., 1928, Introduction and Ch. 1.

CHAPTER 2

WHAT THE CHILD INHERITS

ANYONE WHO ENDEAVORS to deal with problems of child development is concerned with the processes and mechanisms of biological inheritance. Questions touching the extent to which certain physical characteristics and personality qualities may have been inherited arise constantly. Everyone seems interested in the intriguing issue of the relative influence of inborn factors and the social pressures of the environment. A thorough study of the nature and needs of children must necessarily include a consideration of this question. Modern child psychology concerns itself thus with biological heredity as well as with the processes of social development.

The Significance of Biological Inheritance

Even if one should take the position that the child's physical organism is all he inherits from his ancestors, a study of the biological mechanisms of inheritance would loom large in importance. The child's physical equipment is obviously an important part of his personality. He is dependent upon it in matters of health, appearance, muscular ability, and to some extent more personal qualities. The significance of inheritance is further indicated when it is realized that some biologists and psychologists believe that such attitudes and characteristics as ambition, thrift, laziness, sensitiveness, and even moral traits [1] are passed on from parents to children through the germ cells.

Most modern scientists are, however, very doubtful concerning the biological inheritance of attitudes and of character and personality traits. They believe that direct biological inheritance is confined to the infant's organic structures. Thus the

[1] H. S. Jennings, "How Heredity Affects Personality," *The Parents Magazine*, 6: 17, 65, 67 (1931). See also Peter Sandiford, *Foundations of Educational Psychology*, New York, Longmans, Green & Co., 1938, pp. 40-41.

present chapter is devoted to a discussion of the mechanisms of inheritance and to a study of the equipment the newborn infant brings into the world with him. Such an orientation should enable the reader to avoid common errors and faulty conclusions regarding what the child inherits.

The Meaning of Heredity.—Heredity is popularly thought of as providing the inborn characteristics with which the child is equipped at birth. These characteristics are regarded as fixed qualities and are thus contrasted with environmental factors which change with experience. Heredity and environment are believed to be contrasting factors which interact with one another in ways determinative of the developing child's character and personality.

That heredity and environment are mutually exclusive influences is also a widespread belief. Many debates have been concerned with this question. Actually, the two factors have never existed separately. The child's environment begins the instant the *ovum* or germ cell from which it is destined to develop is fertilized by a male *sperm*. Throughout the child's prenatal life hereditary and environmental factors are amalgamated; neither enjoys a separate existence. It should be understood, then, that heredity and environment are interrelated factors and that neither can be thought of as existing without the other. They are related to each other as are the two sides of a piece of paper or the two blades of a pair of scissors.

The biologist Conklin [2] has defined heredity as "the continuing from generation to generation of certain elements of germinal organization. Heritage is the sum of all those qualities which are determined or caused by this germinal organization." A well-known zoologist, Jennings,[3] states his conception of heredity thus, "Experimental biology has shown that at its beginning the organism is a complex thing, containing a great number of *separate substances—what we call the genes.* By the interaction of these thousand substances with each other, with cytoplasm, with materials brought in from the outside, with

---

2 E. G. Conklin, *Heredity and Environment,* Princeton (N. J.), Princeton Univ. Press, 1929, p. 133.

3 H. S. Jennings, "Health Progress and Race Progress, Are They Compatible?" *Journal of Heredity,* 18 : 272 (1927).

the forces of the environment—development takes place, the individual is produced with all his later characteristics."

It is clear that, according to the science of genetics (inheritance), heredity is not synonymous with physical equipment which is present at birth or which is in evidence at any time following fertilization of the ovum (female sex cell) concerned. It is properly defined as the potential influence for future development inherent in the germ plasm and associated structures of sex cells before the time of conception. Thus whatever is transmitted *through the germ plasm* of the race may be regarded as hereditary. After conception the influence of the intrauterine environment is always present, thereby making it impossible to separate the influence of environment from that *determined by the germ plasm.* Only in the case of identical (same inheritance) twins is it possible for one to observe the influence of the social environment as contrasted with biological inheritance.

The Role of Inheritance.—Scientists and others who were convinced of the superior efficacy of heredity in the development of desirable intellectual and personality qualities would not be as likely as others to provide the best possible conditions for child growth. Insofar as they were interested, their logic would lead them to advocate the development of "better stocks." Being concerned with the inherited "potentials" of their children they would lend their energies primarily to the development of individuals of supposed superior ability. Those who regard the child's social and educational environment as being the predominant influence in his growth and development would be motivated to provide conditions conducive to maximum development along all modifiable lines. It is evident, thus, that an individual's attitude toward the education of children is determined by his conception of the nature of inheritance.

As Conklin [4] (and others) has advocated for years, both heredity, as defined above, and environment are important in an understanding of child growth and development. The

4 E. G. Conklin, *op. cit.*, p. 60.

bearers of heredity could not produce a human being without benefit of an environment suited to their work. Similarly, no environment, superior or otherwise, could bring about the development of an individual in the absence of the germ plasm required to initiate life. The two factors must become integrated into a unique influence which is something more than a mere addition.

One psychologist, Gray,[5] has reasoned that the newborn child does not actually possess an original nature. According to him, at any point in its development the child's nature is "what its inherited genes have been able to make it under the control of its environment up to that time." This is comparable to saying that man inherits genes (germ plasm) only, and that they can accomplish only what environmental conditions make possible. Gray goes on to say that "no trait, physical or otherwise, is exclusively inherited. Inheritance and environment become amalgamated in organic life and each loses its identity." From this point of view nothing is "innate" except the germ plasm, and its character is always unknown. This is because germ plasm is affected by the nature of the environmental medium in which it must develop. It is highly probable that many personality characteristics, commonly thought to be biologically inherited, are to a great extent the result of factors present in the environment in which the bearers of heredity are called upon to operate.

It can be concluded, thus, that the facts of biological inheritance are essential in a thorough study of child psychology. It is not necessary to be unduly concerned over the nature-nurture controversy. Apparently one of these factors cannot be singled out and contrasted with the other.

Implications for Child Psychology.—Scientists whose researches are confined largely to the processes of inheritance are inclined to regard heredity as being more influential than environmental opportunities in the determination of both intellectual status and personality qualities. Students of psychology,

[5] J. S. Gray, "A Biological View of Original Nature," *Educational Administration and Supervision,* 16:655-657 (1930).

psy

sociology, and anthropology have been impressed, on the contrary, with the influence exerted by such institutions as the home, the school, the community, the church, youth organizations, mental-hygiene clinics, and other constructive organizations for the education and personality development of children and youths. They believe that these social agencies are potent factors in both the intellectual and behavioral areas of development. In fact, many doubt whether hereditary potentials are as important in child development as are the social institutions mentioned.

It is true, of course, that biologists do not give inherited factors entire credit for child growth and development. They make it clear that inheritance can register its full effects in a favorable environment only. Sandiford,[6] who accepts the biological point of view, reasons as follows: "Imagine two equally intelligent children, one of whom is taught to read, the other not. The differences between them, due to these differing environments, will be pronounced. One may become the greatest scholar of his generation; the other must remain an illiterate in a world of letters. But in the next generation things would tend to even up once more; the children of both the reader and the non-reader will be born with the potential ability to read just as their parents were before them."

Nevertheless, scholars of strong hereditary persuasion frequently write of intellectual, moral, and personality qualities as though they are largely the result of germ plasm influence.[7] Such a belief should be as far as possible investigated, but as yet no one has been able to demonstrate its authenticity. As we shall see later, important social and cultural factors are always present in any instance of character and personality development. However, since biological inheritance is essential to an understanding of at least the body-structure aspects of child growth, it would seem desirable to be well informed concerning its general features. Parents and teachers need to appreciate the inherited limitations, as well as the capacities, of their children.

6 Peter Sandiford, *op. cit.,* p. 43.
7 H. E. Walter, *Genetics,* New York, The Macmillan Co., 1938, pp. 302-309.

The Processes of Inheritance

Little was known concerning the mechanisms of inheritance before the dawn of the present century. The important work of Mendel, which will be reviewed later, was lost for approximately forty years. It was apparent to students of the biological sciences before that time that many characteristics are transmitted from parents to offspring in harmony with some unknown laws. Scientists were puzzled, however, by the observed fact that, although in a general way "like begets like," enough exceptions were in evidence to indicate an apparent lack of consistency in inheritance. Little was known about the intricate processes operating in the cells of reproduction. But with the discovery in 1900 of Mendel's account of his experiments on garden peas, considerable enthusiasm was injected into the search for genetic laws.

Chromosomes as the Bearers of Heredity.—Scientists have long recognized that whatever characteristics are transmitted

Figure 5. Chromosomes in Elongated Threadlike Form Showing Genes Arranged in Linear Order
(From A. F. Shull, *Heredity*, New York, McGraw-Hill Book Co., Inc., 1926, p. 19.)

from parents to offspring must travel by way of the tiny germ plasm cells. It seems apparent that these minute agents initiate whatever processes are responsible for the passing on of physical traits from one generation to another. Laboratory technicians have shown that, when studied under the microscope, these tiny cells are characterized by a complicated nucleus of threadlike particles similar to irregular strings of minute beads. It has also been discovered that when stained with dyes this nucleus becomes more conspicuous than the fatty substance, called *cytoplasm,* surrounding it. It is because of this response to staining that these strandlike particles are called "chromosomes."

Research has shown that although species differ widely in the number of chromosomes possessed, each is characterized by a constant number. In the case of humans, it is known that 24 pairs or 48 chromosomes are present. Half of these are transmitted by the male parent and half by the female.

The mechanisms of inheritance are controlled by the sex cells containing the chromosomes. According to biologists, the chromosomes are the "bearers of heredity." They determine the physical characteristics which the future individual will possess. As Jennings [8] puts it, "the *'laws of inheritance' are essentially the rules of distribution of the chromosomes.*" Some have suggested, however, that since chromosomes are composed of literally hundreds of minute particles called "genes," the latter should be designated as the true bearers of heredity. Combinations of genes are known to be responsible for the inheritance of various physical traits.

The Determination of Sex.—Investigations dealing with the fruit fly (Drosophila) by Morgan [9] have revealed that certain physical features in offspring are associated with the presence of given chromosomes. This scientist has discovered that the germ plasm of the female contains an even number of chromosomes, but that the male sex cell possesses an uneven number, in the sense that one is a small and somewhat shriveled chromosome. Thus he was able to observe the actions of the extra (complete) female chromosome from generation to generation.

---

[8] H. S. Jennings, "How Heredity Affects Personality," *op. cit.,* pp. 64-65.
[9] T. H. Morgan, C. B. Bridges and A. H. Sturtevant, "The Genetics of Drosophila," *Bibliographia Genetica,* 2 : 1-262 (1925).

It subsequently became known that the "X" or extra chromosome is the sex determiner. When the male sperm having an X chromosome (males carry sperm with and without the X) impregnates a female ovum, which always has an X chromosome, the offspring is always a female. A male individual is produced when a male sperm having no X chromosome (only

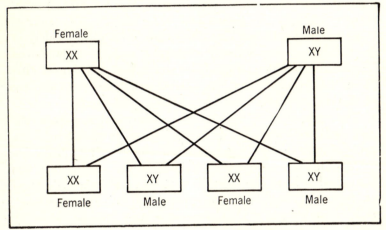

Figure 6. The Mechanics of Sex Determination

the diminutive y) fertilizes an ovum. Morgan found as well that genes for a variety of physical characteristics are linked with the X chromosome or sex determiner. These findings have indicated that, in the main, chromosomes and genes account for the physical processes of inheritance. They also provide an explanation for the presence of consistent laws in inheritance.

The Reduction Process in Sex Cells.—Knowledge of the actions of sex cells and their chromosomal equipment makes it possible to understand the physical differences exhibited by offspring of the same parents. The behavior of these chromosomes as they become mature also indicates how the correct number for the species is maintained in the process of mating and reproduction. When sex cells are multiplying in the body of the developing fetus, all splitting results in the equal division of chromosomes and in constant uniformity of chromosomal equipment. This is similar to that of *mitosis* (splitting of body cells) and is designed to provide the organism with sufficient cells for later reproductive purposes.

However, previous to the onset of puberty (sexual maturity), a decidedly different process of cell division occurs. At this point the sex cells undergo a process of both *maturation* and *reduction.* Chromosomes from paternal and maternal forebears (half originally came from each) arrange themselves in 24 pairs (48 total) and, after becoming considerably enlarged, again divide. This division process is, however, much more complicated than that of mitosis. Here 24 chromosomes gravitate to one cell and 24 to the other as the parent cell divides. However, in this instance the chromosomes go their way to separate cells in *chance combinations.* In the reduction process each germ cell does *not* get half its chromosomes from the paternal and half from the maternal side of the family. The mechanism of cell reduction is nature's way of preparing for mating when fertilization of the female ovum by the male sperm (zygote) will provide the new organism with the appropriate number of chromosomes for its species (48).

The significant feature of the reduction process is that a given germ cell may by chance receive any one of thousands of combinations of paternal and maternal chromosomes. This fact should make it clear that in any union any one of an enormous number of combinations of chromosome patterns may be transmitted. When it is realized that the chromosomes and genes are bearers of whatever characteristics are inherited, it is easy to understand why children of the same parents frequently differ markedly in physical qualities.

Gene Action in Inheritance.—Biologists are generally agreed that the tiny genes and chromosomes contain the potentials for later physical characteristics. Direct biological inheritance is thus often spoken of as *gene* or *germinal inheritance.* As Jennings [10] has said, "The way diverse individuals develop, the peculiarities that they show, the so-called laws of heredity, the extraordinary resemblances and differences between parents

---

[10] H. S. Jennings, "How Heredity Affects Personality," *op. cit.,* p 3.

and offspring—all these things depend largely on the arrangement and behavior of the genes." It is thus evident that the physical characteristics exhibited by an individual are the result of the combinations of genes from which he developed. This biological fact is essential to an understanding of the physical aspects of child growth and development.

An important aspect of gene action is the fact that each parent provides the offspring with a complete set of chromosomes, each with its appropriate "string" of genes. Every human offspring has two parents and thus receives two sets of chromosomes. These arrange themselves in pairs in such a way that genes concerned with the same functions are stationed opposite each other. (See Figure 7.) The child thus inherits two sets of gene-equipped chromosomes, each of which is capable of producing a complete organism.

Nature's provision of paired inheritance has an important bearing on human welfare. This is because each gene (actually a number of genes) in a pair is capable of performing its func-

Figure 7. Schematic Illustration of the Arrangement of the Genes, or Bead-Shaped Bodies, on the Stringlike Chromosomes

As indicated, one string of the pair comes from the father and one from the mother. The genes portrayed as being white are defective; those shown in black are healthy (normal).

tion in the formation of whatever structure is being developed without the assistance of its mate. Thus if one of a pair of genes is defective, its "partner" can perform the function which both would normally exercise. Under such circumstances healthy structure would be produced by the normal gene working alone.

The mechanism described holds for the development of eyes, ears, feet, skin, and other physical structures. It explains why children escape so many physical defects and limitations implicit in their family "tree." Fortunately for mankind, double inheritance enables normal bearers of heredity (genes) to transcend their defective mates and to beget children with healthy physical qualities in spite of family defects. To quote Jennings again, "It appears that this insurance through doubling of the genes is the chief biological ground for our having two parents instead of one. Gene defects are so common that without this doubling—the two genes of each pair coming each from a different source—defective individuals would be far more common than they now are. Organisms reproducing from two parents have a great advantage in this respect over those reproducing from a single parent" (page 9).

How the Genetic System Works.—It is clear from the principle of double inheritance that transmission of defective characteristics is the result of pairing of paternal and maternal defective genes. Such an outcome may occur even when both parents are themselves normal in every observable respect. Biologists have shown that many normal individuals carry defective genes in their sex cells.

It is essential for students of child psychology to observe how the processes of double inheritance produce marked and sometimes unexpected differences between parents and children. If a father had inherited a pair of defective genes for eye material in his make-up, he would in the nature of the case have defective eyes. He might also be a carrier of genes for such a defect. The mother may have inherited normal genes for eye development and thus have escaped eye defects. At the time of mating, the father and the mother each transmit series of genes to the offspring. In this instance the child might receive both a defective and a normal gene potential for eye development and would thus be normal in that respect. Obviously, this is because the dominant normal gene (actually many genes) brought about the formation of normal eyes without help or interference from the defective gene paired with it. The child was protected by the healthy genes transmitted by his mother.

To cite another example, if the father inherited two defective groups of genes for eye structure and was thus himself defective, whereas the mother inherited but one defective gene grouping for eye development, some of their children might inherit defective genes from both sides of the house and thus have defective eyes. By the same token, other offspring of this union may inherit the father's defective gene only and thus have normal eyes. These facts of inheritance may be further clarified by study of Figure 8.

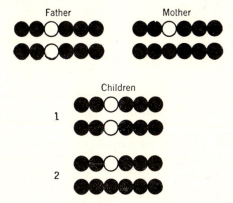

Figure 8. The Hereditary Outcome in Instances Where One Parent (in this case the father) Has Two Defective Genes (white) in a Given Pair, and the Other Parent (in this case the mother) Has One Defective Gene in a Corresponding Pair

Child 1 inherited two defective genes in that particular pair and is therefore defective; child 2 inherited only one such defective gene and is thus not defective.

It would be possible to go on showing how the principle of double inheritance explains the appearance in children of body characteristics not observable in either their fathers or mothers. Offspring may inherit qualities superior to those of their parents or they may be the recipients of inferior characteristics. It has been shown that these processes operate unerringly generation after generation in the rapidly reproducing Drosophila fruit fly.[11]

11 T. H. Morgan, C. B. Bridges, and A. H. Sturtevant, *op. cit.*

A single gene cannot, however, bring about the development of a complicated physical structure such as a foot, a hand, a pair of eyes, or a head of hair. Many genes interact and cooperate to produce any one of these or other structures. In the case of the fruit fly, approximately fifty pairs of genes are said to cooperate in the formation of the typical red eye color. It is common knowledge, also, that one gene may influence the development of a number of physical traits.

Conclusions Concerning Gene Action.—Knowledge of the mechanisms of gene-inheritance has greatly increased man's understanding of the physical differences and likenesses so often noted between parents and their children. Such information also accounts for the unexpected appearance of defective or physically superior offspring. The nature of physical characteristics can now be predicted in some species of lower animals. However, because of the difficulty of observing gene action more directly in their case, little can be said of the probable qualities of unborn human offspring.

Nevertheless, knowledge that a healthy gene is more potent than a defective one in most couplings of the two, makes possible the formation of several practical eugenic procedures. These would include:

1. *Preventing close relatives from marrying and producing offspring.* Since close relatives have immediately common ancestors, hidden family gene defects would be brought to light most readily by such unions. In the case of markedly defective stocks even distant relatives should be prevented from mating. This procedure neutralizes genes rather than improving them but it prevents the unnecessary appearance of defective children.

2. *Discouraging marrying into a family having obvious physical defects.* Some defects, such as extra fingers on each hand (polydactylism), webbed fingers (syndactylism), and baldness are dominant and may appear in children without the pairing of defective genes. Furthermore, both parties to a marriage may possess somewhat similar gene taints. The chances of producing nondefective offspring are reduced when either party to a marriage is handicapped by such defective genes.

3. *Breeding out defects from the genes of a race or races.*
This is the method of *eugenics,* and one that proposes the weeding
out of defective, weak, and otherwise unfit individuals through
controlled mating and breeding. Such a proposal is advancing in
use in the animal realm but is obviously out of the question among
civilized humans. Both the difficulty of determining desirable stocks
and the presence of deep-rooted social and moral cultures make
this type of eugenics untenable, at least for some time to come.
About all that can be done is to sterilize known defectives who
are in a position to procreate. In America, 28 states have steriliza-
tion laws and are making progress with the problem. Other countries are working along similar lines.

The Mendelian Laws of Inheritance

It is an interesting coincidence that the first laws of genetics
(inheritance) were discerned by a man not primarily concerned
with biology. They were originally made known by the ingenuity of the Austrian monk and later Abbot of Königskloster,
Gregor Johann Mendel (1822-1884). Mendel lived at the time
of Francis Galton and Charles Darwin, but his work did not attract the attention of scholars as did theirs. In fact, the report
of his genetic findings was filed away and forgotten about the
time of the Civil War in this country.

Mendel's Experimental Approach.—Not until 1900 was
Mendel's report, published by his teacher, Karl Nageli, in the
Transactions of the Natural History Society of Brunn, re-
covered and presented to European and American scientists.
Although similar investigations had been made in the meantime,
Mendel has been given credit for the discovery of his now
famous laws of inheritance. Bateson [12] has aptly said of him,
"untroubled by any itch to make potatoes larger or bread
cheaper, he set himself in the quiet of a cloister garden to find
out the laws of hybridity, and so struck a mine of truth, in-
exhaustible in brilliancy and profit."

Mendel was impressed with the variety of characteristics
possessed by the sweet peas in his monastery garden. He must

[12] Quoted in H. E. Walter, *Genetics,* New York, The Macmillan Co., 1938, p.
56. By permission.

have been of an inquiring mind and gifted with imagination, because he proceeded to satisfy his curiosity by crossing certain of the flowers artificially and making careful notes of the characteristics of several generations of progeny. As the result of this experimentation, three genetic laws of fundamental importance were made available to science. Mendel's ingenuity led him to study the behavior, generation after generation, or such single characteristics of sweet peas as tallness or shortness, smoothness or wrinkledness of stems, and color of flowers. Other scientists had failed to secure significant results because of their preoccupation with the behavior in inheritance of whole plants or animals. Mendel's approach enabled him to discern the effects of breeding later embodied in his laws.

Mendel's Three Genetic Laws.—Mendel's findings may be formulated as three interrelated principles of inheritance. These have been summarized as follows:

The Law of Segregation. This law grew out of Mendel's experiments in crossing tall and short garden peas. He effected this cross by artificial fertilization; that is, by removing flower

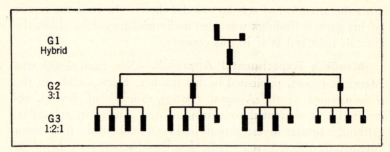

Figure 9. The Results of Crossing Tall and Short Stemmed Sweet Peas
Tallness, which is indicated by the longer heavy lines, is dominant.

stamens to prevent self-fertilization and by placing the pollen of tall pea flowers on the stigma of short pea flowers (and vice versa). The results of several generations of such crossing are illustrated in Figure 9.

As the diagram shows, the first generation of Mendel's peas (*G1*) were all tall, but in the second generation (*G2*) a ratio of three tall to one short appeared. In the third generation ($G3$), a third of the tall peas produced all tall offspring and the short peas bred true by producing all short progeny. The remaining two-thirds of the tall peas produced offspring in the ratio of three tall to one short. As a more elaborate chart would indicate, the ratios obtaining in the first three generations continued indefinitely. Twentieth-century biologists have duplicated Mendel's ratios of inheritance in both the vegetable and animal kingdoms (for example, with black and white guinea pigs).

The explanation of Mendel's results is found in the processes of gene behavior, which were, of course, unknown to him. In the case of peas, only one of the two alternative tall and short characteristics can reside in a given reproduction cell. When two cells containing genes for shortness reproduce, the resulting peas will obviously be short. If, however, a germ cell potential for tallness unites with a cell containing genes for shortness, the vines reproduced will be tall. This is because tallness is *dominant* over shortness in garden peas.

The Law of Dominant and Recessive Traits. Mendel's second law, the principle of *dominant and recessive traits,* was suggested by his finding that tallness dominates shortness as these characteristics segregate generation after generation. It is a generalization of the discovery that some characteristics consistently supersede others when both are present in the genes concerned with reproduction. This principle operates in man and animals, as well as in the vegetable kingdom. It is known, for example, that brown eyes are dominant over blue eyes and that curly hair supersedes straight hair in inheritance. Fortunately, desirable and normal traits are usually dominant over defective characteristics. Dominant and recessive traits in humans may be seen in Table 1.

The Law of Independent Unit Characters. Mendel's third law grew out of his observation that a given "unit character" (physical characteristic) of garden peas is independent of other unit characters in that species of plants. Mendel discovered, for example, that the colored flowers growing on tall pea vines could be produced on short vines (which grew white

TABLE 1. MENDELIAN INHERITANCE IN MAN

CHARACTERS	DOMINANT	RECESSIVE
Normal Characters		
Hair	Curly; dark	Straight; light to red
Eye color	Brown	Blue
Skin color	Dark; normal pigment	Light; albinism
Face	Hapsburg type (thick lower lip and prominent chin)	Normal
Abnormal and Pathological Characters		
General size	Dwarfs with normal bodies but with short limbs	Normal
	Normal	Dwarfs with normal body proportions
Fingers and toes...	Short; webbed; supernumerary	Normal
Skin	Thick; hairless; excessive blisters	Normal
Nervous system ...	Normal	Multiple sclerosis Meniere's disease (roaring in ears) Chorea (St. Vitus Dance)
Eyes	Hereditary cataract, glaucoma; coloboma; displaced lens	Normal
Ears	Normal	Hardness of hearing due to thick tympanum Deaf-mutism
Sex-Linked Characters		
		Haemophilia (slow-clotting of blood) Red-green color-blindness Night-blindness Atrophy of optic nerve

(Adapted from E. G. Conklin, *Heredity and Environment*, Princeton (N. J.), Princeton Univ. Press, 1929, pp. 119-120.)

flowers) by a process of cross-fertilization. This means of course that color of flowers is independent of tallness and shortness in pea stems.

The same mechanism has been found to operate in man. The same ratios of inheritance as those followed in the tall-short vine cross appear in unit character reproduction. The related processes of unit character independence and dominance of some unit characters over others can be depended upon to appear throughout nature where stocks of known gene constitution are involved. As an example of this principle, Morgan [13] cites the inheritance of eye color in humans: "Blue eyes mated to blue give only blues; brown eyes bred to brown give only brown, provided the browns have had only brown ancestry. If a blue mates with a pure brown, the children are brown. If two individuals that have arisen from such a parentage marry, their children will be brown- and blue-eyed in the ratio of 3 to 1."

Unit Characters and the Genes.—The principle of "unit character" inheritance has so many important implications that it may be well to examine it more thoroughly. Even before Mendel's findings were known to scientists, it was believed by such prominent nineteenth-century workers as Darwin and Lamarck that the inheritance of parental characteristics was made possible by the actions of tiny somatic (body) particles called "ids" or "idants." These men felt that inheritance must be explained by the orderly march of such minute body particles into the germ cells, where they would bring about the development of characteristic structures in resulting embryo.

When Mendel's experimental results were brought to light, they appeared to confirm the idea that germ cell particles cause the appearance in offspring of specific characteristics. It was evident that physical traits at least were transmitted in harmony with a mathematical principle of some kind. Certainly shortness in pea vines was distributed in definite ratios, since it reappeared in later generations after having disappeared in the first. The earlier biologists did not realize, however, that germ

13 T. H. Morgan, *The Theory of the Gene*. New Haven, Yale Univ. Press, 1926, p. 10.

cells can carry on such processes without the aid of particles emanating from body cells.

The discovery of chromosomes and their gene equipment soon threw new light on the mechanisms of inheritance. It became evident that genes alone (and their surrounding cytoplasm) are the bearers of heredity. Not long after the detection of chromosomes under the microscope, it became known that, in the case of Drosophila flies at least, genes are arranged in linear order within them.

These findings led to the belief by some that practically all human traits—mental, moral, and temperamental, as well as physical—are passed on from parents to children through the avenue of genes. Science thus entered an era of more or less ardent belief in the inheritance of human characteristics of all kinds. For a time little recognition was given to the fact that not only personal and social traits, but physical structures even, are profoundly influenced by events and pressures in the environment. The doctrine was preached by many that the majority of human inequalities and personality disorders are the inevitable result of tainted genes and that society's principal hope for improvement lay in a long time program of selective breeding (eugenics).

The human race needs improvement but the social and moral involvements of attempting to accomplish it in cultured groups through eugenics are clearly insurmountable. There are practically no pure human stocks with which to experiment, and most social and ethical attitudes are amenable to improvement through educational channels. Furthermore, controlled breeding would run counter to numerous moral and religious principles. It is for these and similar reasons that the earlier belief in the gene-inheritance of *temperamental and social characteristics* is now largely in doubtful repute among critical scholars.

The Phenomenon of Blending.—There are a number of instances in which the principle of segregation of dominant and recessive traits has failed to appear. In short, the offspring of dissimilar parents in some cases inherit characteristics that are clearly intermediate between theirs. For example, when long-eared rabbits are mated with rabbits possessing short ears their offspring exhibit medium length ears. And, contrary to the usual outcome, these hybrid animals breed offspring resembling their intermediate parents; succeeding generations do not follow segregation and the usual 3:1 ratio between dominant and recessive traits.

Everyone is familiar with the appearance of mulattoes, individuals with a skin color intermediate between that of Negroes and whites. This is another case of blending and one which occurs when true black and true white humans are crossed. Scientists have been puzzled over the relation between this phenomenon and Mendel's well-established law of segregation. They have wondered whether blending is not a special and more complicated variety of segregation of unit characteristics. The commonly accepted conclusion is that blacks carry two pairs of genes for black pigmentation and that since whites carry no genes for black pigmentation, cross-mating produces an offspring characterized by half the amount of pigment transmitted by both parents combined.[14] This is thought to be an instance of segregation in which the influence of two or more duplicate or cumulative genes is felt.

Linkage in Inheritance.—Not long after the establishment of Mendel's laws, it was discovered that some characteristics do not appear in the 3:1 ratio typical of the segregation of dominant and recessive traits. Actually, these traits persist together in later generations after being crossed. Since several characteristics stay together in this phenomenon of inheritance, it has been called "linkage." It is believed that linked qualities have their origin in the same chromosome. Thus children receiving this chromosome inherit all the characteristics resident (linked) in it. As an example, if a parent transmits a chromosome containing genes for color, texture, and profusion of hair, the child concerned will inherit all—not one or part—of the characteristics in question. Physical qualities developing from

---

[14] A. Scheinfeld, *You and Heredity*, New York, F. A. Stokes Co., 1939, pp. 66-67. See also C. B. Davenport and F. H. Danielson, *Heredity of Skin Color in Negro and White Crosses*, Carnegie Institution Publications, No. 188, 1913.

a pattern of single chromosome genes are known as a "linkage group."

Probably the best evidence for linkage in inheritance is found in the consistent association of a number of physical traits with sex. These characteristics are evidently grouped in the *X* or sex-determining chromosome.

Haemophilia (bleeding), baldness, color-blindness, and other sex-linked characteristics are transmitted by an affected male through his daughters to his grandsons. In other words, those affected are always males (except in the case of color-blindness), who in turn received their defects from their mothers, themselves free from the taint.

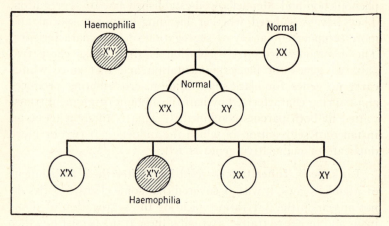

Figure 10. The Inheritance of Haemophilia

As Figure 10 shows, both sons and daughters of a haemophilic father and normal mother will be normal so far as blood clotting is concerned. But the daughters, themselves normal, transmit haemophilia to their sons, who in turn continue to be the fathers of normal children. It will be realized that this outcome is due to the action of paired genes. Since sex-linked traits are recessives, a normal *X* (sex determiner) gene paired with a defective *X* gene (from the father) will result in a normal blood condition. However, when a defective *X* gene from the mother (who is herself not affected) is coupled with a

y gene from the father (who carries both *X* and *y* genes), the
X gene is predominant and thus causes the appearance of haemophilia.

Sex-linked recessives inherited by sons from their mothers
include, in addition to haemophilia, baldness, and color-blindness, muscular atrophy, multiple sclerosis, and forms of myopia
and nystagmus.

Significance of the Laws of Genetics.—The laws of genetics, although based to a considerable extent upon experiments
with plants and animals, offer explanations for many phenomena of difference and likeness between parents and their children. The processes of inheritance explain the appearance of
given body features, texture and color of hair, skin, pigmentation, facial features, and numerous other physical characteristics. They also make possible an understanding of the appearance of such defects as haemophilia, webfingers, and baldhead-
edness. Furthermore, genetic principles explain why defective
children may occasionally appear in families of high cultural
status, and why physically inferior parents may produce offspring decidedly superior in this respect.

The possession of genetic knowledge makes it possible to
understand why mulattoes are intermediate between their parents in skin color and why near-sightedness, baldness, and other
defects are confined to the male sex. Such information also
makes it clear why defective individuals should not procreate
offspring, and why inbreeding involves dangers not apparent
to the uninformed.

It is difficult, in the light of present biological knowledge, to
control or predict the inheritance of strictly physical characteristics. Yet some individuals speak definitely of the transmission
of such complicated and socially influenced factors as mental
ability and moral attitudes. Obviously, one should be cautious
about making declarations in these less thoroughly investigated
realms. As yet no one has demonstrated the presence of genes
for mental or personality characteristics. If these qualities are
transmitted biologically, the mechanisms for their inheritance
are as yet unknown. Until we have made an adequate study

of the influence of various aspects of the social environment upon both the mental and social development of the child, it is probably best to confine our statements regarding what is and is not inherited to the known facts of genetics. It may turn out not to be necessary to drag in genes or chromosomes to explain much of the social pathology so characteristic of an appreciable fraction of society. Child psychology is interested in learning with what assets nature has equipped the individual. It is not willing to accept the many *a priori* declarations pertaining to inheritance of those who have not investigated the problems involved.

The Process of Reproduction

The study of Mendel's laws and related genetic principles leads naturally to a consideration of the phenomenon of human reproduction. The processes of reproduction and embryonic development have much to contribute to an understanding of child psychology. Such information is not widely available in non-technical language and is thus usually welcomed by students of child development. It is presented here in broad outline.

Fertilization of the Ovum.—A new individual has been conceived the instant a male sperm has been successful in penetrating the interior of a female ovum. Such a union of complementary germ cells is commonly referred to as *fertilization*. Following this phenomenon, the intricate but systematic process of *mitosis* gets under way. The original cell (ovum) divides and continues to multiply according to a plan laid down by nature. The process of mitosis or cell multiplication can be observed with laboratory instruments in various of the smaller animals. It is believed by embryologists that human development exhibits a similar order of events.

As indicated in Figure 11, the process of mitosis begins when the tiny sperm penetrates the mature ovum and passes between the two centrosomes which separate as it approaches. The chromosome nuclei of the sperm and ovum then come together and "back up" to each other on a straight plane at the

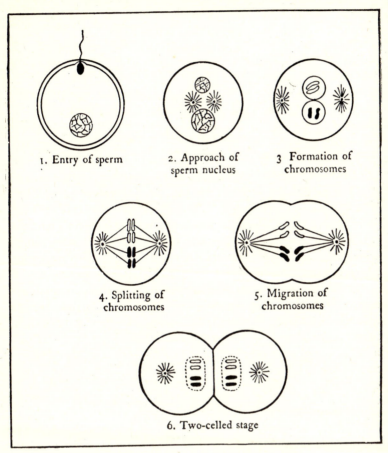

1. Entry of sperm
2. Approach of sperm nucleus
3 Formation of chromosomes
4. Splitting of chromosomes
5. Migration of chromosomes
6. Two-celled stage

Figure 11. The Mechanism of Fertilization

In this diagram it is assumed that four is the number of chromosomes characteristic of the species. Paternal chromosomes are represented as black, maternal
chromosomes as white.

(From H. E. Walter, *Genetics,* New York, The Macmillan Co., 1938, p. 186.)

center of the combined cell. Following this development, the
combined chromosomes divide lengthwise and move in opposite
directions following their respective centrosomes, with which
they are connected by fine strands. As a next step, the cell
lengthens and commences to divide, each chromosome nucleus
gravitating to its own nearby, separate cell. In the end, each

nucleus grows to mature proportions and becomes the chromosomal equipment of the fully developed cell.

The division process illustrated goes on continually and eventuates in the development of appropriate body structures. The solid sphere, which appears first, soon gives way to a hollow sphere or *blastula*. In a remarkably short time specialized organs and other physical structures take form. In two or three months the growing fetus can be identified as belonging to the human species.

It is important to realize that a newly fertilized ovum contains in its chromosomal nucleus all the potential characteristics that the parents in question can pass on to the next generation. The minute sex cell is the "slender but effective thread" that joins one generation with another. Since germ cells are not produced by the persons housing them, but by the same union which developed their bearers, they are credited with providing a never ending "bridge" between succeeding generations.

It should also be remembered that in the mitotic process each new cell receives an equal number of chromosomes from its male and female parent. Thus all cells share alike their paternal and maternal heritage. It follows that all somatic or body cells of a developing embryo are alike in chromosome and gene organization, each getting half its heritage from each parent. It is essential to an understanding of later development that differentiation of structural development must be brought about by forces independent of chromosomal cell nuclei.

In-utero Cell Relationships.—Late nineteenth-century biologists were of the belief that the future structures of an organism were completely determined by inheritance. They reasoned that the development of bodily characteristics was the exclusive task of germ cells. As they saw it, the growing animal or human individual did not participate in the development process until growth had proceeded a considerable distance. These early scientists were almost completely oblivious to the influence of either internal or external environmental forces.

A modern student of genetics, Child, has challenged this almost exclusively hereditarian view of prenatal growth. He believes that such a position neglects important environmental influences and embryonic responses affecting development. Child [15] writes, "This conception is fundamentally preformistic and fails to take account of the facts of physiology. Reaction to environment is occurring at all stages of development, . . . moreover, such behavior or reaction is itself a factor in development and therefore in the construction of the behavior mechanisms of later stages. The behavior of the various developmental stages as well as the specific hereditary constitution of the protoplasm is a factor in determining the behavior of the fully developed organism. . . ." This view of development has been substantiated by studies of the influence of both external and prenatal environments. Thus we turn our attention to an examination of this type of evidence.

The Inner Environment and Development.—Biologists have discovered the principle that "what any particular cell of the individual produces is largely determined by the surroundings of that cell—by the cells in contact with it, and by the hormones that bathe it; in short, by the internal environment—so that the same set of genes produces different results in different cases." [16]

This principle is illustrated by the influence of the environment and of the cytoplasm (fatty material surrounding a chromosome cell nucleus) in the development of the sea urchin. It is a novel fact that when a two-celled sea urchin egg is divided, thus causing each cell to move in a sea water environment instead of being attached to another cell, metabolic activity and the subsequent course of development of the animal is affected. It is also true that the cytoplasmic material of the sea urchin single-egg cell is almost as essential to its normal development as are its chromosomes and genes. If certain zones of the cytoplasm are removed, corresponding structures of the organism being produced do not develop. This happens even when the chromosome nucleus of the egg cell is undisturbed. One inves-

---

[15] C. M. Child, *Physiological Foundations of Behavior,* New York, Henry Holt & Co., Inc., 1924, pp. 1-5.
[16] H. S. Jennings, *The Biological Basis of Human Nature,* New York, W. W. Norton & Co., Inc., 1930, p. 122.

tigator has claimed that the light green stripes in corn are caused by cytoplasm influence.[17]

Child [18] has suggested that it would be to our advantage to recognize "that environmental factors play some part in ordering and unifying the process of realization of heredity potentialities in the development of the individual organism. . . ." The correctness of this view is indicated by a number of demonstrated facts. First, as mentioned, in the case of some embryos, the body-building function performed by any given somatic cell is determined by its surroundings—by the cells, hormone action, temperature, and other influences in its immediate vicinity. For example, if, in the early embryonic stage of development, a small cluster of cells destined to help produce muscle tissue is transplanted to a "sphere of influence" concerned with the growth of bony structure, it participates in the function of its new environment and assists in the production of bone. This process of accommodation enables the developing organism to maintain its structural pattern even when disturbed by accident or surgical manipulation.

It is not long, however, until the developing organism reaches the place where growth trends are sufficiently definite to resist modification. From this point on, cells that chance to be transplanted or otherwise moved, continue to produce the structures with which they were originally concerned. This law of growth may occasionally result in the appearance in animals of such inappropriate body formations as two heads, two tails, extra legs, and eye deformities. It is probable that this phenomenon provides at least a partial explanation for many monstrosities.

External Factors Affecting Growth.—The extent to which external factors influence the development of embryonic physical structures is not generally known. It has been possible to observe such modifications in certain of the lower animals. The salamander, for example, is normally a water animal equipped with finlike legs, a flat tail, and gills. When required by cir-

17 A. F. Shull, *Heredity*, New York, McGraw-Hill Book Co., Inc., 1938, Ch. 16.
18 C. M. Child, *op. cit.*, p. 32.

cumstances to develop on land, the salamander becomes an *Amblystoma* characterized by a round tail, lungs, and legs usable on land. It seems likely that differing environments stimulate the genes involved to develop different body structures, or that land surroundings permit them to prolong growth past the stage possible in watery surroundings.

Another example of external influence on development is afforded by observations on the fruit fly. If, at the hatching stage, this fly is required to live in a lowered temperature, it grows numerous legs instead of the six characteristic of its species. According to Hoge,[19] certain thermal and chemical conditions are essential to normal growth in this and other animal organisms. Some fish, for instance, develop one eye instead of the usual two if incubated in abnormal (for them) temperatures. Others, the squid embryo, for example, become one-eyed when permitted to develop in chemically treated sea water for from 12 to 48 hours.[20] These examples are illustrative of the marked influence of certain environmental factors on the development of physical structures. They suggest the dependence of even the genes and chromosomes upon external stimulating conditions for the realization of inherited physical potentialities. It seems evident that a complex combination of factors, in addition to germinal possibilities, operate to bring about the physical development of young organisms. Many biologists believe that this principle holds in the case of human offspring. They are obviously not at liberty to experiment with the human embryo, but the factors conditioning growth are believed to be similar in many respects to those operating in the animal world.

The Nature of Prenatal Influences

The influences operating in early embryonic development discussed in the previous sections are not the only important forces in the picture of human prenatal growth. A number remain to be presented. Prominent among these are the nature of the

[19] M. Hoge, "The Influence of Temperature on the Development of a Mendelian Character," *Journal of Experimental Zoology*, 18 : 24-285 (1932).

[20] Paul Weiss, *Principles of Development*, New York, Henry Holt & Co., Inc., 1939, p. 146.

connection between the mother and growing fetus (further developed embryo) and the facts of congenital inheritance. The first-mentioned point is crucial to an understanding of popular superstitions concerning the origin of birthmarks, attitudes, and special talents. An unusual amount of credulity exists in this area of child development. In no other field of observation is the principle of causation so hopelessly misinterpreted.

Influencing the Developing Fetus.—When a human ovum has been fertilized and the subsequent process of mitosis initiated, it gravitates toward the uterus of the individual in whom its impregnation took place. At this point the developing ovum becomes enveloped in a chorion sack (membrane), a part of which is destined to imbed itself in the placenta or uterus wall of the mother. This is the manner in which the connection between the originally independent embryo and the appropriate surface of the mother's body is established. As Figure 12 shows, the connection is an indirect one in which minute blood vessel terminals (villi) from the umbilical cord of the fetus become interlaced in the wall of the mother's uterus. It is evident, thus, that the growing child does not receive blood or any form of nourishment directly from the maternal blood stream. Oxygen and nutritive material must get from the maternal to the fetal blood stream by a process of *osmosis* or seepage through the blood vessel walls of villi which are in contact with the mother's blood stream.

It would seem that the possibility of maternal influence on a child during pregnancy hinges on the nature of the physical connection between the two organisms. There is, however, neither a nerve connection nor a direct blood-flow connection between the mother and her unborn child. It is this fact that renders the belief in a mother's capacity to influence her child's mental or moral development a very doubtful one. Without a nerve connection between the two individuals, it does not seem possible to transmit so-called mental influences. Science is not, of course, in possession of final information regarding this problem, but the present status of knowledge goes far toward dis-

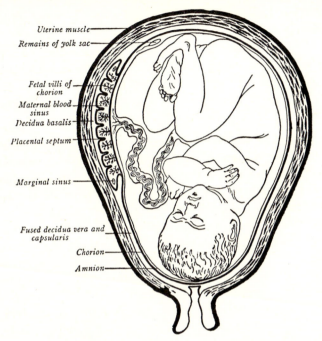

Figure 12. Diagrammatic Section of the Uterus Showing the Relation of an Advanced Fetus to the Placenta and Other Membranes

(From L. B. Arey, *Developmental Anatomy*, Philadelphia, W. B. Saunders Co., 1934, p. 108.)

crediting unconfirmed theories of prenatal marking or influencing.

There is widespread belief, for example, that intense experiences encountered by an expectant mother will result either in birthmarks on her child's body or in the formation of latent attitudes. One woman glibly ascribed a dog-shaped birthmark on her child's back to being frightened by a strange dog in the early period of her pregnancy. Another mother attributed a strawberry-shaped mark on her son to her weariness at having to pick strawberries day after day during his prenatal development. A third woman claimed that her son's later musical success was made possible by the fact that she took music lessons and attended concerts during the gestation period. It apparently never occurred to the latter individual that the musically stimulating environment provided for years after birth could have been in part responsible for her son's excellent musical development. One psychologist has characterized such naive stories as "old wives' tales—mere fabrication or coincidence." This is probably the basis of most such tales.

It should be apparent that the causes some people attribute to birthmarks and special talents could not be true in terms of natural phenomena and the known facts of inheritance. It takes little trained intelligence to realize that even though the experience, during pregnancy, of longing for a new hat preceded the appearance on the subsequently born child of a hat-shaped birthmark, it did not necessarily cause the mark. To suggest such a cause and effect relationship when physiological factors could have brought about the birthmark is to dispense with logical reasoning and scientific caution. Besides, medical doctors report considerable evidence that marks may be caused by disturbances of pigmentation or of blood vessels. Even in these cases the form of the marks is probably a coincidence.

It is interesting to contemplate with Anatole France, in the story of Little Pierre, what might have happened to the boy if during his prenatal period his mother, instead of longing for cherries only, had "hankered after feathers, trinkets, a cashmere shawl, a coach and four, a town house, a country mansion, and a park!" Finally, if certain experiences or influences actually left marks on offspring such results would *always* have to occur when the experiences in question were encountered. There can be little doubt that literally thousands of cases in which such a result did *not* occur have gone unmentioned by the parents concerned. Most people neglect negative evidence and fall into the fallacy of believing that because one event precedes another in time it is necessarily the *cause* of the second event.

Germinal versus Other Forms of Inheritance.—Many individuals hold the mistaken belief that all characteristics or defects possessed by an infant at birth are biologically inherited in the sense of being potential in gene organization. Such individuals have failed to understand the difference between direct *germinal* or gene inheritance and *congenital* or prenatal inheritance. Germinal inheritance obviously refers to growth potentials in the germ plasm of a family tree. Yet it is common knowledge that a variety of undesirable or disturbing influences may play upon the growing child between conception and the birth event. These influences, some of which are to be presented shortly, and their effects upon the unborn child, are referred to as *congenital* inheritance. They occur before birth but are not inherent in gene or chromosome constitution.

Factors in Congenital Inheritance.—The most significant congenital experiences productive of ill effects to a growing fetus have been listed by Schwesinger [21] as:

1. *Malnutrition.* Excessive malnutrition of the mother's organism during the intra-uterine period may deprive the growing child of essential nutritive elements. Such deprivation may hamper the child's physical development.

2. *Disease.* Mothers suffering from such wasting diseases as diabetes, cancer, tuberculosis, and pellagra are likely to affect their unborn offspring adversely. Physical effects similar to those noted in malnutrition may be produced.

3. *Infection.* Infectious diseases, particularly syphilis, frequently attack the nervous system and may result in congenital weakness or instability. An apparently healthy mother may house germs that prey on her unborn child.

4. *Toxins.* The developing child may be affected by toxic poisons that seep through blood vessel walls into the umbilical cord. It was formerly believed that alcohol could affect sex cells before conception but this belief has been largely discredited.

5. *Endocrine imbalance.* A deficiency or excess of endocrine secretion in the mother may seriously hamper the physical and mental development of an offspring. It is well known that cretinism, a disorder marked by general retardation and emotional and mental subnormality, may be caused by a deficiency of the thyroid hormone.

6. *Birth injuries.* Injuries resulting from the use of obstetrical instruments and pressure on the soft skull of a fetus during labor

[21] Gladys C. Schwesinger, *Heredity and Environment*, New York, The Macmillan Co., 1933, pp. 331-332.

and delivery may result in arrested development, feeblemindedness, cerebral palsy, or other abnormal tendencies. Various defects are sometimes erroneously assigned to this cause, but parents naturally prefer to avoid admissions of germinal weakness.

7. *Emotional shock.* It is possible that severe emotional shock may force an excess of the powerful adrenalin hormone into the blood stream going to the fetus (by osmosis). Whether such a process affects adversely the mentality and nervous stability of the developing child is a moot question. Little of a certain nature is known about this problem and it is thus best to suspend judgment regarding it.

The practical implications of the foregoing factors in congenital inheritance should be clear. The majority of the causes of maldevelopment listed can be prevented by mothers sufficiently interested to regulate living conditions during pregnancy. Expectant mothers can prevent most of the unfortunate outcomes mentioned by observing their diet, avoiding diseases and infections, consulting a physician about endocrine and blood conditions, and by securing competent medical assistance at the time of delivery. The child's ultimate well-being and personality integrity warrant careful attention to these and other congenital factors.

Acquired Characteristics and Heredity.—Many people believe that physical, mental, artistic, and other abilities acquired by parents may be transmitted to their children. A variety of unproved ideas regarding the inheritance of parental learning are still common in uninformed circles. Probably the first to promote such a theory of inheritance was the nineteenth-century scientist, Lamarck. He needed such a doctrine to explain the upward progress of man as he saw it. Charles Darwin's theory of organic evolution and the principle of natural selection also needed a biological explanation for the apparent progressive trend of mankind. Quite naturally, he also accepted the idea of the inheritance of acquired abilities. Since the processes of germinal transmission were unknown to them, neither Lamarck nor Darwin were able to give an explanation of how inheritance took place. Darwin proposed the previously mentioned theory, however, that minute somatic cell particles, called *gemmules,* worked their way from all parts of the body into the germ cells and there registered their potential effects on future offspring.

A number of experiments designed to test the validity of the dogma of transmission of learned abilities have been carried out.[22] A study of these will indicate the doubtful nature of the theory. Practically all of the evidence is negative. In view of this situation, biologists and psychologists alike are inclined to regard the germ cells of reproduction as being relatively independent of body cells and acquired abilities. The evidence indicates that child characteristics have their origin either in gene constitution or in the effects of environmental learning activities, or both. Educational and cultural achievements evidently cannot be transmitted biologically to offspring. Every child must start from the beginning in his quest for physical, intellectual, and social development. Present knowledge shows that parents cannot transmit ready-made personalities and achievements to immature children.

The status of the inheritance problem has been summarized by Walter [23] in words indicative of why the theory merits rejection: "First, there is no known mechanism whereby somatic (body) characters may be transferred to germ cells; second, the evidence that such a transfer actually does occur is inconclusive and unsatisfactory; third, the theory of the continuity of the germ plasm is sufficient to account for the facts of heredity without assuming the inheritance of acquired somatic characters." Except for some minor objections, this is about where the problem stands at present.

Summary and Further Implications

If the personality of the growing child is to be regarded as subject to improvement, it is necessary to clear up some common misunderstandings concerning what traits or qualities are and are not biologically inherited. If it could be shown that moral

[22] H. S. Jennings, *The Biological Basis of Human Nature,* New York, W. W. Norton & Co., Inc., 1930, pp. 338-347.
[23] H. E. Walter, *Genetics* (3rd ed.), New York, The Macmillan Co., 1930, p. 71. By permission.

and personality traits are transmitted to offspring by the same genetic (gene) processes that are known to characterize physical inheritance, it would be necessary to admit that little can be done to improve a child's social and moral sense if he has been the victim of defective inheritance.

This type of reasoning is, however, both fatalistic and out of harmony with ascertained facts of child growth and development. It also perpetuates the fallacy of oversimplifying the complex problems of child personality and character. Thus to overlook the important social implications of human development leads to a neglect of needed researches concerning the nature of psychological factors in growth. If it is arbitrarily assumed, for example, that a child inherited his introvertive or antisocial temperament, his parents would have less incentive than otherwise to set up conditions calculated to make him more social. A great many people have no doubt been strongly influenced by extreme declarations concerning the genetic origin of attitudes and social dispositions. As the present chapter has indicated, considerable is known about the inherited basis of physical structures and characteristics. However, scientists have not as yet proved the existence of a process for the gene-inheritance of temperament, moral attitudes, or personality traits. These and other more strictly social characteristics are apparently powerfully influenced by environmental conditions operating in a given child's home, school, and community.

Biologists who work close to the processes of human inheritance are frequently so impressed with the evidence for the gene transmission of physical characteristics that they assume the same genetic mechanism for personality traits. Thus they believe that apparently acquired faults and virtues are germinally inherited. Jennings,[24] for instance, after admitting that even physical gene potentialities require a satisfactory environment for their development, goes on to say that "differences in the set of materials (genes) out of which people are made affect deeply their nature and character in every possible way—phys-

---

[24] H. S. Jennings, "How Heredity Affects Personality," *The Parents Magazine,* 6: 17, 65, 67 (1931).

ically, physiologically, emotionally, mentally, morally. There is no respect in which changes in these materials do not cause changes in the individual." Walter [25] expresses a similar belief that "there is . . . no fundamental scientific distinction that can be drawn between moral, mental, and physical traits, since all . . . are undoubtedly equally subject to the laws of heredity."

Statements of this kind have been so influential that it is difficult to find a single personality trait that has not been regarded by some people as being biologically inherited. Furthermore, few individuals realize the importance of congenital influences for the determination of even physical characteristics. Such attitudes may be accounted for in part by the tendency of many men and women to rationalize their weaknesses as being due to inherited handicaps. Parents who desire to avoid the embarrassment of admitting failure in the rearing of their children often attempt to escape responsibility by blaming the relentless forces of inheritance. Mothers who find it difficult to cope with their troublesome offspring frequently dismiss the matter by declaring that they were "born that way."

In viewing the question of inheritance, it would seem advisable to suspend judgment as to what is and is not inherited. The physical organism of the child, with its structures and autonomic functions, is obviously transmitted through biological channels in harmony with the laws of inheritance. This organism constitutes the child's physical equipment and is the foundation upon which his elaborate structure of personality develops in the social medium. It is well to recognize that if even the physical body of the prenatal child is influenced by the forces surrounding it, postnatal character and personality developments must be powerfully affected by the modifying impact of the social environment. It seems logical thus to regard the child's personal and social characteristics as products of the stream of experience and as having their foundation in the biologically inherited organism.

[25] H. E. Walter (1938 ed.), *op. cit.*, p. 304.

Questions for Discussion

1. Why can it be said that, in the case of human *in-utero* development, heredity and environment have no separate identity? What bearing does this issue have as an understanding of child development?

2. Is it possible to demonstrate that character and personality qualities are inherited by the same processes as physical characteristics? What *pro* and *con* arguments could be brought to bear on this question? What is said about it in scientific literature?

3. In the light of present knowledge concerning gene-inheritance, what predictions can be made about the probable physical characteristics of an expected offspring? Does inheritance operate to make offspring unlike as well as alike? Explain.

4. What is the significance for the child's physical well-being of the principle of double gene-inheritance? What would occur in the physical sense if a child inherited all his characteristics from one parent? Is it known whether pairings of defective genes produce personality defects?

5. Why is it so difficult to determine whether physical traits in humans are transmitted on the basis of Mendelian ratios of inheritance? What phenomena of human inheritance can be used to demonstrate one or more of Mendel's laws? What logical arguments can be presented concerning this question?

6. What is the functional value of understanding the processes involved in linkage, blending, dominant and recessive traits, double inheritance, and other genetic laws? What are the practical advantages, if any, of knowing that the developing embryo is affected by its environment?

7. What arguments have been advanced for belief in the biological transmission of acquired characteristics or learnings? What was Darwin's proposal? What evidence is there that parents cannot pass on to children skills and qualities which they have developed?

8. In view of the nature of the physical connection between an expectant mother and the developing fetus, what can be said about the possibilities of influencing the future mental ability or moral attitude of the latter during gestation? How final is present knowledge concerning this question?

9. What evidence is there for the claims of some writers that

delinquent and criminal tendencies, forms of insanity, immorality, vagrancy, lack of industry, and other such undesirable personality qualities may be biologically inherited? How scientific are the arguments usually advanced?

10. What is the explanation for the appearance in animal offspring of such anomalies as five legs, two heads, one eye, and other such monstrosities? Could deviations of this kind occur in the human species? What is the evidence here?

RECOMMENDED READINGS

Castle, W. E.　*Genetics and Eugenics*.　Boston: Harvard Univ. Press, 1930.

Conklin, E. G.　*Heredity and Environment*.　Princeton (N. J.): Princeton Univ. Press, 1929.

Gilliland, A. R.　*Genetic Psychology*.　New York: The Ronald Press Co., 1933, Chs. 7, 8.

Guyer, M. F.　*Being Well Born*.　Indianapolis: Bobbs-Merrill Co., 1927.

Jennings, H. S.　*The Biological Basis of Human Nature*.　New York: W. W. Norton & Co., Inc., 1930.

Jennings, H. S.　*Genetics*.　New York: W. W. Norton & Co., Inc., 1935.

Morgan, J. J. B.　*Child Psychology*.　New York: Farrar & Rinehart, Inc., 1942, Ch. 2.

Morgan, T. H.　*The Theory of the Gene*.　New Haven: Yale Univ. Press, 1926.

Rosanoff, A. J.　*Manual of Psychiatry and Mental Hygiene*.　New York: John Wiley & Sons, Inc., 1938, Ch. 8.

Scheinfeld, A.　*You and Heredity*.　New York: F. A. Stokes Co., 1939.

Shull, A. F.　*Heredity*.　New York: McGraw-Hill Book Co., Inc., 1938.

Walter, H. E.　*Genetics*.　New York: The Macmillan Co., 1938.

CHAPTER 3

MENTAL ABILITIES: NATURE AND NURTURE

As the discussion in Chapter 2 indicated, considerable progress has been made in unraveling the mysteries of biological inheritance. It is now known with fair certainty that physical attributes and characteristics are transmitted through the processes of gene and chromosome action. The facts of inheritance thus tell how newborn infants come to possess the physical features which stamp them as members of a family and a race.

However, when we come to the equally important question of the inheritance of mental ability the available evidence is not so clear. The problems involved in ascertaining a child's so-called native mental capacity and the extent to which it may have been biologically inherited are exceedingly complex. In the present state of knowledge no one knows the location in the organism of native ability, whether it is transmitted through the avenue of genes, or to what extent it may be influenced by congenital and environmental factors. A study of the available evidence does, nevertheless, throw a great deal of light on these important issues.

Attitudes Toward Mental Inheritance

Views concerning the inheritance of mental ability vary considerably. Some believe that such ability is transmitted from parents to offspring in the same manner as physical characteristics. Others are impressed with the modifications in intellectual achievement that varying environments seem to bring about. Still other views stress the interlocked nature of hereditary and environmental forces and their influence on mental development.

The Fatalistic Attitude Toward Inheritance.—Nevertheless, belief in the all-pervading influence of biological inheritance has influenced the American mind to the extent that practically all traits—physical, mental, and temperamental—are widely regarded as being hereditary. As one writer [1] declares, "we find racial, tribal, and family traits, both physical and mental, transmitted with great regularity." Thus it has been thought that criminal tendencies are inborn and, as brought out in Chapter 1, that infants inherit good or evil natures. It has also been taken for granted that mental defects, special abilities, and personality patterns are products of biological transmission. Practically no human characteristic has escaped the attention of the proponents of inheritance, most of whom have made little or no effort to prove their contentions.

People are often impressed by the fact that a certain mental or emotional characteristic has appeared for several generations in a family. An appreciable proportion of relatives might, for example, have been emotionally unstable or unusually capable in the mastery of language. The layman is quick to conclude that such traits are biologically inherited. It seldom occurs to most people that even if this were true it would be difficult, if not impossible, to demonstrate by what processes such traits are transmitted. Gene-inheritance is never free from the influences of intra-uterine (congenital) and postnatal environmental factors. Thus the possibility that social and emotional conditions in a certain family environment might be highly conducive to the development of given traits has usually been overlooked.

As one volume [2] on child study brings out, "It is easy to assign familiar traits to heredity when their occurrence is due to undiscovered factors in the family environment. Mental characteristics, personality likenesses, and behavior need especial care in their study since they are developed and secondary and may or may not have their basis in heredity." Thus if a child displays a temper similar to that of his father it is well to determine whether home conditions were such as to induce the development of such a trait. Nevertheless, uncritical individuals find it difficult not to assign to heredity a characteristic

---

[1] Arne S. Jensen, *Psychology of Child Behavior,* New York, Prentice-Hall, Inc., 1938, p. 113.

[2] Winifred Rand, M. E. Sweeny, and E. L. Vincent, *Growth and Development of the Young Child,* Philadelphia, W. B. Saunders Co., 1930 (original ed.), p. 83.

that has recurred for two or three successive generations in a family.

Nature of the Evidence for Mental Inheritance.—Those who claim that the hereditary factor is predominant in determining mental ability believe that there is ample evidence to prove their view. They point to the fact that both feeblemindedness and brightness tend to run in families. The superficially studied, but much discussed, Kallikak, Jukes, and Edwards family histories are pressed into service to show the alleged hereditary nature of mental capacity. It has also been suggested that native superiority may be determined by finding how many relatives of a superior person are listed in the pages of *Who's Who*. The fact that many of the above family history investigations were based on uncritical observations and made without the use of quantitative measurements or verifiable techniques appears to have escaped a number of writers.

Other general evidences for mental inheritance include the finding that the closer a "blood" relationship the more likely offspring are to possess similar characteristics. Identical (monozygotic) twins are more alike in physical, mental, and temperamental traits than fraternal (dizygotic) twins. Similarly, siblings (brothers and sisters) are more alike than cousins or even parents and child. These findings, together with the fact that racial groups tend to be more alike than different in most respects, are taken to demonstrate the inherited nature of mental as well as other characteristics.

The above line of logic appears convincing until it is realized that intellectual superiority, for example, could in many instances be accounted for in part by a stimulating social environment and superior educational advantages. Such environmental features are often present in socially and economically privileged families. The same type of reasoning could hold for subnormal intellectual development—it could in some cases be accounted for, in part at least, in terms of a barren environment and non-stimulating (intellectual) experiences. The influences of the social environment cannot be ignored in the development of so flexible an organism as the infant and child.

This is not to say that the hereditary factor, although always an unknown, should be neglected. The effects of environmental influences can, however, be explored, and studies concerning them are providing clues concerning the control of mental development in children. As the biologist Jennings [3] has said, "there has been much misunderstanding, in consequence of the common fallacy that if a characteristic is affected by the environment it cannot be hereditary; that if it is hereditary, it cannot be influenced by the environment." The evidence tends to show that in a very unfavorable environment the most excellent appearing inheritance will fail to bring about superior development.

The Structure-Function Theory of Inheritance.—Some have sought to solve the difficult problem of mental inheritance by assuming that intellectual ability is dependent upon the possession of a superior brain and nervous system. Their belief is expressed in the slogan "a good brain—a good mind." Since the brain is obviously inherited, this view would make possible a theory of mental inheritance. It assumes that mental ability has its basis in the quality of the structure of the nervous system, particularly the cerebrum. On this basis an individual's mental ability would be in direct proportion to the quality and possibly quantity of the neurones making up his cerebral and other neural structures. Differences in native ability could thus be attributed to differences in nervous system structure.

The theory that mental ability is a *function* of brain structure; that is, that the quality of the brain and nervous system will determine the quality of an individual's intellect, is a plausible one, but one that has not been proved. Like the idea that the number of neurone connections parallels mental capacity, it is but a hypothesis. As the psychologist Thorndike [4] has declared, "What is essential to the *hypothesis* is that, by original nature, men differ in respect to the number of connections or associations with ideas which they can form, so that despite outside environments, some of them would have many more than

[3] H. S. Jennings, *Biological Basis of Human Nature*, New York, W. W Norton & Co., Inc., 1930, p. 147.
[4] E. L. Thorndike, *The Measurement of Intelligence*, New York, Teachers College, Columbia Univ., 1927, p. 415. (Italics not in the original.)

others." It is possible that good brains provide superior mental ability, but no amount of reasoning can prove that to be the case. There is no positive evidence that the brain or nervous system constitute the exclusive basis for the appearance of intellectual functions. Some believe that intelligence is a biological function in which the whole organism, including brain, nervous system, endocrine glands, and muscles, participate in a composite way.

Another argument, favorable to the structure-function theory, is that neurones cannot perform their task of transmitting neural energy until such time as they are thoroughly insulated with the fatty covering called *myelin*. According to this point of view, nerves leading from one part of the body to another become *myelinized*, or covered with sheathing, by a progressive process which permits the gradual development of intellectual ability. This theory suggests possible evidence for the structure-function hypothesis of mental inheritance. It, too, is based on the idea that the nervous system is responsible for the appearance and development of mental ability. It is an uncertain hypothesis and one that neglects the influence of environmental factors on intellectual development.

Evidence from Brain Experimentation.—There is considerable evidence in both animal and human realms that the complete brain is not essential to the functioning of consciousness and intelligence. Lashley [5] and others have shown that even when a section of a rat's brain is removed by surgery, thoroughly learned skills are frequently not seriously disturbed. Newly developed abilities are impaired by such surgery but can usually be relearned. In the main, these investigations studied the effects, on well-learned skills in running a maze and escaping from puzzle boxes, of the removal of certain areas of the cerebrum.

In addition to finding that sections of the brain can be dispensed with without appreciable loss of skill, Lashley discovered that the removal of any given area of the cerebrum resulted in a very similar loss of skill. The entire area of the cerebrum

[5] K. S. Lashley, *Brain Mechanisms and Intelligence*, Chicago, Univ. of Chicago Press, 1929.

appears to operate as a unit in the development or impairment of skill. The brain is evidently involved in the learning of skills, since those *recently* learned are lost when a section is removed. However, the fact that older and more thoroughly learned abilities survive the loss of brain tissue indicates that its complete integrity is not necessary to the functioning of the intellectual and neuromuscular activities of an animal. This type of evidence would appear to be damaging to the structure-function theory of mental inheritance.

Results similar to the above have been obtained in tumor operations and head accidents in the case of humans. It appears that here, too, the supposed close relationship between brain integrity and mental status does not always hold. Dandy,[6] a brain surgeon, has removed large sections of the brains of humans in tumor cases without impairing the patient's intellectual life. In one case he removed the individual's right hemisphere, left frontal lobe, and part of the left temporal without disturbing his ability to read, write, remember, or carry on normal mental relations with his friends. Operations of this kind may result in loss of sensory and motor functions or even paralysis, but do not necessarily damage the patient's mental integrity.

Dandy and other brain surgeons have concluded that since only a small area of the brain is responsible for maintaining consciousness and mental normality, too great reliance has been placed on the cortex in explaining the operations of the intellect. Kantor [7] has summed up the problem in these words: "It is indeed unfortunate that psychological [mental] phenomena are still looked upon as general functions requiring some sort of neural substratum [structure]. This, no doubt, is only an exemplary illustration of the weighty influence of tradition upon our thinking."

Changing Conceptions of Mental Deficiency.—Since the publication in 1913 of the Kallikak family history of social degeneracy, there has been a tendency to hold tenaciously to the

6 W. E. Dandy, "Changes in Our Conceptions of Localization of Certain Functions of the Brain," *American Journal of Physiology*, 93 : 643 (1930).
7 J. R. Kantor, "Current Trends in Psychological Theory," *Psychological Bulletin*, 38 : 58 (1941).

belief that heredity is responsible for such an outcome. As the story goes, Martin Kallikak, a Revolutionary War soldier, cohabited with a supposedly feebleminded barmaid, thus bringing into existence a long line of progeny characterized by much feeblemindness, pauperism, criminality, prostitution, and other forms of social degeneracy. Uncritical acceptance of the hereditary interpretation given this and similar loosely studied investigations subsequently led to the almost universal belief that feeblemindedness is biologically inherited. Little recognition has been accorded the possibility that the tavern girl may not have been feebleminded, and that the Kallikak offspring were reared in a barren, isolated community where there was little opportunity to develop either socially or intellectually.

It is evident now that sociological studies, especially those in which modern sampling and measurement techniques were not available, cannot be accepted as proof of the inheritance of mental ability. Such studies may be examples of the influence of an unfavorable environment.

There is considerable evidence that the traditional attitude toward mental inheritance is changing. In 1914 Goddard [8] studied the family histories of 300 feebleminded persons in the Vineland Training School for mental defectives and concluded that 54 per cent of the histories indicated unquestionable inheritance. He further classed 11 per cent as probably hereditary and 12 per cent as having tainted (neuropathic) ancestry. Goddard thus arrived at the conclusion that 77 per cent of his cases probably inherited their mentally deficient status. In 1934, Doll [9], who later followed Goddard as director of research at the Vineland School, reported that, according to his figures, 30 per cent of the inmates appeared to be hereditary cases, 30 per cent secondary (postnatal trauma, infections, and endocrine disorders), and 40 per cent unknown or uncertain.

Thus Doll classified 30 per cent of the cases as being possibly inherited in the same institution where Goddard listed 77 per cent as being similarly tainted genetically. This striking

[8] Henry H. Goddard, *Feeble-mindedness, Its Causes and Its Consequences,* New York, The Macmillan Co., 1914.
[9] Edgar A. Doll, Department of Research Annual Report, 1933-34. *Training School Bulletin,* 31 : 112-123 (1934).

difference reflects the general trend toward making more critical studies of the influence on mental status of social and educational factors.   Doll's findings are concurred in by Penrose,[10] who studied 513 institutional cases and found 29 per cent classifiable as hereditary aments (feebleminded), 9 per cent as postnatal or environmental, and 62 per cent as uncertain.   These findings present the evidence upon which a change in attitude is taking place concerning the causes of mental deficiency.

As already mentioned, many cases of feeblemindedness formerly thought to be biologically inherited have been shown to be the result of secondary or postnatal factors.   These include injuries associated with labor and delivery at birth (trauma), infectious diseases such as spinal meningitis, polioencephalitis (inflammation of the brain), and encephalitis lethargica (sleeping sickness), and dysfunctions of the thyroid (hypothyroidism) and pituitary glands.   Prenatal or congenital factors may also possibly affect the mentality of later offspring.   Malnourishment, infections, and excessive alcoholism occurring during pregnancy may influence adversely the growing fetus.   The evidence for the effects of congenital syphilis is not as conclusive as many have claimed, but it appears to be a factor in mental deficiency in some cases.   According to Davis,[11] studies have revealed that 3.68 per cent of 177,216 child cases of mental subnormality were presumably caused by syphilitic infection.

Constancy of the Intelligence Quotient.—According to most of the early investigations of mental development, the intelligence quotient (I.Q.) of a given individual tends to remain relatively constant from year to year.   This revelation has caused many scientists to believe that the amount of intelligence possessed by a person of given capacity is proportional to his chronological age (up to mid- or late adolescence), and that it is determined by inheritance.   This is comparable to saying that mental development is a growth process dependent upon organic maturation.   But as Blatz [12] has brought out, this is an over-

[10] L. S. Penrose, *Mental Defect,* New York, Farrar & Rinehart, Inc., 1934.
[11] Gertrude D. Davis, *The Behavioral Effects of Congenital Syphilis: A Review of the Literature,* Master's Thesis, Indiana Univ., 1935.
[12] W. E. Blatz, "What Is an Exceptional Child?" *Proceedings of the Sixth Institute on the Exceptional Child of the Child Research Clinic of the Woods School,* Oct. 1939, pp. 39-40.

simple explanation and one that has apparently gotten child psychology on the wrong track in this area. Students of child development have gained little by borrowing concepts from the physical sciences in the mental inheritance field. Yet many have thought that the I.Q. is based on brain and nervous system development, and that it is thus inherently constant. They believe that differences in mental test scores are due largely to differences in inheritance or to degree of "mental maturation." This view sets narrow limits to the improvability of human intelligence.

The above position has some evidence to support it, but has been greatly weakened by recent findings damaging to the contention that mental growth is largely independent of social and educational influences. As a number of psychologists have suggested, a constant I.Q. is not necessarily hereditarily determined. A relatively constant environment might also make for relatively uniform test scores. As Freeman [13] has said, "Constancy in the I.Q. would only be evidence that the I.Q. is determined by heredity if the environment fluctuated enough to lead us to expect marked fluctuation in the I.Q. It is probably more common for the environment of the child to be relatively constant throughout his school career. If this is true, constancy of the I.Q. might merely reflect constancy instead of the effect of the environment." As later discussions in the present chapter will show, I.Q. scores have been known to fluctuate markedly with major and extended changes in the child's intellectual environment. Besides, an individual's mental test scores are conditioned by the extent to which he is motivated, as well as by the capacity he may possess. Industry and the desire to learn are largely functions of a person's social, economic, and intellectual environment.

Even the older studies showed fluctuations when individuals were retested with standard mental tests. The variations were, however, sufficiently limited and centralized to be considered relatively constant. About half the cases varied up or down from 0 to 5 points. Approximately 20 per cent of the cases devi-

[13] F. N. Freeman, "The Effect of Environment on Intelligence," *School and Society*, 31: 623-631 (1930).

ated more than 10 points, a change which was considered significant. When the variations were studied by the correlation method, the coefficients ranged from about .80 to .95, depending on the abilities and homogeneity of the individuals tested. The modest fluctuations found were, as a rule, ascribed to conditions related to the administration of the tests. These included clerical errors, the personality of the examiner, the interest of the examinee, language handicaps, and limitations inherent in the test. Seldom were environmental factors credited with influencing test scores. The more recent investigations of mental development have, however, indicated the influence of favorable and barren educational opportunities on the child's intellectual status. These will be examined in some detail.

Evidence from Twin Studies

Solution of the difficult nature-nurture problem is complicated by the difficulty of holding either of these factors constant while observing the influence of the other. There appears to be no possibility of controlling children's environments in such a way as to determine the actual contribution of inheritance to their development. It is possible, however, to study differences exhibited by "identical" or like twins, whose gene-inheritance was presumably the same.

Difficulties Encountered in Studying Twins.—The difference between identical (monozygotic) and fraternal (dizygotic) twins can be clarified by stating that the former are the result of the fertilization of one ovum which subsequently split into two similar ova, and that fraternal offspring develop when two different ova are fertilized by two equally distinct male sperms. It is obvious, thus, that identical twins develop from one set of chromosomes and genes. This is why they are considered alike in inheritance. Fraternal or unlike twins develop from different sets of chromosomes and are thus no different from ordinary brothers and sisters (siblings) in the matter of inheritance. They are born at approximately the same time but, like siblings, do not necessarily look alike and may be of either the same or the opposite sex.

Since they are offspring from the same ovum, invariably of the same sex, and nearly always enclosed in one chorion sack (membrane) with one placenta, identical twins are evidently alike in inheritance. Such children provide an opportunity for studying the influence of diverse environments, since in their case heredity can be held constant for two persons. It is natural, thus, that identical twins should be utilized as avenues for the determination of the effects of so-called original nature on the intellectual, as well as other forms of development in children. This is one of the most promising methods of attack on the nature-nurture problem because it makes possible the control of the hereditary factor.

However, a number of difficulties confront the investigator in the identical-twin field. First of all, since only about 25 per cent of all twins are identical, it is difficult to secure enough cases for study to satisfy the requirements of scientific accuracy. Furthermore, a relatively small percentage of identical twins are available for extended study in diverse social and economic environments. There is also the problem of ascertaining, in a thorough manner, in precisely what respects environments differ in their effects on children's mental development. It may be that apparently superior homes are sometimes less influential intellectually than those of a more humble but mentally stimulating variety.

Considerable difficulty has also been encountered in determining whether twins located many years after birth are actually identical. Some investigators doubt whether like twins can be detected in later life, but Newman [14] is generally regarded as having developed a technique for such determination. It should also be remembered that prenatal (congenital) influences might bring about dissimilarities even in offspring of identical inheritance. It is not uncommon for one of a pair of like twins to be born dead. In spite of these hazards and complexities, the identical-twin method of studying environmental influences has proved to be a useful one.

[14] H. H. Newman, Studies of Human Twins, I: "Methods of Diagnosing Monozygotic and Dizygotic Twins," *Biologic Bulletin*, 55: 283-297 (1928).

Evidence from Objective Studies of Twins.—It has long been noticed that the closer people are related the higher are coefficients of correlation (degrees of resemblance) calculated from their intelligence test scores. Whereas coefficients of relationship between unrelated children approximate zero, those for cousins run about .25, for siblings around .50, for fraternal or unlike twins about .70 or .75, and for identical twins around .90. Many investigators believed that these increasingly higher figures were due to the mechanisms of heredity. It has been pointed out that identical twins are the recipients of a more common inheritance than fraternal twins and that fraternals probably have a more similar heredity than siblings. It is true that duplicate twins have an identical heritage but fraternal twins apparently have nothing more in common in this respect than brothers and sisters born at different times.

It could be assumed, thus, that the higher intellectual resemblances noted between fraternal twins is associated with the more similar environment which they experience because of their more similar age. It would be premature to claim that nurture is definitely more influential here than nature, but the likelihood that the fraternals will be in the same school grade, have the same teachers, and have identical friends leads rather naturally to the expectation that they will be more alike than ordinary siblings in intellectual and other characteristics. The even more similar environment usually experienced by identical twins makes it plausible that they should exhibit a more marked degree of intellectual likeness. This interpretation is, of course, subject to debate since it has not been definitely proved.

In a study of Canadian children Wingfield and Sandiford [15] secured a coefficient of correlation of .72 between mental test results for 57 pairs of fraternal twins and a coefficient of .91 between 45 pairs of identical twins. Since the reliability coefficient of mental test scores does not exceed this figure appreciably, a relationship of .91 represents a very high degree of intellectual resemblance between the like twin pairs. It would be logical to conclude that for this group each individual re-

[15] A. H. Wingfield and Peter Sandiford, "Twins and Orphans," *Journal of Educational Psychology,* 19 : 410-423 (1928).

sembled his twin practically as much as himself. These data indicate the measurable difference in intellectual resemblance between fraternal and identical twins.

Merriman [16] has investigated the differences between intelligence test scores of twins of the same and the opposite sex. He found that unlike-sex pairs resembled each other to the extent of .50, that all twin pairs (both sexes) correlated with a figure of .78, and that like-sex pairs produced a coefficient of .87. Because of the more similar environment and experiences usually encountered by twins of the same sex, these figures have led to further debates concerning the relative influences of heredity and environment. Like-sex twins of the identical variety receive a similar biological inheritance, but this cannot be said of fraternal twins of the same sex. In spite of this fact, fraternal twins exhibit much higher intellectual resemblances, as revealed by mental test scores, than do siblings. Thorndike has suggested that heredity is responsible for this difference, but his opponents reason that a more similar environment for fraternals is the logical answer to the data secured.

A thorough statistical comparison of the physical and psychological characteristics of 52 pairs of like-sex fraternal twins and 50 pairs of identical twins has been made by Holzinger [17] and associates. In this study twins were judged as being identical on the basis of quantitative physical measurements and the presence of reversed body symmetry or what is called "mirror-imaging." The resemblances may be seen in Table 2.

A good idea of the mental differences among identical twins, fraternal twins, and siblings may be gained from the above and other correlation data. The case for heredity has been made, to some extent at least, by the figures for identical twins. The significant influence of environmental factors has been shown by the higher correlations for individuals enjoying more identical social and educational living conditions. Holzinger has concluded from his investigation that nature and nurture exert approximately equal influence on twin development and

16 C. Merriman, *The Intellectual Resemblance of Twins,* Psychological Monographs, Vol. 33, No. 5 (1924).
17 K. J. Holzinger, "The Relative Effect of Nature and Nurture Influences on Twin Differences," *Journal of Educational Psychology,* 20 : 241-248 (1929).

TABLE 2. CORRELATIONS INDICATING SIMILARITIES BETWEEN IDENTICAL
AND FRATERNAL TWINS

Measures	Identical	Fraternal
Standing height	.93 ± .01	.65 ± .05
Binet I.Q.	.88 ± .02	.63 ± .06
Otis I.Q.	.92 ± .01	.62 ± .06
Word meaning	.86 ± .02	.56 ± .06
Nature study	.77 ± .04	.65 ± .05
History and literature	.82 ± .03	.67 ± .05
Spelling	.87 ± .02	.73 ± .04
Woodworth-Mathews (neurotic inventory)	.56 ± .07	.37 ± .08

(Adapted from K. J. Holzinger, "The Relative Effect of Nature and Nurture Influences on Twin Differences," *Journal of Educational Psychology*, 20:241-248 (1929).)

twin differences. In a study to be reported later, Holzinger has, however, suggested that environmental factors may overshadow the differences produced by genetic (inherited) influences.

Studies of the Dionne quintuplets show that they, too, differ in some respects. In spite of their presumably identical inheritance, these children display mental and emotional differences that Blatz [18] and his associates regard as being environmentally determined. Comprehensive records of their education, daily routine, and behavior suggest that the quints are influenced by slight differences in environment and experience. Each has the other four to whom she must adjust and each encounters somewhat different emotional and social problems. The quints are said to have been slightly retarded in the speech function but this is a common experience among children of multiple birth, who usually find it possible to get along without speech intercourse with adults longer than single-born children. Studies of the Dionne quintuplets have not, however, been carried to a sufficient extent to indicate the degree of their development in comparison to other children of their age.

Testimony from Identical Twins Reared Apart.—It will be seen that up to this point investigations of both fraternal and identical twins have failed to show the extent to which the

[18] W. E. Blatz and D. A. Millichamp, *The Mental Growth of the Dionne Quintuplets*, Child Development Series, No. 16, Univ. of Toronto Press, 1937.

environment affects intellectual and social growth. This outcome can be explained by the fact that most of the studies were concerned with twins living together who were experiencing relatively similar educational and social advantages. Crucial evidence regarding the influence of environmental conditions on the development of children of like heredity must come from investigations of identical twins who have been separated for a number of years. A fair number of such studies have been made and published by competent investigators. These studies have suggested some of the effects on development of general environmental differences, but have presented little evidence regarding the influences of *specific* or detailed environmental experiences on mental, emotional, and social growth. Nevertheless, valuable information concerning the relative effects of nature and nurture may be secured through the medium of carefully conducted identical twin investigations.

Insomuch as Newman [19] has been a leader in this field, we shall present two of his pairs of monozygotic or identical twins. One of Newman's earlier pairs, twin girls A and O, lived in widely separated homes from the time they were eighteen months of age until they were reunited at about eighteen years. During the time in question twin A lived in a crowded, middle-class section of London where the ravages of the first World War resulted in a number of deprivations. Her elementary education, which was of a home-arts nature, was frequently interrupted by war activities. In the meantime she was the victim of a number of childhood diseases which included measles, tonsillitis, whooping cough, and scarlet fever. Twin O was adopted by a socially well-accepted family and taken to the quiet of Chelsea, Ontario (Canada) to live. Unlike her less fortunate sister, O went to school in an uncrowded environment and enjoyed the advantages of a thoroughgoing academic education. In the end both girls experienced nine years of schooling, which culminated in a secretarial course leading to employment as a stenographer.

[19] H. H. Newman, "Mental and Physical Traits of Identical Twins Reared Apart," *Journal of Heredity*, 20: 49-64, 97-104, 153-166 (1929).

When studied by Newman and his assistants, this identical pair were found to be very similar in temperament and emotional status, but considerably unlike in educational and intellectual development. Twin O, who was reared in an apparently superior environment in North America, surpassed her London educated sister by one year and eleven months in mental age (M.A.) and one year and seven months in educational age (E.A.). On the Stanford-Binet mental test O exceeded her less developed twin by 12 I.Q. points, and on the International Group test she excelled by 62 score points. It is evident from these data that marked differences in education and social environment can bring about a difference in intellectual achievement in two individuals presumably similarly endowed by nature. It is also clear that apparently dissimilar environments need not result in noticeable differences in emotionality or temperament. Unlike environmental conditions may evidently result in the development of both likenesses and differences in identical twins.

In the most comprehensive investigation of twins yet carried out, Newman, Freeman, and Holzinger [20] reported data for 50 like-sex fraternal twins and 50 identical twins reared together. They also presented important evidence regarding differences between 19 pairs of identical twins reared apart. The majority of the latter twin pairs had been separated for a long period of years (from 11 to 53) and were studied when they were fully developed adults. More than half had been separated during the first year of life and seven others had been parted before they were five. No outstanding differences in religion or racial composition were present among these twins and the range of home environments was not radical.

The outcome of one pair of identical sisters, H and G, in this series of investigations was especially noteworthy. G's early years were spent with a family that moved about so much that she did not go beyond the third grade in school. She was able, however, to prepare herself for a career as a saleswoman and later as an office worker. She was required to work hard

[20] H. H. Newman, F. N. Freeman, and K. J. Holzinger, *Twins; A Study of Heredity and Environment.* Chicago, Univ. of Chicago Press, 1937.

and never enjoyed the advantages of economic security or cultural opportunities. Twin H was reared in a modest home, but was given much better educational advantages and ultimately finished a college course. She subsequently became a teacher of history and English. H also enjoyed many social and cultural opportunities.

At thirty-five both girls were married and the mothers of families. Both were considered normal and reasonably well adjusted. G, however, lacked social poise and was not successful in competing with women who knew the details of proper grooming and social entertaining. H, on the other hand, was unusually confident and charming in manner. She was also an excellent conversationalist and leader in social affairs. In harmony with her superior advantages, H was three years and ten months, or 24 I.Q. points, superior to her sister G. She had many of the characteristics of a much more intelligent woman than her less fortunate sister.

Not all identical twins reared apart show marked intellectual differences, even when their respective educational environments are diverse in this respect. Both Müller [21] and Burks [22] have reported such cases. However, one can usually discern certain factors in the home or school conditions of such investigations that might account for the apparent discrepancies found. In other instances the inconsistency is not easily explained.

Interpretations Growing Out of Twin Studies.—It is not easy to generalize concerning the effects on intellectual development of diverse environments. It is possible, however, to discern certain trends from such studies as Newman's (and collaborators) and the others mentioned. It can be concluded, for example, that physical traits are not often appreciably affected by the environment, that mental development and school achievement are noticeably influenced by differing environments, and that temperament and personality are affected most of all by diverse living conditions.

[21] H. J. Müller, "Mental Traits and Heredity," *Journal of Heredity,* 16 : 433-448 (1925).
[22] Barbara S. Burks, "Personality Determinants in a New Case of Identical Twins Reared Apart," *Psychological Bulletin,* 57 : 522 (1940).

In the case of identical twins, some have turned out to be strikingly alike in nearly all respects while others have developed extensive differences in both intelligence and personality traits. According to Newman, his 19 pairs of identicals reared apart manifested an average difference of 8.21 I.Q. points, with a range of differences from 0 to 24 points. These figures are slightly larger than those obtaining before the publication of Newman's classical study. Schwesinger [23] has estimated that the former average difference for identicals reared apart was 7.7, with a range of 0 to 17 points.

In summarizing these and other findings concerning the 19 twin pairs under discussion Curti [24] writes, "On the extent and personal significance for the individuals concerned of the unfavorable effect of poor social status or poor family background the authors do not dwell, but the facts speak eloquently of the important influence for general development of a good and happy social environment. When we see two people whom we know to be equally gifted by nature, so different in their response to the world and in their ability to enjoy life, we need no statistics to prove to us the importance of environment. Had some of these separated twins been brought up in a remote hamlet in East Tennessee or in certain orphanages, the differences both in intelligence and social adaptability would almost certainly have been more striking."

An examination of the 19 twin pairs in Newman's study reveals that significant differences in mental ability were *always in the same direction* as differences in educational opportunity. Only one case showed a large difference in education that was not accompanied by a similar difference in ability. Marked differences in mental ability were in every case associated with similarly marked differences in educational and other opportunities. In fact, differences in educational advantages, as rated by five independent judges, correlated .79 with Stanford-Binet I.Q. scores. The relationship between educational ratings (en-

23 Gladys C. Schwesinger, *Heredity and Environment,* New York, The Macmillan Co., 1933, pp. 225-231.
24 Margaret W. Curti, *Child Psychology,* New York, Longmans, Green & Co., 1938, p. 175.

vironment) and educational age on the Stanford Achievement Test was even higher, being .90.

Figures for unseparated and separated identical twins suggest further the influence of environmental differences. As Table 3 shows, whereas physical traits are hardly affected by

TABLE 3. CORRELATIONS FOR UNSEPARATED AND SEPARATED IDENTICAL TWINS

Trait	Unseparated Identicals	Separated Identicals
Standing height	.98	.96
Sitting height	.96	.96
Weight	.97	.88
Head length	.91	.91
Head width	.90	.88
Binet mental age	.92	.63
Binet I.Q.	.91	.67
Otis I.Q.	.92	.72
Stanford Achievement	.95	.50
Woodworth-Mathews	.56	.58

(Adapted from H. H. Newman, F. N. Freeman, and K. J. Holzinger, *Twins; A Study of Heredity and Environment,* Chicago, Univ. of Chicago Press, 1937, p. 347.)

diverse living conditions, mental ability as indicated by the I.Q. shows noticeable differences in varying environments. Identical twins who grow up together apparently do not differ as much in intelligence and school achievement as those who are separated for a period of years. In the case of nervous symptoms, differences in living conditions are evidently not influential. Perhaps all the homes were fairly similar in their effects in this area of development. At any rate, it seems clear that since appreciable differences in intelligence occurred in a setting where the environments of the separated twins were said to be not greatly dissimilar, living conditions operating over a period of years may influence an individual's intellectual status noticeably. As a number of investigators have noted, one accurately measured case of marked difference in intelligence between identical twins reared apart would indicate the possibilities of nurture. This would be especially true in cases where aspects of intellectual development most susceptible to environmental influence are the recipients of favorable conditions.

It is well to be careful about assuming that because children have been separated, their intellectual environments are necessarily totally different. It is entirely possible that homes of similar social and economic level may differ greatly in ability and willingness to present children with the detailed patterns of experience necessary to insure later success with mental tests. It is also possible that what appear to be similar environments, even within one home, may possess decided differences of an unnoticed nature that result in dissimilar mental development. Students of child psychology have only recently begun to develop measures of *specific environmental factors* designed to detect these differences.

The Testimony of Barren Environment Studies

The nature-nurture controversy has long been concerned with the question of whether country children are as bright intellectually as city boys and girls. It has been recognized that country children and youths know many things that are foreign to their city "cousins," but students of child development have wondered to what extent they could compete with the latter on tests of intelligence. Thus a number of studies designed to measure the comparative mental ability of rural and urban children have been made. Most of these agree that rural children are more retarded than urban children in their ability to cope with mental tests.

Comparisons of Urban and Rural Children —In a comparison of the mental test scores of 321 country children with city children of the same age, Pressey and Thomas [25] found the latter distinctly superior. According to their figures, the percentage of rural children of from ten to thirteen years of age exceeding the average for city children of similar ages was only 29, 33, 21, and 25, respectively. Children from barren and hilly districts were also intellectually inferior to those residing in

[25] S. L. Pressey and J. B. Thomas, "A Study of Country Children in (1) a Good and (2) a Poor Farming District, by Means of a Group Scale of Intelligence," *Journal of Applied Psychology*, 3 : 283-286 (1919).

more prosperous farming districts. A similar situation was found in England where Thomson [26] measured the relative ability of city and country dwellers in Northumberland County. This investigator was inclined to believe that cities make the better showing because they drain off the more superior intellects in their vicinity.

Book [27] made a number of comparisons between rural and urban high school seniors in Indiana. His findings confirmed the intellectual superiority of city youth. This difference held in all sections of the state. However, students in the southern part of the state made relatively lower average scores than those in the north. This finding has been regarded both as the result of the immigration of inferior white stock to Southern Indiana and as the result of barren educational opportunities.

In their comparative study of rural and urban children, Baldwin, Fillmore, and Hadley [28] found no significant difference in intelligence between them *at the lower age levels*. Until approximately the age of three the country children did as well on the tests as those living in cities. However, from the fifth year on they fell behind on the Detroit Kindergarten test. Both groups did about equally well in manipulating concrete materials. According to the authors, the inferiority of the country children in the verbal tests could have been due to a lack of suitable pictures, books, and other intellectually stimulating factors.

Earlier interpretations of the uniform intellectual superiority of urban children have stressed the probability that the country's best stocks have been migrating steadily to the cities. Investigators of former decades regarded this logic as constituting a plausible explanation. But the question has arisen whether city children are not actually stimulated to greater achievements by superior educational opportunities. Thus this controversy again raises the long debated issue of whether intellectual ability is

[26] G. W. Thomson, "The Northumberland Mental Tests," *British Journal of Psychology*, 12: 202-222 (1921).
[27] W. F. Book, *The Intelligence of High School Seniors*, Boston, Ginn & Co., 1922.
[28] B. T. Baldwin, E. A. Fillmore, and L. Hadley, *Farm Children: An Investigation of Rural Child Life in Selected Areas of Iowa*, New York, D. Appleton-Century Co., Inc., 1930.

largely innate (inherited) or whether at any given point in a child's life it is the natural result of the specific educational advantages he has enjoyed.   It may be that the average city offers relatively superior opportunities for the mastery of the more abstract and linguistic skills so essential to the comprehension of mental test problems and questions.   Since the previously mentioned investigation of Indiana seniors indicated that the intellectual superiority of city youths became less as the amount of training experienced by their country "cousins" increased, some have ascribed the superiority of city children to superior training.

Evidence from Barren Environment Studies.—There is available considerable evidence suggesting that a child's mental ability is influenced both positively and negatively by the kind of educational environment encountered.   Much of the evidence points to the intellectually depressing effects of barren and isolated living conditions.   The presentation of a few investigations in this field will show the extent to which children's I.Q. scores are influenced by the type of environment in which they live.

One of the first studies was made by Gordon [29] in connection with the mental development of English canalboat and gypsy children.   Gordon first administered Stanford-Binet tests to a group of children living with their parents on canalboats. He found in substance that whereas the I.Q.'s of those under six years of age ranged between 90 and 100, children over nine averaged less than 70 I.Q.   The latter score, which is considered on the borderline of feeblemindedness, was thus made by children who had attended school only about 5 per cent of the normal time for English children.   Gordon found a correlation of —.755 between the children's age and their I.Q.'s.   Gypsy children, who had received about 35 per cent of the usual amount of school experience, showed a lower negative correlation of —.566.   This means, of course, that the older these underprivileged children became, the lower were their mental test scores.   The investigator did not believe that the children in

---

[29] H. Gordon, *Mental and Scholastic Tests Among Retarded Children,* Bureau of Education, Educational Pamphlets (London), No. 44, 1923.

question became progressively duller with age. He concluded, rather, that mental tests do not measure native ability independently of educational opportunities.

An investigation by Stroud [30] of 1,079 public school children in primitive districts of the Blue Ridge mountains also showed a decline in I.Q. scores with advancing age. The average for first graders was 90 I.Q., but the scores for each succeeding grade fell until the seventh and eighth, where the average I.Q. declined to the low 70's. The same situation was found by Wheeler [31] in the case of Eastern Tennessee mountain children. In a test of (Dearborn scale) 1,147 children he secured scores ranging from 94.7 at age six to 73.5 at age sixteen. A midpoint of 80.0 I.Q. was found at age eleven. In this instance a follow-up investigation, carried out ten years later, showed the children in the same locality to be eight months younger chronologically and nine months older mentally for their grades. However, in spite of improved social and educational conditions, the pupils still experienced a decrease of approximately 2 I.Q. points per year from ages six to sixteen. In a study employing a reversal of the above procedures, Nietz[32] noted that formal city schooling raised the intelligence test scores of a group of pupils from backward mountain districts. One year (in some instances two or three) of high school training enabled a group of Tennessee pupils from isolated districts to raise their I.Q.'s from approximately 70 to normal standing.

Perhaps the most extensive study of isolated children was the one by Sherman and Henry [33] in mountain hollows (Virginia) not far from the Nation's capital at Washington, D. C. They, too, found that in primitive and isolated communities, five- and six-year-old children enjoyed normal I.Q.'s, but that their older siblings earned progressively lower mental test scores as their ages advanced. These investigators made a careful

[30] J. B. Stroud, *Educational Psychology*, New York, The Macmillan Co., 1935, pp. 252-253.

[31] L. R. Wheeler, "The Intelligence of East Tennessee Mountain Children," *Journal of Educational Psychology*, 23 : 351-370 (1932). Also, by the same author, "A Comparative Study of the Intelligence of East Tennessee Mountain Children," *Journal of Educational Psychology*, 33 : 321-333 (1942).

[32] J. A. Nietz, "What Does the Terman Group Test of Mental Ability Measure?" *Univ. of Pittsburgh, School of Education Journal*, Jan.-Feb. 1928.

[33] Mandel Sherman and T. R. Henry, *Hollow Folk*, New York, T. Y. Crowell Co., 1933, pp. 121-137, 193-208.

check of the extremely primitive social and educational conditions under which the children lived and reported that the less progressive and more isolated the district, the greater was the decline in intelligence quotients. The older children were inferior to their younger classmates even in tests of performance (form boards). The investigators do not believe that the evidence points to inherent differences in intellectual ability between children of different ages, or between city and country children. They reason that the apparent differences may be to a great extent spurious in the sense that they are caused by the absence in the children's environment of educational opportunities essential to intellectual development as measured by mental tests.

The inference may be drawn from studies of this kind that mental ability, at least as indicated by test scores, is not determined primarily by inherited factors. Apparently favorable and unfavorable environmental conditions have much to do with a child's intellectual status. This view represents an optimistic attitude toward the improvability of children's intelligence and suggests the importance of adequate schools and other educational opportunities. It does not, however, settle the question of the inheritance of mental ability. It is obvious that even innate mental capacity would be handicapped in its expression by markedly limited educational facilities.

Further Influences of Limited Opportunities.—An attempt has been made by a group of investigators at the University of Iowa [34] to compare the I.Q. changes in two groups of orphanage children, ages eighteen months to five and one-half years, who did and did not attend a model preschool. The orphanage selected for study was described as being decidedly non-stimulating intellectually. Thirty-five children were housed in one cottage under the care of an untrained matron who provided no play materials, pictures, or other educational facilities. The development of each child who attended the preschool (experi-

[34] Harold M. Skeels, Ruth Updegraff, Beth L. Wellman, and H. M. Williams, "A Study of Environmental Stimulation," *Univ. of Iowa Studies in Child Welfare,* Vol. 15, No. 4 (1938).

mental) was compared with that of another child (control) of similar sex, age, I.Q., and length of residence in the orphanage. In the end 46 preschool and 44 control children were studied over a period of three years. Both groups lived in the same barren environment, but the members of one attended the model orphanage preschool.

On the average, children who attended the preschool gained in I.Q. points. Their average gains were also proportional to the number of days spent in the school. Those who attended 400 or more days achieved an average gain of 4.6 I.Q. points. The control group, which did not attend the preschool, lost an equal amount, or 4.6 I.Q. points, during the same 400 days. The Iowa psychologists have been inclined, however, to stress the large *individual* losses experienced by certain of the children in the control group. It is their contention that since several originally normal (I.Q. scores) children declined to a borderline status below I.Q. 70, a markedly barren environment can be expected to bring about such a result. Evidence is introduced to show that one child lost 43 I.Q. points (103 to 60), another 37 points (98 to 61), a third 24 points (86 to 62), and a fourth 23 points (83 to 60). These and other figures have led the authors of the Iowa study to conclude that when environmental conditions are especially unfavorable over a period of years, I.Q. changes from average intelligence to apparent feebleminded status may be expected.

A number of psychologists [35] have criticized the Iowa orphanage study on the grounds that selected cases favorable to the influence of environment have been overemphasized, that evidence damaging to the authors' point of view has been suppressed, and that the experiment was not carefully conducted. It has been pointed out, for instance, that while a few children did decline from 25 to 43 I.Q. points in the barren environment of the orphanage, the average loss was only 4.6 I.Q. points.

[35] Quinn McNemar, "A Critical Examination of the University of Iowa Studies of Environmental Influence Upon the I.Q.," *Psychological Bulletin*, 37:63-92 (1940); Florence L. Goodenough, "Look to the Evidence! A Critique of Recent Experiments on Raising the I.Q.," *Educational Method*, 19:73-79 (1939); Lewis M. Terman, "Intelligence: Its Nature and Nurture," *Thirty-Ninth Yearbook, National Society for the Study of Education*, 1940, Part I, pp. 460-467.

Furthermore, critics have shown that five out of seven of the children whose mental deterioration seemed to be so great were less than twenty-four months of age when diagnosed as "average" intellectually. It is known, of course, that infant mental tests are the least reliable of all such instruments. Even with the use of these tests, seven control (did not attend preschool) children gained more than 14 I.Q. points. It is believed, thus, that although a number of children in this experiment declined markedly in test intelligence, evidence for the influence of the barren environment involved is conflicting. There is need for more such investigations emphasizing better techniques for testing infants, more adequate sampling methods, more refined statistical procedures, and more thorough attention to the influence of what is known as the phenomenon of *regression*.

Contrasting Interpretations of Evidence.—The general evidence from barren environment investigations seems clear. Because of their weighty emphasis upon schooling, especially language skills, mental tests are more difficult for rural than for city children. It appears that the more adequate schooling and cultural contacts provided by the typical city home and school enable children to develop the verbal and other language abilities necessary for success with mental tests. This seems especially true in the case of older children whose age presupposes several years of formal education.

Some investigators believe that mental ability is biologically inherited and that fluctuations in I.Q. scores merely mean temporary environmentally induced retardations or accelerations of native capacity to learn. Others feel that variations in I.Q. of children from different social-economic levels of society and of country versus city pupils may be accounted for largely by differences in opportunity *per se*. The latter conclusion has been reached by a number of students of child development.[36] These individuals reason that the progressive decline in I.Q. scores so evident in barren environment studies, when not due to errors of measurement or statistical procedures, may logically be

---

[36] See, for example, Walter S. Neff, "Socio-economic Status and Intelligence: A Critical Survey," *Psychological Bulletin*, 35 : 727-757 (1938).

ascribed to the intellectually stifling influences of such surroundings. This means, of course, that if a child is to be successful with mental tests he must be exposed to such academic schooling, language experiences, and other sources of information as the tests require.

A careful study of the evidence marshaled in this section apparently leads to the conclusion that children in diverse communities should be compared with norms (averages) for *their own group*. Such a practice would be fair to the children and consistent with the logic of comparative testing. It is evident that, as measured by tests, mental ability is not based on innate power to learn that matures automatically and that can express itself in spite of adverse educational conditions. It seems equally clear, however, that the idea of general inheritance of potential mental ability has not been disproved. Nearly everyone is aware of the existence of feebleminded children whose defective status defies efforts at improvement and intellectually brilliant youngsters whose unusual capacities it is almost impossible to explain.

Neither has it been shown that children of any social-economic status can decline to feeblemindedness or rise to the level of genius. Extravagant claims of this nature are not supported by evidence and should thus be avoided. The very concept of comparative testing involves reasonably common experiences on the part of children whose futures are to be determined on the bases of the intellectual ability they display.

The Effects of Foster Home Placement

To be sure of the relative influence of the general environment on I.Q. scores, it would be necessary in any given instance to know the potentiality for intellectual development resident in the child's inheritance. Since such knowledge can obviously not be obtained, it becomes necessary to secure evidence concerning the nature-nurture problem from whatever sources are available. Having canvassed the twin field and the evidence for barren environments we come to a study of the effects on intellectual development of foster home placement.

Evidence from the Chicago Investigation.—Freeman [37] and his collaborators conducted a pioneer study that has done much to stimulate interest in the influence of foster home adoption on the intellectual development of children. These investigators abandoned the difficult problem of determining so-called "innate" intelligence and proceeded to measure 401 children's intellectual status before and after placement in two types of foster homes. The study was designed to provide evidence concerning the much debated question of whether I.Q. scores remain relatively constant or whether they fluctuate with prolonged social and intellectual changes in the environment.

A summary of the Chicago investigation will disclose the extent of its findings. One group of 74 children for whom mental test scores had been obtained were placed in homes of known cultural and educational status. At the end of four years those placed in superior homes showed an average gain of 10.4 I.Q. points, while those placed in more modest homes improved to the extent of 5 I.Q. points. Thus the average gain for the entire group of children was 7.5 I.Q. points. For the most part, children placed at an early age gained more in test scores than those placed at a more mature age.

A number of other findings indicated the extent of the influence exerted by foster homes on the intellectual status of adopted children. It was learned, for example, that unrelated children whose mental test scores would normally be unlike developed a resemblance (correlation) of from .25 to .37 after living together four years in a foster home. On the other hand, a group of siblings whose I.Q. scores usually correlate approximately .50, dropped to a coefficient of .25 when separated before six years of age and reared in foster homes for a similar four-year period. The I.Q.'s of the adopted children also became more like those of their foster parents in proportion to the length of time spent in their homes. During the four-year adoption period, original coefficients of .34 for this relationship rose to .52. This finding suggests that an approximately common

[37] F. N. Freeman, K. J. Holzinger, and B. C. Mitchell, "The Influence of Environment on Intelligence, School Achievement, and Conduct of Foster Children," *Twenty-Seventh Yearbook, National Society for the Study of Education*, 1928, Part I, pp. 103-211.

environment exerts a leveling influence as far as test-intelligence is concerned.

An important phase of the Chicago study concerned itself with the intellectual status of 26 children whose parents had been diagnosed as feebleminded. After a foster home stay of four years these children achieved an average I.Q. of 81, and all but one made a score of 70 or above. Since an I.Q. of 70 is commonly considered the differentiating point between feeble-mindedness and the lower levels of "dull normal" status, it is evident that most of these children were either not feebleminded originally or that their foster homes exerted a beneficent influence intellectually. Their average I.Q. score of 81 was much higher than former evidence would lead one to expect.

In the end, the relationship between home rating as determined by material, cultural, and educational advantages and intelligence test scores of foster children turned out to be .48. In the case of the 74 children for whom preplacement I.Q. scores were available, four years in a superior home resulted in a final average I.Q. score of 95, and the same length of time spent in a relatively poorer foster home eventuated in an average I.Q. of 86. Freeman and his associates do not believe that these differences in intelligence can be accounted for by the claim that the brighter children were selected by the more superior homes and foster parents. They have, in fact, suggested that the higher test scores made by children in the superior homes represent significant evidence of the influence for intellectual growth of a favorable environment.

Like all nature-nurture studies, this investigation has been criticized on several counts. First, it has been pointed out that more definite results would have been secured if original I.Q. test scores had been obtained for all the children concerned, especially those from supposedly feebleminded parents. As suggested above, the chief objection has been that selective factors may have operated to bring about the adoption of the brighter children in the more superior homes, thus obviating the likelihood that very favorable environmental opportunities produced the relatively higher test scores noted. Critics have pointed out that the original coefficient of relationship between foster parents and adopted children in this group was .34, whereas in the population at large it would normally be zero. It is on this point that they base their claim of selective placement.

Evidence from the Stanford Study.—An investigation similar in many respects to the Chicago study has been reported by the late Barbara Burks, formerly of Stanford University. Burks [38] made a critical study of the mental development of 214 California children who had been placed in foster homes by child-placement agencies before they were one year of age. This investigator made a number of measurements of the children's home environment, as well as of their intellectual progress. Mental ages, vocabulary ages, and incomes of parents were ascertained in an effort to select a homogeneous group of homes for the foster children. To secure a comparative check on mental development Burks included a control group of 105 children of similar social-economic status living with their own parents. She felt that the two groups of similar home environment would provide a basis for determining the relative influences of nature and nurture.

The investigation disclosed that in the end foster children's I.Q. scores correlated .42 with a combination of father's mental age, father's vocabulary age, mother's vocabulary age, and family income. I.Q.'s of the control children, who had been living with their own parents, correlated with the same home factors to the extent of .61. Furthermore, the foster children's I.Q.'s had risen from an assumed average of around 103 to an average of 107.4. Since the control children improved from the same estimated 103 I.Q. average to one of 115.4 during the same period of time, Burks concluded that the difference in gain must be attributable to differences in native ability. On the basis of these data, and in view of the fact that variations of around five I.Q. points are to be expected in individual retests, this investigator came to the conclusion that home environment is much less efficacious than heredity in the determination of mental development. Burks aroused a veritable storm of criti-

[38] Barbara S. Burks, "The Relative Influence of Nature and Nurture upon Mental Development," *Twenty-Seventh Yearbook, National Society for the Study of Education,* 1928, Part I, pp. 219-316.

cism by announcing that "Home environment contributes about 17 per cent of the variance in I.Q." and that "The total contribution of heredity (i.e., of innate and heritable factors) is probably not far from 75 or 80 per cent."

Conflicting Interpretations of Data.—In spite of the fact that Freeman and Burks carried out very similar investigations and that they found almost identical I.Q. increases in superior home environments, their interpretations have been considerably at variance. It seems evident from Burks' conclusions that she had been influenced by the hereditarian view so characteristic at the time of the psychology department of the institution which she represented. She apparently regarded her findings as being thoroughly in harmony with belief in the inheritance of mental ability. She has consistently maintained that the most favorable or unfavorable environmental conditions can raise or depress the I.Q. a maximum of only 20 points. Burks has claimed that "heredity can produce alike the idiot of twenty and the genius of two-hundred I.Q." As for the environment, it is said to contribute a mere average variance of 3 to 6 I.Q. points. On this basis the chief function of the environment is that of providing a medium in which the dominant factor, heredity, may have an opportunity to exert its superior influence.

The interpretations advanced by Freeman reflect by contrast the view of a psychologist who apparently appreciates the evidence for hereditary forces but who is willing to explore the possibilities of superior homes and educational facilities for the social and intellectual development of children. According to him, the I.Q. gains in the Chicago investigation indicate the importance of superior cultural opportunities, of early placement in the case of foster children, of the educational level of parents, and of nurtural factors in general. Freeman's conclusions strike an optimistic note and suggest that children with an apparently unfavorable heredity may, if properly assisted, compete successfully with the typical run of school children. He believes that even greater mental development of dormant ability may be anticipated when the exact environmental factors requisite to such growth become better known.

Leahy [39] has endeavored to check the discrepancy between the Stanford and Chicago studies by means of an investigation in which the factor of selective placement was apparently carefully controlled. She compared the mental development of a group of 194 children who had been placed in foster homes before they were six months of age with children living in their own homes who were matched with them on the basis of age and occupational status of parents. In the end, Leahy found only low correlations between I.Q. scores of adopted children and their foster parents. When the children's I.Q.'s were correlated with the cultural status of their homes the coefficient for foster children was .21 and that for "own" children .51. These correlations led Leahy to conclude that, in the Chicago study at least, the factor of selection exerted a more significant influence than had formerly been thought. It must be recognized, however, that this investigator was not able to match the two groups of children on many important traits that might condition desire to learn, also that she could have little knowledge of the specific factors in each child's environment which influenced its development most effectively. The outcome of this study has been regarded as somewhat inconclusive because of the statistical difficulties involved and because of its divergence from the evidence of so many other nature-nurture investigations.

It is believed that further progress in foster home adoption studies must await the development of better methods of evaluating the effects on intellectual growth of various aspects of a child's environment. It is one thing to claim that a child is enjoying a general so-called "superior environment" and another to show the *specific* effects on development of such home factors as books, pictures, stories, pets, trips, educational games, blocks, and assistance in the mastery of the tools of reading. So far, most investigators have lumped all social, cultural, economic, and educational factors into one supposedly favorable or unfavorable environment. An apparently superior environment does not necessarily provide the exact stimulating experiences

[39] Alice M. Leahy, *Nature-Nurture and Intelligence*, Genetic Psychology Monographs, Vol. 17, No. 4 (1935), pp. 235-308.

so necessary to satisfactory intellectual development or mastery of the facts and skills implied in mental tests.

New Testimony from the Iowa Studies.—A recent series of foster home placement studies which appear to have eclipsed earlier investigations in uniqueness and outcome, have been reported by psychologists working at the University of Iowa. The major contribution to this series, by Skodak,[40] will perhaps be of most interest to students of child psychology. Skodak reports the results of the placement before they were six months of age of 154 foster children, 140 of whom were illegitimate, in superior foster homes for a period of between four and five years. The children were secured from socially inferior mothers whose I.Q.'s averaged 87.7 and who had completed an average of ten grades of schooling. Sixteen and three-tenths per cent of the mothers were borderline cases intellectually and 13.8 per cent were said to be feebleminded. The true fathers of these children, 88 of whom were known, had also completed ten grades and represented an occupational status of 5.4, or .6 of a class (professional, clerical, skilled labor, common labor, etc.) below that of the population in general. The I.Q.'s of the true fathers were not determined.

The foster children were adopted into homes in which both fathers and mothers had, on the average, completed twelve grades of schooling. The foster fathers rated 3.1 occupationally, a status which is 1.7 points above the general population. It was in this more superior environment that the children were tested when they were one year and seven months of age (on the average), and again when they had reached a mean age of four years and one month. Children under three and one-half years were measured with the Kuhlmann individual test and those above that age with the Stanford-Binet. In spite of the plebeian social status and low I.Q. scores of their mothers, the children averaged 116 I.Q. on the first test (after approximately a year in the foster home) and 111.5 on the second test (following about three and one-half years' residence). On the first

---

[40] Marie Skodak, "Children in Foster Homes: A Study of Mental Development," *Univ. of Iowa Studies in Child Welfare,* Vol. 16, No. 1 (1939). Also Marie Skodak and H. M. Skeels, "A Follow-up Study of Children in Adoptive Homes," *Journal of Genetic Psychology,* 66: 21-58 (1945).

test 65 per cent of the children scored above 110 I.Q. and 41 per cent made scores of 120 or above. Only 4 per cent were below 90 I.Q. and none went below 80. Furthermore, a follow-up study conducted when the children were seven years of age provided no evidence of mental deterioration. The I.Q.'s became increasingly stable with increasing age. This was a surprising outcome and one that has occasioned a number of refutations and many an argument.

According to Skodak, such findings show that the I.Q. improves most in the better class homes where foster parents are socially, educationally, and occupationally superior, and that the mentality of the true parents does not materially affect children's chances of achieving superior mental status. She refers to the findings of Skeels,[41] another Iowa investigator, whose study of 147 foster children (in some instances the same children as Skodak's) preceded and corroborated hers. Skodak [42] has also reported a subsidiary study of 16 foster children whose mothers were claimed to be definitely feebleminded. Startlingly enough, these children, too, achieved an average I.Q. score of 116 after approximately a year's residence in superior foster homes. In this instance the known fathers (7 of the 16) had attained an average education of nine school grades. Critics have doubted the criteria by which the mothers were adjudged feebleminded, but Skodak concludes that "The mental development of children of feebleminded mothers and the most inferior true family backgrounds is indistinguishable from that of children whose mothers are not feebleminded."

As in the case of the Iowa orphanage preschool project, a number of critics have pointed to conclusions which they regard as doubtful in the Iowa foster home studies. McNemar's [43] criticisms seem especially pertinent, albeit they are at times unnecessarily caustic. In the first place, there has been some doubt regarding the accuracy of the true mother's average

[41] Harold M. Skeels, "Mental Development of Children in Foster Homes," *Journal of Consulting Psychology,* 2 : 33-43 (1938).
[42] Marie Skodak, "The Mental Development of Children Whose True Mothers Are Feebleminded," *Child Development,* 9 : 303-308 (1938). Also Harold M. Skeels, "Children with Inferior Social Histories: Their Mental Development in Foster Homes," *Psychological Bulletin,* 38 : 594 (1941).
[43] Quinn McNemar, *op. cit.,* pp. 74-79.

I.Q. of 87.7. Had the chronological age divisor been 15 instead of 16, as the World War I figures indicated were probably fairer in the case of uneducated adults, the mothers would have achieved an average I.Q. of 93.5, which is approximately normal. And, as McNemar brings out, if the tests were administered immediately before or after the birth of the illegitimate child, the scores could be regarded as questionable (on emotional grounds). The mothers were also apparently the victims of an impoverished environment. Secondly, it was not clear what social and occupational status the true fathers represented. They may have been too young to have attained their potential occupational level. There is also the possibility that the thirty-five unknown true fathers may have been of better stock than the Iowa investigators supposed. This point is, however, uncertain.

In the third place, children on whom the Kuhlmann test was standardized made a higher average score than the usual 100. Those below eighteen months of age averaged 115 I.Q., and two- and three-year-olds averaged 107. The scores made by Skodak's foster children were not much higher than these figures. Fourth, it has been shown repeatedly that intelligence test scores for infants and young children are highly unreliable. They are not usually predictive of the degree of intelligence of the Stanford-Binet variety that a child will display even as early as ages four or five. Finally, both Skodak and Skeels are accused of failing to take full account of the phenomenon of *regression,* which indicates that children with high I.Q.'s are likely to decline in standing on retest scores and that, by the same token, those of low I.Q. status are likely to improve on later tests. The Iowa investigators [44] have refuted McNemar's (and others') criticisms on the ground that they have been misquoted and misunderstood. At present the controversy is far from having been settled. Students of child development are thus confronted with the necessity of viewing the pros and cons of the debate in the light of other evidence and of coming to their own conclusions.

[44] Beth L. Wellman, Harold M. Skeels, and Marie Skodak, "Review of McNemar's Critical Examination of Iowa Studies," *Psychological Bulletin,* 37 : 93-111 (1940).

Conclusions on Foster Home Placement.—The extent of differences in the I.Q.'s of foster children and true parents in the more recent studies is certainly significant. Such differences suggest the presence of intellectually motivating factors in some foster homes at least that have formerly not been suspected. It has been pointed out, however, that since adopted children are in the nature of the case "wanted" children, their new-found parents are likely to be zealous in their efforts to provide a sympathetic and stimulating environment designed to promote intellectual and social development. In short, it is possible that foster parents provide not only an affectionate attitude but the type of games, toys, pictures, books, trips, stories, and other educational influences calculated to create "readiness" for success with mental tests.

Whatever the influences may be that bring about such favorable scores in the case of foster children, it is apparent that I.Q.'s are modifiable to an extent not formerly suspected. Here again favorable opportunities seem to be associated with mental development in children. It seems fair, thus, to conclude that, so far as intelligence is concerned, inheritance is not as limiting a factor as was once supposed. It may be that the genes provide an original innate mental capacity, but certainly children's measurable ability fluctuates with educational and social conditions in their home and immediate community. Apparently children are sufficiently flexible intellectually to adjust to a wide variety of living conditions.

If nature provides an inherited mental capacity the range within which it can fluctuate is apparently relatively wide. As evidence from identical twins reared apart and from barren environment studies show, such deviations may extend 25 I.Q. points or more. Some writers, Neff, for example, have gone so far as to suggest that the high relationship between children's social status and their intelligence test scores demonstrated in foster home studies requires no other explanation than an environmental one. Neff [45] writes, "we have tried to show that although individuals at birth may differ in native endowment (a still incompletely settled question), it has defi-

45 Walter S. Neff, *op. cit.,* p. 755.

nitely not been proved that social status of the parent has any-thing to do with the native endowment of the infant."

So far as the Iowa investigations [46] are concerned, the following broad social implications have emerged from their foster home studies:

1. Intelligence as commonly defined and measured is much more susceptible to environmental changes than had formerly been supposed.
2. Any hereditary constitutional factor that may exist permits mental development to operate within broad limits.
3. Children's mental development is significantly related to the social, educational, and cultural level of their home environment.
4. Because of the low predictive value of the child's true family history, its value as a basis for placement is doubtful.

The Influence of Formal Schooling

It is commonly believed that a well-supervised education is essential to intelligent citizenship and to life adjustment in general. The question arises, however, whether systematic schooling actually raises the child's intellectual capacity—his ability to reason and otherwise to cope with the abstract symbolism of mental tests—or whether it results merely in increasing his stock of information, practical or otherwise. There is a distinct difference between raising the intelligence quotients of children and enabling them to master the subject matter requirements of formal schooling. It can be seen that this question is but another aspect of the nature-nurture or constancy of the I.Q. problem. Although it is in some instances conflicting, evidence concerning the effectiveness of schooling in raising the I.Q. is not lacking.

The Effect of Schooling on Test Scores.—It has been contended by some investigators that approximately one-half of an elementary school child's ability to cope with standardized

[46] Harold M. Skeels, "Some Iowa Studies of the Mental Growth of Children in Relation to Differentials of the Environment: A Summary," *Thirty-Ninth Year-oook, National Society for the Study of Education,* 1940, Part II, pp. 305-307.

mental tests is attributable to formal schooling. Even such a well-developed individual mental test as the Simon-Binet is said to be extensively influenced by linguistic ability as learned in school. Other psychologists have reasoned that these investigators failed to make a clear distinction between *cause* and *effect* in the question of innate mental capacity versus school achievement. They believe that inherited mental ability can account for both success with intelligence tests and superior school achievement. However, no matter which point of view one takes, there is always the question of whether formal schooling enhances mental ability or whether, on the contrary, native mental capacity is responsible for success in school subjects.

In a study of all fifth grade children in 273 health areas in New York City, Maller [47] found extensive differences in average I.Q. among groups of children from different parts of the city. The mean group I.Q.'s ranged from 74 in the lowest area to 118 in the two highest areas. These differences were said to be seven times greater than one would have expected if each group represented a typical (random) sample of the total population tested. It has been claimed that the differences found in Maller's investigation can be accounted for by the factor of selection; that is, that the superior groups contained children who were superior in native ability to begin with and who were thus not necessarily influenced by a culturally and educationally stimulating school environment. This may be true but the contention has not been proved.

R. L. Thorndike [48] and associates studied the retest scores of about 3,000 children attending three equally superior private schools in New York City—Ethical Culture, Horace Mann, and Lincoln. In no instances were increases in I.Q. proportional to the time spent in the school environment. However, whereas only small average gains were noted in two of the schools, the third yielded an average improvement of over 6 I.Q. points. Thorndike is at a loss to explain this difference but suggests

[47] J. B. Maller, "Vital Indices and Their Relation to Psychological and Social Factors," *Human Biology*, 5 : 94-121 (1933).

[48] R. L. Thorndike and associates, "Retest Changes in the I. Q. in Certain Superior Schools," *Thirty-Ninth Yearbook, National Society for the Study of Education*, 1940, Part II, pp. 351 361.

that it could be due to the more mentally stimulating nature of the environment in school B. Other explanations have included chance fluctuations of the samplings tested in each of the three schools and the possibility that different investigators may have administered the tests somewhat differently.

It should not be supposed that all school environment studies indicate marked influence on mental test scores of superior educational advantages. Reymert and Hinton [49] have, for example, reported an investigation in which the mental test scores of 100 children six years of age and over was not affected by a four-year stay in the superior environment of the Mooseheart home and school in Illinois. These authors conclude that, "Indications from our study, then, seem to be that if the removal of children from a relatively inferior to a relatively superior environment is to have an advantageous effect on their I.Q.'s, such change should be made before they reach the age of six, because, for children from school-entrance age on, the I.Q. remained constant over five annual examinations following upon a change to a relatively superior environment."

It should be noted, however, that a younger preschool group in the same school showed a significant improvement in I.Q. status. Reymert and Hinton's findings have, nevertheless, been corroborated by Lamson,[50] who found no gains in mental test scores for children in attendance in the fourth grade of a demonstration school characterized by an educationally enriched environment. Lamson concluded that a vital school curriculum is not influential in determining a child's intellectual status.

Nursery Schooling and the I.Q.—From the foregoing evidence it is obvious that school age children who do not attend school decline markedly in I.Q. status as they grow older. The evidence for children who attend an average or superior school is not, however, so definite. According to objective findings, the data are conflicting here. Some children and groups of

[49] Martin L. Reymert and Ralph T. Hinton, "The Effect of a Change to a Relatively Superior Environment Upon the I.Q.'s of One Hundred Children," *Thirty-Ninth Yearbook, National Society for the Study of Education*, 1940, Part II, pp. 255-268.

[50] Edna E. Lamson, "To What Extent Are Intelligence Quotients Increased by Children Who Participate in a Rich Vital School Curriculum?" *Journal of Educational Psychology*, 29 : 67-70 (1938).

children show marked gains in I.Q. while others appear to be uninfluenced in this respect by the advantages of systematic schooling. With the evidence as conflicting as it is, it may be well to turn to studies of the mental development of preschool children who, because of their plasticity, might be considered ideal candidates for the stimulating influences of schooling.

Jones and Jorgensen [51] conducted a study of the mental development of 54 children in attendance at the University of California Nursery School as compared with that of several control groups of matched age, I.Q., and education of parents. A comparison of their mental growth curves showed that the nursery school children made no more improvement than the various control groups. It was also noted that no significant relationship existed between mean I.Q. changes and length of attendance in the preschool. The investigators did not believe that the outcome of the study was attributable to the unreliability of the tests used or to any lack of scientific technique on the part of the nursery school personnel. They concluded that "nursery school attendance has, under the conditions of this study, no demonstrable significance for mental growth."

In another investigation [52] of the effects on I.Q. status of preschool education, it was found that 114 graduates of the Winnetka Nursery School made slightly higher, but statistically insignificant, mental test scores than a larger group of Winnetka school children who had not attended. The nursery school children were said to resemble the general population in both central tendency and scatter of I.Q. scores. The author concluded that "as far as this evidence goes, experience in the Winnetka Nursery School does not tend to raise the I.Q.'s of the children." This result is said to have occurred in spite of the fact that the nursery school in question was well equipped and considered to be modern in most respects.

Lest it be believed that nursery schooling is always ineffective in raising the mental status of its members, it may be well to

[51] Harold E. Jones and Ada P. Jorgensen, "Mental Growth as Related to Nursery-School Attendance," *Thirty-Ninth Yearbook, National Society for the Study of Education*, 1940, Part II, pp. 207-222.

[52] William H. Voas, "Does Attendance at the Winnetka Nursery School Tend to Raise the I.Q.?" *Thirty-Ninth Yearbook, National Society for the Study of Education*, 1940, Part II, pp. 363-376.

examine investigations which appear to testify otherwise. Barrett and Koch [53] compared the mental development of 17 children from the Chicago Orphan Asylum who attended a nursery school for one year with a control group from four orphanages matched on the basis of age and initial test-status. Merrill-Palmer mental tests given at the beginning and end of the first year of nursery-school training showed a much greater gain for the experimental group than for the children not in attendance at the school. Fifteen of the seventeen pre-school children gained more I.Q. points than the average for the control groups and every pupil improved more than the control child with whom he was matched. The nursery school children also made the greater improvement in personality development.

Similar results have been reported by Starkweather and Roberts [54] at the Merrill-Palmer School in Detroit. Two hundred and ten children were given mental tests upon entrance to the nursery school and re-examined after an interval of six to forty months. Seventy-two of the children were again retested one year to eight years after withdrawal from the nursery school. According to the investigators, "Children attending the Merrill-Palmer Nursery School gain in I.Q. . . . as measured by the Stanford-Binet and Merrill-Palmer retests." Sixty per cent gained an average of 14.1 I.Q. points, 34 per cent declined an average of 10.4 points, and 6 per cent remained constant mentally. Twelve per cent of the preschool children gained 20 I.Q. points or more. The retests after withdrawal from the nursery school indicated that I.Q. changes attained during attendance at the nursery school tended to be maintained.

A more recent investigation by Rinehart [55] has corroborated these findings. Of a group of three-year-old children from the lower middle class population of Cleveland, the half (21) who

[53] H. E. Barrett and H. L. Koch, "The Effect of Nursery School Training Upon the Mental-Test Performance of a Group of Orphanage Children," *Pedagogical Seminary and Journal of Genetic Psychology*, 37 :102-122 (1930).

[54] Elizabeth I. Starkweather and Katherine E. Roberts, "I.Q. Changes During Nursery-School Attendance at the Merrill-Palmer School," *Thirty-Ninth Yearbook, National Society for the Study of Education*, 1940, Part II, pp. 315-335.

[55] Jesse B. Rinehart, "Some Effects of a Nursery School-Parent Education Program on a Group of Three Year Olds," *Journal of Genetic Psychology* 61 : 153-161 (1942).

attended nursery school, although originally 7 I.Q. points below the control group, averaged 2 I.Q. points higher at the close of their nursery school experience. The investigator regarded these results as positive evidence of the value of early schooling.

From these studies it is evident that there is little agreement as to the effectiveness of nursery schooling in raising the I.Q. of children. Those who supposed that because of their impressionable and plastic nature, very young children would automatically make large and permanent gains in a modern nursery school are evidently due for a disappointment. Yet data from a number of investigations have suggested the possibility of appreciable and fairly lasting increments of mental improvement. Whether the conflicting findings from the various studies were occasioned by differences in the mentally stimulating nature of the schools in question, to the social-economic status of the children studied, or to mere differences in measuring technique and statistical procedures is not clear. The fact remains, however, that, according to the evidence, some schools have succeeded in motivating preschool children to improve their mental test intelligence.

Results from the University of Iowa.—Through a series of papers, Wellman [56] has reported rather remarkable and permanent improvements in I.Q. status as the result of attendance at the University of Iowa Elementary School. Certain children have apparently not only gained as much as 30 and 40 I.Q. points during preschool years but have maintained much of this increment throughout high school and into college. One child is said to have increased his I.Q. score of 98 at age three and one-half to 167 at age five. This score dropped, however, to 143 at age ten. Another gain of from 89 at age three to 149 at age ten and one-half with a drop to 130 at age eleven is reported. Average gains were not stressed to the same extent as individual increases. This procedure is no doubt intended to impress the reader with the fact that important individual gains

[56] Beth L. Wellman, "The Effect of Preschool Attendance Upon the I.Q.," *Journal of Experimental Education*, 1:48-69 (1932-33). See also in the same journal, "Growth in Intelligence Under Differing School Environments," 3:59-83 (1934-35), and "Mental Growth From Preschool to College," 6:127-138 (1937-38).

are obscured by the presentation of average increases in mental development.

R. L. Thorndike [57] has summarized the findings of the Iowa preschool studies as follows:

1. "The Binet I.Q. of children from generally superior homes rose markedly during a period in nursery school, but did not rise during the summer spent in the general home environment."

2. "The gains in Binet I.Q. were maintained by a sample of children located and tested after several years of attendance at other than University schools."

3. "The gains in Binet I.Q. were further added to by a sample of children who remained in the University school and were tested at a later time."

4. "Length of attendance at the University school was related to intelligence test score in high school and at college entrance."

5. "Gain from attending preschool was not related to the occupational level of the parent."

6. "The greatest gain in preschool was for those who originally received the lowest scores, and the smallest gain for those who received the highest" (regression effect).

The Iowa reports have been rather severely criticized by a number of psychologists, particularly Goodenough [58] and McNemar.[59] The general trend of criticism is that the studies were not accurately carried out and that interpretations of the evidence collected were not always justified. Some feel that the Iowa preschool studies need verification by unbiased investigators working under similar conditions and utilizing similar but more accurate experimental and statistical procedures. These investigators believe that the use of more precise testing pro-

[57] R. L. Thorndike, " 'Constancy' of the I.Q.," *Psychological Bulletin*, 37 : 167-186 (1940).
[58] Florence L. Goodenough, "New Evidence on Environmental Influence on Intelligence." *Thirty-Ninth Yearbook, National Society for the Study of Education*, 1940, Part I, pp. 311-316.
[59] Quinn McNemar, "A Critical Examination of the University of Iowa Studies of Environmental Influence Upon the I.Q.," *Psychological Bulletin*, 37 : 79-92 (1940).

cedures, thoroughly adequate samplings, and more accurate statistical methods, including recognition of the regression effect for high and low I.Q. scores, would do much to clear up the partial uncertainty that pervades studies of the influence on intelligence of nursery and elementary school experiences.

The Possibilities of Systematic Schooling.—Throughout the investigations of the influence of schooling on mental development there has been evident a general assumption that, except for isolated school situations, early school experiences are roughly similar in their effects on intellectual status. In short, schooling has been evaluated in a broad, blanket sense and not in terms of the influence of *specific* educational experiences on equally specific mental skills. The inadequacy of this practice has been criticized by many students of child development who make a distinction between *casual* influences of the environment and *systematically planned* school activities.

In commenting on this situation, both educators and psychologists have stressed the point that schools well qualified in the techniques of child rearing could provide genuinely stimulating experiences and instruction designed to secure much greater improvement in mental ability than is usually witnessed. To quote one such individual,[60] "Nobody knows what any child could do if presented with facts and principles in an orderly, ascending sequence with full attention to his motivational needs." Another authority [61] has the following to say regarding reading: "In recent years . . . we have come to realize that it is desirable to prepare children somewhat for reading, to provide them with experiences which will:

1. Awaken in them a sensitiveness to reading symbols and their use.
2. Enable them to put meanings into and to get meanings out of reading symbols before any definite instruction in books is undertaken.
3. Establish in them a readiness for reading, and a desire to read.

[60] George D. Stoddard, *The Meaning of Intelligence,* New York, The Macmillan Co., 1943, p. 9. By permission.
[61] Nila B. Smith, *Trends in Reading Readiness* (Teacher's Guide for the First Year), New York, Silver, Burdett & Co., 1936, p. 63.

It will be recalled that while children did not, on the average, improve in intellectual status in some of the nursery and elementary school investigations, in other instances increases in I.Q. scores were appreciable. The specific reasons for the more desirable outcomes in certain schools might well be studied in some detail. Child psychology needs to know precisely why and in what respects some schools are so productive of mental development. If this were done there is no reason why *types of schools* (including teaching personnel) cannot be established that would stimulate a degree of intellectual development beyond that now commonly regarded as satisfactory. In the mental growth sense, much present-day schooling is probably not worthy of the name, being largely an ineffective routine of lesson learning and apathetic memorization. The failure of many schools to function satisfactorily in the mental development of children may thus be due, in part at least, to a lack of systematic and stimulating educational experience.

Summary and Further Implications

Singularly enough, the testimony of a rather impressive array of nature-nurture investigations has led to conflicting conclusions. Some feel that the evidence amassed points to the efficacy of the cultural and social environment so far as the mental development of children is concerned. Others seem equally convinced that a critical interpretation of the data leads to a case for inheritance. Students of child psychology are thus thrown upon their own resources in coming to valid conclusions on this important question. Perhaps the status of the controversy may best be summarized by quoting conflicting views.

Wellman,[62] for example, believes that the evidence points to a *functional* view of intelligence; that is, that mental status is a function of the type of educational and other environmental influences experienced during childhood. She says, "The fact that the concept of innateness must be broadened to allow for extreme changes during the lifetime of the child leads to the necessity of adopting a functional view of intelligence. The

[62] Beth L. Wellman, "Our Changing Concept of Intelligence," *Journal of Consulting Psychology,*" 2 : 97-107 (1938). By permission.

only alternative is to believe in what I prefer to call a mystical intelligence. It is mystical because nobody has ever demonstrated that it really exists. . . . The only way the degree of this intelligence can be gauged, however, is by functional tests such as our present tests of intelligence. The validity of a test I.Q. will be judged in terms of whether the test I.Q. coincides with the so-called 'real' intelligence. But here a dilemma arises because this 'real' intelligence cannot be measured. Hence, it is never known whether test I.Q. and 'real' I.Q. do coincide."

1 point of view

Somewhat in corroboration of this point of view Curti [63] writes, "Not only is the doctrine of inherited intelligence illogical; it is also, in so far as it may lead either to a fatalistic or to an overoptimistic attitude toward any one child, misleading. In one child hereditary factors may be more important in determining the developed trait, in another, environmental factors. For example, in one an I.Q. of 60 may possibly be due largely to an inherited defective cortex, while in another child the same I.Q. may be due to malnutrition in infancy. In one child an I.Q. of 85, indicating 'dullness,' may be due to hereditary conditions different from normal, while another child may make an I.Q. of 85 rather than 100, because he has lived in a social environment much inferior to the average. Each child must be judged as an individual. An I.Q. carefully obtained will, if conditions are favorable, and especially if the same result is obtained in a succeeding year or years, give a rough measure of his present intellectual capacity as compared with that of other children of his age. But it will not tell what the I.Q. might have been had other environmental conditions prevailed since conception. Nor will it in all cases enable us to predict future intelligence status. The I.Q. is roughly constant from year to year, but there are many individual exceptions."

In contrast to these conclusions is the one stressing the biological inheritance of mental ability. This assumption appears to be somewhat on the wane but there are still those who believe in it implicitly. Thorndike,[64] for instance, has proposed that

[63] Margaret W. Curti, *Child Psychology,* New York, Longmans, Green & Co., 1938, pp. 183-184.
[64] E. L. Thorndike, *Human Learning,* New York, D. Appleton-Century Co., inc., 1931, pp. 198-200.

since intellectual differences are so marked among adults, those apparently possessing *genes potential for intellect* (and other qualities) should be encouraged to improve the status of the race by reproducing better gene-equipped stocks. Contrary to the view of those who believe that the evidence suggests the importance of superior educational opportunities, this scientist contends that if the intelligence of the race is to be materially improved such an outcome must be sought through selective breeding. Like others who hold this view, Thorndike believes that better laws, customs, and society in general must await the generation of intellectually superior stocks. On this basis, it is the duty of society, through the avenue of eugenics, to improve the native capacity of children to learn.

In conclusion we can but say that it is probably not possible in the light of present knowledge to settle the question of intellectual or any other kind of human potentiality on positive grounds. We can, however, engage in a critical analysis of the implications of the various beliefs advanced and should be willing without undue *a priori* commitment to weigh impartially the evidence for and against opposing and compromise theories. We might, nevertheless, be pardoned for leaning, in the absence of certainty, toward the more socially hopeful interpretations which stress the child's educability and the possibilities of a stimulating environment.

QUESTIONS FOR DISCUSSION

1. What criticisms can be made of the belief that mental tests measure *native* ability? In view of the fact that all responses to mental tests have been learned, how can basic differences in intelligence among children be determined?

2. What objections can be advanced against the assertion that a child's intelligence represents an accumulation of learnings which is relatively independent of the quantity or quality of his brain and other neural structures? Is such a position in harmony with modern theories of intelligence?

3. Why, in your judgment, are the interpretations of the Chicago and the Stanford nature-nurture (foster-home placement) researches so different? How could one investigator be so im-

pressed with the limitations presumably set by heredity when the other believed that he had found evidence for the superior influence of educational opportunities?

4. How would you defend the assumption that an apparently superior environment does not necessarily provide the specific stimulating factors necessary either to general intellectual growth or high intelligence-test scores? What kind of environment do you think would be suitable for ensuring such development?

5. When reared apart, why do some identical twins become unlike intellectually and others grow unlike temperamentally instead? To what extent do such findings argue for a connection between specific environmental factors and the outcomes noted? Explain.

6. What reasons can you give for the apparently conflicting evidence concerning the influence of formal schooling upon the intellectual status of children? To what extent do you think psychologically sound "systematic instruction" can influence children's I.Q. scores?

7. How are we to explain the consistently superior intelligence-test showing (average) of urban over rural children? Defend, first, the view that cities tend to "drain off" the cream of the rural stock and, second, that urban environments provide educational opportunities better designed to stimulate intellectual growth. Which position harmonizes the better with the facts?

8. If intelligence tests measured native ability, how would one explain the evidence from studies of "mountain hollow" children indicating that their I.Q.'s decline progressively from about ages four or five to ages nine or ten? Does such evidence disprove individual differences in native ability? Defend your answer with evidence.

9. Why is the question of the intellectual improvability of children such an important one? Is it not true that the race is sufficiently intelligent now for all practical purposes? Support your conclusion with data and sound logic.

10. What are the implications for child psychology of the belief in an intellectual caste system as being inherent in man's genetic constitution? What might be the undesirable results of adopting a fatalistic attitude toward the educability of children in general?

RECOMMENDED READINGS

Louttit, C. M. *Clinical Psychology.* New York: Harper & Bros., 1936, Chs. 4, 7.

McHugh, Gelolo. *Changes in I. Q. at the Public School Kindergarten Level.* Psychological Monographs, Vol. 55, No. 2 (1943).

McNemar, Quinn. "A Critical Examination of the University of Iowa Studies of Environmental Influence Upon the I.Q." *Psychological Bulletin,* 37:79-92 (1940).

Morrison, H. C. *Basic Principles in Education.* Boston: Houghton Mifflin Co., 1934, pp. 346-354, 386-422.

Neff, Walter S. "Socio-economic Status and Intelligence; A Critical Survey." *Psychological Bulletin,* 35:727-757 (1938).

Newman, H. H., Freeman, F. N., and Holzinger, K. J. *Twins; A Study of Heredity and Environment.* Chicago: Univ. of Chicago Press, 1937.

Schwesinger, Gladys C. *Heredity and Environment.* New York: The Macmillan Co., 1933, Ch. 4.

Sherman, Mandel, and Henry, T. R. *Hollow Folk.* New York: T. Y. Crowell Co., 1933.

Stoddard, G. D. *The Meaning of Intelligence.* New York: The Macmillan Co., 1943.

Thirty-Ninth Yearbook, National Society for the Study of Education. Parts I and II, Bloomington (Ill.): Public School Pub. Co., 1940.

Thorndike, R. L. "'Constancy' of the I.Q." *Psychological Bulletin,* 37:167-186 (1940).

Thorpe, Louis P. *Psychological Foundations of Personality.* New York: McGraw-Hill Book Co., Inc., 1938, Chs. 3, 4.

Wellman, Beth L. "Our Changing Concept of Intelligence." *Journal of Consulting Psychology,* 2:97-107 (1938).

Wellman, Beth L., Skeels, Harold M., and Skodak, Marie. "Review of McNemar's Critical Examination of Iowa Studies." *Psychological Bulletin,* 37:93-111 (1940).

CHAPTER 4

after Birth

POSTNATAL LIFE BEGINS

ALTHOUGH THE NEWBORN INFANT is obviously helpless, he possesses physical equipment and potentialities for growth that make possible a future adaptive capacity far beyond that of the lower animals. In comparison with many other species, the human infant seems poorly prepared for the life of continual physical and psychological adjustment which confronts him. Yet within the living cells of the human offspring are resident possibilities of genetic development marvelous to contemplate. This original equipment includes, in addition to the skeletal framework and body organs, a nervous system, an intricate series of duct and ductless glands, a set of immature muscles, and a variety of sensory channels through which the developing child will make contacts with the outside world. It is with this, and other more detailed physical equipment, that the newborn infant sets out to adjust to a none-too-benign environment.

Physical Characteristics at Birth

General Features of Physical Equipment.—The nervous, glandular, and muscular systems probably loom largest in a discussion of the infant's native equipment. The functioning of these structures holds many implications for the more strictly psychological reactions associated with later development. They may be said to represent the base upon which the child's developing personality will be built. The principal functions of these primary physical structures may be stated somewhat as follows:

THE NERVOUS SYSTEM. The human nervous system is composed of two major but closely interlocked divisions, the *central* and the *autonomic*. The central nervous system regulates the actions of skeletal muscles and is commonly believed to represent the physical basis, in part at least, of all mental processes. The autonomic nervous system, consisting of a series of ganglia in the vicinity of the spinal cord, controls the organs and glands of the trunk. Since the autonomic regulates digestive, metabolic, circulatory, and other such vital processes, the infant's physical well-being is dependent upon it. At any rate, fetal development of the autonomic system precedes that of the central nervous system both structurally and functionally. Many physiologists believe that the central nervous system serves the autonomic, the latter being primarily concerned with the maintenance of bodily tonus and well-being.

The autonomic division of the nervous system is almost fully developed at birth. The central system is, however, immature when postnatal life begins, and thus requires a maturing process, including that of *myelinization,* before it can function in the development of childhood neuromuscular skills. Such growth is not achieved through the development of new nerve structure cells, but by the maturation of nerve cells present at birth but as yet unable to function. Muscular maturation, which occurs even later, must await the growth of nervous structures. The nervous system maintains a continual lead in the growth of the organism, both prenatally and postnatally. In view of its prominent role in the control of glandular and muscular tissues, it is not surprising that the nervous system takes precedence in the development of the organism.

The Glandular System. Endocrinologists have shown that many important physical functions, including digestion, metabolism, bodily growth, and sexual development, are vitally affected by the hormones secreted into the blood stream by the duct and ductless glands. These agents, which cooperate with and influence the nervous system itself, are to a considerable extent determiners of both childhood and adult behavior. In short, it is believed that endocrine secretions participate in regulating the rhythm and intensity of most, if not all, of the vital processes of living.

The glands of internal secretion do not, according to physiologists, function independently; instead they cooperate in such a way as to make the action of any given gland dependent upon the extent or intensity of activity of every other gland. The action of each gland is also influenced by situations obtaining in such closely cooperating agencies as the blood stream, chemical affinities in adjacent organs, and the nervous system itself. In fact, the physical organism, including the endocrine system, operates as an integrated unit in which every process is more or less influenced by every other vital activity. It is possible, nevertheless, to describe the unique function or functions of some of the ductless glands.[1]

Probably the most potent drug secreted by the endocrine system is that produced by the suprarenal medulla. This hormone, called *adrenalin,* plays a prominent role in exciting the infant or child to respond emotionally. The adrenalin autocoid, which has been synthesized artificially from the formula $C_9H_{13}O_3N$, is responsible both for stimulating the heart, lungs, and other visceral organs, and for limiting the activities of the digestive system during high emotional states.

The *pineal* gland, located in the brain back of the eye level, and the *thymus,* embedded in the thorax, are both influential in controlling growth during infancy and childhood. These glands appear to regulate growth processes sufficiently to control both rate of growth and the appearance of secondary sex characteristics at adolescence. Closely associated with the pineal and thymus endocrines are the *gonad* glands, which not only secrete the germ cells concerned with reproduction, but produce the secondary sex hormones responsible for the development at adolescence of either masculine or feminine bodily characteristics. Children whose gonad glands function improperly or insufficiently may fail to develop characteristic sex qualities before or at the time of adolescence.

Another gland essential to the child's physical growth and sexual development is the *pituitary,* an endocrine located in a recess on the under side of the brain. If the child's pituitary gland becomes overactive, its hormones may stimulate the body to excessive growth. Hypoactivity of the anterior lobe of the

---

[1] For a fuller account of endocrine functions the reader is referred to R. G. Hoskins, *Endocrinology, The Glands and Their Functions,* New York, W. W. Norton & Co., 1941.

pituitary may result in the individual's becoming a symmetrical dwarf (midget) with normal intelligence, but marked by
subnormal sexual development. Since the posterior pituitary is
concerned with the control of body fat, underactivity of its
hormone may bring about the marked obesity so noticeable in
some children.

The best known and probably most readily regulated ductless
gland is the *thyroid,* a small (when normal) endocrine located

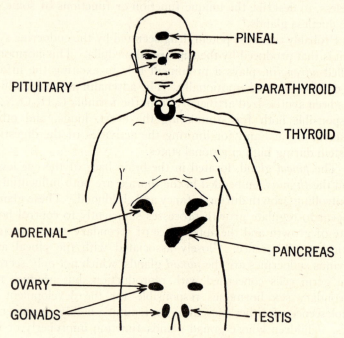

PINEAL

PITUITARY

PARATHYROID

THYROID

ADRENAL

PANCREAS

OVARY

GONADS

TESTIS

Figure 13. Bodily Position of the Endocrines

in the lower part of the neck close to the windpipe. This gland
is vested with the task of regulating the vital process of metabolism. A marked deficiency of the thyroid hormone almost
invariably brings about a sluggish and apathetic manner,
coupled with indifference concerning activities going on in an
individual's environment. Overactivity of the thyroid gland
usually results in irritability, nervousness, and general emo-

tional instability. When the functioning of the thyroid gland is seriously impaired before birth, the result is sometimes the development of a *cretin,* a child marked by a stunted body, pasty skin, weak physical powers, a disinterested attitude, and considerable mental deficiency. The adult equivalent of cretinism, *myxedema,* may be developed as the aftermath of a goiter operation in which the thyroid gland is partially or wholly removed. Children suffering from thyroid dysfunction may, however, sometimes be successfully restored to health through the administration of sheep's thyroid or a recently developed synthetic substitute called *thyroxin* (formula $C_{15}H_{11}O_4NI_4$). Thyroxin contains a considerable amount of iodine, a deficiency of which contributes to thyroid gland disorders. Pediatricians (medical child specialists) have been able to correct imbalances in thyroid functioning more adequately than in any other endocrine field. Both hypo- and hyperthyroidism can be alleviated to some extent by the use of the glandular therapy.

MUSCULAR EQUIPMENT. According to Brooks,[2] the total muscular equipment of a newborn child weighs less than one-fourth (23.4 per cent) as much as its entire body. This ratio increases to an average of 27.2 per cent at age eight and 44.2 per cent at sixteen. Such muscles as the infant possesses are extremely immature, so far as possibilities of skillful functioning are concerned. Muscles regulating the heart, lungs, digestive system, and other organs controlled by the autonomic nervous system function sufficiently well at birth to maintain the infant's organic well-being. Skeletal muscles are, however, so undeveloped that only massive, gross movements of the body are possible. The larger muscles only are capable of reacting to stimuli, and they do so in a very rudimentary manner. At this stage of maturity the extremities of the body possess little or no independence of action, being unable to affect detailed movements which will later become a matter of course. Even cursory observation of a newborn infant will show that all early movements involve large muscle responses of the whole body. Detailed movements must await the maturation (growth) process

[2] Fowler D. Brooks, *The Psychology of Adolescence,* Boston, Houghton Mifflin Co., 1929, p. 30.

which enables muscles concerned with more definite and localized responses to operate adequately. As will be shown in more
detail later, muscular development in infants proceeds from the
general to the specific, the massive to the detailed.

Bodily Proportions of the Newborn.—Anyone who has
observed a newborn infant will recognize how extensively it differs in bodily proportions from an older child or an adult. Its
legs are extremely short in relation to its trunk, and its head,
which is proportionately twice as large as that of an adult, gives
the infant a top-heavy appearance. Whereas at birth the total

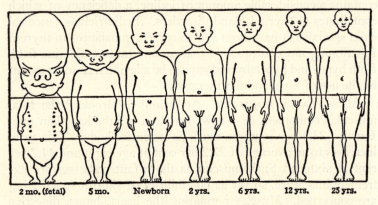

2 mo. (fetal)   5 mo.   Newborn   2 yrs.   6 yrs.   12 yrs.   25 yrs.

Figure 14. Showing Changes in Body Form and Proportion During Prenatal
and Postnatal Growth

(From C. M. Jackson (Editor), *Human Anatomy,* 9th ed., Philadelphia, P. Blakiston's
Son & Co., 1933, p. 25.)

height of the infant is approximately four and one-half times
the length of its head, at fifteen years stature has increased to
about seven times head length. The total height of an adult is
about three and one-half times his stature at birth, but his head
has merely doubled in length. A close view of the upper part
of an infant's skull will also reveal that it is proportionately
much larger in relation to the face (8:1) than it will be at
adulthood (2:1).

In keeping with the presence of a proportionately very large
skull, the upper part of the infant's face is more completely

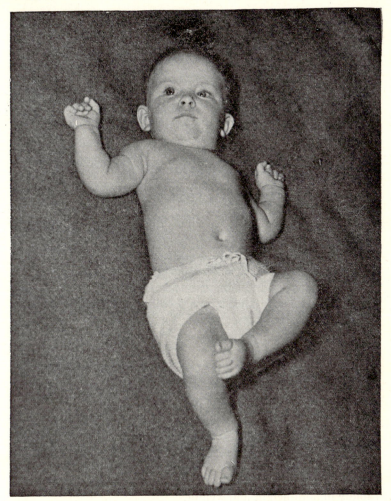

Figure 15. Bodily Proportions of a Five-Months-Old Infant

Indicates length of the trunk in relation to that of the arms and legs, also proportionate length of head.

developed both posteriorly and laterally than the lower part. The forehead is prominent in relation to the base of the skull, which is small. Because of a large nasal aperture, the infant's nose appears broad and flat. His upper and lower jaws are relatively low in his face and both contain elevated structures for the later development of "baby" teeth.

The infant's arms are also relatively shorter than the adult's. The bones of his forearm (radius and ulna), unlike those of the adult, are not markedly unequal in thickness. Much the same is true of the infant's legs, but their growth rate is unusually rapid during the early years. In three years the child's legs increase in length one-half as much as they will in the next nine years. At maturity, an individual's legs are approximately five times as long as they were at birth. The infant's trunk, which is relatively large at birth, becomes approximately three times as long and wide, and about two and one-half times as thick at maturity.

The bones of the newborn infant are soft and cartilaginous. This fact explains the child's relatively low susceptibility to bone fractures and dislocations. When a young child does suffer a fracture, the bone splinters much after the fashion of green wood, not sharply as in the case of a dry stick. Some bones, although destined to join later, are still unconnected in infancy. Other bones ossify slowly, making it impossible for the structures in their vicinity to perform their functions. The first bone in the infant's body to ossify, the clavicle or collarbone, is short, thus giving the shoulders their sloping appearance.

The newborn infant is, on the average, approximately 1 foot and 8 inches in length, and weighs about 7½ pounds. These figures vary a great deal, but it is uncommon for a child to weigh less than 4 or 5 or more than 9 or 10 pounds at birth. Cases of infants weighing from 1 to 3 pounds have been reported, but their mortality rate is high. Following a loss of several ounces during the first week of life, most infants grow rapidly in both height and weight.

Other Physical Characteristics of the Infant.—The flesh of an infant is solid, but its skin is surprisingly soft. In color, the skin soon changes from a reddish pink to a soft "rose petal" pink. Some infants are born with a downy growth of fine hair on some parts of the body which, however, soon disappears. A fatty substance secreted by glands associated with the skin covers the infant at birth, but does not reappear after the latter is washed and oiled.

The child's mouth is well adapted at birth to perform the sucking function. The tongue, cheeks, hard and soft palate, gums, and lips are sufficiently developed to cooperate satisfactorily in this important act. Small pads of adipose tissue in each cheek facilitate nursing by distributing pressure and supporting the cheeks. Except in rare instances, the newborn infant has no teeth. He is able, nevertheless, to suck and to take in liquid food with the use of the mouth "shoulders" on which teeth are destined later to appear.

The infant's head is usually covered with a soft, downy growth of hair which often falls out during the first months of postnatal life. This original crop of hair, which is sometimes quite heavy, may be different in color from that which develops later. The infant's eyes, which also change color in harmony with gene potentials, are almost black at birth. The child's eyes are also adapted to the release of tears, but these do not usually appear until a number of weeks after birth.

The average weight of a newborn child's heart is said to approximate 25 grams. By the sixth year this weight has increased to four or five times such a figure, and by adulthood it is twelve times as heavy. However, the heart does not commence its steady growth until somewhat more than a month after birth. In the matter of heart beat the infant's rate is much faster than that of the adult. Beginning with a rate of from 130-135 at birth, the heart gradually decelerates in this respect during childhood days. Tensions associated with crying and physical discomforts may result in acceleration up to 175-185, but in general heart beat decreases in rate noticeably during the first three or four years. By the twelfth year, the rate is approximately 85, a figure not far from the adult average.

Sensory Equipment of the Infant

The sense organs, and the central nervous system which they serve, are among the most completely developed structures possessed by the newborn infant. The further growth of the child's sensory equipment is so rapid that by approximately the end of the third year it is as sensitive to environmental stimuli as it will be in adulthood. However, sight, hearing, taste, smell, and touch do not function with full efficiency at birth. The rate at which these functions mature has been shown, to some extent, by both laboratory studies and infant biographies.

Degree of Maturity at Birth.—Since infants cannot cooperate in evaluating the effect of even a simple stimulus, it is difficult to secure accurate evidence concerning their sensory acuity. Direct techniques for measuring infant sensitivity have not been developed. Thus impressions made by sensory stimuli must be judged from responses made by infants under controlled conditions. The experimenter can never be quite certain, however, whether failure to respond, for example, to the touch of a hand on his leg, means that the infant is insentitive to the stimulus or that particular body structures are insufficiently mature to make possible an adequate reaction to the stimulus. It may be that sensory acuity precedes development of capacity to make motor (muscular) responses. Newborn infants display marked differences in physical maturity and consequently in capacity to respond adaptively.

The average infant will make a distinct response to touch stimulations a few days after birth, and may also react negatively and positively to unpleasant and sweet taste stimulations, respectively. It requires a much greater amount of added bitterness or sweetness (in the stimulus) to bring out a discriminatory response in infants than is the case with adults. Infants are less annoyed, for instance, by a strong quinine solution than are adults. Discriminatory response differences between infants and adults are explicable in terms of both increased maturity of sensorimotor structures and the influence of learning, which obviously takes place soon after birth. The original reactions of infants are commensurate with their degree of physical maturity, but are as a rule so diffuse as to be devoid of definite recognizable patterns.

The Newborn Child's Visual Acuity.—Although the average infant is able to make a number of movements with his eyes almost from the moment of birth, his original sense of sight is too immature to react to any but sudden and marked changes of light. According to Chase,[3] among the simplest methods of determining whether infants are sensitive to differences in brightness are those of observing their pupillary reactions and the movements of their eyes in relation to moving visual stimuli. Such reactions are not present at birth, but develop within the first days or weeks of postnatal life. The age at which infants are able to sense or to react to brightness differences is not known.

Ability to fix the eyes on an object and watch it for a time suggests that the infant is reacting to some kind of visual impression. The capacity to fixate on a stimulus object varies considerably from child to child, but may appear a few hours after birth. The peak of a sustained fixation pattern is reached in from four to five weeks. Preyer [4] reported that his infant son was able to fix his gaze upon a light on the eleventh day. A second baby biography, by Shinn,[5] revealed that the infant gazed "interestingly" at a bright surface near the end of its second week. Evidently the ability to attend visually to objects is developed by the typical infant during the first two to four weeks.

Judging from Valentine's [6] studies, most infants can open and close their eyes (as well as blink) when certain stimuli, such as touching or blowing the eyelids, are presented. Some infants fail to blink, however, when a moving object is brought close to their eyes. Response of the eyes to a succession of mechanically regulated moving objects, called *optic nystagmus* by the investigator,[7] was found to occur, though somewhat unsuccessfully, during the first twelve hours after birth. It was not until the third and fourth weeks that successful "ocular

[3] W. P. Chase, "Color Vision in Infants," *Journal of Experimental Psychology*, 20 : 203-222 (1937).

[4] W. Preyer, *The Mind of the Child* (trans. by H. W. Brown), New York, D. Appleton-Century Co., Inc., 1882.

[5] Millicent W. Shinn, *Biography of a Baby*, Boston, Houghton Mifflin Co., 1900.

[6] C. W. Valentine, "Reflexes in Early Childhood: Their Development, Variability, Evanescence, Inhibition and Relation to Instincts," *British Journal of Medical Psychology*, 7 : 1-35 (1927).

[7] J. M. McGinnis, *Eye-movements and Optic Nystagmus in Early Infancy*, Genetic Psychology Monographs, Vol. 8, No. 4 (1930), pp. 321-430; B. C. Ling, "A Genetic Study of Sustained Visual Fixation and Associated Behavior in the Human Infant from Birth to Six Months," *Journal of Genetic Psychology*, 61: 227-277 (1942).

pursuit" was in evidence with the most precocious infants. By the sixth week all of the young subjects showed adequate photographic records.

More elaborate data regarding eye movements of infants have been secured by the Shermans.[8] These investigators

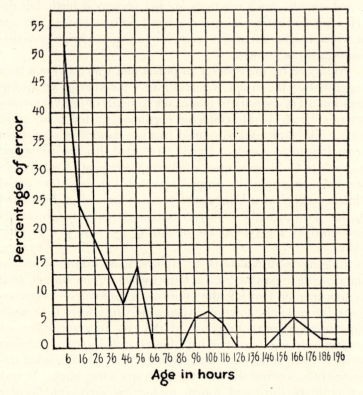

Figure 16. Coordination of the Eyeballs in Following a Light

(From Mandel Sherman and I. C. Sherman, *The Process of Human Behavior,* New York, W. W. Norton & Co., Inc., 1929, p. 78.)

studied 88 infants by the method of moving a dim flashlight back and forth in front of them in a darkened room about 15 inches from their faces. To quote the Shermans, "The number of eye movements observed in each test was limited to fifteen. Dur-

[8] Mandel Sherman and I. C. Sherman, "Sensori-Motor Responses in Infants," *Journal of Comparative Psychology,* 5 : 62-65 (1925).

ing the test, the number of coordinated eye movements in the process of fixation was counted, and the ratio obtained of the number of uncoordinated movements to the total number of movements made. The resulting ratio was taken as a percentage of error in the test. For example, if an infant made five uncoordinated movements in fifteen the per cent of error was 33." These investigators report that none of the 68 infants who were above thirty-four hours of age made any errors in fixation. As the ages went below thirty-four hours, the number of errors in fixation tended to increase proportionately. As Figure 16 shows, development of eyeball coordination is rapid during the first fifteen to forty-five hours. It is believed that not only learning but inner maturation of both cortical and visual structures, which began in fetal days, account for the improvement noted.

A study [9] of responses to color, as determined by the relative strength of eye fixations on a gray versus a colored (red, yellow, blue, or green) disk, has shown that infants ranging from 69 to 143 days of age are slightly more responsive to the colors mentioned than they are to gray. In the case of 239 children, five and one-half to twenty-four months of age, the investigator found a steady increase with advancing size in reaching for the colored disk. It is thus likely that definite chromatic acuity is not well established until the third or fourth month. Even then the child may not be discriminating among colors in the adult sense.

Auditory Acuity of the Infant.—Unlike infant visual responses, those resulting from auditory stimulation are uncoordinated and diffuse. It is thus difficult to secure accurate measures of auditory acuity. Investigators are consequently uncertain concerning the time of appearance of original reactions to auditory stimuli. Pratt [10] states that many investigators believe infants are deaf for a number of hours after birth, but that the majority respond overtly to sudden noises, whistles, the tick of a watch, and the like within the first few days. The

[9] Ruth Staples, "The Responses of Infants to Color," *Journal of Experimental Psychology*, 15 : 119-141 (1932).

[10] K. C. Pratt, "The Neonate," in *Handbook of Child Psychology* (edited by Carl Murchison), Worcester, Clark Univ. Press, 1933, pp. 163-208.

bodily responses observed include eye movements, blinking, cessation of crying, jerking movements of the arms and legs, modified breathing, and change in body movements. Blanton [11] has reported, for example, that one infant responded with a convulsive start when subjected to sudden loud sounds during the first few days of life. Bryan [12] found no evidence in his study of neonates of hearing during the first two days, but concluded that many children begin to hear by the third day and that by the tenth day they are able to detect voice sounds. Wide individual differences in auditory acuity among infants suggests that some may have been born with defects of the hearing apparatus or that certain gelatinous fetal tissue in the middle ear cavity has not yet been absorbed.

It is nevertheless possible, as suggested by Stubbs,[13] that some of the differences in neonate auditory acuity may be due to differentials in strength and character of the stimuli applied. This investigator has accordingly recorded the reactions of newborn infants to sounds of different pitch, duration, and intensity. The findings show that hearing increases with amplifications of either the duration or the intensity of a sound stimulus, but that variations in pitch produce much less striking variations in hearing response. It may thus be that failure to respond to a sound stimulus is indicative of its inadequate duration or intensity rather than of the infant's capacity for response.

Studies intended to "condition" infants to sound stimuli have led to interesting, if uncertain, implications. Working with a child who did not respond to sounds but who, like most infants, reacted to stroking of the sole of the foot, Aldrich [14] found that it could "learn" to move its foot when a bell was rung. Aldrich's method was that of stroking the baby's foot with a pin, at the same time that an unseen bell was being rung

[11] Margaret G. Blanton, "The Behavior of the Human Infant During the First Thirty Days of Life," *Psychological Review*, 24 : 456-483 (1917).

[12] E. S. Bryan, "Variations in the Responses of Infants During the First Ten Days of Post-Natal Life," *Child Development*, 1 : 56-77 (1930).

[13] Esther M. Stubbs, "The Effect of the Factors of Duration, Intensity, and Pitch of Sound Stimuli on the Responses of Newborn Infants," *Univ. of Iowa Studies in Child Welfare*, Vol. 9, No. 4 (1934).

[14] C. A. Aldrich, "A New Test for Hearing in the Newborn: The Conditioned Reflex," *American Journal of Diseases of Children*, 35 : 36-37 (1928).

at half-hour periods during one night and until the next mid-morning. The infant came to withdraw its leg even though it was untouched when the usual bell was rung. In a later study, Marquis [15] found that infants who were subjected to the sound of a buzzer at each bottle-feeding soon (from three to six days) came to respond with such feeding movements as sucking, mouth-opening, and crying when the buzzer alone was sounded.

Both infant biographies and experimental investigations suggest that the structures responsible for auditory acuity are less mature at birth than those concerned with visual responses. Evidence shows that infant's reactions to loud sounds are diffuse and spasmodic rather than coordinated. These immature, undifferentiated emotional responses become much more detailed and specific, however, as the child develops definite ways of responding to certain sounds.

Gustatory and Olfactory Responses.—Investigators are not agreed concerning the acuity of the newborn infant's sense of taste. Judging from their sucking and other facial and bodily responses to either mother's or cow's milk, most infants react with a feeling of satisfaction to this type of food. Babies also respond positively to sweet flavors and negatively to bitter, sour, or salty solutions.[16] Fenton [17] administered castor oil to a six-day-old infant with the result that it was vigorously rejected. Shinn [18] reported, on the other hand, no indication of gustatory (taste) acuity several days after birth.

Jensen [19] measured the responses of newborn infants to such gustatory stimuli as sweet, sour, bitter, and salt solutions, as well as to air, by the use of a device for the recording of sucking movements. Sucking reactions to most of these stimuli differed little from those usually made under ordinary feeding condi-

[15] Dorothy P. Marquis, "Can Conditioned Reflexes be Established in the New-born Infant?" *Journal of Genetic Psychology,* 39 : 479-492 (1931).

[16] K. C. Pratt, A. K. Nelson, and K. H. Sun, *The Behavior of the Newborn Infant,* Columbus, Ohio State Univ. Press, 1930.

[17] Jessie C. Fenton, *A Practical Psychology of Babyhood,* Boston, Houghton Mifflin Co., 1925.

[18] Millicent W. Shinn, *op. cit.*

[19] Kai Jensen, *Differential Reactions to Taste and Temperature Stimuli in Newborn Infants,* Genetic Psychology Monographs, Vol. 12, Nos. 5-6 (1932), pp. 361-479.

tions. Unusual sucking reactions were elicited only by salt solutions and by air. In this investigation sweet, sour, and bitter stimuli did not bring out differential sucking responses in infants.

Studies of infants' olfactory acuity, or sense of smell, have shown that strong odors, such as those emanating from ammonia, acetic acid, cloves, and petroleum, cause a discomfort or avoidance reaction in about half (48 per cent) of the stimulating situations presented.[20] Of the odors presented, ammonia and acetic acid produced the greatest number of overt reactions. Stern [21] found that the odor of milk or of perfume caused some infants to stop crying. Many odors, regarded as mild by adults, do not appear to affect newborn babies. Although the olfactory apparatus is well developed at birth, sensitivity to odors is not thoroughly developed in infants, and the sense of smell is thus dependent upon a certain degree of additional structural growth for its mature functioning.

Responses to Touch and Thermal Changes.—The sense of touch appears to be well developed at birth, and is utilized by the infant to enjoy sensations by the time he is a month old. Since a slight touch of its lips sets up sucking movements, the baby's mouth is evidently sensitive to touch stimuli. This appears to be true as well of his nose, eyes, hands, and the soles of his feet. Shinn [22] reported that her niece drew her tongue back and forth through her lips, apparently to enjoy the sensations produced, at the age of five weeks. Other investigators have found that infants respond to a touch on the nose by closing the eyes, and that vigorous blowing on their face often results in crying or withdrawal.

Sensitivity to pain is not marked at birth, and usually develops somewhat slowly, with the head region leading in vulnerability to such feelings. This is especially true of skin pain. A number of workers in this field have found that skin scratches

[20] K. C. Pratt, A. K. Nelson, and K. H. Sun, *op. cit.*
[21] William Stern, *Psychology of Early Childhood*, New York, Henry Holt & Co., Inc., 1924, pp. 73, 78.
[22] Millicent W. Shinn, *op. cit.*

do not seem to disturb the infant's comfort.[23]   Dearborn [24] has stated that even on the seventy-ninth day, pinching an infant's finger to a degree that would cause pain to adults, does not elicit signs of discomfort. However, the infant's sensitivity to gas pressure, colic pain, and other internal disturbances is marked during the first postnatal weeks.

Infants respond with signs of discomfort to temperatures above or below normal, and most of all to extremes of cold. According to Crudden,[25] localized responses make up 33.8 per cent of the total response to thermal stimulation (ranging from 16 to 45 degrees Centigrade) of the leg in the case of sleeping neonates (offspring ten days to three weeks of age) from 41 to 1,045 hours of age. However, responses of extreme magnitude were more likely to be non-localized than localized. "Scratch" responses appeared to bear a relation to the age of the infant. It was suggested that the infant's responses might have been less diffuse and more localized if they had been stimulated by varying temperatures when awake. Koffka [26] has reported that a young baby will attempt to get out of bath water that is not heated to the right temperature. Infants do not, however, seem to be sensitive to applications of heat or cold to small areas of the body.

In a study by Jensen,[27] newborn infants reacted differently in their sucking movements when the temperature of milk was 55 degrees Centigrade than when it was heated to only 15 degrees. This tendency was in evidence as early as the second day in eight out of a total of seventeen infants studied. In a similar investigation,[28] in which infants ranging in age from birth to eleven days were stimulated with drops of water (on the tongue) heated to a temperature of 8 to 53 degrees Centigrade, greater sensitivity was found in one-day-old subjects than was the case

[23] Mandel Sherman, I. C. Sherman, and C. D. Flory, *Infant Behavior*, Comparative Psychology Monographs, Vol. 12, No. 4 (1936), pp. 1-107.
[24] George V. N. Dearborn, *Motor-Sensory Development*, Baltimore, Warwick & York, Inc., 1910, p. 38.
[25] Charles H. Crudden, "Reactions of Newborn Infants to Thermal Stimuli Under Constant Tactual Conditions," *Journal of Experimental Psychology*, 20 : 350-370 (1937).
[26] Kurt Koffka, *The Growth of the Mind*, New York, Harcourt, Brace & Co., 1925, p. 120.
[27] Kai Jensen, *op. cit.*
[28] K. C. Pratt, A. K. Nelson, and K. H. Sun, *op. cit.*

with older infants. The authors also reported more pronounced reactions in the case of colder-than-body temperature stimuli than with those heated to a warmer-than-body status.

It can be concluded that the infant is equipped with a moderately mature set of sensory channels through which he makes contacts with his physical environment. Until his neuromuscular structures become much more developed than they are at birth he cannot, however, make the adjustive responses that more mature organisms are called upon to effect. The infant's original reactions to sensory stimuli, as well as his motor responses, are for the most part general and indeterminate, and must await the processes of both physical and experiential maturation.

Responses of the Newborn Child

The developing fetus' responses make their appearance not long after conception and well before the mother can detect their presence. By the beginning of the third month of intra-uterine life, fetal muscles will react to directly-applied electric currents, and by the fourth month cases have been observed in which the toes will flex when the sole of the foot is stimulated. Later prenatal movements include sucking movements of the mouth (six months), a clearly observable knee jerk (seven months), and grasping reactions (eight months).[29]

The nature of postnatal responses is more adequately understood if one realizes that earlier development follows a phenomenon known as the *physiological gradient*.[30] Just as metabolic activity is at its height in the head and shows a progressive decline in intensity toward the lower part of the body (gradient) so fetal growth proceeds from head region to the lower extremities. As evidence of this trend of development, one can point to the fact that, after birth, the infant is much more able to use his arms in reacting than he is to utilize his legs for walking. The fact that the infant can also make general movements with his arms before he can control his fingers and wrists, shows

[29] Leonard Carmichael, "Origin and Prenatal Growth of Behavior," in *Handbook of Child Psychology* (edited by Carl Murchison), Worcester, Clark Univ. Press, 1933, pp. 31-159.
[30] C. M. Child, *Physiological Foundations of Behavior*, New York, Henry Holt & Co., Inc., 1924, Ch. 7.

that the direction of body development is from its center (axis) toward the periphery (extremities).

It is possible, under certain conditions, to stimulate movements in a fetus by external means. Sontag and Wallace [31] induced responses of fetal muscles by vibrating a door-bell buzzer against a wooden disk attached to the mother's abdomen. Responses were noted as early as the beginning of the eighth month of intra-uterine development. The investigators believe that their technique can be used as an index of fetal development.

Research workers have also found that experiences of the mother may bring about an unusual amount of activity in the fetus.[32] This finding has led to some speculation as to whether the physical condition and activities of the mother exert any influence on the behavior trends of the child subsequent to birth. These investigators have reported, for example, that fetal movements are affected by whether the mother is tired or rested, emotional or calm, quiet or active. They conclude that evidence on this point is inconclusive and that too many factors are involved to make possible a determination of the influence on later behavior or prenatal conditions.

The Child's Postnatal Responses.—The nature of the newborn infant's basic behavior patterns can perhaps best be understood in connection with evidence concerning the development of the young of lower animals. Outstanding among investigations of this kind is Coghill's [33] study of the behavior of the *Amblystoma,* a variety of water lizard. The initial movements of this little amphibian are characterized by massive, unspecialized responses. Its first swimming movements develop out of a broad general flexing of the entire body. In short, the *Amblystoma's* first responses represent movements of the whole body, not of its specialized parts; independent action of parts of the body must await an inner growth process that makes such

[31] L. W. Sontag and R. F. Wallace, "The Movement Response of the Human Fetus to Sound Stimuli," *Child Development,* 6 :253-258 (1935).
[32] L. W. Sontag and T. W. Richards, *Studies in Fetal Behavior,* I: *Fetal Heart Rate as a Behavioral Indicator,* Monographs of the Society for Research in Child Development, Vol. 3, No. 4 (1938).
[33] G. E. Coghill, *Anatomy and the Problem of Behavior,* New York, The Macmillan Co.. 1929.

responses possible. The front limbs develop independence of action before those in the rear of the body. Furthermore, the animal's limb responds as a whole before its knee action or foot and toe movements are able to operate autonomously. This phenomenon of gradual emergence of independent action of specialized body parts is known as *individuation*. According to Coghill, the direction of such development is from the animal's *head to his tail* and from the *axis of his body to its periphery*.

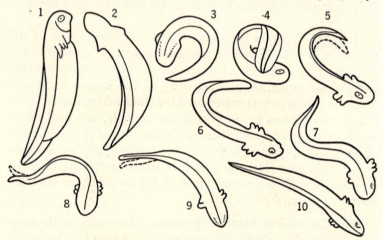

Figure 17. Tracings of Motion Pictures of *Amblystoma Tigrinum* Performing the Early Swimming Movements.

(From G. E. Coghill, *Anatomy and the Problem of Behavior*, New York, The Macmillan Co., 1929, p. 6.) By permission.

The observations of Coghill and others have led to the formulation of several important generalizations relating to growth which seem as applicable to human infants as to the lower animals. These principles may be summarized as follows:

1. Initial behavior is characterized by *mass* reactions of the entire organism. Specific responses emerge later from this general pattern.
2. Behavior patterns emerge in regular sequences of movement in a manner made possible by the development of the nervous system.

3. Physiological functions follow embryological growth in a relatively precise way in the development of feeding and locomotion (on land or in water).

4. "Behavior develops from the beginning through the progressive expansion of a perfectly integrated total pattern and the individuation within it of partial patterns which acquire various degrees of discreteness."

Just as the water lizard (and other animals) progresses from mass behavior to discrete responses as it becomes more mature, so infants begin with diffuse, uncoordinated movements of the body as a whole and progress to those of a more specialized or differentiated nature. A variety of stimuli will cause an infant

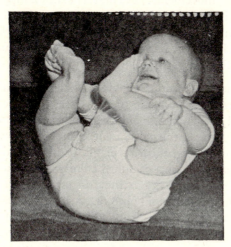

Figure 18. Activity Involving the Whole Body
The infant uses head, arms, and legs in gross reactions
(Courtesy of Barney Katz)

to thrash about, wave his arms, kick with his legs, squirm, vocalize, and otherwise respond diffusely. In short, any stimulus may apparently bring about movements in many parts of the infant's body at once. As Pratt,[34] who has made extensive studies of infant behavior, says, most responses involve move-

[34] K. C. Pratt, "The Organization of Behavior in the Newborn Infant," *Psychological Review,* 44:470-490 (1937).

ments of the major part of the body, including the smaller and sometimes unnoticed parts. This investigator has also reported that there is no evidence for the former assumption that a marked degree of specificity obtains in the behavior of the new-born.

Even when the child has learned to walk and to make adaptive hand-eye coordinations, he still exemplifies a form of diffuse behavior. He now shows interest in every aspect of his environment by "getting into everything"; that is, by walking toward, looking at, or handling almost any object within his range of stimulation. It should not, however, be supposed that all infant reactions are too gross and unorganized to make possible adaptive movements. A child will suck a nipple when hungry, move his leg when pinched on a toe, and close his eyes when air is blown in his face. Infant behavior is marked by much generalized behavior, but some degree of individuation is possible from the earliest days.

Tropisms in Infant Behavior.—Scientists have for years been endeavoring to explain the processes by which organisms, both animal and human, make their more elementary adjustive responses. More specifically, man wishes to know why moths gravitate toward lights, why plants bend toward rays of the sun, why animals have a chemical affinity for certain foods, and why human infants react as they do to loud sounds, to being dropped, and to hot or cold objects. Various investigators have endeavored to account for these and other apparently mechanical responses on the basis of what is called a *tropism*. According to the author of the term, Loeb,[35] it means *to turn* in response to an external stimulus. As Loeb explains it, a moth, for example, would be compelled to move toward a light once it had been stimulated on some part of its body by a light. If one side of the moth was stimulated by the light, muscular contractions on that side would cause the animal to turn toward the light in such a way as to enable both sides of its body to receive equal stimulation from the light. On this basis, the moth would be forced to fly directly toward the light. Loeb believes that worms

[35] J. Loeb, *The Mechanistic Conception of Life*, Chicago, Univ. of Chicago Press, 1912.

gravitate toward food (olfactory stimulus), that plants turn toward the sun, and that infants make their simple approaches to stimuli in this mechanical way.

Many modern psychologists regard this explanation as being too simple to account for the extreme *variability* of even animal behavior. Some believe, as well, that the tropism theory fails to reckon with the intelligent contribution that a human individual may make to a given stimulus-response situation. Wheeler,[36] for instance, rejects the mechanistic conception of elementary behavior, and proposes the explanation that organisms turn toward lights, retreat from cold, and the like in an effort to maintain a state of body equilibrium designed to insure feelings of well-being. This is the *Gestalt* view of behavior, and one that proposes to account for infant, as well as animal, reactions on the basis of holistic adjustive capacity.

If defined as characteristic approach or avoidance responses to heat, cold, sounds, odors, and similar external stimuli, tropisms are present in both children and adults. In early life they tend to bring about reactions of the organism as a whole, not of independent parts. Adults have, as a rule, become too civilized and modified by education to respond in a primitive chemical way to stimuli in their environment. Man's cultural development has apparently enabled him to transcend many of the simple tropistic responses of childhood.

The Problem of Reflex Behavior.—In addition to displaying mass activity and a repertoire of general tropisms, the newborn infant (neonate) enacts a large number of specific movements commonly called *reflexes*. Reflexes are ordinarily defined as specific responses of a limited part of the organism, as exemplified by the eye wink or the knee jerk, and are regarded as being unlearned, involuntary, and relatively fixed in their mode of operation. Many reflexes are present at birth, others are believed to develop later. It is common knowledge, for example, that the typical infant swallows, sneezes, coughs, chokes, gasps, and yawns with the utmost spontaneity. Reflexes which are more readily modified with age include biting,

[36] R. H. Wheeler, *The Science of Psychology*. New York, T. Y. Crowell Co., 1940, pp. 103-105.

coughing, stretching, crying, clasping, turning the head, and vocalizing.[37]

The physical basis of reflex action is not known with certainty. The usual supposition is that such action is made possible by the presence in the infant of preformed (connected) neural pathways. It is believed that since, in the case of reflexes, connections are already established between sensory and motor nerves (via the central nervous system), the child can

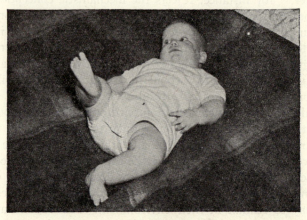

Figure 19. The Babinski Reflex
(Courtesy of Barney Katz)

respond only in a stereotyped way determined by the nature of these connections. On this basis, later learned responses would be thought of as chains of original reflexes. More recent physiological findings suggest, however, that nervous action is too diffuse and widespread in the body to warrant the older concept of simple, localized activity. Mature behavior, instead of representing a combination or synthesis of early reflexes, is apparently a refinement of original general, mass activity.

Two original (present at birth) reflexes, which disappear later—the Babinski (plantar) and the so-called Darwinian—have attracted considerable attention among students of child development. The Babinski reflex, which involves a fan-shaped

[37] Wayne Dennis, "A Description and Classification of the Responses of the Newborn Infant," *Psychological Bulletin,* 31 : 5-22 (1934).

spreading of the toes and the bending back of the great toe
when the sole of the foot is stimulated, is most in evidence from
birth to about the end of the sixth month, but disappears after
the first two years. Some authorities state that this reflex is
not present in every infant. The Darwinian or suspension-grasp
reflex is also present at birth but declines in strength by the end
of the first month and is usually gone by the fourth month.
The grasping reflex, which some believe represents an evolu-

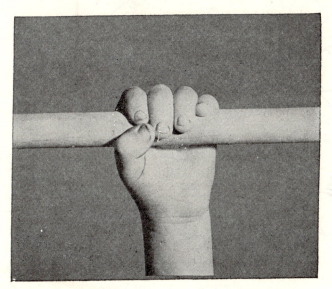

Figure 20. The Suspension Grasp or Darwinian Reflex
(Courtesy of E. Toral Seat)

tionary survival, is sufficiently marked in certain infants to
enable them to support their entire weight while holding on to a
rod with one hand. According to Watson,[38] the grasping reflex is present to some degree in practically all infants. The
physical basis for the appearance of both the Babinski and Darwinian reflexes is uncertain. Earlier investigators believed that
their presence indicated an immaturity of spinal centers.

[38] John B. Watson, *Psychology from the Standpoint of a Behaviorist,* Philadelphia, J. B. Lippincott Co., 1924.

Others have suggested that high synaptic resistance in the nervous system might account for the phenomena observed.

A number of investigators have studied the nature and duration of the Moro or "startle" reflex. According to Wagner,[39] this reflex is comparable to the "body jerk" response, which is defined as a sudden tensing or jerking of the body and limbs. The startle (body jerk) reflex occurs most often during the

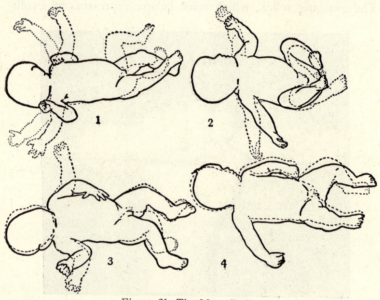

Figure 21. The Moro Reflex

(From Myrtle B. McGraw, *Growth: A Study of Johnny and Jimmy*, New York, D. Appleton-Century Co., Inc., 1935, p. 48.)

infant's first few days. The Moro reflex cannot be elicited unless the infant is relaxed, and usually takes place during deep sleep. It has been commonly believed that the Moro response disappears at about the end of the third month. However, Dennis[40] has presented evidence suggesting that, instead of waning, the Moro reflex becomes inhibited by other responses.

[39] I. F. Wagner, "The Body Jerk of the Neonate," *Journal of Genetic Psychology*, 52 : 65-77 (1938).
[40] Wayne Dennis, "A Psychologic Interpretation of the Persistence of the So-called Moro Reflex," *American Journal of Diseases of Children*, 50 : 888-893 (1935).

The difficulty of observing older children under thoroughly re-laxed conditions may also account for the alleged disappearance of this reflex.

Criticisms of the Reflex Theory.—The traditional reflex theory has been criticized on a number of points, at least three of which seem pertinent to child psychology. First, Wheeler and other Gestalt psychologists maintain stoutly that reflexes have no properties or functions of themselves, but that they are sub-servient to and receive their direction from the organism as a whole. To quote Wheeler,[41] "walking is not a combination of local reflexes of the limbs; each limb is integrated with the trunk. Local movements emerge through an individuation proc-ess and not as an integration of independent units. . . . The central organization develops with reference to the special pat-tern (walking) long before the latter makes its appearance in behavior." In short, this point of view holds that so-called reflexes are specialized responses that have developed out of gross patterns (in some cases before birth) of action; it denies that reflexes have any local independence.

Second, reflexes have been explained as equalization proc-esses by means of which the organism maintains its internal balance. Instead of being mechanical responses to stimulation of certain parts of the body, such as the eye or the knee, reflexes are said to be nature's way of equalizing body tensions. A tap on the knee causes muscle tension and the ensuing contraction (knee jerk) equalizes the tension set up, thus bringing the structures concerned back to a state of balance. As Goldstein [42] puts it, by the use of such an equalization process "the organism is capable of coming to terms with the stimulus." Reflexes can thus be explained on the basis of the maintenance of body equi-librium. The eye winks to restore the disequilibrium caused by a gust of wind; the throat goes through swallowing movements to equalize tensions set up by food or excess saliva; and cough-ing is utilized to reduce stresses caused by throat irritation.

[41] R. H. Wheeler (1929 ed.), *op. cit.*, p. 495.
[42] Kurt Goldstein, *The Organism*, New York, American Book Co., 1939, pp. 162-163.

In the third place, some psychologists maintain that there is a learned element in all responses, reflex or otherwise. Morgan,[43] for example, believes that in animals well-coordinated reflexes develop out of more diffuse uncoordinated body movements during the fetal period. In the case of humans, much of this development is said to occur after birth, thus making possible considerable flexibility of behavior even in the so-called reflex reaction. To quote Morgan's view, "To be sure, there are some pathways in the nervous system which are readily established. Stimulation of the eye with a bright light will cause the pupil to change more readily than it will cause a flexion or extension of the toe. Nevertheless, if it were of value to have the child flex his toe upon being presented with a bright light such a reaction could probably be learned. . . . Reflexes are not inviolable. . . . The chief characteristic of the human infant is his flexibility and this is present even in his reflex behavior."

Emotional Behavior at Birth

The newborn infant is capable of making a variety of complicated, although only vaguely definable, emotional responses to both intra-organic and external stimuli. Psychologists have for years endeavored to determine the nature of these reactions and the conditions under which they may be aroused. Agreement appears to be limited to the conclusions that infant emotion is elicited by few types of stimuli, and that such responses are for the most part diffuse. An examination of the emotional life of infants shows that it, too, develops from undifferentiated to differentiated levels, and that considerable confusion has resulted from efforts to associate definable emotional reactions with specific stimulating situations.

The Nature of Emotional Behavior.—In the case of infants, emotion is regarded as a more or less widespread affective response to some form of external stimulation such, for example, as a loud sound produced at close range. This, and a variety of other stimuli, elicit undirected and undifferentiated

---

[43] J. J. B. Morgan, *Child Psychology*, New York, Farrar & Rinehart, Inc., 1942. pp. 101-102.

but nevertheless violent, reactions from very young children. Reactions of this kind, which are noted for their intensity and for the scope of muscular activity involved, are regarded as being characteristically emotional. As will be indicated more extensively later, emotional experiences involve widespread and explosive changes in the individual's glandular and visceral organs. Even infant emotion involves a thoroughly stirred up state of the organism characterized by a flood of sensations in which muscles, glands, abdominal organs, and the nervous system are involved. Although subject to considerable modification, emotional behavior is much in evidence throughout life. It is one of the most important factors in child nature and one that requires careful regulation if desirable personality development is to be achieved.

Considerable speculation has been expressed concerning the emotional background of the so-called "birth cry." Some have attributed this original outburst to the child's feeling of helplessness and inferiority in the face of reality and its problems. Others would have us believe that the child is angry at being disturbed in its comfortable fetal environment. More realistic investigators have reminded us that a newborn infant must be stimulated, by jostling or mild blows if necessary, to vocal activity if he is to begin inhaling air into his lungs. It may be, thus, that the birth event has considerable import for the character and development of subsequent emotional patterns. Shaffer's [44] interpretation of this issue is illustrative: "Certainly at birth there is an intensive overstimulation and undoubtedly a resulting visceral upheaval, which has adaptive value in getting the infant started on his worldly existence. The typical cry is part of this reaction. It is interesting to note that at birth the infant first experiences noise, violent restraint of movement and loss of support which appear as emotional stimuli early in life. Perhaps a conditioning or learning process occurs at this time by which these stimuli become especially attached to the emotional response."

[44] Laurance F. Shaffer, *The Psychology of Adjustment*, Boston, Houghton Mifflin Co., 1936, p. 46.

Early Views on Original Emotions.—Both students of child development and laymen have long wondered which, if any, of the numerous and complex emotions experienced by adults are present at birth. Little progress was made toward a solution of this problem until John B. Watson [45] inaugurated his epoch-making investigations of the original emotional nature of infants. According to Watson's findings, the newborn infant is capable of experiencing only three distinct emotional states, i.e., *fear, anger,* and *love.* These supposedly clearly discernible emotional responses could be evoked only by an extremely limited list of specific stimuli.

Fear, as expressed by crying and struggling, is aroused, says this investigator, by loud sounds such as those from a steel bar or the slamming of a door, and by the loss of support experienced when dropped a short distance or toppled over by the jerk of a blanket. Anger is elicited only by restraint of movements, such as pinning the infant's arms to his sides or holding his head in a rigid position, and is expressed by stiffening of the body and, when possible, slashing movements of the arms and legs. The love emotion (interpreted by Watson in the general sense referred to as sex by Freud), expressed by cooing, smiling, gurgling, and cessation of crying, is stimulated by tickling, rocking, and the stroking of such sensitive zones as the face, lips, breast, and other more erogenous (sex) areas of the body.

Watson has assumed from his experiments that, since only three emotional patterns can be shown to be original in infant responses, many others formerly believed to be native must have been acquired. He found, for example, that infants under six months of age made no emotional response to the presence of a rabbit, a white rat, a black cat, or a large dog. The infants showed no fear of the dark, and would reach toward a nearby fire. Later studies have shown that even snakes arouse no sign of fear in infants of this age. There is believed to be justification, thus, for assuming that adult emotional reactions to these and similar stimuli must have been learned by direct condition-

---

[45] John B. Watson, *op. cit.,* Ch. 6.

ing or by a vicarious (knowledge from the experience of others)
process.

Conflicting Views of Native Emotions.—Because of the
apparently clear-cut nature of Watson's pioneer classification of
infant emotions, it has been widely accepted in child development circles. Watson has been successful in creating the belief
that his three basic infant emotions are thoroughly differentiated and, in the main, mutually exclusive in pattern. This
view is not, however, shared by all students of child psychology,
many of whom object to it on both experimental and theoretical
grounds.

Ragsdale [46] has suggested that much of the organization
and definiteness noted might have been *read into* the infant's
emotional responses by the investigator. This writer believes
that the responses associated with fear are largely a collection
of *avoiding* reactions; that those noted in anger are in actuality
the beginnings of more definite *approach* responses; and that
movements related to love are the forerunners of mild *approaches* to the love object. On this basis, fear, rage (anger),
and love are group names for a variety of infant reactions which
can be more adequately classified as avoidance or approach movements. By such a two-fold classification, infant behavior might
conceivably be measured on a scale from marked avoidance
or retreat to positive approach to a stimulus. Most modern
investigators regard Watson's postulation of three distinct emotions as a tentative hypothesis, and some have subjected it to
further examination employing careful controls and more precise observations.

Probably the most extensive refutation of Watson's belief in
the existence of definite, inherited emotional patterns is that
made by the Shermans.[47] These investigators did not secure
clear-cut love, fear, and rage responses from stroking, loss-of-
support, and restraint-of-movement stimuli, respectively. In
fact, they report that many infants failed to respond emotionally
when dropped through several inches of space. Some of the

---

[46] Clarence E. Ragsdale, *Modern Psychologies and Education,* New York, The
Macmillan Co., 1932, p. 126.

[47] Mandel Sherman and I. C. Sherman, "Sensory-Motor Responses in Infants," *Journal of Comparative Psychology,* 5 : 53-68 (1925).

infants displayed an emotional reaction to puffs of air blown against the cheek. The Shermans concluded that infant emotional reactions are at first generalized and that their differentiation must await experience and maturity. They, too, noted that infant emotional responses are marked by two general but opposite tendencies—"rejecting the stimulus, and accepting the stimulating conditions."

Such studies point to the organismic principle that general, undifferentiated responses antedate specific, differentiated ones in the development of young organisms. Except for general withdrawing or approaching tendencies, infants display few if any definite patterns of emotional response. As Jersild [48] says, "From the viewpoint of emotional expression, the child's reactions group themselves on the one hand as reactions of apparent withdrawal or rejection, such as squirms, twists, tensions, movements of the trunk and the arms and extremities, turning of the head and cries. On the other hand, there are reactions of apparent acceptance, quiescence, passivity, and rudimentary form of pursuit, such as is found when the child turns his head and opens his mouth to suckle when an object is brought into contact with his lips. His overt behavior during the early days of his life does not show organized responses to which a particular label, such as anger, fear, or joy, can confidently be attached."

The Modifiability of Infant Emotions.—The fact that infants' emotional responses evolve from early unorganized movements to later more or less definable patterns of behavior, points to their extreme modifiability. The infant responds to disturbing situations in indiscriminate ways, some of which may eventually lead to satisfying results. In this way the child learns that certain movements or outcries are effective in overcoming distress-producing conditions. Eventually, the growing child develops more precise methods of relieving his various stresses. Early pliable emotional reactions thus develop into relatively recognizable patterns of response. Although emotional behavior may become somewhat set in later childhood,

[48] Arthur T. Jersild, *Child Psychology,* New York, Prentice-Hall, Inc., 1940, pp. 17-18.

there is the possibility throughout life of changing such behavior in favor of more socially desirable patterns.

How the Infant Adjusts Himself

If it were not for his extended and pliable infancy, man would be unable to make the many intricate adjustments so imperative to successful living. The significance of human infancy lies in the foundation it affords for flexibility of development and for adaptability to the galaxy of requirements encountered in the modern world. With all its hazards, human infancy is essential to the development of the variations in attitude, preference, and skill that make possible diverse adult social and vocational adjustments.

Helplessness of the Infant.—The extremely dependent nature of human infancy can perhaps best be portrayed by contrasting it with the relative maturity of infrahuman (animal) offspring. A calf, for example, is able to move about on all fours soon after birth and can, in addition, locate the source of food in its mother's udder. In a remarkably short time this young animal learns to explore its environment and to adjust itself to the requirements of vegetative living. The calf soon becomes independent of its mother, even to the extent of foraging for food and other necessities of life. Like most other young animals, the calf needs little assistance and soon becomes relatively self-reliant.

In contrast to the young of infrahuman organisms, the human infant is helpless indeed. For months he must be held with great care lest his fragile neck and other structures suffer injury. The neonate's food must also be watched for a long period of time if his health is to be adequately guarded; it is years before he can eat solid foods with the abandon exhibited by very young animals. The average child is unable to walk until after the first year and even then he does so with considerable uncertainty. Obviously, infancy for the human offspring is an extended period characterized by much dependency and helplessness.

Scientists have long noted that the period of immaturity of a given species is inversely proportional to its position on the animal scale. To quote Gesell,[49] "Infancy is a period of formative immaturity which tends to lengthen (and to involve more deeply one or both parents) as the organism becomes more complex.

TABLE 4. CHRONOLOGICAL TABLE COMPARING THE ONTOGENETIC AGES OF SIMILAR DEVELOPMENTAL ITEMS IN MACACUS RHESUS AND IN MAN

Development Items	Age of Appearance in Macaque	Age of Appearance In Man
Crying, sneezing, suckling, winking............	1 day	1 day
Response to sound (unadaptive)................	2 days	. .
Head and eyes turn to follow object............	3 days	2-3 mos.
Grasp at object seen (visual stimulus).........	5 days	5-6 "
Recognitive responses to sound................	11 "	. .
First attempt to walk.........................	12 "	12 "
Solid food first eaten........................	4 wks.	6-12 "
Scoops objects with palmar prehension.........	3 "	6 "
Opposes thumb and fingers....................	5 "	7-10 "
Sustains weight by reflex clasping.............	0-3 days	0-3 wks.
Plucks pellet (or grain of corn) opposing thumb and fingers	6 wks.	10 mos.
Attempts to draw mother into play............	5 "	10-18 "
Holds head up steadily and gazes about........	5 days	3-4 "
Follows moving hand with eyes................	6 "	3-4 "
Attempts to crawl............................	12 "	9 "
Runs (trots)	14 "	18-24 "
Weaned......................................	7 wks.	6-12 "
Crumpling explorative play with paper.........	8 "	6-9 "
Attains virtually all adult vocalizations.........	by 9 "	12-24 "
Duration of gestation.........................	168 days	280 days

(From Arnold Gesell, *Infancy and Human Growth,* New York, The Macmillan Co., 1928, p. 345.) By permission.

Although infancy itself denotes incompleteness and imperfection, there is an evolutionary premium upon it, with the paradoxical result that infancy is most prolonged and intensified in the species which stands highest in the life scale."

The striking differences in postnatal development between a human infant and a subhuman offspring (in this case a

[49] Arnold Gesell, *Infancy and Human Growth,* New York, The Macmillan Co., 1928, pp. 335-336. By permission.

monkey) may be seen in Table 4. The relative precocity of the young animal is impressive, yet it is destined to live on a scale of attainment infinitely below that of the young child with which it has been compared.

The value of prolonged plasticity in infancy lies in the potentialities for later learning and adaptability which it makes possible. Man's cultural development has been made possible by the pliability of his organism and the many verbal and neuro-muscular adaptations that such flexibility has assisted in bringing about. Animals may be born with certain well-developed behavior patterns based on inner nervous and muscular structures, but man must await for his adaptive skills upon the processes of physical maturation and learning. Infancy thus possesses an important significance for human progress. The development of fixed skills is not the function of infancy; nature has apparently designed it as a flexible foundation for later adjustment to a complex environment.

Variations in Infant Behavior.—The range of individual differences among human infants is much greater than that obtaining in any animal species. It has been found that very young children differ considerably in motor ability, adaptive capacity, and behavior in relation to people. One two-months-old infant will follow an object with his eyes before another seems sufficiently interested to react at all. Similarly, one nine-months-old child may attempt to crawl, whereas an eleven-months-old playmate may decline to do so. Infants learn to eat solid food, pick up blocks with thumb and fingers, combine cup and spoon in play, and similar functions at different age levels. They may also cry, laugh, coo, and hold out their arms to be picked up at different ages and under different conditions.

Many differences in behavior, although seemingly insignificant in infancy, may forecast variation of considerable magnitude in adulthood. Although infant tests are admittedly unreliable in the prediction of later intelligence and adaptive capacity, marked childhood differences are believed to be indicative of even greater variability in later life. When early deviations from average behavior are suggestive of intellectual

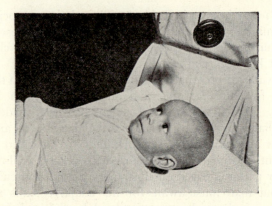

Shiny tape measure gets the child's alert attention. He is also able to follow the tape measure with his eyes.

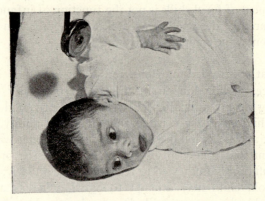

Tape measure is ignored by the child.

Figure 22. Normal and Subnormal Responses to a Shiny Object
(From *Life,* Aug. 18, 1941, p. 37. Courtesy of A. R. Gilliland.)

or structural defects, parents are justified in being concerned about them. However, differences of a purely personal or otherwise not undesirable nature might well be encouraged. Very active children could, with possible profit to society, be given opportunities for expending their energies in constructive ways. Children who show a keen interest in musical instruments or mechanical tools could be directed into channels designed to utilize their capacities along these lines.

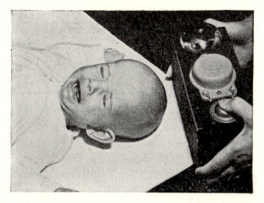

Ringing of bell at close range makes child cry.　This child can search out the source of sounds with his eyes.

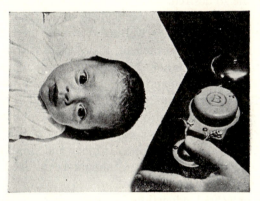

The child hears bell, but not with such acute perception.　Because she is slow, sound makes no emotional impact.

Figure 23.　Normal and Subnormal Responses to the Ringing of a Bell
(From *Life*, Aug. 18, 1941, p. 37.　Courtesy of A. R. Gilliland.)

The Development of Adaptability.—When an infant is experiencing tensions occasioned by hunger, cold, isolation, and the like he will usually react in a vigorous, undifferentiated manner until something is done to relieve him.　In a remarkably short time he will begin to utilize the responses which appear to result in the reduction of his tensions.　The infant will also modify such responses as prove to be futile in his quest for bodily satisfactions.　It is in this manner that he develops an increasing ability to make satisfying adaptations to situations for which he has no fixed mode of response, and which prove to be annoying to him.

The infant may, for example, kick aside his bedcovers and react to the succeeding stresses of cold by crying, squirming, and making thrashing movements with his limbs. When his mother comes to his rescue and restores his feeling of well-being, his symptoms of distress are discontinued. At another time, the infant may find that kicking and squirming alone do not bring his mother to his side. It is usually not long until he comes to manage his mother by expressing vocal signals of discomfort when he is in the mood for attention. Many an infant has utilized this adaptive technique to have himself picked up whenever he so desired.

It is well to encourage the development of adaptability along lines conducive to the child's welfare. It is to the child's advantage to explore his environment, to associate with a number of people, to play with other children, and to manipulate toys and articles requiring adaptive responses. Even the infant should be given the opportunity of being active and of adjusting to novel situations in his environment. Inactive children, whose behavior is relatively stereotyped, do not as a rule become effective and well-adjusted adults. Infancy and childhood constitute an exploratory period and should be utilized for the development of adaptive capacity.

Modern preschool education is capitalizing on the young child's exploratory interests. Here the pupil is encouraged to develop, not only verbal skill and social cooperation, but a problem-solving attitude. The child is given an opportunity to play with blocks and other articles requiring manipulation, to learn about and care for pets, to participate in simple games, to listen to interesting stories concerning the world about him, and to care for his personal clothing and toilet. The pupil thus learns that he is surrounded by a complex environment in which new problems requiring continual readjustments of old methods constantly arise. Childhood education should utilize the pupil's flexibility and avoid the establishment of fixed responses. Even the infant's responses are not determined by structural organization alone, and should thus be led into adaptive channels.

How Learning Occurs in Infancy.—Most infant learning is of the "conditioned response" variety, a simple form in which a new or substitute stimulus comes to bring out a response which it did not natively elicit. For example, when the sight of a rabbit, which does not frighten an infant at birth, comes to do so upon being associated with a loud sound, the child is said to be "conditioned" against rabbits. Most of the original experiments on conditioning were carried out by Russian physiologists and psychologists, a majority of whom concluded that because of the immaturity of the cortex such learning cannot be established in infants less than three or four months of age. However, a number of investigations have shown that this generalization is not borne out by the facts.

The Russian experimenters Denisova and Figurin [50] succeeded in establishing a true conditioned response in which sucking movements were made by three- and four-weeks-old infants when they were seated in the mother's lap, but before being given the breast. Tests showed that neither the sight or odor of the mother's breast, nor her voice, face, or body warmth were responsible for the conditioned sucking movements. The infants responded with sucking reactions even when placed in the position of nursing on a man's lap, provided the latter's face was covered and he did not speak.

In the United States, several investigators, one of whose researches will be reported, have studied the possibilities of conditioning infants. Working at the University of Iowa, Wenger [51] carried on a series of carefully controlled experiments designed to determine what type of conditioned responses can be established in newborn infants. In the first experiment a flash of light, which normally causes closure of the eyelid, was presented simultaneously with a tactual vibration on the infant's body. In the case of several infants, the lid closure

[50] Reported in Margaret W. Curti, *Child Psychology*, New York, Longmans, Green & Co., 1938, pp. 212-213.

[51] M. A. Wenger, "An Investigation of Conditioned Responses in Human Infants," *Univ. of Iowa Studies in Child Welfare*, Vol. 12, No. 1 (1936).

became conditioned to the tactual body stimulus in from five to six days. When a group of infants (second experiment) were stimulated by a mild electric shock applied to the foot simultaneously with a flash of light, two became conditioned to the shock by the sixth day. In Wenger's third series, no success was achieved in an attempt to condition sucking responses to the sound of a buzzer.

Although these and other experiments have demonstrated the possibility of establishing conditioned responses during the first few weeks of life, such conditioned learning requires considerable repetition of both natural and "shifted" stimuli. Furthermore, infant conditioned responses are, as a rule, very unstable. Infants also vary widely in susceptibility to various types of conditioning. With older children, evidence has shown that the more intelligent they are, the more readily they respond to the requirements of conditioned learning. Some investigators believe that the immaturity of cortical and subcortical tissue in neonates explains, at least in part, their relative slowness in learning. The plasticity of infants and children should, nevertheless, stimulate parents and teachers to guide them toward the attainment of behavior patterns which will be of value as they progress toward maturity. Learnings acquired in infancy may be vital in the determination of later personal and social adjustment.

Summary and Implications

The newborn infant displays a wide variety of responses to both intra-organic and environmental stimuli. Although the processes concerned with his metabolic and other vegetative (digestion, heart action, respiration, etc.) activities are well coordinated, his bodily responses are characterized by much mass action and unorganized movement. The infant exhibits much reflex behavior, but it, too, may be regarded as an expression of undifferentiated action designed to reduce various body stresses. Some reflexes, such as the Darwinian, soon fade out in the child's behavior; others become inseparably merged with learned reactions and thus lose their distinctiveness. Infant emotions have been shown to be diffuse; they cannot be listed accurately under such categorized names as love, fear, and anger. Most infant emotional behavior can be described more objectively as constituting acceptance or rejection tendencies. Stimulation of the neonate's sense organs brings into play much indefinite response. He neither sees, hears, tastes, nor smells with the definiteness and acuity so characteristic of more mature human organisms. The infant must await the processes of growth and experience before he can use his sensory and muscular equipment in making specialized and adaptive movements.

Postnatal life begins with sensorimotor equipment the potentialities of which are truly remarkable, but which at first constitute the raw material out of which will develop all of the complex aspects of the child's personality. The infant inherits his physical structures, his equipment for registering emotions, and his potential capacity for making physical adaptations to the requirements of his environment. However, the attitudes he develops, the degree of socialization he attains, and the manner in which he achieves satisfaction of his needs are apparently determined by the way his development is "engineered." The infant becomes what his inherited structures and environmental opportunities make possible.

QUESTIONS FOR DISCUSSION

1. In what ways is the doctrine that the newborn child is a miniature adult incompatible with known facts? How does the neonate differ from the adult in physical proportions? In relative muscular weight? In blood pressure? In contour of the head?

2. What are the advantages of the human infant's relatively long period of physical helplessness? What effects on the child's ultimate development would the possession of ready-made adaptive capacity, such as that characteristic of the puppy or the calf, probably have? Why?

3. By what process (or processes) do infants develop more adequate sensory acuity? Would they probably achieve such development if no environmental stimuli were encountered? What difference does it make whether infants are sensitive to thermal conditions or whether they experience pain?

4. What is meant by development from "gross, undifferentiated" to "specialized, differentiated" behavior responses? Why can it be said of the infant's physical responses that he reacts "all over"? To what extent can the infant display discrete or localized reactions?

5. What are some of the criticisms of the concept of discrete, independent reflexes in infant behavior? What more "organismic" (whole organism) view can be advanced to explain reflex behavior? What are the disadvantages of viewing infant reflexes as semi-independent responses?

6. What is meant by the assertion that tropisms are "mechanistic" concepts? Why are tropisms not used more widely as explanations of infant and child behavior? If it could be shown that animals behave tropistically, would it follow that human offspring do the same?

7. To what extent has it been demonstrated that infants display clear-cut fear, love, and rage reactions? What criticisms could be advanced against the view that their emotional responses are largely undifferentiated, and that infants tend merely to *move toward* or *retreat from* emotion-evoking stimuli?

8. How do you explain the fact that several other investigators' findings do not agree with Watson's in experiments dealing with the emotional behavior of infants? Could it be that Watson's experimental conditions were too limited or that he did not check his results carefully? Explain.

9. To what extent do infants' emotional responses appear to be modifiable? Would it be preferable to contend that children's emotional responses should be *regulated* than that conditions should be so arranged that children are not frequently aroused to a high pitch of emotional excitement? Elaborate.

10. By what process do infants learn (acquire) new ways of responding to environmental stimuli? What is meant by the development of adaptability? What can be done to hasten such development? Where does education enter the picture here?

Recommended Readings

Dennis, Wayne. "Description and Classification of the Responses of the Newborn Infant." *Psychological Bulletin,* 31:5-22 (1934).

Hooker, Davenport. "Reflex Activities in the Human Fetus," in *Child Behavior and Development.* (Edited by Roger G. Barker *et al.*) New York: McGraw-Hill Book Co.. Inc.. 1943, Ch. 2

Hoskins, R. G. *Endocrinology, The Glands and Their Functions.* New York: W. W. Norton & Co., Inc., 1941.

Nagge, Joseph W. *Psychology of the Child.* New York: The Ronald Press Co., 1942, Ch. 2.

Pratt, K. C. "The Organization of Behavior in the Newborn Infant." *Psychological Review,* 44:470-490 (1937).

Pratt, K. C. "The Neonate," in *Handbook of Child Psychology.* (Edited by Carl Murchison.) Worcester: Clark Univ. Press, 1933, pp. 163-208.

Rand, Winifred, Sweeny, M. E., and Vincent, E. L. *Growth and Development of the Young Child.* Philadelphia: W. B. Saunders Co., 1940, Ch. 1.

Shaffer, Laurance F. *The Psychology of Adjustment.* Boston: Houghton Mifflin Co., 1936, Ch. 2.

Sherman, Mandel, and Sherman, I. C. "Sensory-Motor Responses in Infants." *Journal of Comparative Psychology,* 5:53-68 (1925).

Sherman, Mandel, Sherman, I. C., and Flory, C. D. *Infant Behavior.* Comparative Psychology Monographs, Vol. 12, No. 59 (1936).

Stern, William. *Psychology of Early Childhood.* New York: Henry Holt & Co., Inc., 1924.

Watson, John B. *Psychology from the Standpoint of a Behaviorist.* Philadelphia: J. B. Lippincott Co., 1924, Ch. 6.

CHAPTER 5

THE DYNAMICS OF CHILD NATURE

CHILD PSYCHOLOGY HAS FOR DECADES been interested in determining the dynamics of behavior in human offspring. Students of child development are constantly in search of the motivation underlying the activity of infants and children. The quest is for an understanding of why young organisms act as they do, and of the nature of the motives that impel them to carry on their ceaseless behavior. Such a study of the dynamics of behavior is essential to insight into the many problems of adjustment of the developing child.

A widespread belief still exists that most of man's tendencies at birth are of an innate, biologically inherited nature. It is further supposed that many characteristic forms of behavior are potential in the human species. Until recently little interest has been shown in explaining the mechanisms of human nature and the external forces acting upon the child that might offer a more concrete explanation of the dynamics that underlie behavior. Many people are content to assume that such personality disorders, for example, as delinquency and emotional instability are inevitable expressions of an innately perverse nature. Relatively few individuals have endeavored to investigate the influence of the galaxy of ever-present environmental pressures in their quest for an explanation of child behavior. A study of this important problem should yield a better understanding of the characteristics of child nature.

The Instinct Controversy

Primitive man was noted for his tendency to ascribe the natural phenomena operating about him to the caprice of good or evil spirits. These spirits were thought to inhabit otherwise inanimate objects and to cause them to behave in certain unpredictable ways. Storms and earthquakes presumably arose and subsided at the behest of the gods. Famines, floods, and diseases were regarded as expressions of the ill-will of evil agencies. Early man was apparently unable to understand the principle of natural causation which we now know to be at work when the phenomena described are in evidence. *Animism,* as this doctrine has been called, was, however, apparently not the exclusive property of primitive man. There are still those who believe that evil tendencies, not to mention delinquent and criminal dispositions, are manifestations of an innately evil nature. The mode of operation of such an immaterial force could not be determined by any method known to science, and is thus generally regarded as a modern version of the older doctrine of animism.

Early Conceptions Concerning Instincts.—Following the rise of the inquiring attitude and the coming of more concrete knowledge concerning processes of the human body, belief in animism in its more naive form began to decline. The more objective thinkers of the day began to associate dynamics, or motives to action, with body functions. Such seventeenth-century scholars as Bacon, Descartes, and Hobbes endeavored to draw distinctions between tendencies of original nature and products of experience. Eighteenth-century philosophers, such as Locke, Condillac, and Reimarus, proceeded a step farther by attempting to analyze and catalogue the innate tendencies of man. The last-named scholar went so far as to compare the inherited tendencies of man with those of animals.

Some of these and other early thinkers were inclined to locate inherited tendencies to action in the operations of the physical body. Others considered such a step too materialistic and suggested the existence within man of a group of psychic (immaterial) forces capable of driving the body into action. Each of these groups, one emphasizing innate behavior tendencies of the physical organism and the other stressing so-called mental or spiritual forces, came to call their respective unlearned tendencies by the well-known term "instincts." The instinct idea gained in popularity until practically every form of behavior in both animals and humans has been called instinctive by someone. Infant responses, especially, have been regarded as strictly determined by innate unlearned factors of one kind or another. Scholars even have assured parents that the complexities of childhood behavior can be explained in terms of instinctive tendencies.

Instincts in Modern Child Psychology.—The psychologist William James is generally credited with being the first modern scholar to define and classify instincts as specific, inherited forms of behavior. James was anxious to make the psychology of his day less vaguely philosophical, and thus endeavored to place human motivation on a more definite physiological basis. He defined instinct as "the faculty of acting in such a way as to produce certain ends, without foresight of the ends, and without previous education in the performance," and insisted that such unlearned capacity was based on the inheritance of elaborate *nervous system connections.* James believed that there were twenty-eight instincts, ranging from the infant's biting and sucking to hunting and parental love.[1]

Thorndike, a pupil of James, gave added impetus to the instinct theory by associating it even more specifically with the functioning of the nervous system, and by applying it to the education of children. He early expressed his views on the inheritance of unlearned behavior in the following vein: "We inherit certain connections between nerve-cells which make us act in certain circumstances in definite ways, without our learning how, or thinking about the matter at all, or hearing what we are going to do. . . . We call such unlearned activities *instincts, or native reactions.* Such activities may appear before birth or at birth or be delayed until after birth." [2] Thorndike enlarged on his predecessor's lists of instincts by breaking them down into more specific divisions. His view of the instinct problem is practically the same as that in vogue today among those who still believe in the strict inheritance of so-called universal behavior patterns.

[1] William James, *Principles of Psychology* (Briefer Course), New York, Henry Holt & Co., Inc., 1892, p. 403.
[2] E. L. Thorndike, *The Human Nature Club,* New York, Longmans, Green & Co., 1900, pp. 27-28.

Instinct psychology was stimulated to added popularity by the doctrines of another early twentieth-century scholar, William McDougall, who regarded instincts as the "essential springs or motive powers of all thought and action." McDougall refused, however, to regard instincts as the behavioral counterpart of inherited neural connections, and insisted instead that they were *innate mental driving forces* or "native springs of action." This psychologist has consistently held that, in addition to a physical body, man possesses independent mental forces which are capable of influencing the body in such a way as to satisfy their instinctive demands. He admits, however, that in man instincts can be modified by intelligence; that is, by the proper training of infants and children. McDougall has published several lists of instincts conceived of as the prime movers of all activity, and believes that each is characterized by an *emotional* core. Perhaps the best known of these formulations is the one published in 1923.[3] In this list each instinct is accompanied by its emotional counterpart:

Parental—protective and tender feeling.
Combat—anger.
Curiosity—questioning attitude.
Food seeking—appetite.
Escape—fear.
Gregariousness—loneliness.
Primitive passive sympathy—shared feelings.
Mating—sex feeling.
Acquisitive—possessiveness.
Constructive—feeling of creativeness.
"Appeal"—distress.
Laughter—amusement.

McDougall's published works indicate that he believed that child behavior, as well as the social, economic, and political activities of adults, is motivated, indirectly at least, by the major instinctive urges. On this basis, it would be necessary to admit that both child and adult action is determined, in the last analy-

[3] William McDougall, *Outline of Psychology,* New York, Chas. Scribner's Sons, 1923, pp. 135-165.

sis, by instinctive rather than by rational forces. McDougall has contended that such a limitation of the intellectual factor in man (and child) is warranted by the "facts."

Criticisms of the Instinct Concept.—Objections to the instinct idea tend to center on two alternative, but less mysterious, explanations of child (and adult) behavior: (1) that so-called instincts have been developed through the process of learning, and (2) that instinct is merely a name for the responses of body structures as made possible *by their mechanical design.* With reference to the first point, Watson [4] says, "Everything we have been in the habit of calling an instinct today is a result largely of training—belongs to man's learned behavior." It has been claimed, for example, that because of the well-nigh universal tendency of man to defend himself against every form of danger, everyone displays an instinct of self-preservation. This may be true, but infants, who have had no opportunity to learn to avoid danger in the many flexible ways utilized by adults, do not appear to fear most forms of danger. According to the evidence examined in Chapter 4, about all newborn infants seem to fear are loud noises and disturbances of equilibrium of a kind calculated to create tensions in their sensitive nervous systems. An infant would offer no objections to the approach of a wild animal, would make no attempt to escape from the path of an oncoming train, would willingly place sweet-tasting poison in his mouth, and would not hesitate to grasp a sharp knife placed within his reach. The concern of older children about these and similar dangers are apparently learned from parents, teachers, companions, and to some extent from concrete experience. So it is with many other so-called instincts—whereas they are supposedly innate, in actuality they have been learned in the course of intellectual development and education.

As for responses appearing at birth, such as crying or kicking, they have been called the mechanically necessary reactions of body structures to either intra-organic or external stimuli. This view denies the existence of innate behavior tendencies that are independent of neuromuscular possibilities or environ-

[4] John B. Watson, *Behaviorism,* New York, W. W. Norton & Co., Inc., 1930, p. 94.

mental influences. In discussing the nature of such original responses as sucking, smiling, sneezing, and love, fear, and rage,
Watson [5] reasons, "Can we not say that man [the infant] is
built of certain materials put together in certain complex ways,
and as a corollary of the way he is put together and of the material out of which he is made—he must act (until learning has
reshaped him) as he does act?" This position regards infant
behavior as being a function of the way the organism is designed, and thus dispenses with the need of instincts as elaborate
unlearned adaptive responses. It recognizes that original behavior is determined by the mechanical possibilities of the
infant's body, but that such responses are soon modified by
learning. Facility in nursing (sucking) must be learned, but
in this instance the form of mouth and throat structures is so
appropriate to sucking, and the experience of swallowing warm
milk so satisfying, that the skill involved is soon learned. The
same logic holds for learning to crawl, walk, play, and vocalize.
These and other childhood functions depend upon the intelligent
utilization of adequately mature physical structures.

The notion that instincts are innate mental forces, the removal of which would render the individual powerless to act,
has been criticized as constituting a kind of glorified animism,
or belief in spirits. Where such forces would be located in the
human organism is a problem beyond the ken of man.
Shaffer's [6] comments on this issue are apropos, "Unfortunately,
some persons have taken instincts to mean forces within the
individual which cause or compel him to do things. Such a
conception is even worse than useless. It peoples the organism
with a host of little *daemons* who prod and urge and drive it to
activity. This is a very primitive type of explanation."
Shaffer's words may be a bit severe, but, as the present author
has written elsewhere, belief in mystic mental forces "perpetuates the scientific fallacy of assuming that a spiritual force, itself
outside the circuit of physical cause and effect, can exercise
a tangible effect on material substance (the body)." [7] In short,

[5] *Ibid.*, pp. 112-113.
[6] Laurance F. Shaffer, *The Psychology of Adjustment*, Boston, Houghton
Mifflin Co., 1936, p. 84.
[7] Louis P. Thorpe, *Psychological Foundations of Personality*, New York,
McGraw-Hill Book Co., Inc., 1938, p. 186.

the theory that human dynamics, child or adult, are associated with intangible entities, is considered untenable to science, of which child psychology is a branch.

Breakdown of the Instinct Hypothesis.—The great popularity of the instinct theory during the first two decades of the twentieth century can probably be attributed to the prestige of such exponents as James, Thorndike, McDougall, and Woodworth. These and other psychologists of the day gave the instinct hypothesis an impetus that made it an almost universally accepted doctrine in education, psychology, sociology, and related social sciences. It was not until the lists of alleged instincts became suspiciously large, and various scientists began to point out both physiological and psychological flaws in instinct theories, that "the elaborate theoretical structure broke beneath its own weight." [8]

A number of psychologists have stressed the fact that classifications of specific instincts are out of harmony with the findings of physiologists, and that considerable confusion and disparity has existed among instinct enthusiasts themselves. An avalanche of criticisms, particularly from those who were doubtful of all theories of innate, inherited behavior tendencies, finally reduced the instinct hypothesis to a position of relative unimportance. Today, few psychologists subscribe to its tenets. It is recognized that animals display some apparently unlearned behavior suggestive of inherited nervous system connections.[9] However, so far as humans (especially children) are concerned, the instinct hypothesis is being disregarded in favor of an intensive search for more tenable physiological and psychological bases of motivation to behavior. Instead of dealing with instincts, which *describe* rather than *explain* child behavior, psychologists are endeavoring to ascertain the dynamic factors which account for the child's tendencies to act in certain ways, and subsequently to control his environment in such a manner as to guarantee the emergence of socially desirable behavior.

[8] Percival M. Symonds, "Human Drives," *Journal of Educational Psychology,* 25 : 682-683 (1934).

[9] K. S. Lashley, "Experimental Analysis of Instinctive Behavior," *Psychological Review,* 45 : 445-471 (1938).

The Structure-Function Principle

Genesis of the Structure-Function Idea.—In an effort
to avoid founding child development programs on the dubious
instinct concept, some students of the subject have developed
a substitute proposal which they feel meets many of the objections usually leveled at instincts. This proposal is sometimes
referred to as the *structure-function* principle, but is also often
discussed as the *maturation* theory. According to the structure-
function concept, motor abilities such as crawling or walking,
and even vocal functions, appear in the developing child at a
time and rate determined by the growth of body structures concerned with such responses. Gesell,[10] a leader in this field,
speaks of maturation as the "intrinsic component of development (growth)" or the ripening of inner structures that makes
possible the performance of their life functions. Gesell's strong
emphasis on the inner, inherited factor in growth is indicated by
the following words, "The nervous system grows according to
its own intrinsic pattern and thereby establishes the primary
forms of behavior. These forms are not determined by stimulation from the outside world. Experience has nothing specifically to do with them." On this basis, maturation is a regulatory
mechanism, inherent in the child's organism, which stimulates
and determines the direction of growth.

Maturation may be contrasted with learning by regarding
the former as being controlled from within the organism, and
the latter as being occasioned by factors operating in the environment. Maturation refers to development brought about
by internal growth factors; learning is concerned with modifications of behavior made possible by training and education.
Gesell[11] recognizes this contrast when he says, "Learning
. . . may be regarded as that aspect of growth (or development) which is a functional perfecting of behavior adaptations
to specific situations, present or past." Although it is true that
the child's physical structures must await the process of maturation, the detailed ways in which they will function are deter-

---

[10] Arnold Gesell, "Maturation and the Patterning of Behavior," in *Handbook
of Child Psychology* (edited by Carl Murchison), Worcester, Clark Univ. Press,
1933, p. 210.
[11] *Ibid.*

mined to a surprising extent by the ever-present learning process. Although considering the evidence for innately determined growth, some psychologists, even, are persistently prone to minimize the effects of environmental influences.

Maturation Experiments with Children.—A number of important researches in child maturation have been reported, but those by Gesell and by McGraw are perhaps the most illustrative.

Gesell and Thompson [12] studied the stair climbing skill of a pair of identical infant twins who were very similar in all measurable mental, physical, and other characteristics. When forty-six weeks of age, twin T (training twin) was given systematic training in stair climbing ten minutes per day for a period of six weeks. At the conclusion of the training period, when she was fifty-two weeks of age, this twin was regarded as being a "relatively expert climber." Twin C (control twin) could not, at this age, climb the stair even with assistance, but was able to do so without help one week later. At this point twin C (fifty-three weeks) was given a two-weeks' course in climbing which culminated when the sisters were fifty-five weeks of age. As motion pictures of the experiment showed, twin C became as proficient after two weeks' practice as her sister T, who had been given an earlier six-weeks' course of training. Twin C's training period was much shorter than that accorded T, but since it was instituted several weeks later, the maturation process was in a position to make its effects felt.

Gesell has concluded from this and other experiments that the development of infant behavior patterns is a function of the maturation of appropriate neural and muscular structures. Gesell is aware of the influence of education in the development of verbal ability, and in connection with personality trends, but believes that there is danger of overestimating the learning possibilities of infants. As he puts it, "He [the infant] grows in accordance with endowment as well as environment. Training cannot transcend maturation, but must respect it." To

---

[12] Arnold Gesell and H. Thompson, *Learning and Growth in Identical Infant Twins: An Experimental Study by the Method of Co-twin Control*, Genetic Psychology Monographs, Vol. 6, No. 1 (1929) pp. 1-124.

this psychologist, maturation is an intrinsic stabilizing agency which gives direction to the mechanics of growth. He concludes that "the growth characteristics of the infant are primarily determined by hereditary and constitutional factors which undergo their basic organization in the uterine period." [13]

McGraw has made an extensive growth study of a pair of male twin infants in which one was given extra exercise and taught such motor skills as swimming and roller skating at as early an age as possible, and the other restricted somewhat less along exercise lines than the average child. Their behavior development was carefully compared with each other and with that of a group of 68 infants whose physical activities were in no way restricted. According to this investigator, activities of a phyletic (inherent in structural design) nature, such as crawling and walking, were not noticeably affected by practice. In fact, the twin who had not been stimulated to learn to swim and skate was able to perform these skills at a later date about as well as his more active brother. Skill in games involving insight was in some instances improved by exercise. However, training in motor skills appeared to bring about a more persistent and cooperative attitude on the part of the learner.

McGraw found that, to be effective, training must be given at a time appropriate to the infant's or child's degree of physical development and experience. To quote her, "The comparative development of these infants in relation to each other and to the larger group indicates that in general the somatic aspect of the behavior-patterns . . . was not materially influenced by exercise of the performance during postnatal development. However, even from the earliest, more extensive experience appeared to develop a more acquiescent attitude. In some instances the attitude determined the persistence of duration of a particular somatic pattern though it did not alter the essential sequential phases observed in the growth of a behavior-pattern." [14] Thus, like Gesell's infants, Johnny and Jimmy could function in any skilled sense only to the extent that their physical struc-

---

[13] Arnold Gesell, C. S. Amatruda, B. M. Castner, and H. Thompson, *Biographies of Child Development,* New York, Paul B. Hoeber, Inc., 1939.
[14] Myrtle B. McGraw, *Growth: A Study of Johnny and Jimmy,* New York, D. Appleton-Century Co., Inc., 1935, p. 118.

Figure 24. Behavior on Slides (Johnny)

Top. Johnny begins ascending a slide placed at an angle of 11 degrees when 8½ months old. *Center left.* At 10 months he ascends a slide placed at an angle of 48 degrees. *Center right.* At 21 months he scales the 70-degree slope. *Bottom.* Johnny at 13 months walks up and down an incline of 32 degrees. (From Myrtle B. McGraw, *Growth: A Study of Johnny and Jimmy*, New York, D. Appleton-Century Co., Inc., 1935, p. 138.)

tures were mature. Although training (learning) yielded certain dividends, it was allegedly not able to transcend the maturation factor.

Criticisms of the Structure-Function Principle.—Critics of the strict structure-function or maturation principle feel that it represents to a great extent a disguised form of determinism reminiscent of the older inheritance theories. Taken at its face value, the theory would lead one to believe that infants and children are endowed by nature with elaborate behavior patterns that need only to be stimulated in some specific way to set them in motion. In the eyes of Gesell and his associates, maturation looms so large that in comparison with it experience and learning apparently occupy a minor role. To these psychologists the infant's destiny appears to be mapped out by the inevitable forces of biological inheritance; he will become to a large extent what the germ plasm and other determiners of development dictate in advance. Advocates of such a developmental view recognize the influence of the physical and social environment, but they apparently do not regard these factors as being of more than superficial importance in the determination of child behavior.

Proponents of the maturation theory believe that inherited mechanisms provide the infant's sequence of behavior forms. They insist that experience is not fundamentally necessary to the appearance of adaptive behavior in the growing child. They have thus revived the earlier emphasis on innate endowment in a more modern form. Ardent environmentalists, while not denying the importance of the structure-function principle, contend that no distinction should be made between unlearned and learned activities. They believe that a majority of the infant's acts are influenced by both the structural design of his body and the demands of the physical and social environment. They feel that no useful purpose is served by making a distinction between the hereditarian's "structure-maturation" responses and behavior brought about by experience and training. These factors are believed to be interlocked and thus inseparable. To give too much emphasis to behavior basically determined by maturation is to lose sight of the fact that experience itself influences the performance of bodily responses.

Investigators in both the human and animal fields have reported researches which throw doubt on the assertion that body responses mature automatically at a given rate. The Sher-mans [15] found that infants' reflexes are dependent for their development upon practice as well as growth, and that such body-structure activities as crawling, reaching, and walking also become better coordinated through training. They also noted that infants' trial-and-error responses could be noticeably improved by stimulating them to more continuous adaptive activity. The Shermans conclude: "This indicates that many of the responses usually attributed to organic maturation are in reality products of learning, since such a speeding up of adaptive behavior could not take place were maturation necessary for its growth." It is possible that learning plays a more important role in the development of infant adaptive behavior than strict maturationists have supposed.

It should be recognized when an infant performs some act which appears to be a function of maturation, the exercise of that act influences its pattern and may lead to even more adaptive behavior. Maturation and learning are thus not two contrasted factors; they are, rather, aspects of an inseparable integration whose effect explains the development of adaptive behavior in infants and children. It could be said, thus, that such be-havior develops fundamentally as the counterpart of maturing body structures, but that the details of its expression, the time of its appearance, and the rapidity of its development are sub-ject to the modifying influences of the individual's environment, i.e., *learning*.

The Concept of Fundamental Needs

As an explanation of the nature and temporal appearance of child behavior, the structure-function principle seems definitely more adequate than the older instinct theory. The maturation-of-structure approach to child development has not, however, provided an answer to the quest for the real motivators of be-havior—the dynamics of child nature. Such an approach may indicate in what sequence functional abilities develop and what direction they take under given circumstances, but it does not

---

[15] Mandel Sherman and I. C. Sherman, *The Process of Human Behavior,* New York, W. W. Norton & Co., Inc., 1929, pp. 62-84.

provide an explanation of why children behave as they do, why they eat, drink, play, work, and seek affection, recognition, and approval. In short, neither the instinct nor structure-function theories solved the problem of motivation, the fundamental question of *why* the child acts at all. It is to this quest that the present section is devoted.

Behavior as Stress-Relieving Activity.—Students of child psychology have in recent years come to realize that infants and children probably behave as they do in an effort to secure certain forms of satisfaction. Young organisms are characterized by physical and psychological *needs* which tend to direct their actions and which provide the clue to why they react as they do. The child, like mature man, is so constituted that a minimum fulfillment of his organic and psychological needs is necessary to the maintenance of his personal integrity. On this basis behavior, such as eating, sleeping, and seeking attention, would be designed to reduce the stresses set up by hunger, fatigue, and the desire for recognition, respectively. As Chapman and Counts [16] wrote some years ago, "Man spends all his days in a valiant struggle to satisfy his imperious wants. On entering the world the first inner tension is relieved by crying; he eats, drinks, fights, loves, mates, and thinks to relieve other tensions; and on his death bed, in the act of blessing his family, he relieves a last tension."

The fundamental need concept of child dynamics is much more understandable than the vague instinct theory, and does not require a solution of the endless nature-nurture controversy. If the child is characterized by a number of irreducible *needs*, it seems logical to reason that excessive frustration of these needs would result in the creation of certain tensions. Furthermore, since tensions (stresses) seek release in the form of restoration to a state of balance or equilibrium, the child is motivated to do something to relieve his ever-recurring stresses. He seeks food when hungry, endeavors to secure attention when neglected, and daydreams or rebels when rejected. In short, the

[16] J. C. Chapman and G. S. Counts, *Principles of Education*, Boston, Houghton Mifflin Co., 1924, p. 55.

child must receive reasonable fulfillment of his fundamental needs if he is to escape maladjustment.

Murray [17] has summarized the need concept by defining a need as "An electro-chemical process of some sort which is invariably felt as the force of a desire . . . and that tends to propel thought and action in a certain direction." By this reasoning, child behavior, be it food-seeking or falsehood to a companion, is brought about by tensions. To put the matter in Lewin's [18] "topological" phraseology, when a child's state of equilibrium has been disturbed in some respect (hunger, thirst, anger, rejection, etc.), he will endeavor to respond in the direction of establishing a new state of equilibrium (secure food, overcome an obstacle, or gain acceptance). This process of adjustment may be viewed schematically in Figure 25.

Lewin conceives of motivation in terms of stresses or tensions which initiate movement in a relational, social field of force. The dynamic relationships involved affect the child in terms of the environmental setting in which he is situated. The child will thus behave in ways that are commensurate with his needs at the time and the existing situation as it appears to him. Whether he requests his teacher, for example, for permission to get a drink of water will depend on the state of his organism (stress) and the nature of the activities going on about him (field force). If the child were listening to a favorite story or enjoying a pleasant game, he would probably not be driven to action by slight stresses of thirst.

The stress-reducing explanation of child behavior claims no mysterious unlearned origin. It is based upon biological processes and upon acquired patterns of behavior calculated to secure the satisfaction of basic needs. Such an explanation of the nature of child motivation is concerned with the ways in which the young organism reacts to frustrations of its organic and psychological needs.

[17] H. A. Murray, "Facts Which Support the Concept of Need or Drive," *Journal of Psychology*, 3: 27-42 (1937).

[18] K. Lewin, *A Dynamic Theory of Personality*, New York, McGraw-Hill Book Co., Inc., 1935, p. 58. See also, by the same author, "Environmental Forces," in *Handbook of Child Psychology* (edited by Carl Murchison), Worcester, Clark Univ. Press, 1933, Ch. 14.

ANNOYING SITUATION – STRONG REWARD

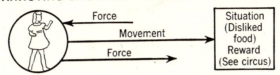

PLEASING SITUATION – STRONG PUNISHMENT

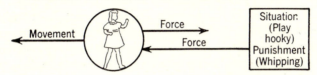

ANNOYING SITUATION – STRONG PUNISHMENT

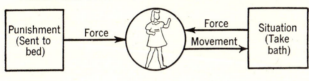

OR

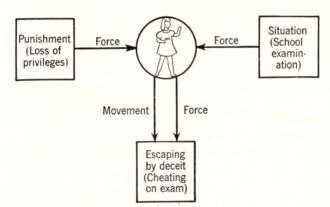

Figure 25. Diagram Showing Some Possibilities in the Operation of Field Forces or Stresses

Stimulating situations may involve opposing forces, in which event the direction and intensity of a child's movement will be determined by the interplay of these forces.

Development of the Fundamental Need Concept.—A brief account of the evolution of the fundamental need (as motivation) concept should serve to show how child behavior, formerly regarded as being instinctive, has come to be interpreted more naturalistically. In 1918, Kempf [19] developed a concept of human dynamics based upon the biological functions of the autonomic nervous system. It was Kempf's belief that, since the vegetative functions of the body (breathing, heart beat, digestion, metabolism, etc.) are under the control of the autonomic system, organic cravings provide the motive power for activity. The central (cerebro-spinal) nervous system is said to serve the autonomic by providing environmental conditions suitable for the fulfillment of its self-centered demands. Thus tensions created by such autonomic processes as digestion, elimination, and the maintenance of body temperature are said to stimulate the child's central nervous system to the initiation of such physiologically satisfying activities as his maturity and experience make possible. This is admittedly a pleasure-pain theory of human motivation, but it possesses the advantage of providing a tangible biological basis for the tension-relieving concept. Its greatest weakness is that it regards the child as being a mechanical organism governed almost wholly by the principle of self-preservation.

In the following year, 1919, Thomas,[20] a sociologist, concluded that human behavior is impelled by forces experienced in the form of "wishes." Thomas classified his dynamics as: (1) the wish for recognition, (2) the wish for response, (3) the wish for security, and (4) the wish for new experience. According to this thesis, a child could not enjoy normal adjustment unless all four wishes were satisfied in some measure. The predominance of one or more wishes would depend upon the child's temperament, which would in turn be contingent upon the condition of his glandular and nervous mechanisms. Thomas' concept of wishes as motivators to action has been widely publicized, and has enjoyed considerable acceptance.

[19] K. J. Kempf, *The Autonomic Functions and the Personality,* Nervous and Mental Disease Monograph, No. 28 (1918).
[20] W. I. Thomas and F. Znaniecki, *The Polish Peasant in Europe and America,* Richard G. Badger (Boston, Chapman & Grimes), 1919.

A few years later the psychologist Tolman [21] further clarified the dynamics problem by presenting the concept of *fundamental drives,* regarded as *appetites* and *aversions* (not as innate forces). Appetites were said to be drives in the sense that they represent internal physiological disturbances or states of disequilibrium which lead to overt activities designed to secure such food or other necessities as would restore harmony. As the word implies, aversions have reference to retreating behavior, the tendency to avoid experiences involving fear, pain, injury, and similar unpleasant states. Tolman has characterized stresses brought about by organic needs and autonomic nervous system processes as "first-order" drives, and learned urges, which have proved useful in satisfying these needs as "second-order" drives. Self-assertion, for example, is said to make possible the more adequate satisfaction of physiological drives. Tolman [22] has classified his fundamental drives in the following fashion:

First-Order Drives		*Second-Order Drives*
Appetites	Aversions	Curiosity
Food-hunger	Fright (injury-	Gregariousness
Sex-hunger	avoidance)	Self-assertion
Excretion-hunger	Pugnacity (in-	Self-abasement
Specific-contact-hunger	terference-	Imitativeness
Rest-hunger	avoidance)	
Sensori-motor-hunger		
Aesthetic and play		

Following Tolman's proposal of organic (first-order) and learned psychological (second-order) drives, other psychologists have formulated somewhat similar lists and have characterized them as "tissue needs," "distresses," "human wants," "human desires," "basic needs," and other such dynamic demands.[23]

The appetites, aversions, and desires are present in children and adults alike. Each individual learns to satisfy them in accordance with the demands of his personality pattern and in

21 E. C. Tolman, "The Nature of the Fundamental Drives," *Journal of Abnormal and Social Psychology,* 20: 349-358 (1926).
22 E. C. Tolman, *Purposive Behavior in Animals and Men,* New York, D. Appleton-Century Co., Inc., 1932, Chs. 18-19.
23 Percival M. Symonds, "Human Drives," *Journal of Educational Psychology,* 25: 681-694 (1934).

ways made possible by the circumstances of his physical and social environment. Thus child dynamics may be thought of as involving organic needs and the psychological satisfactions growing out of security, affection, and a general sense of personal worth.

The Basic Needs of the Child.—In more recent years there has been a tendency to classify child dynamics in terms of as few and comprehensive groups as possible. Since basic needs impel the child to behave in ways calculated to satisfy their demands, his nature is most readily understood from the standpoint of fundamental motivating factors. The child's happiness is dependent upon a balanced fulfillment of certain irreducible requirements. Thus it is important that parents and others appreciate the nature and extent of these dynamic forces.

From the standpoint of both child development and desirable personality adjustment at higher levels, fundamental needs may be classified as follows: [24]

THE ORGANIC NEED—the need to safeguard one's physical well-being by satisfying the stresses of hunger, thirst, temperature changes, fatigue, and pain. Children are aware of these ever-recurring demands and are almost continuously active in their efforts to satisfy them. A hungry child will, for example, endeavor to secure and consume food. A thirsty child will make an effort to find and consume water or other liquid. Avoidance of pain-producing situations is practically a universal activity among infants and children.

Men, women, and children engage in endless adjustive activities in their efforts to satisfy physical needs. Hospitals, restaurants, hotels, food stores, and homes are all operated, in part at least, for the purpose of reducing the stresses set up by body needs. In the case of infants, it is obvious that they enjoy and develop satisfactorily on a program of nursing, stroking, bathing, caressing, and erotic satisfaction in general. If the Freudians are to be believed, such a regime of organic pleasure is essential to the child's psychological adjustment. Certainly excessive frustration of the child's need for food, shelter, and the

---

[24] Louis P. Thorpe, *Personality and Life*, New York, Longmans, Green & Co., 1941, pp. 8-10.

material necessities of life can lead to such emotional reactions as depression, anxiety, resentment, or inferiority.

THE SELF OR EGO NEED—the need for recognition, response, personal autonomy, and of being regarded as an individual of worth. Children of all ages continue to strive for some form of favorable notice, social approval, distinction, or individuality. Children as well as adults possess a keen sense of personal importance and at no time do they abandon their efforts to support their integrity as autonomous personalities. Although this primary need is not regarded as being inherited, it is apparently developed very early in life. It is almost universally recognized that the behavior of all human beings, be they normal or abnormal, is powerfully influenced by the stresses occasioned by the need for maintaining a sense of personal worth.

The need for status, or feeling of belonging, is essential to the child's personal integrity, thus its excessive frustration may lead to serious emotional maladjustments. The child cannot live adequately without recognition and response from those who mean something to his welfare. Just as body tissues disintegrate when deprived of nutritive and other vegetative needs, so the child's emotional stability is imperiled when his fundamental ego need suffers excessive frustration. Continual failure in school may, for example, so thwart the child's need for being regarded as worthy and capable as to lead to antisocial behavior of a character designed to relieve his stresses of insecurity.

Like adults, children resent being shunned, ignored, or disparaged. Continued experience of this kind may result in considerable unhappiness and in some cases may lead to neurotic disorders or other pathological behavior. As Allen [25] has stated, children wish to appear capable to those about them, to be loved, and to be considered distinctive. Realization of the wish to *belong* establishes a feeling of equilibrium within the child which enables him to turn his attention to satisfactory relationships with other children and associates. In short, when the child's need for a feeling of worth and belonging is main-

[25] S. Allen, "The Wish to Belong," *Bulletin of the Menninger Clinic,* 4:74-81 (1940).

tained by friendly and tolerant treatment, he is motivated to make progress toward the all-important need of becoming socialized.

THE SOCIAL OR MUTUALITY NEED—the need to extend respect, recognition, and generous service to other members of society, particularly to those with whom one associates. In the adult field, the social motive is served both in connection with the rearing of a family and in treating associates with respect as *individuals of worth*. Such mutuality may also be expressed in social service and in contributions made through socially constructive vocations and professions. Fisher [26] has stressed the importance for balanced living of extending sympathy and aid to those in distress, and of adopting a humanitarian attitude toward unfortunate and underprivileged individuals. Mutuality also includes an understanding of peoples' needs and the use of sincere social skills in dealing with them in everyday relations. In brief, the social motive involves the extending to other individuals of the same recognition and status that one needs for the support of his own personal integrity.

Unfortunately for society and for the individuals concerned, many apparently do not recognize the importance for human happiness and adjustment of the social need. Organic and self-enhancement needs are seldom neglected, but the value for mental health and social harmony of mutuality in human relations is easily lost sight of. In spite of the emphasis accorded it in religious teachings and in the biographies of heroes, the social motive has to a great extent been overlooked. Psychologists even have sometimes neglected to present mutuality as the core of personal adjustment and socialization in their lists of human dynamics. It is nevertheless obvious that well-adjusted individuals and the better societies are characterized by a disposition to live in harmony with the principle of mutuality in human relations.

So far as infants and young children are concerned, they are primarily individualistic and too immature to cater to the well-being of other organisms. It should be recognized, however,

---

[26] V. E. Fisher, *Auto-Correctivism: The Psychology of Nervousness*, Caldwell (Idaho), The Caxton Printers, 1937, Ch. 3.

that they must eventually come to do so if they are to maintain mental health in a world of interpersonal obligations. The process of growing up socially and emotionally is one of becoming *less and less individualistic or egocentric and increasingly mutual or sociocentric in disposition.* As Figure 26 depicts, maturity represents a balance or integration of self-striving and social living.

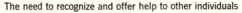

The need to recognize and offer help to other individuals

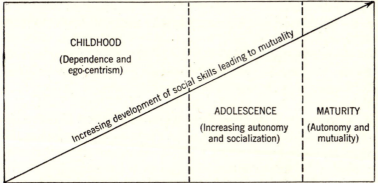

The need for recognition, response, and the feeling of belonging

Figure 26. Schematic Representation of the Development of Mutuality or Balance Between Ego-striving and Social Living

Whereas the infant must in the nature of the case make constant demands on his parents without giving service or recognition in return, the mature individual is required to give some form of payment for services rendered. To put the matter in another way, whereas the young child is dependent upon his elders for recognition and support for his sense of personal worth, the older child (and adolescent) must *win his status and approval through the avenue of social skills.* The acceptance of social obligations is essential to development beyond the infant stage, thus one of the most fundamental needs of children is that they become independent but reciprocal personalities within the larger social framework.[27]

---

[27] H. G. Miller, "The Transformation of the Self in Children," *American Journal of Mental Deficiency,* 48 : 374-378 (1944).

The basis for adequate personality growth may thus be said to be laid in childhood. As the child develops, he must adjust to increasingly complex social situations in which mutuality in the giving and getting of ego-recognition becomes more and more essential. If parents, in addition to providing security and affection, teach the child how to make himself liked, his sense of personal worth is maintained. If he fails to develop the social skills requisite for acceptance he encounters stresses of insecurity and may dislike people or become afraid of them. Such a threat to the child's feeling of personal importance is likely to eventuate in introspection, jealousy, boasting, fighting, belittling others, or other such psychological "mechanisms" designed to build up defenses by means of which his infantile personality may be kept intact.

Consequences of the Existence of Needs.—The concept of basic psychological needs does much toward clarifying the nature of child personality. The child is seen as a dynamic, constantly changing individual who stands continually in need of both physical and psychological satisfactions. The well-adjusted child is one who has found realization of his needs in ways acceptable to himself and to his associates. Normality of behavior may therefore be thought of as stemming from a balanced fulfillment of physical, egoistic, and social needs. Under such conditions the child's sense of personal worth is adequately maintained. However, since his dynamic nature motivates him to seek a feeling of worth, threats to his personal integrity in this area will almost invariably result in *efforts to restore it by socially undesirable means.* There are thus grounds for maintaining that delinquent and antisocial behavior, as well as neurotic trends, represent efforts to escape the stresses of insecurity and to bolster a sense of personal importance. Figure 27 suggests the nature of undesirable ego-supporting mechanisms.

From the above discussion it can be seen that the art of child rearing involves harmonization with the needs of the individual as they are at present understood. If the child is to achieve personal happiness and facility in human relations he

must be enabled to live in accordance with the requirements of
his own nature and of the social environment in which he is
imbedded.

The concrete nature of a program of good adjustment as
related to stress-producing needs has been adequately set forth
by Trow [28] in the following words: "If enough good food, rest,
sunshine, and so forth, are obtainable, so that the physiological
organism is strong and healthy, if there is sufficient opportunity
for free activity, for striving for ends which he considers de-

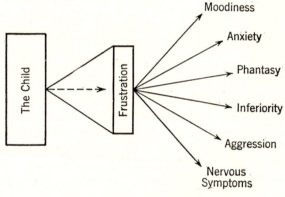

Figure 27. Typical Effects of Frustration

sirable, and for the appreciation of things which are to him
beautiful; and if, in the eyes of his comrades, there is something
of respect for him; and if there are those in whom he can confide and those whom he can in some way serve, man [and the
child] may experience that feeling of happiness which has been
the goal of life for untold generations."

Those who deal with children should thus seek the basic
causes of antisocial or egocentric behavior with a view to
assisting them in finding more socially desirable forms of recognition—more acceptable outlets for active interests, and more
adequate satisfaction of their organic and psychological needs.
Such a point of view in child development represents a logical

[28] W. C. Trow, *Educational Psychology,* Boston, Houghton Mifflin Co., 1931,
p. 41.

refutation of the older dogma of innate depravity which regarded the child as being essentially sinful by nature.

Psychoanalytic Views of Motivation.—Students of child psychology who are interested in the problem of personality dynamics frequently wonder to what extent psychoanalytic views do or do not harmonize with the more conventional psychological concepts of motivation. Such individuals are also concerned with the adequacy of psychoanalytic explanations of the adjustment processes of human nature. Perhaps a brief account of the three principal psychoanalytic systems will enable the reader to compare them with the balance-among-needs proposal described in previous sections.

FREUDIAN PSYCHOANALYSIS. It was the contention of Sigmund Freud, the founder of psychoanalysis, that the primary motivating force in child life is the desire for sexual gratification. However, Freud interprets the term sex in a broad pleasure-seeking sense. Thus the infant finds sexual or erotic satisfaction in such vegetative processes as sucking at the breast, eliminating, sleeping, and moving his body freely. The child also finds pleasure in thumb-sucking, the caresses of his mother, and in the manipulation of the erogenous (sex) areas of his body. According to Freud, all such experiences provide the child with satisfaction of his "libido" or innate desire for erotic gratification. However, as he develops, the child learns that many social regulations and morals stand in the way of continued free expression of his pleasure drive. This situation soon makes the child conscious of the necessity of maintaining the approval of people while still attempting to pursue his sensual pleasures.

Such a dual requirement is said to bring about a conflict in the emotional life of the child which leads at first to resistance of social demands, but which ultimately causes him to repress many of his erotic desires into the unconscious. The child thus is faced with the necessity of continually choosing between the desire for social approval (recognition) and a craving for sensual, but largely taboo, bodily pleasures or love attachments with adults. Children who enjoyed sufficient sex satisfactions in infancy to feel secure and accepted, are said to get along very well except for a minimum of wishful dreams and erotic desires. Children who were unfortunate enough to be frustrated in their sex needs in infancy are said, on the other hand, to find the conflict between the ideals of social living and the cravings of love satisfactions too intense to be resolved by methods other than that of continual repression into the unconscious. The latter individuals thus become victims of anxiety, nervousness, depression, symbolic dreams, hysterical illnesses, and similar symptoms of inner conflict.

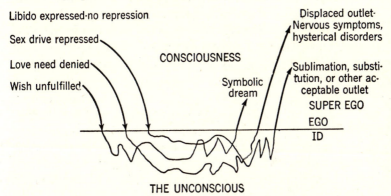

Figure 28. Diagram Showing Freud's Conception of the Results of Repression of Libidinal Needs

Psychoanalysis has suggested several avenues through which conflicts between suppressed desires and social regulations may "drain off" when the tension becomes too great. These dynamisms, as they are called, include (1) *repression,* or the relegating to the unconscious of disturbing thoughts and wishes; (2) *rationalization,* or the covering up of unacceptable behavior by way of excuses; (3) *sublimation,* or the substitution of socially approved pleasures for tabooed sexual impulses; (4) *symbolization,* or the substitution of dream symbols for unobtainable sexual satisfactions; (5) *projection,* or the transference of blame to others or to obstacles in a manner designed to preserve one's ego status; and (6) *conversion,* or the release of emotional tensions caused by the repression of strong impulses throughout the body, as in cases of hysteria.

According to Freud, the child's emotional status is dependent upon the extent to which his ego, or sense of social conformity, is successful in controlling the dormant desires of the unconscious.

ADLERIAN PSYCHOANALYSIS. Alfred Adler,[29] a colleague of Freud, has consistently maintained that, although each individual encounters a conflict between opposing desires, neither of these is of a sexual or love nature. As Adler puts it, every developing child is caught between the cultural demands of society and a powerful desire for mastery over others. The life drive or libido is for *power*, not sex. The newborn infant soon realizes his helplessness and inferiority in relation to those about him, and is thus led to develop ways and means of affecting some type of superiority. Inevitable failures to achieve such distinction bring about efforts at *compensation*, or attempts to atone for deficiency, which may assume either desirable or antisocial directions.

Desirable examples of compensation include the child who, though partially deaf, becomes adept in lip reading and school work in general; also the frail boy who atones for his inability to excel in athletics by learning to play an instrument in the school orchestra. Bullies, braggarts, and chronic juvenile delinquents provide examples of socially undesirable methods of compensating for feelings of inferiority. These and similar behavior dynamisms represent efforts to attain power in social relations and are properly interpreted in the light of the extent to which they serve to reduce stresses of personal insecurity. Since he believes that the "style of life" is set in the early years, Adler emphasizes the importance of enabling children to meet their problems with an assurance that will prevent the appearance of unnecessary inferiority feelings. This point of view has gained wide acceptance in psychology, and is utilized extensively in the field of child development.

JUNGIAN PSYCHOANALYSIS. The doctrine of motivation advocated by C. G. Jung,[30] another colleague of Freud's, re-

---

[29] Alfred Adler, *Problems of Neurosis*, Cosmopolitan Book Corp. (New York, Farrar & Rinehart), 1930.
[30] C. G. Jung, *Contributions to Analytical Psychology*, New York, Harcourt, Brace & Co., 1928.

sembles Adler's except that, according to him, the primary life force is the desire to make progress—the urge to make a success of cherished plans. This libido is more fundamental than sex, and includes such universal interests as religion, esthetics, and social acceptability. Failure to succeed in the struggle for self-hood and achievement may lead to what Jung calls "infantile regression," or the disposition to give up the battle for adult satisfactions in favor of the protections of childhood. A defeated individual may thus abandon attempts to carve out a career and develop a neurotic disorder designed to bring him sympathy and protection. Jung has accordingly emphasized the fact that problems arising at any given age may be just as influential "infantile repressions" in bringing about nervous disorders. Jung is also the author of the now famous concept of contrasted introvertive and extrovertive personality types.

SUMMARY OF PSYCHOANALYSIS. It can be seen that psychoanalysts hold various views concerning the nature of child dynamics. As they see it, infants and children are characterized by powerful innate desires [for love (sex), power, or success] that soon come into conflict with social ideals and requirements, but which are sufficiently dynamic to influence behavior in considerable detail when not adequately satisfied. The general psychoanalytic point of view is somewhat reminiscent of instinct psychology, but has nevertheless enjoyed widespread popularity. Regardless of one's position in this field, it must be acknowledged that the explanations of behavior, especially of neurotic disorders and so-called dynamisms, offered by this school of thought have profoundly influenced child psychology. Few textbooks on either normal or abnormal psychology have escaped the influence of the doctrine so confidently advocated by the various proponents of psychoanalysis.

However, in spite of its emphasis upon love (sex) and security in childhood, desirable compensation for inferiorities, and the insurance of successful achievement, psychoanalysis does not appear adequately to have comprehended the principle of mutuality as a basis for personality development. In short, although they recognize the importance of adjustment to social requirements, psychoanalysts say that neurotic and other undesirable forms of behavior arise as a result of repression of the child's desire for erotic pleasures or for power to dominate others. As has been mentioned previously, there is considerable evidence that neurotic disorders grow out of failure to combine in an adequate balance the need for status (self or ego need) and for contributing to the welfare of other human beings (social or mutuality need). Satisfactory child development may be said to result from harmony among apparently antagonistic (self and social) but actually complementary motives, not necessarily from the expression of sex or power desires alone. The avenue to personality adjustment is a mutual one in which the growing child is taught to exemplify a type of social living that enables associates to enjoy an equal degree of recognition and response.

The Psychology of Play

Play in some form is said to be universal among the young of all races. This observation has led psychologists to conclude that play must represent some important dynamic function. In modern education bodily activity in the form of unrestrained play is considered not only desirable but essential to the physical, emotional, and social development of children. Such a genetic point of view is a far cry from the New England dogma of play as an expression of the child's innate tendency toward evil doing. The following quotation from the early eighteenth century is illustrative of such a position: "Play must be forbidden in all of its forms. The children shall be instructed in this matter in such a way as to show them, through the presentation of religious principles, the wastefulness and folly of all play. They shall be led to see that play will distract their hearts and minds from God, the eternal Good, and work nothing but harm to their spiritual lives." [31] Fortunately, a more comprehensive and realistic conception of the characteristics of child

[31] Quoted in C. H. Judd, *Genetic Psychology for Teachers,* New York, D. Appleton-Century Co., Inc., 1911, p. 72.

nature has freed mankind from such an unverified assumption concerning the implications of play.

Modern students of child development have come to understand that, from a biological point of view, children's spontaneous activities provide a wholesome outlet for energy acquired through metabolic and other vital organic processes. It is also through play that the child learns the many neuromuscular skills, such as grasping, throwing, drawing, and other hand-eye coordinations, so imperative to the development of more mature functions. Furthermore, it is becoming increasingly apparent that happy childhood, including the development of social attitudes, is dependent upon at least a minimum amount of freedom to engage in untrammeled activity purely for the sake of the physical and emotional enjoyment which it provides.

The Child's Tendency to Play.—It is to be expected that theories concerning the function of play in child development should arise. The child's tendency to play has been a continuous source of interest to both philosophers and psychologists, a number of whom have proposed reasons for the appearance of this phenomenon. A brief résumé of the principal theories purporting to explain the forces underlying play activities should orient the reader to the complexities of this phase of child psychology.

Prominent among theories of play is the one proposed by Herbert Spencer [32] who, in harmony with the poet Schiller's earlier suggestion, believed that play was designed to drain off the child's surplus energy. Proponents of this view reason that since healthy children possess an abundance of energy, nature has provided play as an outlet for its release. They also point out the fact that neither frail children nor adults tend to play as much as healthy children. Spencer's theory has, however, been criticized on three counts: (1) that it does not explain the various forms of play activity, (2) that it fails to show why release of energy in the form of work would not be as effective with children as play, and (3) that it cannot account for children's frequently observed willingness to continue to play when

[32] Herbert Spencer, *The Principles of Psychology*, New York, D. Appleton-Century Co., Inc., 1873, Vol. II, pp. 627-635.

almost completely exhausted. It is common knowledge today that work is often not a satisfactory substitute for play, and that both children and adults frequently find great pleasure in physical play after much of their energy has been consumed. No amount of rationalizing would convince an athletically inclined boy that he could have as much fun beating a rug as he could playing baseball.

Karl Gross,[33] a Swiss psychologist, has endeavored to explain play as preparation and training for the later more serious business of life. Gross's study of the play of animals, primitive people, and children led him to conclude that children intuitively play at what is later to become their life work. On this basis the child who plays vigorously at an activity suitable for later specialization ultimately gains the advantage over his less active associates. Like other theories, the "preparation for life" point of view has been subjected to logical criticisms. It has been termed an effort on the part of adults to interpret in utilitarian fashion activity that would otherwise appear to be relatively useless. It has also been accused of confusing what is *cause* with what is *effect* by neglecting to realize that preparation for life results from rather than brings about the child's tendency to play. Furthermore, some forms of play have no apparent future value; others, such as fighting and playing robber, may even be harmful to the child's development.

The pioneer American psychologist G. Stanley Hall[34] has attracted much attention with his *recapitulation* theory of play. According to Hall, instead of looking forward in his play, the child re-enacts the activities of his primitive ancestors. This is the doctrine that child play parallels the evolution of man from earlier forms of animal life. On this basis, when small boys climb trees, build caves, and inhabit swimming holes they are recapitulating similar activities on the part of their remote progenitors. This is a picturesque theory, but it neglects to point out that many forms of play, such as bicycle riding, playing marbles, and enjoying card games, could hardly have stemmed

---

[33] Karl Gross, *The Play of Man*, New York, D. Appleton-Century Co., Inc., 1901.
[34] G. Stanley Hall, *Youth*, New York, D. Appleton-Century Co., Inc., 1920 Ch. 6.

from the prehistoric activities of lower animals. In addition, Hall's theory assumes the unverified hypothesis that acquired characteristics can be biologically transmitted.

In harmony with his other teachings, McDougall [35] has insisted that the tendency to play rests upon an *instinctive* basis. Although not present at birth, the instinct to play is said to "ripen" with development and is usually present when there is serious need for it. McDougall believed that, like any other instinct, play should be utilized in the education of children, especially in connection with rivalry. Such a theory of play is, of course, subject to the usual criticisms leveled at instinct doctrines. Instead of explaining play, it merely describes it while hiding behind the uncertain hypothesis of inherited tendencies.

Other more modern theories of play include Appleton's [36] biological view of play as a stimulus to growth, Robinson's [37] belief that play provides a compensatory make-believe activity for children (such as playing house or going hunting), and Dewey's [38] doctrine of play as life itself in the process of becoming socialized. Most present-day views in this field are founded upon the knowledge that the child is an active dynamic being whose fundamental physical and psychological needs can be met in part through the medium of play. Play itself may be regarded as a need which, when intelligently directed, brings in its wake not only physical well-being, but a sense of acceptance and emotional tonus as well. Properly supervised play is believed to involve many potentialities for the growth and development of children and youths.

Children's Play Interests.—With the coming of the project method and the so-called experience curriculum in preschool and elementary education, much interest has been displayed in the play life of children. Both parents and educators are anxious to determine what play materials are most appropriate for

[35] William McDougall, *Social Psychology*, Boston, John W. Luce & Co., 1918, pp. 111-113.

[36] L. E. Appleton, *A Comparative Study of the Play of Adult Savages and Civilized Children*, Chicago, Univ. of Chicago Press, 1910.

[37] E. S. Robinson, "The Compensating Function of Make-Believe in Play," *Psychological Review*, 27 : 429-439 (1920).

[38] John Dewey, *Human Nature and Conduct*, New York, Henry Holt & Co., Inc., 1922, pp. 90-93.

children of different ages, and how these may be used to further wholesome child development. Fortunately, a number of investigations have been made which go far toward answering these inquiries. A brief presentation of their findings should serve to clarify the problem of children's play interests.

In an effort to avoid reading adult views into child interests, Bott [39] permitted nursery school children to play with a variety of classified toys with a minimum of supervision. Trained observers kept a careful record of both play material preferences and the attention span, or length of time occupied with each toy, of each child. The play materials in question were classified as: (1) *pattern toys,* such as beads, puzzles, tinker builders, peg boards, and wooden dolls, whose construction tended to determine the manner of their use; (2) *raw materials,* such as beans, blocks, color cubes, blackboards, and spools, whose use depended largely upon the ingenuity of the child; (3) *locomotor toys,* such as trains, tricycles, wagons, kiddy-kars, doll carriages, and dump trucks, whose design lent itself to the transportation function; and (4) *small mechanical toys,* such as animals and automobiles which could be pushed or wound up and watched as they ran down, whose structural design did not lend itself to imaginative functions.

On the basis of the aggregate time spent with each toy, Bott came to the following conclusions concerning nursery school children's play interests: (1) Children two or three years of age spend about the same amount of time with all type toys, but tend to discriminate among toys as they grow older. (2) Pattern toys become more popular with children as they grow older. According to Bott, "In pattern toys, where structure largely prescribes use, a child must not only have an idea of what he is trying to make but must be able to adapt his idea to his materials." (3) Raw materials are most popular with three- and four-year-old children, but are still enjoyed by those who are older. They make possible considerable originality in their use. (4) Locomotor toys are extensively used at all ages, but preference for certain types in this class varies with age. Younger children are interested in kiddy-kars and older ones in the tricycle. It is common knowledge that locomotor interests persist throughout life. (5) Mechanical toys are the least interesting to all nursery school children. Such toys make less of a demand on either amount or kind of activity and thus diminish in popularity with children as they grow older. These data suggest why children so often desert expensive mechanical toys in favor of those which require greater display of ingenuity and sustained activity.

An investigation by Van Alstyne [40] of over a hundred children, ranging in age from two to five years, has corroborated the finding that "raw material" toys are preferred to all other kinds, including pattern and locomotor toys. This research demonstrated as well that a gradual change in play interest takes place between the ages of two and five. The two-year-olds showed greatest interest in clay, painting, blocks, and doll corners, the three-year-olds in books and wagons, the four-year-olds in balls, scissors, beads, and small cars, and the five-year-olds in crayons. Although there was considerable overlapping between the play interests of boys and girls, the former tended to be interested in wagons, small cars, and dump trucks, and the girls in crayons, scissors, cubes, beads, and doll corners. Van Alstyne's findings also showed that from around 70 to 90 per cent of the preschool children played by themselves without making active efforts to cooperate with one another.

A study of the play interests of older children, ranging in age from six to thirteen, by Foster [41] has shown that both boys and girls prefer outdoor games to indoor games, and that play activities change noticeably during the first six school grades. Foster reports, "Of the outdoor games, those of the types of catching and throwing, chasing and fleeing, and hiding and seeking games were most popular with boys and girls of all ages. Boys show more interest than girls in certain games such as the catching-throwing games, while girls show more interest in the jumping-hopping games. Of the indoor games, the same types

[40] Dorothy Van Alstyne, *Play Behavior and Choice of Play Materials of Preschool Children*, Chicago, Univ. of Chicago Press, 1932.
[41] Josephine C. Foster, "Play Activities of Children in the First Six Grades," *Child Development*, 1 : 248-254 (1930).

appear popular as for the out-of-door games with the addition of table games and games involving simple dramatization." This investigation also suggested that inactive types of play, such as sewing, painting, and listening to the radio, were of little interest at the elementary school level.

Undoubtedly the most extensive study of play interests of both elementary and high school children is that by Lehman and

TABLE 5. RANK IN FREQUENCY OF GAMES AND OTHER PLAY ACTIVITIES MOST COMMONLY ENGAGED IN BY BOYS AND GIRLS EIGHT TO FIFTEEN YEARS OF AGE

Activity	Ages							
	8	9	10	11	12	13	14	15
BOYS:								
Look at the Sunday "funny paper"....	1	1	1	1	1	1	1	1
Reading books	2	3	2	3	4	7	5	5
Just playing catch	3	2	2	2	3	3	3	3
Reading the newspapers	10	8	3	3	2	2	2	2
Chewing gum	7	7	3	5	5	4	5	7
Drawing with pencil, pen, chalk, or crayon	4	5	10	13	19	19	17	27
Whistling	5	6	4	8	13	14	11	14
Just running and romping..............	8	4	6	20	19	21	..	..
Football	15	8	6	4	8	6	8	7
Riding in an automobile	16	11	5	7	6	5	5	4
Going to the "movies"	26	17	8	6	5	6	4	4
GIRLS:								
Look at the Sunday "funny paper"	1	1	1	1	1	1	1	1
Reading books	2	2	2	3	3	3	3	2
Jumping or skipping rope	3	6	4	10	13	17	30	..
Reading short stories	6	3	3	4	5	5	6	3
Reading the newspapers	13	8	3	2	2	2	2	1
Drawing with pencil, pen, chalk, or crayon	4	4	7	7	11	15	20	20
Just singing	7	5	5	6	7	10	10	12
Chewing gum	12	5	6	5	6	4	4	5
Riding in an automobile	13	11	9	10	8	8	5	3
Cutting paper things with scissors.....	5	6	8	12	14	25	29	..
Gathering flowers	10	10	5	9	4	9	12	10
Reading jokes or funny sayings........	21	16	11	9	8	6	7	4

(Adapted from H. C. Lehman and P. A. Witty, The Psychology of Play Activities, New York, A. S. Barnes & Co., 1927, pp. 51, 53.)

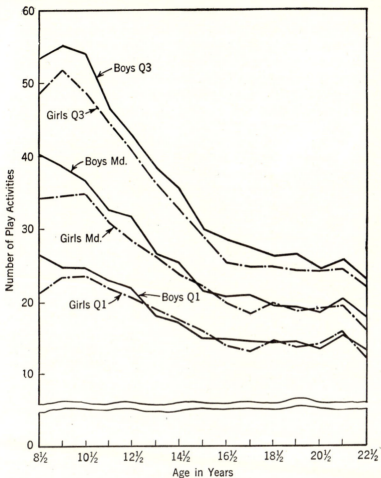

Figure 29. The Number of Different Play Activities Engaged in by Boys and Girls of Various Ages

(Adapted from H. C. Lehman and P. A. Witty, *The Psychology of Play Activities,* New York, A. S. Barnes & Co., 1927, p. 58.)

Witty.[42] These investigators administered the Lehman Play Quiz, which calls for the extent to which a child has engaged in any of 200 different play activities during the preceding week,

[42] Harvey C. Lehman and Paul A. Witty, *The Psychology of Play Activities,* New York, A. S. Barnes & Co., 1927.

to approximately 7,000 pupils. The principal findings were that: (1) The number of play activities engaged in decreases with age. This number dropped from 40 for boys and 34 for girls at age eight to 20 for both boys and girls at age sixteen. A further but less marked drop occurs up to age twenty-two. (2) That changes in play activities occur gradually with age. "Previous investigators of play . . . have tended to obscure the most important characteristic of play behavior, namely, its continuity . . . the obvious characteristic traits of each period have their beginning in preceding stages and merge gradually into succeeding ones." (3) That the great majority of play activities reach the peak of their popularity before the age of eleven. Three-quarters of the 200 play interests mentioned had reached the height of their popularity by this age. Approximately one-third had reached such a peak during the eighth year.

Table 5 presents some of the popular games and activities in this investigation, as well as the frequency with which boys and girls of various ages engaged in them. The extent of interest in the Sunday comics is obvious from this table, and is shared in alike by children of average and superior intelligence. The validity of such a large number of interests of an inactive type at the ages noted has been further substantiated by a more recent research by Dimock,[43] made in connection with a group of 200 Wisconsin boys.

It can be seen from the studies reported that childhood is most certainly the playtime period in life. It is further evident that a child who does not display such interests is not developing according to a normal pattern. A child whose play interests are either retarded or radically dissimilar to those of his associates is probably the victim of inadequate home or school conditions which are thwarting the legitimate expression of his fundamental physical or psychological needs.

Life-Adjustment Values of Play.—Considerable evidence can be marshaled in favor of the assertion that play is essential to child development. The child knows nothing of the value of play, neither does he question its outcome. To him play is a

[43] H. S. Dimock, *Rediscovering the Adolescent,* New York, Association Press, 1937.

joyous experience, an opportunity to express himself freely and without undue restraint. The benefits of spontaneous play per, meate the child's entire life and do much to prepare him for adjustment to the requirements of his environment, as well as to the needs of his own nature. As one writer [44] on play has said, "To the child play is life itself, serious, all-absorbing, self- validating. By it he lives and grows. Through it he develops his own personality and his ability to get along successfully in society."

For convenience, the more important benefits of play may be classified as (1) physical, (2) educational, (3) social, (4) those concerned with personality building, and (5) therapeutic.

PHYSICAL BENEFITS OF PLAY.   Since the trend in physical development is from gross structures to those of a more detailed nature, it seems evident that play activities are valuable for the promotion of large muscle growth. Vigorous outdoor exercise also increases blood circulation, assists in the elimination of body waste matter, promotes the digestion of food, and other- wise aids in building sound health. It is believed that such play activities as running, jumping, throwing, and bending stimu- late the organs of the body to vigorous activity, thus insuring a desirable physical tonus. The playing child is almost certain to breathe deeply and to strengthen the muscles concerned with posture. Desirable play activities may thus benefit the child physically by making his organism less susceptible to disease, by stimulating vigorous muscular development, and by insuring general good health.

EDUCATIONAL BENEFITS OF PLAY.   It is through the ave- nue of play that the child secures much of his information con- cerning the material and social world in which he lives. Play also provides many opportunities for the exercise of potential creative abilities. Insofar as constructive imagination is pos- sible for a child of a given age, play is an admirable channel for its development. Certainly a variety of interests are capitalized upon in the play approach to education.

44 J. E. Rogers, *The Child and Play*, New York, D. Appleton-Century Co., Inc., 1932, p. 12.

Modern preschool, and to a considerable extent elementary, education has capitalized on the young child's spontaneous interest in play. Thus activities involving construction, knowledge of animals, becoming acquainted with foreigners, caring for gardens, avoiding traffic accidents, learning to read, and similar enterprises are utilized on a play basis in the child's educational development. By synchronizing with the young learner's tendency to play, educators are securing a degree of motivation and practical accomplishment unknown to the proponents of the older more regimented school. The modern school provides its children with opportunities to pursue purposeful activities and thus places education on a functional level. Such a program utilizes play, not as a lazy or inefficient activity, but as one requiring effort and persistent planning. Guided play provides a dynamic orientation to the serious business of learning.

SOCIAL BENEFITS OF PLAY. It is through the medium of play that many children first develop the sense of fairness and cooperation which makes possible adequate social growth. Play situations require the child to share his toys and to hold his own wishes in abeyance sufficiently to merit the companionship of playmates. The child who insists on usurping a toy soon learns that others will not play with him until he is willing to take turns in enjoying it. Since most play is essentially social in nature, participation in play activities leads to the development of social attitudes. Furthermore, social cooperation and adaptability in childhood are natural avenues to development of the bonds of fellowship and trust so essential to success in adult social life.

Children who have little or no opportunity to play usually find it difficult to adjust satisfactorily with other children. Such boys and girls are likely to seek outlets for approval and recognition in the less frustrating world of phantasy and daydreaming. Unsocialized children are also often shy, moody, sensitive, and suspicious. Joyous play is believed to be one of the antidotes for such attitudes, as well as for the development of skill in dealing with people.

PERSONALITY DEVELOPMENT AND PLAY. In a previous section the point was made that a well-adjusted personality is marked by balance between ego striving and social living. The mentally healthy individual possesses a sense of personal worth, at least part of which he has achieved through the avenue of social skills. Even the child must secure status and acceptance if he is to maintain his personal integrity. And it is through play that he often learns the first lesson of mutuality in social relations. Whether the developing child is to be introvertive or extrovertive, dominant or submissive, emotionally stable or unstable, depends to a considerable extent upon the social attitudes developed in his early years. While it is true that parental handling is a major factor in shaping the child's social and emotional attitudes, play occupies an important role in such development.

The feelings of well-being and exhilaration engendered by untrammeled, spontaneous play are conducive to a sense of good morale and happiness. The satisfaction experienced by participation in vigorous social play assists in the formation of a framework of morale upon which an adjusted personality may most readily be developed. Play is also an effective activity for the development of tactfulness in getting along with people. Thus it can be said that the child's personality is to a considerable extent conditioned by the type and extent of joyous play experiences encountered.

THE THERAPEUTIC VALUE OF PLAY. A variety of techniques for utilizing play as a therapeutic measure in the release of emotional tensions have recently been developed. Prominent among these is Levy's [45] program for problem children whose maladjustments are traceable to unsatisfactory relations with siblings and other members of the family. The child is given dolls representing his own siblings and parents and is permitted to play with them in any way he may desire. Having identified dolls with members of the family toward whom he feels antisocial, the child may release his stresses by mutilating certain of them. Such freedom to express pent-up feelings and

[45] David M. Levy, "Hostility Patterns in Sibling Rivalry Experiments," *American Journal of Orthopsychiatry*, 6: 183-257 (1936).

antagonisms often results in improved attitudes toward the individuals involved. It is believed that the emotional release afforded by "taking it out" on the dolls is conducive to a more satisfactory adjustment.

Newell [46] has advocated both spontaneous and controlled types of play therapy, and believes that the maladjusted child derives at least three kinds of benefits from such activity: (1) the constructive relationship he develops with the therapist, (2) the opportunity to act out his conflicts, and (3) the understanding of his problems which he may gain from the experience. Kanner,[47] another psychiatrist, has, however, warned that such therapy may be too haphazard to be of value and that it may be one of the psychoanalyst's methods of "foisting a limited set of one-sided and unproved 'interpretations' on playing children." It is widely believed, nevertheless, that intelligently-guided play activities are of considerable value in the readjustment of problem children.

Summary and Implications

The instinct concept, which enjoyed such popularity during the early part of the present century, has apparently thrown little light on the problem of child dynamics. Being concerned with descriptions of behavior rather than with its causation, the instinct explanation failed to provide the *why* of child activity. It has thus been largely discarded in favor of the more concrete, understandable concepts of learning and structure-function development. It is now believed that child responses of the variety formerly regarded as instinctive have been learned or are the reactions of maturing bodily structures. Although explanatory of such functions as eating, drinking, crawling, walking, and vocalizing, the structure-function principle has not solved the problem of why the child seeks certain satisfactions in preference to others.

It remained for the concept of fundamental needs to clarify the problem of childhood dynamics. According to this prin-

[46] H. W. Newell, "Play Therapy in Child Psychiatry," *American Journal of Orthopsychiatry*, 11: 245-252 (1941).
[47] Leo Kanner, "Play Investigation and Play Treatment of Children's Behavior Disorders," *Journal of Pediatrics*, 17: 533-546 (1940).

ciple, the child's nature is so constituted that it demands at least a minimum of fulfillment of its irreducible organic, egoistic, and social motives. As one writer [48] has summarized it, "The child has certain emotional cravings, such as the need for affection and understanding, the need for respecting his parents and teachers, the need for security, the need for attention and approval, the need for successful achievement, the need for friends and companions, the need for varied and interesting outlets of his energies in work and play. If the circumstances of the child's home and school are such that they tend habitually to thwart or to deprive him of any or all of these legitimate satisfactions, or to overaccentuate any of them, the results show themselves in nervousness, in the development of unhappy personality traits, or in misbehavior. Thus, the misbehavior is merely a symptom of hidden maladjustments, and the purpose of the child's behavior is usually a blind and misguided effort to secure satisfactions which are entirely natural and to which he is entitled."

Play is now regarded as one of the avenues through which the child finds satisfaction of his need for self-expression and a sense of untrammeled freedom. It is also at least partially through play that physical health, educational progress, social growth, and personality development are realized and maintained. Various theories of the purpose of play have been proposed, but the explanation most widely accepted today is that children play because they enjoy it and because play to a child is life itself—indeed "self-validating" life.

QUESTIONS FOR DISCUSSION

1. Why do you suppose that such capable pioneers in psychology as William James and Edward L. Thorndike considered the instinct idea so superior to previous doctrines of personality dynamics? Were they justified in adopting such a position? Why?

2. Why did the instinct hypothesis cause such confusion in psychological circles? Have instincts given us a tangible explana-

[48] Clara Bassett, *The School and Mental Health,* New York, The Commonwealth Fund, 1931, pp. 10-11.

tion of motivation so far as children and youths are concerned? Justify your answer as you would to a specialist in
child psychology.

3. Could one dispense with instincts and explain child behavior in
terms of the responses of physical structures as conditioned by
(1) their mechanical design, (2) their degree of maturation,
and (3) modification brought about by learning? Try it.

4. Why do some psychologists decline to accept the proposals of
the psychoanalysts in the matter of motivation of behavior?
Are they unscientific or do some psychologists fail to appreciate
their value? Why have we borrowed so many psychoanalytic
concepts in mental hygiene?

5. Refute the accusation that the maturation concept is merely a
disguised substitute for the old instincts. In what way is the
maturation idea a superior explanation of the development of
motor ability? Linguistic growth?

6. What difference does it make whether we think of personality
dynamics as being inner forces which drive us to behave or
as learned dispositions to act which have resulted from environmental influences? Explain the implications of each position
for child development and endeavor to show the feasibility of
a compromise position.

7. On what grounds did such investigators as the Ohio group, the
Shermans, and others take issue with Gesell, Coghill, and other
maturationists who contend that behavior is for the most part
a function of neural structures as determined by their degree
of maturation? Give the pros and cons of this interpretation.

8. What justification do psychologists have for postulating organic, self, and social needs as motivators to action? Should
we not seek for a deeper source of motivation as being implicit
in purposing and planning? What are the objections to the
latter position?

9. Assuming that insufficient satisfaction of physical needs results in a state of organic imbalance (stresses), could it be
reasoned that excessive frustration of ego and social needs will
result in a similar condition? What are the implications here
for the personality development of the child?

10. What are the objections to calling the desire for independence
of action and the desire for freedom to carry out purposeful
activity basic needs of children? Are these needs sufficiently

universal and fundamental to merit such a position in the dynamics field? Justify your answer.

RECOMMENDED READINGS

Bassett, Clara. *The School and Mental Health.* New York: The Commonwealth Fund, 1931.

Fisher, V. E. *Auto-Correctivism; The Psychology of Nervousness.* Caldwell (Idaho) : The Caxton Printers, 1937, Chs. 1-4.

Gesell, Arnold, and Thompson, H. *Infant Behavior.* New York: McGraw-Hill Book Co., Inc., 1934.

Lehman, Harvey C., and Witty, Paul A. *The Psychology of Play Activities.* New York: A. S. Barnes & Co., 1927.

McGraw, Myrtle B. *Growth; A Study of Johnny and Jimmy.* New York: D. Appleton-Century Co., Inc., 1935.

Mitchell, E. D., and Mason, B. S. *The Theory of Play.* New York: A. S. Barnes & Co., 1934.

Morgan, J. J. B. *Child Psychology.* New York: Farrar & Rinehart, 1942, Ch. 12.

Shaffer, Laurance F. *The Psychology of Adjustment.* Boston: Houghton Mifflin Co., 1936, Ch. 4.

Skinner, C. E., and Harriman, P. L. (Editors). *Child Psychology.* New York: The Macmillan Co., 1941, Ch. 14.

Symonds, Percival M. "Human Drives." *Journal of Educational Psychology,* 25:681-694 (1934).

Thorpe, Louis P. *Psychological Foundations of Personality.* New York: McGraw-Hill Book Co., Inc., 1938, Ch. 5.

Thorpe, Louis P. *Personality and Life.* New York: Longmans, Green & Co., 1941, Ch. 1.

Trow, W. C. *Educational Psychology.* Boston: Houghton Mifflin Co., 1931, Ch. 2.

CHAPTER 6

EFFECTS OF EARLY HOME CONDITIONS

IN VIEW OF THE FACT that the growing child's nature is characterized by certain irreducible needs which must be met if he is to develop satisfactorily, it becomes essential to consider the influence of early home conditions upon his personal and social adjustment. It becomes imperative to know the specifications of a good home, the nature of desirable parental functioning, what child needs the home can satisfy, how children may develop happily together, and under what conditions the child will acquire a social outlook as he develops physically and intellectually. Answers to these and similar questions should enable the student of child development to gain insight, not only into the influence of home conditions on the child's personal integrity, but into ways and means of guiding the destiny of children who may come under his care and direction.

Influences of Early Home Life

Modern psychology is vitally concerned with the determination of conditions under which the child will develop physically, emotionally, socially, and morally. Since it is so often claimed that early family life lays the foundation for later adjustments, the question of the effects of specific home conditions becomes an acute one. The discussion will thus begin with a scrutiny of the extent to which the home may be expected to meet the primary psychological needs of infants and children.

Psychological Significance of the Family.—It is commonly recognized that parents should make provision for the physical care and nourishment of their children. It is not so clearly understood that satisfactory family life is indispensable to the psychological welfare of the child. It is in the home that the young child encounters the initial experiences which are to determine whether he develops a sense of personal security and of being loved and accepted.   It will be recalled from the discussion of child dynamics that such a feeling of personal worth is regarded as being imperative to mental health and social development.

The fundamental significance for the child's welfare of early family life is indicated by the outcomes of institutional care. An institution operated by well-trained nurses and supervisors could provide care superior, so far as housing, feeding, clothing, and the control of temperatures are concerned, to that extended by most private families.   Children in such a "home" would be assured of regularity and punctuality in all activities concerned with their physical care and development.   Yet students of child psychology are largely agreed that institutional care, no matter how systematic, is inadequate for the psychological needs of either infants or young children.

Zachry [1] tells of a hospital in which babies were fed perfunctorily, changed on a table, dressed as quickly as possible, and left to their own resources when they cried.   A pediatrician, who apparently understood the needs of infants, remarked that babies treated in this way did not smile or respond socially as readily as those who were reared in their own homes.   Thus a regulation was adopted requesting all nurses to go through the wards and cuddle the babies regularly.   After they had enjoyed a reasonable amount of such intimate treatment the infants not only responded to adults with smiles, but actually gained more weight than usual.   It was noted that babies and young children are dependent for their welfare upon affectionate physical contacts with those who care for them.   Such a need points clearly to the importance for child development of a loving mother and adequate home care.   Although no controlled experiments have been made relative to the specific difference between home and institutional care of children, it is generally recognized that the properly disposed home has most of the advantages in this respect.   In fact, one of the most extensive studies of child life

[1] Caroline B. Zachry, "The Child's Emotional and Social Adjustment," *Proceedings of the Sixth Conference on Education and the Exceptional Child of the Child Research Clinic of the Wood's Schools* May 1940, p. 10.

of recent times reported its findings concerning institutional children with the words, "Institutional care for the most part has produced uninspired individuals poorly adjusted to the outside world." [2]

In a study of the relationship between personality development and family conditions of children from varying environments, Stott [3] found a distinct tendency for those from homes in which parents welcomed their friends, had enjoyable times with them, shared their joys and troubles, and participated in recreational activities with them outside the home to be well-adjusted both personally and socially. The children were marked by "personal adequacy" and a sense of "personal responsibility in maintaining satisfactory relationships with others." Stott concluded that: "The most important function of modern family life is psychological in nature. Family life meets certain basic human requirements more directly than is possible in any other area of life. In the family situation are provided the setting, the stimulation, and guidance which determine, very largely, whether the child shall develop into a personally well adjusted and socially useful individual."

Studies dealing with the causes of juvenile delinquency have also suggested the psychological significance of early family life. Healy, a leader in this field, has traced thousands of offenses to undesirable home situations, and believes that less than 10 per cent of delinquents come from good homes. Healy [4] and his associates have also shown that maladjusted children may become socially desirable individuals if placed for a few years in foster homes where their fundamental physical and psychological needs are met. These and other specialists in child development have found that the personality qualities requisite for success in a social world are not likely to be developed adequately outside of a home marked by interest in the child's need for affection and security.

[2] *White House Conference on Child Health and Protection,* New York, D. Appleton-Century Co., Inc., 1931, p. 134.
[3] Leland H. Stott, *Personality Development in Farm, Small-Town, and City Children,* Univ. of Nebraska Agricultural Experiment Station, Research Bulletin No. 114 (1939), pp. 28-34.
[4] William Healy, A. F. Bronner, E. M. H. Baylor, and J. P. Murphy, *Reconstructing Behavior in Youth,* New York, Alfred A. Knopf, Inc., 1929, Chs. 22-24.

Basic Influences of Family Life.—The foremost influences exerted by early family life relate to their effect upon the fundamental needs of the child. It will be recalled that these dynamics include (1) the need for physical satisfactions necessary to the well-being of the body, (2) the need for psychological security or a feeling of personal worth, and (3) the need for social competence or facility in winning acceptance from associates. Other less crucial but nevertheless important needs include a legitimate sense of freedom to play and to consummate purposeful tasks. Children also need to develop a sense of values or identifications with activities and interests which provide them with an acceptable social outlook. The relation between these needs and the child's satisfactory development will later be discussed in some detail. It is sufficient here to point out the importance of family life for the adequate fulfillment of the child's needs. Thus the basic influences of family life will be presented in terms of: (1) influences relating to physical well-being, (2) influences pertaining to self or ego security, (3) influences relating to social growth, and (4) influences touching the development of social values.

INFLUENCES PERTAINING TO PHYSICAL WELL-BEING. The human infant is one of the most helpless of offspring. If no one were to provide him with warm clothing or water bottles when he is cold, or remove him from the intense heat rays of the sun or of an artificial heater, the babe would obviously perish. It is upon the home that the child must depend if he is to remain alive. But the home does more than protect the child from the elements; it provides food, as much insurance as possible against pain, and when illness demands, appropriate medical care. The child's family protects him from accidents and injuries, and usually (to the best of its ability) from health-destroying physical diseases. The home is thus the child's defense against forces of destruction, and his buffer against problems too complex for his ability to make adjustments. The adequate home endeavors to guarantee the child's survival and to provide him with every possible form of physical security.

INFLUENCES PERTAINING TO SELF OF EGO SECURITY. Since the human offspring is so constituted, even in infancy and early childhood, that he needs warm acceptance and intimate responses of both a physical and psychological nature, it is evident that the home is the original determiner of his sense of personal well-being and security. The child's family is thus in a crucial position to support or threaten his feeling of personal worth. If the conditions of the child's home enable him to maintain his self-esteem, he will make satisfactory personality development. Under such circumstances he will experience a minimum of emotional stress and will tend to cooperate happily with his family. If however, the home fails to provide the child with affectional responses and a secure sense of status, he is in the nature of the case required to adopt socially undesirable defense mechanisms designed to bolster his threatened ego.

The critical position of the family in this phase of development may be seen from the following analysis by Frank: [5] "This conception of the family as cultural agent which . . . attempts to socialize him [the child] and in so doing fosters a personality and a private world, enables us to understand that whatever individuals do are symptoms of their feelings toward life, derived from their early experience as children, when they were undergoing this family training and socialization. Thus we can interpret their conduct, especially their antisocial, destructive activities, as the outward, overt expressions of their own inner insecurity, unhappiness, anxiety, and the distortions and frustrations they have suffered." This statement is indicative of the attitude of modern social scientists toward the home as the builder of children's personalities.

INFLUENCES RELATING TO SOCIAL GROWTH. Infants and young children are dependent upon their families for a sense of personal security and autonomy. However, as they grow older children must win the approval and acceptance of persons outside the family circle through their own social behavior. Personal status can only be secured by way of sincere respect

[5] Lawrence K. Frank, "The Family as Cultural Agent," *Living,* Feb. 1940, p. 18.

for people and by the use of intelligent social skills. *In a social world the growing child's personal integrity is dependent upon mutuality in social relations, and cannot be insured on an egocentric program which leads to indifferent treatment of people.* Thus the child's ultimate social adjustment depends upon the extent to which he respects the rights, feelings, and property of those with whom he associates. The well-adjusted individual is the socialized individual, and socialization is a product of home treatment marked by tolerance, respect, and affection. It is in the inner circles of his home that the child acquires both the feeling of personal acceptance which lays the groundwork for being well disposed toward other human beings and the expanding social attitudes which insure cooperation with the larger environment outside of his home. Family experiences determine whether the developing child will evolve from an individualistic infant to a socialized adolescent and adult, or whether he will retain an infantile self-centeredness which will prevent him from becoming integrated with the society of which he should be a part. The adequate home lays the foundation for social growth, and social growth is fundamental to the maintenance of mental health.

INFLUENCES TOUCHING THE INCULCATION OF SOCIAL VALUES.   An individual's attitudes toward such important social institutions as manners, customs, morals, religion, and even political beliefs are for the most part inculcated during the early years of home life. It can thus be said that the pattern of a person's likes and dislikes, prejudices and preferences, and beliefs and disbeliefs is largely the aftermath of the type of home life he experienced in childhood. The home of today shares its responsibility for the education of the child with other agencies, but it is nevertheless the dominant influence in determining the development of social and cultural values.

The sociologist Nimkoff [6] has summarized the function of the family in equipping the child with social values and attitudes in the following words: "The home provides the child with fundamental *tastes*. It is interesting to note that however much

---

[6] Meyer F. Nimkoff, *The Child*, Philadelphia, J. B. Lippincott Co., 1934, pp. 151-152.

food tastes may alter with the years, people continue to relish most of those foods which were enjoyed at home in childhood and youth. Likewise, basic *attitudes* are engendered at home. One's true feeling towards such matters as sex, marriage, religion, and even life itself, more frequently than not, trace back to family experience. Also, the home furnishes the child with *mannerisms.* The inflection of his speech he often derives from his parents. . . . The whole division known as *manners* betray family influence. A child's bearing, the way in which he conducts himself, the style in which he dresses—these and similar acquirements show clearly their source in the example of the home." It should be evident that the home is virtually the "pattern maker" of the man. The family exerts a powerful influence in the development of social values and practices, be they desirable or undesirable.

The Family and the Child's Needs.—Even the infant has psychological needs, the fulfillment of which are essential to satisfactory personality development. It should thus be realized that *just as adequate food and appropriate hygienic surroundings are necessary to physical health and development, suitable psychological experiences are imperative to mental health and adjustment.* If they are to be free from the stresses of insecurity, infants and children need a variety of both organic and psychological satisfactions.

A few years ago John B. Watson,[7] the founder of behavioristic (mechanistic) psychology, created considerable confusion in the realm of infant training by declaring that babies should be treated objectively and not subjected to the kisses and caresses of fond but naive mothers. It was Watson's contention that children would develop self-reliant and independent qualities if permitted to grow without the inhibiting influences of feminine demonstrations of affection. This doctrine was widely heralded and enjoyed considerable acceptance in some quarters.

Subsequent developments have, however, caused many, perhaps most, students of personality and child development to conclude that Watson's theoretical hypothesis did not work out

[7] John B. Watson, *Psychological Care of Infant and Child,* New York, W. W Norton & Co., Inc., 1928.

in practice. It is now widely agreed that the mother's love and physical affection are essential to the infant's ultimate mental health. The infant needs the warmth and firm tactual contact of the mother or nurse as much as he does the physical nourishment resulting from suckling. It is by way of such experiences that the baby develops a needed sense of security and of being protected. To quote a recent writer,[8] "In this respect the human infant is like the young of all mammals, who thrive when nursed and cuddled and derive much needed emotional security from the oral activity of sucking and the close contact with the mother."

As the result of extensive studies of infants and their parents, one pediatrician-psychiatrist [9] has come to the conclusion that even after birth mother and child are psychologically still a unit, and that a close physical relationship is as essential for early mental and emotional development as was the fetal connection for physiological development. Intimate mothering was found to be fundamental to the fulfillment of basic infant needs such as oxygen hunger, sucking, sleep, elimination, stimulation, and life rhythms. In fact, the investigator was convinced that fondling stimulates the infant's nervous system into normal action and growth, that capacity for mature emotional relationships is a direct outgrowth of caressing, maternal love, and that such experiences as sucking, being rocked, and being sung to satisfy the infant's deepest psychological requirements. Infants who experienced such consistent mothering tended to develop attitudes of trust and confidence, as well as an outgoing personality responsive to social stimulation and affectional relationships. Young babies who had not been adequately "mothered" tended to become either negativistic and tense (screamed or refused to suck) or regressive (were quiescent or fell into stupor-like sleep).

Clinical observations have shown that infants are especially sensitive to maternal attitudes. Of all the intimate influences to which the infant is exposed, that of emotional climate is one

[8] Lawrence K. Frank, "The Fundamental Needs of the Child," *Mental Hygiene, 22*: 353-379 (1938).
[9] Margaret A. Ribble, *The Rights of Infants,* New York, Columbia Univ. Press, 1943.

of the most contagious. Psychologists and others have in fact found that "exposure to intense adult emotions is traumatic to the developing personality of the infant." [10] This is true whether the mother overstimulates the child, constantly entertains it compulsively, or inhibits its growth through overtraining.

Children of nursery school age, particularly those who have been denied affection in the home, need teachers who are willing and capable of giving them a warm emotional response and the all-important feeling of "belonging." Some may feel that such an attitude is "unscientific," but if it results in improved mental health it can hardly be classified as anything but constructive handling. Some teacher-training institutions have, in fact, inaugurated a program of therapy along this line for children from approximately eighteen months to six years of age. Many children come to school who have experienced, among other cultural stresses, a deprivation of cuddling experiences. Under such circumstances the teacher might well offer these children the affectionate response which has been lacking in the home. The teacher may take the child on her lap and cuddle him to an extent which seems appropriate to his needs. Physical contacts are lessened as the child adjusts, but he continues to receive some attention from the teacher, especially when he is hurt or is in distress. Although it is difficult to determine the contribution made by such a program it would seem safe to conclude that treatment of this kind serves children well so far as mental health is concerned.

Modern educators have thus advocated that nursery schools endeavor to readjust children whose behavior is marked by fear and resentment as the result of arbitrary and destructive domination in the home. It is felt that unless something is done for these children they are destined to encounter much unhappiness, if not outright mental disorders or criminality. Harsh authority thwarts the child's need for acceptance and a feeling of adequacy, thus resulting in introspective, antisocial, or out-and-out

10 F. Dunbar, "Effect of the Mother's Emotional Attitude on the Infant," *Psychosomatic Medicine,* 6: 156-159 (1944).

neurotic behavior.   Wittels,[11] a Freudian, has declared that the only way to relieve the young child of the feeling that he is the slave of his superiors is for them to extend him wholehearted love.   These statements are not intended to mean that no authority over children should be exercised, but rather that their regulation should be benevolently and intelligently directed.   All competent students of child psychology recognize that over-indulgence of children leads to excessive selfishness, to unruly behavior, and to feelings of egocentrism and superiority calculated to bring about much friction with associates.   It is *cuddling* and not *coddling* that children need for the preservation of their mental health and for the development of satisfactory socialization.

The Ideal Parent-Child Relationship.—Although some homes have failed to provide satisfying childhood experiences to which adults can look back with appreciation, there appear to have been many in which children enjoyed adequate security and stimulating comradeship with their parents.   According to Nimkoff,[12] many biographies and autobiographies reveal little in their early home experiences that stimulated the individuals concerned to constructive living.   It may be true that many children and youths must look to sources other than the family circle for stimulation to self-realization, yet others will testify to the adequacy of their childhood home.

Nimkoff has described a good home as one in which the child has two parents who (1) love each other, (2) love him, (3) understand his interests, capacities, and aspirations, and (4) who do what they can to help him realize them and thus achieve adequate selfhood.   Such a home will enable the child to satisfy his dynamic needs for physical well-being and for a feeling of belonging.   As has already been indicated, such a regime seems admirably designed for the stimulation of happy, well-adjusted personalities.   It is difficult to find examples of resentful, antisocial, or delinquent children coming from such homes.

[11] Fritz Wittels, *Set the Children Free!* New York, W. W. Norton & Co., Inc., 1933, p. 151.
[12] Meyer F. Nimkoff, *op. cit.,* p. 166.

They care for the needs of the child's nature and thus tend to guarantee adequate personality development.

There are, however, a few practical aspects of the ideal parent-child relationship which deserve mention. These may be said to include (1) carrying on activities together, (2) developing mutual interests, (3) stimulating the child to effort, and (4) encouraging self-reliance.[13]   In the adequate home parents share experiences with their children.   They win the confidence and good will of their children by showing a sincere interest in their activities.   Louis Pasteur's father studied diligently to keep pace with his talented son and was able to converse intelligently with him about chemical matters.   Such fellowship could hardly result in anything but mutual trust and confidence. Many a father or mother has also insured a child's allegiance by sharing his recreational interests, be they swimming, skating, baseball, or stamp collecting.   The same may be said for sharing mutual interests.   The parent who discusses events of the day or current family problems with a son or daughter is establishing a basis for common bonds that will defy the ravages of occasional parent-child friction.

Adequate parents are also quick to encourage their children to constructive effort.   If a child demonstrates an aptitude for music, such parents will endeavor to provide facilities for instruction and stimulation along musical lines.   One father went so far as to plan a musical education abroad for his gifted son and is consequently now the proud parent of a well-known symphony orchestra violinist.   Desirable parental functioning will also strive for the development of self-reliance in children. Intelligent parents encourage children to solve their own problem and to become independent of their family.   Abraham Lincoln developed a strong sense of self-determination early in life by doing such things for himself as were appropriate to his age.   Such a process of rearing is essential to adult self-reliance.

In an investigation of the personality development of farm, small-town, and city children of Nebraska, Stott[14] found a

13 *Ibid.,* pp. 167-171.
14 Leland H. Stott, *op. cit.,* pp. 28-30.

significant degree of relationship between personality scores and certain items of a home-life questionnaire dealing with inter-actions between parents and children. The home-life items which correlated most highly with good personality scores are shown in Table 6.

TABLE 6. COMPARISONS OF THREE RESIDENCE GROUPS AS TO PERCENTAGE OF "FAVORABLE" REPORTS REGARDING EACH OF TEN HOME-LIFE ITEMS WHICH WERE FOUND MOST FREQUENTLY TO CORRELATE SIGNIFICANTLY WITH SCORES ON PERSONALITY TESTS

Home Life Item	Total Significant Correla- tions	"Favorable" Answers			CR [1]
		City	Farm	Town	
	No.	Pct.	Pct.	Pct.	
1. Parents "always" welcome child's friends in the home	20	69	65	66	
2. "Often" have enjoyable times together in the home	20	47	52	37	Farm>town, 5.54 City >town, 3.40
3. "Often" go on picnics, visits, and other recreational excursions outside home	17	50	60	43	Farm>town, 6.25 Farm> city, 3.42 City >town, 2.35
4. No punishment during previous week	17	65	75	62	Farm>town, 5.12 Farm> city, 3.70
5. Shares joys and troubles with mother "almost always"	13	48	45	44	
6. Shares joys and troubles with father "almost always"	13	25	24	25	
7. Kisses mother "occasionally" or "every day"	12	83	57	75	City >farm, 10.28 Town>farm, 7.03 City >town, 3.33
8. Nothing in mother's behavior criticized	11	65	63	59	City >town, 2.08
9. Meals at regular hours "almost always"	10	66	73	70	Farm> city, 2.57
10. Nothing in father's behavior criticized	9	64	62	56	City >town, 2.21 Farm>town, 2.21

[1] The CR in each case is the difference between the two percentages divided by the standard error of that difference. CR's of less than 2.00 are regarded as insignificant and are not shown in the table.

(From Leland H. Stott, *Personality Development in Farm, Small-Town, and City Children,* Univ. of Nebraska Agricultural Experiment Station, Research Bulletin No. 114, 1939, p. 29.)

It is evident that the home-life items in this table are the kind that synchronize with the standards of desirable parent-child relationship discussed above. It can thus be agreed that "the security which the child may feel, the extent to which he may become self-reliant, self-directing, and independent, and the ease and skill with which he may successfully assume personal and social responsibilities, depend to a large degree upon these relationships." [15]

The Significance of Parent-Child Relationships

Havelock Ellis once made the remark "there ought to be no reason, and under happy conditions there is no reason, why the relationship between parent and child, as one of mutual affection and care, should ever cease to exist." One might well wish that the happy conditions referred to were more universally provided. It appears to be true, however, that many parent-child relationships are marked by a degree of friction that militates against adequate development on the part of the child. It is to a consideration of the probable causes and results of such friction that this section is devoted.

Parental Attitudes and Children's Behavior.—So far as resulting child behavior is concerned, undesirable parental attitudes may be said to include (1) rejection of the child, (2) dominant behavior on the part of parents, (3) submissive behavior on the part of parents, (4) overacceptance of the child, and (5) various forms of friction between parents. An understanding of the general outcomes of each of these forms of parental malfunctioning is essential to an appreciation of the problems faced by many children.

REJECTION OF THE CHILD. It is not easy to define rejection as it is here used. Instead of employing such uncertain criteria as dislike for a child or the allegation that he was not wanted, most investigators present a concrete list of indications of rejection as shown by parents. Fitz-Simons [16] has suggested the

---

[15] Ernest W. Tiegs and Barney Katz, *Mental Hygiene in Education,* New York, The Ronald Press Co., 1941, pp. 232-233.

[16] M. J. Fitz-Simons, *Some Parent-Child Relationships as Shown in Clinical Case Studies,* New York, Teachers College Contributions to Education, No. 643, Columbia Univ., 1935

following items (and others) as being sound clinically: (a) parent sees mostly shortcomings, (b) parent uses severe punishments, (c) parent deserts child, (d) parent evicts child, (e) parent puts child in an institution to avoid trouble, (f) parent does not provide financial support, and (g) parent deliberately frightens child.

A number of investigations have disclosed the results of such rejection, particularly when perpetrated by the mother. Newell [17] found from a study in the Cleveland public schools that rejected children "feel more insecure than the average child, are impelled by the necessity of extracting from their parents and other adults experiences of being welcome and important. Thus they are peculiarly sensitive to attention. They derive a certain satisfaction from having their mothers upset about them and much of their specific behavior represents a discovery on their part of what their mothers fear the most." These findings have been corroborated by Walberg,[18] who reports from an intensive study of thirty-three emotionally unstable children that parental rejection generates "tension, rage, and anxiety that flood the immature ego and jeopardize normal security feelings. Rejection undermines the self-esteem of the child and . . . induces catastrophic feelings of helplessness and a persistent sense of frustration." One investigator [19] has indicated, however, that rejected children may develop a degree of independence and special interests which make it possible for them to effect satisfactory social adjustments outside the home.

Probably the most thorough investigation of the effects of parental rejection on child personality is that by Symonds,[20] in which a detailed analysis was made of the personal and social characteristics of thirty-one rejected children (as contrasted with an equal number of accepted children). The children in the two groups were equated on the basis of sex, age, school

17 H. W. Newell, "The Psychodynamics of Maternal Rejection," *American Journal of Orthopsychiatry*, 4 : 387-401 (1934). See also Alexander Reid Martin, "A Study of Parental Attitudes and Their Influence Upon Personality Development," *Education*, 63 : 596-608 (1943).

18 L. R. Walberg, "The Character Structure of the Rejected Child," *The Nervous Child*, 3 : 74-88 (1944).

19 M. Bergum, "Constructive Values Associated with Rejection," *American Journal of Orthopsychiatry*, 10 : 312-327 (1940).

20 Percival M. Symonds, *The Psychology of Parent-Child Relationships*, New York, D. Appleton-Century Co., Inc., 1939, Ch. 2.

progress, intelligence, and socio-economic status. Evidences of rejection included (a) no interest in child, (b) no time for child—neglect, (c) unfavorable comparison with siblings, (d) verbal punishment—nagging, scolding, (e) failure to support child, and (f) physical punishment or cruelty. Many areas of inquiry, such as "Is he *frank, open, and communicative?*" "What are some of his *friendships, attachments,* or *crushes?*" and "Does he resent parental authority?" were included in the study.

According to Symonds, children who were rejected by their parents tended to be unfriendly, to resent authority, to be rebellious, to feel persecuted, to feel inferior, to indulge in self-pity, to be discouraged, to evaluate themselves unrealistically, and to face the future with misgivings. Accepted children for the most part displayed the opposite dispositions. The investigator believed that the rejected children's behavior was not only a response to thwarting situations, but to inner attitudes created by them.

DOMINANT BEHAVIOR ON THE PART OF PARENTS. The nature of hostile or dominant parental behavior is better understood than is the case with acts of rejection. Fitz-Simons [21] has also offered a list of specific dominating parent's actions which includes the following: (a) parent "pushes" child, (b) parent threatens punishment, (c) parent nags child, (d) parent spanks, whips child, (e) parent holds child to unsuitable standards, (f) parent criticizes child, and (g) parent threatens to evict child.

In a questionnaire study of the outcomes of such severity, Goodwin Watson [22] writes that "The picture given us by these data is that of old-fashioned homes, economically underprivileged with poor marital adjustments leading to *severity* in handling children which produced, thirty years later, adults who hated their parents, quarreled with associates, were unable to live on a mature and independent basis, were socially maladjusted, full of overconscientiousness, guilt, and fears, were in-

---

[21] M. J. Fitz-Simons, *op. cit.*
[22] Goodwin Watson, "A Comparison of the Effects of Lax Versus Strict Home Training," *Journal of Social Psychology,* 5: 102-105 (1934).

clined to be sickly, and definitely unhappy." A more recent and better controlled investigation by Newell [23] has shown that boys become disobedient, rebellious, quarrelsome, and otherwise aggressive when either or both parents' behavior is consistently hostile. Girls develop similar aggressive attitudes when either or both parents' behavior is ambivalent (inconsistent), or when the father is hostile.

Symonds [24] also has made an analytical study of the effects of parental dominance. In this case he used 28 pairs of children who were dominated by one or both parents, and whose parents were submissive to them, respectively. Again the children were equated as to sex, age, school progress, intelligence, and socio-economic status. The same areas of behavior as those utilized in the previously mentioned study of parental rejection were investigated. Children were considered to be dominated when their parents (a) insisted on complete obedience, (b) supervised their choice of activities closely, (c) superimposed ideals upon them, (d) supervised them too much, (e) protected them from harm, and (f) were overanxious about trifles.

The research disclosed that, in comparison with children who are given little supervision, "the dominated children tend to be humble, shy. They feel slightly more inferior and less adequate. They tend to be somewhat confused and bewildered. They are, on the whole, more tolerant of others, fair, and broadminded. . . . They identify themselves with and are devoted to members of the family." These findings have been corroborated in a study by McKinney,[25] in which students who made "poorly adjusted" scores on the Thurstone *Psychoneurotic Inventory* were found to have been reared in homes characterized by dominating attitudes on the part of parents, little opportunity for bearing responsibilities, a repressive type of discipline, and a meager amount of outside social activities.

SUBMISSIVE BEHAVIOR ON THE PART OF PARENTS. Fitz-Simons [26] has defined submissive behavior as that in which (a)

[23] H. W. Newell, "A Further Study of Maternal Rejection," *American Journal of Orthopsychiatry,* 6: 576-589 (1936).
[24] Percival M. Symonds, *op. cit.,* Ch. 3.
[25] F. McKinney, "Personality Factors of College Students as Related to Factors in Personal History," *Journal of Applied Psychology,* 23 :660-668 (1939).
[26] M. J. Fitz-Simons, *op. cit.*

parent indulges child—cannot refuse requests, (b) parent gives in to child, (c) parent does not provide financial support, (d) parent deserts child, (e) parent neglects child, (f) parent does not spend time with child, and (g) parent pays no attention to child—gives no money, toys, or treats. The previously mentioned investigation by Symonds [27] showed that submissive parental behavior tends to develop attitudes marked by self-importance, conceit, overconfidence, disobedience, and disrespect for authority. Such children also tend to identify themselves with individuals outside the family circle. They are, however, somewhat self-confident and independent.

OVERACCEPTANCE OF THE CHILD. Overacceptance has been defined and categorized by Levy [28] as follows: (1) Excessive contact of mother with child. Mother may sleep with child, regardless of sex, for many years, and may fondle him excessively. (2) Prolongation of infantile care. Mother may nurse or bottle-feed child for an unnecessarily long period, or may bathe and dress him long after he can perform these functions for himself. (3) Prevention of development of self-reliance. Mother may supervise child's activities excessively, may solve his problems for him, and may defend him from individuals outside the home. (4) Lack or excess of maternal control. Here the mother may either overindulge and wait upon the child or insist upon strict obedience designed to produce so-called "good" behavior.

A number of studies have suggested the outcomes of oversolicitude on the part of parents. In a study of the relationship between nursery school and kindergarten children's behavior and the attitude of parents, Hattwick [29] found that "children whose homes reflect overattentiveness are liable to display infantile, withdrawing types of reactions." This investigator also noted that "asking for unnecessary help (in school) was, in the case of children with an overattentive parent, associated with staying near the adult and with various infantile reactions.

[27] Percival M. Symonds, op. cit.
[28] David M. Levy, "Maternal Overprotection and Rejection," Archives of Neurology and Psychiatry, 25 : 886-894 (1931). Also, by the same author, Maternal Overprotection, New York, Columbia Univ. Press, 1943.
[29] B. W. Hattwick, "Interrelations Between the Preschool Child's Behavior and Certain Factors in the Home," Child Development, 7 : 201-226 (1936).

In this case the behavior seems largely the result of lack of experience or of opportunities to 'grow up.' " Hattwick reported further that "babied" children were inclined to encounter more than the normal amount of social difficulties, and to develop progressively poorer work habits in school.

Blanchard [30] tells the story of a ten-year-old boy whose widowed mother centered her affections upon him to the extent of giving him his baths and having him sleep with her at night. This overacceptance resulted in unusual intimacies which in turn made it practically impossible for the boy to develop normal moral attitudes and emotional responses. He was unhappy at school because of the necessary separation from his mother, and was as an apparent consequence very inattentive. He also preferred staying with his mother to playing with more socially active boys in the neighborhood. As an upshot of his excessive mother-attachment, the boy fell to daydreaming of the time when he could provide his mother with the fine clothes and other luxuries which she had been denied in real life. The boy's maladjusted condition, which precluded the experiences and social activities of normal living, thus constituted a threat to his chances of becoming an independent, self-reliant member of society.

FRICTION BETWEEN PARENTS. In a study of the relationship between children's personality adjustments and the marital relations of their parents, Baruch [31] was able to ascertain certain hithertofore little known home-life concomitants of young children's emotional tensions. In the main, it was found that dominance-submission relations and sex adjustments of parents are primary factors in the determination of children's personality status. The children were noted on a special scale designed to measure self-adjustment, as well as reciprocal relations with the family and with social (school) groups. The parents were interviewed on a confidential basis regarding marital friction.

[30] Phyllis Blanchard, *The Child and Society*, New York, Longmans, Green & Company, 1928, pp. 51-53.

[31] Dorothy W. Baruch, "A Study of Reported Tension in Interparental Relationships as Co-Existent with Behavior Adjustments in Young Children," *Journal of Experimental Education*, 6 : 187-204 (1937) ; Dorothy W. Baruch and J. A. Wilcox, "A Study of Sex Differences in Preschool Children's Adjustment Coexistent with Interparental Tensions," *Journal of Genetic Psychology*, 64 : 281-303 (1944).

The nature of the children's maladjustments was not reported, but the interparental relationships involved were summarized by Baruch as follows:

"Certain of the items reported in the interparental relationships were significantly related to child adjustment. These were: Tension over sex, over ascendance-submission, over lack of consideration, lack of cooperation on the upbringing of the child, extramarital relations, tension over health, inability to talk over differences to mutually acceptable solution, tension over insufficient expression of affection, tension over friends, over work, and over relatives.

"Considering the material in the light of the various types of analysis that were made, the tensions over sex and over ascendance-submission appeared to be those most appreciably related to child adjustment.

"The following items reported in the interparental relationship did not appear significantly related to child adjustment: Tension over leisure pursuits, criticalness of the partner, tension over finances, and over differences in tastes."

These findings have to some extent been verified in a study by Stott [32] of the personality development of children from a variety of home backgrounds. It was found that children who had been reared in home life patterns marked by family discord or parental misconduct were inferior in personal adjustment, attitude toward home life, and general personality development to those from home patterns characterized by confidence, affection, and companionability. This investigation suggested the importance for desirable social development of cordial and compatible home relations.

Although it would be unsafe to make sweeping generalizations concerning causal relationships between parental attitudes and children's behavior on the basis of data presented in these and other studies, the conclusions reached by the various investigators have certainly suggested the effects of certain home conditions upon child personality. The data should be inter-

[32] Leland H. Stott, "Some Family Life Patterns and Their Relation to Personality Development in Children," *Journal of Experimental Education*, 8 : 148-160 (1939). Cf. James H. S. Bossard and Eleanor S. Ball, *Family Situations*, Philadelphia, Univ. of Pennsylvania Press. 1943. Chap. 6.

preted on a tentative basis, but may be regarded as a point of departure for further researches in this important phase of child psychology.

Other Varieties of Parental Mishandling.—Other unfortunate parent-child relationships, the apparent results of which should be known to the student of child psychology include: (1) projection of parental ambitions upon the child, (2) preference for a child of a given sex, and (3) parental jealousy of the child. Like other undesirable parental attitudes, these often result in types of mishandling which militate heavily against the child's chances of achieving personal and social adjustment.

PROJECTION OF PARENTAL AMBITIONS UPON THE CHILD. It is not uncommon to find unaccomplished parents who regard their children as avenues through which they may achieve thwarted ambitions. Other parents, who have acquired considerable ego over their own achievements, expect their children to perpetuate the family's "name" through similar accomplishments. Such attitudes influence parental handling of the child. Bassett [33] has reported the case of a boy whose father, a highly successful business executive, became alarmed when his son failed to do well in school work and seemed unable to compete with his classmates. Repeated urgings on the part of both the father and the boy's teacher only resulted in his becoming discouraged and introspective. A clinical examination disclosed that the boy was in some way defective and that he was too dull intellectually to succeed with the more abstract content of upper elementary school subjects. Unfortunately, the excessive demands of a too-proud father had in the meantime caused the child to develop serious neurotic trends. His elders had failed to recognize his limitations and had endeavored to drive him beyond his ability to achieve.

Some parents seem determined to relive their lives more successfully through their children's careers, and thus project an offspring's vocation or profession without regard to its suitability to his interests or abilities. One such mother made the mistake of insisting that her son become a minister after he

[33] Clara Bassett, *The School and Mental Health,* New York, The Commonwealth Fund, 1931, pp. 27-28.

had already developed a deep-seated interest in medicine. The boy made a serious attempt to achieve the goal set for him by his mother, but became increasingly dissatisfied and anxious about his future. Before finishing the pre-ministerial course, he became careless about both his conduct and his studies. It required the understanding counsel of a friendly teacher to get this young man settled in the line of work for which he was suited. In spite of the mother's remonstrances and disparagement of the medical profession, the boy ultimately became a successful physician. However, the mother's insistence that her son carry on his deceased father's work as a minister had come perilously close to wrecking his career.

It can thus be seen that trouble arises when parents' wishes for their children are centered on self-perpetuation. As the collaborators [34] of a discussion of this problem have written, "When the major drive behind the wish is gratification of the parental ego or a desire to live again one's own life through the child parents rob the child of individuality, and force the development of interests that are not native or dwarf capacities that should be dominant." Actually, both parents and teachers should give the child every opportunity to explore his interests and abilities, and to work out his career along lines suggested by them. In this way the child's sense of personal worth and general feeling of well-being can be enhanced.

PREFERENCE FOR CHILD OF A GIVEN SEX. A parent who expresses a strong preference for a child of either sex is in danger of making one of the undesired sex feel unwanted. Children soon discover whether they are welcome by father and mother. As previous discussions have indicated, rejected children are almost certain to experience feelings of insecurity, resentment, and loneliness. Thus when a child of unwanted sex is born into the family, the disappointment encountered is likely to influence the treatment the child will receive. This is especially true in cases where parents are not emotionally well adjusted.

34 Winifred R. Rand, M. E. Sweeny, and E. L. Vincent, *Growth and Development of the Young Child*, Philadelphia, W. B. Saunders Co., 1940, p. 413. See also J. W. Macfarlane, "Inter-personal Relationships Within the Family," *Marriage and Family Living*, 3 : 25-31 (1941).

It is not uncommon for prospective parents to manifest an unwavering preference for a son, especially if the child is the "first-born." This preference is probably a perpetuation of the ancient ambition of practically every woman to give birth to a "man-child." It is, nevertheless, a serious handicap to girls, who must in some cases emulate boys' traits to the extent of becoming tom-boys if they hope to enjoy a semblance of the feeling of acceptance that every child craves. Other girls do what they can to win their parents' approval, only to be neglected when a male child is born.

Being unable to change their sex—and some children have been known to long for such transformation—many boys and girls must suffer the pangs of being unloved and of feeling insecure in the home. It is believed that such "hybrid" feminine names as Georgianna, Augusta, Alberta, Pauline, and Josephine are evidence of the wish at some time, on the part of parents of girls, that they had been favored by the birth of a son. When a child comes to realize that his only chance for parental acceptance lies in a change in sex, he is almost certain to develop feelings of hopelessness and inferiority. Such a child's principal hope lies in the development of satisfying contacts with children and others outside of the home.

PARENTAL JEALOUSY OF THE CHILD. A parent who feels insecure in the love of his marital partner may resent the appearance of a child and feel that the attention accorded it is depriving him of his security. Such feelings are seldom expressed, but are nevertheless influential in determining the parent's treatment of the child. This treatment may, unfortunately, be detrimental to the child's development.

The father may, for example, be jealous of the child because of the mother's excessive attention to it, a devotion which may stem from the mother's need for a love attachment which she does not experience with her husband. Under such conditions, the father may become indifferent to the child, and may treat him with a severity that can only result in strained and resentful relations. Children of this kind usually dislike their father intensely and tend to compensate by seeking security and affection from the mother. If the mother is jealous of the father's devotion to the child she may treat the child with coolness, but is more likely to hide her real feelings by demonstrations of great fondness for it. Such a mother usually endeavors to take complete charge of the child, in the meantime trying to disparage the husband's attentions as being inadequate for the child's care.

Children recognize such subtle conflicts early in life, and may feel that they are the cause of the difficulty. Some have been known to wish that they could be adopted into other homes and thus bring their parents together. Others have developed the phantasy that they have real parents elsewhere who love them, and that their present parents are not their own. This is, of course, an extreme instance of wishful thinking, but it is a natural security-seeking mechanism for a child of jealous parents. In such instances the parents alone can rectify the situation; the child is merely trying in an immature way to find substitute satisfaction for his need for affection and for being considered worthy. No child is free from the stresses of insecurity who fails to receive warm recognition and response from his parents.

The Etiology of Parent-Child Relationships.—It is probably not generally recognized that parents tend to treat their children in ways *designed to satisfy their own needs and attitudes,* and that they do not as a rule rear them on the basis of logical reasoning or in terms of the children's dynamic needs. Recognition of this unfortunate but nevertheless common situation does much toward creating an understanding of why some parents behave toward their children as they do. Such insight also makes it possible to determine, in part at least, the origin of a variety of parental attitudes.

In his study of the attitudes of accepted and rejected children's parents, Symonds [35] was able to determine the nature of the home attitudes which they in turn had encountered in childhood. According to the findings, there was a "close correspondence between the conditions considered favorable for childhood

[35] Percival M. Symonds, *op. cit.,* pp. 98-103.

(of the parents) and the parents' tendency to accept their children." It was also ascertained that " 'good' fathers [who accepted their children] grew up with a kindly, intelligent, friendly, hardworking father and an intelligent, non-dominating mother. Father and mother were compatible and happy together and they were wise and consistent in their discipline. 'Bad' fathers [who rejected their children], on the other hand, were somewhat spoiled by domineering mothers in a poor home environment. The parents were poorly mated and quarreled and the discipline of the children was harsh and inconsistent. The evidence further suggests that the mother is more important than the father in determining what kind of parent the boy will later be. 'Good' mothers had intelligent, kind, stable fathers with scant indication that the personality of the father is more important than that of the mother. The home atmosphere is friendly and cheerful as well as orderly and tidy. The parents are compatible and the discipline of the children is consistent. There is early sex instruction. 'Good' mothers had good relations with brothers and sisters as children. 'Bad' mothers, on the other hand, had irritable mothers and austere fathers. There is friction and nagging in the home and the discipline is inconsistent, with excessive punishment and criticism."

A study by Field [36] has corroborated the principle that unhappy childhood leads to later mishandling of children. This investigation was made to determine the maternal attitudes of mothers of twenty-five maladjusted children who had been committed to the New York State Psychiatric Institute and Hospital. The children, whose difficulties included conduct disorders, habit disorders, and neurotic traits, were of normal intelligence and came from homes in which both parents were alive and living at home. Here again it was found that mothers who had experienced an unhappy childhood developed neurotic attitudes which apparently caused them to reject their own children.

As for parents who dominated their children or who were submissive in dealing with them, Symonds [37] says, "My own

[36] M. Field, "Maternal Attitudes Found in Twenty-five Cases of Children with Primary Behavior Disorders," *American Journal of Orthopsychiatry,* 10 : 293-312 (1940).

[37] Percival M. Symonds, *op. cit.,* pp. 136-140, 169.

TABLE 7. DIFFERENCE BETWEEN THE FREQUENCY WITH WHICH ITEMS IN MOTHER'S BACKGROUND WERE CHECKED FOR MOTHERS OF ACCEPTED AND REJECTED CHILDREN

Differences in Favor of Accepted Group	Children Accepted	Differences in Favor of Rejected Group	Children Rejected
8	Home atmosphere friendly and cheerful	7	Educational opportunities limited
6	Father intelligent	5	Excessive punishment or criticism
5	Home located in good residential district		Fear used as a method of control by parents
	Mother well educated	4	Meager home environment
	Parents compatible		Mother irritable
4	Consistent discipline	3	Backward in school
	Early sex instruction and favorable attitudes toward sex		Bad companions
	Father emotionally stable		Disliked work as a child (disliked helping in home)
	Father kind		Erratic enforcement of discipline
	Good companions during childhood		Father austere
	Good relations with brother and sister		Inconsistent training
	Home orderly and tidy		"Nagging" parents
	Nutrition good as a child		Overprotected
	Parents very moral		
	Successful in school		

(From Percival M. Symonds, *The Psychology of Parent-Child Relationships*, New York, D. Appleton-Century Co., Inc., 1939, p. 101.)

study of dominance and submission in parents suggests the occurrence of an interesting apparent reversal of character in the child of dominant parents (or submissive parents). The child of dominant parents is docile, conforming, somewhat insecure personally, nonaggressive. These are the surface manifestations of their personalities. But these children are much repressed—and they have strong aggressive and compulsive trends underneath. When they mature and become parents these unconscious aggressive trends assert themselves and as parents they become authoritative, strict, dominant. Children of submissive parents, on the other hand, are rebellious, authority-resisting, aggressive. But when later they become parents they suffer from a lack of superego or compulsive trends. They are lax housekeepers, happy-go-lucky as parents, and repeat the pattern set by their own parents by being weak and submissive."

These findings have been substantiated by other investigators. An intensive analysis,[38] for example, of 25 life histories selected from 100 cases of apparently normal college-educated women showed that "what each was to be in adulthood became clear in fairly early childhood." The authors state that women who enjoyed a happy childhood were well adjusted socially, relatively physically fit, used insight in solving their problems, and that, regardless of the size of their income, they got along satisfactorily on the money they had. In comparison with women with an unhappy home background, they were more understanding with people, experienced more satisfactory relations with men, and were less inclined to have inferiority feelings. Although inferior in all of the above respects, the women from unhappy childhood homes were more active in church affairs and seemed better able to withstand criticism and teasing. The criteria of happy (and unhappy) childhood homes were much the same as those presented in Table 7. It was concluded that the home exerts a powerful influence on the development of personality.

It may thus be said that, although generalizations based on somewhat meager findings must be made with caution, there is room for believing that, in general at least, parents are markedly influential in their treatment of children by the way in which they were reared. Judging from accumulating evidence, many parents behave toward their children in ways calculated to *reduce their own stresses of resentment, inferiority, or insecurity,* rather than in terms of their children's best interests. This situation suggests the importance for parents of gaining insight into their own state of adjustment and subsequently of making an intelligent effort to be guided by their children's rather than their own needs, insofar as they can effect a reasonably satisfactory personal adjustment in this way. It is all too common for maladjusted parents unwittingly to raise stresses of insecurity in their children.

[38] Katherine E. Roberts and Virginia V. D. Fleming, *Persistence and Change in Personality Patterns,* Monographs of the Society for Research in Child Development, Vol. 8, No. 3 (1943), Ch. 4.

The Problem of Sibling Relations

Much interest has been evidenced in the probable influence of a child's position in the family upon his behavior and personality development. Although little reliable clinical and experimental evidence concerning this question is available, the importance of the problem demands the presentation of such tangible data as are extant. Students of childhood are anxious to know what the probable consequences are of being a first, an intermediate, a last, or, perchance, an "only" child. In attacking this question it is well to remember that such position is only one of many factors operating in the treatment of children in the family circle, and that no two children, including twins, reared in the same family ever encounter exactly the same environment.

Effects of Child's Position in the Family.—It should be recognized at the outset that a child's position in the family may involve attitudes on the part of parents and siblings (brothers and sisters) which lead to overacceptance, rejection, or other forms of mishandling. Such maltreatment of children may, of course, result in a variety of undesirable behavior trends, regardless of the child's position in the family. To say that position alone determines behavior trends is to ignore cause and effect relationships in the treatment of children.

THE OLDEST CHILD. It has been claimed, nevertheless, by Adler [39] and others that there is a clearly discernible relationship between the child's family status and his personality pattern. This psychoanalyst claims, for example, that the *oldest* child will develop a dependence upon his parents which makes it difficult for him to adjust to children and others outside of the home. The oldest child is also said to so resent the unwillingness of school children to allow him the center of the stage, to which he is accustomed, that he either adopts tricky attention-getting mechanisms or develops a feeling of inferiority. The arrival of a new baby means his overthrow as the object of

[39] Alfred Adler, *Problems of Neurosis*, Cosmopolitan Book Corp. (New York, Farrar & Rinehart), 1930, pp. 151-178.

affection, and may also result in the emotional pain of feeling unloved and isolated.

Adler is no doubt correct in stating that a great many first-born children develop these attitudes, but it should be evident that there is nothing inevitable about their appearance. Parents can, and some do, avert such outcomes by the simple expediency of avoiding the types of treatment mentioned in favor of those conducive to the development of independence and self-reliance. If the oldest child is dependent it is because his parents have treated him in such a way as to encourage such development instead of giving him responsibilities and teaching him to share with playmates and friends. Resentment at the arrival of a new addition to the family can easily be averted by teaching the child to look forward to it as a future playmate and companion. If parents permit the oldest child to remain the favorite and thus overaccept him, he becomes maladjusted accordingly, and not necessarily because he is a first-born child.

A number of researches have provided valuable information concerning the personality status of oldest children, but without regard to the nature of the home treatment encountered. Levy [40] found from a study of 576 problem cases, who had been brought to a juvenile research institute, that the first-born constituted a behavior problem more often than later-born children. The same was true of a larger number of normal children of similar age taken from the general population. A study by Ross [41] indicated that under present conditions of parent-child treatment, oldest children are more likely than others to manifest jealousy. The principal reason for this outcome has already been touched upon. In an investigation concerned with more marked deviations, Katz [42] found that the incidence of mental disorders is greater among first-born than among other children. This outcome was not substantiated by Wile and Noetzel,[43]

[40] John Levy, "A Quantitative Study of Behavior Problems in Relation to Family Constellation," *American Journal of Psychiatry*, 10: 637-654 (1930-31).

[41] B. M. Ross, "Some Traits Associated with Sibling Jealousy in Problem Children," *Smith College Studies in Social Work*, 1: 364-378 (1931).

[42] Barney Katz, *The Etiology of the Deteriorating Psychoses of Adolescence and Early Adult Life*, Doctoral Dissertation, The Univ. of Southern California, 1939.

[43] Ira S. Wile and Elinor Noetzel, "A Study of Birth Order and Behavior," *Journal of Social Psychology*, 2: 52-71 (1931).

whose study of 500 hospitalized children disclosed no significant relationship between order of birth and neurotic or other serious maladjustment.

Although the above data are conflicting, it seems reasonable to conclude that the outcome of being an oldest child is largely contingent upon the kind of treatment received at the hands of parents or their equivalent. Unless parents understand the difficulties involved and provide the conditions essential to the development of independence, self-reliance, a sense of personal worth , and a social outlook an oldest child is in danger of being overaccepted, overprotected, and, of becoming self-centered. Such a child may turn out to be timid, dependent, or crude in his treatment of people, as the case may be. Such outcomes could, however, be averted if the parents concerned treated their child in ways calculated to engender desirable personality qualities.

THE YOUNGEST CHILD. It is often said that the *youngest* child in a family is certain to be "spoiled" or to be so "bossed" that he becomes defiant and irritable. It is true that a child who has no need to share with a successor may be continually babied and thus led to retain infantile habits. He may be deprived of the opportunity of assuming a normal amount of responsibility and of holding his desires in abeyance for the good of the family, and thus develop a dependent, irresponsible personality. The youngest child may also be subjected to the pressure of so many demands from older siblings that he becomes resentful and antagonistic. It has been shown, for instance, that, next to "only" and first-born children, the incidence of delinquency is greatest among youngest children.[44] However, many youngest children are well adjusted and possess desirable social qualities. Intelligent parents can bring about such an outcome by avoiding the mishandling mentioned above and by according the "baby" of the family opportunity for becoming self-reliant and for maintaining a feeling of belongingness in the family.

[44] M. Parsley, "The Delinquent Girl in Chicago: The Influence of Ordinal Position and Size of Family," *Smith College Studies in Social Work*, 3: 274-283 (1933).

THE INTERMEDIATE CHILD. Other sibling relationships may, if not properly guarded by parents, contribute to the development of unwholesome personality trends. The *middle* child (or children) may, by virtue of receiving neither the attention of the oldest nor the recognition of the youngest, be allowed to fall into the background of parental notice and affection. Such a situation would naturally lead to feelings of inferiority and insecurity. One such child of the author's acquaintance complained that since she was neither as attractive as her older sister nor as cute as her little brother, there was not much that she could do to gain recognition and response from her parents. Such a situation is aggravated when parents fail to sense the child's need for status and a sense of personal worth. Being an intermediate child apparently invites conditions conducive to neglect and the development of feelings of inadequacy, but the obstacles in question can readily be overcome by understanding parents who sense the dangers involved. Again it is the treatment a child receives and not his ordinal position in the family *per se* that determines his personality development.

Socialization of the Only Child.—A strongly intrenched tradition exists that "only" children are certain to possess undesirable personality qualities. It is further believed that an only child who does succeed in developing adequate social adjustment does so in spite of the handicap of being reared without benefit of brothers and sisters. Such a point of view was stressed in the writings of G. Stanley Hall, and has been reiterated by many theoretical writers since his time.

It is true that in the case of parents who do not understand the difficulties involved, the fact of being an only child incurs the danger of becoming individualistic and egoistic. Many parents lavish a degree of attention and affection upon an only child that would hardly be possible where there are siblings with whom it must be shared. Furthermore, the child who is deprived of contacts with brothers and sisters with whom he would have to share playthings and attention is in danger of becoming egocentric and demanding. In this sense brothers and sisters are a great help to a child whose parents might otherwise permit him to become extremely selfish. However, it should be obvious that intelligent parents could avert this unhappy outcome by the relatively simple expediency (where possible) of providing the child with neighborhood playmates, of sending him to a nursery school or other preschool institution and, perhaps most important of all, of teaching him not only to share good things with his parents but to respect the rights and property of everyone within the range of his social contacts. Only children who are handled in this way, and who receive a judicious degree of attention, are unlikely to develop the dependent and unsocial traits so commonly associated with their ordinal position in the family.

Recent studies in this field have not substantiated the views of either early writers or research workers. In 1928, Fenton [45] presented evidence contrary to the idea that only children are inferior socially. This investigator found, in fact, that only children tended to be superior in some traits. Later studies by Ward [46] and by Guilford and Worcester [47] revealed no marked differences between the personality traits of only and non-only children. These and other researches have, however, been criticized as involving conspicuously small samplings of children, as having made poorly equated comparisons between only and non-only children, and as having used young or very young subjects. [48]

In an effort to correct the weaknesses mentioned, and the additional limitation of failure to take into consideration the place of residence and general environmental setting of the home, Stott [49] has made a comprehensive study of the personality qualities possessed by only versus non-only farm, small-town, and city children. Personality data obtained from the

---

[45] Norman Fenton, "The Only Child," *Journal of Genetic Psychology,* 35: 546-556 (1928).

[46] A. Ward, "The Only Child: A Study of One Hundred Only Children Living at Home with Both Parents, Referred to a Child Guidance Clinic," *Smith College Studies in Social Work,* 1: 41-65 (1930).

[47] R. B. Guilford and D. A. Worcester, "A Comparative Study of the Only and Non-only Child," *Journal of Genetic Psychology,* 38: 411-426 (1930).

[48] Paul A. Witty, "Only and Intermediate Children in the Senior High School," *Journal of Experimental Education,* 6: 180-186 (1937).

[49] Leland H. Stott, "General Home Setting as a Factor in the Study of the Only Versus the Non-only Child," *Character and Personality,* 8: 156-162 (1939).

CHILDREN, MATCHED FOR SEX, OTIS I. Q., AND ECONOMIC AND CULTURAL LEVEL OF FAMILY

(Positive critical ratios favor the Only Group, negative the Non-only.)

Personality Variable	Only		Non-Only		Diff.
	Mean	σ	Mean	σ	σDiff.
Farm home setting					
Rationality of thinking	36.1	6.4	38.1	5.7	−1.47
Personal adjustment	36.5	6.6	35.8	6.7	+0.44
Honesty	7.4	2.5	7.0	2.3	+0.47
Independence in personal matters	36.4	10.2	39.2	8.3	−1.35
Resourcefulness in group situations	19.6	9.8	19.2	8.5	+0.20
Personal responsibility	20.3	5.9	20.6	4.7	−0.25
Small-town home setting					
Rationality of thinking	36.2	6.3	36.9	5.3	−0.58
Personal adjustment	33.9	6.5	35.6	8.8	−1.06
Honesty	8.0	1.8	7.2	2.4	+1.82
Ethical judgment	26.2	4.5	24.7	3.8	+1.55
Independence in personal matters	36.9	10.1	38.4	9.6	−0.73
Resourcefulness in group situations	23.5	11.3	23.0	10.9	+0.22
Personal responsibility	20.5	5.7	20.8	5.9	−0.25
City home setting					
Rationality of thinking	38.2	5.0	40.8	4.9	−2.63
Personal adjustment	41.1	5.1	36.9	6.7	+3.65
Honesty	7.2	2.4	7.7	1.9	−1.19
Ethical judgment	25.4	4.0	25.7	4.7	−0.31
Independence in personal matters	43.4	9.4	39.2	9.3	+2.33
Resourcefulness in group situations	22.7	9.0	22.8	11.0	−0.06
Personal responsibility	25.4	5.6	20.6	5.5	+2.62

(From Leland H. Stott, "General Home Setting as a Factor in the Study of the Only Versus the Non-Only Child," *Character and Personality*, 8: 160 (1939).)

Maller *Case Inventory* and a self-reliance inventory devised by the investigator were secured for an equated group of 150 children matched as to sex, I.Q., and economic and cultural level of family (Sims' Socio-economic Scale). As Table 8 shows, even in such traits as resourcefulness in group situations, personal responsibility in social relationships, and honesty in classroom situations—"traits in which only-child deficiencies might theoretically be expected to appear"—the differences between only and non-only children were negligible. However, among the city children the only group was reliably superior (statistically) in personal adjustment, independence in personal matters, and personal responsibility. The non-only group was definitely superior in rationality of thinking.

Stott has concluded that the former confusion regarding the effects of "onliness" upon personality development resulted from the failure of investigators to recognize that "onliness may not be properly regarded as a factor constant in its effects in all types of home setting and in all cultures, or that its significance may change with the march of general social change." In other words, limitations in transportation, communication, and general social living were such in earlier days as to require the only child frequently to be reared in comparative isolation from other children. Finally, "Conclusions regarding the effects of having or not having brothers and sisters may legitimately be drawn only in terms of the particular environmental setting and the particular culture in which the study was made."

Causes of Jealousy Between Children.—A child becomes jealous when he feels that his security with a loved one is threatened. Like other symptoms of disturbance of the child's sense of personal importance, jealousy has an antecedent cause, but cannot logically be regarded as inevitable. When a sibling shows evidences of being jealous it is probably because a newborn baby has deprived him of privileges and parental attention, because unfavorable comparisons have been made between him and brothers or sisters, because illness of a sibling has caused the loss of much desired care and affection, or because parents, teachers, or relatives have shown recognizable favoritism.

A study by Sewell [50] of the behavior of 70 children who had recently been displaced to some extent by the arrival of a new addition to the family, showed frequent tendencies to ignore the infant, to deny any connection with it, or to make overt attacks upon it. In some cases the arrival of the new sibling brought about marked changes in the personality of the supplanted child. The changes noted included increased shyness and timidity, tendencies toward daydreaming, and the development of negativistic attitudes. Sewell believed that these attitudes were symptoms of jealousy brought about by a sense of loss of parental preferment.

The plight of the child who is summarily supplanted by a new baby has been graphically portrayed as follows: "The arrival of a younger child in the family also may create acute anxiety when the older child has not been prepared for it. The shock of waking up one morning to find the mother absent, to be told that she has gone to the hospital to have a baby, and then to have her return with an infant who engrosses her time and attention is the unhappy fate of many children whose parents either ignore their need for preparation and reassurance or else deny it because they cannot face the questions about sex and procreation involved. So many children suffer unnecessarily from the arrival of a younger brother or sister when that arrival could be the occasion for happy expectations and enjoyment!" [51] Certainly, such a plight can be avoided. One mother managed the problem nicely by assuring her three-year-old son that when the little brother or sister came he could have good times with it, that he could help care for it, and that he could be its protector. He was neither asked to "give up" anything nor to dispense with his mother's love and attention. Needless to say no jealousies of serious magnitude arose between these siblings as they grew up together.

[50] M. Sewell, "Some Causes of Jealousy in Young Children," *Smith College Studies in Social Work,* 1 : 6-22 (1930).
[51] Lawrence K. Frank, "The Fundamental Needs of the Child," *Mental Hygiene,* 22 : 353-379 (1938).

Children who are subjected to enforced generosity, loss of needed attention, and odious comparisons are obviously hampered in their social development. Being frustrated in their efforts to secure affection and status, such children tend to remain emotionally immature. Some gain the much desired attention by such mechanisms as refusal to eat until coaxed or threatening to harm a disliked sibling, others become negativistic, destructive, overactive, self-centered, restless in their sleep, or addicted to nail-biting and enuresis. These and other symptoms of insecurity arise when the child's fundamental need for parental affection is frustrated.

The Development of Sibling Cooperation.—Children who are prepared for the coming of a younger brother or sister, and whose parents continue to recognize and care for them while nurturing the new arrival, are in a favorable position to develop cooperative attitudes toward members of the family. It is a cardinal principle that a child learns cooperative ways of behaving most naturally in concrete situations controlled in such a way as to insure the satisfaction of his basic needs. Thus, if a child continues to receive recognition and love while assisting in the care of an infant or helping a sibling protect himself from neighborhood bullies, he will in the nature of the case find satisfaction in such cooperation. Parents can readily use this fundamental technique in building sibling teamwork. Desirable results cannot be gained by asking the immature child to "sacrifice" basic satisfactions in favor of adult ideals of cooperation. Both the child's psychological nature and his level of maturity must be recognized in any program of socialization.

Children who are reared in accordance with psychologically sound principles readily develop cooperative behavior trends. Just as one mother taught her son to protect his younger brother from unfair attacks by larger boys at school, others can inculcate habits of cooperation in activities involving work, play, and routine home life. Many a small boy or girl has learned to speak proudly of an infant sibling as "my baby sister." Others have learned to share toys, sweets, and privileges with both siblings and playmates outside the home.

Behavior Patterns Inculcated by Adults

The child is not equipped by nature with the capacity to adapt himself to social situations, neither is it longer believed that he possesses a so-called instinct of imitation. Evidence tends to show that the child learns to adjust himself to the requirements of social demands, and that characteristic patterns of behavior result from responses to the actions of parents and other members of the family. Since the individuals comprising his family are the principal models to which he is exposed during the early years, it is natural that the child should respond to the types of social stimuli which they present.

How the Child Reflects Parental Behavior.—The questions are often asked, why behavior problems run in families, why children's temperaments reflect their father or mother, why there are so many more stutterers in some family "trees" than in others, and why children act so much like their parents. The general answer to these queries given by most psychologists is not that children inherit these tendencies and patterns, but that they reflect parental behavior and adopt defense mechanisms utilized by their parents.

In a study of the relationship between parental and child defense behavior, Levy and Patrick [52] found that children of parents subject to fainting spells are more likely to utilize such spells than other forms of defense behavior. Children of parents given to periodic headaches also more often experience headaches than fainting spells or other such nervous symptoms. There is likewise some evidence that parents who dislike or distrust people tend to engender the same attitudes in their children. Such findings show that young children pattern their behavior after that exemplified by their parents. Children tend to be neat, clean about their person, courteous to strangers, punctual at appointments, and the like somewhat to the extent portrayed by their fathers and mothers. Clinical evidence has suggested, however, that exceptions to this tendency occur when a

---

[52] David M. Levy and H. T. Patrick, "Relation of Infantile Convulsions, Head-Banging, and Breath-Holding to Fainting and Headaches in the Parents," *Archives of Neurology and Psychiatry,* 19 : 865-887 (1928).

mother continues to bombard the child with admonitions, for example, to be neat and clean. Under such circumstances the child may eventually develop untidy personal habits in an unrecognized attempt to *declare her independence* of an overshadowing and dominant parent. This is probably a means by which some children maintain their selfhood and personal autonomy.

In an informal discussion of the subtle ways in which parental attitudes may be inculcated in children through the medium of social inheritance, Travis [53] has described the case of a boy, Kenny, whose educated and able mother was concerned over the boy's tendency to emulate his father's timid, self-conscious personality. As this psychologist explained it, "Kenny is not asocial just because his father is. Kenny is asocial and his father is asocial because of a common factor, or common factors, in the home environment of the two. Kenny introjected the attitudes of his father, Kenny's father introjected the attitudes of Kenny's grandfather . . . and so on back. Before Kenny's two-year-old brother was born Kenny wasn't so bad. True, he was a little shy, a little insecure. So was his father. The father didn't say, 'Now Kenny, I'm a little insecure, so you must be too! Or, I'm a little insecure, you mustn't be.' No. He didn't say anything like this. Yet, he said everything like this. He said everything in tensions, in voice quality, in touching Kenny, in silent intervals, in voice inflections, in the way he held Kenny, in the way he played with Kenny. . . . He gave his attitudes to Kenny in elementary, fundamental, and subtle ways—the ways Kenny understood." It might well be added that this boy's timidity is almost certain to be transferred to numerous social situations outside his family circle.

Developing Habits of Eating and Sleeping.—A widespread belief seems to be in evidence that a child's feeding problems are solved if a physician has prescribed how much he should eat, how often he should eat, and what kind of foods he should eat. Yet many mothers complain that even though they follow such a schedule, their apparently well-fed children not only do not

[53] Lee Edward Travis, "Personality Hazards and Potentialities of the Modern Home," *Education,* 61 : 601-607 (1941).

relish their food, but are on occasions positively stubborn in their refusal to eat. Only recently have pediatricians (medical child specialists) come to realize that feeding, like all other child problems, has important psychological implications.

Roberts [54] has reported a series of researches on child feeding designed to suggest conditions most conducive to spontaneous eating and a wholesome attitude toward food. In one study careful observations were made of the eating reactions of 100 city children from comfortable homes, 50 farm children, and 100 children from the underprivileged section of a large city. Records were made of the kinds of food served, the amounts of each eaten, the time required for eating, and of the children's attitude toward the food. Whereas only 19 per cent of the privileged city children showed normal hunger, 100 per cent of the children from poor homes reacted with a high degree of hunger. Approximately two-thirds of the country children seemed normally hungry. A mere 5 per cent of the poor children required the coaxing to eat demanded by 40 per cent of the prosperous group. A study by Davis [55] showed that newly weaned infants eat a variety of natural foods, both vegetable and animal, when these are placed before them with no restrictions as to amount eaten, manners used, and time involved. The combinations of food chosen by the children were of such nature as to result in adequate nourishment. Furthermore, in the case of young children, eating behavior may serve as a sensitive indicator of emotional adjustment.[56]

These and similar findings have led pediatricians and other child specialists to realize that rigid attitudes toward children's diet that do not take into account individual variations lead to feeding difficulties; that the transition from breast to bottle, or from bottle to other utensil may, if made too rapidly, cause emotional tensions; that psychological problems appear if parents require the child to eat solid foods before it is mature

[54] Lydia A. Roberts, "A Review of Recent Literature on Certain Phases of Nutrition Research and its Significance in Child Development," *Report of National Research Council, Third Conference on Child Development,* 1929.
[55] C. Davis, "Self Selection of Diet by Newly Weaned Infants," *American Journal of Diseases of Children,* 36 : 651-679 (1928).
[56] S. K. Escalona, "Feeding Disturbances in Very Young Children," *American Journal of Orthopsychiatry,* 15 : 76-80 (1945).

neuromuscularly or delay such eating after the child is ready to function adequately; and that children will not necessarily suffer from physical infirmities in later life if they do not eat freely such popularly recommended foods as spinach, carrots, oatmeal, and the like.[57]

The following paraphrased statement of the views of a leading pediatrician [58] expresses the more modern attitude toward child feeding: "Babies need not be fed every four hours on the dot, but when they are hungry. They should be allowed to eat as much or as little as they want. When left to their own hunger pangs, most babies stick to an even schedule, eat the right amount necessary for growth and health. Pediatricians used to vie with each other to see who could find the earliest age to give infants solid foods. One even fed meat to toothless three-months-olds. But now doctors generally stick to milk, wait for a few teeth before feeding babies solids. As for the transition from bottle to cup, [they] suggest placing a cup on baby's feeding tray, waiting till he starts to play with it and tries to drink out of it."

It is essential, of course, for parents to provide the proper kind of food for their children at all levels of development. For infants, human milk is regarded as the most natural food. Babies can be nourished by other methods but breast feeding provides the chemically most adequate food for most infants during the first six or eight months of postnatal life. When it is necessary to resort to artificial feeding, only such a formula as may be recommended by a physician who specializes in infant feeding should be selected. Appropriate foods for older children may be ascertained by consulting volumes devoted to this problem. The two brief references cited below provide general instruction in this phase of child care.[59]

---

[57] W. S. Langford, "The Psychological Aspects of Feeding in Early Childhood," *Journal of American Dietitians Assn.*, 17 : 208-216 (1941) ; L. S. Selling and M. A. S. Ferraro, *The Psychology of Diet and Nutrition*, New York, W. W. Norton & Co., 1945.

[58] Charles A. Aldrich, "Let Your Children Alone," *Time*, Oct. 20, 1941, p. 42.

[59] Paul L. Boynton, *Psychology of Child Development*, Minneapolis, Educational Publishers, Inc., 1938, pp. 449-454 ; Winifred Rand, M. E. Sweeny, and E. L. Vincent, *Growth and Development of the Young Child*, Philadelphia, W. B. Saunders Co., 1940, pp. 247-252.

Like feeding methods, some of those practiced in an effort to induce children to sleep may eventuate in undesirable attitudes that carry over into adult life. During the first six months the infant sleeps most of the time. As he grows older situations appear that tend to militate against the enjoyment of sleep. For example, if a child is rather suddenly required to leave an interesting game or say good-night to a group of visitors who are apparently planning to continue an attractive social evening, he may come to feel that sleep is a detriment to his fun and to regard it as an indirect form of punishment. Under such conditions a child will long to stay up and may resort to innumerable subterfuges to accomplish his purpose. Many a child who was forced to go to bed in this way has bothered his mother for some time afterward by calling for a glass of water, complaining about the temperature, requesting permission to go to the toilet, or saying that he has something important to confide in her.

Modern students of the subject advocate that parents avoid clashes over bedtime rules by creating quiet, relaxed conditions conducive to drowsiness at that time. It is best to avoid all hustle or excitement when bedtime comes around. Such a program is conducive to the elimination of sleep-disturbing tensions. No intelligent parent will expect a child to look forward to being put to bed when exciting things are going on around him. Neither will such a parent require the child to drop some interesting game or pastime instantly without a chance to bring his activity to a close. Such arbitrary domination would further intrench in the child a dislike for sleep. Sleep should be made a privilege, not a punishment, to the developing boy or girl.

Undesirable Results of Arbitrary Discipline.—The great majority of parents no doubt desire to discipline their children fairly and intelligently. Such a desirable training program can only be carried out, however, where there is reasonable understanding of the needs of child nature. Many parents still believe that corporal punishment is the principal avenue to the development of character, and thus fail to realize that their children's undesirable behavior may often be traced to their own inadequate management. Others labor under the assumption that children's behavior tendencies are inherited and thus not amenable to modification. Still other parents decline to attempt training because of a belief that children cannot be influenced in their behavior trends before they are able to converse and understand what they are told. Such damaging practices as bribing children to behave and threatening them with visits from a policeman or an irate father are not uncommonly utilized. Unfortunately, many parents also assume that the birth of an offspring brings in its wake intuitive knowledge concerning the intricacies of child care and discipline.

Until recent times, punishment was practically the only method of administering discipline. Since the child was considered to be sinful by nature, it was thought necessary to punish him vigorously for every deviation from adult-determined standards of moral behavior. The maxim "spare the rod and spoil the child" was advanced on the theory that vigorous suppression of evil tendencies was necessary to the development of piety and respect for social endorsements.

The modern interpretation of discipline does not dispense with punishment, but utilizes it only when there are reasonable indications that it will result in the ultimate personal welfare of the child. Punishment is no longer regarded as an end in itself, or as a repressive measure, but as a means for the development of socially desirable behavior. The child who is subjected to continual harsh treatment experiences little fulfillment of his need for a sense of freedom and may become morbidly sensitive or rebellious. Such attitudes are clearly inimical to social growth. It is for this reason that disciplinary methods are now directed toward the determination of *causes* of bad behavior and to the building of adequate character and personality qualities.[60] Also growing out of these objectives of discipline is the development of self-reliance and personal responsibility. The heart of the disciplinary technique of today is not, as some have supposed, unlimited freedom or "self-ex-

<hr>

[60] Leo Kanner, "Work with Psychobiological Children's Personality Difficulties," *American Journal of Orthopsychiatry,* 4 : 402-412 (1934).

pression" resulting in such uncontrolled impulses as striking other children, breaking the neighbor's window, or throwing stones at passing automobiles, but stimulation to concern with wholesome work and play activities. Instead of advocating the extremes of domination or license, child psychology suggests the utilization of disciplinary methods designed to satisfy the child's personal and social needs.

Unless punishment is administered in a just way that makes it clear to the child that his well-being rather than retribution is involved, nothing but harm can come from its use in child training. The intelligent disciplinarian is concerned with the offender's readjustment, not with the offense as such, and does not complicate matters by inflicting pain in proportion to the alleged seriousness of the "crime." To proceed on any other basis is to encourage an offender to commercialize morals by deceiving his elders regarding the magnitude of his misdemeanors. Other evils growing out of arbitrary punishment include: (1) hatred of the one who overdoes the punishment, (2) trickery to avoid being caught, (3) a tendency to seek revenge from the perpetrators of the punishment, and (4) a degree of fear that may lead to nervous manifestations.

As Davis's [61] data show, corporal punishment has declined in favor in American public schools. Whereas the St. Louis school system administered 141.1 corporal punishments per 1,000 pupils in 1881, the figure had dropped to 1.7 such punishments per 1,000 pupils in 1924. Today, most school systems are prohibited by law from inflicting such harsh treatment upon children. The kind of present-day punishments utilized in a sampling of children from a variety of environments is shown in Table 9.

Perhaps the most important generalization involved here is that the administering of punishment should at all times be consistent. If a child is told that disobedience or the destruction of property, for example, will be followed by certain punishments, such treatment should ensue as a matter of course with no delay, excuses, or exceptions. Any other practice will

[61] H. H. Davis, "Corporal Punishment and Suspension," *School and Society*, 28 : 630 (1928).

be met with disrespect for authority and schemes for outwitting the negligent parent. The administration of punishment should be just but sure. The child, for example, who is told four or five times by his apparently helpless mother that if he

TABLE 9. METHODS OF PUNISHMENT USED BY PARENTS AS REPORTED BY FARM, SMALL-TOWN, AND CITY SUBJECTS

| | Boys | | | | Girls | | | |
| | By mother | | By father | | By mother | | By father | |
Method	N	%	N	%	N	%	N	%
Farm subjects								
Scolded	44	46.3	38	40.0	61	67.0	16	17.6
Made to stay home	4	4.2	4	4.2	5	5.5	3	3.3
Slapped	3	3.2	1	1.1	2	2.2	1	1.1
Whipped					1	1.1	1	1.1
Cussed			1	1.1				
"Went out and stayed"							1	1.1
Total	51	53.7	44	46.3	69	75.8	22	24.2
Town subjects								
Scolded	62	50.8	44	36.1	90	70.9	17	13.4
Made to stay home	3	2.5	6	4.9	11	8.7	3	2.4
Slapped	2	1.6			3	2.4		
Privileges taken away	1	0.8	2	1.6				
Made to do work over					1	0.8	1	0.8
Allowance cut			1	0.8				
No supper			1	0.8				
No dates					1	0.8		
Total	68	55.7	54	44.2	106	83.5	21	16.5
City subjects								
Scolded	43	44.8	28	29.2	56	62.9	10	11.2
Made to stay home	7	7.3	10	10.4	9	10.1	3	3.4
Slapped	1	1.0	2	2.1	1	1.1	1	1.1
Allowance stopped	1	1.0	1	1.0			1	1.1
Sent to bed	1	1.0					1	1.1
Talking to							1	1.1
Cutting insults					1	1.1		
(Not reported)			2	2.1	4	4.5	1	1.1
Total	53	55.2	43	44.8	71	79.8	18	20.2

(From Leland H. Stott, "Home Punishment of Adolescents," *Journal of Genetic Psychology*, 57:423 (1940).)

repeats a certain misdemeanor he will be sent to bed, is almost certain to develop an arrogant attitude. Children whose parents fail to agree in the treatment of undesirable behavior are thrown into frequent confusion and may use every possible means to pit one parent against the other. Furthermore, parents who fluctuate from strictness to indulgence, and who threaten punishment for minor infractions at one time while permitting them to go unnoticed at others, are giving their children no opportunity to anchor themselves to a consistent policy. These and other vacillations in child care can only result in the development of undesirable behavior.

Summary and Implications

The positive effects of desirable early home conditions have been summarized by Symonds.[62] To quote him, "Emotional security depends in the first place on physical contact. The physical touching, the fondling, and the cuddling of the child by mother and father furnish the baby his first feelings of support and assurance. His sense of security is further enhanced by the care which he receives and by the promptness and completeness with which his needs are met. Good parents are generous . . . generous with food, toys, and with their own time and attention. They frequently give the child presents. Good parents show their fondness for the child by including him in their activities, by being interested in him, and by showing pleasure at his growth and development. Both parents express their pleasure in the child not only by deeds, but also by words, and reveal their fondness for and pride in him directly to him both in the family circle and also to relatives and friends outside the home. When the child grows older the parents are interested in his plans and ambitions, in his accomplishments in school, in his special interests and hobbies, and they give him every encouragement along these lines."

The constructive home provides the child with the feeling that he can always return to it with full assurance that he *belongs* there. It also *accepts* him in spite of any physical defects, deficiencies in intelligence, or social immaturities he may display. The adequate home aids the child in developing a normal, well-adjusted personality by accepting him as he is, and does not demand that he measure up to arbitrary adult standards. It also makes the child so certain of his parents' warm affection that a moderate amount of punishment causes

[62] Percival M. Symonds, *The Psychology of Parent-Child Relationships*, New York, D. Appleton-Century Co., Inc., 1939, p. 151.

no resentment or bitterness. Successful parents have learned that sincere expressions of regard are more effective in insuring the child's sense of security than any number of superficial demonstrations of generosity.

The value to society of an increase in the number of individuals reared in such homes should be apparent. It would mean a decline in emotional instability and other maladjustments so characteristic of our civilization. Other improvements to which constructive home life should lead include a stemming of the tide of lawlessness and a reduction of the national burden of chronic neuroticism. Good home conditions are the natural avenue to the maintenance of individual integrity and to the development of a social outlook. It can thus be said that the welfare of the nation depends to a great extent upon the effectiveness with which parents regulate the early experiences of their children. Personalities do not, as a rule, transcend the conditions under which they develop.

QUESTIONS FOR DISCUSSION

1. What evidence is there that early home conditions and parental handling tend to determine the direction of the child's personality development? Is it true that the family is the most significant psychological influence in the child's early life? Explain.
2. Explain the probable effects on the child's emotional development of parental *rejection* versus parental *overacceptance*. Show how either of these forms of treatment block the child's chances of later social adjustment. Cite one or more examples.
3. To what extent can one depend on Symonds' findings concerning the effects of parental dominance or submission on child personality? Is there a direct cause and effect relationship here? Why do you suppose that dominated children tend to become dominating parents?
4. Describe the ideal parent-child relationship. Would it seem preferable for a girl to have a dominant but kind father and a submissive but loving mother than a dominant mother and a retiring father? Justify your contention with both logic and examples.

5. Name several forms of parental mishandling of a child in terms of his fundamental needs and show the probable outcome in each instance. Cite researches which tend to corroborate your statements. Suggest the basis for a defensible science of child rearing.

6. Why is it impossible to predict a child's personality development with precision on the basis of his position in the family? How could the disadvantage of being a first or last child be overcome by understanding parents? What are the effects of parental preference for a child?

7. What are the fallacies in the assumption that an "only" child is invariably "spoiled"? Cite evidence to the contrary from Stott's investigation of city and country children. Support the contention that in a sense every child is an "only" child.

8. Support the assertion that siblings can be influenced to love each other, hate each other, or to be jealous of each other. Indicate the home conditions under which each of these results would be most likely to obtain. Show how any one of them could be prevented.

9. What psychological reasons can you give for the frequent refusal of some children to eat, to go to sleep, or otherwise to conform to ordinary health habits? What does a child probably gain by such negativism? What kind of parental handling might be at fault?

10. What are the principal differences between the older and newer views concerning the function of discipline? How can discipline be administered in such a way as to further a child's personal and social adjustment? What are the dangers of arbitrary and inconsistent disciplinary methods?

Recommended Readings

Anderson, John E. *Happy Childhood*. New York: D. Appleton-Century Co., Inc., 1933.

Blanchard, Phyllis. *The Child and Society*. New York: Longmans, Green & Co., 1928, Ch. 2.

Brill, A. C., and Youtz, M. P. *Your Child and His Parents*. New York: D. Appleton-Century Co., Inc., 1932.

Chittenden, G. E. *Living With Children*. New York: The Macmillan Co., 1944.

Foster, J. C., and Anderson, John E. *The Young Child and His Parents*. Minneapolis: Univ. of Minnesota Press, 1930.

Frank, Lawrence K. "The Fundamental Needs of the Child." *Mental Hygiene*, 22:353-379 (1938).

Hart, H., and Hart, E. B. *Personality and the Family.* New York: D. C. Heath & Co., 1935.

Myers, G. C. *Modern Parenthood.* New York: Greenberg, Publisher, Inc., 1931.

Nimkoff, Meyer F. *The Child.* Philadelphia: J. B. Lippincott Co., 1934, Ch. 8.

Rand, Winifred, Sweeny, M. E., and Vincent, E. L. *Growth and Development of the Young Child.* Philadelphia: W. B. Saunders Co., 1940, Ch. 9.

Ribble, Margaret A. "Infantile Experience in Relation to Personality Development," in *Personality and the Behavior Disorders.* (Edited by J. McV. Hunt.) New York: The Ronald Press Co., 1944, Vol. II, Ch. 20.

Selling, L. S., and Ferraro, M. A. S. *The Psychology of Diet and Nutrition.* New York: W. W. Norton & Co., 1945.

Symonds, Percival M. *The Psychology of Parent-Child Relationships.* New York: D. Appleton-Century Co., Inc., 1939.

Tiegs, Ernest W., and Katz, Barney. *Mental Hygiene in Education.* New York: The Ronald Press Co., 1941, Ch. 11.

CHAPTER 7

PHYSICAL GROWTH AND HEALTH

FEW ASPECTS OF CHILD DEVELOPMENT have enjoyed the attention recently accorded problems associated with physical growth and health. Educators, clinicians, and pediatricians have sought to determine the rate and rhythm with which children grow, the maturation levels at which motor acts can most economically and safely be learned, what programs of diet, exercise, and health conservation are most conducive to bodily vigor, and to what extent individual differences in physical constitution require specific educational planning. Students of child psychology are also interested in knowing what long-range studies in physical development have revealed, what factors cause individual differences in growth rate, and what practical applications to educational problems can be made of growth data in general.

In an effort to find answers to these and related questions, child research agencies have been established in such well-known institutions of learning as Yale, Harvard, and the universities of Iowa, California, Michigan, and Minnesota. These and other institutions have for some time been making exhaustive year by year measurements of children's physical, mental, social, and personality development. Child foundation clinics and guidance centers have also amassed cumulative records of individual growth. Journals and societies devoted to the publication of scientific findings in this field have made their contributions both to the public and to child specialists. There is thus every indication that the facts of physical growth and health will be increasingly utilized by those charged with safeguarding the development of the Nation's children.

General Aspects of Child Growth

The general aspects of physical growth are becoming increasingly well understood. Researches in this field have provided a reasonably clear picture of the changes a child undergoes in his development from infancy to adulthood. Such growth is apparently made possible by a none-too-well understood general deterministic factor [1] in the body which, under satisfactory circumstances, appears to guarantee the cooperative development of all parts of the organism.

Factors in Physical Growth and Development.—Although acknowledging that nature (maturation) plays an indispensable role in physical development, Courtis [2] has described *growth* as "progress toward a defined maturity brought about in an immature organism by the action of appropriate environmental forces under constant conditions." This investigator's point is that the living organism responds in its growth to changes in the conditions under which it is called upon to develop. That is to say, if appropriate minerals and vitamins are not absorbed into the system, basic structures will be unable to grow satisfactorily; and if disease-carrying organisms are not prevented from entering the body, tissues may be prevented from developing in a normal manner. Chemical and endocrine dysfunctioning during prenatal days are apparently also responsible for many physical defects appearing in the newborn. Birth trauma (injuries) also play their part in the generation of abnormal structural development. And, as will be noted in more detail later, the maturing of sex glands has an important bearing on the rate of physical growth.

In any consideration of physical growth it is well to recognize that both nature and nurture are involved—nature in the form of the living organism with its self-actuated nervous, muscular, glandular, and bony structures, and nurture with its environmental factors of food, water, heat, light, cold, pain, and

1 George D. Stoddard, "Research in Child Development," *American Council on Education Studies,* 3 : 21 (1939).
2 S. A. Courtis, "Major Growth Concepts," in *Pupil Development and the Curriculum,* Bureau of Educational Reference and Research, Univ. of Michigan, 1937-38, p. 61.

emotion-producing experiences. No useful purpose is served, however, by debating the *relative* influence of nature and nurture in the physical development of the individual. Both factors lose their separate identity when the fertilized ovum is sent on its way in the development of a future human organism, and both participate as a fusion of factors in the determination of bodily growth. The crucial problem here is the control of general physical development in ways designed to insure a desired degree of body symmetry, physical health, neuromuscular efficiency, and longevity.

Longitudinal versus Horizontal Measurements.—Until recent years, practically all researches in child growth concerned themselves with securing cross-sectional data; that is, with determining the *average* height, weight, or other physical measures of large groups of children. Such findings made it possible to construct representative curves of physical growth for a number of developmental factors. However, with increased interest in the growth and development of the *individual child* it became necessary to make *longitudinal* (year after year measurements) studies of given children. It had become apparent that cross-sectional data were misleading in the prediction of individual growth rhythms. In short, curves of average growth had obscured the pattern of individual growth by cancelling out individual differences and cycles of development. Cross-sectional and longitudinal measurement procedures serve different yet complementary purposes. One (cross-sectional) provides a background for discerning growth tendencies within groups, races, populations, and either of the sexes. The other (longitudinal) makes it possible to compare an individual with himself at different stages of growth and with groups of which he may be a member.[3]

Thus far practically every extensive growth study in which the longitudinal method has been used has reported that growth is somewhat cyclic (proceeds by cycles or accelerations and decelerations) rather than being strictly gradual in nature. In

---

[3] Harold E. Jones, "Resources for the Consultant," *Journal of Consulting Psychology*, 3: 157-159 (1939).

discussing the twelve-year Harvard Growth Study,[4] Rothney [5] writes, "Enough longitudinal studies have now been conducted to enable us to describe the general form of linear physical growth curves. We can say with a great deal of assurance that growth is very rapid from birth to the age of two, that it tends to continue at a diminishing rate until a period of approximately three years before the advent of puberty, rises rapidly (more rapidly than previous cross-sectional studies had revealed) until puberty is reached, and then falls away quickly to end points (where the increase is smaller than the errors of measurement) at ages between seventeen and nineteen. The shape of the curves for both sexes is almost identical but the timing of the adolescent spurt disturbs the parallelism of the growth curves."

Courtis,[6] who has been active in both the theory and practice of longitudinal growth measurement, maintains that there are at least four distinct cycles of growth. These are described as:

1. The *prenatal,* during which development proceeds *in utero* as in the case of animals who live in water.

2. *Infancy* (on the average from birth to five or six years of age), during which the sensory channels begin to function and the child learns to creep, walk, and speak.

3. *Childhood* (on the average from five to twelve), during which permanent teeth appear, the child learns to read, write, and care for himself, and marked changes in personality take place.

4. *Adolescence* (on the average from twelve to eighteen), during which the development of sex organs brings about the appearance of physical sex characteristics.

According to Courtis, these cycles are associated with changes in *rates* of growth in height and weight, ossification of

[4] W. F. Dearborn and J. W. M. Rothney, *Predicting the Child's Development,* Cambridge (Mass.), Sci-Art Publishers, 1941.

[5] J. W. M. Rothney, "Recent Findings in the Study of the Physical Growth of Children," *Journal of Educational Research,* 35 : 161-182 (1941).

[6] S. A. Courtis, "Maturation as a Factor in Educational Diagnosis," in *Educational Diagnosis, Thirty-Fourth Yearbook, National Society for the Study of Education,* 1935, pp. 177-178.

bony structure, intelligence (mental age), educational achievement, and interest in play, social activities, and vocations. The
cycles also occur at different ages for different children and
produce results of different degrees of intensity. Each child's
development is strictly unique and should be appraised in terms
of his own tempo of growth, not with reference to mass data
for groups of children. Figure 31 indicates the importance
of making such longitudinal studies of individual children.

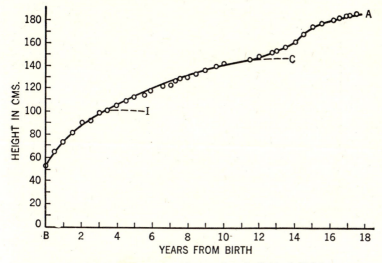

Figure 30. The Growth Curve of an Individual Child

(From R. E. Scammon, in J. A. Harris *et al., The Measurement of Man,* Minneapolis,
Univ. of Minnesota Press, 1930, p. 176.)

In spite of the difficulties involved in obtaining them, longitudinal growth data will probably displace many of the grosser
mass methods in the scientific study of children. The difficulties referred to include great expense, the problem of avoiding
population change, the number of years needed for completion,
the maintenance of constant conditions of measurement, and the
necessity of using new statistical techniques. The advantages
of such individual long-range studies have been summarized as
follows: [7]

[7] S. A. Courtis, *The Importance of Longitudinal Studies of Children's Growth,*
unpub. ms., 1939, p. 13.

They reveal the natural patterns of growth which "average
out" in mass data.

They make possible the interpretation of a child's growth curve
in terms of his own natural standards.

They increase the reliability of interpretations of test scores.

Fewer cases are needed for a given reliability.

They are powerful diagnostic instruments.

They eliminate the effect of selective factors.

They permit comparisons and correlations between different
types of measurement.

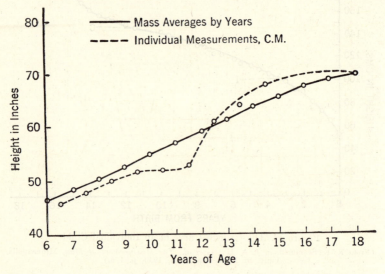

Figure 31. Comparison of Mass Average and Longitudinal Data for Growth
in Height of School Children

(From S. A. Courtis, *The Importance of Longitudinal Studies of Children's Growth,*
unpub. ms., 1939, p. 5.)

Individual Differences in Growth Rates.—It has already
been stated that each child grows according to a unique pattern
peculiar to his organism and influenced by the shifting combinations of experience which he encounters. Although physical
growth curves apparently tend to follow the same general pattern, children of the same age differ by virtue of the facts that
one may be destined to reach a *higher maximum growth* than

another, that one may *grow at a more rapid rate* than another, and that different parts of the body grow at different rates *within* the same individual. It is well known that the height, weight, and other physical characteristics of mature men and women differ extensively, but it is not so well understood that, because of possessing unique physical patterns, children of a given age need not and often should not be expected to conform

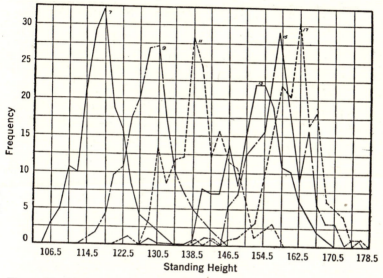

Figure 32. Overlapping of Distributions of Standing Height Measurements of 167 Girl Subjects of the Harvard Growth Study Measured at Alternate Years from Ages 7 to 17 Inclusive

(From J. W. M. Rothney, "Recent Findings in the Study of the Physical Growth of Children," *Journal of Educational Research*, 35:170 (1941).)

to an arbitrary height-weight classification. As Figure 32 shows, it is extremely difficult to classify a child by age as far as physical height is concerned. In view of the fact that eleven- and twelve-year-old children overlap in height to the extent of 59 per cent, there is no point in being concerned about a child who is not up to the average in this respect for his age.[8]

The Harvard Growth Study has also shown that prediction of standing height from earlier height figures is so uncertain

[8] J. W. M. Rothney, *op. cit.*, p. 170

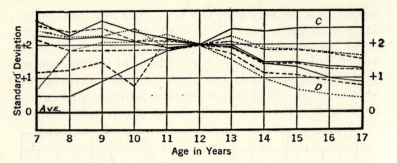

Figure 33. Variability from Average at Each Age of Eight Girls Whose
Standing Height Measurements Were Identical at Age 12

(From J. W. M. Rothney, "Recent Findings in the Study of the Physical Growth of
Children," *Journal of Educational Research*, 35:174 (1941).)

as to possess little value. As may be seen in Figure 33, the differences in growth in height displayed by eight girls whose height was identical at age twelve are sufficiently great at other ages to make it unlikely that anyone measuring them at any previous age level would have expected such identity at that age. As Rothney [9] puts it, "The variability in deviation from averages for age and from previous patterns . . . indicate the futility of attempting to predict future growth of individuals in standing height at any other age." A scrutiny of cases C and D in Figure 33, whose height curves cross at age twelve, will demonstrate the truthfulness of this statement. Meredith [10] has shown, however, that prediction of height of boys of North European descent (Harvard Growth Study data) may be made with errors of not more than 2.5 centimeters in 95 per cent of cases, if such prediction is made at the relatively stable age of seven for height at age eleven.

Basic Principles of Organism Growth.—Since the advent of individual longitudinal studies of physical and mental growth, it has become necessary to revise, somewhat, former statements of the laws of human development. This is because

9 *Ibid.*, p. 174.
10 H. V. Meredith, "The Prediction of Stature of North European Males Through the Elementary Years," *Human Biology*, 8 : 279-283 (1936). See also Katherine Simmons, *The Brush Foundation Study of Child Growth and Development*. II. *Physical Growth and Development*, Monographs of the Society for Research in Child Development, Vol. 9, No. 1 (1944).

growth curves based on average figures obscured the specific patterns of individual development, and thus led to fallacious interpretations of individual growth in terms of averages for a given age, sex, or group. Some of the earlier statements [11] of the laws of growth were carefully formulated on the basis of evidence then available, but suffered from the belief that successive measurements of the same children would yield results similar to those based on averages for groups of children.

Care should be exercised not to interpret the newer longitudinal data as overthrowing entirely the findings of group growth investigations. Although it is true that the nature of both physical and mental growth has been clarified by studies of individual development, the basic principles or so-called "laws of growth" have been modified by them only in certain instances and in some cases to only a moderate degree. The discussion of principles of organism growth presented here is not intended to be exhaustive, but should serve to orient the reader to the principal facts and controversies of this important phase of child psychology. Some of the principles are the same as those mentioned in Chapter 1 in connection with the genetic method of child study.

GROWTH IS MARKED BY FLUCTUATIONS IN PACE. As the Harvard Growth Study and the reports of Courtis,[12] Shuttleworth,[13] Bunak,[14] and others have shown, individual growth does not proceed at a gradual rate, but is characterized by accelerations and decelerations—that is, by discernible cycles of development. Although development is *continuous* and cycles are closely merged, especially between infancy and childhood, investigators have noted postnatal periods of growth comparable to *infancy, childhood, and adolescence* (and possibly preadulthood). Curves of individual development illustrate this law of growth (see page 265). As Figure 34 shows, mass

[11] See, for example, Florence L. Goodenough and John E. Anderson, *Experimental Child Study*, New York, D. Appleton-Century Co., Inc., 1931, Ch. 2.

[12] S. A. Courtis, "What Is a Growth Cycle?" *Growth*, 1 : 155-174 (1937).

[13] Frank K. Shuttleworth, *The Physical and Mental Growth of Girls and Boys Age Six to Nineteen in Relation to Age at Maximum Growth*, Monographs of the Society for Research in Child Development, Vol. 4, No. 2 (1939).

[14] Viktor V. Bunak, "Topology of Growth Curves of the Human Body," *American Journal of Physical Anthropology*, 26 : 69-85 (1940).

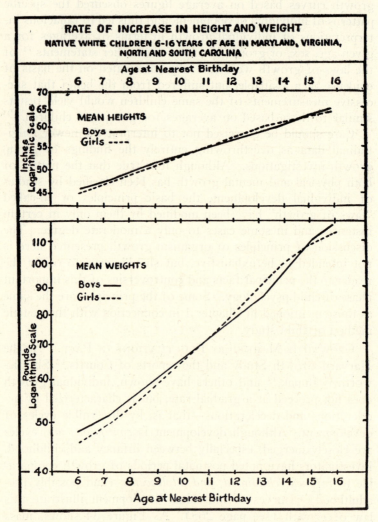

Figure 34. Rate of Increase in Weight and Height of 14,335 Native White Children 6 to 16 Years of Age in Maryland, Virginia, North and South Carolina

(From *Public Health Report* of the United States Health Service, Vol. 37 (May 19, 1922).)

curves for height and weight have tended to obscure the variable nature of such physical growth.

ORGANISM FACTORS INCREASE WITH AGE.   As curves for physiological, neuromuscular, anatomical, and other aspects of physical development show, these and other factors develop with age until maturity is reached. The various parts of the body do not, however, grow at the same rate or reach their ma-

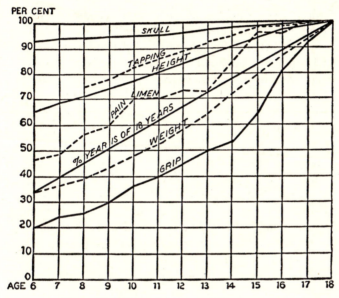

Figure 35. Differential Rates of Development

(From A. T. Poffenberger, *Applied Psychology*, New York, D. Appleton-Century Co., Inc., 1932, p. 108.)

turity simultaneously. As the Harvard Growth Study revealed, an individual child may deviate from the mean of a group more, for example, in standing height than in chest depth, and more in weight than in leg length. This finding indicates that muscular coordinations may fluctuate in degree of facility from one age to another. It also shows the futility of endeavoring to determine the maturity level of one factor (for example, speed of tapping) by recourse to figures for another factor (height or weight).

INDIVIDUALS DIFFER IN RATE OF GROWTH. Although every child apparently develops according to a general pattern of growth, each proceeds at a rate peculiar to himself. Accelerations occur at different age levels for different children and produce results unique to their varying physical constitutions. The timing of the adolescent growth spurt is also different in each individual and between the sexes. The growth rate of each child is affected by modifying influences and must therefore be studied in relation to them. External factors influencing growth include diet, health habits, bacterial invasions (if any), and thermal conditions. Constitutional factors, particularly those of an endocrine nature, are thought to play a dominant role in the determination of both pattern and rate of growth.

CORRELATION AND NOT COMPENSATION IS THE RULE. It has been commonly believed that a child who is superior in one aspect of development is doomed to be correspondingly inferior in another. The physically well-developed boy has, thus, often been suspected of being retarded intellectually. Although there is no scientific justification for such a theory, it has been expressed in such slogans as "big but dumb" and "a strong body but a weak mind." Actually, Terman [15] and others have shown that many desirable qualities tend to be found together in the same individual (theory of correlation). In the physical realm height, weight, motor skill, resistance to disease, longevity, and similar factors most often exist as positively related clusters in the same individual.

Postnatal Bodily Growth

It is evident that young children grow rapidly. As they increase in stature children become heavier, their shoulders broaden, their legs become longer in relation to the trunk, their hips and waistline become more contrasted, and their hands and feet are much more in evidence. It is not so well known, however, that specific aspects of growth within the same child proceed toward maturity in ways that are not as apparent as gen-

[15] Lewis M. Terman, *Mental and Physical Traits of a Thousand Gifted Children, Genetic Studies of Genius,* Vol. I: Stanford University, Stanford Univ. Press, 1925.

eral skeletal growth. The processes of growth are complicated and cannot be understood without recourse to a careful study of individual development.

Types of Data on Bodily Growth.—Students of physical growth have become accustomed to discussing such development in terms of *general* and *specific* growth.[16] General growth has reference to over-all skeletal development and to the integrative action of the organism as a whole. Although various parts of the body grow at somewhat different rates, they all develop in harmonious relation to each other, and at a tempo made possible by centralized action of the organism as a unit. Unity and integration (oneness of action) characterize all biological development. As Wheeler [17] has expressed it, the human organism (the child) does not *achieve* biological integration or oneness in the process of growth, it *maintains* an originally present integration at increasingly more complex levels of growth and development. General growth may thus be thought of as being unified and interlocked.

It should be recognized, nevertheless, that, although tissues and organs develop in relation to each other, bodily growth is marked by a certain degree of specificity of development. For example, the central nervous system, certain lymphoid tissues, and the genital (sex) organs progress toward maturity at different rates of growth. Brain and nervous system structures grow rapidly from birth to early childhood, but exhibit a marked decrease in rate of development as the individual nears maturity.[18] Lymphoid tissues exhibit a similar pattern of growth from birth to early childhood, but continue to develop slowly to the time of puberty, at which point they decline in rate of growth. By contrast, the genital system develops slowly through infancy and childhood to the onset of adolescence (puberty), at which time its growth is sharply accelerated.

16 White House Conference Report, *Growth and Development of the Child,* Part II, "Anatomy and Physiology," New York, D. Appleton-Century Co., Inc., 1933, pp. 610-617.

17 R. H. Wheeler, "The Problem of Integration," in L. Thomas Hopkins et al., *Integration: Its Meaning and Application,* New York, D. Appleton-Century Co., Inc., 1937, Ch. 3.

18 J. A. Harris, C. M. Jackson, D. G. Paterson, and R. E. Scammon, *The Measurement of Man,* Minneapolis, Univ. of Minnesota Press, 1930, pp. 187-193.

Neural, sensory, and optic apparatus development experience greatest acceleration during the prenatal period of growth. It appears, thus, that various structural systems experience unique patterns and rhythms of growth.

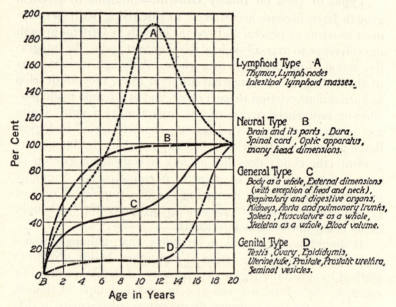

Figure 36. The Major Types of Postnatal Growth of the Various Parts and Organs of the Body

The several curves are drawn to a common scale by computing their values at successive ages in terms of their total postnatal increments (to twenty years). (From J. A. Harris *et al.*, *The Measurement of Man*, Minneapolis, Univ. of Minnesota Press, 1930, p. 193.)

A notable difference between boys and girls in rate of general bodily growth has been ascertained. Growth acceleration occurs among girls sufficiently early to make them taller (on the average) than boys between the ages of ten and thirteen or fourteen. Boys experience their most rapid growth between approximately the years thirteen and sixteen. Although marked individual differences obtain among both sexes, the above differential in rate of growth is apparently well nigh universal. It is followed in later adolescence and early adulthood by a gradual decline in rate of development on the part of both sexes, with the girls reaching physical maturity (although not superiority in height) well in advance of boys. Palmer and Reed [19] have concluded that adolescent acceleration in height is a function of attained height rather than one of age. According to them, male acceleration begins when the boy has attained a height of 52 or 53 inches and continues until he has reached a status of 60 to 61 inches. Feminine adolescent acceleration is said to begin at 50 or 51 inches and to continue until the girl has reached a status of 55 to 56 inches. These data do not, however, invalidate earlier figures of differences between rate and rhythm of male and female growth.

It can thus be said that physical growth in children is both general and specific, that various bodily structures develop at their own rate, that acceleration follows general cycles of growth, that boys and girls experience periods of acceleration in height at different ages and reach maturity at different points, and that development of specific structures (brain, nervous system, etc.) occurs much earlier in life than general bodily maturity.

Factors Influencing Physical Growth.—Many opinions have been expressed concerning the accelerative or retardative effects on physical growth of certain constitutional and environmental factors. However, only a limited number of scientific investigations are available for the support of views of this kind. Common among the factors often credited with influencing physical growth are race, family health history, economic status, care of health, physical defects, diet, illness, excessive exercise, birth conditions, endocrine balance, geographic location, and factors associated with sex. Objective studies have been concerned largely with relationships between height or weight and state of health or of nutritive practices. The relationships between many other factors and growth have, however, been studied.[20]

[19] C. E. Palmer and L. J. Reed, Anthropometric Studies of Individual Growth, I: "Age, Height, and Rate of Growth in Height of Elementary School Children," *Human Biology*, 7: 319 (1935).

[20] For a summary of such studies see American Educational Research Assn., *Review of Educational Research*, Vol. 14, No. 5 (1944), pp. 429-432.

In commenting on the alleged increased height of present-day young people, particularly college students, Sanders [21] declares that there is evidence for such a trend and that it can be attributed to improved standards of living, better health practices, more nourishing food, and increased attention to physical exercise. Retarding factors are said to include poor housing, inferior food, child labor, and lack of medical care. Another investigator [22] has attributed the improved physical status of American school children to superior nutrition. He says, "Large physique no doubt means on the whole better nutrition at all ages and especially at the younger ages, and better nutrition means comparative freedom from defects. We have good evidence in unpublished statistics from the United States Public Health Service that superior height and weight go with comparative freedom from common defects."

In a study of over 400 Joliet, Illinois, elementary school children, Hoefer and Hardy [23] concluded that good health is a significant factor in the determination of rate of physical growth. In every case, healthy children showed relatively greater increments of growth in height, weight, and breadth of skeletal frame than did children characterized by poor health. Differences in these respects between the two groups were said to be marked. Evidence was also presented that the robust children had had parents who were themselves in good health at the time of conception, as well as during pregnancy and the infancy period.

In summarizing the factors influencing growth for which there seems to be some supporting evidence, Rugen [24] lists the following:

[21] Barkov Sanders, *Environment and Growth*, Baltimore, Warwick & York, Inc., 1934, pp. 296-297. See also Georg Wolff, "Further Results on the Trend of Weight in White School Children," *Child Development*, 12 : 183-205 (1941).
[22] James F. Rogers, *Physique of School Children*, U. S. Office of Education, Leaflet No. 37 (no date), p. 13.
[23] Carolyn Hoefer and Martha C. Hardy, "The Role of Health in the Child's Development," *Elementary School Journal* 35 : 423-439 (1935). See also Vernette S. Vickers and Harold C. Stuart, "Anthropometry in the Pediatrician's Office. Norms for Selected Body Measurements Based on Studies of Children of North European Stock," *Journal of Pediatrics*, 22 : 155-170 (1943).
[24] Mabel E. Rugen, "The Physical Growth of the Child," in *Pupil Development and the Curriculum*, Bureau of Educational Reference and Research, Univ. of Michigan, 1937-38, p. 75.

1. Socio-economic status as illustrated in improved standards of living.
2. State of nutrition and the particular value of milk as a growth food.
3. General state of health as determined by the physician's examination supplemented by various measures of vital capacity, muscular strength, and nutritional status.
4. Physical defects when they are of such a nature as to produce strain or drain on the child.
5. Lack of proper medical care in time of illness and for the correction of handicapping defects.
6. Child labor and employment when under non-ideal conditions.
7. Sleep, rest, and relaxation.
8. Play, exercise, and athletics.
9. Health of parents and genetic stock.
10. Health of child during infancy.

From the standpoint of inheritance and on the basis of Harvard Growth Study data, Shuttleworth [25] has proposed the theory that "the patterns of physical growth shown by different dimensions and different groups from conception to maturity are the resultant of a progressive balancing of endocrine factors, of the timing of endocrine stimulation, of factors determining mature size, and of factors associated with sex." In short, Shuttleworth believes that inherent glandular and related constitutional factors determine the rate of growth and the timing of growth cycles. As may be seen from Figure 37, the postnatal growth rate of various ductless glands lends support to the belief that they, perhaps more than other body structures, determine the pattern of bodily growth. He makes it clear, however, that the five factors mentioned operate interdependently and that each represents "an exceedingly complex set of forces some of which operate for only limited intervals and at different ages." This investigator does not fail to mention environ-

[25] Frank K. Shuttleworth, *op. cit.*, pp. 216-221. Also George B. Dorff, "Gonadotropins and Linear Growth: The Pituitary—Gonadal Mechanism and Its Relation to Linear Growth and Sexual Development," *American Journal of Diseases of Children*, 64: 661-673 (1942).

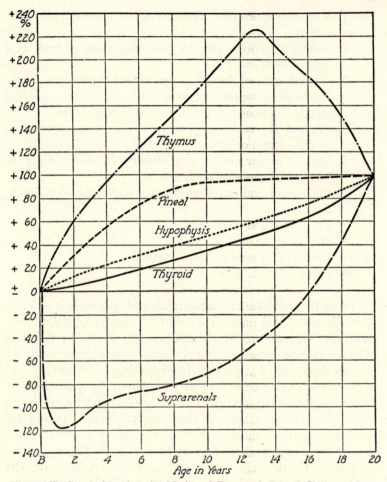

Figure 37. Graph Showing the Modes of Postnatal Growth Followed by a Number of the Organs Usually Described as Ductless or Endosecretory Glands

The curves are reduced to a common scale by computing their values at year intervals as per cents of their total postnatal increments (to twenty years).

(From J. A. Harris *et al.*, *The Measurement of Man*, Minneapolis, Univ. of Minnesota Press, 1930, p. 200.)

mental agencies affecting child growth but emphasizes the importance of further explorations of the constitutional factors involved. In this he is encouraged by Sheldon,[26] who points

[26] W. H. Sheldon, *The Varieties of Human Physique*, New York, Harper & Bros., 1940, pp. 230-234.

out that body form is closely associated with endocrine action, particularly of the thyroid, pituitary, adrenal, and gonadal glands. Sheldon suggests the possibility that instead of being "caused" by endocrine action, body form may be determined by inherent constitutional factors underlying all physical development, including glandular balance.

Data on Growth of Body Structures.—Having considered the child's patterns and rhythms of growth, it becomes necessary briefly to present pertinent data touching actual increases in height, weight, dentition, and a variety of other forms of physical development. An understanding of the magnitude of these changes at progressive ages is essential to intelligent child care.

Growth in Height and Weight. Although it is of the utmost importance to consider the physical growth of a given child in the light of his ancestry and constitutional pattern of development, average growth figures for groups of children are considered useful as a point of reference for making general comparisons. Unfortunately, however, tables of norms for growth in height and weight disagree to a disconcerting extent. As Boynton [27] has pointed out, at age six and a half (school entrance age) there exists a variation among tables of norms of almost 4 inches in height and approximately 7 pounds in weight. There is thus no way of determining with certainty how tall or how heavy a given child should be at any given age. In the light of these facts it is probably best to be skeptical of arbitrary height-weight tables and to develop, as Faber [28] has done, normal *weight ranges* for boys and girls of designated ages. On this basis, no child is considered abnormal in height or weight unless he falls outside of a range which has been so computed as to include, from a sampling of several thousand children, the middle 80 per cent of weights for his age.

[27] Paul L. Boynton, *Psychology of Child Development,* Minneapolis, Educational Publishers, Inc., 1938, pp. 100-107. Also Meinhard Robinow, "The Variability of Weight and Height Increments from Birth to Six Years," *Child Development,* 13 : 159-164 (1942).

[28] H. K. Faber, "A Weight Range Table for Children from 5 to 15 Years of Age," *American Journal of Diseases of Children,* 38 : 758-761 (1929).

Table 10. Weight Ranges for Specified Heights and Ages (Boys)

Height in Inches	AGE IN YEARS										
	5	6	7	8	9	10	11	12	13	14	15
39	34-40	34-40									
40	35-41	35-41									
41	36-42	36-43	37-44								
42	37-44	38-45	38-45	39-46							
43	38-45	39-46	39-46	40-47							
44	40-47	41-48	41-48	41-49	42-51						
45	42-49	43-50	43-50	43-52	44-53						
46	44-51	45-52	45-52	45-54	46-55						
47	46-53	47-54	47-55	47-56	48-57	48-58					
48		49-58	49-58	49-58	50-59	50-60	50-62				
49		51-60	51-60	52-62	52-62	52-63	52-64				
50		54-63	54-63	54-65	54-65	55-66	55-67	55-68			
51			57-66	57-68	57-68	57-69	57-69	57-71			
52			60-70	60-71	60-71	60-72	60-74	60-74	60-75		
53			62-73	62-74	63-75	63-75	63-76	63-77	63-78		
54				63-76	64-77	65-80	65-80	66-81	66-81		
55				65-78	67-80	67-81	67-83	68-84	68-85	66-82	
56					70-84	71-85	71-87	71-87	71-88	69-86	74-92
57					73-87	74-89	74-91	74-91	75-93	76-95	77-96
58					76-91	77-93	77-95	77-95	78-97	80-99	81-101
59						80-98	80-99	81-101	82-102	83-103	84-104
60						84-101	84-103	85-104	86-106	86-107	87-108
61							87-107	88-109	89-111	90-112	91-113
62							91-112	92-113	94-116	95-118	96-119
63							95-117	96-118	97-121	99-123	101-125
64								99-122	101-125	104-129	106-131
65								104-128	106-131	107-133	110-137
66									110-137	112-139	115-142
67									115-142	117-146	119-148

(Adapted by P. L. Boynton, Psychology of Child Development, Minneapolis, Educational Publishers, Inc., 1938, p. 108, from H. K. Faber, "A Weight Range Table for Children from 5 to 15 Years of Age," American Journal of Diseases of Children, 38:758-761 (1929).)

TABLE 11. WEIGHT RANGES FOR SPECIFIED HEIGHTS AND AGES (GIRLS)

Height in Inches	AGE IN YEARS										
	5	6	7	8	9	10	11	12	13	14	15
39	33-38	33-39									
40	34-41	34-41									
41	35-41	35-42	36-43								
42	37-44	37-44	37-44								
43	38-45	38-45	38-46	38-46							
44	40-47	40-47	40-48	40-48							
45	42-49	42-49	42-50	43-50	43-52						
46	44-51	45-53	45-53	45-54	45-54						
47	46-53	46-55	46-55	46-56	46-57	45-56					
48		47-57	48-58	48-58	48-59	46-58					
49		50-59	51-61	51-62	51-62	48-60	49-62				
50		53-63	53-63	53-64	53-66	51-64	51-66				
51			55-67	55-67	56-69	54-67	54-69	56-72			
52			58-71	58-72	58-72	56-70	57-72	58-74			
53			61-73	61-74	62-76	58-73	59-75	59-76	62-82		
54				63-77	64-79	62-78	62-78	62-80	66-85		
55				66-81	67-82	64-81	64-82	65-83	69-90	70-91	
56					70-86	67-84	67-86	68-88	73-95	74-96	
57					73-89	70-88	70-90	71-92	77-99	78-102	82-106
58						73-91	74-94	75-96	80-103	83-108	86-111
59						76-95	77-98	78-100	84-109	86-112	90-117
60						80-100	81-104	82-106	87-113	90-117	95-123
61						84-105	85-108	86-110	91-118	94-122	98-128
62							89-114	90-116	95-124	97-126	102-132
63							94-120	95-122	100-130	101-131	105-137
64								99-128	104-135	105-137	108-140
65								103-132	108-140	110-143	111-144
66								106-137	112-145	113-147	114-149
67									116-151	117-152	118-152

(Adapted by P. L. Boynton, *Psychology of Child Development*, Minneapolis, Educational Publishers, Inc., 1938, p. 109, from H. K. Faber, "A Weight Range Table for Children from 5 to 15 Years of Age," *American Journal of Diseases of Children*, 38:758-761 (1929).)

Since height-weight ranges for infants are not given in the above table, it may be well to mention that, according to a recent study,[29] the average birth weight regardless of race or sex is 7.13 pounds. In this case male infants weighed, on the average, 0.2 pounds more than female newborn. White newborn infants weighed 0.25 pounds more than Negro infants, but socio-economic status exerted no effect on the birth weight of the child. An earlier investigation [30] showed that 85 per cent of the newborn weigh between 6 and 9 pounds and vary between 17 and 22 inches in height. An idea of the rapidity with which the infant grows may be gained from the facts that infant boys grow, on the average, $7\frac{1}{8}$ inches by the age of nine months, and that infant girls grow $6\frac{3}{4}$ inches by the time they have reached the same age. Even more marked is the infant's increase in weight, which is doubled by the average child during the first six months. By the time the average boy has reached a height of $28\frac{1}{4}$ inches, his weight has increased to $19\frac{11}{16}$ pounds. The average baby girl of $28\frac{1}{4}$ inches will have attained a weight of $19\frac{5}{16}$ pounds.[31]

Growth in Dentition and Ossification. A child's degree of physical development may be ascertained in a number of ways. Height, weight, chronological age, and sexual growth are among the most common measures for determining such development. It is possible, nevertheless, to secure useful criteria of physical development by recourse to data concerning (1) the extent of skeletal ossification (maturity of bony structure) and (2) the number of permanent teeth erupted.

According to the Cattell [32] Dental Age Scale, a child's stage of physical maturity can be determined in terms of the number of permanent teeth cut at any age between five and approximately fourteen. This scale, which provides data for both

29 M. A. Perlstein and A. Levinson, "Birth Weight: Its Statistical Correlation with Various Factors," *American Journal of Diseases of Children,* 53 : 1645 (1937).

30 B. T. Baldwin, "Physical Growth of Children From Birth to Maturity," *Univ. of Iowa Studies in Child Welfare,* Vol. I, No. 1 (1922).

31 Winifred Rand, M. E. Sweeny, and E. L. Vincent, *Growth and Development of the Young Child,* Philadelphia, W. B. Saunders Co., 1940, pp. 78-81.

32 Psyche Cattell, *Dentition as a Measure of Maturity,* Harvard Monographs in Education, No. 9 (1928). Also Carl R. Doering and M. F. Allen, "Data on Eruption and Caries of the Deciduous Teeth," *Child Development,* 13 : 113-129 (1942).

boys and girls, suffers from the same limitations inherent in all cross-sectional mass-data instruments—average growth figures obscure individual growth patterns. It is preferable thus to consult *individual* curves of development or mass-data tables which present *ranges* of growth at any given age. Such indices for growth in dentition may be viewed in Table 12 and Figure 38.

TABLE 12. INTERNATIONAL COMPARISONS IN TOTAL NUMBER OF PERMANENT TEETH CUT BY BOYS OF SPECIFIED AGES

(Italy, Switzerland, England, Scotland. Total, 7,288)

Age*	63	75	87	99	111	123	135	147	159	171	183	195	207	219	231	243
T.R.	90	424	670	752	899	969	1086	771	743	439	228	109	62	27	16	3
D.R.	7	15	22	26	46	46	40	22	18	7	9	15	11	3	1	0
E.R.	83	409	648	726	853	923	1046	749	725	432	219	94	51	24	15	3
32													2	1	1	
31													2		2	1
30													2	4	1	
29							1	1	2	1	2	3	4	5	2	
28						7	57	98	263	202	117	56	31	11	8	1
27						4	35	95	112	79	41	13	5	1		1
26					1	14	55	70	104	68	28	7	3			
25						15	57	57	52	24	16	5	2	1		
24			1			2	23	77	78	73	19	11	4	1		
23						4	26	62	59	33	15	2	3			
22						5	29	86	57	22	8	2	2			
21						7	31	64	50	20	7					
20				1		9	40	65	50	12	4			§		
19					13	46	71	30	10	3		1				
18					21	64	64	23	5	1						
17				4	30	67	57	23	7							
16				9	55	88	73	21	4	1						
15				13	68	87	62	14	1							
14			5	43	108	118	57	11	3							
13			10	49	123	87	46	7	1							
12		1	35	154	210	128	49	3								
11			27	84	85	23	5	2	1							
10		16	118	182	76	18	3									
9		3	45	55	15	3										
8		18	97	50	12	4										
7		26	45	23	4											
6	1	73	128	37	4	1										
5	1	32	31	8	1											
4	5	62	48	7												
3	2	30	9	4												
2	7	51	23	2												
1	3	20	11													
0	64	76	15	1												
Mean	1.2	4.4	7.9	11.0	13.7	16.7	20.4	23.6	26.2	27.1	27.5	27.5	28.6	28.9	28.9	29.2
S.D.	1.37	2.96	3.03	2.50	2.78	4.05	4.66	3.95	2.82	2.01	1.35	1.76	1.38	1.58	2.60	1.70

(First column label: Number of Teeth)

* Age—Age in months; T. R.—Total records; D. R.—Defective records; E. R.—Effective records.
(From S. A. Courtis, "Major Growth Concepts," in *Pupil Development and the Curriculum*, Bureau of Educational Reference and Research, Univ. of Michigan, 1937-38, p. 65.)

The fact of individual uniqueness in acceleration and deceleration of growth in dentition is shown in the figure for an individual child, which also shows two cycles corresponding to childhood and adolescence (arrow pointing to the onset of adolescence). It can be seen that fourteen teeth were cut during each of these growth periods. The table portrays the tremendous spread of development in dentition that characterizes

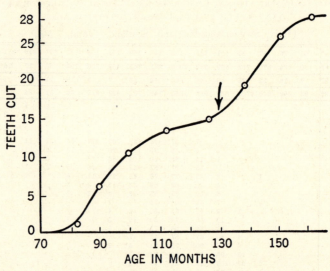

Figure 38. Individual Growth Curve for the Cutting of Permanent Teeth (Girl)

(Adapted from "Harvard Growth Study" by S. A. Courtis, *op. cit.,* p. 65.)

every childhood age (boys). For those who desire mean (average) figures for this type of development, the summary data at the bottom of the table should be adequate. They should not, however, be used as standards of growth for boys of varying constitutional patterns.

The growth of skeletal structures has for years been determined by X-ray studies of bone ossification, a hardening process which is under way before birth and which continues to the time of maturity. Certain bones and sections of bones are well along toward complete ossification at birth. The femur, or

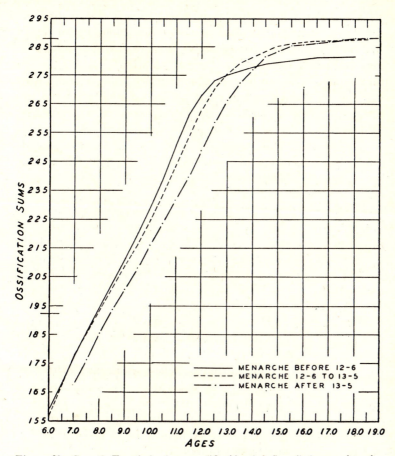

Figure 39. Growth Trends in Average "Ossification Sums" (sums of twelve linear measurements taken from X-rays of the right hand) of Three Groups of Girls Menstruating at Different Ages

(From Frank K. Shuttleworth, *Sexual Maturation and the Skeletal Growth of Girls Age Six to Nineteen,* Monographs of the Society for Research in Child Development, Vol. 3, No. 5 (1938), p. 4.)

bone of the upper leg, is at least partially ossified in most full-term infants, a condition which is not true of bones of the lower leg. The most profitable skeletal areas for the determination of bone development are the shoulder, hip, elbow, hand, knee, and foot. The carpal bone of the wrist has also been extensively utilized as an index of physical development.[33] Available evidence proves that girls' bones ossify more rapidly than boys', and that the former are likely to be a year or two more advanced than boys in this aspect of physical development. Figure 39 shows that rate of ossification in girls is in direct relation to the time of onset of menstruation.

GROWTH RATES OF OTHER BODY STRUCTURES. A number of investigations have been made concerning the growth rate of various parts and dimensions of the body other than height, weight, and skeletal development. These aspects of total organism growth include sitting height, leg length, chest breadth, chest depth, breathing capacity, head circumference, shoulder width, hip width, arm length, and other anthropometric measurements. However, since fewer studies have been made of these measures than of data for height and weight, it is not possible to state how much reliance can be placed in them.

An anthropometric study by Bayley and Davis [34] of 61 babies born in Berkeley, California hospitals shows the average progressive physical development of infants from birth to the thirty-sixth month in body length, weight, stem length, head circumference, chest circumference, chest width, hip width, and shoulder width. Although the small number of cases involved and the possibility of selection of non-typical children tend to invalidate the data disclosed by these investigators, the ranges of development presented are perhaps indicative of the bodily development of preschool children.

An investigation by Boynton and Parsons [35] of the physical development of pupils attending the Peabody College Demonstration School provides average data for children between the ages of five and one-half and seventeen and one-half. In

[33] Psyche Cattell, "Preliminary Report on the Measurement of Ossification of the Hand and Wrist," *Human Biology,* 6 : 454-471 (1934). See also Frank K. Shuttleworth, *Sexual Maturation and the Skeletal Growth of Girls Age Six to Nineteen,* Monographs of the Society for Research in Child Development, Vol. 3, No. 5 (1938), Ch. 3.
[34] Nancy Bayley and F. C. Davis, "Growth Changes in Bodily Size and Proportions During the First Three Years," *Biometrika,* 27 : 26-87 (1935).
[35] Paul L. Boynton and Rosa F. Parsons, "Pupil Analysis in the Peabody Demonstration School," *George Peabody College Bulletin,* 1935.

TABLE 13. MEANS AND NORMAL RANGES * FOR EIGHT ANATOMICAL CHARACTERISTICS

Age in Mos.	Sex	Body Length Av.	Body Length N. Range H.	Body Length N. Range L.	Weight Av.	Weight N. Range H.	Weight N. Range L.	Stem Length Av.	Stem Length N. Range H.	Stem Length N. Range L.	Head Circumf. Av.	Head Circumf. N. Range H.	Head Circumf. N. Range L.	Chest Circumf. Av.	Chest Circumf. N. Range H.	Chest Circumf. N. Range L.	Chest Width Av.	Chest Width N. Range H.	Chest Width N. Range L.	Hip Width Av.	Hip Width N. Range H.	Hip Width N. Range L.	Shoulder Width Av.	Shoulder Width N. Range H.	Shoulder Width N. Range L.
1	B	21.8	23.0	20.6	9.6	10.8	8.4	14.2	14.8	13.6	15.2	15.8	14.6	14.4	15.2	13.6	3.9	4.3	3.5	4.3	4.7	3.9	5.8	6.1	5.5
1	G	21.0	22.2	19.8	8.8	10.3	7.3	13.7	14.6	12.8	14.6	15.2	14.0	14.0	14.8	13.2	3.8	4.2	3.4	4.2	4.7	3.5	5.5	5.8	5.2
2	B	23.2	24.1	22.3	11.6	13.0	10.2	15.2	16.3	14.1	15.8	16.4	15.3	15.3	16.3	14.3	4.1	4.6	3.6	4.8	5.3	4.3	6.3	6.7	5.9
2	G	22.4	23.5	21.3	10.6	12.4	8.8	14.6	15.2	13.9	15.3	15.9	14.7	14.9	15.7	14.1	4.0	4.3	3.7	4.7	5.2	4.2	5.8	6.4	5.2
3	B	24.3	25.1	23.5	13.3	15.2	11.4	15.9	16.5	15.3	16.4	17.0	15.8	15.9	16.8	15.0	4.2	4.8	3.6	5.1	5.7	4.5	6.6	6.9	6.3
3	G	23.5	24.6	22.4	12.1	14.0	10.2	15.3	16.1	14.5	15.8	16.3	15.3	15.6	16.5	14.6	4.0	4.4	3.6	5.1	5.6	4.6	6.3	6.6	6.0
4	B	25.2	26.1	24.3	14.9	16.8	13.0	16.5	17.0	16.0	16.8	17.3	16.3	16.5	17.6	15.4	4.2	4.7	3.7	5.3	5.8	4.8	6.9	7.3	6.5
4	G	24.5	25.4	23.6	13.7	15.7	11.7	16.1	17.0	15.2	16.3	16.9	15.7	16.2	17.0	15.4	4.2	4.6	3.8	5.3	5.8	4.7	6.7	7.1	6.3
5	B	26.2	27.2	25.2	16.5	18.7	14.3	17.1	17.9	16.5	17.3	17.9	16.7	17.1	18.1	16.1	4.4	4.9	3.9	5.6	6.1	5.1	7.2	7.7	6.7
5	G	25.4	26.6	24.2	15.2	17.6	12.8	16.5	17.5	15.5	16.7	17.3	16.1	16.8	17.8	15.8	4.2	4.5	3.9	5.5	6.1	4.9	7.1	7.6	6.4
6	B	27.0	28.1	25.9	17.9	20.0	15.8	17.6	18.4	16.8	17.7	18.3	17.0	17.5	18.3	16.7	4.4	4.9	3.9	5.8	6.3	5.3	7.5	8.0	7.0
6	G	26.1	27.2	25.0	16.2	18.7	13.7	17.0	17.7	16.3	17.0	17.6	16.4	17.3	18.6	16.0	4.3	4.8	3.8	5.6	6.1	5.1	7.3	7.9	6.7
7	B	27.5	28.7	26.3	19.3	21.3	17.3	17.9	18.7	17.1	18.0	18.7	17.5	18.1	19.2	17.0	4.5	4.9	4.1	6.0	6.5	5.5	7.8	8.2	7.2
7	G	26.8	28.1	25.5	17.6	20.3	14.9	17.4	18.4	16.4	17.5	18.2	16.8	17.6	18.7	16.5	4.3	4.7	3.9	5.8	6.4	5.2	7.5	8.0	7.0
8	B	28.3	29.5	27.1	20.5	22.8	18.2	18.3	19.2	17.4	18.3	18.9	17.7	18.4	19.0	17.4	4.5	5.0	4.0	6.1	6.6	5.6	7.8	8.4	7.2
8	G	27.4	28.8	26.0	18.6	21.4	15.8	17.8	18.7	16.9	17.7	18.3	17.1	18.0	19.0	17.0	4.3	4.9	4.1	6.0	6.6	5.4	7.6	8.1	7.1
9	B	28.7	29.8	27.6	21.5	23.6	19.4	18.6	19.4	17.8	18.5	19.1	17.9	18.6	19.5	17.7	4.6	5.1	4.1	6.1	6.5	5.7	8.0	8.5	7.5
9	G	27.7	29.0	26.4	19.3	21.5	17.1	17.9	18.5	17.3	17.9	18.5	17.3	18.2	19.3	17.1	4.5	5.0	4.0	6.1	6.6	5.6	7.7	8.3	7.1
10	B	29.2	30.3	28.1	22.6	25.1	20.1	18.9	19.8	18.0	18.8	19.4	18.0	18.8	19.8	17.8	4.7	5.2	4.2	6.2	6.6	5.8	8.2	8.8	7.6
10	G	28.2	29.5	26.9	20.2	23.1	17.5	18.2	19.1	17.3	18.0	18.7	17.3	18.4	19.5	17.3	4.6	5.1	4.1	5.9	6.6	5.2	7.8	8.4	7.2
11	B	29.7	31.0	28.4	23.4	26.2	20.6	19.2	20.0	18.4	18.9	19.5	18.3	19.0	20.0	18.0	4.7	5.1	4.3	6.5	6.7	6.3	8.3	8.8	7.8
11	G	28.8	30.2	27.4	21.0	24.0	18.0	18.5	19.5	17.5	18.3	19.1	17.5	18.4	19.4	17.4	4.6	5.0	4.3	6.0	6.6	5.4	8.0	8.7	7.3
12	B	30.3	31.6	29.0	24.1	27.0	21.2	19.3	20.3	18.3	19.1	19.8	18.4	19.2	20.3	18.1	4.8	5.3	4.3	6.6	6.9	6.3	8.3	8.8	7.8
12	G	29.3	30.6	28.0	21.6	24.8	18.4	18.8	19.7	17.9	18.4	19.1	17.7	18.8	19.7	17.6	4.7	5.1	4.3	6.1	6.6	5.6	8.1	8.6	7.6
15	B	31.7	33.1	30.3	25.9	29.1	22.7	20.2	21.1	19.3	19.4	20.1	18.7	19.6	20.8	18.4	4.8	5.3	4.5	6.6	7.1	6.1	8.5	9.2	7.8
15	G	30.6	32.0	29.2	23.2	26.3	19.5	19.3	20.2	18.4	18.7	19.3	18.1	18.8	19.9	17.8	4.8	5.3	4.5	6.3	6.8	5.8	8.2	8.7	7.7
18	B	32.8	34.5	31.1	27.3	30.8	23.8	20.5	21.4	19.6	19.6	20.3	18.9	19.9	21.2	18.6	4.9	5.3	4.5	6.8	7.3	6.3	8.7	9.2	8.2
18	G	31.8	33.2	30.4	24.5	28.0	21.0	19.6	20.5	18.7	18.9	19.5	18.3	19.2	20.1	18.3	4.8	5.3	4.5	6.4	6.9	5.9	8.4	8.8	8.0
24	B	34.8	36.5	33.1	29.8	35.2	24.4	21.1	22.0	20.2	20.0	20.7	19.3	20.7	21.9	19.5	5.0	5.5	4.5	6.9	7.4	6.4	8.9	9.5	8.3
24	G	33.9	34.9	32.9	26.9	30.2	23.6	20.1	20.7	19.5	19.3	19.9	18.7	19.5	20.6	18.4	4.8	5.1	4.5	6.6	7.1	6.1	8.7	9.2	8.2
30	B	36.6	38.7	34.5	32.5	37.1	27.9	21.3	22.3	20.3	20.1	20.8	19.4	21.3	22.6	20.0	5.0	5.4	4.6	7.0	7.6	6.4	9.0	9.5	8.3
30	G	35.7	37.3	34.1	29.8	33.6	26.0	20.7	21.7	19.7	19.4	20.0	18.8	20.4	21.5	19.5	5.0	5.1	4.6	6.8	7.3	6.3	8.8	9.2	8.3
36	B	38.3	40.5	36.1	34.7	39.8	29.6	21.9	23.1	20.7	20.2	20.9	19.6	21.6	22.9	20.3	5.1	5.5	4.7	7.2	7.6	6.8	9.3	9.8	8.8
36	G	37.4	39.1	35.7	32.0	35.8	28.2	21.0	21.9	20.1	19.6	20.1	19.1	21.0	21.9	19.4	5.2	5.2	4.6	7.0	7.5	6.5	9.1	9.5	8.7

* The normal range is developed here by P. L. Boynton, *Psychology of Child Development*, Minneapolis, Educational Publishers, Inc., 1938, pp. 110-111, from the data given by N. Bayley and F. C. Davis, "Growth Changes in Bodily Size and Proportions During the First Three Years," *Biometrika*, 27:26-87 (1935). It is based on the same assumptions of normality as were set up by H. K. Faber (see page 280). It was computed in this instance by taking 1.28 standard deviations around the mean,

TABLE 14. CERTAIN PHYSICAL MEASUREMENTS FOR CHILDREN OF DESIGNATED AGES

Item Measured	Sex	AGE IN YEARS												
		5.5	6.5	7.5	8.5	9.5	10.5	11.5	12.5	13.5	14.5	15.5	16.5	17.5
Height Sitting	B	25.00	25.93	27.15	28.36	29.03	29.21	30.00	30.81	31.47	33.58	35.13	36.07	36.56
	G	24.88	25.82	26.88	26.91	28.45	29.05	30.17	31.29	32.65	33.15	33.38	33.72	33.56
Breathing Capacity	B	64.38	82.50	97.00	110.08	120.50	131.00	143.00	159.62	173.89	204.17	233.33	255.84	257.50
	G	64.50	73.75	87.50	93.44	107.50	117.50	135.00	152.06	166.67	180.42	180.42	181.80	186.67
Chest Circumf.	B	22.08	22.65	23.58	24.50	24.41	25.36	25.60	27.03	27.83	29.93	30.92	31.75	32.11
	G	21.46	22.14	22.82	23.18	24.13	25.15	26.25	27.88	28.69	29.59	29.71	29.70	29.56
Chest Width	B	7.48	7.55	7.93	8.16	8.21	8.45	8.79	9.16	9.27	9.95	10.32	10.74	10.71
	G	7.32	7.37	7.83	7.84	8.02	8.36	8.63	9.12	9.15	9.55	9.71	9.71	9.80
Chest Depth	B	5.51	5.68	5.81	6.05	6.16	6.12	6.29	6.48	6.71	7.15	7.31	7.52	7.49
	G	5.36	5.38	5.56	5.62	5.88	5.93	6.14	6.40	6.65	6.79	6.83	6.83	6.84
Head Circumf.	B	20.81	21.00	21.11	21.13	21.33	21.21	21.36	21.58	21.70	21.75	22.02	22.38	22.16
	G	20.30	20.39	20.68	20.65	20.90	20.98	21.05	21.15	21.46	21.49	21.62	21.65	21.65
Total Arm Span	B	44.75	48.00	49.79	53.55	55.33	56.43	58.17	60.00	63.00	67.17	69.30	71.07	70.50
	G	44.36	46.45	49.94	51.17	53.43	54.95	58.41	60.63	62.71	63.84	64.28	64.18	64.38
Shoulder Width	B	10.54	10.84	11.31	12.10	12.47	12.41	12.63	13.31	13.97	14.75	14.96	15.65	15.73
	G	10.58	11.05	11.32	11.50	11.75	12.33	12.68	13.50	13.54	14.06	14.13	14.06	14.00
Shoulder Front Wd.	B	9.44	10.10	10.35	10.75	11.23	11.42	12.05	12.32	12.93	13.78	14.38	14.91	14.88
	G	9.59	10.03	10.35	10.66	10.94	11.47	11.94	12.47	12.76	13.36	13.35	13.42	13.67
Hip Width	B	7.51	7.79	8.05	8.39	8.63	9.05	9.25	9.47	9.86	10.42	10.72	10.98	11.22
	G	7.43	7.71	8.06	8.20	8.54	8.86	9.28	9.58	10.22	10.75	10.98	11.04	10.99
Arm Length	B	18.55	19.04	19.90	21.23	22.17	22.56	23.43	24.28	25.47	26.95	28.16	28.69	28.03
	G	18.00	18.68	20.14	20.54	21.13	22.04	23.42	24.33	25.23	25.62	25.71	25.46	25.80
Abdominal Circumf.	B	21.25	21.80	22.75	23.63	23.20	24.00	24.21	24.75	25.35	26.41	26.94	27.46	27.78
	G	21.23	21.70	22.38	22.67	23.25	24.36	24.79	25.55	25.75	26.57	27.27	27.04	27.21
Ankle Circumf. R.	B	6.59	6.82	7.01	7.23	7.50	7.65	7.56	8.01	8.34	8.91	8.98	9.19	8.98
	G	6.23	6.52	6.74	6.96	7.25	7.57	7.71	8.05	8.15	8.19	8.11	8.13	8.10

(From P. L. Boynton, *Psychology of Child Development*, Minneapolis, Educational Publishers, Inc., 1938, p. 113.)

view of the fact that these children are accelerated in growth in comparison with other groups of similar age, the authors have suggested that they may constitute a select group socially, economically, and physically. Their anthropometric measurements compare favorably, however, with figures secured at the University of Iowa Child Welfare Station by Meredith and by Boynton.[36]

No doubt the most extensive *longitudinal* investigation of various aspects of physical growth yet attempted is the previously mentioned twelve-year Harvard Growth Study. Typical of the physical factors measured annually are those for girls presented in Figure 40. As can readily be seen, increments of growth in all the factors measured are greatest between the ages of approximately ten and twelve, with sharp deceleration in rate of growth following soon after the latter age. These curves are in harmony with those for growth in height, and make it clear again that growth curves do not follow a straight line. In fact, the peak of the curve for leg length in the figure comes sufficiently close to the second S L G (straight line growth) line to show that increments for such growth are nearly twice as great at age twelve (approximately) as would be expected from straight line growth.

It can be added that organs of digestion, circulation, and respiration grow in much the same fashion as other body structures, but are about one-half as large in relation to the size of the rest of the body at maturity as they were at birth. The brain and nervous system grow most rapidly during the fetal period and during the first three or four postnatal years. By the age of four the brain has attained approximately four-fifths its adult weight.[37] From this time on nervous system growth is relatively slow, and is marked by neurone development rather than by the growth of new cells.

THE ONSET OF PUBERTY.   Degree of sexual maturity, or status with respect to pubescence, has been used as an index of

[36] H. V. Meredith, "The Rhythm of Physical Growth," *Univ. of Iowa Studies in Child Welfare,* Vol. 11, No. 3 (1935). B. Boynton, "The Physical Growth of Girls," *Univ. of Iowa Studies in Child Welfare,* Vol. 12, No. 4 (1936).
[37] A. R. Gilliland, *Genetic Psychology,* New York, The Ronald Press Co., 1933, p. 154.

anatomical development with only moderate success. This is because the time of onset of puberty varies extensively among both boys and girls. Individual differences in degree of sexual maturity are so great as to make practically useless tables of

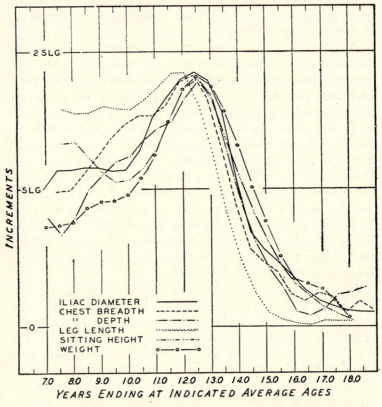

Figure 40. Generalized Patterns of Annual Increments in Sitting Height, Leg Length, Iliac Diameter, Chest Breadth, Chest Depth, and Body Weight
(From Frank K. Shuttleworth, *op. cit.,* p. 44.)

puberty norms based on averages of hundreds or thousands of developing youths. There are few areas of development in which individual differences are more in evidence.

A number of factors have been advanced as influencing the time of pubertal beginning. It has been claimed that the onset of adolescence is determined (1) by climatic conditions, with warmer temperatures encouraging early maturation; (2) by racial background, with Southern European stocks developing earlier than those from the more northern countries; (3) by economic conditions, with those having access to abundant suitable food maturing earlier than less favored classes; and (4) by place of dwelling, with urban residence being more conducive than rural living to precocious sexual development. It is probable, however, that a combination of these and other factors such as health status, emotional outlook, and especially endocrine timing, influence pubertal onset. Shuttleworth [38] has, in fact, concluded from his examination of Harvard Growth Study results that "the nature of the findings reinforces the endocrine interpretation of the data." According to this investigator, in the case of girls "the probable sequence of events in each individual is pituitary [endocrine] stimulation, followed by the initiation of the processes of sexual maturation and of accelerated physical growth, followed in turn by endocrine mechanisms dependent on ripening ovaries which bring the period of accelerated growth to a close and somewhat later initiate the cycle of menstruation."

Efforts to determine the average age at which puberty (called the *menarche* in the case of girls, who enter the period at the time of first menstruation) is reached have resulted in conflicting findings. Investigators have reported averages ranging from age twelve almost to age seventeen, with extensive individual differences. Hardy and Hoefer [39] determined the time of onset of the menarche for 109 girls in the municipal schools of Joliet, Illinois and have reported that "the average age of the first appearance of the menstrual flow was thirteen years seven months, the onset for 52 per cent of the girls occurring between the ages of twelve years eight months and fourteen years three months." Mills [40] made a study of the onset of puberty in the

---

[38] Frank K. Shuttleworth, *op. cit.*, pp. 52-54.

[39] M. C. Hardy and C. H. Hoefer, *Healthy Growth; A Study of the Influence of Health Education on Growth and Development of School Children,* Chicago, Univ. of Chicago Press, 1936. See also Leona M. Bayer, "Build Variations in Adolescent Girls," *Journal of Pediatrics,* 17 : 331-344 (1940).

[40] C. A. Mills, "Geographic and Time Variations in Body Growth and Age at Menarche," *Human Biology,* 9 : 43-56 (1937).

case of entering freshmen girls at the University of Cincinnati and claims to have found an average menarchial age of 12.9 years. Dimock [41] examined 1,406 boys between the ages of ten and eighteen years with the "Crampton criteria" (pigmentation and kinkiness of hair in pubic regions), and found the average age of pubescence to be thirteen years one month. This finding is somewhat out of harmony with former studies which placed the average onset of puberty in the case of boys around age fourteen, or approximately one year later than for girls.

It is obviously difficult to ascertain average ages for such a complicated and perhaps multiple-caused growth phenomenon as the advent of puberty. Some have claimed that the average girl matures at thirteen or thirteen and one-half years and that the typical boy comes to the same stage of development from six months to a year later. Disregarding dramatic cases in which children have become pubescent at such tender ages as eight, six, or even four,[42] it is probably best to view the onset of pubescence in terms of age ranges for representative groups of boys or girls. On this basis, Shuttleworth [43] has reported that among 248 girls between six and nineteen years of age "3.2 per cent menstruated while ten years old, 12.1 per cent while eleven, 33.5 per cent while twelve, 36.3 per cent while thirteen, 10.5 per cent while fourteen, 3.2 per cent while fifteen, and 1.2 per cent between sixteen and nineteen." It is evident that knowledge of a boy's or girl's chronological age does not indicate the extent of his or her sexual development. One twelve-year-old girl, for example, may be well into the pubescent period while a classmate of similar age is unaffected by any physiological changes concerned with the advent of sexual maturity.

Implications for Childhood Education.—Modern school systems are concerned with the development of all aspects of

[41] H. S. Dimock, *Rediscovering the Adolescent*, New York, Association Press, 1937.

[42] C. P. Stone and Lois Doe-Kulman, "Notes on the Mental Development of Children Exhibiting the Somatic Signs of Puberty Praecox," *Journal of Abnormal and Social Psychology*, 22 : 391-324 (1927-28).

[43] Frank K. Shuttleworth, *Sexual Maturation and the Physical Growth of Girls Age Six to Nineteen*, Monographs of the Society for Research in Child Development, Vol. 2, No. 5 (1937).

child growth. An adequate school program will thus take into account the facts of physical growth and the extent of individual differences in physical development among its pupils. Education aims, in short, to meet the physical as well as other important needs of growing children. A few suggestions, based for the most part on tangible findings, may be helpful in implementing the physical education program of the school.[44]

1. Since each child grows at a unique rate, it seems best that his progress toward physical maturity be determined in the light of his own constitutional make-up, and not in relation to average height-weight tables. Educators and medical men should recognize that pupils who mature late and who have not acquired the secondary sex characteristics (change of voice, growth of pubic hair, development of body, etc.) noticeable in classmates of the same chronological age are likely to wonder whether they are physically normal. The same may be true of those who mature early. Mental health problems related to concern over height-weight status may often be prevented if pupils are made acquainted with the individual nature of growth.

2. In view of the fact that different parts of the body grow at different rates, it should be recognized that one aspect of development cannot be inferred from the degree of maturity attained in another. Skeletal development may, for example, be somewhat in arrears of genital growth. Teachers should seek to determine the stage of maturity reached by any part or function of the body by observing (or securing data concerning) that particular aspect of growth.

3. With growth being characterized by periods of acceleration, it is possible, as some educators have suggested, that physical tasks should be harmonized more closely with the child's level of development. Since various body structures grow at their own rates even during periods of acceleration (at pre-adolescence, for example), it is best not to judge the strength or endurance of a youth by his physical proportions or body weight. More evidence is needed here, but it may be that certain levels of physical development are

[44] Mabel E. Rugen, *op. cit.*, pp. 75-76; Willard C. Olson and B. O. Hughes, "Concepts of Growth—Their Significance to Teachers," *Childhood Education*, 21: 53-63 (1944); and *Child Growth and Development Emphasis in Teacher Education*, The American Assn. of Teachers Colleges, 1944, pp. 21-27.

more susceptible to fatigue and loss of emotional poise than others.

4. Since girls mature physically somewhat earlier than boys, it is logical to raise the question whether this difference should be taken into account in physical education programs. It is possible that girls might benefit from a more strenuous (for them) program of play than would be appropriate for boys of the same age. The matter of a too vigorous athletic program at the time of greatest acceleration (pre-adolescence) in growth also needs more consideration.

5. The school should look into the possible causes for seasonal fluctuations in physical growth. With rate of growth increasing in late summer and early fall [45] there may be reasons over which the school has some control for the less rapid growth during the school term. The extent to which factors associated with attendance at school are operating in the phenomenon of physical development is not known. No controlled experiments have as yet been conducted in this area of child study.

6. Both the child's health status and the standard of living enjoyed by his parents are closely associated with growth rate. Children suffering from poor health tend to be less active on the playground, less proficient in school work, and less able to cooperate in group activities than their healthier classmates. It follows that the school should do everything within its power to improve the health of its pupils, and to influence parents to raise their standards of living as well as to safeguard the physical well-being of their children.

7. In view of the fact that appropriate rest, sleep, sunshine, fresh air, play, exercise, and proper nutrition are associated with physical growth, the school should inaugurate a health education program sufficiently comprehensive to encourage both pupils and their parents to adopt desirable attitudes and practices toward essential health habits. Such a program would involve frequent opportunity for rest, relaxation, and supervised play. School lunches and instruction regarding proper dietetic practices should also do much to promote both adequate health and physical development.

45 James F. Rogers, *op. cit.*, p. 9.

8. Both the construction of school buildings and the selection of furnishings should be influenced by the facts of pupil growth. It is becoming increasingly customary to construct classrooms in harmony with standards of healthful living and to use movable furniture of correct height, as well as to provide colorful, well-lighted surroundings in the education of small children. Cots, sleeping rooms, cafeterias, and sanitary wash rooms are also provided in modern schools. Both physical growth and social development are apparently promoted by such equipment.

Physical Health of the Child

It is becoming recognized that a child's psychological well-being (mental health) is dependent upon the possession of a healthy physical organism. The problem of child health thus looms large in the home, the school, and in society in general. These and other agencies are vitally concerned with the maintenance of a satisfactory state of adjustment in the highly intricate but frequently imperfect machine called the human body. Good health for every child is the goal of both medical workers and educators. The value to society of a generation of children characterized by high physical vitality and efficiency would be difficult to overestimate.

Probably the most dramatic evidence of the lack of physical fitness of the young men of America was that disclosed by physical examinations in connection with both World War I and World War II. Approximately 40 per cent of the men drafted for military service—young men who would be expected to possess a maximum of vigor and good health—were suffering from physical disabilities of a nature that made them doubtful candidates for active service in the defense of their country. From 6 to 10 per cent of the men were so seriously defective physically as to be wholly unfit for military service. An examination of Civil War records has disclosed much the same situation. Health data from the nation-wide White House Conference on Child Welfare in 1930 have shown that the health situation in the case of children is also a precarious one. It is for these reasons that any discussion of child psychology and development should concern itself with physical health problems.

Caring for the Child's Nutritional Needs.—Laporte [46] has stated that the principal nutritional needs of the human body relate to (1) *basal metabolism* or energy output of the individual; (2) *growth,* which is greatest in children; (3) *muscular activity,* which is also at a maximum in children; and (4) *values lost in excreta,* which fluctuate greatly from individual to individual. The same writer has noted that nutritional needs vary with (1) *age,* with children needing the most tissue-building food; (2) *sex,* with the more active boys needing relatively more food than girls; (3) *temperature,* with summer and winter requiring their appropriate foods; and (4) *type of activity,* with individuals engaged in sedentary activities requiring less food than those doing work of a more physically strenuous variety. It should be evident that the child's growth and health are dependent upon the consistent intake of foods appropriate to his sex and age, and upon the activities in which he is engaged.

Students of child development are interested in the relationship obtaining between nutritional status and behavior tendencies. Although few definite cause-and-effect sequences have been ascertained with respect to this relationship, if he has not been denied affectionate responses, a well-nourished infant tends to smile, coo, and take an interest in the activities going on around him. A poorly nourished infant is often restless, fretful, difficult to put to sleep, and indifferent to the presence of people. Older children suffering from malnutrition are often negativistic and may display attitudes of shyness, self-centeredness, depression, and lack of confidence. Behavior trends of this kind are most likely to develop when the child concerned is also denied fulfillment of his need for affection and status with parents.

It is generally conceded that human milk is the most desirable food for infants and that it possesses the additional advantage of immunizing the baby against certain diseases during

[46] Wm. Ralph Laporte, *Hygiene and Health,* Los Angeles, The Caslon Printing Co., 1939, p. 57.

the first few months of postnatal life.   As Stuart [47] has written, "Breast feeding is the natural method of providing food for the newborn infant. It is no longer the only successful method, as it was not many years ago, but it is still the best method for the greater majority of infants during their first six or eight months of life. Breast milk is physically and chemically a better food for young infants than cow's milk. The chief physical advantages of breast milk are the smaller and softer protein curds which form from it in the stomach, the smaller fat globules which it contains, and the shorter time which the stomach requires to digest and pass it on to the intestines. The chemical advantages of breast milk have to do with the nature of its proteins, the amount of digestive acids needed to utilize those proteins, and the relative amounts of fats, carbohydrates, and protein which it contains. In addition, breast milk has the advantage of passing directly from the mother's breast into the baby's mouth, without any possibility of becoming contaminated. This is a most important consideration, for a very large proportion of the nutritional upsets which occur in infants is due to bacterial infection, acquired from contaminated foods." These considerations point to the desirability of breast feeding. When coupled with affectionate cuddling, such feeding does much toward insuring wholesome physical and psychological development.

Even children who have the benefit of a mother's milk diet need to supplement this source of nutriment as they develop. Orange juice is often added around the beginning of the second month since it gives the child the benefit of scurvy-resisting vitamins. Cod liver oil is also an important food at this stage of growth as a preventive of rickets. It is advisable to introduce the child to such solid foods as eggs and cereals at approximately the age of six months. These foods should be well cooked and should be administered in amounts commensurate with the child's degree of hunger and taste for them. Later foods should include soup, vegetables, fruit, and beef broth. The child's diet should at all times be varied and should be ad-

[47] H. C. Stuart, *Healthy Childhood*, New York, D. Appleton-Century Co., Inc., 1933, p. 174.

ministered in such a way as to prevent the development of dislike for nutritive foods or a general distaste for nourishment. The White House Conference Report [48] on child develop-

TABLE 15. AN ADEQUATE DIET FOR PRESCHOOL AND KINDERGARTEN CHILDREN

COST UNRESTRICTED

| Age | Percentage of total calories from each class of food | | | | | |
	Milk	Foods from cereal grains	Vegetables and fruits	Egg yolk *	Fats †	Sugar
1–2 years	60–70	10–20	10–15	2–3	1–3	0–1
2–3 years	50–60	16–20	15–20	3–5	3–5	1–3
3–4 years	45–55	18–22	16–22	4–6	5–7	2–4
4–5 years	40–50	20–24	16–22	4–7	6–8	3–5

* Chiefly egg and liver.
† Chiefly butter and cod liver oil.

COST RESTRICTED

| Age | Percentage of total calories from each class of food. | | | | | |
	Milk	Foods from cereal grains	Vegetables and fruits	Egg yolk *	Fats †	Sugar
1–2 years	65–75	10–20	5–10	1–2	1–3	0–1
2–3 years	55–60	20–22	10–12	2–3	3–4	1–3
3–4 years	50–55	20–24	12–14	4–5	4–5	2–3
4–5 years	45–50	23–25	14–18	5–6	5–8	2–5

* Chiefly egg yolk and liver.
† Chiefly butter and cod liver oil.

(From W. Rand, M. E. Sweeny, and E. L. Vincent, *Growth and Development of the Young Child*, Philadelphia, W. B. Saunders Co., 1940, p. 222.)

ment has described a four-year investigation in which children were given a controlled diet in both home and school which conformed closely to the best-known practices for feeding young children. Returns from the health records of 58 two- to three-year-old children and 92 three- to four-year-olds

[48] White House Conference Report, *Growth and Development of the Child*, New York, D. Appleton-Century Co., Inc., 1933, Part III, pp. 442–443.

showed that their diet was apparently well chosen so far as the distribution of calories was concerned. The investigators have consequently suggested the diet program shown in Table 15 as a useful guide in the feeding of young children. Where costs prevent the most ideal combination of foods, a reduction in the amount of vegetables and fruits has been proposed.

Evidence that the supplying of needed vitamins in the diet of malnourished children improves their physical status is found in a comprehensive study [49] of 404 elementary school pupils, many of whom were suffering from a deficiency of vitamin A. According to the authors, all malnourished children who were given carotene or halibut liver oil were restored to normal health within a month's time. It is apparent that minor but crucial additions to a child's diet may improve his health and increase his weight.

Safeguarding the Child's Special Organs.—Few children possess perfect sensory and other special organs. Physical defects in this area are more often the rule than the exception. Furthermore, many of the handicaps involved are not recognized sufficiently soon to prevent serious physical maladjustments. This is particularly true in the case of physical handicaps of a borderline variety which so easily escape detection. It seems important, thus, to consider implications for the child's welfare of handicaps associated with his eyes, ears, nose and throat, and teeth. It is in connection with these special organs that children encounter a major share of their physical handicaps.

DEFECTS OF VISION. Defects of vision are uncommon among very young children, but become alarmingly prevalent during the elementary school period. It has been estimated that from 20 to 30 per cent of all school children are suffering from visual impairment of a serious nature. A larger per cent are handicapped by less evident but nevertheless deficient visual acuity. According to a recent writer,[50] one of every 500 school

[49] P. C. Jeans and Z. Zentmire, "The Prevalence of Vitamin A Deficiency Among Iowa Children," *Journal of the American Medical Assn.*, 66 : 996-997 (1936). See also Ruth F. Harrell, "Effect of Added Thiamin on Learning," Teachers College Contributions to Education, No. 877, Columbia Univ., 1943.
[50] C. M. Louttit, *Clinical Psychology*, New York, Harper & Bros., 1936, p. 568.

children needs to be placed in special sight-saving classes, while one in 2,000 is blind. It is of the utmost importance that children be taught the value of their eyes and how to protect them most adequately.

The most common eye defects have been listed by Laporte [51] as: (1) *astigmatism,* or irregularity of the surface of either the cornea or the lens; (2) *hypermetropia,* or far-sightedness; (3) *myopia,* or near-sightedness; and (4) *muscular imbalance,* or tendency of the eyes to turn inward or outward and sometimes upward or downward unequally. Children afflicted with astigmatism are constantly under the strain of trying to bring seen objects into clear focus, and thus frequently develop headaches, eyeache, watering of the eyes, and even stomach disorders and similar nervous symptoms. Hypermetropia appears to be an inherited structural defect, and if not corrected by appropriate glasses may lead to much squinting and eye strain.

Myopia (nearsightedness) is not present at birth but frequently develops with advancing age. It is believed to be associated with academic school requirements, and thus suggests the hazards of poor lighting, faulty print, extensive homework, insufficient rest, and general excessive close use of the eyes. Muscular imbalance, one form of which is called "cross eyes," may in mild cases be partially relieved by exercises directed by a specialist (ophthalmologist). In severe cases, surgical correction is necessary. Fortunately, most visual defects, with their train of headaches, eye smarting, inflammations, abnormal fatigue, and nervous manifestations, can be corrected by the relatively simple prescription of properly fitted eyeglasses and adherence to the common rules of physical hygiene. Thus every school child should be given a careful visual examination and appropriate remedial treatment at the beginning of each school year. Such a practice would tend to eliminate not only the disabilities already mentioned, but the plight of handicapped pupils who suppose that all their classmates are struggling with the same blurred or double vision reading experiences with which they are afflicted.[52]

51 Wm. Ralph Laporte, *op. cit.,* p. 43.
52 George F. Meyer, "The Visually Handicapped," *The Phi Delta Kappan,* 23 : 57-60 (1940).

DEFECTS OF HEARING.   Defects of hearing are less prevalent than eye defects and are much more frequently overlooked.
In view of the importance of hearing for school work and other
communication activities, handicaps in this area should be accorded immediate and serious consideration.   Nevertheless, superficial observers frequently overlook symptoms of partial
deafness which are still in the curable stage.   Since pain is not
present in cases of auditory deficiency the afflicted child may not
be cognizant of his handicap.   Many who do recognize the presence of such a disability become classified as being dull because
of their efforts to conceal the defect and their sensitiveness concerning it.   In fact, many hard-of-hearing pupils defend themselves against detection as supposed defectives by sitting far
from the front of the classroom where hearing would not be
difficult, but where they would feel self-conscious.   Many a
hard-of-hearing child has also resorted to antisocial behavior in
an effort to atone for a feeling of inferiority and to draw the
teacher's attention away from his physical defect.   Such ego-
inflating behavior is indulged in by both bright and dull children.

It is estimated that approximately 10 to 20 per cent of school
age children are suffering from sufficient auditory impairment
to require "front seat attention" and special help by the teacher.
An additional 2 to 4 per cent are so handicapped in this respect
as to need systematic lip-reading instruction, as well as special
class work in speech and language skills.   For those who fall as
low as 45 or 50 per cent in hearing efficiency, special classes or
special schools are required.   In the better schools, degree of
hearing deficiency is determined not only by medical checks and
group audiometer methods, but by accurate individual testing
instruments.   According to Lefever [53] et al., such care is essential to detection of the hearing acuity of borderline cases.

Most cases of deafness have their origin in childhood.   Boynton [54] believes that such a condition is due to three basic causes;
namely, "congenital deafness with which the child is born; diseased conditions of the nose and sinuses; and lastly, deafness

[53] D. Welty Lefever, A. M. Turrell, and H. I. Weitzel, *Principles and Techniques of Guidance,* New York, The Ronald Press Co., 1941, p. 411.
[54] Paul L. Boynton, *Psychology of Child Development,* Minneapolis, Educational Publishers, Inc., 1938, pp. 458-459.

resulting from infectious children's diseases such as measles, whooping cough, diphtheria, scarlet fever, and severe chills which are permitted to continue without proper treatment." It is evident that many cases of deafness could have been prevented if the diseases mentioned had been detected in time and properly cared for. One student of the subject [55] has reported that when treatment is administered in the early stages of hearing loss, 50 to 75 per cent of the children concerned may be re-

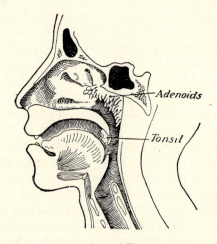

Figure 41. Internal View of Tonsils and Adenoids
(From C-E. A. Winslow, *Healthy Living, Book II,* New York, C. E. Merrill Co., 1920, p. 108.)

stored to hearing normality or greatly improved in this respect. When it is realized that an additional number of seriously handicapped children can be materially assisted by the wearing of hearing aids, it becomes evident that the plight of the hard-of-hearing can be alleviated to an extent not formerly realized.

NOSE AND THROAT DEFECTS. Children's nose and throat abnormalities are most commonly in the form of adenoids and defective tonsils. Examination of a sampling of 535 children disclosed the fact that 50.7 per cent were suffering or had suffered from tonsillar defects, but that less than 1 per cent were

[55] F. M. Cuckles, "The Hard of Hearing Child," *Nevada Educational Bulletin,* Sept. 1940, pp. 16-19.

afflicted with nasal disorders.[56]   An investigation by Payne [57] of 5,000 city elementary school children showed that adenoids and diseased tonsils ranked third in frequency among physical defects, and that their highest incidence occurred at age nine.

As can be seen in Figure 41, tonsils are circular-shaped organs which lie on each side of the throat.   Adenoids may be described as spongy growths which develop in the throat at the point where the passages from the nose converge with it.   Diseased tonsils provide a favorable breeding ground for germs, which may subsequently find their way into the blood stream and cause heart disease, rheumatism, and other serious disorders.   Enlarged adenoids may obstruct the passage of air which would normally go from the nose to the throat and thus cause unhealthy mouth breathing.   Children suffering from such adenoid growths are frequently restless in their sleep and are inclined to be irritable, inattentive, and apathetic about school work.   Diseased tonsils, and to some extent adenoids, are among the serious menaces to a child's physical health.

Most medical men recommend the surgical removal of diseased tonsils and would make a similar disposition of adenoids if they do not disappear of their own accord.   However, there is some evidence for increased susceptibility to such respiratory diseases as laryngitis and pneumonia following the removal of infected tonsils.[58]   It is not uncommon for symptoms of disease usually laid at the door of defective tonsils to be caused by other pathological conditions.   It is for this reason, and the fact that so many parts of the human organism operate together in the causation of disease, that tonsillectomies are not always successful so far as the cure of diseases is concerned.

DENTAL DEFECTS.   Teeth are among the most susceptible organs of the body to the ravages of disease.   As one medical authority [59] stated several years ago, "If bitter experience had

[56] Jan Downes, "Sickness Records in School Hygiene," *American Journal of Public Health,* 20: 1199-1206 (1930).

[57] C. C. Payne, "Physical Handicaps of the Present Day Child," *Ohio State Medical Journal,* 32: 24-27 (1937).

[58] A. D. Kaiser, "Results of Tonsillectomy," *Journal of the American Medical Assn.,* 95:837-842 (1930).

[59] C-E. A. Winslow, "The Prevalence and Treatment of Sense Defects," in *The Child: His Nature and His Needs* (M. V. O'Shea, Editor), Valparaiso (Ind.), The Children's Foundation, 1924, pp. 222-223.

not taught us otherwise, we should probably have supposed these hard, shining, ivory-like structures to be among the most resistant portions of our anatomy; yet they yield with peculiar readiness to the decaying influence of microbe life. When a cavity is formed in the enamel, a hard protective outer coating of the teeth, the softer dentine underneath is rapidly attacked and ultimately an abscess may be formed at the root. The final result of such a decay (known as 'dental caries') may be exceedingly serious since the bacteria from a tooth abscess are likely to pass on to the general circulation and cause rheumatism, heart disease, and other grave conditions." This writer adds that since abscesses are not always painful, they may work severe damage to general health without the victim knowing the real cause of the trouble.

The prevalence of dental defects in children is probably not realized by either parents or teachers. An extensive study [60] of this problem by public health officials has disclosed a situation that obviously demands attention. It was found, for example, that 87.7 per cent of six-year-old and 91.7 per cent of ten-year-old children were suffering from some dental abnormality (at least one tooth decayed or missing). Yet in the face of these figures, only 4.8 per cent of ten-year-olds had been given appropriate treatment (tooth filled). It is evident that a large percentage of school children, especially in the elementary grades, are afflicted with dental cavities which may harbor bacteria conducive to the contraction of scarlet fever, diphtheria, and other disorders which flourish when body resistance is low. Decayed teeth also exact a toll in the form of pain or discomfort, as well as in appearance.

Although the cause of tooth decay is not entirely known, nutrition experts and dentists are apparently agreed that inadequate diet is to a considerable extent at fault. Careful attention to principles of nutrition on the part of the mother during pregnancy and in the later care of the child should do much to reduce the danger of dental decay. When coupled with cleanliness and repair of defects as they appear, such a program will

[60] A. L. Stoughton and U. T. Meaker, "Dental Decay and Correction Among School Children of Different Ages," *U. S. Public Health Service Reports*, Vol. 46, No. 44 (1931), pp. 2608-2623.

insure the best possible results in the prevention of dental disorders.

A study by Lewis and Lehman [61] of the dental development of 170 children, eighteen months to fifteen years of age, at the Merrill-Palmer School in Detroit brought out the fact that occlusion (the fitting of the upper and lower teeth so that food may be chewed) is affected by both growth changes and by the factors which influence growth. One jaw may grow more rapidly than the other so that the teeth of the two jaws do not

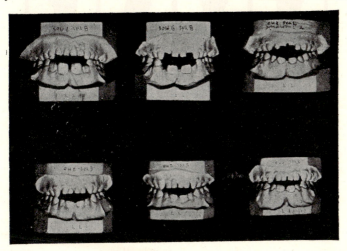

Figure 42. The Effects of Thumb-Sucking on the Alignment of Teeth

(From W. Rand, M. E. Sweeny, and E. L. Vincent, *Growth and Development of the Young Child*, Philadelphia, W. B. Saunders Co., 1940, p. 149.)

fit together properly. Such a condition is designated as "malocclusion." Since malocclusion interferes with the chewing of food it represents a threat to child health. The investigators found that thumb-sucking also causes such a condition and that if the habit is not broken in early childhood the protrusion of the upper front teeth may cause serious mastication difficulty as well as disfiguration. In some cases self-correction of malocclusion has been observed in school-age children. It is not

[61] Samuel J. Lewis and I. Lehman, "Observations on the Growth Changes of the Teeth and Dental Arches," *The Dental Cosmos*, 71 : 5 (1929).

likely to occur, however, in children who continue to suck their thumbs after the fifth or sixth year.

Establishing Desirable Body Posture.—It is becoming increasingly clear that good body posture is essential to health, and that faulty posture can bring about curvature of the spine,

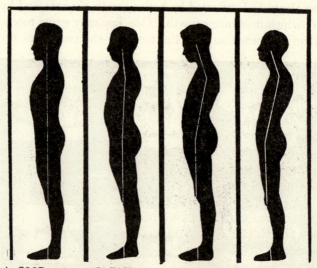

A. GOOD	B. FAIR	C. POOR	D. VERY POOR
1. Head, trunk, and thigh in straight line.	1. Head forward.	1. Relaxed (fatigue) posture.	1. Head forward badly.
2. Chest high, and forward.	2. Abdomen prominent.	2. Head forward.	2. Very exaggerated curve upper back.
3. Abdomen flat.	3. Exaggerated curve in upper back.	3. Abdomen relaxed.	3. Abdomen relaxed.
4. Back curves normal.	4. Slight hollow back.	4. Shoulder blades prominent.	4. Chest flat-sloping.
		5. Hollow back.	5. Hollow back.

Figure 43. Types of Posture in Men (and Boys)

(From Wm. Ralph LaPorte, *Hygiene and Health*, Los Angeles, The Caslon Printing Co., 1939, p. 26.)

deformities of the bony structure, and serious disturbances to the functioning of organs of the trunk. Poor posture may in turn be caused by malnutrition, low body vitality, and such structural deformities as broken arches (flat feet) and lateral curvature of the spinal column. In any case, it is essential to recognize that stooped shoulders, a flat chest, a forward-tilted head, a round or hollow back, and deformities of the feet all militate, not only against an individual's appearance, but against his health and vitality as well. Continual sagging of the body, as illustrated in Figure 43, causes the structural system and the internal organs to be thrown out of alignment and thus to disturb the normal distribution of stress within the organism.

Lowman,[62] a specialist in orthopedics, has stressed the relationship between defective feet and general organic welfare. When the foot arches are improperly formed the various organs of the body experience stresses of a character calculated to disturb their functioning and thus to cause widespread disorders. Poor posture, which may be associated with defective feet, also contributes in some cases to serious organic malfunctioning. Siemsen and Dolan [63] found that bow legs and curvatures of the spine tended to increase in frequency with age in children, but that knock knees and flat feet were less in evidence as pupils entered high school. They also noted a higher percentage of postural defects in girls than among boys of similar age.

It seems vital that children be given properly fitting clothes, shoes that are broad enough to permit free movement of the toes, school seats which make possible good posture, and a regime of healthful living designed to encourage bodily vigor and posture. In the case of structural deformities which already exist, recourse should be had to exercises prescribed by a specialist, or to orthopedic surgery. In no case should children or youths suffering from marked postural defects, which may be caused by spinal deformities or seriously defective arches, be permitted to participate in a program of athletics on the assumption that such activity will correct their postural difficulties. Such a procedure may aggravate rather than alleviate structural disorders.

Preventing and Caring for Childhood Diseases.—There are a number of communicable diseases whose victims are for the most part children. Measles, mumps, whooping cough, and chickenpox are so common among elementary school pupils that

[62] C. L. Lowman, "Feet and Body Mechanisms," *Journal of Health and Physical Education*, 11 : 137-138, 192-193 (1940).
[63] W. J. Siemsen and G. K. Dolan, "The Problem of Body Mechanics," *Journal of Health and Physical Education*, 3 : 10-12, 78-79 (1935).

TABLE 16. SPECIFICATIONS FOR THE

	DIPHTHERIA	MEASLES	SCARLET FEVER	CHICKEN-POX
CAUSE	Diphtheria bacillus	A virus. No specific germ yet isolated	Streptococcus hemolytic	Unknown. Probably filterable virus
SEASON	Usually winter and spring	Most cases in spring	Usually fall, winter, or spring	Most cases in spring or fall
CHIEF SOURCE OF INFECTION	Discharge from mouth or nose. Coughing, sneezing	Discharge from mouth or nose. Coughing, sneezing	Discharge from mouth or nose. Spitting, talking	Emanation from mouth with or without contact
SUSCEPTIBILITY	Highest 9 months to 3 years. Still quite high at 7	After 6 months. Most children	Highest between 4th and 7th years	Very widespread
INCUBATION PERIOD	Usually 3 to 5 days	Seven to 10 days	Two to 5 days	Fourteen to 21 days
ONSET	Often fever, sore throat, and neck swelling	Fever, sneezing, cough, with "running" nose and eyes	Usually some temperature, sore throat, and vomiting	Usually mild with or without fever. Eruptions on body
ISOLATION	About 2 weeks and until culture negative	Usually one week after rash gone	Usually 4 weeks. Longer if discharge from infected parts	Until blisters are completely dried up
TREATMENT AND PREVENTIVE MEASURES	Early injection of diphtheria antitoxin	Rest in bed. Injection of convalescent serum	Isolation Scarlet fever antitoxin	Prevention of infection from scratching

(From Béla Schick and William Rosenson, *Child*

parents have been inclined to regard them as temporary but inevitable inconveniences which might just as well be contracted and "gotten over with." Scarlet fever, diphtheria, spinal meningitis, and infantile paralysis are much more fearsome diseases and have usually been guarded against or shunned with considerable care. As a matter of fact, the first-mentioned group of childhood diseases have serious import for the child's future, as well as present, health and should as far as possible be avoided. A case of measles, for example, may result in bronchial pneu-

MORE COMMON DISEASES OF CHILDHOOD

MUMPS	WHOOPING COUGH	CEREBRO-SPINAL MENINGITIS	TYPHOID FEVER	INFANTILE PARALYSIS
Unknown	Bordet-Bengou bacillus	Meningo-coccus	Typhoid bacillus	Virus in nervous system and secretion of nose
Any season	Most cases in winter and spring	Winter and spring	Summer and fall	Summer and fall
Discharge from mouth in coughing and spitting	Discharge from mouth or nose. Sneezing, spitting	Discharge from nose and sometimes mouth	Infected drinking water or food, especially milk	Not definitely known
Highest between 5th and 15th years	Very widespread. May occur in infants	Widespread	Widespread	Greatest during first 4 years
Fourteen to 21 days	Seven to 14 days	Three days to two weeks	One to two weeks	Two to 14 days
Usually slight fever and swelling about ear. Some pain	Mild-sounding cough. Whoops after 10 to 14 days	Sudden with fever, headache, vomiting, and stiff neck	Sometimes sudden rise in temperature with headache and prostration	Usually sudden with fever, vomiting, and slight stiffness of neck
Until all swellings have subsided	At least 6 weeks or until cough has stopped	Until complete recovery	Until temperature normal for 10 days, and feces free from bacilli	Two weeks
Disease usually mild. No specific treatment	In bed for week or two. Sedative to relieve cough	Injection of antimeningococcus into spine	No specific treatment. High caloric diet	Early orthopedic care to prevent deformities. Sometimes blood serum

Care Today, Cleveland, World Pub. Co., 1945.)

monia, a respiratory ailment which causes approximately 75 or 80 per cent of deaths resulting from measles.

The childhood diseases mentioned are known as infectious diseases. "The germ causing the disease enters the body either through the skin or mucous membrane. Mucous membrane is the tissue which forms the lining of various organs of the body such as the nose, mouth, intestine, and bronchial tubes. A small injury to the skin or mucous membrane, so small that it is frequently invisible, is sufficient to allow the germs to enter the underlying tissue. Disease germs are transmitted to the body by contact, by the air, through contaminated water or food, and by insects. After the microbes enter the body they may remain localized near the portal of entry or they may travel via the blood or lymph stream to distant parts where they may lodge and cause an inflammation. Even when the microbes remain confined to one area, other parts of the body may be irritated by harmful substances produced and excreted by them and distributed by the blood." [64]

An infectious disease is thus an adjustive reaction of the body to the *toxins* produced by invading germs. Such a disease will continue until the organism has been able to generate sufficient antibodies (antitoxins) to combat or neutralize the harmful effects of the disease-producing germs. The extent to which the body of a child will be able to accomplish such a task is contingent upon its reserve of vitality and its degree of immunity to the disease in question. Assistance is now available from laboratory-prepared *antitoxins* which may be injected into the blood and thus create immunization against certain infectious diseases. Great success has been achieved by this method in the prevention of smallpox and diphtheria. Most modern school systems have been using it for years in their health programs.

A brief summary of the causes, symptoms, and treatment of the most common childhood infectious diseases is presented in Table 16. A thorough treatment of these diseases would occupy a complete volume, but a study of the table will indicate the principal features and implications of the childhood ailments with which most parents are called upon to cope. [65]

Recent years have witnessed much progress in the diagnosis, control, and treatment of both the milder and more virulent infectious diseases of childhood. Medical men have done a great deal to remove the superstitions and mysteries formerly associated with these physical disorders. The future will undoubtedly bring new discoveries leading to more adequate prevention and control of diseases that prey on children. The im-

[64] Béla Schick and William Rosenson, *Child Care Today,* Cleveland, World Pub. Co., 1945, pp. 286-287.

[65] A more technical discussion of childhood diseases and other health problems may be found in *Synopsis of Pediatrics,* by John Zahorsky, St. Louis, The C. V. Mosby Co., 1937.

portant procedure at present is for parents and all others concerned with the protection and welfare of children to utilize such knowledge as is available in the struggle against the ravages of disease. Widespread attention to the principles and practices of healthful living will do much to safeguard the rising generation against needless physical ailments and handicaps.

Summary and Implications

With the realization that children grow at individual rates rather than in harmony with mass height-weight scales, that growth is characterized by periods of acceleration and seasonal fluctuation, and that different parts of the child's body grow at different rates, educators should obviously develop physical education and athletic programs commensurate with physical status at any stage in the growth curve. Parents also should come to realize that a child's physical development must be taken into account in the regulation of his diet, his sleep, rest, and relaxation, and his schedule of play and exercise. It is possible that overtaxation of physical energy at certain points on the growth curve may result in more or less serious health problems.

Physical health is of sufficient importance to warrant lifelong attention. It should be safeguarded in every possible way beginning with prenatal life, through infancy and childhood, to adulthood and the declining years. The health program should include emphasis upon rest, sleep, and exercise, the development of good posture and structural balance, the maintenance of an adequate diet, proper care of special organs—eyes, ears, nose, throat, and teeth, the prevention of organic and infectious diseases, and habits of cleanliness in the care of hair, teeth, nails, skin, and other parts of the body. Such a constructive program would provide a foundation not only for physical well-being, but for the maintenance of emotional health and the development of socially desirable personality qualities.

QUESTIONS FOR DISCUSSION

1. What fallacy (or fallacies) appears to have grown out of efforts to interpret the nature of individual physical growth from curves showing average growth for groups of children?

What erroneous ideas concerning growth in height have originated in this manner?

2. What are the advantages and limitations of making long-term longitudinal investigations of the physical growth of children? Discuss principles of development which have emerged from such studies. What new light have longitudinal researches shed on physical growth?

3. How early can individual differences in rates and patterns of physical growth be charted? How were such differences obscured by earlier studies? Do these variations in growth express themselves in both rates and patterns or in rates alone? Discuss.

4. On the basis of the Harvard and other growth studies, to what extent can the ultimate growth in height of a child be predicted? Are the variations so great here that no prediction can be made? Consult the conclusions of investigators.

5. Why are height-weight scales unreliable for determining the adequacy of a given child's status (as to physical growth)? To what extent can this situation be alleviated by using height and weight *ranges* for the different ages? Clarify this issue.

6. What are the limitations of Courtis' belief that mental and educational development follow the same so-called cycles as physical growth? To what extent does Courtis' more theoretical view of physical growth agree with evidence from the Harvard Growth Study?

7. What internal factor is usually given most credit for regulating physical development? Is the cause and effect relationship here theoretical or has it been demonstrated beyond reasonable doubt? What external factors are believed to influence the physical growth of the child? Can each of these be regulated? How?

8. Is it possible that a child's nutritional needs might be seriously neglected in a well-to-do home? If your answer is in the affirmative, explain how this could be. Indicate as well why children from underprivileged homes are likely to relish their food more than those from more favored economic groups.

9. How do you explain the fact that so many American parents fail to attend to the visual and auditory handicaps possessed by their children? What were the figures for such disabilities according to the White House Conference on child welfare? Are these handicaps on the increase?

10. Name the six or seven most common childhood diseases and
show from medical works how serious they are. Report as well
on the extent to which these diseases can be both prevented
and controlled. Suggest what good it does parents and teachers
to be informed about childhood diseases.

RECOMMENDED READINGS

Boynton, Paul L. *Psychology of Child Development.* Minneapolis: Educational Publishers, Inc., 1938, Chs. 5, 14.

Breckenridge, Marion E., and Vincent, E. L. *Child Development.* Philadelphia: W. B. Saunders Co., 1943, Ch. 4.

Child Growth and Development Emphasis in Teacher Education, The American Assn. of Teachers Colleges, 1944.

Dearborn, W. F., and Rothney, J. W. M. *Predicting the Child's Development.* Cambridge (Mass.): Sci-Art Publishers, 1941.

Hardy, M. C., and Hoefer, C. H. *Healthy Growth: A Study of the Influence of Health Education on Growth and Development of School Children.* Chicago: Univ. of Chicago Press, 1936.

Meredith, Howard. "The Rhythm of Physical Growth." *Univ. of Iowa Studies in Child Welfare,* Vol. 11, No. 3 (1935).

O'Shea, M. V. (Editor). *The Child: His Nature and His Needs.* Valparaiso (Ind.): Children's Foundation, 1924, Chs. 9, 11.

Rand, Winifred, Sweeney, M. E., and Vincent, E. L. *Growth and Development of the Young Child.* Philadelphia: W. B. Saunders Co., 1940, Chs. 2, 3, 4.

Sanders, Barkov. *Environment and Growth.* Baltimore: Warwick & York, Inc., 1934.

Schick, Béla, and Rosenson, William. *Child Care Today.* Cleveland: World Pub. Co., 1945.

Simmons, Katherine. *The Brush Foundation Study of Child Growth and Development. II. Physical Growth and Development.* Monographs of the Society for Research in Child Development, Vol. 9, No. 1 (1944).

Stuart, H. C. *Healthy Childhood.* New York: D. Appleton-Century Co., Inc., 1933.

Terman, Lewis M., and Almack, J. C. *The Hygiene of the School Child.* Boston: Houghton Mifflin Co., 1929.

White House Conference Report, *Growth and Development of the Child.* Part II, "Anatomy and Physiology." New York: D. Appleton-Century Co., 1933.

CHAPTER 8

INTELLIGENCE AND HOW IT DEVELOPS

EVERYONE IS INTERESTED in the manifestations of intelligence displayed by children, and in observing their development along intellectual lines. This aspect of growth is fraught, however, with many problems difficult to solve even by those who have devoted years to their solution. The nature of intelligence itself has eluded the search of both biological and psychological science. The rate at which intelligence develops and the extent to which it varies from year to year are also questions the solution to which many research workers have given much attention. Students of child development are interested as well in the relation between mental and physical growth, and in modern objective methods of measuring expressions of intelligence. A comprehensive study of the growing child will thus concern itself with all identifiable factors affecting mental growth.

Theories of the Nature of Intelligence

It is difficult, if not impossible, to understand the nature of mental growth in children unless various current definitions and descriptions of intelligence are first comprehended. Although marked differences in point of view regarding the basic nature of human intelligence exist among those most competent to judge, a brief survey of these differences should serve to clarify the discussions of mental development which follow. Intelligence is not a concept to be dealt with lightly. Though indefinite, what is known concerning it throws much light on problems of child growth and development. It is essential that every effort be made to determine of what intelligence consists and what forces may be marshaled in promoting its fullest development.

Controversies Concerning Intelligence.—Students of child development regard intelligence as being an important component of personality and have as a result given it a prominent place in their discussions. As one writer [1] has said, "Intelligence is one of the aspects of an individual's personality that is of great importance in modern civilized life." If this be true the question naturally arises whether intelligence is an inner agency or mental factor which directs behavior or whether it is perchance a name for the adaptive quality of an individual's observable acts. There is also the previously mentioned (Chapter 3) problem of whether intelligence, regardless of its ultimate nature, is a biologically inherited factor or whether the extent of its development is largely a function of environmental conditions. It is on the solution of the latter problem that the much debated question of the modifiability of the I.Q. (intelligence quotient) hinges.

As was brought out in Chapter 3, there is a strong present-day tendency to think of intelligence in terms of what an individual is able to do rather than as a disembodied inborn mental force. This point of view has been aptly presented in the following words: [2] "We may first refute any assumption that mental tests have any mysterious power of detecting intelligence as an entity apart from life performance. There is no such measure at present, and the probability is that there will never be any direct measure of intelligence. In fact, it is very doubtful if there is any such entity as intelligence. It is much more defensible to say that a person *acts intelligently* than to say that he has *intelligence*. The term 'intelligent behavior' is a description of behavior under certain conditions. We can generally agree on what behavior is intelligent even though we might never agree about the existence of some mysterious 'intelligence' within the individual. By analogy we apply the term intelligent to the person who acts intelligently. People are considered more or less intelligent on the basis of their behavior and

[1] Rudolph Pintner, *Intelligence Testing,* New York, Henry Holt & Co., Inc., 1931, p. vi.
[2] Carroll A. Whitmer, "Has Man Measured His Intelligence?" *Pitt, Univ. of Pittsburgh Quarterly,* Nov. 9, 1941 (autumn), pp. 38-39.

in the practical world past behavior is considered to be the best basis for predicting future behavior."

Psychologists have called attention to the fact that intelligence tests have their greatest predictive value in the scholastic field. This is because mental test materials are so closely related to the language, mathematical, and other symbolic content of elementary and high school courses of study. The tests are, in fact, often referred to as measures of academic ability; most of them are not, as many have supposed, measures of ability in non-scholastic fields of endeavor. As Stoddard [3] states, "there is no higher validity for mental testing than its tendency to parallel school achievement. Under cultural conditions that make school work dominant from ages six to eighteen, and highly important at younger and older ages, this is to be expected. . . . In brief, the meaning of intelligence, as it emerges from all child testing Binet [individual mental test] in type, is *scholastic aptitude.*" On this basis intelligence connotes the ability to do good school work and mental test results refer to the quality of a sampling of scholastic performances which have been made possible, in part at least, by the stimulating influence of an educational environment. The making of wise decisions and the socially desirable ordering of one's life involve important adjustive acts which do not come within the scope of ordinary tests of intelligence. Intelligence, at least as now measured, refers to a limited area of child behavior. It does not include ability to develop socially acceptable behavior traits, moral attitudes, or personal qualities which make for popularity.

Varying Conceptions of Intelligence.—The above conception of intelligence as capacity to learn—especially to learn school subjects—while widely held, is not the only one that has been brought forward. The widespread use of intelligence tests has tended to popularize the idea that intelligence represents "the ability to think in terms of abstract ideas," [4] but has minimized the capacity for intelligent behavior of individuals whose abilities do not run along academic or abstract lines.

[3] George D. Stoddard, "On the Meaning of Intelligence," *Psychological Review,* 48 : 250-260 (1941).
[4] Lewis M. Terman, in the symposium "Intelligence and Its Measurement," *Journal of Educational Psychology,* 12 : 123-147, 195-216 (1921).

Intelligence as the *ability to adjust* to novel life situations has been advanced by a number of early workers in this field. According to Stern,[5] "Intelligence is a general capacity of an individual consciously to adjust his thinking to new requirements: it is general mental adaptability to new problems and conditions of life." This view of intelligence broadens its scope to include dealing with problems of a non-academic variety—problems of a mechanical, artistic, and social nature, and does not give the bulk of credit to those who are especially facile in the use of language and symbolic materials. It also harmonizes with the social objectives of modern schools which are more vitally interested in the personality development and social adjustment of their pupils than in the acquisition of academic knowledge for its own sake.

The adjustment view of intelligence is likewise in harmony with that advanced by Alfred Binet, the father of mental tests. Binet [6] believed that intelligence involves the ability not only to adjust but "to take and maintain a definite direction" in so doing. He also proposed that an individual's intelligence could be determined by the extent to which he could *comprehend* problems, *invent* ways of solving them, follow a *direct* line of procedure in making adjustments, and *criticize* "the accuracy of what he said and did." As Binet once said, "Comprehension, invention, direction, and criticism—intelligence is contained in these four words." This view discounts the intelligence of individuals who are unable to recognize their own weaknesses, who use little reflection in planning their activities, who are apparently unable to evaluate the consequences of their acts, and who fluctuate and deviate when attacking an adjustment problem.

A third view evaluates intelligent behavior in terms of its *practical results* to the individual concerned and to society. This definition is often called the *empirical* conception of intelligence. It has been stated by Thorndike [7] as the "power of good

[5] William Stern, *Psychological Methods of Testing Intelligence,* Baltimore, Warwick & York, Inc., 1914, p. 3.
[6] Alfred Binet, quoted in Lewis M. Terman, *The Measurement of Intelligence,* Boston, Houghton Mifflin Co., 1916, p. 45.
[7] E. L. Thorndike, in the symposium "Intelligence and Its Measurement," *op. cit.*

responses from the point of view of truth or fact." Pintner,[8] a former colleague of Thorndike's, has declared that "We must free ourselves from the idea that there is a specific faculty of intelligence. We must remember that intelligence is merely an evaluation of the efficiency of a reaction or a group of reactions under specific circumstances." Thorndike has also stressed what he believes to be three important aspects of intelligence, i.e., (1) *altitude,* or degree of ability to perform difficult tasks; (2) *breadth,* or the number of tasks of equal difficulty that can be mastered in a given period of time; and (3) *speed,* or the quickness with which responses to problems can be made. Many intelligence tests are so organized that their questions and problems become increasingly more difficult, and are so timed that only the brightest individuals have a chance of completing them in the time allotted. In this way both intellectual altitude and speed of response are measured. Here again intelligence is evaluated in terms of the efficiency and speed of mental reactions.

In an effort to assemble the most functional and logical qualities of the three views of intelligence portrayed above, Stoddard [9] has described *intelligence* as "the ability to undertake activities that are characterized by (1) difficulty, (2) complexity, (3) abstractness, (4) economy (speed), (5) adaptiveness to a goal, (6) social value, and (7) the emergence of originals (inventiveness), and to maintain such activities under conditions that demand a concentration of energy and a resistance to emotional forces." It can thus be said by way of summary that an individual is intelligent (at his age level) to the extent that he is able to think in the abstract, to discern relationships within difficult and complex problems or activities, to maintain a steady direction toward a goal with reasonable speed, to invent new solutions when necessary, to keep his activities within the range of normal social values, and to resist the pressures of emotional bias.

[8] Rudolph Pintner, "An Empirical View of Intelligence," *Journal of Educational Psychology,* 17 : 608-616 (1926).

[9] George D. Stoddard, *op. cit.,* p. 255. See also, by the same author, *The Meaning of Intelligence,* New York. The Macmillan Co., 1943.

Theories of the Nature of Intelligence.—The foregoing definitions of intelligence have stressed its function of enabling children to learn school subjects, to solve difficult problems with dispatch, and to adjust to the requirements of an orderly society. They have not, however, solved the fundamental problem of the nature of intelligence. Since both classroom practice and the selection of curricular materials to be learned are affected by the child's intellectual organization, much theorizing and considerable statistical research have been carried on. Three major points of view regarding the nature of intellectual functions have emerged as a result of such study. These will be briefly described.

SPEARMAN'S TWO-FACTOR THEORY. Spearman,[10] an English statistician, held that intelligence is for the most part a *general* ability, but that certain *special* abilities also exist. According to him, the general or *G* intellectual factor accounts for the positive relationships (correlations) which obtain between the mastery of the various school subjects (reading, arithmetic, language, etc.). Special abilities, called *s,* account for the lack of high relationships between musical, artistic, or motor or athletic skill and facility with language and other symbolic materials. Such special abilities are said to have little in common with the general or more closely integrated intellectual factor. The general factor is, however, fundamental to all intellectual activity and makes possible the discernment of relationships in problem solving. Spearman believed that his *G,* or general intellectual factor, measures a form of energy which is derived from the whole cortex or even wider area of the brain, and that the *s,* or special factors, measure the efficiency of different parts of the brain in which fractions of this energy may be concentrated.

Critics of the two-factor theory have maintained that a general factor is not necessary to an explanation of the observed relationships among intellectual abilities. They also believe that Spearman's doctrine of inherited general ability fails to make sufficient allowance for the influence of educational factors in

[10] C. Spearman, *The Nature of "Intelligence" and the Principles of Cognition,* New York, The Macmillan Co., 1923.

a child's environment. Some psychologists are also skeptical of the idea of brain localization of intellectual energy. The two-factor theory has, nevertheless, enjoyed wide recognition.

THORNDIKE'S QUANTITY OR SYNTHESIS THEORY. Thorndike, a leading American psychologist, has discounted the assumption that a general unitary factor underlies all mental ability, and has advanced the theory that intelligence is a summation of many specific and varied abilities. The high relationships (correlations) between various scholastic and other abstract aptitudes are explained by the presence of "common elements," or inner nervous system pathways, among them. Intelligence depends upon the quantity or number of physiological connections in the individual's brain. As Thorndike [11] reasons, "The person whose intellect is greater or higher or better than that of another person differs from him in the last analysis in having, not a new sort of physiological process, but simply a larger number of connections of the ordinary sort." This is the theory that intelligence, instead of representing a general ability, is a synthesis of mental capacity made possible by the presence of an adequate quantity of nerve connections.

While this theory explains the finding that many specific mental abilities are closely related and places intelligence on a physiological basis, it, too, suffers from a number of shortcomings. Probably most serious of these is the claim that amount of intelligence is dependent upon the number of brain and nervous system connections possessed. This deduction has been criticized for its attempt to assemble a total intellectual pattern from numerous discrete physiological connections. It has also been regarded as too mechanical to account for the flexible nature of even a child's intellectual activities.

THE MULTIPLE-FACTOR THEORY OF INTELLIGENCE. A number of modern statisticians have found what they believe to be groupings or clusters of more specialized mental abilities within the total pattern of intelligence, and have thus concluded that Spearman's G factor is not as unified as it has been al-

[11] E. L. Thorndike *et al.*, *The Measurement of Intelligence*, New York, Teachers College, Columbia Univ., 1927, p. 415.

leged to be. Kelley,[12] for example, has detected what he calls *multiple factors* within the so-called general intellectual factor. His statistically determined groupings of mental ability include (1) facility with numbers, (2) memorizing ability, (3) skill with verbal or reading materials, (4) facility with spacial (visual) relationships, and (5) speed of comprehension.

A later factor analysis study by Thurstone [13] has disclosed the presence of thirteen group factors, the following seven of which are said to represent "primary mental abilities": (1) visual or spacial ability, (2) logical or verbal-relations ability, (3) memory, (4) inductive ability, (5) perceptual speed, (6) ability to solve problems, and (7) deductive ability. These factors should not be confused with the older so-called "faculties" of the mind which assumed the presence of separate compartments for attention, reason, memory, imagination, and other functions. They are, rather, clusters of related abilities possessing degrees of uniqueness and independence somewhat similar to the uniqueness and independence of arms, legs, eyes, and ears in the total unity of the body.

Although popular at the present time, the multiple-factor theory of the nature of intelligence has been accused of going back by a statistical route to the outmoded notion of mind faculties. It is also said that, instead of being real groupings of ability, the factors represent mere statistical manipulation of Spearman's general factor. Some psychologists have doubted, as well, the adequacy of the basis for labelling seven of the factors "primary mental abilities."

The So-Called Kinds of Intelligence.—It has been noted that mental tests are concerned almost exclusively with the manipulation of language and other abstract symbols. There are, however, many other areas of endeavor—social, political, mechanical, artistic, and the like—in which problems requiring intelligent solutions constantly arise. Many individuals who appear mediocre in academic performances possess unusual abilities in mechanical pursuits or in dealing with people. Since

12 Truman L. Kelley, *Crossroads in the Mind of Man,* Stanford University, Stanford Univ. Press, 1928.
13 Louis L. Thurstone, *Primary Mental Abilities,* Chicago, Univ. of Chicago Press, 1938.

these areas of adjustment often involve problem solving ability of a high order which is not measured by traditional mental tests, it has been proposed that various kinds of intelligence be recognized. One such formulation by Thorndike, which includes *abstract, mechanical,* and *social* intelligence, has been widely accepted.

Abstract intelligence refers to ability to deal successfully with such symbolic materials as numbers, words, codes, geometric figures, and abstract principles. The academic curriculum of the school makes heavy demands upon this kind of intelligence and has thus come to dominate the content of mental tests. Mental tests are therefore not tests of "general" intelligence, they are rather measures of one area of intelligent behavior—the abstract or academic. This type of ability is highly essential in scientific, political, and financial activities where educational ideas, monetary systems, social orders, religious views, and political ideologies have their source.

Mechanical intelligence refers to ability to deal with concrete objects rather than with the words associated with them. Individuals of high mechanical aptitude often surpass their more "scholarly" colleagues in manipulating machinery and in coping with tests of mechanical ability. Such persons may be said to possess the mechanical type of ability. They are not, however, necessarily deficient in academic intelligence. It is probably from the ranks of such individuals that society recruits its inventors, engineers, surgeons, and soldiers.

Social intelligence refers to the use of psychological principles in problems involving human relations and the ability to influence people in desirable ways. Sincerity and discretion in dealing with people, the ability to make good impressions and to gain social acceptance, and skill in making others feel worthy and successful are among the criteria of social intelligence. Although everyone needs this type of ability, it is especially important to teachers, ministers, salesmen, public officials, and all others vested with the responsibility of leadership in social relations. Many people of moderate academic intelligence possess high social ability.

The Process of Intellectual Development

Theoretical discussions of intelligence have added little to knowledge concerning the actual course of mental development in infants and children. It is obvious, however, that the growing child makes increasingly complex and adaptive responses to his physical and social environment. His mental development is reflected in his performance of new acts, in his mastery of verbal skills, in his improved judgments, and in his increased capacity to make intelligent adjustments to social requirements. Children differ widely in rate of mental development but nearly all display improvements that can be observed and to some extent measured.

Until comparatively recently little information other than subjective judgments and empirical observations has been available touching this important aspect of child development. Much has been said about "stages" of mental growth and about the relative brightness of children, but it remained for objective studies to map the course usually taken by intellectual growth. There is, nevertheless, still considerable disagreement concerning the true nature of mental development.

Growth Curves of Intelligence.—Although it is impossible to ascertain the exact rate of mental development by the plotting of test scores, such a procedure provides important information regarding children's intellectual growth. Line graphs of this kind may be constructed from mental test norms for the various chronological ages or from data for individual tests repeated over a period of years.

Curves of Infant Development. Bayley [14] has made a study of mental development in infancy (first three years) in the case of 31 males and 30 females that is suggestive of the course of intellectual growth. The yearly increases in point scores on 185 items taken from scales by Kuhlmann, Gesell, and Jones are shown in Figure 44.

It can be seen that the mental growth of these infants was rapid to about the ninth or tenth month, after which a degree

[14] Nancy Bayley, *Mental Growth During the First Three Years,* Genetic Psychology Monographs, Vol. 14, No. 1 (1933), pp. 1-92.

of deceleration set in which was maintained to the third year. Bayley was not able, however, to predict individual infant development from one age to another, and thus concluded "that the behavior growth of the early months of infant development has little predictive relation to the later development of intelligence." This finding is based on the fact that the tasks required in infant tests are largely of a motor nature and thus unlike the more verbal problems included in tests of the Binet

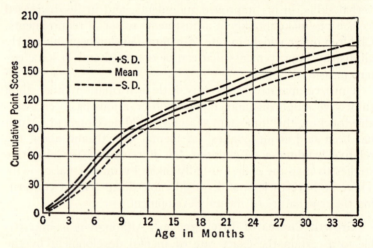

Figure 44. Mental Growth Curve in Terms of Cumulative Point Scores
(From Nancy Bayley, *Mental Growth During the First Three Years*, Genetic Psychology Monographs, Vol. 14, No. 1 (1933), p. 39.)

type for older children. Some psychologists [15] have also questioned whether infant tests are reliable at the extremes of the age ranges for which they are designed. It is thus possible that, in spite of the recent finding that certain individual test items located at six and at twelve months points on the scale correlate better with later I.Q. than total test scores, there are no reliable tests of infant mental development.

Curves constructed from mental test norms for older children frequently show a tendency toward deceleration after the

[15] Virginia L. Nelson and T. W. Richards, "Studies in Mental Development: Performances of Twelve-Months-Old Children on the Gesell Schedule, and Its Predictive Value for Mental Status at Two and Three Years," *Pedagogical Seminary and Journal of Genetic Psychology*, 54 : 181-191 (1939).

sixth or seventh year. This is particularly true of the Detroit First-Grade Intelligence Test shown in Figure 45. Similar growth curves have been found in the case of such measures as the Dearborn and the Haggerty intelligence tests. The norms for a number of other intelligence tests do not, however, yield the type of curve noted in Figure 45. It is believed that such a discrepancy can be explained by methods used in the selection of test items and by selective factors which may have crept into the sampling of children upon which a given test was standardized.

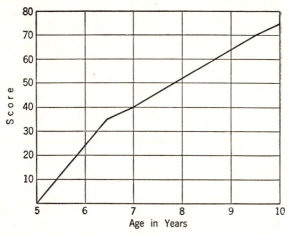

Figure 45. Norms for Children Aged Five to Ten on the Detroit First-Grade Intelligence Test

MASS VERSUS INDIVIDUAL LONGITUDINAL GROWTH CURVES. As in the case of growth in height, curves derived from averages of the mental development of a group of children and those for repeated tests of individual children display somewhat different characteristics. As can be seen from Figure 46, curves indicating the mental development of a group of over two hundred children tend to proceed in a fairly straight line with slight accelerations at about ages ten or eleven for superior boys and girls and somewhat later for those of average I.Q. But again, as in the case of physical growth, more marked fluctuations of individual children are obscured by the leveling influence of average mental age figures. This tendency was in

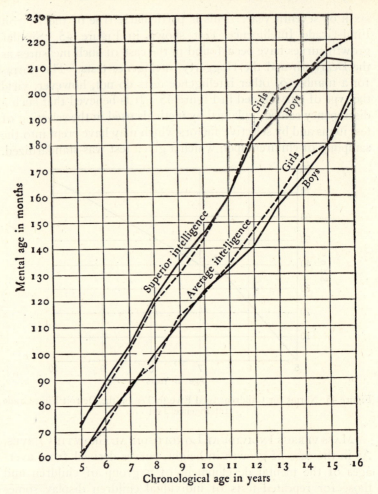

Figure 46. Growth in Mental Age as Shown in Consecutive Stanford-Binet Tests of 207 Average and Superior Children

(From B. T. Baldwin and L. I. Stecher, "Additional Data from Consecutive Stanford-Binet Tests," *Journal of Educational Psychology,* 13:558 (1922).)

evidence in a more recent study [16] of English children ranging from six to fourteen years of age (extended by extrapolation

[16] C. A. Richardson and C. W. Stokes, *The Growth and Variability of Intelligence,* British Journal of Psychology, Monograph Supplement No. 18, Cambridge Univ. Press, 1933.

from birth to age twenty-four), who showed an inflection point around four years of age and a fairly marked deceleration at about thirteen.

That individual mental development fluctuates more than mass data curves would indicate has been demonstrated by Free-

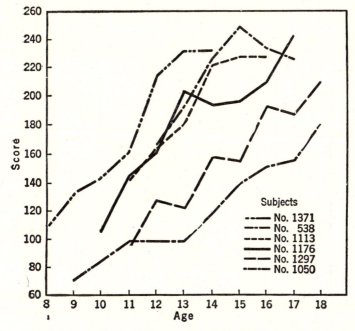

Figure 47. A Miscellaneous Group of Individual Growth Curves of Six Subjects

(From F. N. Freeman and C. D. Flory, *Growth in Intellectual Ability as Measured by Repeated Tests,* Monographs of the Society for Research in Child Development, Vol. 2, No. 2 (1937), p. 62.)

man and Flory [17] in a study utilizing repeated individual tests (Figure 47). The individual curves display marked differences in pattern of intellectual development. They also show marked deviations from the traditional average-for-a-group mental age growth curves.

[17] F. N. Freeman and C. D. Flory, *Growth in Intellectual Ability as Measured by Repeated Tests,* Monographs of the Society for Research in Child Development, Vol. 2. No. 2 (1937).

Courtis [18] has asserted that individual mental development parallels growth in height, manifesting the same growth cycles and showing roughly similar degrees of acceleration and deceleration. According to him, it is the cyclic nature of mental growth and not the unreliability of intelligence tests that makes the I.Q. vary at given stages of growth. General growth determines the rate of intellectual development, except as extraneous (environmental) forces operate to change the *biologically potential rate of growth*. How much evidence Courtis can bring

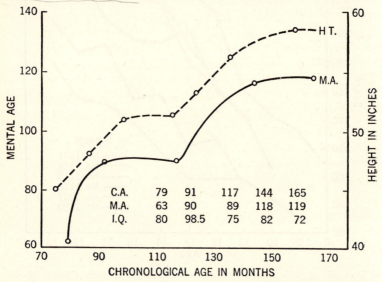

C.A.	79	91	117	144	165
M.A.	63	90	89	118	119
I.Q.	80	98.5	75	82	72

Figure 48. The Relation Between Physical and Mental Development

(From S. A. Courtis, "Major Growth Concepts," in *Pupil Development and the Curriculum*, Bureau of Educational Reference and Research, Univ. of Michigan, 1937-38, p. 63.)

to bear on his theory of concomitant development is not clear. He has, nevertheless, presented a number of such individual cases as the one shown in Figure 48.

CONCLUSIONS CONCERNING GROWTH CURVES.   In spite of the apparent reliability of the indices of mental growth pre-

18 S. A. Courtis, "Maturation as a Factor in Diagnosis," in *Educational Diagnosis, Thirty-Fourth Yearbook, National Society for the Study of Education*. 1935, pp. 169-187.

sented in the above figures, it is a question whether the true rates of such development can be inferred from them. This is because scores yielded by mental tests do not represent absolute measurements in which the size of units of measurement at various points on the scale are necessarily equivalent. In other words, a year's mental growth, even in the case of a normal child, may not be the same between any two successive years. Since mental test norms (average performances) are based on the demonstrated abilities of children of various ages, it may be that a year's gain, for example, between eleven and twelve represents a greater (or smaller) intellectual increment than that between five and six. Young children are measured in relation to mental activities much less complicated than those demanded of older children, thus the possibility exists that the difficulties of different units on the measurement scale are far from being equivalent. If this be true, repeated tests and curves representing scores made on them do not reflect the actual amount of intellectual development made by the subjects concerned. Thurstone,[19] a statistician, has devised a method of "absolute" scaling which promises to obviate some of the shortcomings of the cruder measures of development. Such a technique was utilized in the previously mentioned study of childhood and early "teen age" development by Richardson and Stokes.

Although no definite pattern of the mental development of children has been established, a few trends appear to have emerged from the researches reported in this field. It can be said that individual children differ markedly in both rate and pattern of intellectual growth, and also that curves of individual development diverge noticeably from those depicting the average increments of growth of groups of children. It can, however, be stated that, in a very general sense, infancy and the preschool years are characterized by rapid mental development, that growth is fairly even but with some deceleration during the elementary school years, and that slight acceleration is in evidence around the time of the onset of puberty.

[19] Louis L. Thurstone and Luton Ackerson, "The Mental Growth Curve for the Binet Tests," *Journal of Educational Psychology*, 20: 569-583 (1929).

Theories Concerning the End of Growth.—There has been considerable controversy over the question of when mental growth, or the ability to solve increasingly more difficult intellectual problems, comes to its complete fruition. It has been maintained for years by some psychologists that the peak of mental growth (Thorndike's mental *altitude*) is reached at approximately ages fourteen to sixteen. On this basis adolescents in their early teens would be as capable intellectually (though much less experienced) as normal adults. That such is the case has been claimed by a number of investigators. Yerkes [20] believed, for example, that the mental test records of 93,965 white soldiers (World War I) pointed to an average adult mental age of 13.08, and that intellectual maturity is thus reached in the early phases of adolescence.

In connection with his first revision of the Binet mental scale, Terman [21] for years maintained that age sixteen marks the upper level of intellectual development. Because of considerable criticism directed against this conclusion, and as a result of researches leading to the publication of a second revision (1937) of the Binet scale, Terman [22] has recently placed the upper limit of development at age 15, with the assertion that only one year's growth occurs between ages thirteen and fifteen. In harmony with these hypotheses is the contention of Spearman,[23] author of the two-factor theory of the nature of intelligence, that "evidence clearly indicates that the growth of *G* certainly does not continue to any appreciable amount after the ages of fourteen or sixteen, and perhaps even ceases some years earlier."

Contrasted with these conclusions are those of an equally able group of investigators who believe that their evidence points to a greater prolongation of mental development. A

[20] Robert M. Yerkes, "Psychological Examining in the United States Army," *Memoirs of the Academy of Sciences,* Vol. 15, Washington, D. C., Government Printing Office, 1921.
[21] Lewis M. Terman, *The Measurement of Intelligence,* Boston, Houghton Mifflin Co., 1916.
[22] Lewis M. Terman and M. A. Merrill, *Measuring Intelligence,* Boston, Houghton Mifflin Co., 1937.
[23] C. Spearman, *The Abilities of Man,* New York, The Macmillan Co., 1922. p. 364.

study by Jones and Conrad,[24] employing the same Army Alpha test utilized by Yerkes, but in this case with something over 1,000 rural subjects, suggested that mental growth is linear to approximately age sixteen, with some deceleration to a culmination at about twenty, and, as shown in Figure 49, with a slow decline in mental ability through adult life. Freeman's [25] study of the upper limits of mental development also showed

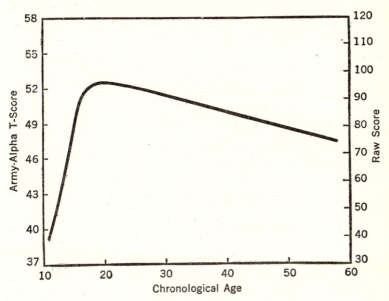

Figure 49. Smoothed Curve of Growth and Decline of Army Alpha Test Scores for 1,191 Subjects, Aged 10 to 60

(From Harold E. Jones and H. S. Conrad, *The Growth and Decline of Intelligence: A Study of a Homogeneous Group Between the Ages of Ten and Sixty,* Genetic Psychology Monographs, Vol. 13, No. 3 (1933), p. 241.)

that (1) the intellectual growth curve diminishes only slightly in rate from eight years to fifteen or sixteen years of age, and that (2) intellectual growth continues at least to twenty years

[24] Harold E. Jones and H. S. Conrad, *The Growth and Decline of Intelligence: A Study of a Homogeneous Group Between the Ages of Ten and Sixty,* Genetic Psychology Monographs, Vol. 13, No. 3 (1933), pp. 223-298. See also, by the same authors, "Mental Development in Adolescence," *Forty-Third Yearbook, National Society for the Study of Education,* 1944, Part I, pp. 146-163.

[25] F. N. Freeman and C. D. Flory, *Growth in Intellectual Ability as Measured by Repeated Tests,* Monographs of the Society for Research in Child Development, Vol. 2, No. 2 (1937).

and probably beyond. (page 86) An elaborate investigation of both child and adult intelligence by Miles [26] corroborated the thesis that development continues to at least age eighteen and shows a slight decline to the time of senescence.

Probably the most widely publicized research on intellectual growth and decline is the one by Thorndike [27] in which he found increased support for the hypothesis of prolonged development. He concludes that there is no basis for the claim that "gain in altitude of intellect of the sort measured by existing intelligence tests is zero after fourteen, . . . or even after sixteen. It decreases, but it should not become inappreciable until eighteen or later. According to our results, the decrease from fourteen to eighteen is not an abrupt slowing up of a gain that has been made hitherto, but is part of a general negative acceleration (deceleration) which began long before the age of six and one-half." Thorndike's study, which also suggested that mental development reaches well into the twenties, has been criticized for allegedly not eliminating a selective factor which gave his older and more experienced candidates an advantage that could not be measured by test of so-called "pure" intelligence.

It is apparent that psychologists are not agreed on the time of cessation of mental growth. This is not surprising when it is realized that mental test scores are markedly influenced by educational opportunities or a lack thereof, and in view of the uncertainty of the nature of intelligence. It seems logical to conclude, however, that those who have found evidence for development to the age of eighteen and possibly the early twenties, merit as much consideration as those who believe that ages fourteen to sixteen represent the peak of altitudinal growth. A scrutiny of Figures 47 and 48 will show that individual growth curves sometimes continue their upward trend at least to age eighteen, and that some curves (of averages) for both normal and superior children are for the most part still continuing their

[26] C. C. Miles and W. R. Miles, "The Correlation of Intelligence Scores and Chronological Age from Early to Late Maturity," *American Journal of Psychology,* 44 : 44-78 (1932).

[27] E. L. Thorndike *et al., op. cit.* See also by the same author, *Adult Learning.* New York, The Macmillan Co., 1928.

linear rate of acceleration at age sixteen, with no indications of suddenly becoming horizontal. It is perhaps safe to say, thus, that intellectual maturing continues to the eighteenth year and possibly into the early twenties.

Data on Fluctuations in Mental Development.—Turning to recent objective studies, we find many of them testifying that mental growth is not as a rule steady.[28] Prominent among longitudinal studies is that by Freeman and Flory[29] in which 469 children were tested at yearly intervals from ages eight to sixteen with a specially selected group of mental tests which were so organized as to involve practically uniform units of difficulty over the age range in question. The investigators found marked individual differences in patterns of mental growth in the case of children who were available for testing for a period of six or more years. Relationships between test scores for the same individual given five to ten years apart were so low that it was impossible to predict later mental ability (I.Q.) from test scores made at an early age. The brighter children tended to develop more rapidly than those of either average or dull status in the preadolescent period, but not at later ages.

Wellman[30] has published similar data pertaining to the fluctuations in I.Q. of a group of children who were tested repeatedly from preschool days through high school and in college. As Table 17 shows, not only marked individual differences in rates of mental growth but great fluctuations in I.Q. scores occurred. According to Wellman, "These children illustrate some of the more extreme amounts of gain, but otherwise they are not atypical. They were members of a fairly large group in which most of the children made large gains in I.Q."

[28] Ralph H. Ojemann, K. C. Garrison, and Kai Jensen, "Mental Development from Birth to Maturity," *Review of Educational Research,* Vol. 11, No. 5 (Dec. 1941), Ch. 2. See also Ch. 2 of the same journal in Vol. 9, No. 1 (Feb. 1939).

[29] F. N. Freeman and C. D. Flory, *op. cit.* See also F. N. Freeman, "Intellectual Growth of Children as Indicated by Repeated Tests," *Psychological Studies of Human Variables,* Psychological Monographs, Vol. 47, No. 2 (1936), pp. 20-34.

[30] Beth L. Wellman, "Our Changing Concept of Intelligence," *Journal of Consulting Psychology,* 2: 97-107 (1938). By permission.

TABLE 17. CHANGES IN I.Q. OF CHILDREN ATTENDING AN "UNUSUALLY" STIMULATING ELEMENTARY SCHOOL

Age at Test, Years	Intelligence Quotient			
	Child 1	Child 2	Child 3	Child 4
3	89			
3½	118	98	98	124
4	128	120		135
4½	129	145	109	137
5	119	167		146
5½			126	144
6	117		125	143
6½				
7	140		134	
7½				
8				
8½	135			
9		155		148
9½				160
10		143	153	
10½	149			165
11	130	152		
11½				
12	139	143		154
12½				
13		(100C)		
13½	132			
14				(99C)
14½				
15	(99C)		(99C)	
15½				
16				
16½				
17			(93U)	
17½				
18	(99U)			

(From Beth L. Wellman, "Our Changing Concept of Intelligence," *Journal of Consulting Psychology,* 2:98 (1938).) By permission.

In connection with the Harvard Growth Study, Lincoln [31] showed that there is a greater tendency for I.Q. changes to occur when the time interval between the two tests is relatively long. The average fluctuation, when retests were given within one year, was 6 points; within six years, it was 9 points. The

[31] Edward A. Lincoln, "Stanford-Binet I.Q. Changes in the Harvard Growth Study," *Journal of Applied Psychology,* 20: 236–242 (1936).

greater average change, 9 points, was made by superior children of above 120 I.Q. Marked fluctuations in individual gains were also made by a group of 140 elementary school children studied by Pintner and Stanton,[32] who were tested annually for periods of from two to six years. Such fluctuations, as well as individual differences in fluctuation, are graphically represented by another author in Figure 50.

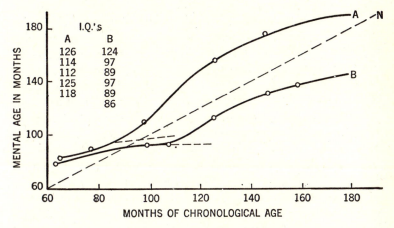

Figure 50. Comparison of the Mental Development Curves of Two Children Showing How Cycles Occur at Different Times

(From S. A. Courtis, "Major Growth Concepts," in *Pupil Development and the Curriculum,* Bureau of Educational Reference and Research, Univ. of Michigan, 1937-38, p. 64.)

It should not be supposed, however, that all investigators point to marked fluctuations of the intelligence quotient with repeated tests. A number of recent researches have reported in favor of constancy.[33] Gesell[34] has, in fact, concluded from a ten-year longitudinal mental growth study of 30 children that

[32] Rudolph Pintner and Mildred Stanton, "Repeated Tests with the CAVD Scale," *Journal of Educational Psychology,* 28 : 494-500 (1937).

[33] See, for example, Irving Lorge and Leta S. Hollingworth, "Adult Status of Highly Intelligent Children," *Pedagogical Seminary and Journal of Genetic Psychology,* 49 : 215-226 (1936) ; Grace Arthur, "The Predictive Value of the Kuhlmann-Binet Scale for a Partially Americanized School Population," *Journal of Applied Psychology,* 21 : 359-364 (1937) ; and Arnold Gesell, "Some Observations of Developmental Stability," *Psychological Studies of Human Variabilities,* Psychological Monographs, Vol. 47, No. 2 (1936), pp. 35-46.

[34] Arnold Gesell, "The Stability of Mental Growth Careers," *Thirty-Ninth Yearbook, National Society for the Study of Education,* 1940, Part II, pp. 149-160.

their infant behavior patterns were "prophetic" of later growth careers. While such investigations should be examined with care they cannot entirely outweigh conflicting evidence that I.Q. scores do, under certain conditions, change from year to year.

The reader will perhaps have noticed that the mental development of preschool children presents more fluctuations than that of older children. The reason for this finding is not entirely clear, but may be due to the relative unreliability of infant intelligence tests or to the difficulty of setting up standard testing conditions in their case. It is much more difficult to secure maximum effort and to control such influential factors as timidity, negativism, and lack of interest in the case of younger children than it is with those whose additional maturity enables them to behave in a more socialized and cooperative way. Fluctuations in mental age during the early years exert more influence on the I.Q. than do those appearing at a later age. It has been calculated, for example, that a mental age fluctuation of six months at the age of three results in an I.Q. change of 17 points, whereas at the age of eight, only a 6-point difference results from such a change. Many would contend, nevertheless, that both the increased fluctuations in mental growth and the more rapid development noted in the first four or five years are the logical result of the young child's relatively greater susceptibility to stimulating educational influences. It should thus be apparent that we have no reliable means of measuring the growth of intelligence during the first or even the first two years of life.[35]

Interpretations of Mental Development.—An individual's interpretation of the nature of mental growth is to a considerable extent contingent upon his views concerning what is and what is not biologically inherited. Those who believe that intelligence is an innate, inherited capacity dependent upon quality and quantity of nervous structure (brain and central ner-

[35] See G. P. Driscoll, *The Developmental Status of the Preschool Child as a Prognosis of Future Development*, Child Development Monographs, No. 13 (1933). Also P. H. Furfey and J. Muehlenbein, "The Validity of Infant Intelligence Tests," *Pedagogical Seminary and Journal of Genetic Psychology*, 40 : 219-223 (1932).

vous system) are likely to think of mental age at any point of development as an accompaniment of nervous system maturation (growth). This is the previously mentioned view advanced by Courtis when he maintained that mental growth patterns parallel physical growth (in height) cycles as a matter of innate tendency. It is also implicit in Gesell's often mentioned declaration that maturation, as inner growth, is principally responsible for the orderly appearance, not only of motor abilities, but of linguistic skills as well.

It will be recognized that the above view minimizes the influence of schooling and other favorable experiences on mental development. Considerable evidence was presented in Chapter 3 touching the doubtfulness of such a position. Furthermore, as the next section of the present chapter will indicate, only slight relationships have been found between various aspects of physical and mental growth. It is for these reasons, and the further fact that knowledge is not innate no matter how great a child's heritage may be claimed to be, that an increasing number of investigators are considering the possibility that mental age may represent primarily the accumulation of all such information of the mental test variety as has been made possible by the type of educational environment encountered by the individual from infancy.

Such a point of view permits the possibility that under unusually favorable circumstances a child's mental growth might be stimulated to progress somewhat beyond the limits supposedly set by maturational factors. Intellectual immaturity could, on this basis, be ascribed, in part at least, to lack of experience and educational opportunity. Barring defects of nervous, glandular, or other structures, mental development would go forward to the extent that social and scholastic opportunities permitted, while physical growth proceeded in harmony with age, nutritional status, and inner growth potentials. A glance at the five individual growth curves plotted in Figure 51 suggests that this probably is what actually happens.

This is not to say that nature sets no limits to a given child's intellectual possibilities or that no mental defects exist which cannot be overcome by the stimulating effects of a favorable

home and school environment. That such limitations are sometimes in evidence is well known to all, and these should be taken
into account by parents and teachers in their plans for child
guidance. But for the great majority of children it appears
likely that achievements, scholastic and otherwise, are somewhat

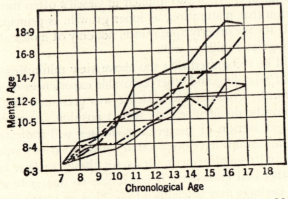

Figure 51. Variability in Mental Growth of Five Boys Whose Mental Test
Scores and Intelligence Quotients Were Equivalent at Age 7

(From W. F. Dearborn and J. W. M. Rothney, *Predicting the Child's Development*,
Cambridge (Mass.), Sci-Art Publishers, 1941, p. 329.)

below capacity as it would be determined by a vital educational
environment. This statement can be made whether the environment hastens the tempo of mental development or whether it
merely operates to assist the child in accumulating the kind of
information demanded by most verbal intelligence tests.

The Relation Between Physical and Mental Growth

A great many studies have been made concerning the degree of relationship existing between mental development and
various aspects of physical growth. As in related fields, practically all of the older investigations [36] were conducted by the
method of finding averages and computing cross-sectional relationships among groups of children. The trend of the evidence secured was toward positive but low correlations, usually

[36] Donald G. Paterson, *Physique and Intellect*, New York, D. Appleton-
Century Co., Inc., 1930. See also Harold E. Jones, "Relationships in Physical
and Mental Development," *Review of Educational Research*, Vol. 3 : 150-162
(Apr. 1933) ; also Vol. 6 : 102-123 (Feb. 1936) and Vol. 14 : 394 (Dec. 1944).

below .30, and very commonly between .10 and .20. This finding was in evidence whether one measure of physical growth (height, weight, dentition, etc.) or a combination of physical developmental data was compared with one measure of mental status. All of the figures were so low as to suggest little relationship. That is to say, knowledge of a child's degree of physical development was of practically no value in determining his present or future mental status or vice versa. Paterson,[37] who has made a thorough review of the studies to 1930, concluded from his findings that, "Our detailed survey of available quantitative evidence has demonstrated that prevalent notions regarding the intimacy of the relationship between physical traits and intellect have been greatly exaggerated. Search in the realm of gross anatomy for a physical correlate of intellect has yielded uniformly negative results. It appears that such structural characteristics as height and weight are correlated only slightly with intelligence, narrowly defined."

Structural Development and Intelligence.—A scrutiny of the newer studies concerning physical-mental growth relationships shows that they tend to use longitudinal methods, also that they have utilized more refined statistical techniques than was formerly the case. These investigations have not, however, resulted in any particularly new or startling findings.

Boynton and Parsons [38] have reported a research in which relationships between intelligence and height, weight, morphological index (height-weight ratio), lung capacity, and head circumference were determined for four groups of children from nine to twelve years of age. It was believed that these children were old enough to be studied with a high degree of accuracy and young enough to have missed the greater increments of growth associated with the onset of puberty. The correlations computed, of which there were forty, were all low, with an average (median) of .175. This meager relationship, although positive, was rightly considered too slight to be of value in individual diagnosis or prediction. A graphic representation

[37] Donald G. Paterson, *op. cit.*, p. 269.
[38] Paul L. Boynton and R. F. Parsons, "Pupil Analysis in the Peabody Demonstration School," *George Peabody College Bulletin*, 1935.

of such interlocked but loosely related development is provided in Figure 52, which illustrates (by the longitudinal method) the diverse patternality of various forms of physical growth as these are related to mental development.

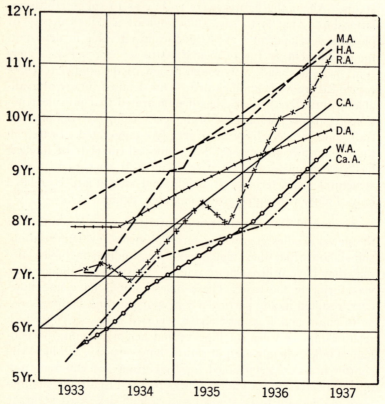

Figure 52. "Average" Growth with Rapid Change in an Extroverted Boy

Abbreviations refer to mental age, height age, reading age, chronological age, dental age, weight age, and carpal age.

(From Willard C. Olson, "The Concept of the Organism as a Whole," in *Pupil Development and the Curriculum*, Bureau of Educational Reference and Research, Univ. of Michigan, 1937-38, p. 97.)

An extensive longitudinal research dealing with correlations between mental and physical growth among 178 girls and 179 boys in the Laboratory Schools of the University of Chicago, in which measurements were obtained at successive birthdays, has been published by Abernethy.[39] From ages eight to seventeen correlations between intelligence test scores and height were all positive but low, with an average of .26 for boys and .16 for girls. Of the various measures studied, standing height was the most closely related to intelligence. Coefficients of correlation for intelligence as related to sitting height, weight, ossification ratio, chest girth, and lung capacity were all positive but slight. Although the pattern of mental development was similar for boys and girls, they differed in rate of physical maturing and in degree of relationships between physical and mental development (girls being lower than boys). Mental-physical growth relationships for students of college age were close to zero, thus suggesting that such relationships become smaller with advancing age.

Both of these findings were corroborated and supplemented by a similar investigation [40] at the University of California utilizing 127 boys and 125 girls ranging in age from twenty-one months to seven years. Scores from the California Preschool Mental Scale (used to age five) and the Stanford-Binet scale (used for six- and seven-year-olds) correlated only slightly with physical growth. At age seven, intelligence test scores correlated .19 with height and .16 with weight, with no sex differences in evidence. Dennis [41] has also found that, contrary to popular belief, gifted children begin to walk at approximately the same age as those of normal mental ability. There was again no significant relationship between structural and mental development.

Relationships between intelligence and athletic ability also tend to be low. In a study of 290 college students, one investigator [42] found practically zero correlations (ranging from

[39] M. E. Abernethy, *Relationships Between Mental and Physical Growth,* Monographs of the Society for Research in Child Development, Vol. 1, No. 17 (1936).

[40] Marjorie P. Honzik and Harold E. Jones, "Mental-Physical Relationships during the Preschool Period," *Journal of Experimental Education,* 4 : 139-146 (1937).

[41] Wayne Dennis, "On the Possibility of Advancing and Retarding the Motor Development of Infants," *Psychological Review,* 50 : 203-208 (1943).

[42] Vincent G. Di Giovanna, "A Comparison of the Intelligence and Athletic Ability of College Men," *Research Quarterly of the American Assn. for Health and Physical Education,* 8 : 96-106 (Oct. 1937). Also J. C. Seegers and O. Postpichal, "Relation Between Intelligence and Certain Aspects of Physical Ability," *Journal of Educational Research,* 30 : 104-109 (1936).

In interpreting investigations relating to the greater incidence of physical defects of various kinds among mentally retarded children, it should not be supposed that the relationships found are high. They are, in fact, usually low. However, no evidence is available proving that physical defects contribute to the lowering of intelligence. No *cause and effect* relationship has as yet been found between these factors. It may be that neither intelligence nor physical abnormality affects the other, but that a more fundamental factor (or factors) is responsible for both physical abnormalities and mental retardation. It could be reasoned that children suffering from physical deficiencies tend to come from the more impoverished communities where less attention is given to the correction of such defects than would be the case with more economically and socially favored groups. It is further possible that the more barren environments fail to provide the kind of nutrition, child care, and educationally stimulating experiences calculated to engender both physical development and intellectual growth. In short, a multiplicity of factors and agencies may cause either physical defects or mental retardation, or both. No simple one-for-one or factor-to-factor relationship can be found in these areas of child development.

A few general relationships have, nevertheless, been noted between birth injuries and subsequent intellectual status. In summarizing the apparent effects of birth trauma, Doll *et al.*[48] state that they include early mortality, minor physical damage which is later outgrown, motor (neuromuscular) handicaps of varying degrees of severity, serious behavior disorders, and mental deficiency. To this evidence has been added that found by Katz [49] in a study of cerebral birth trauma sustained during labor and delivery. According to this investigator, such injury may be associated with not only feeblemindedness, but disturbances such as spastic paralysis, epilepsy, convulsions, and schizophrenia.

[48] Edgar A. Doll, W. M. Phelps, and R. T. Melcher, *Mental Deficiency Due to Birth Injuries,* New York, The Macmillan Co., 1932.
[49] Barney Katz, *The Etiology of the Deteriorating Psychoses of Adolescence and Early Adult Life,* Doctoral Dissertation, The Univ. of Southern California, 1939.

Implications for the Study of Growth.—The finding that relationships between the various aspects of physical and mental growth are almost uniformly low has led students of child development to seek explanations in harmony with the concept of the unitary nature of the human individual. Psychologists have endeavored to reconcile the indifferent relationship between children's intelligence and their degree of physical development at any point on the growth scale with the fact that the child as a whole is always an organic unity.

Some psychologists,[50] have suggested an *organismic* approach in which changes in magnitude and relationship of the various body structures and their functions be determined as accurately as possible in relation to growth. According to this view, all forms of growth, although apparently developing at somewhat different rates, are interrelated on the basis of an internal *dynamic balance.* H. E. Jones [51] has offered a somewhat similar hypothesis—that a common factor or group of factors may favor the development, though uneven, of the *total* organism. To these explanations may be added the hypothesis that educational opportunities and other social stimuli may influence the development of intelligence while exerting little effect on structural growth. The presence or absence of satisfactory nutrition and other health factors could also affect physical development in a variety of ways. When the extent of fluctuation in the experience of a given child of both social and physical factors is concerned, it is little wonder that coefficients of correlation between mental and physical development are low.

These considerations have tended to discourage the tendency to regard the child's organism as an aggregation of parts having little effect upon one another's growth and function. They have led to a recognition of the fact that growth, in spite of its diversity, is unitary in the sense that a dynamic balance of some kind maintains its organismic nature. A quotation

---

[50] Lawrence K. Frank, "Structure, Function, and Growth," *Philosophy of Science,* 2 : 210-235 (1935) ; Willard C. Olson and Byron O. Hughes, "Growth of the Child as a Whole," in *Child Behavior and Development* (edited by Roger G. Barker *et al.*), New York, McGraw-Hill Book Co., Inc., 1943, Ch. 12.

[51] Harold E. Jones, "Relationships in Physical and Mental Development," *Review of Educational Research,* Vol. 9, No. 1 (1939), p. 91.

children (who have no congenital or other defects which prevent development) have the capacity for change and adaptation, and that much can be done under favorable conditions to promote their development. As one psychologist [53] has stated the matter, "If I have a healthy infant in front of me, I can prepare him for life without knowing about his heredity. Just what effect heredity had in determining the nature of the organism is beside the point. Here is an organism which is capable of many changes, and if I supply the right kind and amount of environmental stimulation, I can accomplish a given end result." Such a statement is not intended to imply that there are no limits to a given child's educability, but rather that pliability and adaptability are primary characteristics of young organisms.

THE UNRELIABILITY OF INFANT TESTS.   Many misunderstandings have arisen because of failure to recognize the unreliability of infant mental tests. The many controversies concerning the intellectual benefits of foster home placement of young children hinge in part on this question. It is therefore important that the facts in the case be as thoroughly ascertained as possible. Some of these have already been mentioned on previous pages. It might well be added that the unreliability of infant tests is relatively proportional to the length of the time-span between their administration. One investigator,[54] for example, noted that the Bühler [55] *Baby Tests* were fairly consistent when given within a few days of each other but that they yielded very inconsistent results when administered several months apart. The same was true [56] of the Linfert-Hierholzer [57] scale when given to three groups of six-, nine-, and twelve-months-old infants—the scores correlated only to the

[53] Milton Metfessel, "Relationships of Heredity and Environment in Behavior," *Journal of Psychology*, 10 : 177-198 (1940).
[54] Amanda Herring, "An Experimental Study of the Reliability of the Bühler Baby Tests," *Journal of Experimental Education*, 6 : 147-160 (1937).
[55] Charlotte Bühler and Hildegard Hetzer, *Testing Children's Development from Birth to School Age* (trans. by H. Beaumont), New York, Farrar & Rinehart, Inc., 1935.
[56] Paul H. Furfey and J. Muehlenbein, "The Validity of Infant Intelligence Tests," *Journal of Genetic Psychology*, 40 : 219-223 (1932).
[57] Harriette E. Linfert and Helen M. Hierholzer, "A Scale for Measuring the Mental Development of Infants During the First Year of Life," *Studies in Psychology and Psychiatry*, Catholic Univ. of America, Vol. 1, No. 4 (1928).

extent of —.11, —.34, and —.20 with the Stanford-Binet scale administered to the same children when they had reached the age of four.

These results should not be surprising when it is realized that infant tests are necessarily largely confined to the measurement of sensorimotor responses. Reactions of this kind have never been adequate as indices of intelligence in the case of older children (and youths), and can thus hardly be expected to

Figure 53. Three-Months-Old Infant Inspects His Fingers—Watches the Movement of His Own Hands

(From W. Rand, M. E. Sweeny, and E. L. Vincent, *Growth and Development of the Young Child*, W. B. Saunders Co., 1940, p. 32.)

yield results similar to those elicited by verbal tests of the Binet type. This point has been well summarized by Bayley,[58] a student of infant development, in these words: "Infant intelligence tests have been devised and standardized on the assumptions that the maturation in sensorimotor functions and simple adaptations are intellectual and should be predictive of later intellectual performances. However, it does not necessarily follow that individuals whose sensory acuity is great and whose simple coordinations are perfected more rapidly will eventually

[58] Nancy Bayley, *Mental Growth During the First Three Years*, Genetic Psychology Monographs, Vol. 14, No. 1 (1933), pp. 1-92.

be able to respond more adequately to complex [intellectual] situations."

A recent test of infant intelligence by Cattell [59] has been patterned after the revised Stanford-Binet scale (ages two to adult), and is said to secure results more nearly comparable to those obtained in the case of older children. It consists of five regular test items (and one or two alternates) at each of fourteen difficulty levels appropriate for infants ranging from two to thirty months in age. The examinations upon which the scale is based were part of a series of comprehensive observations of children enrolled from birth in the child hygiene department of a university. The test is said to be a downward extension of the Terman-Merrill revision of the Stanford-Binet Scale, which yields comparable mental ages and intelligence quotients. Test items include following a ring in horizontal motion, inspecting fingers, folding sheets of paper, and the like.

DETERMINING RELIABILITY AND VALIDITY.   A valid mental test is so constructed that its questions and problems avoid the influence of specific training, sex differences, technical information, special talents, and other specialized factors. Well-standardized tests are constructed from materials believed to be common to the general environment of the children to whom they are to be administered.

This means that in addition to possessing other criteria, a good mental test must be both reliable and valid. Its *reliability* is indicated by the extent to which it yields a consistent estimate of a child's (or other individual's) mental ability when administered more than once with a short interval intervening. Test reliability may also be ascertained by consistency of results when two halves (split halves or odd versus even numbers) or two comparable forms of a test are given separately. A test is regarded as being *valid* if it measures what it purports to measure in relation to some criterion outside of itself. In the case of mental tests, the usual criterion has been success in school subjects or in other activities of a distinctly linguistic or symbolic nature. Other criteria of test validity include inter-correlations between one test and the averages of others, and the extent to which a test produces an average I.Q. of 100 for the various school grades. Current standards of validity do not approximate perfection, but data for reliability have frequently indicated relatively high statistical relationships between two administrations of a test.

THE HETEROGENEITY OF CHILDREN WITH IDENTICAL I.Q.'s. It has commonly been supposed that children of identical or approximately the same I.Q. possess similar mental ability. Elementary school pupils grouped in classifications varying from five to ten points in range have been regarded as being

TABLE 18. THE HETEROGENEITY OF 25 PUPILS WITH IDENTICAL I.Q.'s OF 106

Factors	Ranges in Months
1. Memory ability.......	120 months M.A. to 180 months M.A., or 60 months of M.A.
2. Spacial or visualization ability	101 months M.A. to 180 months M.A., or 79 months of M.A.
3. Reasoning ability.....	130 months M.A. to 159 months M.A., or 29 months of M.A.
4. Verbal ability........	98 months M.A. to 156 months M.A., or 58 months of M.A.
5. Language ability......	120 months M.A. to 149 months M.A., or 29 months of M.A.
6. Non-language ability..	121 months M.A. to 156 months M.A., or 35 months of M.A.
7. Chronological age.....	121 months C.A. to 139 months C.A., or 18 months of C.A.

(From Ernest W. Tiegs, *Tests and Measurements in the Improvement of Learning,* Boston, Houghton Mifflin Co., 1939, p. 271.)

highly homogeneous. Critical analysis has, however, revealed the fact that such children may actually be very heterogeneous intellectually. Diagnostic tests of mental ability have shown that children of identical I.Q. may vary greatly *in certain aspects* of mental ability. As Table 18 reveals, children may differ extensively in such specific factors within the framework of general mental maturity as memory ability, spacial or

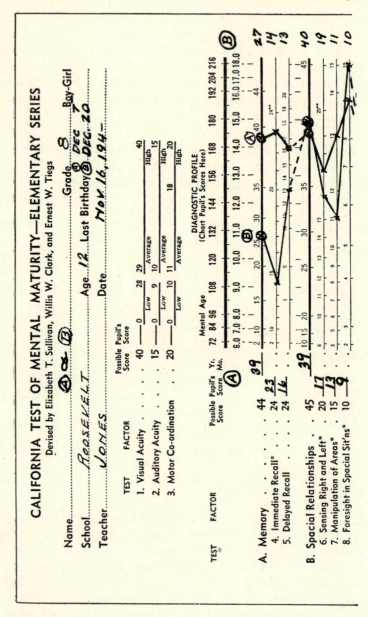

CALIFORNIA TEST OF MENTAL MATURITY—ELEMENTARY SERIES

Devised by Elizabeth T. Sullivan, Willis W. Clark, and Ernest W. Tiegs

Name .... (A) or (B)

School .... ROOSEVELT .... Grade 8 Boy-Girl

Teacher .... JONES .... Age 12 Last Birthday (A) DEC 7 (B) DEC 20

Date MOV 16, 194—

TEST FACTOR	Possible Score	Pupil's Score				
1. Visual Acuity	40	0	28	29		40
			Low 9	Average 10	High 15	
2. Auditory Acuity	15	0	9	10		15
			Low	Average	High	20
3. Motor Co-ordination	20	0	10	11	18	20
			Low	Average	High	

DIAGNOSTIC PROFILE
(Chart Pupil's Scores Here)

Mental Age
6.0 7.0 8.0 9.0 10.0 11.0 12.0 13.0 14.0 15.0 16.0 17.0 18.0
72 84 96 108 120 132 144 156 168 180 192 204 216

TEST FACTOR	Possible Score	Pupil's Score	Yr. Mo.
A. Memory	44	39	
4. Immediate Recall*	24	23	
5. Delayed Recall	24	16	
B. Spacial Relationships	45	39	
6. Sensing Right and Left*	20	17	
7. Manipulation of Areas*	15	13	
8. Foresight in Spacial Sit'ns*	10	9	

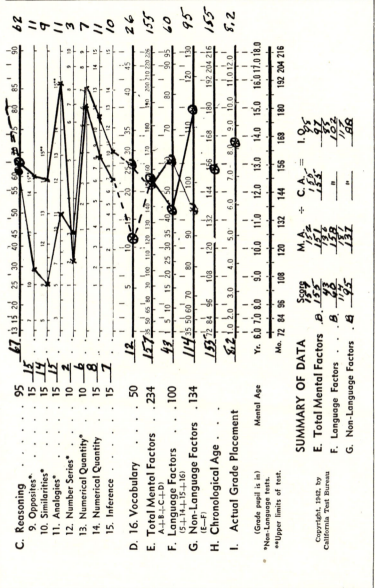

Figure 54. Showing the Intellectual Heterogeneity of Two Twelve-Year-Old Children of Approximately Identical I.Q.'s (98 and 97)

visualization ability, reasoning ability, verbal ability, and both language and non-language ability. As Tiegs [60] has said, such abilities "appear to be more or less independent factors in mental maturity, and all . . . have in the past been hidden in a single or total M.A. or I.Q. which obscured their nature and varying manifestations." This means, of course, that children can achieve the same I.Q. score by widely different intellectual routes. As can be seen from Table 18, children (fifth grade) of 106 I.Q. may vary in memory ability from 120 months (average for ten-year-olds) to 180 months (average for fifteen-year-olds), a range of five years. Much the same situation holds for visualization ability, reasoning ability, and the rest.

As will be noted in Figure 55, a given child may also vary considerably in his ability to cope with language and non-language materials. In the case presented, two verbal group tests —the Otis and the language section of the California Test of Mental Maturity—yielded mental scores considerably out of harmony with the results of the non-language section of the California test and the relatively valid Stanford-Binet scale. It can thus be seen that verbal (language) group tests are likely frequently to misrepresent a child's status so far as non-language ability is concerned.

Mental Growth as Shown by Test Scores.—A variety of mental tests for infants and children have been constructed in recent years. These may be classified as: [61]

1. *Baby Tests,* or tests concerned with infant sensorimotor responses such as following an object with the eyes, holding the head erect, grasping cubes, and the like. Baby tests usually measure development during the first year or two of postnatal life.

2. *Developmental Scales,* or tests designed to determine the rate at which infant activities "unfold" along both sensorimotor and social and personality lines. Such scales represent a variation from

---

[60] Ernest W. Tiegs, *Tests and Measurements in the Improvement of Learning,* Boston, Houghton Mifflin Co., 1939, pp. 270-272.

[61] A more detailed description of mental tests may be found in Edward B. Greene, *Measurements of Human Behavior,* New York, The Odyssey Press, 1941.

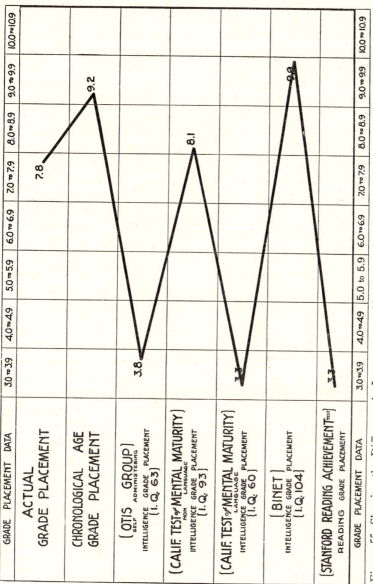

Figure 55. Showing the Difference in Language and Non-language Mental Ability of a Junior High School Boy (From Esther Grace Nolan, "Reading Difficulty Versus Low Mentality," *California Journal of Secondary Education*, 17:34-39 (1942).)

ordinary baby tests which Dr. Arnold Gesell, their greatest exponent, believes to be superior to tests yielding intelligence quotients.

3. *Verbal Tests,* or individual tests of the Binet type which ascertain a child's mentality chiefly through the avenue of language and abstract problem solution. Here the higher mental processes are examined on an age norm basis from ages two or three through childhood and adolescence.

4. *Performance Tests,* or tests utilizing form-boards, blocks, picture-puzzles, pencil mazes, and other non-language materials suitable to the detection of ability to discern spacial and form relationships. Such tests are usually adapted to children four or five years of age and older.

5. *Group Tests,* or tests designed to save time and expense by measuring, in relatively large groups, the mental ability of children who are able to read. These tests are not in all cases as reliable as individual scales but can be used with children from the third or fourth grade and up. In the case of younger children, group tests employing pictures may be used.

6. *Achievement Tests,* or standard measures of school accomplishment in subject matter fields, are often used to determine children's academic ability. Although they are not strictly mental tests, these instruments correlate fairly highly with I.Q. scores.

7. *Special Ability Tests,* or tests designed to ascertain aptitude for such specific skills as drawing, music, mechanics, athletics, and social ability. It is believed that skill in any one of these areas involves the possession of certain forms of mental ability.

DEVELOPMENT DURING INFANCY. An idea of the rate and manner in which infants mature in ways indicative of mental development is afforded by several tests devoted to the measurement of such growth. The following excerpts from the *Baby Test,* by Charlotte Bühler, present monthly norms for the first year. The sample responses for alternate months (the test contains monthly norms) given below are suggestive of the types of reactions used to measure infant development.

Two Months

Focuses attention on shiny object approximately a foot from head.
Makes searching head movements when rattle is shaken a foot and a half from head.

Four Months

Looks about actively in a new situation.
Looks at an object while manipulating it.

Six Months

Is expectant in response to repetition of a stimulus.
Smiles in a general way.

Eight Months

Is persistent in reacting to the removal of a toy.
Makes deliberate choice of a toy.

Ten Months

Removes cover from a covered object.
Imitates the ringing of a bell.

One Year to One Year Two Months and Twenty-nine Days

Observes image of self in a mirror.
Endeavors to grasp reflection of a cracker seen in mirror.

Another widely known scale of early development, the Linfert-Hierholzer Scale (Table 19), portrays infant development during the first year of life.

It is apparent that the above and similar infant tests (Kuhlmann, for example, beginning at three months, and Merrill-Palmer, ranging from eighteen to seventy-two months) reflect the work of Gesell and his developmental schedule which, incidentally, is designed to measure motor-manipulation, adaptive behavior, and social growth rather than mental development *per se.*[62] Gesell's infant norms (average performances for the ages given) include lashing the arms, turning the head and eyes 90 degrees to watch rings and rattles, and listening to a bell at four weeks; smiling, bringing ring or rattle to mouth, and holding head up when held upright at sixteen weeks; recognizing strangers, shaking a rattle, sucking toe, and playing with image in mirror at twenty-eight weeks; and sitting up, creep-

---

[62] For additional infant tests see Anna M. Shotwell and A. R. Gilliland, "A Preliminary Scale for the Measurement of the Mentality of Infants," *Child Development,* 14 : 167-177 (1943), and R. V. D. Campbell and A. A. Weeck "Measures Which Characterize the Individual During the Development of Behavior in Early Life," *Child Development,* 12 : 217-236 (1941).

TABLE 19. PERCENTAGE OF SUCCESSES IN TESTS BY VARIOUS AGE-
GROUPS, LINFERT-HIERHOLZER SCALE

SERIES I

Test	1 Month	2 Months	4 Months
1. Rolls to side	6	10	58
2. Rolls from side to back	36	78	94
3. Notices ball on string	62	90	96
4. Follows ball with eyes	52	68	82
5. Follows ball with head	14	36	64
6. Notices blue ball	58	76	96
7. Follows blue ball with eyes	48	66	75
8. Follows blue ball with head	20	26	56
9. Distaste to salt	50	74	98
10. Head held erect and firm	30	34	46
11. Regards teaspoon quietly, then flourished	4	10	36
12. Toe reflex—extension	22	44	54
13. Socially stimulated smile	60	82	100
14. Attention to voice	90	92	98
15. Clasps cube	10	16	66

SERIES II

Test	6 Months	9 months	12 Months
1. Sits alone	36	100	100
2. Creeps	19	71	88
3. Climbs	0	0	90
4. Stands with help	10	92	100
5. Stands alone	0	37	84
6. Walks with help	0	37	94
7. Walks alone	0	0	30
8. Builds with blocks	0	2	38
9. Plays peek-a-boo (pat-a-cake)	0	83	94
10. Recognizes name	65	100	100
11. Salutes	0	45	94
12. Says "bye-bye"	0	20	56
13. Says more than one word	0	47	64
14. Inhibits forbidden acts	0	0	50
15. Uses spoon	0	8	44
16. Removes shoes	0	4	50
17. Controls bowel	0	2	40
18. Asks for things	0	0	54

(Condensed from Harriette E. Linfert and Helen M. Hierholzer, "A Scale for Measuring the Mental Development of Infants During the First Year of Life," *Studies in Psychology and Psychiatry*, Catholic Univ. of America, Vol. I, No. 4 (1928).)

ing, pulling self to feet, and saying "mama," "dada," and one other word at forty weeks. On what basis such responses can be regarded as manifestations of mental ability is not clear. As has been noted, they are unlike the more verbal and abstract questions upon which mental tests for older children are based. Gesell has, however, solved the problem involved to his own satisfaction by regarding his scale as a developmental schedule of growth, and by causing it to yield a D.Q. (developmental quotient) rather than the more questionable (at this age) I.Q. (intelligence quotient).

DEVELOPMENT DURING CHILDHOOD. Experience has shown that mental tests designed for children of post-infant age are much more valid than the previously presented baby tests. After reaching the age of three or four years, children begin to participate in increasingly more intellectual and linguistic activities. It is the measurement of such higher mental processes that has enabled investigators to predict a given child's probable growth in intelligence. Following the work of Binet (and Simon) in France, a number of Americans have constructed reliable scales for the measurement of the mental ability of elementary school children. Outstanding among these is the Stanford-Revision (of the Binet Scale), constructed in 1916 and extensively revised in 1937, whose range encompasses age two (six months' tests to age five) to superior adult status. Excerpts from various of its age levels (norms) will indicate the typical performances of children of average ability.

STANFORD-BINET (TERMAN-MERRILL 1937 REVISION)

YEAR II

Identifies by name such objects as kitty, button, thimble, cup, engine, and spoon.
Identifies parts of the body such as hair, mouth, ears, and hands.
Manipulates three-hole form board.

YEAR III

Puts beads on a string.
Copies a circle.
Repeats three digits.

YEAR IV

Completes picture of a man.

Repeats simple twelve-syllable sentence.
Comprehends the concept of *two*.

Year V

Defines the words "ball," "hat," and "stove."
Memorizes ten-word sentences.
Counts four specific objects.

Year VI

Locates deficiencies in mutilated pictures.
Counts thirteen specific objects.
Traces pencil maze.

Year VII

Copies a diamond-shaped figure.
Tells similarity between wood and coal, apple and peach, etc.
Repeats five digits.

Year VIII

Tells difference between baseball and orange, aeroplane and kite, etc.
Repeats sixteen-syllable sentences.
Solves such problems as difference between stopping train and automobile.

Year IX

Finds words that rhyme with "bat" and "tree."
Repeats four digits reversed.
Makes change, such as 10 − 4, and 15 − 12.

Year X

Detects absurdities in pictures.
Repeats six digits.
Reports memory of short story read.

Year XI

Repeats twenty-syllable sentences.
Defines abstract words such as "connection," "compare," revenge," etc.
Tells similarities between snake—cow—sparrow, rose—potato—tree, etc.

Year XII

Detects absurdities in sentences.
Interprets a simple picture.
Repeats five digits reversed.

Test items for adolescents tend to become more and more symbolic and abstract. They involve defining increasingly difficult words, abstracting lessons (generalizations) from fables, detecting subtle absurdities in statements, rearranging scrambled sentences, and solving "mental arithmetic" problems. None of the test item placements in the Stanford-Binet Scale have been subjectively determined; all have been experimentally established by the responses of representative samplings of children. As the child grows older he is required to make more intricate responses of a reasoning and discriminatory nature.

Values in Using Intelligence Tests.—When used judiciously, with full knowledge of their limitations as well as the functions they can logically perform, mental tests constitute an invaluable tool to the student of child psychology. In the field of education, objective tests are no longer regarded as being ends in themselves or as instruments designed to solve all of the intricate problems of mental growth and adjustment. Mental tests are rightfully looked upon as useful tools which, although not substitutes for the judgment of teachers and clinicians, are nevertheless indispensable to the adequate diagnosis and guidance of children. Tests of the Binet type are essential to the determination of a child's skill in the use of words, as well as his ability to cope with abstract concepts and materials. They are in part indicators of the educational opportunities a given child has previously experienced, and of his probable future success in school as well. Tests of a less linguistic nature, such as form boards, pencil mazes, and figure patterns, provide an insight into the intellectual possibilities of children suffering from language handicaps who have not enjoyed the opportunity of adequate systematic schooling.

Mental tests may furnish information regarding the status of a given child's intellectual development which is much more precise, and certainly more readily secured, than that obtainable from ordinary observation. Such tests can also be used to guide the child or youth along lines commensurate with his mental capacity or future promise. It is through the use of a battery of tests and an intelligent interpretation of their disclosures, as well as a knowledge of the child's general qualifications, that adequate educational and vocational guidance is made possible. It is in this way that the science of child psychology hopes to enable children to avert the tragedy of attempting to prepare for activities for which they are not suited.

The more specific uses to which mental test results may, under favorable circumstances, be put have been mentioned by a number of writers and may be summarized briefly. In each instance intelligence test scores should be utilized in the light of a comprehensive factual and anecdotal picture of the child's assets, limitations, and physical and mental qualifications. The test uses referred to include: (1) an analysis of mental growth, (2) appraisals of the influence of varying educational environments, (3) the classification of pupils into ability groups, (4) educational guidance, (5) vocational guidance, (6) the mental diagnosis of problem cases (both educational and "behavior"), (7) the measurement of results of varying educational procedures, (8) the study of patterns of delinquency, and (9) the determination of the intellectual status of prospective members of the professions and various vocations.

It should not be supposed, however, that adequate test intelligence is sufficient equipment to insure success in a career or even in academic pursuits. Such strictly personal qualities as "drive," perseverance, emotional stability, and social intelligence are essential factors in successful achievement in both professional and vocational areas. From two-thirds to three-fourths of those who are dismissed from remunerative positions are released because of more or less marked personality weaknesses. Such results are even in evidence among men and women who are intellectually (according to test scores) highly competent. This phenomenon is explained by the fact that there is, on the average, little correspondence between an individual's intellectual status and his personality qualities. It is therefore imperative that children be enabled to develop the emotional stability and social skills requisite for both vocational security and social acceptance. Good mentality can be made an asset to such a program.

Summary and Implications

A determination of the nature of human intelligence is one of the most baffling questions confronting psychologists. It is not surprising that a variety of conceptions concerning both the nature and functioning of the intellectual factor in man should have arisen. Principal among these theories are the beliefs that intelligence is : (1) a unitary factor, (2) a synthesis of numerous specific factors, and (3) a grouping of clusters of ability. The primary function of intelligence has been variously interpreted to be : (1) adjustment to the requirements of the environment, (2) the mastery of abstract concepts, (3) the learning of school subjects, and (4) ready adaptation to the demands of new experiences. The construction of mental tests has made it possible to chart the genetic development of intelligence. Questions concerning the innateness of mental ability and the improvability of intellectual status have, however, proved to be difficult of solution. In the appraisal of intellectual status only manifestations (behavior) of adaptive capacity, not an intellectual entity, have been measured. Such ability has been found to be relatively unrelated to physical development during the infancy and childhood periods.

Judging from the testimony of studies dealing with the relation between educational opportunities and I.Q. scores, intellectual development is to a considerable extent a function of education and stimulation. To the degree that this relationship holds, it seems logical that educators should do everything in their power to develop instructional techniques and methods of motivation most conducive to mental development. The fact that some nursery school programs have resulted in marked increments in intellectual growth while others have brought about no such improvement may mean that the factors involved have as yet been touched upon largely by chance. Formal schooling does not automatically connote adequate intellectual stimulation. The "casual influence" of a school or other educational environment does not guarantee the systematic acquisition of insight, understandings, or similar intellectual adaptations. Only when *blanket* school regimes and more or less fruitless programs of "lesson learning" are dispensed with in favor of experimentally validated educational activities can we expect to witness a degree of intellectual development commensurate with children's potentialities. It would appear to be to the advantage of society to encourage such growth, with the provision that the program involved be accompanied by efforts to insure the personal and social development of its children.

QUESTIONS FOR DISCUSSION

1. What fallacy is involved when nature-nurture studies are attempted with children who are already from one to four or more years of age? How, if at all, can this handicap be overcome? What would you do about it?

2. What logical criticisms could one make of the claim that mental tests measure native ability? Since all responses to mental-test situations are obviously learned, how can we compare the basic mental differences among children? What bearing do these questions have on the child's educability?

3. In view of the fact that intelligence tests are often contrasted with personality inventories, how can we justify the practice of including intelligence as a component or part of child personality? Is intelligence a major personality "trait"? Take a position on this question and defend it.

4. Why are individual curves depicting the growth of intelligence in children often so different in shape? What logical explanation can you give for the fluctuations in development over a period of years of a given child? What implications do such findings have for childhood education?

5. Why do mental tests for preschool children yield such uncertain predictions of future intellectual status? What is the principal difference between infant "intelligence" tests and those designed for children of elementary school age? Support your answer with evidence.

6. What are the chief objections to the idea of intellectual status as being an accumulation of learning or nurtural influences, all of which are relatively independent of the quality or quantity of brain and nervous system structures inherited?

7. Compare the various definitions of intelligence given in this chapter. Which seems most useful in the case of children? Which regards intelligence as a function of neural activity, and which sees it as adaptive capacity?

8. Which conception of the nature of intelligence appears to be most acceptable from a scientific point of view? Prepare a defense of your answer that would be acceptable to a modern

psychologist. Why did you choose it in preference to the others?

9. Why is the two-factor theory of the nature of intelligence distasteful to followers of the Thorndike school of thought? Give the *pro* and *con* arguments in your answer. Do factorial analyses such as those by Kelly and Thurstone tend to corroborate either Thorndike's or Spearman's position?

10. Does evidence damaging to the notion of "localized mind" also render doubtful the idea of gene-inheritance of mental ability? Support your answer. In case you object to the concept of mental inheritance, how do you account for the intellectual differences among children?

RECOMMENDED READINGS

Bayley, Nancy. *Mental Growth During the First Three Years.* Genetic Psychology Monographs, Vol. 14, No. 1 (1933).

Boynton, Paul L. *Psychology of Child Development.* Minneapolis: Educational Publishers, Inc., 1938, Ch. 6.

Brooks, Fowler D. *Child Psychology.* Boston: Houghton Mifflin Co., 1937, Ch. 9.

Curti, Margaret W. *Child Psychology.* New York: Longmans, Green & Co., 1938, Ch. 7.

Freeman, F. N. *Mental Tests.* Boston: Houghton Mifflin Co., 1939.

Gesell, Arnold, and Amatruda, C. S. *Developmental Diagnosis.* New York: Paul B. Hoeber, Inc., 1941.

Green, Edward B. *Measurements of Human Behavior.* New York: The Odyssey Press, 1941.

Sherman, Mandel. *Intelligence and Its Deviations.* New York: The Ronald Press Co., 1945, Chs. 1-4.

Shock, N. W., and Jones, H. E. "Mental Development and Performance as Related to Physical and Physiological Factors." *Review of Educational Research,* Vol. 11, No. 5 (1941), Ch. 3.

Skinner, C. E., and Harriman, P. L. *Child Psychology.* New York: The Macmillan Co., 1941, Ch. 8.

Stoddard, George D. *The Meaning of Intelligence.* New York: The Macmillan Co., 1943.

Terman, Lewis M. *The Measurement of Intelligence.* Boston: Houghton Mifflin Co., 1916.

Terman, Lewis M., and Merrill, Maud A. "The Stanford-Binet Scales for Measuring Intelligence," in *Child Behavior and Development.* (Edited by Roger G. Barker *et al.*) New York: McGraw-Hill Book Co., Inc., 1943, Ch. 10.

Wellman, Beth L. "Our Changing Concept of Intelligence." *Journal of Consulting Psychology,* 2:97-107 (1938).

CHAPTER 9

REGULATING EMOTIONAL BEHAVIOR

AN EXAMINATION OF THE PSYCHOLOGICAL LITERATURE in either its technical or popular forms makes it evident that emotional behavior is regarded as being an extremely important phase of child nature. It is, in fact, commonly believed that the emotions represent nature's provision for the motivation of behavior—that they are, in the last analysis, man's springs to action. Although not always in agreement as to the ultimate function of emotional forces, practically all writers on child development devote considerable space to an account of their origin, as well as to methods by which they may be regulated. Any serious consideration of the problems of human development must take into account the processes associated with emotional reactions.

Theories of the Nature of Emotional Behavior

Like many other psychological terms, the word *emotion* lends itself to a variety of definitions and concepts. It has been confused, in the discussions of both psychologists and laymen, with feelings, motives, biases, instincts, and, to some extent, with dynamic needs. The emotion concept has, in fact, become almost as ambiguous as that associated with the instinct hypothesis. It is this situation that makes necessary an explanation of diverse theories of the nature of emotions and of the function of emotional forces in the personal and social adjustment of growing children.

Views on the Role of Emotions.—Before proceeding to a discussion of the more prominent concepts and theories of emotive behavior, it should prove profitable to consider the implications of primary emotional responses, defined as *intensely* *stirred-up states of the organism,* for personal adjustment. Such an analysis involves a consideration of the four questions: (1) Are emotions *causal* agents (of behavior) or are they primarily *effects* of intense stimuli? (2) Are emotions dynamic drives or are they results of need-frustration? (3) Are emotions synonymous with attitudes or are they associated with the expression of attitudes? (4) Are emotions (as defined) advantageous to personality adjustment or are they conducive to increased organism stress? A brief consideration of these questions should throw considerable light on the function and utility of the emotional factor in child behavior.

ARE EMOTIONS CAUSAL AGENTS? It is well to realize at the outset that emotions are not innate forces capable of bringing about the appearance of well-coordinated patterns of response such as love, fear, and rage. These forms of behavior are obviously responses, the *results* of specific forms of external stimulation of a type and intensity calculated to bring them out. Love (in children) is characteristically elicited by satisfying body contacts, rage by frustration of intense desire or need; neither emotion is an explanation for the appearance of the behavior associated with it. As one writer [1] has said, "if one is asked why a man is throwing his arms about, clenching his fists, and using abusive language, the reply 'rage makes him do it,' is no explanation." In such an instance the term rage merely describes a pattern of behavior; it does not purport to explain its origin. It is evident that emotional states are not causal agents except insofar as they bring about *subsequent* mental or motor behavior of a chaotic or attempted-adjustment nature. Emotions involve widespread visceral disturbances, but these are in turn caused by frustrations or exciting environmental stimuli of varying degrees of intensity.

ARE EMOTIONS DYNAMIC DRIVES? Related to the preceding question is that whether emotions are dynamic drives or whether they are merely reactions to frustrations of fundamental needs. It should be evident that, being effects of external stimulating situations, emotions cannot qualify as basic drives.

[1] J. J. B. Morgan, *Child Psychology,* (2nd ed.), New York, Farrar & Rinehart, Inc., 1934, pp. 144-145.

The child needs recognition, response, a sense of personal worth, and the like, and is driven to emotional behavior when denied reasonable satisfaction of these dynamic needs. Nevertheless, some writers have committed themselves to unqualified statements apparently purporting to place emotions in the primary drive category. Boynton [2] has stated, for example, that "emotions are the greatest motivating factors in human experience." Freud's concept of repression, which in reality teaches that emotional tensions in children are *created* by the denial of a fundamental need for physical gratification and affection, is given as a case in point. Another psychologist, Perrin,[3] has declared that "just as hunger impels the organism to obtain and devour food, so fear prompts it to flee from danger, and anger spurs it to belligerent activity." This view does not take account of the fact that the word fear, for example, instead of explaining a pattern of response, merely describes it. The child flees from danger because he realizes that his security is being threatened—he sees a wild animal, a railroad train, or a snake— and becomes frightened in the process. The stress occasioned by hunger will usually initiate food-seeking actions; fear is a state of stress brought about by some type of security-threatening situation.

ARE EMOTIONS SYNONYMOUS WITH ATTITUDES? Emotions, which are by definition regarded as temporarily stirred-up states of the organism, have been confused with attitudes, prejudices, and values. Textbooks [4] and journal articles have devoted much space to discussions of "emotionalized attitudes." Children are said to be manifesting emotional states when they sing songs, carry flags, and portray patriotic attitudes in general.[5] Adults are allegedly doing likewise when they assist in political or religious causes, when they express sentiments of loyalty to their Alma Mater, or when they support a war effort. Actually, these and similar activities are not by definition emo-

[2] Paul L. Boynton, *Psychology of Child Development,* Minneapolis, Educational Publishers, Inc., 1938, p. 227.

[3] F. A. C. Perrin, *Psychology: Its Methods and Principles,* New York, Henry Holt & Co., Inc., 1932, pp. 158-159.

[4] See, for example, Thomas H. Briggs, *Secondary Education,* New York, The Macmillan Co., 1933, Chs. 18-23.

[5] Paul L. Boynton, *op. cit.*

tions, they represent rather strong dispositions to behave in accordance with personal *values* that have been developed as a result of childhood and adolescent experiences. In the objective sense, attitudes are organism "sets" acquired in the genetic stream of affective experience. Certain attitudes, such as dislike for animals or distrust of members of the opposite sex, may have been formed as the result of emotional experiences, but they are not themselves emotional states. It should be recognized, however, that emotional responses may readily be aroused by the blocking or frustration of strong dispositions (attitudes) to behave in preferred ways.

ARE EMOTIONS ADVANTAGEOUS TO ADJUSTMENT? Psychologists disagree as to the utility of true emotional experiences in personal and social adjustment. Some hold that the impulsive and disorganized nature of most emotional reactions render them worse than useless in a civilized society in which so many situations call for socialized and tactful responses. They point out the fact that although emotions may be valuable for crude defensive and adjustment purposes under primitive conditions, they all too frequently lead to chaotic responses poorly adapted to the exigencies of present-day circumstances. One writer [6] maintains that nature abhors emotions and that, since they are so overwhelming in their effects on both children and adults, they are actually dangerous under the conditions usually encountered in the modern world. It is evident, for example, that emotional stress may paralyze action in dangerous situations, that it may force rational thinking into the background, and that extreme grief or temporary infatuation may cause an individual to focus his attention on a very restricted area of adjustment. The shooting frays of jilted lovers and the drinking bouts of frustrated career men constitute illustrations of the maladaptive reactions sometimes resulting from emotional stress.

Some psychologists [7] feel, nevertheless, that high emotions lead both children and adults to make adjustment-seeking re-

---

[6] Henry C. Morrison, *Basic Principles in Education*, Boston, Houghton Mifflin Co., 1934, pp. 174-184.
[7] See, for example, J. J. B. Morgan, *op. cit.*, pp. 148-149.

actions that may ultimately lead to the overcoming of restraints for which no adequate response has been learned. A child who is being held by a bully may, for example, rid himself of the restraint by an emotionally induced degree of vigor and energy not available under more serene conditions. An emotionally aroused adult might, by the same token, reduce his stresses through a verbal tilt with an antagonist who has attempted to defame his reputation. To quote one pair of collaborators [8] on this subject, "the chief function served by these tendencies (emotions) in promoting adjustment to a complex environment is to initiate activities which, through conflict, lead to new forms of behavior."

Definitions of Feeling and Emotion.—Thus far in the discussion emotion has been presented as a *highly stirred-up state of the organism* and as involving extensive visceral disturbances. There has been considerable discussion, however, as to whether emotive experience differs essentially from that commonly called *feeling*. According to one view, feeling and emotion are simply relative degrees of the same affective type of experience. On this basis feeling, whether pleasant or unpleasant, would represent a state of body equilibrium characterized by a moderate amount of affective tonus. True emotion, being marked by more violent visceral stresses, would be a quantitative extension of the feeling experience; that is, excess or more intense feeling. This position is illustrated by the contention that "Emotion bears the same relation to ordinary feeling that the swell bears to the ordinary ripple of the sea. It is composed of feeling, but of an accumulation of feeling." [9] Feeling, as thus conceived, usurps the major role in determining the direction a child's behavior will take.

Some psychologists and biologists regard feeling as being a unique experience of pleasantness or unpleasantness which accompanies man's entire gamut of experience. The exact nature and physiological correlates of such affective tonus are not,

---

[8] J. C. Chapman and G. S. Counts, *Principles of Education*, Boston, Houghton Mifflin Co., 1924, p. 62.
[9] Meyer F. Nimkoff, *The Child*, Philadelphia, J. B. Lippincott Co., 1934, pp. 100-101.

however, well understood. Troland [10] has advanced the theory that feelings are closely related to bodily well-being, and that they are intimately tied up with physiological equilibria. Nafe [11] is even more explicit concerning the probable physiological nature of feeling. He writes, "Pleasantness, as a psychological experience, consists of a pattern of discrete bright points of experience in the general nature of a thrill, but usually is much less intense. It is vaguely localized about the upper part of the body. Unpleasantness is similar, but characteristically duller, heavier, more of the pressure type of experience, and is localized toward the abdomen or the lower part of the body."

These and other views relating to the nature and function of feeling are well summarized in the following words: "If one were permitted a very broad generalization based upon an examination of the above and other hypotheses about feelings, it would be that these affective experiences are closely related to the physiological state of the organism. Feelings might be called the indicators of whether or not conditions are optimum for the maintenance of those dynamic physiological processes that are characteristic of the organism." [12] As this writer further suggests, this is probably as far as one should go in speculating about the nature of feeling.

In discussing the emotions, Prescott [13] subscribes to the view that, although they may vary greatly in degree of intensity, emotions are essentially different from the milder feelings. Whether this difference is strictly one of degree or of quality is not clear from the experimental findings. As yet little evidence has been presented disproving the seemingly logical contention that feelings and emotions represent but different degrees of intensity on the affective scale of experience. As Meyer [14] has pointed out, vascular-muscle functions, skeletal-muscle functions, and

[10] L. T. Troland, *The Fundamentals of Human Motivation,* New York, D. Van Nostrand Co., 1928, pp. 284-300.

[11] J. P. Nafe, "Pressure, Pain and Temperature Senses," in *Handbook of General Experimental Psychology* (edited by Carl Murchison), Worcester, Clark Univ. Press, 1934, p. 1076.

[12] Daniel A. Prescott, *Emotion and the Educative Process,* Washington, D. C., American Council on Education, 1938, p. 13.

[13] *Ibid.,* pp. 17-30.

[14] Max F. Meyer, "The Whale Among the Fishes—the Theory of Emotions," *Psychological Review,* 40: 292-300 (1933).

the regulatory chemical action of the glands of internal secretion are all present in both so-called feeling and emotional behavior. Since these responses apparently differ only in degree of intensity, it is practically impossible to determine at what point one ceases and the other begins. Meyer illustrates by writing, "How red must a person be in his face before he is said to have lost the unemotional (feeling) character? Why is he not slightly emotional while taking his afternoon nap? Who can decree that such and such an intensity of glandular and neural function is an emotional state and that below that intensity level the glandular and neural functions are unemotional? In other words, why make a sharp distinction when none exists?"

It should be profitable, thus, to consider emotions in terms of levels of physiological disturbance (intensity). This is the approach utilized by Dumas [15] in his discussion of three levels of emotional behavior, which he interprets as (1) *mild* emotion, (2) *strong* emotion, and (3) *disintegrative* emotion. Each of these emotional levels is accompanied by widespread visceral disturbances of varying degrees of intensity, the extent of which is associated in each instance with the type of stimulating situation eliciting them. Dumas has shown, for example, that *mild* emotional shocks, involving a moderate increase in intensity of normal physiological functions, follows such stimulating experiences as the threat of being pricked by a pin, seeing broken glass, reading erotic literature, being exposed to cooked beefsteak, and being "kidded."

Strong emotions, as previously indicated, involve affective reactions of an intense character, and are marked by violent visceral and all-over physiological changes. Strong anger, fear, joy, and sexual excitement, for instance, are accompanied by highly vivid sensations, and usually lead to vigorous bodily action designed to reduce the stresses entailed. Emotions involving despair, deep sorrow, or remorse lead, on the other hand, to a passive or inactive type of behavior. Strong negative emotions are obviously caused by significant threats to physical or

[15] Georges Dumas, *Nouveau Traité de Psychologie,* Paris, Felix Alcan, 1932, Vols. I-III.

ego security or by the frustration of fundamental needs and desires. Furthermore, as Dunbar [16] has shown, disorders affecting the skin, the bones, the genito-urinary system, the sense organs, and the respiratory system are sometimes produced by strong and persistent emotions.

Disintegrative emotions are said to be involved in cases of serious physical and mental pathology in which powerful stresses and conflicts of long duration, rather than organic factors, lie at the root of the difficulty. Many individuals suffering from psychoneurotic disorders, and even from psychotic states, have developed such conditions as the result of overwhelming and persistent emotional stresses. Such individuals are frequently victims of hysterical manifestations, simulated (functional) physical disorders, delusions, hallucinations, and other symptoms of personality disorganization. Cases of this kind may not only be caused by high emotional stresses, they also tend to develop distorted patterns of emotional reaction to normal life situations. Such responses may vary all the way from violent rejection of food to complete apathy concerning the welfare of former loved ones.

In the light of the foregoing discussion of levels of emotive behavior, it seems logical to assume that "a continuum of affective experience exists, varying from vague feelings of pleasantness or unpleasantness up to profound experiences which greatly disturb both mental and physical functions." [17] We could add that this continuum, or *gradient,* of emotional intensity, is sufficiently gradual to make it difficult if not impossible to differentiate among distinct "levels" of affective response.

Theories of the Nature of Emotion.—There has been much discussion concerning whether emotion, as a confused and intense state, *follows directly* upon an exciting stimulus, such as an insult or a scene of disaster, or whether it is aroused by the flood of sensations incidental to a visceral upheaval, which upheaval is believed by some to intervene between the external stimulus and the emotion proper. According to the James-

---

[16] H. Flanders Dunbar, *Emotions and Bodily Changes,* New York, Columbia Univ. Press, 1935.

[17] Daniel A. Prescott, *op. cit.,* p. 30.

Lange theory,[18] "the bodily changes follow directly the perception of the exciting fact, and . . . our feeling of the same
changes as they occur IS the emotion." On this basis there
could theoretically be no emotion unless an externally aroused
bodily upheaval was first experienced. James illustrated this
point of view by declaring that "we feel sorry because we cry,
angry because we strike, afraid because we tremble, and not that
we cry, strike, or tremble, because we are sorry, angry, or fearful, as the case may be." Although this theory has been widely
accepted, it suffers from the dual criticism that it fails to provide any criteria for differentiating physically among such
emotions as fear, anger, and joy, and that it cannot refute several experimental studies (to be discussed) damaging to its
major claims.

A more recent theory by Cannon [19] maintains that reactions
involving high emotion may occur in animals whose visceral
organs have been completely disconnected (by surgery) from
the central nervous system, and that a widespread bodily upheaval is thus not essential to the occurrence of an emotional
experience. Although Cannon has ascertained in considerable
detail the nature of the visceral disturbances associated with
emotive behavior, he has been more interested in studying the
function of the thalamus (lower brain) as the distributor of
neural discharges, of an exciting nature, to the cortex. He believes his experimental evidence supports the contention that
thalamic discharges give emotions their characteristic quality
and provide a basis for their differentiation as satisfying or distressing experiences. As he sees it, nerve impulses resulting
from an external stimulus are relayed to the thalamus, there to
be redirected both *to the autonomic system,* responsible for the
arousal of glandular and smooth-muscle visceral organs, and
to the cortex of the brain, where the consciousness of the emotion is supposedly registered.

Much of Cannon's experimental work has been devoted to a
determination of the functions of the autonomic nervous system

18 William James, *Principles of Psychology,* New York, Henry Holt & Co.,
Inc., 1908, Vol. II, pp. 449-450.
19 W. B. Cannon, *Bodily Changes in Pain, Hunger, Fear and Rage,* New
York, D. Appleton-Century Co., Inc., 1929, Ch. 19.

and of the endocrine secretions in emotional stress. In one instance he severed the autonomic sympathetic trunks from the superior cervical to the pelvic ganglia in a number of cats in an effort to learn the effect on emotional behavior of such removal of the physical basis for a visceral flood of sensations. Surprising as it may seem, the cats, in spite of the operation, displayed the usual signs of emotion in the forms of hissing, lifting the paws to strike, baring the teeth, and growling when confronted with barking dogs. The animals were evidently able to emote despite the removal of the visceral mechanisms formerly considered indispensable to such behavior. This experiment, which has been duplicated with dogs by Sherrington,[20] an English physiologist, and with cats by Bard,[21] appears to prove Cannon's contention that emotional experiences are produced by powerful neural discharges emanating from the region of the thalamus and directed toward the higher, cortical areas of the brain. A case reported by Dana [22] has shown that human emotions apparently operate in the same manner. A woman had, as the result of a spinal cord injury, been reduced to complete paralysis of both trunk and limbs. In spite of such loss of sensitivity, this individual responded as before to events calling for manifestations of grief or joy.

One of Cannon's chief contributions to the science of psychology, including child development, has been his clarification of the operations of the autonomic nervous system during emotional excitement. He has shown that, although all organs and glands of the viscera are connected with the three sections of the autonomic ganglia—the cranial (upper section), the thoracico-lumbar or "sympathetic" (middle section), and the sacral (lower section)—the sympathetic is in the ascendency during intense emotional experiences. During the excitement of high anger or fear, for example, the sympathetic division of the autonomic system stimulates the entire organism to intense activ-

[20] C. S. Sherrington, *The Integrative Action of the Nervous System*, New Haven, Yale Univ. Press, 1923.

[21] P. Bard, "The Neuro-humoral Basis of Emotional Reactions," in *Foundations of Experimental Psychology* (edited by Carl Murchison), Worcester, Clark Univ. Press, 1929, Ch. 12.

[22] C. L. Dana, "The Anatomic Seat of the Emotions; A Discussion of the James-Lange Theory," *Archives of Neurology and Psychiatry*, 6:634-639 (1921).

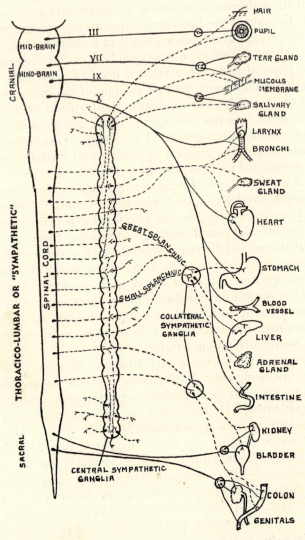

Figure 56. Diagram Showing the Autonomic Nervous System

The nerves of the cranial and sacral divisions are shown in full lines, while those of the sympathetic are shown in broken lines.

(From F. H. Lund, *Psychology*, New York, The Ronald Press Co., 1933, p. 207.)

ity marked particularly by greatly increased heart action, higher blood pressure, and accelerated breathing rate. Such intense stress also causes the adrenal glands to secrete the potent *adrenalin* hormone into the blood stream, where it is enabled to release sugar from the liver for speedy delivery to needy muscular tissues. As a result of such dynamic physiological activity, which is normally accompanied by excessive perspiration and a flushing of the face, as well as cessation of digestive processes, the pulsating organism is enabled quickly to defend itself with a show of strength not available under ordinary conditions.

It is this capacity of the human organism readily to adapt itself to conditions of combat by developing increased strength, by bringing about rapid coagulation of escaping blood, and by banishing fatigue, that has led Cannon to formulate his Emergency Theory of the function of emotions. He believes that primitive man's capacity for survival was greatly aided by the evolutionary development of the emotional mechanisms which made possible his more adequate defense against the attacks of both animals and hostile humans. This view is, of course, embarrassed by the necessity of explaining why modern man, who enjoys relative freedom from unarmed personal combat, continues to be so well equipped with emotion-producing physical mechanisms.

Conclusion on Views of Emotion.—Cannon's theory, especially his notion of thalamic determination of emotional quality, has been challenged by a number of his contemporaries. Gray,[23] for example, believes that the nature of each emotion is caused by a characteristic *blood chemistry* combination resulting from the combined action of all the endocrine glands. Lashley,[24] who subscribes to the visceral-sensations basis of the expression of emotions, declares that he can find no evidence for the contention that thalamic discharges bring about the characteristic quality of each emotional episode. It can be said, however, that, although Cannon's experimentally developed theory of emotive action has been subjected to scholarly criti-

[23] J. S. Gray, "An Objective Theory of Emotion," *Psychological Review,* 42 : 108-116 (1935).

[24] K. S. Lashley, "Experimental Analysis of Instinctive Behavior," *Psychological Review,* 45 : 445-471 (1938).

cisms, it is at present the most widely known and accepted point of view. When supported by the commonly acknowledged belief that the pattern of an emotion, be it fear, anger, joy, or the like, is determined by the circumstances of the external situation eliciting it, Cannon's systematic treatise seems reasonably well adapted to the interpretation of childhood affective behavior.

The Experimental Study of Children's Emotions

It will be recalled from Chapter 4, which dealt with the original responses of newborn infants, that there has been considerable controversy concerning the nature and patterning of so-called native emotional responses. The experimental work conducted by J. B. Watson [25] and his associates, as well as criticisms of the resulting conclusions, were presented in brief in that connection. A summary of these and other experimental findings is presented at this point to indicate the present state of knowledge concerning the development of emotional behavior in infants and children. When considered in the light of the above discussion of the physical basis of emotional functioning, such information should be of value in the regulation of child behavior.

Criticisms of Early Conclusions.—It will be remembered that Watson concluded from his experimentation with infants at the Johns Hopkins University Hospital that they are characterized by three primary emotions—fear, rage, and love —which represent complex but recognizable patterns of overt behavior. Fear, which can presumably be elicited only by the removal of support or by a loud sound, is exemplified, says Watson, by "a sudden catching of the breath, clutching randomly with the hands, the sudden closing of the eyes, and the puckering of the lips followed in some cases by crying." Rage, which is said to result only from hampering of the infant's movements, is shown by slashing movements of the arms and hands, by stiffening of the body, and by holding the breath until the face becomes flushed. Love, the third of Watson's

25 John B. Watson and R. Rayner, "Studies in Infant Psychology," *Scientific Monthly,* 13: 493-515 (1921).

postulated innate emotions, and which is described as being elicited by rocking, patting, and stroking of erogenous body areas, is marked by "cessation of crying, smiling, attempts at gurgling and cooing." In older children, extension of the arms is also often in evidence. According to his writings, Watson believes that the emotional patterns described are implicit in infant organization, and that they alone can be discerned in their emotional reactions.

In view of the widespread belief that Watson's pioneer findings are valid, it should be profitable to review the principal factual criticisms that have been leveled against them. One of the first of these was by Pratt, Nelson, and Sun,[26] who conducted an experiment in which more than 60 infants were subjected to Watson's methods of inducing rage. The pronounced difference in results is indicated by the following findings: (1) The so-called defense reactions of striking the experimenter's hands when the nose was held occurred in only 1 per cent of the cases. (2) In instances where infants were held by the arms, (a) 58 per cent remained passive even after the restraint was removed, (b) 26 per cent became inactive after a brief period of activity, (c) 13 per cent exhibited flexing and other activity, and (d) 3 per cent became active after being quiet for a time. With so many cases making passive responses, these experimenters concluded that quiet, not "rage," is the most characteristic response to restraint of movement. They also reported that in many instances there was either no response or merely a "pacifying" one to loud sounds. Similar results were obtained by another Ohio State University study,[27] in which Watson's stimulus conditions were carefully employed. The author reported: "Those conditions which Watson described do not initiate constant pattern responses in the infants used in this study; and, since Watson's findings are considered basic by those who hold that emotional responses are innate, the entire theory is placed on the defensive."

[26] K. C. Pratt, A. K. Nelson, and K. H. Sun, *The Behavior of the Newborn Infant,* Ohio State Univ. Studies, No. 10, 1930.
[27] J. H. Taylor, *Innate Emotional Responses in Infants,* Ohio State Univ. Studies in Infant Behavior, No. 12, 1934, p 81.

Curti [28] has made the point that fear may not be a function of a loud sound alone, but that it may occur to an extent determined by the circumstances under which a given child is stimulated. Subsequent to mentioning that one of her own children exhibited no fear of thunder, and that another psychologist [29] had reported a similar instance, she writes, "apparently whether a fear occurs or not is a function not merely of the intensity of the sound but of the kind of sound, and also of the condition of the organism at the time, and of the total behavior situation at the time. A baby in his mother's arms may not fear thunder, but one playing alone may." Curti goes on to say that, Watson's declarations notwithstanding, young children sometimes show fear of both sudden or unexpected movements on the part of acquaintances, and of strange situations for which they have no previously developed response. The first phenomenon is illustrated by the response of a five-months-old child who made a violent start when her mother stood up suddenly and approached her crib at an angle which made it impossible for the child to see her plainly. The second response was in evidence when a twenty-one-months-old girl ran joyfully to greet her father at his accustomed morning chair, only to find that a stranger, an unknown (to her) friend of the family, had established himself there and was reading a magazine. At this sudden shift of a stimulating situation for which she had been originally emotionally prepared, the little girl's lip went down, whimpering began, and soon she was crying openly. This response occurred in spite of the friendly greeting accorded the child by the visitor.

In a brief review of investigations concerning native emotions, Dennis [30] has attempted to reconcile conflicting data and to clarify the situation by proposing the three conclusions: (1) that the classical rage response might better be classified as restlessness and crying, and that it can be elicited in infants by any intense and enduring stimulus; (2) that restraint of move-

[28] Margaret W. Curti, *Child Psychology*, New York, Longmans, Green & Co., 1938, pp. 109-110.
[29] C. W. Valentine, "The Innate Bases of Fear," *Pedagogical Seminary and Journal of Genetic Psychology*, 37 : 393-421 (1930).
[30] Wayne Dennis, "Infant Reactions to Restraint: An Evaluation of Watson's Theory," *Transactions of the New York Academy of Science*, 2 :202-218 (1940).

ment, if accomplished without intense stimulation, does not necessarily lead to a negative response (here prenatal restraint of movement and postnatal infant binding are suggestive) ; and (3) that as the child grows older any interference with his customary behavior or ongoing activity may elicit a negative reaction. Whether restraint of movement or any other stimulus constitutes a frustration depends upon the state of the child's organism at the time and upon the type of response he has previously learned. Dennis concludes that reactions to frustration are not innate behavior patterns, but that they represent the degree to which a given child has or has not learned to adjust to the situations bringing them out.

Difficulties in Judging Infant Emotions.—A number of research workers have endeavored to ascertain the extent to which infant emotions are accompanied by differentiated and readily recognizable facial expressions and other patterns of reaction. Such researches are intended, of course, to check the validity of Watson's assumption of the existence of innate infant emotions. Outstanding among these experiments is the series conducted by Sherman,[31] in which the ability of observers to name infant emotional responses without benefit of knowledge of the stimuli involved was investigated. Subsequent to showing motion pictures of infants, in which their emotional responses to having the head and face restrained, being suddenly dropped, being pricked on the cheek with a needle, and being delayed in feeding, were shown, Sherman reorganized the film in such a way as to separate the respective responses from the stimuli which originally produced them. Graduate and undergraduate students in psychology, nurses, and medical students were then asked to identify the emotions presumably registered on the film. With students of psychology naming from twelve to twenty-five different emotions as emanating from the four Watsonian type stimulations, it is evident that these observers were unable to find a basis for differentiation among the infant responses.

[31] Mandel Sherman, "Differentiation of Emotional Responses in Infants," *Journal of Comparative Psychology*, 7 : 265-284, 335-351 (1927).

Other series in Sherman's research included the task of naming an emotion when it was associated with an irrelevant stimulus which had been interchanged in the film, and identifying an emotional pattern while viewing the living infant as he was being stimulated from behind a screen. A final study involved the naming of unseen stimuli responsible for given

TABLE 20. JUDGMENTS OF GRADUATE STUDENTS IN PSYCHOLOGY OF MOTION PICTURES OF THE REACTIONS OF INFANTS WHEN THE STIMULI WERE NOT SHOWN

JUDGMENTS	STIMULI CALLING OUT THE REACTIONS				
	"Hunger"	Dropping	Restraint	Sticking with Needle	Total
	Number of Students Naming the Emotion				
Hunger	7	6	2	2	17
Anger	11	14	13	8	46
Fear	7	5	5	9	26
Pain	3	3	4	2	12
Grief	1	1		1	3
Hurt				1	1
Rage	2	1	3	1	7
Discomfort			1		1
Sleepy			1		1
None				1	1
Consternation	1	1			2
Nausea		1			1
Physical discomfort			1		1
Total *	32	32	30	25	119

* The totals are not the same because not all observers made judgments of every reaction shown.
(From Mandel Sherman, "Differentiation of Emotional Responses in Infants," *Journal of Comparative Psychology*, 7:268 (1927).)

infant cries. In all these investigations agreements tended to be close when the nature of the stimuli involved was known. When stimuli and responses were transposed as shown on the films, the medical students tended to name an emotion which they believed should "go with" the stimulus shown. In the case of crying responses for which the stimuli were not known, no better success was achieved by the observers—nurses regarded them as being due to hunger, medical students associated them with colic pains, and students of psychology named a dozen

stimuli which they presumed might elicit them. Sherman concluded that "the emotional responses of the newborn infant to
the types of stimuli employed . . . are undifferentiated, and
the success of the individual observer in recognizing and differentiating the emotional character of these responses is due to a
knowledge of the causative stimulating conditions."

A number of other investigators and writers have concurred
with Sherman's conclusions. After failing to find any such
well-defined emotions as fear, love, or rage, Bridges [32] came to
the conclusion that definable emotional patterns evolve later
from the originally undifferentiated behavior of infants. Not
until they were three months of age or older did Bridges' infants display recognizable "pleasure" and "anger" responses.
Pratt [33] has summed up the above and other evidence for alleged innate patterns of emotional behavior in neonates by
declaring that "there seems to be little utility in the term emotion as applied to the behavior of newborn infants." Landis,[34]
after discussing a comprehensive group of investigations touching emotional behavior, declares that it is a matter of extreme
doubt whether true patterns of emotional expression appear in
the human infant or in higher animal forms. This writer also
stresses the point that even when emotions are accompanied by
facial and other reactions said to be somewhat characteristic
of them, such responses will vary with situations and from
individual to individual.

The Maturation of Emotional Behavior.—Psychologists
differ considerably in their emphasis on the role of maturation
in the development of emotional behavior. Gesell,[35] the titular
head of the maturation group, feels that this intrinsic factor is
responsible for the gradual evolution of emotional experience
in both infant and child. This investigator disagrees with those
who advocate that emotional development is a phenomenon

[32] K. M. B. Bridges, "Emotional Development in Early Infancy," *Child Development*, 3 : 324-341 (1932).
[33] K. C. Pratt, "The Neonate," in *Handbook of Child Psychology* (edited by
Carl Murchison), Worcester, Clark Univ. Press, 1933, p. 195.
[34] Carney Landis, "The Expressions of Emotion," in *Handbook of General
Experimental Psychology* (edited by Carl Murchison), Worcester, Clark Univ.
Press, 1934, pp. 326-327.
[35] Arnold Gesell, *The Guidance of Mental Growth in Infant and Child,* New
York, The Macmillan Co., 1930 p. 289.

largely of social stimulation. He writes, "The role of maturation in the control of emotional behavior has had scant recognition. The primary emotions have been discussed as though they were elementary stable phenomena subject only to the changes in social conditioning. This is the implication in much that has been written about the emotion of fear. It seems to us that the problem has been oversimplified. Fear may be an original tendency, but it is subject to the genetic alterations of organic growth, as well as to organization by environmental conditioning. Such conditioning may determine the orientation and reference of fears, but the mode of fearing undergoes change as a result of maturation."

As evidence for his position, Gesell [36] describes the behavior of infants when confined in a small enclosed "pen." At ten weeks such confinement is usually accepted with complete complaisance; at twenty weeks mild apprehension in the form of head turning and dissatisfaction is often in evidence; while at thirty weeks intolerance with the situation may be expressed by vigorous crying of the type characteristic of fear or fright. On the assumption that emotional patterns are "shaped by intrinsic maturation as well as by experience," Gesell thus again takes the stand that evolving innate forces predominate in practically every phase of the growth and development of children.

It is true that the infant's neural and sensorimotor equipment, which is relatively undeveloped at birth, becomes more and more mature with growth, also that he becomes progressively more capable of responding to environmental stimuli which did not at first influence him. This is comparable to saying that structural development makes possible a wider variety and more complex reactions to emotion-producing situations— not that specific, innate emotional patterns emerge as a function of maturation *per se*. With the development of additional insight, more knowledge of the world about him, greater control of bodily and facial movements, changes in endocrine functioning, and with social experience in general children are logically in a position to express themselves more adequately emo-

---

[36] Arnold Gesell, "The Individual in Infancy," in *Foundations of Experimental Psychology* (edited by Carl Murchison), Worcester, Clark Univ. Press, 1929, pp. 628-660.

tionally. As Prescott [37] has stated the case, "such information as we have seems to support the concept that maturation influences the expression of emotion by the development of capacities rather than (through) the ripening of specific innate response patterns."

H. E. Jones and M. C. Jones [38] write that their experimental evidence points to the importance of maturation in the genetic development of affective behavior. However, unlike Gesell, they interpret such maturation as involving the development of *organism capacities* and *intellectual insights,* rather than the sequential emerging of specific emotional behavior patterns. As an illustration of this interpretation, these investigators describe the reactions of children of various ages and of adults to the presence of a six-foot, but nevertheless harmless, snake which was permitted to glide about in their presence. In spite of the snake's agile movements and frequently protruded forked tongue, children of less than two years of age showed no fear of it. Children three and one-half years of age paid closer attention to the snake and showed more caution in getting near and touching it. The four-year-olds (and older) were much more inclined than the younger children to avoid the snake altogether. Adults were even more disturbed and disposed to keep their distance. The younger children were apparently not conscious of any danger when they reached for the snake moving about in their presence. Just as such children do not realize the menace that lurks in fire, they are unaware of the possible consequences of endeavoring to play with potentially dangerous animals. But with increasing age comes an accompanying clarified conception of the nature of objects in the environment. It is probably as a result of the development of this more adequate conception of the real world about him that the child comes to experience what is called fear.

The Joneses point out the part played by experience and learning in such emotional development when they write: "As a child develops, his intelligence innately matures, and his perceptions become enriched through experience. New things

[37] Daniel A. Prescott, *op. cit.*, p. 69.
[38] Harold E. Jones and M. C. Jones, "A Study of Fear," *Childhood Education,* 5 : 136-143 (1928).

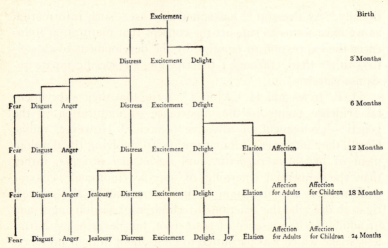

Figure 57. The Approximate Ages of Differentiation of the Various Emotions
During the First Two Years

(From K. M. B. Bridges, "Emotional Development in Early Infancy," *Child Development*, 3:340 (1937).)

startle him because of his keener perception. . . . Fear arises
when we know enough to recognize the potential danger in a
situation but have not advanced to the point of complete comprehension and control of the changing situation."

A comprehensive series of studies of the progressive development of emotional behavior in nursery school children by
Bridges [39] has also suggested that affective behavior patterns
differentiate with physical growth and social experience. As
may be seen in Figure 57, Bridges believes it possible to identify
the emotion of *distress* at about the third month of life. The
more satisfying emotional experience commonly known as *delight* also appears at this age. By approximately the sixth
month, recognizable responses indicative of *fear, disgust,* and
anger are believed to have become differentiated from the more
general pattern of *excitement*. Similar results were secured by
Washburn [40] in a study of the smiling response in infants, and

[39] K. M. B. Bridges, *Social and Emotional Development of the Pre-school Child*, London, Kegan Paul, 1931.
[40] Ruth W. Washburn, *A Study of Smiling and Laughing of Infants in the First Year of Life*, Genetic Psychology Monographs, Vol. 6, Nos. 5-6 (1929), pp. 397-537.

by Bayley [41] in an investigation of the crying behavior in standardized situations of infants who are less than one year of age.

Bridges recognizes that children's emotions are relatively variable and superficial but feels that they develop fairly systematically as an accompaniment of experience. A particular emotion is determined by circumstances, both internal and external, of the situation which elicits it. General *distress,* which in infancy is marked by muscle tension, difficulties in breathing, change in facial color, and crying, becomes differentiated with experience and bodily development into *anger* at interference and *fear* at sudden shocks. Bridges believes that "although children vary considerably in their emotional reactions, certain groups of them show elements in common in their behavior. This is probably due to the fact that children have many emotional experiences in common. They are subject to similar emotion-producing situations both at home and at school." (page 187) This is a somewhat different interpretation from Gesell's, which, it will be recalled, maintains that emotional growth is in the main a function of emerging innate patterns of a specific nature.

Methods of Studying Children's Emotions.—The difficulties involved in studying the emotional aspects of child development are increased by the inability of infants and young children to report their affective experiences. This fact has made it necessary to utilize carefully controlled objective methods, as far as it is possible to do so, in the determination of the nature and intensity of childhood affective reactions. Some investigators [42] have attempted to utilize the principle of the Keeler polygraph or "lie detector," an instrument designed to register changes in breathing and blood pressure, in the measurement of infant emotional responses. Such a method is suggestive, but is largely vitiated by the inability of young subjects to understand and cooperate in its application. The results secured

[41] Nancy Bayley, "A Study of the Crying of Infants During Mental and Physical Tests," *Journal of Genetic Psychology,* 40 : 306-329 (1932).

[42] M. C. Jones and Barbara S. Burks, *Personality Development in Childhood,* Monographs of the Society for Research in Child Development, Vol. 1, No. 4 (1936), pp. 64-65.

have thus been too variable to lend themselves to quantitative interpretation.

Standardized tests [43] of the questionnaire variety have been found useful in ascertaining how children feel, think, and act about problems pertaining to their personal and social adjustment. Such instruments can be used by clinicians and teachers as check lists in the determination of the extent of emotional stresses in children who are too young to read. They have been found useful for detecting feelings of security, self-reliance, sense of belongingness, withdrawing tendencies, antisocial inclinations, nervous symptoms, and similar "weather vanes" of emotional status. A more detailed account of these and other types of social adjustment tests will be given in a later section devoted to the measurement of personality adjustment. A scrutiny of their design will reveal the present tendency to study emotional reactions in relation to personality development.

A parallel trend is that of endeavoring to ascertain the emotional status of normal children, and of supplying the needs of those who are maladjusted through observation of their play activities.[44] Investigators hope to utilize this avenue of untrammeled self-expression as a means of effecting the emotional readjustment of children. Somewhat similar efforts are being made to diagnose children's basic attitudes and state of emotional development through their interpretations of paintings, drawings, pictures, ink blots, and other art materials.[45] This medium has provided data relating to children's frustrations, defense mechanisms, compensatory activities, and phantasies.

Children's Fears: Their Nature and Control.—A controlled investigation by Jersild and Holmes [46] has disclosed new

[43] See, for example, Walther Jöel, "Behavior Maturity of Children of Nursery School Age," *Child Development*, 7 : 3 (1936). Also Louis P. Thorpe, Willis W. Clark, and Ernest W. Tiegs, *The California Test of Personality*, Primary and Elementary Series, California Test Bureau, Los Angeles, 1939-40.

[44] Erik H. Erikson, *Studies in the Interpretation of Play, I: Clinical Observation of Play Disruption in Young Children*, Genetic Psychology Monographs, Vol. 22, No. 4 (1940), pp. 557-671. Also Leo Kanner, "Play Investigation and Play Treatment of Children's Behavior Disorders," *Journal of Pediatrics*, 17 : 533-546 (1940).

[45] Elizabeth W. Amen, *Individual Differences in Apperceptive Reaction: A Study of the Response of Preschool Children to Pictures*, Genetic Psychology Monographs, Vol. 23, No. 2 (1941), pp. 319-385.

[46] Arthur T. Jersild and Frances B. Holmes, *Children's Fears*, Child Development Monographs, No. 20 (1935).

evidence concerning children's fears. Employing eight experimental situations which have been known to elicit fear reactions in young children, these psychologists endeavored to ascertain the characteristic types of fear behavior displayed by them at the various preschool ages. Data from a total of 105 subjects netted the following results: "Animals (dog and snake) elicited signs of fear most frequently; next in order of effectiveness was a dark room, followed by a high place, a strange person, and a loud sound; least effective were situations representing insecure footing and being left alone. The order of effectiveness changed with age. In the study as a whole, the results show a sharp decline with age in the frequency of fear in response to the specific situations that were used." (page 301)

These investigators thus found that up to the fifth year, fear may often show a decline, rather than an increase, with age. Fear of dogs, for example, declined slightly from age two to three, but remained constant through the age of four. Fear of being left alone and of a dark room increased between the ages of two and three, but declined at four and disappeared at five. Fear of snakes showed a gradual decline after the fourth year. The rate of these and other fear fluctuations are indicated graphically in Figures 58a and 58b.

A significant feature of this research was the negative finding relating to Watson's doctrine of consistent and permanently conditioned fears. The evidence suggested that it is hazardous to predict under what conditions a given child will display fear. As the authors write, "the same child may face a given situation at a certain time without showing fear but at a later time, with no grossly apparent intervening causal factors, the same situation gives rise to fear. Further, the data show again and again that a child may be afraid on his first contact with a certain event and show no fear when he meets it a second time. . . . The picture of conditioning that has sometimes been proposed—a child, a rat, a sudden noise, the rat leaps, the child starts, the child subsequently fears rats and other furry things—is a decided oversimplification of what occurs in daily life."

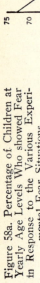

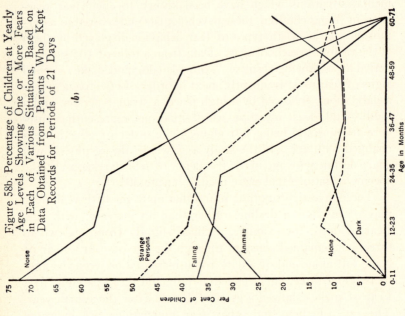

Figure 58b. Percentage of Children at Yearly Age Levels Showing One or More Fears in Each of Various Situations, Based on Data Obtained from Parents Who Kept Records for Periods of 21 Days

Figure 58a. Percentage of Children at Yearly Age Levels Who showed Fear in Response to the Various Experimental Fear Situations

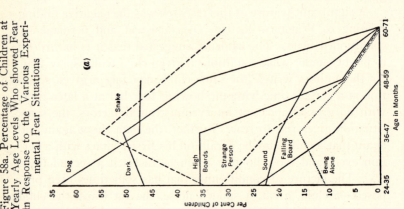

(From Arthur T. Jersild and Frances B. Holmes, *Children's Fears*, Child Development Monographs, No. 20 (1935), p. 230.)

In a study [47] in which parents reported the objects and situations which elicited fear in their children, it was found that for those less than one year of age the greatest fears were associated with: (1) noises and events revolving about them; (2) strange situations, objects, or persons; (3) falling objects, sudden movement, threats of bodily pain or harm; and (4) animals. Except for fear of injury or bodily harm and the fear of animals, the fear value of all these situations had decreased by the age of five. As these children grew older they tended to show an increasing fear of such less tangible factors as ghosts, death, supernatural events, skeletons, corpses, and being left alone in the dark.

After the fifth year a variety of new situations become effective in producing fear reactions.[48] In the typical child's sixth year he begins to be afraid of imaginary situations such as kidnapers, dreams, imaginary creatures, queer people, and being abandoned by parents. This trend represents a transition from fear of concrete objects and situations to concern about unreal, intangible experiences. Even feared animals are not as a rule ones with which children have encountered frightening experiences or injury.

It should perhaps be pointed out that a certain amount and kind of fear is a valuable asset to children; it helps keep them out of trouble and away from danger. An individual is not necessarily immature emotionally if he is afraid of certain objects and situations. If he had no fear, a child might readily step in the way of fast moving trains, endeavor to pet wild animals, jump off high roofs, and perhaps step into swift running streams. Fear enables the child to avert many a catastrophe; it causes him to run, hide, or fight when inaction might result in serious injury, as in the case of being caught in a burning building or a bombing raid. When experienced in moderation and when it leads to adaptive action, fear is a valuable regulator of the child's safety.

[47] Arthur T. Jersild and Frances B. Holmes, "Some Factors in the Development of Children's Fears," *Journal of Experimental Education*, 4: 13-141 (1935).
[48] Arthur T. Jersild, F. V. Markey, and C. L. Jersild, *Children's Fears, Dreams, Wishes, Daydreams, Likes, Dislikes, Pleasant and Unpleasant Memories*, Child Development Monographs, No. 12 (1933).

CAUSES AND KINDS OF FEAR.[49]   Although it is not always clear from whence fears come, a few sources have been determined, a knowledge of which may help a child or his parents better to cope with them. An understanding of the origin of an unreasonable fear will not necessarily eliminate it, but may lead to its more intelligent conquest later on. The following five sources of fear are suggestive:

1. *Ignorance or Superstition.* Children are often relatively ignorant of cause and effect relationship, and they may thus believe that unseen forces of an intangible nature are trying to harm them. It pays to be well informed because knowledge dispels fear.

2. *Fixed Ideas or Illogical Beliefs.* Some children are taught to believe that vaccination will bring sure death, that a broken mirror will bring disaster, that thirteen is an unlucky number, and that there is no escaping ghosts. They may also develop the idea that they are doomed always to be inferior. Such fixed ideas cause unreasonable fears.

3. *Forgotten Childhood Experiences.* A child may have an inordinate fear of automobiles but be unable to remember how he acquired it. He may also be afraid of water, policemen, elevators, cats, or members of a certain race. This is the "conditioned" fear so often associated with frightening experiences in early childhood.

4. *The Feeling of Insecurity with People.* Some children feel that their classmates do not care for them and that they are unpopular and more or less unwanted. This is the anxiety form of fear but it is none the less inimical to the development of emotional maturity.

5. *The Fear Behavior of Parents.* The child who sees his father cringe at the sound of thunder or his mother act as though she is being tortured in the dentist's chair is likely to develop these fears. Judging from the resemblances between children's and parents' fears (especially the mother's), the former must introject (take into himself) his parents' emotional behavior.

COPING WITH FEARS.   There need be no concern with the conquest of reasonable fears. Children might well be afraid

[49] Louis P. Thorpe, *Problems of Personality* (unpub. ms.), The Univ. of Southern California, 1945, pp. 34-37.

of getting their hands near fire, of grasping sharp metal objects, or of devouring the contents of attractive looking bottles housed in the bathroom medicine closet. Irrational fears should, however, be conquered before they make too great inroads on the child's sense of security. There are a number of procedures that have proved helpful in coping with such fears. These include the following:

1. *Becoming Better Informed.* Children are likely to be less fearful if they have a fair understanding of the laws of nature. The child who knows that accidents, misfortunes, and diseases are caused by natural events (careless driving, forgetting to turn out the gas, violating quarantine laws, etc.) is not concerned with fear of the mysterious or the unknown. Plato once said, "Better to be unborn than untaught because ignorance is the root of misfortune."

2. *Learning to Relax.* Tension is an ally of fear; relaxation is its mortal enemy. Since fear is a state of tension it would pay parents to learn to relax and to enable their children to do the same. Muscle tensions are associated with irrational fears and with nervous disorders. A feeling of security is promoted by learning to relax the body and by developing a relaxed outlook on life.

3. *Unlearning Childhood Fears.* This is the "unconditioning" process to be described more in detail later. By its method the child is led to become accustomed to the things he fears by *gradual degrees* and under *pleasant* and reassuring conditions. A child who is afraid of water could, for example, participate in a picnic near the water and later wade in a shallow section with good friends who provide an atmosphere of pleasure and security. Fears of people, animals, and objects could be overcome in a similar manner.

4. *Doing the Thing One Fears.* It is best neither to avoid nor fight a fear. With the help of an adult the child should be led to find out what is causing his fear and subsequently to work toward its removal. If he is afraid of certain people, the child should be given the probable reasons for such a situation and taught to meet these people under reassuring circumstances. Insofar as possible it is well to take an "I don't care" attitude toward unreasonable fears.

5. *Removing Feared Objects.* This is sometimes called the method of disuse, and involves keeping the child away from fear-evoking situations. If he is afraid of snakes, he can be shielded from exposure to either real or pictorial reproductions of such creatures. This procedure will not, of course, prevent the child from being afraid of imaginary snakes. A related method is that of providing distractions when fear situations arise. It is illustrated by playing games while a thunderstorm is in progress.

Other Emotions.—The emotion of fear has been discussed at length because of its major role in the determination of maladjustment in children. *Worry* and *anxiety* may be regarded as milder forms of insecurity but as being related to fear. The child is afraid of people or objects that are present to his senses, but worries about those he expects to be confronted with at a later time. Anxiety is as a rule a general or "free-floating" condition in which the child lives in a state of insecurity. *Hatred* and *anger* are emotions elicited by threats to the child's self-esteem and, like anxiety states, are discussed in a later section in connection with mental hygiene problems (Chapter 15). The positive emotion of *joy* is, of course, a reaction to success or good news and represents a state marked by adequate physiological tonus and psychological well-being. *Love,* an indefinite term, is used to mean an affectional relationship between the child and some other person based on the fact of having been accorded close recognition and response. Since all of these emotions (or feelings) are reactions to stimuli having a bearing on personal integrity or security, it is probably better that they be considered in connection with the child's flow of experiences and general development than as detached topics as such. This plan has in the main been followed throughout this book.

Experiments in Emotional Conditioning

The conditioning process, an explanation of which is given in the pages to follow, is believed to provide the key to the origin of many of children's emotionally charged biases, beliefs, preferences, prejudices, and even an appreciable share of their general attitudes. To some psychologists, the process of conditioning represents the very foundation of child development and personality formation. Some would, in fact, contend that the growing child's psychological life is but an elaborate organization of chains of conditionings which together constitute his uniqueness as a member of society.

Definition of the Conditioned Response.—The apparently simple but actually involved form of learning traditionally known as the *conditioned response* may be defined as that in which a reaction comes to be elicited by a stimulus which was not originally effective in evoking it. This means that a great many childhood reactions, both desirable and undesirable, come to be causally connected with stimulating conditions which did not natively arouse them. A child may, for example, exhibit marked fear of the water in a bathtub, a stimulus-response connection which is not present in infants who have experienced no frightening situations in relation to water.

The implications for the growing child's welfare of this phenomenon of learning should be evident. Even older children may be conditioned to fear objects and situations which are known to be harmless, and may come to distrust people who are merely associated with unpleasant events in their past life. Many a child has apparently come to be fearful of dark rooms or of furry animals as a result of encountering these objects simultaneously with certain originally terrifying stimuli. Furthermore, a great many conditioned fears and biases become so spontaneous and so deeply entrenched in an individual's repertoire of responses that they are believed by many to be biologically inherited. It is thus apparent that considerable confusion has arisen concerning the origin of irrational and efficiency-disturbing emotional tendencies.

PAVLOV'S FAMOUS STUDY OF DOGS. Our most tangible information concerning the conditioned response phenomenon stemmed originally from the experimental work of the Russian physiologist, Pavlov.[50] This inventive investigator secured his data from extensive studies of dogs carried on in soundproof

---

[50] I. P. Pavlov, *Conditioned Reflexes*, New York, Oxford Univ. Press, 1928.

laboratories so constructed that they could be controlled from the outside by means of pneumatic and electrical conductors, thus eliminating the presence of the experimenter. Early in the course of his work, Pavlov noticed that, whereas saliva would ordinarily begin to flow in a dog's mouth only upon the presentation of food, it later came to do so at the sight of someone bringing food or even at hearing the steps of an approaching keeper. As a result of this clue, Pavlov entered upon the long series of experiments which eventuated in the establishment of the now famous "conditioned reflex" and "conditioned stimulus" principles of learning.

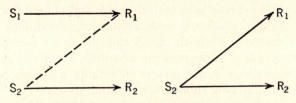

Figure 59. The Conditioned Response

Originally, S_1 evokes only R_1, and S_2 elicits only R_2. When these reactions occur simultaneously a sufficient number of times, stimulus S_2 becomes capable of calling forth R_1.

Pavlov's principal contribution to psychology was his discovery that when two stimuli—for example, meat, which natively evokes the flow of saliva, and the ringing of a bell, which elicits no definite reaction—are presented *simultaneously* (approximately) a certain number of times, the sound of the bell (conditioned stimulus) comes to evoke the saliva-flowing reaction (conditioned response) which was originally brought out by the unconditioned stimulus (meat-securing situation). Other experiments with the conditioned response led this seemingly tireless scientist to perform many astounding feats with dogs, among which were the ability to discriminate between high and low musical sounds and to delay responses to conditioned stimuli for a number of minutes.

Early Experiments on Child Conditioning.—The outcomes of pioneer experiments on animal conditioning early led psychologists to recognize the import for child development of this relatively simple method of learning. There are several features of the conditioned response that make it especially useful in child psychology. These apparently well-established phenomena include the following: (1) Conditioned responses are so easily established that they may be established in the lower forms of animal life, even in insects.[51] This fact suggests the facility with which they may be inculcated in infants and children. (2) As previously mentioned, conditioned associations may occur without the individual concerned being aware of their presence or origin. A child may come to fear dogs because of having encountered a frightening noise several times while handling, for example, a pet rabbit. In such a case, whereas the child was the unwitting victim of an uninvestigated and unnoticed conditioning in connection with a furry animal, his parents may naively believe that his dislike for dogs is an "innate" personality trait. A great deal of unconscious learning may take place in this way throughout infancy and early childhood.

(3) Conditioned responses may, under appropriate circumstances, become associated with any stimulus whatsoever. Investigators [52] have been able, for example, to condition dogs to respond positively to food when the right hind leg was extended forward, but to react negatively when the leg was placed in any other position. It is not uncommon for infants who have become accustomed to being fed every few hours to begin making sucking movements when feeding time comes around, even before the food stimulus is presented. In such instances internal physiological stresses constitute a substitute or conditioned stimulus. This and similar examples make it evident that the conditioning process is an important factor in the course of early development.

(4) Any response from any part of an organism may become attached to a given conditioned stimulus. This principle is illustrated by an experiment reported in Pavlov's writings in which the reactions of dogs to hypodermic injections of morphine were later elicited by the sight of the preliminary prepara-

---

[51] E. R. Hilgard and D. G. Marquis, *Conditioning and Learning,* New York, D. Appleton-Century Co., Inc., 1940.

[52] E. S. May and J. A. Larson, "Posture-Sense Conduction Paths in the Spinal Cord," *American Journal of Physiology,* 50 : 204-208 (1920).

tions (exposing skin area, disinfecting with alcohol, and bringing out hypo needle) for such an operation. A similar experiment by Menzies [53] with humans further portrays the possibilities of this principle. Subjects who had previously experienced a rise or fall in skin temperature as the result of having a hand immersed in a jar of warm water or of "ice" water, were so conditioned that a similar response came to be evoked by the sound of a buzzer, postures of the subject's hand or arm, the whispered repetition of a word by the subject, and a visual stimulus made up of illuminated crosses. This outcome suggests the possibility of the conditioned origin, in childhood, of later neurotic symptoms, especially those of a hysterical nature.

RUSSIAN INVESTIGATIONS WITH CHILDREN. Most of the early experiments on conditioning in children were carried out in Russia by pupils of Pavlov. Although these investigations were originally published in the Russian language, a few translations of the principal findings are available.[54] In 1907 Krasnogorski entered upon the task of applying Pavlov's conditioning method to the study of children. He soon found that when a blindfolded child is fed chocolate candy (unconditioned stimulus) at the same time that a bell is rung (conditioned stimulus), the latter stimulus (bell ringing) comes, after a few trials, to bring out the swallowing movements originally elicited only by the organically satisfying chocolate stimulus. This investigator thus established the fact that children as well as animals readily learn to respond to "shifted" stimuli. Krasnogorski also found that the more intelligent children acquired the modification of behavior involved in conditioning much more readily than did their less able associates.

Mateer,[55] an American psychologist, has made an extensive check of Krasnogorski's findings. In an experimental investigation involving fifty normal children, ranging from one to

[53] R. Menzies, "Conditioned Vasomotor Responses in Human Subjects," *Journal of Psychology*, 4: 75-120 (1937).
[54] See, for example, the German report by N. I. Krasnogorski, *Bedingte und unbedingte Reflexe im Kindesalter und ihre Bedeutung für die Klinik*, Berlin, Springer, 1931. Also G. H. S. Razran, "Conditioned Responses in Children: A Behavioral and Quantitative Critical Review of Experimental Studies," *Archives of Psychology*, No. 148 (1933).
[55] Florence Mateer, *Child Behavior*, Richard G. Badger (Boston, Chapman & Grimes), 1918.

seven years of age, and fourteen children of low intelligence, she secured results comparable to the Russian outcomes. Mateer's method was that of attaching a pneumatic tambour to a blindfolded child's throat in such a manner as to record, on a moving strip of paper, any movements made by the throat in swallowing.   A series of trials was then carried out in which a piece of sweet chocolate was dropped into the child's mouth ten seconds after the bandage was slipped down over his eyes. Every experimental child eventually came to make swallowing movements after the blindfold was attached but *before* the chocolate was administered. Thus, with the application of a blindfold and the later feeding of sweets, swallowing eventually came to be the *delayed* conditioned response to the blindfold alone.   Mateer, too, found that mentally deficient (intelligence test scores) children frequently require two or three times as many repetitions as do normal subjects to fix the conditioned association firmly.

Other results secured by Krasnogorski [56] seem equally significant for personality development in children. Following Pavlov's technique in conditioning his dogs to discriminate among differences in tone waves, he found that children can learn to react, for example, to a metronome beat of 144 strokes per minute, while declining to do so when the rate for the same length of time is but 92 strokes.   Krasnogorski also noted that when the difference in metronome beat rate is reduced to a minimum of 144 versus 132 strokes children either become nervous and irritable or actually go to sleep. Excited responses or deep relaxation were also in evidence when children were required to respond after certain periods of delay. Many of the subjects were able to delay their responses to a conditioned stimulus, such as the ringing of a bell, for as long as several minutes, but when pressed to do so beyond a certain point, became unable to continue. This investigator believes that such results point to a plausible method for differentiating among stable and nervously unstable children.

[56] N. I. Krasnogorski, "The Conditioned Reflexes and Children's Neuroses," *American Journal of Diseases of Children,* 30: 753-768 (1925).

RECENT AMERICAN EXPERIMENTS. The presentation of a few of the more recent and representative American experiments on infant conditioning should make this phenomenon of behavior modification sufficiently clear to indicate its import for child psychology. A study by Jones,[57] for example, showed that infants can be conditioned to respond to a light or to a sound in much the same manner as they do to a slight electric shock. By administering the mild shock to the skin of infants three to nine months of age at the same time that light, a touch, or a sound was presented, Jones was able to secure a response, as registered by deflections on a galvanometer, resembling emotional reactions in adults to these conditioned stimuli. It should perhaps be mentioned that one infant became so thoroughly conditioned to a sound stimulus that the tendency to respond as he would in the case of an electro-tactual stimulus was still present in marked form six weeks after the last experimental administration.

Wenger [58] has found that, although marked individual differences exist and results are neither stable nor easily obtained, conditioned responses can be established in infants in the first week of life. By presenting a tactual stimulus simultaneously with an unconditioned stimulus in the form of a flash of light, this investigator was able to condition the eyelid closure to the tactual stimulus by the infant's fifth day. She also succeeded in some instances in conditioning a withdrawal response (to a mild shock) to a flash of light by the sixth day. Even more striking results were secured in a series of conditioning experiments conducted by Kantrow.[59] Through the use of motion pictures and records of crying and other bodily activity, she conditioned infants between one and four months of age to respond with sucking movements to the sound of a buzzer. As a bottle (nipple) was inserted into the infant's mouth, a buzzer

[57] Harold E. Jones, "The Retention of Conditioned Emotional Reactions in Infancy," *Pedagogical Seminary and Journal of Genetic Psychology*, 37 : 485-498 (1930).
[58] M. A. Wenger, "An Investigation of Conditioned Responses in Human Infants," *Univ. of Iowa Studies in Child Welfare, Studies in Infant Behavior*, Vol. 12 (1936), pp. 8-90.
[59] Ruth W. Kantrow, "An Investigation of Conditioned Feeding Responses and Concomitant Adaptive Behavior in Young Infants," *Univ. of Iowa Studies in Child Welfare, Studies in Infant Behavior*, Vol. 13, No. 3 (1937).

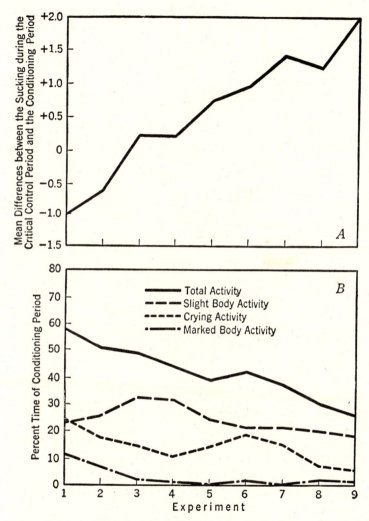

Figure 60. Curves of Sucking (*A*) and Activity (*B*) of Fifteen Infants for Nine Consecutive Experiments

(From Ruth W. Kantrow, "An Investigation of Conditioned Feeding Responses and Concomitant Adaptive Behavior in Young Infants," *Univ. of Iowa Studies in Child Welfare, Studies in Infant Behavior,* Vol. 13, No. 3 (1937), p. 32.)

was sounded for 15 seconds. In from one to five days the infants came to suck as vigorously at the sound of the buzzer as they did during a control period lasting from 25 to 75 seconds during which spontaneous sucking movements were recorded photographically. As Figure 60 shows, the infants exhibited a steady increase in amount of conditioned sucking movements and a steady decrease in amount of general activity associated with such conditioning.

These and other experiments offer factual evidence that both emotional and physiological conditioned reactions may be induced in infants and children during the early months and years. There is also evidence for the assertion that such modifications of behavior are sometimes retained for long periods of time.

Watson's Investigations of Conditioning.—Probably the most widely publicized experiments on emotional conditioning are those conducted by J. B. Watson and associates at Johns Hopkins University. The reader will perhaps remember that it was Watson who encountered the opposition of certain psychologists by declaring that his researches had demonstrated the inherited nature of three so-called original emotions, i.e., love, fear, and rage.

It will be recalled that it is Watson's [60] contention that newborn infants display fear responses to loud noises and loss of support only, and that the multitude of other fears so evident in the behavior of many adults must thus have been developed through some form of learning. As he says, "We know that hundreds of children are afraid of the dark, we know that many women are afraid of snakes, mice and insects, and that emotions are attached to a person and to places and to general situations, such as the woods, the water. . . . How do such attachments grow up? How can objects wh:ch at first do not call out emotions come later to call them out and thus greatly increase the richness as well as the changes of our emotional life?"

60 John B. Watson, *Behaviorism,* New York, W. W. Norton & Co., Inc., 1930, p. 158.

It was in an attempt to answer the critical question of the origin of fears and other emotionally charged responses that Watson entered upon his well-known experiments in child conditioning. In the end, he believed that his results warrant the conclusion that all affective reactions of major intensity, other than love, fear, and rage, are built in—"home made"—by the same conditioning process in evidence in Pavlov's experiments with dogs. In his book on child care Watson [61] stresses the point, for example, that whereas an unconditioned child is not afraid if placed in a dark room, he will come to be so if loud slamming of doors is permitted to occur simultaneously with such placement. Similarly, fear of a thunderstorm is engendered, not by flashes of lightning, but by the frightening claps of thunder which are associated with it. The child is unaware of the linkage, and may not even remember the incident (or incidents), but the tendency to display fear is nevertheless in evidence when darkness or storms are encountered. As conditioned stimuli they have come to evoke emotional responses which they did not originally elicit.

PROCEDURES IN EMOTIONAL CONDITIONING.   Watson's [62] conditioning technique is well illustrated in his account of the experiences of Albert B., an even-tempered infant of eleven months. After making certain that the child was not afraid of white rats and other furry animals, the investigator and his associates set out to determine whether they could condition the little fellow experimentally against these pets through the method of associating their presentation (simultaneously) with a loud noise produced by striking a heavy steel bar. Having previously ascertained the fact that Albert's response to such a noise was characterized by crying, throwing movements of the arms, and efforts to get away, Watson reasoned that he could condition the child against furry animals by substituting one of their number for the noise stimulus. Albert was accordingly subjected to the sound produced by the striking of the bar just as he reached for a friendly white rat. The result

[61] John B. Watson, *Psychological Care of Infant and Child,* New York, W. W. Norton & Co., Inc., 1928, pp. 45-56.
[62] John B. Watson and R. Rayner, "Conditioned Emotional Reactions," *Journal of Experimental Psychology,* 3: 1-14 (1920).

was a fear reaction on the child's part. At the next presentation of this dual stimulus he reacted as before except that he
now displayed some apprehension at the sight of the rat.

After three joint presentations of the rat and the sound stimulus a week later, little Albert exhibited distinct signs of fear
when the rat alone was shown. A few more double stimulations caused the boy to become what Watson regarded as permanently afraid of the rat. He further claims that the child's
fear had spread to include other small furry animals, even fur
coats, rugs, and wool material.

The Technique of Unconditioning.—Since children are
likely to develop conditioned attachments of varying degrees
of intensity between objects or people and fear, anger, or
anxiety responses, the question arises as to whether those
of an undesirable nature can be successfully broken. It
would appear to make considerable difference whether a child
who has fallen heir via the conditioning route to an irrational
fear can or cannot be relieved of such a handicap. Furthermore,
the conventional methods of reasoning with children, explaining the apparent origin of their conditioned fears, and pointing
to the fearlessness of other children to the objects of their own
concern, have not been successful in relieving them of their
more thoroughly intrenched conditioned tendencies. It was
for this reason that Watson and his assistants continued to
experiment with infants until they hit upon the method of "unconditioning."

Mary Cover Jones,[63] an associate of Watson's, has written
a graphic account of her experiences in unconditioning little
Peter, a child of approximately three years, who had come to be
terrified at the sight of rabbits, dogs, white rats, and even
feathers. Having learned the futility of insisting that the child
become accustomed to being near rabbits, Jones experimented
with the principle of associating the feared rabbit (conditioned
stimulus) by easy stages with the pleasurable activity of eating. Thus the feared stimulus was gradually attached to the

[63] Mary Cover Jones, "A Laboratory Study of Fear: The Case of Peter," *Pedagogical Seminary*, 31: 308-315 (1924). See also, by the same author, "Conditioning and Unconditioning Emotions in Infants," *Childhood Education*, 1: 317-322
(1925).

pleasurable activity by permitting Peter to see the rabbit at diminishing "safe" distances while engaging in the satisfying occupation of eating. On one or two occasions a day the rabbit was brought slightly nearer the child at eating time, until he became accustomed to its presence (under secure conditions). Finally, after watching a fearless playmate play happily with the rabbit for a time, Peter forgot his remaining fears and followed suit. In the end the little fellow came to hold the animal on his lap and to play with it much as he had done before becoming conditioned against it. Further experimentation disclosed the fact that he was no longer afraid of other furry animals or of feathers.

It can readily be seen that this type of reeducation is important for safeguarding the emotional development of young children. It must, however, be used with discretion, since in a case such as Peter's, the fear emotion might become attached to the food eating activity instead of the pleasurable element involved becoming conditioned to the sight of the rabbit. It is well to realize, further, that the number of experiences required for thorough unconditioning depends upon such factors as a given child's intelligence, age, physical condition, and the intensity and recency with which the conditioned response was established. Even when apparently thoroughly established, the unconditioned response is believed by some psychologists to fade over a period of years, if not properly reinforced.

Specific Applications to Child Life.—Many deeply imbedded behavior patterns are apparently built into the child's personality by way of the conditioning process. It is possible that unfortunate conditioning may cause an infant to become fretful, restless, and given to much crying; intelligently planned conditioning may, by the same token, bring about relatively stable behavior and a sense of well-being. It is normal, for example, for a baby who has been awakened gently regularly for approximately a week a certain number of hours after feeding, to continue to become active at the time the arousals were made. If adequately fed and safeguarded as to health, such a systematically trained child will not tend to awaken and cry (especially the latter) before the usual time. Habits of eating and sleeping are developed in the same way—regular routine and controls tend to condition the child's organism to respond in characteristic ways. It is probable that in the case of such physiological functions as sleeping, feeding, and eliminating, substitute stimuli in the form of muscle tonicity, kinesthetic sensations, and tensions of the visceral organs are principally involved.

Watson [64] has much to say concerning the manner in which fears are produced in the home. As he explains it, parents practically encourage the development of conditioned fears of the dark by permitting doors to slam, window shades to fall down, or screens (near an infant's crib) to fall over when their children are presumably safely asleep in a darkened room. The dropping of pots and pans and the slamming of doors are said to be "sledge hammers" in the shaping of children's fears. A peal of thunder, when occurring in connection with the occupancy of a dark room, may cause a young child to be afraid of the dark for weeks. Watson also emphasizes the influence of continual "don'ts," uttered in a loud voice, upon a child's sensitive nervous system. The powerful word "don't" is comparable to the steel bar in the laboratory and thus comes to elicit fear reactions in situations in which it is used as a stimulus. It is in this manner that many children are said to be conditioned to fear, for example, dogs, water, fire, and even such abstract concepts as devils, enemies, and wickedness.

The numerous ways in which a child may become conditioned for or against people, beliefs, attitudes, and objects in the environment is illustrated in the following summary: "The attachments formed early in childhood for certain persons—parents, relatives, or others—are almost invariably due to some conditioning process. The love for the mother is due to the constant pleasure received from the feeding and petting of the infant. . . . Later in life [he] may have a dislike for a person for no other reason than his name; that is, in all probability, due to some earlier experiences whereby the name has come to stand

[64] John B. Watson, *Psychological Care of Infant and Child*, New York, W. W. Norton & Co., Inc., 1928, pp. 54-68.

for some unpleasant contact. We may not in all cases be able to trace this attitude back to the original natural stimulus; the response, when once made, as conditioned from some original setting, may in itself become the cause of a new conditioning, and thus the chain may be spun out endlessly. The odor or sight of certain flowers may to some people be the cause of poignant grief, even though the cause of the emotion may be absent or forgotten; to others the same flowers may be the harbinger of happy thoughts and good fortune. Early conditioning and reconditionings have caused those emotional attitudes." [65]

The Maintenance of Emotional Control

The safeguarding of children's emotional life involves the intelligent regulation of stimulating conditions, not a course of training in emotional control *per se*. Children learn to adjust to frustration of their needs and to the requirements of their social and material environment, rather than to control their emotions as such. Emotions, defined either as intensely stirred-up states of the organism or as persistent stresses leading to personality disintegration, are *effects* of frustrating experiences.

Emotion and the Frustration of Needs.—Emotion arises primarily as a result of the blocking of behavior designed to satisfy either a dynamic need or a desire that contributes to the individual's sense of personal worth and security. Since children, like adults, are characterized by irreducible needs, it follows that the excessive denial of one or more of these dynamic factors will tend to bring about either disorganized emotional behavior or a gradual disintegration of mental health. The maintenance of emotional control thus involves the control of personality development in such a way as to guarantee the *balanced* realization of the fundamental needs in question. This is comparable to acknowledging that if we would improve the art of child rearing we must avoid the ravages of frustration and emotional maladjustment through harmonizing with

[65] Arne S. Jensen, *Psychology of Child Behavior,* New York, Prentice-Hall, Inc., 1938, p. 159.

the known facts of human development. Such a program would implement the quest for stability, not by way of so-called emotional control, but through the progressive fulfillment of the child's needs.

Evidence supporting the view that much emotional behavior represents a disorganized response to conditions of stress is offered in the researches conducted by Luria.[66] Reasoning that "emotional behavior actually depends upon how freely the tension which is produced in the nervous apparatus as a result of one or another conditions is discharged," this investigator proceeded to study (1) the reactions of university students awaiting examinations, (2) the behavior of criminals (including murderers) immediately after capture, and (3) the responses of subjects suffering from artificially induced neuroses and conflicts. Luria concluded that emotional behavior is a response to frustrating and other stress-producing conditions. He believes further that emotional behavior varies according to the circumstances of a thwarting situation and that it is not patterned in accordance with so-called innate tendencies.

Lewin [67] has also emphasized the dynamic nature of affective behavior in children. As he interprets it, the child is a functional part of the social field (group) in which he develops. The child's needs and dominant objectives are the sources of the energy tensions (called *vectors* by Lewin) which arise as he reacts to both goal-satisfying and goal-frustrating situations in the structural field of which he is a part. Emotions arise as the child's needs and goals—the vectors of force within his psychological field—are denied by frustrating factors. Lewin [68] (and associates) has illustrated his field theory of emotional stress by an experiment involving 30 children, ranging in age from twenty-eight to sixty-one months, designed to demonstrate the results of controlled frustration. Each of the children was observed under two situations: *first,* while playing in

[66] A. Luria, *The Nature of Human Conflicts,* New York, Liveright Pub. Corp., 1932.
[67] Kurt Lewin, "Environmental Forces," in *Handbook of Child Psychology* (edited by Carl Murchison), Worcester, Clark Univ. Press, 1933, Ch. 14.
[68] Roger G. Barker, Tamara Dembo, and Kurt Lewin, "Frustration and Regression: An Experiment with Young Children," *Univ. of Iowa Studies in Child Welfare,* Vol. 18, No. 1 (1941).

a standardized playroom where he could enjoy his toys without restriction and, *second*, after being placed in a situation in which a number of more attractive toys had been put beyond his reach by the insertion of a wire net partition through which he could see but not play with them (frustrating situation). The children varied greatly in the amount of time and energy they spent in attempting, by physical or social means, to overcome the barrier to the toys. Their behavior was marked by (1) efforts to kick, lift, or climb over the barrier; (2) attempts to influence the experimenter, through requests, threats, and coaxings, to remove the barrier; and (3) passive observation of or talking about the desired objects. Among other findings, the experimenters report that:

1. The frequency of happy actions decreases and that of unhappy actions increases in frustration. This change is positively related to the strength of the frustration.
2. The frequency of restlessness and of aggressive (emotional) actions is positively related to the strength of the frustration.
3. The amount of negative emotionality increases with the strength of the frustration.

Building Desirable Emotionalized Attitudes.—It is widely recognized that attitudes determine behavior, that they represent dispositions to behave in characteristic ways in certain stimulating situations. According to Allport,[69] "An attitude is a mental and neural state of readiness, organized through experience, exerting a directive or dynamic influence upon the individual's response to all objects and situations with which it is related." Attitude is not behavior, but is preparatory to behavior; it is a "precondition" to action which enables the individual to live reasonably consistently.

Allport has suggested four processes by which attitudes may be formed, all of which operate in the child's social and physical environment: (1) through the accretion and integration of numerous specific experiences of a similar type; (2) through the individuation of specific action-patterns out of originally

[69] Gordon W. Allport, "Attitudes," in *Handbook of Social Psychology* (edited by Carl Murchison), Worcester, Clark Univ. Press, 1935, pp. 810-811.

diffuse, mass-action behavior; (3) through the results of dramatic (traumatic) incidents of childhood which were of a more or less shocking nature; and (4) through "imitation of parents, teachers or playmates." If these be the true avenues of attitude development—and there is evidence that they are—it follows that the guaranteeing of emotional control becomes in the main a matter of desirable attitude building in childhood days. Emotionally stable attitudes in adulthood are apparently the result of satisfactory surroundings and experiences in childhood.

Since the emotional control exhibited by children is apparently the result of the way they have been treated in relation to their dynamic needs, it is imperative that those concerned with children's care understand how to deal with them effectively. The childhood conditions which contribute most to the maintenance of emotional stability in later life have been to some extent ascertained and may be listed as follows:

Adequate Material Facilities. The child who enjoys sufficient nourishing food, who is permitted to sleep to an extent commensurate with his needs and age, and whose health is intelligently safeguarded is more likely than one who does not enjoy these advantages to be characterized by emotional stability. When such a child also possesses adequate clothing, a few cherished toys, and other essential forms of economic security, he is likely to experience a sense of well-being that is foreign to fretfulness, inferiority, and other such expressions of emotional stress.

Secure Home Life. The child whose need for affection and personal status is adequately, but not excessively, satisfied in the home, will tend to develop a secure, stable outlook on life. Having been provided with a feeling of "belonging," the secure child is free from anxiety states concerning his place in the scheme of things. Since his fundamental needs have been given adequate expression, such a child is not often motivated to make emotional responses to frustrating situations. Wholesome parental attitudes are thus productive of spontaneous emotional control.

OPPORTUNITY FOR SELF-EXPRESSION. There is considerable clinical evidence suggesting that the child who is given reasonable opportunity for autonomous action, such as choosing his friends, assisting in the selection of his clothes, cooperating in the management of the home, and deciding, in part at least, how to spend an allowance, is more likely than a dominated child to react in a stable way to minor and, to a considerable extent, major frustrations. He is also relatively free from feelings of resentment at unnecessary restraint. When carried on in moderation, such a program of self-expression and self-reliance leads to the maintenance of emotional poise and control.

PROTECTION FROM HIGH EMOTIONAL STRESSES. Young children should be safeguarded against highly exciting events of two kinds. Serious nervous symptoms can arise from such intense experiences as being bitten by a dog, seeing a pet animal run over, or strangling in the bathtub. Every effort should be made to protect children from these and other horrifying (traumatic) episodes. Equally disastrous, although less intense, are emotions resulting from exposure to continual parental quarreling and dissension. Children feel the lash of such chronic insecurity and usually display the results in the form of anxiety and nervous symptoms.

OPPORTUNITY FOR SOCIAL LIVING. Young children should be provided with the opportunity of playing and socializing happily with associates of their own age. It is through social intercourse that children learn to express their feelings and emotions in approved ways. Such experience teaches them to inhibit, as well as to express, emotional stresses in a manner acceptable to those with whom they mingle socially. Since personal status and self-realization are contingent upon social acceptance, harmonious group activity is essential to the maintenance of emotional poise. The socially oriented child learns to consider the well-being of playmates and thus builds the foundation for emotional stability.

The Development of Emotional Maturity.—It is not uncommon to hear it said of an adult that he "acted like a child." Such an expression is taken to mean that chronological age does not guarantee the presence of a concomitant degree of emotional maturity. It suggests, rather, that the type of individual concerned has been arrested in his development and that he is still reducing his emotional stresses in infantile ways. Like the infant, he endeavors to influence his associates by explosive and irrational antics. The emotionally immature person is still using the methods of getting what he wants that he found productive of results when he was a child. Infantilisms which provided him with satisfactions at that period were continued and have now come to dominate his behavior.

If it were possible to regulate the experiences of children in such a way that socially desirable responses resulted in acceptance and a sense of well-being, and undesirable actions resulted in failure and unpleasantness, it is probable that such infantilisms as temper tantrums, pouting, and sensitiveness would not develop. Unfortunately, many individuals have been the victims of childhood conditions which led them to adopt false social values and to continue to indulge in emotionally immature behavior. Society is thus afflicted with an appreciable number of adults who exhibit such undesirable emotional responses as anger, resentment, suspicion, hatred, fear, not to mention bizarre beliefs and values concerning which they are highly emotional. *It is because of such emotional instability and immaturity that so many conflicts arise and that personal attributes condemned by society develop.*

The evidences of infantilism mentioned do not, of course, cover the entire range of acts which might properly be regarded as symptoms of failure to become mature emotionally. A list of infantilisms encountered in everyday life was recently offered by a group of 100 psychology students as including: (1) rationalization, or the tendency to give plausible reasons for inconsistent behavior; (2) showing-off, or attempting to attract undue attention by bluffing, posing, or wearing loud clothes; (3) anger when thwarted and resentment against authority and advice; (4) refusal to face reality, or conditions as they exist; (5) lack of consistency in conduct and emotion; (6) selfishness; (7) avoidance of difficult tasks; (8) jealousy; (9) decided crushes on individuals of the same sex; and (10) hero worship.[70] These and similar childish egocentric behavior patterns account for the social isolation of many otherwise capable children and youths. They suggest as well that individuals who are grown up emotionally are both more contented and more useful to society than those who are stunted in this respect.

So far as child development is concerned, "there is evidence that 'sets' or attitudes have developed at certain periods of life which have caused some individuals to retain a type of behavior fairly characteristic of certain ages in childhood. Records of workers in the field of mental hygiene are available showing that fixations of this kind often occur when some questionable infantile or adolescent behavior, such as crying or pretended illness, appears to pay dividends. Self-centeredness is developed in early childhood by example and by lack of experience concerning the advantages of generosity." [71] It is apparent that the development of emotional maturity is a result of intelligent child rearing.

Summary and Further Implications

Emotions may properly be regarded as highly stirred-up states of the organism and as emergency reactions to frustrating situations. Emotions have, however, been classified as being mild, strong, or disintegrative. Disintegrative emotions are said to develop when one or more of the individual's basic needs are consistently blocked over a period of time. Strong emotions are by definition disruptive and are often characterized by more or less maladaptive reactions to situations for which no satisfactory responses have been learned.

Feelings of well-being, sometimes called mild emotions, are conducive to morale and may be thought of as providing zest and "color" to experience. Feelings are not, however, by definition true emotions (highly stirred-up organic states). It could be reasoned thus that, whereas feelings are valuable (up to a certain point) as motivators to activity and to personality well-being, emotions are too high on the scale of intensity to

[70] Louis P. Thorpe, *Personality and Life,* New York, Longmans, Green & Co., 1941, p. 53.
[71] *Ibid,* p. 52.

avoid a shattering of efficiency. Even a state of "love" may, when sufficiently intense, render an individual incapable of judicious behavior. Man must acquire poise and rational control if he is to make an intelligent disposition of the many problems which continually confront him. Extreme expressions of emotion might thus well be avoided.

Investigations of conditioned response have provided valuable data concerning the origin and development of fears, prejudices, biases, anxieties, and emotionalized attitudes in general. Such studies have done much to change naive beliefs regarding the so-called instinctive and hereditary nature of emotional differences among individuals and between the sexes. Although it has been forced to share the credit for pointing out the origin of fears, antipathies, and other attitudes both with evidence for emotional maturation and with more complex theories of learning, the conditioned response principle has been influential in the development of child psychology as a science.

The statement is often made that modern society does not make sufficient provision for either the expression or the sublimation of strong emotions. It is also said that since individual physical struggle is not the usual mode of adjustment in modern civilization, emotional responses represent a menace rather than a benefit to man. So far as the rearing of children is concerned, it is probably logical to conclude that, instead of emphasizing either the expression or the repression of emotions, parents and others might well provide the types of experience that enable children to satisfy their organic and psychological needs and thus avoid, in the main, the repercussions of emotional upheavals. Well-balanced, emotionally stable children and youths who have developed wholesome attitudes toward the necessary sanctions of their social group experience relatively little difficulty about emotional control. Such emotional upheavals (crying, slang expressions, swearing, etc.) as they do encounter are usually of a mild and temporary nature and are characteristically controlled in harmony with their stable outlook.

These considerations strike an optimistic note concerning the important questions of character and personality develop-

ment in children. They suggest that those vested with the care
and education of the Nation's offspring concern themselves both
with alleviating the causes of excessive emotional behavior and
with creating conditions designed to prevent the appearance of
strong or disintegrative emotional stresses.

QUESTIONS FOR DISCUSSION

1. What fundamental fallacy is involved in regarding emotions
   as basic drives in children, i.e., as causal agents? How do emotions, as stirred-up states of the organism, operate in the chain
   of behavioral cause and effect?
2. Can it be said that emotions as such tend to dominate the
   intellectual processes in children and youths? What confusion
   arises when intelligence is thought of as a drive? What are the
   implications for child psychology of Dumas' theory of disintegrative emotions?
3. On what grounds could one argue that full-fledged emotions
   (not feelings) are adjustive agents in the life of a child? Suggest a more defensible view of the nature of adjustment and
   be prepared to meet arguments against your position.
4. Do you agree that Cannon's Emergency Theory of emotion
   is preferable to the James-Lange and other views? Why?
   What would be the value for child psychology of defining
   emotion as a stirred-up state of the entire organism? Explain
   your position clearly.
5. Why is it that in spite of so much experimental evidence to
   the contrary many people continue to believe that there are
   present at birth a few clearly differentiated emotional patterns
   such as love, fear, and rage? Defend the organismic view that
   original emotional responses are generalized and undifferentiated.
6. Defend the view that a free expression of pent-up emotions
   on the part of older children might contribute to the very
   emotional instability which it is intended to forestall. By way
   of what psychological processes could this unfortunate state
   of affairs come about? Illustrate.
7. What is the practical advantage of understanding the details
   of Watson's and others' experiments in conditioning children
   if no laboratory facilities are ordinarily available? Is it true
   that most conditioned responses are "picked up" unnoticed in

the flow of everyday experience? What can be done about this? Give examples.

8. In what way could the material presented in this chapter be said to constitute an optimistic view of child development? Has it opened up avenues for the possible acquisition of desirable personality traits? Explain.

9. What evidence can you advance indicating that the suppression of emotions is likely to cause serious maladjustment? Would it be better to encourage suppressed children to give vent to their emotions regardless of social consequences? Offer an answer that would be acceptable to parents and teachers.

10. Name two or three ways other than those mentioned in the text to prevent the development of emotional instability in children. What proof do you have that "controlling the emotions" means the prevention of prolonged emotional stress rather than the repression of immediate emotional expression? Elaborate.

Recommended Readings

Cannon, W. B. *Bodily Changes in Pain, Hunger, Fear and Rage.* New York: D. Appleton-Century Co., Inc., 1929.

Dunbar, H. Flanders. *Emotions and Bodily Changes.* New York: Columbia Univ. Press, 1935.

Jersild, Arthur T., and Holmes, Frances B. *Children's Fears.* New York: Bureau of Publications, Teachers College, Columbia Univ., 1935.

Jones, M. C. "Emotional Development," in *Handbook of Child Psychology.* (Edited by Carl Murchison.) Worcester: Clark Univ. Press, 1933, pp. 271-302.

Landis, Carney. "The Expressions of Emotion," in *Handbook of General Experimental Psychology.* (Edited by Carl Murchison.) Worcester: Clark Univ. Press, 1934, pp. 312-351.

Luria, A. *The Nature of Human Conflicts.* New York: Liveright Pub. Corp., 1932.

Prescott, Daniel A. *Emotion and the Educative Process.* Washington, D.C.: American Council on Education, 1938.

Ruckmick, Christian A. *A Psychology of Feeling and Emotion.* New York: McGraw-Hill Book Co., Inc., 1936.

Senderling, Ellwood, W. "Emotional Problems," in *Encyclopedia of Child Guidance.* (Edited by Ralph B. Winn.) New York: The Philosophical Library, 1943, pp. 135-138.

Taylor, J. H. *Innate Emotional Responses of Infants.* Columbus: Ohio State Univ. Studies, Contributions to Psychology, No. 12 (1934).

Thorpe, Louis P. *Personality and Life.* New York: Longmans, Green & Co., 1941, Ch. 3.

Watson, John B. *Psychological Care of Infant and Child.* New York: W. W. Norton & Co., Inc., 1928.

CHAPTER 10

THE DEVELOPMENT OF MOTOR ABILITIES

IF HE IS TO ENJOY THE MANY SATISFACTIONS available to him, the infant must learn to control his body. The fulfillment of organic and psychological needs, as well as the avoidance of harmful experiences, are contingent upon the acquisition of motor skills. The ability to effect such movements as crawling, sitting, standing, walking, running, jumping, and throwing is in turn requisite to intellectual and social growth. The mastery of handwriting and the utilization of language are both basically motor processes which can only be achieved insofar as the organism is physiologically developed and its musculature adapted to such communicatory skills. It should thus be realized that throughout infancy and childhood the mental, social, and personality development of the child are all closely allied with his sensorimotor behavior. The significance of motor activity for all-round development is thus of great moment.

Sequences in Motor and Sensory Development

The Nature of Sensorimotor Growth.—As recent researches dealing with the maturation of body structures have shown, the development of motor abilities follows an orderly sequence. The growing child does not gain control of various parts of his body in haphazard fashion. Development does not proceed, for example, from control of the feet to control of the hands, or from ability to bend the back to capacity for managing the neck muscles. As Shirley[1] and others have shown, the order of development of motor abilities follows a sequential schedule which begins with the head and neck, proceeds to the arms and other portions of the upper trunk, and concludes with

[1] Mary M. Shirley, *The First Two Years,* Vol. I: *Postural and Locomotor Development,* Minneapolis, Univ. of Minnesota Press, 1931.

the control of the lower part of the trunk, the legs, and the feet. This order of development, called the *cephalo-caudal* sequence, operates in postnatal motor growth in much the same manner as in prenatal structural development.[2]

Shirley's report of early motor growth demonstrated just such a schedule of development. One of the first orderly movements noted was that of the neonate following bright moving objects with his eyes. Then came the turning and lifting of

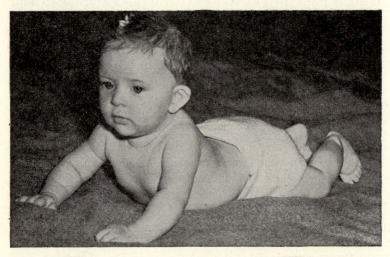

Figure 61. Holding Herself Up by Her Arms Is a Feat for the Five-Months-Old Baby. She greatly enjoys her newfound ability.

the head through the utilization of neck muscles. The three-months-old infant was able to raise his head from the floor when in a prone position with considerable facility. Following this sequence came the control of shoulders, arms, and hands. The typical child begins to notice his hands, to grasp objects in his vicinity, and, by the fifteenth week, to manipulate toys placed in his hands. Added maturity enables the infant finally to gain control of his lower trunk, legs, and feet. After learning to sit up by himself and to move his legs slightly, he begins to play

[2] For a brief account of prenatal motor development see Chapter 4, pp. 144-145.

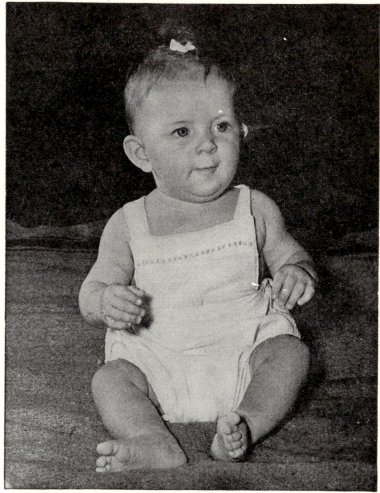

Figure 62. At Seven Months This Child Has Been Able to Sit Up Alone for Over a Month. She appears to like this form of independence.

with his toes and to control his legs more adequately. Subsequent to such development, it is not long until the healthy child creeps forward and backward, stands alone, walks independently, and runs about in play. It is also evident that postnatal control of a given part of the body precedes the ability to control its movements. The infant holds his head erect before being able to turn it and always stands before attempting to walk. And as Shirley [3] has pointed out, satisfactory motor development also involves a decreased weight-body ratio, an in-

Figure 63. Standing Alone While Holding on to a Sofa Has Been Mastered for Some Time by This Eleven-Months-Old Child. She is now able to pull herself up to this position.

creased leg-trunk ratio, and a shift in the center of gravity in the growing child's body.

Application of the Structure-Function Principle.—It is a recognized axiom that motor functions appear in a sequence and at a rate commensurate with the maturation of such structures as make possible their operation. As previously mentioned, it is necessary for body organs, muscles, nerve tissue, and their interlocking connections to reach a certain stage of de-

[3] Mary M. Shirley, *op. cit.*, p. 175.

velopment before specific types of motor skills can be exercised. As one writer [4] has expressed this principle, "all structures of the body must attain adequate differentiation before they are capable of highly specialized reactions. This fact of essential specialization is particularly clear in the nervous system. Individual nerve cells acquire differentiation in their bodies, in their cell processes (axones, dendrites) and in their intercellular connections. Adequate differentiation of this kind in nerve cells is a result of the gradual process of maturing."

Maturation may be regarded as an aspect of anatomical growth, as being intrinsic in the growing organism, and as constituting a necessary prerequisite to the appearance of a variety of forms of motor behavior. Such functions as running and sustained swimming could not, for example, be exercised before the maturing process had performed its task of "ripening" the inner structures concerned with such motor skills. Although learning is probably involved to some extent in the development of all motor skills, nervous system (and other structures) growth is apparently responsible, in harmony with a fundamentally intrinsic pattern, for the establishment of primary forms of behavior. According to Gesell,[5] maturation is an intrinsic regulatory mechanism which preserves the balance of structural growth and lays the basis for motor development. Only when the appropriate body structures reach the required state of maturity can stimuli initiate the complicated motor functions of which the organism is capable.

It is apparent that the development of motor abilities is contingent upon the rate of maturational processes as well as upon learning. Motor ability progresses with growth, which, when coupled with appropriate practice, may result in the development of a repertoire of skilled performances. Such progress is illustrated by the child's transition from walking to skating, from stair climbing to locomotion on a 60- or 70-degree inclined plane, and from manipulation of a small cube to baseball play-

[4] Frederick Tilney, in the introduction to Myrtle B. McGraw, *Growth: A Study of Johnny and Jimmy,* New York, D. Appleton-Century Co., Inc., 1935, p. vii.

[5] Arnold Gesell, "Maturation and the Patterning of Behavior," in *Handbook of Child Psychology* (edited by Carl Murchison), Worcester, Clark Univ. Press, 1933, p. 210.

ing. It follows from these facts that the growing child should be given every opportunity to exercise his muscles as they gain in maturity, also that he should not be required to attempt skilled acts until it is evident that his maturational status is adequate for their development. Any other procedure would usually be relatively futile, and might result in harm to the child.

Mass Action to Specialized Responses.—The organism of the neonate presents an almost continuous state of great activity. It is this flow of apparently spontaneous movements that has led psychologists to designate the infant's behavior as *mass activity*. It should not be supposed, however, that all such responses are random and chaotic, or even that all are entirely generalized. As Pratt [6] has shown, many supposedly random actions are organic continuations of fetal responses and are elicited by intraorganic stimuli having their origin principally in the gastro-intestinal tract. Other internal conditions are believed to lead to fairly specific responses which have perhaps erroneously been regarded as chaotic and non-localized.[7] Furthermore, observation will show that the initial response to almost any external stimulus, such as a touch of the foot or slight pressure of the arm, occurs first at the point stimulated, but that it spreads to other parts of the body sufficiently to give the appearance of chance and generalized activity.[8] As Dennis [9] has stressed, a number of neonate activities, such as sucking and smiling, are more or less specific and involve rhythmic, well-coordinated, and somewhat localized actions. The child may be observed, for instance, contracting and extending his nostrils in response to the demands of respiration, and narrowing and opening his eyes as he adjusts to changing light conditions in his immediate vicinity. The infant's early reflexes, such as the Babinski or toe-spreading response, the Moro or clasping reaction, and the Darwinian or grasping reflex, although not per-

[6] K. C. Pratt, "The Neonate," in *Handbook of Child Psychology* (edited by Carl Murchison), Worcester, Clark Univ. Press, 1933, Ch. 3.

[7] Kai Jensen, *Differential Reactions to Taste and Temperature Stimuli in Newborn Infants,* Genetic Psychology Monographs, Vol. 12, Nos. 5-6 (1932), pp. 361-479.

[8] L. Delman, "The Order of Participation of Limbs and Responses to Tactual Stimulation of the Newborn Infant," *Child Development,* 6 : 98-109 (1935).

[9] Wayne Dennis, "The Role of Mass Activity in the Development of Infant Behavior," *Psychological Review,* 39 : 593-595 (1932).

manent, are also instances of relatively specific forms of behavior.

It appears, nevertheless, that much of the newborn infant's
behavior, no matter how stimulated, is of the mass action (diffuse) variety. To quote Irwin,[10] who has made a detailed
study of neonate behavior during the first postnatal days: "The
most striking characteristic exhibited by infants during the first
ten days is the large amount of energy expended while mass
activity is in progress. It appears during hunger, previous to
belching, during regurgitation, intestinal disturbances, defeca-
tion, and occasionally during micturition [urination] . . . The
body squirms, twists, rolls, and bends. The back arches, the
hips sway, and the head rolls side to side or is thrown back.
The arms slash vigorously or are flexed sharply at ankle, knee,
and hip. Hands, feet, toes, and fingers are in continuous movement. Sucking and smacking sounds frequently occur, while
loud crying is usually coincident with mass activity. All of this
activity is more or less simultaneous and comes and goes with
periodicities which appear in intervals of a few seconds to
several minutes."

That much adaptive (differentiated) motor behavior evolves
from mass action is another axiom of child psychology. The
importance of this principle will become increasingly apparent
as the facts of development along postural and locomotion lines
are presented. It can be illustrated at this point, however, by
the experience of a typical child in learning to write. "He
grasps the pencil awkwardly, and not only moves his hand and
arm but contracts the muscles of his face, twists his body into
unnatural positions and clenches his left hand. . . . As the child
matures under stimulation, the wholes which he can perceive
and write as completed units become larger, and as they become
larger, the greater differentiation of the pattern that comes with
expansion gives a more precise direction to each line."[11]   Thus
does the child's motor skill develop from crude massive responses to detailed, adaptive movements.

[10] O. C. Irwin, *The Amount and Nature of Activities of Newborn Infants
Under Constant External Stimulating Conditions During the First Ten Days of
Life*, Genetic Psychology Monographs, Vol. 8, No. 1 (1930), pp. 1-92.
[11] R. H. Wheeler and F. T. Perkins, *Principles of Mental Development*,
New York, T. Y. Crowell Co., 1932, p. 474.

The rapidity with which progress in relatively simple motor skills may be made by preschool children is indicated in a study by Stutsman [12] in which a number of such children were required to button strips of flannelette three by six inches in size. The various tests involved buttoning a one-button, a two-button, and a four-button size strip of material. None of the eighteen-months-old children were able to manipulate the one-button test. Ten per cent of the two-year-olds and 80 per cent of the two-and-one-half-year-olds were able, however, to button the one-button flannelette strips. Ability with the two-button test increased most rapidly between the ages of two and one-half to three years. Ability to manipulate the more difficult four-button test increased most markedly between the ages of three and three and one-half. Other investigations have corroborated the facility with which infants and young children learn well-coordinated movements when given the benefit of physical maturity and a modicum of experience.

Development in Posture and Locomotion.—The capacity for locomotion, or getting from place to place, is an important function in the life of the child. The infant whose contacts are confined to the spot where he happens to be left and to the individuals who chance to come his way is handicapped in intellectual and social growth as well as in motor development. Crawling and walking lead to an enlargement of the child's environment and thus to an expansion of experience with both people and material objects. Locomotor activities are essential as well to the development of the skeletal muscles in relation to the sensory channels and neural structures which serve them as receptors of stimuli. Regardless of whether creeping and walking are natural products of neuromuscular maturation or whether their development is partially dependent upon the learning process, locomotion itself provides the basis for continued stimulation to growth in motor ability.

Apparently children do not always intuitively tend to walk or even stand in an upright position when the processes of inner maturation have made possible such motor activities. Some

12 Rachel Stutsman, *Performance Tests for Children of Preschool Age*, Genetic Psychology Monographs, Vol. 1, No. 1 (1926), pp. 1-67.

children develop the tendency, under certain circumstances, to get from place to place by running "on all fours." [13] Such children seem content to get about in positions other than the usually upright one. In support of this apparent anomaly of locomotion, Gesell [14] reports the case of a so-called "wolf child" who had been nurtured in a state of nature by wolves and who, when captured, continued to walk and run on all fours. Several

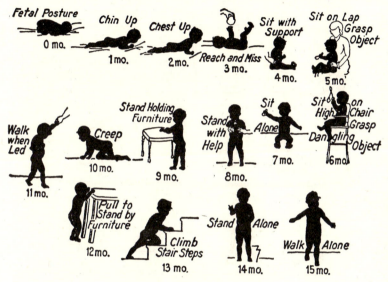

Figure 64. The Motor Sequence

(From M. M. Shirley, *The First Two Years,* Vol. II: *Intellectual Development,* Minneapolis, Univ. of Minnesota Press, 1933, p. iv.)

years were required to teach this child to walk in the upright position; even then she persisted in running as she had done as an inhabitant of the animal world. Regardless, however, of such findings or the extent of innateness of the tendency to get about in the upright position, it is safe to assume that the normal child will come to walk by the use of his legs (1) when he is sufficiently mature structurally, (2) when there is a recognized

[13] Ales Hrdlicka, *Children Who Run on All Fours,* New York, McGraw-Hill Book Co., Inc., 1931.
[14] Arnold Gesell, *Wolf Child and Human Child,* New York, Harper & Bros., 1941. See also J. A. L. Singh and Robert M. Zingg, *Wolf Children and Feral Man,* New York, Harper & Bros., 1942.

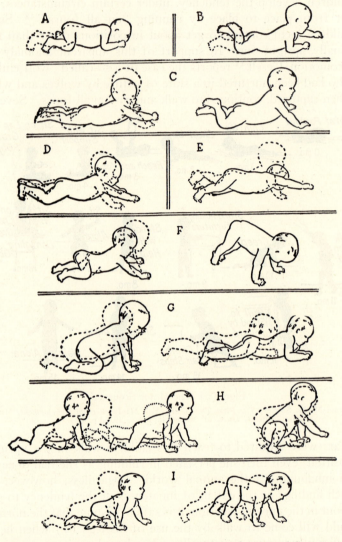

Figure 65. Illustrating Nine Phases in the Development of Crawling

(From Myrtle B. McGraw, "Development of Neuro-muscular Mechanisms as Reflected in the Crawling and Creeping Behavior of the Human Infant," *Journal of Genetic Psychology,* 58:86 (1941).

need for such locomotion, and (3) when an appropriate pattern of upright walking has been present in his visual field.

POSTURAL AND LOCOMOTION SCHEDULES. Motor development apparently never proceeds in random fashion. As can be seen from Figure 64, postural and locomotor growth, like other motor functions, unfold in an orderly sequence. Although there exists a general uniformity among infants in the order of this sequence, considerable variation obtains from child to child in the rate of appearance of patterns of locomotion. Such individual differences are believed to be due to variations in maturation ratio, to differences in criteria of development used by observers, and in some instances to lack of opportunity for engaging in motor activities.

A number of controlled observational studies of postural and locomotor development have made available data touching the genesis and sequence of these functions. Prominent among such investigations are those by Gesell,[15] Shirley,[16] Bühler and Hetzer,[17] Bayley,[18] Thompson,[19] and McGraw.[20] Although there are discrepancies among these developmental schedules (for average infants), the comparative figures in Table 21 portray the general rate and sequence of early motor development. Even after discounting the effects of differences in criteria of development and in the socio-economic status of the infants studied, it is evident that considerable agreement obtains concerning the sequences and tempo of motor growth.

From the foregoing facts and figures, the child's postural and locomotor development can be summarized as follows: by three or four months he can push or pull his hands and feet

[15] Arnold Gesell, *Infancy and Human Growth*, New York, The Macmillan Co., 1928; also Arnold Gesell and H. Thompson, *The Psychology of Early Growth*, New York, The Macmillan Co., 1938.

[16] Mary M. Shirley, *The First Two Years*, Vol. 1: *Postural and Locomotor Development*, Minneapolis, Univ. of Minnesota Press, 1931.

[17] Charlotte Bühler and H. Hetzer, *Testing Children's Development from Birth to School Age*, New York, Farrar & Rinehart, Inc., 1935.

[18] Nancy Bayley, *The Development of Motor Abilities During the First Three Years*, Monographs of the Society for Research in Child Development, Vol. 1, No. 1 (1935).

[19] Helen Thompson, "The Development of the Upright Posture," *Journal of Experimental Education*, 4: 103-111 (1935).

[20] Myrtle B. McGraw, *Growth: A Study of Johnny and Jimmy*, New York, D. Appleton-Century Co., Inc., 1935. See also Myrtle B. McGraw and Kenneth W. Breeze, "Quantitative Studies in the Development of Erect Locomotion," *Child Development*, 12: 267-303 (1941).

TABLE 21. THE DEVELOPMENT OF UPRIGHT POSTURE AND OF LOCOMOTION

Behavior item	Age in weeks as found by				
	Gesell	Shirley	Bühler and Hetzer	Bayley	Thompson
Lifts head when held to shoulder	4	—	—	2	—
Lifts head in prone position	4	3	2	—	4
Turns head laterally, prone position	4	—	—	3	—
Makes postural adjustment when lifted	4	—	—	2	—
Head bobbingly erect, upright position	8	—	8	7	8
Lifts head when suspended dorsally	8	—	—	11	—
Lifts chest, prone position	8	9	12	16	—
Holds head erect and steady, upright position	12	—	—	11	16
Elevates self by arms, prone position	12	—	20	14	16
Lifts foot when held erect	—	13	—	—	12
Legs extend recurrently, held erect	—	—	—	—	20
Sits with support	16	—	—	14	16
Lifts head and shoulders, dorsal position	16	—	20	20	—
Definite anticipatory adjustments to being taken up	16	15	—	13	—
Sits with slight support	20	19	—	18	20
Rolls from back to stomach	20	—	—	—	—
Rests momentarily on abdomen and chest, prone position	—	—	20	—	24
Rests on thighs, abdomen, chest, and hands, prone position	—	—	20	—	24
Sits alone momentarily, back rounded	30	25	—	23	24
Sits erect, briefly	32	—	—	—	24
Held erect, stands firmly	—	29	—	—	32
Stands, holding furniture	—	29	—	—	32
Regresses, lying prone	—	40	—	—	40
Rests on thighs, lower abdomen, and hands	—	—	—	—	36
Attains sitting from prone position	—	—	—	—	44
Attains creeping position from sitting	—	—	—	—	44
Pulls self to knees	—	—	—	—	44
Pulls self to standing	40	47	44	—	48
Creeps	—	45	32	38	48
Walks with help	48	45	48	44	—
Lowers self from standing to sitting	48	—	—	—	—
Stands alone	60	62	48	50	52
Walks alone	60	64	48	50	—
Achieves standing unaided	—	—	—	—	56–60
Walks sideways	—	—	—	66	—
Climbs stairs or chair	72	—	—	—	—
Walks backward	84	—	—	68	—
Goes up and down stairs	120	—	—	—	—
Tries to stand on one foot	120	—	—	—	—

with considerable coordination, hold up his head without support, and, when prone on his stomach, lift the upper half of his body. Although somewhat wobbly, the average six-months-old child can sit upright for a short time; he can also propel himself by hitching himself along on his stomach, and make stepping movements when held under the arms. By eight or nine

Figure 66. This Eight-Months-Old Infant Is Making Rapid Progress Toward His Goal (at least that of his parents) of Walking
(Used by permission of Hollywood Press Service, Inc.)

months the typical child has learned to go from place to place by one method or another. He may creep, crawl, push himself with his heels, or move along on one hip using his hands and one foot as propellers.

In his second year the developing child achieves the most spectacular accomplishment of his brief career—the ability to walk. After months of prerequisite training in muscular co-

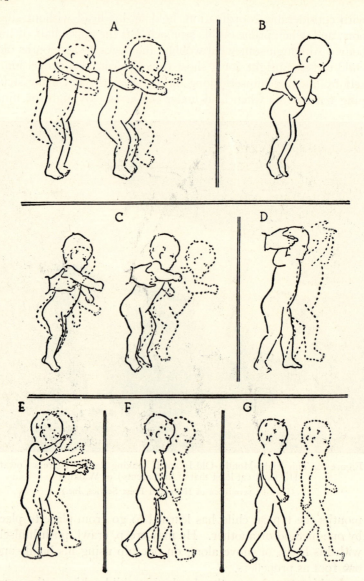

Figure 67. Drawings Illustrating Seven Phases in Learning to Walk

(From Myrtle B. McGraw, "Neuromuscular Development of the Human Infant as Exemplified in the Achievement of Erect Locomotion," *Journal of Pediatrics*, 17:750 (1940).)

ordination he is able to get from place to place in the upright position at from twelve to fifteen months of age. In subsequent months he learns to walk sideways, to climb stairs and articles of furniture, to walk backwards, and to walk up and down stairs. During the third year he develops the ability to stand on one foot, to jump with both feet, to jump from and over low objects, to turn somersaults, and to run with facility. The fourth year brings capacity for more elaborate jumping, for galloping and hopping, and for more skillful running. By the time he reaches school age the average child has become skilled in the fundamental types of locomotion—he can run, jump, hop, dance, and skip.

RECENT RESEARCH ON LOCOMOTION. Considerable attention has been focused during the last few years on studies of infant motor development in the areas of crawling and creeping, postural adjustments, swimming, upright locomotion, and stair climbing. An appreciable number of these investigations have been made by McGraw [21] in connection with the Columbia University Normal Child Development Study. Typical of the researches in question are those concerned with progression in walking and in stair climbing. Samples of these reports, together with interpretations concerning the maturational basis of development, will indicate the trends in motor research.

McGraw and Weinbach [22] have come to the conclusion, after an analysis of cinema records of infants' footprints with reference to their width, pressure, contacts, shifts from isolated to integrated movements, and spacing and timing of steps, that such factors constitute more adequate criteria of progress than do the number of steps taken by the child. The investigators found that the infant just learning to walk places one foot before he begins to move the other, but that the older child starts to raise the second foot before completely placing the first. It was further noted that when walking begins the child's whole sole is placed in contact with the floor, whereas by approxi-

[21] Reported in Nancy Bayley and Anna Espenschade, "Motor Development from Birth to Maturity," *Review of Educational Research*, Vol. 11, No. 5 (Dec. 1941), pp. 562-572. Also (same authors and Journal) Vol. 14, No. 5 (Dec. 1944).

[22] Myrtle B. McGraw and A. P. Weinbach, "Quantitative Measures in Studying Development of Behavior Patterns (Erect Locomotion)," *Bulletin of Neurological Institute of New York*, 4 : 563-572 (1936).

mately six months stepping movements involve contact with the floor of only the toes and the ball of the foot. With further development the contact becomes a heel-toe progression.

A later study [23] of the walking movements of infants ranging in age from birth to five years has disclosed several distinct phases in the development of upright locomotion. These have been characterized as (a) the newborn or reflex stepping, (b) the integrated mature phase of erect locomotion. According to the author, progressive changes in locomotor functions reflect reorganization of the neural centers involved in such activity. The original inhibitory influence of the cortex changes to cortical participation in motivation to motor behavior and later to control of the movements essential to bipedal locomotion.

A motion picture investigation [24] of stair climbing and progress in the prone position, involving twelve one to three-year-old infants, suggested that the two activities are similar in pattern. In stair climbing the child begins by placing his left foot on the first stair, after which the left hand and right foot advance practically simultaneously. Further climbing brings into play similar pairings of contralateral limbs (right foot-left hand, etc.). In creeping the child proceeds much the same as in climbing except that the initial movement involves both an arm and a leg (contralaterally) in place of the leg alone. By the age of three most children can climb stairs in the manner described. By the age of four, the majority go up and down stairs in much the same fashion as adults, only occasionally resorting to handrails or other supports.

Most recent researches point to the importance of the maturational factor in the development of postural and locomotor skill and to the interpretation that neonate coordinations, being both massive and reflex in nature, are under subcortical control. It is believed that with the adequate development of the cortex,

[23] Myrtle B. McGraw, "Neuromuscular Development of the Human Infant as Exemplified in the Achievement of Erect Locomotion," *Journal of Pediatrics,* 17:747-771 (1940).
[24] Louise B. Ames, "Some Relationships Between Stair Climbing and Prone Progression," *Journal of Genetic Psychology,* 54:313-325 (1939). Also Arnold Gesell and Henry M. Halverson, "The Daily Maturation of Infant Behavior: A Cinema Study of Postures, Movements, and Laterality," *Journal of Genetic Psychology,* 61:3-32 (1942).

reflexes disappear, voluntary motor responses emerge, and the maturing process goes forward in the cephalo-caudal direction. Students of the subject declare as well that the acquisition of motor skill is to a marked extent influenced by practice, by freedom from inhibitions, and by the child's attitude toward the activities concerned.

Causes of Retardation in Walking. Most children learn to walk between the ages of twelve and fourteen months. Unless they are feebleminded (defective rather than retarded mentally), few fail to accomplish this essential skill by eighteen months. There are, however, a number of factors other than mental status which may condition or retard a child's progress in this respect. There is some evidence that children from the higher economic classes are precocious in learning to walk and that those enjoying breast feeding walk earlier than bottle-fed children. The most crucial reasons for delayed development in this area have, however, been listed as (1) nutritional deficiency (rickets), (2) overweight, (3) illness, (4) slippery or cold floors, (5) tight clothing and unsuitable shoes, (6) subnormal mentality, (7) emotional blocking, and (8) lack of incentive.[25]

The first two factors obviously militate against the child's chances of adequately supporting himself in an upright position. They can, however, be alleviated by a more satisfactory diet and by attention to the child's health habits. Improvement of the child's general health and, when possible, the generation of more strength and energy, will in the nature of the case compensate for the lack of interest and practice induced by illness. Factors (4) and (5) can be overcome by providing the child with one or more rooms free from drafts and slippery floors, and by equipping him with shoes the soles of which are sufficiently firm to support his feet and at the same time prevent skidding. Tight and unnecessarily long clothing, both of which hamper free walking movements, should be avoided.

[25] Winifred Rand, M. E. Sweeny, and E. L. Vincent, *Growth and Development of the Young Child,* Philadelphia, W. B. Saunders Co., 1940, pp. 127-128. See also Wayne Dennis, "On the Possibility of Advancing and Retarding the Motor Development of Infants, *Psychological Review,* 50 : 203-218 (1943).

Many parents believe that the age at which a child begins to walk is indicative of his mental status. It has thus been believed that retardation in walking is proof of intellectual inferiority. Actually, investigations [26] have shown that, except in the case of definitely feebleminded children, there is little or no relationship between mental age and motility or time of walking. Although it is true that the majority of children can walk by the thirteenth or fourteenth month, some intellectually normal children do not achieve such locomotion until several months later. Although feebleminded children are late (25.08 months on the average) [27] in walking, the reverse is not true—not all children who are retarded in walking are feebleminded.

Emotional factors also apparently operate to retard walking. Slight accidents may produce fear and thus cause the child to avoid the risks involved in getting around in the upright position. This is especially true when parents are oversolicitous of his safety. Laughter at the child's first attempts at walking and ridicule of his immature gait may lead to self-consciousness and thus to reluctance to proceed with walking. The last factor mentioned—lack of incentive—is likely to be present when parents or nurses are too attentive in caring for the child's needs. The child should be given incentives to action in the form of locomotion. A ball with which to play and a toy dog toward which to crawl represent motives for activity and struggle. The excitement of recovering such an object by his own efforts may spur the infant on to greater motor achievements. It is not conducive to effort on the part of a child to hand him everything for which he seems to be asking.

Growth and the Development of Skills.—The growing child develops many motor skills other than those concerned with locomotion. Early in his experience he becomes concerned with activities involving arm-hand coordinations (grasping, throwing, etc.), speed and accuracy of movement, steadiness of control, and the manipulation of objects in the environment.

[26] J. D. Teicher, "Preliminary Survey of Motility in Children," *Journal of Nervous and Mental Diseases,* 94: 277-304 (1941).
[27] Lewis M. Terman, *Genetic Studies of Genius,* Vol. I: *Mental and Physical Traits of a Thousand Gifted Children,* Stanford University, Stanford Univ. Press, 1925, p. 187.

To what extent such development is made possible by maturational factors and to what degree it is a function of learning is difficult to determine. The safest position is probably that of recognizing the interlocked role played by each of those influences, according the major place to learning in the case of the more complex sensorimotor skills.

HAND-ARM COORDINATIONS.   Studies dealing with the ability of infants to grasp objects have led to discovery of the so-called *proximo-distal* law of development. This principle holds that cube-grasping (prehension) skill, for example, develops from gross shoulder and upper arm movements to control of the pincer muscles of the elbow, wrist, and fingers. Grasping reactions evolve from the clumsy squeezing of objects to finer movements involving graceful coordinations of the thumb and the ends of cooperating fingers. It is through such manipulation of his hands, which are richly supplied with sensory nerve endings, that the growing child establishes adaptive sensory contacts with his material world.

Investigations of infants' reaching and grasping behavior, notably those by Halverson [28] and by Castner,[29] have illustrated admirably the sequences of development in this type of motor skill. According to their findings, very young infants made no effort to notice cubes (blocks) placed before them on a table. At sixteen weeks the experimental infants gazed at the cubes for approximately 5 seconds, but made no contacts with them. By the twenty-fourth week, one-half of the children reached for and managed to touch a cube. Between twenty-eight and forty weeks sufficient eye-hand coordination had developed to permit all of the infants to touch a cube. The amount of time devoted to gazing at a cube when attempting to reach it increased from 4.75 seconds at sixteen weeks to 18 seconds at twenty-eight weeks.

The infant's manner of reaching for an object undergoes distinct modifications as it is influenced by maturational and ex-

[28] H. M. Halverson, *An Experimental Study of Prehension in Infants by Means of Systematic Cinema Records,* Genetic Psychology Monographs, Vol. 10, Nos. 2-3 (1931), pp. 107-286.

[29] B. M. Castner, *The Development of Fine Prehension in Infancy,* Genetic Psychology Monographs, Vol. 12, No. 2 (1932), pp. 105-193.

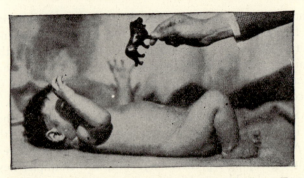

Figure 68. This Three-Months-Old Infant Sees the Proffered Toy and Is Trying to Get It

Control over his hands is not yet established and his first attempts to obtain the object pull his hands away from it rather than guide them to it.

(From W. Rand, M. E. Sweeny, and E. L. Vincent, *Growth and Development of the Young Child,* Philadelphia, W. B. Saunders Co., 1940, p. 36.)

periential factors. Indeed, reaching evolves from massive movements of one or both arms to direct skillful reaching by the fifty-second week. Whereas a backhand sweep characterizes such movements between the sixteenth and twenty-eighth weeks, a circuitous one is in evidence from thirty-two to thirty-six

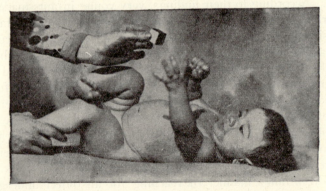

Figure 69. This Six-Months-Old Infant Has Progressed in His Reaching Technique

He is pulling toward the object with both hands and both feet, but has already specialized to the extent that one hand is slightly in the lead. His gaze is clearly directed upon the object.

(From W. Rand, M. E. Sweeny, and E. L. Vincent, *Growth and Development of the Young Child,* Philadelphia, W. B Saunders Co., 1940. p. 38.)

weeks. By the fortieth week, the typical child is able to effect a straight approach to a cube or other object. Although the factor of speed fluctuates with development, accuracy of movement shows a consistent and steady improvement after approximately the sixteenth week.

The growing infant's *grasping* (prehension) movements also undergo a series of developmental changes. As can be seen in Figure 70, they progress from whole hand closure to scissors type closure and finally to pincer prehension. As Halverson found, the twenty-weeks-old infant, instead of gripping the cube, "corrals" it with his hand and presses it against his

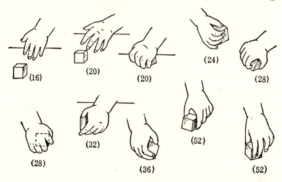

Figure 70. The Development of Prehension in the Infant

(Adapted from H. M. Halverson, *An Experimental Study of Prehension in Infants by Means of Systematic Cinema Records*, Genetic Psychology Monographs, Vol. 10, Nos. 2, 3, pp. 212, 215 (1931).)

body or other hand ("primitive squeeze"). By twenty-four weeks the infant is able to grasp an object clumsily between the fingers and the palm of the hand in a manner characterized as the "squeeze grasp." He has reached the so-called "hand grasp" stage when his fingers encircle the cube more effectively (twenty-eighth week). Between this point and the thirty-second week the average infant comes to utilize the "palm grasp," in which position the thumb and fingers cooperate in holding the cube against the palm of the hand. By the fifty-second week the more mature pincer movement ("forefinger grasp") is established—the child now grips the cube between the thumb and the ends of the fingers. The child can now also hold a crayon.

In six months he will be able to scribble with considerable enthusiasm. At thirty months he is skillful enough to copy either a horizontal or vertical line. His motor development is well on its way to maturity.

EVIDENCE FOR HAND PREFERENCE. Most children show a preference for one hand or the other by their first birthday in reaching, throwing, and handling objects. The great majority of these children, as well as those whose hand preference is not clearly developed until the second or third year, are unquestionably right-handed. The findings of investigations differ considerably, but where the same criteria of handedness are used the percentage of left-handed children varies from approximately 2 to 8. Haefner,[30] for example, found 6.3 per cent presumably pure left-handed children and 4.9 per cent mixed. As shown in Table 22, Cuff's [31] study disclosed a percentage of 6.3 for left-handedness among elementary school children and one of 7.3 in the case of college students.

As might be expected, the causes of hand preference have been attributed to both heredity and environment. On the inheritance side are the beliefs that handedness may be assigned to (a) the superior development of one cerebral hemisphere, (b) the visceral distribution and attendant displacement of the center of gravity to one side of the body, and (c) ocular dominance (that a preferred eye leads to development of the corresponding hand). In fact, Ramaley [32] declared in 1913 that left-handedness is a Mendelian recessive and that it appears in families showing no such characteristics for generations for genetic reasons. There is, nevertheless, a strong tendency today to ascribe handedness, like so many other preferences, to parental and social training. It is believed that if early environmental forces stressed the use of a given hand it is more likely than not to become preferred. This could be true even if an inherent disposition to favor one hand were involved in some cases.

30 Ralph Haefner, *The Educational Significance of Left-handedness,* Teachers College Contributions to Education, No. 360, Columbia Univ., 1929.
31 N. B. Cuff, "A Study of Eyedness and Handedness," *Journal of Experimental Psychology,* 14 : 164-175 (1931).
32 Francis Ramaley, "Inheritance of Left-Handedness," *American Naturalist,* 47 : 730-738 (1913).

There has been much speculation concerning the effects on speech of requiring children who show a preference for the left hand to learn to write with the right hand. Although opinions differ on this point, considerable evidence is extant that such individuals (called *dextrosinistrals*) are more likely than others to suffer from speech disorders.[33] It is believed by many psychologists, however, that it is not the change from left to right hand itself that causes stuttering, but the antagonizing methods

TABLE 22. THE INCIDENCE OF HANDEDNESS IN ELEMENTARY SCHOOL AND COLLEGE

Grade	Cases	Right-Handed			Left-Handed		
		Male	Female	Total	Male	Female	Total
1	34	11	18	29	1	4	5
2	33	17	14	31	1	1	2
3	24	15	8	23	0	1	1
4	26	12	10	22	2	2	4
5	33	15	17	32	1	0	1
6	29	14	14	28	0	1	1
7	29	18	11	29	0	0	0
8	29	13	15	28	0	1	1
Total		115	107	222	5	10	15
Percent		95.9	91.4	93.6	4.2	8.5	6.3
College		16	85	101	1	7	8
Percent		94.1	92.4	92.7	5.9	7.6	7.3

(Adapted from N. B. Cuff, "A Study of Eyedness and Handedness," *Journal of Experimental Psychology*, 14:170 (1931).)

so often employed to bring about the reversal. As Scheidemann,[34] among others, has suggested, such methods often include scolding, unfavorable comparisons, and other stress-producing stimuli. There is also involved the feeling of uncertainty accompanying continual blocking of left-handed motor skills established over a period of years, and the necessity of having to hesitate in order to make sure that the right response is being executed. The child who is constantly reminded that

[33] Lee Edward Travis, "Speech Pathology," in *Handbook of Child Psychology* (edited by Carl Murchison), Worcester, Clark Univ. Press, 1933, Ch. 16.
[34] Norma V. Scheidemann, *The Psychology of Exceptional Children*, Boston Houghton Mifflin Co., 1931, pp. 151-153.

he must use the "other hand" is apt to be antagonistic and irritable.

It is considered questionable today whether parents should require a child with a left-hand preference to use his right hand in writing or in other motor activities. Many skilled technicians are left-handed, and in the case of such a vocation as baseball, such hand preference may be a definite asset. Certainly there is no social discrimination among understanding people against left-handed or ambidextrous individuals. If, however, change of handedness is undertaken, it should be done early in life and in a positive and reassuring way. If a child is made to feel that his interests are being safeguarded and that the change is being made for his benefit, there is apparently no reason why speech defects or any other nervous symptoms should develop.

GENERAL MOTOR DEVELOPMENT. Studies of general motor development may be longitudinal in type, involving repeated observations of the same children as they grow older, or cross-sectional, recording the performances of different children at different ages. Most of the recent investigations are longitudinal and are concerned with the intensive study of relatively few children. They include data concerning development in throwing, swimming, climbing, sliding, tricycling, catching balls, and other motor activities. A sampling of these researches should serve to point out the general nature of maturation and motor learning.

According to Gesell,[35] the typical child can throw in simple fashion from a sitting position at six months, give definite direction to a thrown ball at eleven months, and in about two-fifths of the cases play cooperative ball at approximately thirteen months. During his second year, the developing child improves his throwing both as to distance and direction and can under the most simple circumstances catch a ball. A study by Wild [36] of the manner of throwing a ball, utilized by children two to seven years of age, disclosed the following sequence:

[35] Arnold Gesell and H. Thompson, *Infant Behavior: Its Genesis and Growth*, New York, McGraw-Hill Book Co., Inc., 1934, Ch. 3.
[36] Monica R. Wild, "The Behavior Pattern of Throwing and Some Observations Concerning Its Course of Development in Children," *Research Quarterly of the American Assn. for Health and Physical Education*, Vol. 9 (Oct. 1938), pp. 20-24

"Two to three years. There is no shifting of the body; the arm is drawn backward and directly over the shoulder, or obliquely in some cases, and the delivery is made by swinging the arm forward directly over the shoulder.

"Three and one-half to five years. Rotation of the whole body above the feet is present, and there is a forward shift of the body during the delivery. The backswing of the arm is flatter than at earlier ages, but the delivery is still over the shoulder."

Wild's study included a determination of sex differences in ball throwing and the expected finding that girls stop at a lower level of development than boys in this skill. It also showed that after the fifth year a variety of reverse swings of the arm may be used, that body rotation is often present, and that partial or complete stepping forward with the left foot occurs. The basic throwing pattern is, however, well established by approximately the sixth year.

The development of swimming skill in children has been graphically reported by McGraw [37] in her previously mentioned account of Johnny, who was the recipient of much special motor training, and Jimmy, his fraternal twin, who was permitted to develop ontogenetically without benefit of such stimulating advantages. As was the case with a number of other infants studied by McGraw, Jimmy, the restricted twin, could not hold his head above the water when suspended in it by a strap around his chest. This was on his 231st postnatal day. By the 283rd day he was still inclined to clutch the experimenter's hand and frequently coughed and gagged when placed in the water. Not until he was 597 days old (approximately one year and eight months) could this twin make progress in the water by systematic swimming movements. Johnny, the specially trained twin, was given daily swimming experience from the 231st day in a shallow tank, suspended by a strap similar to Jimmy's, and observed as his strap was lowered and he learned to make regular movements toward a toy placed at the end of the tank.

[37] Myrtle B. McGraw, *Growth: A Study of Johnny and Jimmy*, New York, D. Appleton-Century Co., Inc., 1935, pp. 122-136.

When he was about ten months of age (308 days) Johnny was making good progress in this respect and by approximately his first birthday (360 days) he could release his hold on the edge of the tank and swim its length. Three phases of the movements involved in learning to swim are illustrated in Figure 71.

Retests [38] of Johnny and Jimmy at school age designed to discover the degree of retention of their various skills revealed that some abilities were retained better than others. McGraw

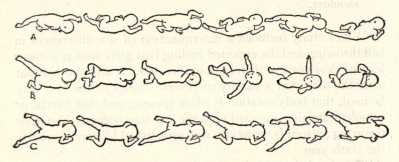

Figure 71. Drawings Showing Three Phases in the Development of Swimming by the Human Infant

(A) Reflex swimming movements. (B) Disorganized behavior. (C) Voluntary or deliberate movements.
(From Myrtle B. McGraw, "Swimming Behavior of the Human Infant," *Journal of Pediatrics*, 15:488 (1939).)

concluded that the maintenance of a skill, especially when accelerated, is determined by the thoroughness with which it was originally learned and integrated, on growth changes in body size and proportion, and on the child's interest in the activity.

A recent study [39] of the general motor achievements of 1,973 kindergarten and primary school children suggests the development that may be expected to the age of seven. According to the investigator, 92 per cent were proficient in climbing ability by the age of six, 81 per cent were facile in jumping by the

[38] Myrtle B. McGraw, "Later Development of Children Specially Trained During Infancy: Johnny and Jimmy at School Age," *Child Development*, 10 : 1-19 (1939). See also, by the same author, *The Neuromuscular Maturation of the Human Infant*, New York, Columbia Univ. Press, 1943.
[39] Mary V. Gutteridge, "A Study of Motor Achievements of Young Children," *Archives of Psychology*, Vol. 34, No. 244 (1939). Also Doris M. Hartman, "The Hurdle Jump as a Measure of Motor Proficiency of Young Children," *Child Development*, 14 : 201-211 (1943).

fifth year, and 63 per cent were skillful in tricycling at age three. Basic galloping movements were in evidence by the latter part of the fourth year, but it was not until age six and one-half that the great majority (92 per cent) displayed skilled responses in this area. The same age (6½) also brought ability to bounce a ball.

The Development of Musical Ability.—Musical expression involves a variety of activities and may be said to have many aspects. Participation in musical enterprises is contingent upon the possession of motor skill, but may lead to considerable enjoyment, esthetic appreciation, and social experience. It seems logical, therefore, to approach this aspect of development from the standpoint of its neuromuscular or motor basis.

Children express themselves in musical and rhythmic forms very early in life. Nearly all children can sing and many apparently do so before they have learned to talk. Whether such ability is primarily an expression of germinally inherited factors or whether it is a product of special training is a moot question. Claims in this respect vary all the way from assertions that any child who is not physically defective can learn to sing or play an instrument to belief that all forms of musical performance and enjoyment are primarily functions of innate capacity. Data pertaining to the nature of musical ability are also conflicting. Judging from the work of Seashore,[40] a leader in the field, such ability is not general but consists, rather, of specialized capacity for discerning musical pitch, intensity, consonance, time, rhythm, and tonal memory. On this basis the possession of one of these abilities does not guarantee the presence of any of the others. Mursell and Glenn [41] have, however, contended that capacity for musical performance and expression is an all-round ability, and one that is most likely to be in evidence in families of relatively high cultural status and musical interest.

[40] Carl E. Seashore, *The Psychology of Musical Talent,* New York, Silver, Burdett & Co., 1919.
[41] J. L. Mursell and M. Glenn, *The Psychology of School Music Teaching,* New York, Silver, Burdett & Co., 1931.

Musical expression may be said to begin with the baby's babbling and the rhythm which he injects into it. With added maturity the child comes to pattern such expressions after the simple melodies sung to him by his elders. Most children can, by the age of four or five, sing melodies, recognize simple tunes, and make rhythmic movements. A study by Williams [42] has suggested a general developmental schedule for young children in musical activities. According to his findings, the eighteen-months-old child is attracted to music, shows signs of liking it, does some vocalizing himself, and indicates by signs that he wants more music. At thirty months he experiments with musical sounds, imitates short musical phrases, and enjoys listening to music. By the age of forty-two months the average child can vocalize four-note melodies with moderate accuracy, can invent rhythmic activities, and enjoys singing with a group. This investigator recognized the presence of marked individual differences in musical development, but believes that the developmental sequences noted hold roughly for children in general. Drexler's [43] finding that the ability to carry a melody increases with age has tended to corroborate belief in such genetic growth.

An investigation by Boynton [44] of the song preferences of 4,473 boys and 4,423 girls in a widely distributed group of elementary schools (grades 1-6) has disclosed the sequences of development in this musical category. School songs are the most popular in the first four grades, but they drop consistently in this respect after that. Interest in classical, folk, and patriotic songs increases with advancing age. Religious, holiday, and nursery rhyme songs, which loom fairly large in interest in the early years, give way later to decided preferences for popular songs and dance music. Practically all the children showed a preference as well for simple, "singable" songs that could be learned without much effort even by those of meager singing ability. Boynton believes that changes in musical choice

[42] Harold M. Williams, *Musical Guidance of Young Children*, Child Welfare Pamphlet No. 29, Bulletin of the Child Welfare Research Station, Univ. of Iowa, New Series, No. 707, 1933.

[43] E. N. Drexler, "A Study of the Development of the Ability to Carry a Melody at the Preschool Level," *Child Development*, 9:319-332 (1938).

[44] Paul L. Boynton, *Psychology of Child Development*, Minneapolis, Educational Publishers, 1938, pp. 297-303.

are to some extent correlated with maturity and with such factors as increasing intelligence, breadth of experience, and opportunity to study and hear good music properly played or sung.

THE INFLUENCE OF SPECIAL TRAINING.   Children are very much interested in both the motor and the musical aspects of rhythm. They enjoy hopping, skipping, running, jumping, rolling hoops, swinging, jumping rope, see-sawing, and other such rhythmic motor activities. Children also like to keep time to music with their hands or feet. They find it easier, however, to walk or step rhythmically than to keep time by clapping their hands.[45] Although they tend to prefer the slower types of songs, children are better able to follow the rhythm of music played at a rapid tempo. Investigations have also shown that while training in making rhythmic movements results in some improvement, this type of motor ability is apparently dependent more upon structural organization than upon experience. A study by Jersild and Bienstock [46] revealed the fact that even when children (aged two to five years) listened to experimenters play the piano, clapped their hands to emphasize the beat, and walked to the time of the music, their gains were small in comparison to their improvement in singing. Preschool training in rhythm apparently does not result in much improvement in the child's ability to keep time to music.

Several investigations have shown that training leads to improvement in children's singing. There is disagreement, however, concerning the amount and permanence of the gains made. In a study by Jersild,[47] the equivalent-group method was used to ascertain the effects of special practice on children's (aged thirty-one to forty-eight months) ability to sing tones and intervals. Tests designed to determine initial ability consisted of the reproduction by the children of sounds made by the experimenter vocally, or on a piano, organ, or pitch pipe. Subsequent practice for ten minutes at a time two or three times per

[45] Arthur T. Jersild, *Music, Thirty-Eighth Yearbook, National Society for the Study of Education*, Bloomington (Ill.), Public School Pub. Co., 1939, Part I, pp. 135-151.

[46] Arthur T. Jersild and S. F. Bienstock, *Development of Rhythm in Young Children*, Child Development Monographs, No. 22 (1935).

[47] Arthur T. Jersild, *Training and Growth in the Development of Children*, Child Development Monographs, No. 10 (1932).

week for a period of six months enabled the training group to make far greater gains in the musical abilities exercised than was the case with the control group. The gains were such, in fact, as to bring those children up in number of tones sung to the average score for unselected eight-year-olds. Much of the improvement noted was maintained during the following summer vacation period. The investigators were convinced that "training in singing at an early age can tap potentialities that are not usually utilized by the average child."

A similar but somewhat more extensive study confirmed the above findings by demonstrating that special practice enables preschool children to make noticeable gains in the singing of not only tones and intervals, but of phrases as well.[48] It was also noted from systematic observations and ratings that the children's improvement in ability to sing was accompanied by increased interest and enthusiasm for singing. An investigation[49] of the effects of systematic training on the singing ability of children afflicted with severe lack of pitch discrimination pointed out that this type of sensory disability can also be improved by training. That such improvement cannot, however, be anticipated with preschool children in the case of performance on an instrument was suggested in a study by Colby[50] in which extended instruction was given in playing a small tin fife. This experimenter came to the conclusion that "specialized instrumental training at too early an age costs far more patience than it is worth, and that the same amount of effort applied to *vocal* acquisition of folksongs, folk games, 'kinderlieder,' etc., would produce greater results because it would capitalize on a natural response and an easier technique."

AFFECTIVE VALUES OF MUSICAL ACTIVITIES. Even though it is, in the case of young children, primarily a motor activity, musical expression is apparently very enjoyable. Affective re-

48 Ruth Updegraff, L. Heiliger, and J. Learned, "The Effect of Training upon Singing Ability and Musical Interest of Three-, Four-, and Five-Year Old Children," *Studies in Preschool Education*, Bulletin of the Child Welfare Research Station, Univ. of Iowa, New Series, Vol. 1, No. 346 (1938).
49 Manuel Wolner and W. H. Pyle, "An Experiment in Individual Training of Pitch-Deficient Children," *Journal of Educational Psychology*, 24 : 602-608 (1933).
50 M. G. Colby, "Instrumental Reproduction of Melody by Preschool Children," *Journal of Genetic Psychology*, 47 : 413-430 (1935).

Figure 72. Musical Development of the Dionne Quints at Age Seven. Annette, most musical, plays the organ for her sisters.

(Copyrighted by King Features Syndicate, Inc.)

actions to musical activities are as a rule on the pleasurable side. "Producing music, whether by striking keys of a musical instrument, winding a music box, or turning on a victrola or radio, is very popular with young children. While they enjoy listening to music produced by others, the enjoyment that they derive from their own music, even though it be of a vastly inferior caliber, is far greater. They enjoy rhythms and dancing, which is often little more than walking to music. Because music in all forms in which the child may take part is such a pleasing, as well as wholesome, form of self-expression, it is strongly encouraged by parents, nursery schools, and kindergartens." [51]

As children grow older they experience a decrease in interest in spontaneous singing. It is believed by some that this phenomenon is due to increasing self-consciousness and frequently to the formal atmosphere or stereotyped requirements of the school. As Kwalwasser [52] has stressed, the skills and musical concepts recommended for courses of study by music authorities are frequently far in excess of the accomplishments usually achieved by children in the time allotted to instruction in school. However, there is at present a strong trend toward making musical activities means of expression and enjoyment as well as avenues to accomplishment.[53] There is also in vogue a tendency to encourage children who prefer instrumental production in the study of instruments adapted to their abilities and aspirations. Music teachers are also largely agreed that the possibilities of musical activities for socialization are among their most trenchant values.

CONCLUSIONS ON MOTOR DEVELOPMENT.—It should be evident that motor abilities result from both structural maturation and opportunity for learning. Superior motor ability may in some cases be the outcome of stimulation to concentrated practice, not primarily of phylogenetic (racial) factors. The child's physical and social environment apparently has much to do with the extent to which native motor ability will be developed. As Jones [54] has concluded from her study of childhood motor development, minimum performance of motor skills depends upon an appropriate degree of neuromuscular maturation, "but the development of the skill into graceful, coordinated performance

[51] Elizabeth B. Hurlock, *Child Development*, New York, McGraw-Hill Book Co., Inc., 1942, p. 416.
[52] J. Kwalwasser, *Problems in Public School Music*, New York, M. Witmark & Sons, 1932.
[53] R. Minor, *Early Childhood Education*, New York, D. Appleton-Century Co., Inc., 1937, Ch. 18.
[54] Theresa D. Jones, *The Development of Certain Motor Skills and Play Activities in Young Children*, Child Development Monographs, No. 26 (1939).

depends upon continued practice. . . . Merging of activities
that previously took place as separate performances seemed to
begin as soon as each activity had reached a stage at which the
child's entire attention was not required for its performance."
Ample space, adequate equipment, and intelligently supervised
stimulation to constructive motor activities should thus as far
as possible be provided the developing child.

Principles of Motor Learning

The Nature of Learning in Childhood.—It is essential in
any discussion of child growth to distinguish between the related
concepts of maturation and learning as they affect the child's
ongoing motor development. Gesell [55] has made such a distinction by insisting that whereas *learning* has reference to that
aspect of growth which involves the making and perfecting of
adaptations to the requirements of environmental situations,
maturation refers to an inner intrinsic factor which determines
the physical and mental development of the child and his life-
cycle. Such a differentiation no doubt has merit but represents
an attempt to separate two interlocked factors in terms of the
nature-nurture controversy. Maturation and learning are actually not contrasting influences, but represent two aspects of an
inseparable integration whose composite effect is in evidence
throughout the child's development. The growing individual
matures and learns at the same time and in such complex ways
as to make it undesirable, if not impossible, to distinguish between the two influences. It is on such a basis that modern
students of childhood endeavor to determine the conditions
under which learning, as the development of adaptive behavior,
takes place most economically and effectively.

Such a conception of learning is in harmony with the previously discussed (Chapter 5) structure-function principle,
which indicated that functions (activities), motor or otherwise,
cannot be performed until such time as the structures concerned
with their exercise are sufficiently mature to so operate. The
structure-function concept is thus important in the study of

[55] Arnold Gesell, "Maturation and the Patterning of Behavior," in *Handbook
of Child Psychology* (edited by Carl Murchison), Worcester, Clark Univ. Press,
1933, Ch. 4.

child development. It does not, however, necessarily involve the belief, so ardently postulated by some, that structures mature practically independently of the learning factor. Physical activities, not to mention environmental influences, are in themselves stimuli to further structural development. The learning process is not one of exclusive internally determined physical development (maturation) followed by environmentally effected motor skills. Structure and function are complementary aspects of an inseparable process of motor development as exemplified by crawling, walking, throwing, climbing, and similar activities.

It should be remembered as well that motor skills, like simple motor functions, emerge as increasingly refined and precise responses from originally massive reactions of the organism. Just as the infant is able to crawl after experiencing many ineffective mass activities with various parts of his body, so he learns to write as the end product of much crude and general crayon wielding which involved many structures other than those of the arm, wrist, and fingers. In the parlance of psychology, differentiated motor skills evolve out of originally general, undifferentiated movements. The child learns through making overt efforts, for example, to swim, to skate, to operate a kiddy-car, to climb, or to ride a tricycle. But these and other motor skills must be learned as whole activities, with the more skilled aspects coming after preliminary general exploration and mass action.

Practically all principles and concepts of learning, although couched in explanatory terms, are actually but *descriptions* of how learning goes forward. In spite of years of both physiological and psychological research in this field, little is known today regarding the internal physical correlates of progress in learning. One school of thought endeavors to explain learning in terms of chains and syntheses of simple physiological conditionings, another supposes that learning bonds are developed by the formation of functional connections between situations and responses made to them, while a third group insists that learning is accompanied by "fluid" action in the so-called "energy field" of the organism. All of these proposals are hypotheses.

not explanations based on known facts. Each one may be utilized, however, as a frame of reference for explaining what the physical basis of observed learning may be. In the meantime it is possible to determine the external conditions under which modification of behavior—that is, learning—is most readily accomplished.

Modern Principles of Motor Learning.—Volumes have been written on the psychology of learning, both motor and verbal. Conflicting schools of thought have presented equally conflicting principles and theories relating to the learning process. All tend to agree, however, that motor skills are learned according to approximately the same general principles as other forms of acquired responses. It is possible, for present purposes, to reconcile a number of views regarding economical methods of learning and to reduce these to a relatively few fundamental interlocked principles of motor-skill development. These may be listed as: (1) motivation through utilization of child interests, (2) the gearing of skills to the child's maturation level, (3) teaching skills as pattern activities, (4) utilizing evaluation for the directing of learning, and (5) insuring an integrated, symmetrical development. Each of these principles will be presented with a minimum of detail.

Motivation Through Child Interests.—*Learning proceeds most effectively and tends to be most permanent when the learner is motivated; that is, when he has an interest, a stake as it were, in the activity being undertaken.* The child who desires, for example, to join his associates in playing on a schoolground slide will be keenly desirous of learning to climb the necessary steps. Motivation lies at the very base of the learning process and of the development of skill. As Woodworth [56] has said, "achievement equals ability times motivation" which latter term is defined as "a state or set of the individual which disposes him for certain behavior and for seeking certain goals."

It should thus be recognized that children learn motor skills, such as ball throwing, roller skating, bicycle riding, and even

[56] Robert S. Woodworth. *Psychology* (4th ed.), New York, Henry Holt & Co., Inc., 1940, p. 366.

writing most effectively when such activities represent personal aspirations, or desired achievements. Cherished personal goals tend to set up stresses leading to activity, as well as to govern the direction and regulation of the ensuing behavior. The same may be said of the results of responses—if they lead toward realization of the child's objective, motivation to further activity is secured. In fact, a recent writer [57] has concluded that the *effects* of responses on the individual's aspirations are of first importance in motivating learning. Positive rewards in the form of desired achievement or added status are primary in determining the direction of learning activity.

Adjustment to Maturation Levels.—If a child is to learn a new motor skill such, for example, as climbing an incline, he must be sufficiently mature physically and experientially to make such an activity possible. In short, *learning proceeds most rapidly and tends to be most permanent when the activity involved is geared to the learner's physical and mental ability to perform that activity.*[58] It is also essential that the skill to be learned bear some relation to both the child's past experience and his present level of aspiration. As the previously mentioned stair-climbing experiment reported by Gesell showed, more adequate physical maturation enabled a fifty-three-weeks-old child to learn to climb stairs in one week as efficiently as his twin had been able to do in six weeks at the more tender age of forty-six weeks. A certain degree of physical and mental maturity is required for the economical learning of any given activity, motor or otherwise. To attempt to develop a motor skill in advance of adequate maturity is thus obviously wasteful, and may result in loss of interest. Just as the child must possess a given degree of mental age (maturity) if he is to be successful in learning to read, so he must be adequately mature physically if he is to master efficiently the intricacies of such motor skills as climbing, sliding, swimming, ball-catching, skating, and turning somersaults.

[57] Arthur I. Gates, "Connectionism: Present Concepts and Interpretations," in *The Psychology of Learning, Forty-First Yearbook, National Society for the Study of Education,* Bloomington (Ill.), Public School Pub. Co., 1942, Part II, Ch. 4.
[58] Kurt Lewin, "Field Theory of Learning," in *ibid.,* Ch. 6.

Successful adjustment to maturation level involves the application of two subsidiary principles, which may be labelled *vertical pacing* and *horizontal pacing*. The problem of the parent or teacher is not merely to require drill and practice in motor skills, but to make as certain as possible that the task at hand is sufficiently simple to permit an early solution by the learner. A subsequent step is that of providing progressively more difficult motor goals in such gradual fashion that the child comes to master more and more complex skills without being defeated by requirements that are clearly beyond his maturity level. Such a teaching and learning procedure is called *vertical pacing*. It suggests more than the usual attention to a given child's program of motor development.

Horizontal pacing has reference to the intelligent distribution of work and rest in the child's educational program. It involves the question of concentrated versus distributed practice or drill. According to research findings, better results are secured from properly paced or distributed work periods than from those carried out on a massed basis. This is particularly true in the early stages of motor learning. This point is illustrated by the results of an experiment [59] in which sixth grade boys were required to practice throwing darts at a target on both a distributed and massed basis. Although all subjects threw approximately 300 darts each, one group practiced throwing twenty darts a day for two days of the week and the other ten darts a day for four days of the same week. Records of the scores achieved showed that distributed or paced practice eventuated in more efficient results in this type of motor learning.

It is necessary, however, to determine in the case of each child and with each type of motor activity what the most advantageous distribution appears to be. It is essential, especially in the case of such more mature motor activities as writing, typing, piano playing, and singing, to distribute practice sufficiently to avoid the ravages of fatigue, boredom, and loss of incentive.

[59] E. D. Long, "The Acquisition of Skill by Children as Affected by Distribution of Practice," reported by Joseph Peterson in *Handbook of Child Psychology* (edited by Carl Murchison), Worcester, Clark Univ. Press, 1933, Ch. 10.

Teaching Skills as Patterns.—*Learning proceeds most effectively and tends to be most permanent when the learner is provided with the opportunity of perceiving meaningful relationships among the elements of the goal toward which he is working.* Learning is no longer regarded as being a slow process of consolidating discrete skills into a synthesized total activity. It is, rather, a matter of discerning the involvements of a skill (or problem) which is within the ability of the learner to grasp, and of differentiating part-skills out of the whole activity (problem or skill). The small boy learns to play baseball by engaging in some form of the entire game, not by combining catching, hitting, running, etc. He may practice such discrete parts of the total game, but could never play baseball as such unless the relationships among these parts were discerned as a complete pattern of motor activity. It is thus logical that learning should be concerned with meaningful units out of which part activities would be abstracted, rather than with the building of a so-called hierarchy of skills.[60] Learning involves goal-striving, thus the more clearly the pattern of the objective is understood, the more the learning process is facilitated.

It has been claimed that children learn motor skills by a process of trial-and-error; that is, by repeating satisfying acts, eliminating unsuccessful movements, and consolidating the selected responses into a complex skill. Such a statement is, however, descriptive rather than explanatory of behavior in attempts to master a difficult skill. Trial-and-error learning is but a process of making explorations and discoveries in an effort to master motor activities which are beyond the child's present capacity (physical or mental maturation level, or both) to adapt himself. When motor activities are adapted to the child's maturity status he has a maximum chance of learning by the process of gaining an understanding of the requirements of the situation, be it a motor act or a problem involving the discernment of relationships. Learning is completed when such relationships are perceived or a skill in question mastered.[61]

[60] Arthur I. Gates, A. T. Jersild, T. R. McConnell, and R. C. Challman, *Educational Psychology*, New York, The Macmillan Co., 1942, pp. 355-357.
[61] T. R. McConnell, "Reconciliation of Learning Theories," in *The Psychology of Learning, Forty-First Yearbook, National Society for the Study of Education,* Bloomington (Ill.), Public School Pub. Co., 1942, Part II, Ch. 7.

Such a mode of learning has been designated as *insight,* or the "sudden clarification of a problematic situation." Actually, learning through insight means either that a problem has been closely adjusted to the child's level or capacity or that a more or less elaborate process of exploration and discovery finally culminated in the discernment of what acts to perform.[62]   Like early physical development, the learning of complex skills pro-

Figure 73. Four-Year-Old Child Demonstrating Inability Adequately to Discern Relationships in a Situation.   Her own platform is more dangerous than the climb to the top of the slide.

(From W. Rand, M. E. Sweeny, and E. L. Vincent, *Growth and Development of the Young Child,* W. B. Saunders Co., 1940, p. 268.)

ceeds from vague undifferentiated understandings and movements to adequately planned and precise acts.   Insight, which has also been characterized as *hindsight,* is not a method of learning, it is rather the end product of a process of learning through practice or understanding.   Such economical learning is best guaranteed through (1) activity directed toward a goal in relation to which the child is under stress (interest), (2) the presentation of problems and skills in pattern form, with the relationships among parts being clear, and (3) the adjustment of learning problems to the child's level of maturity.

62 W. N. Kellogg, "An Eclectic View of Some Theories of Learning," *Psychological Review,* 45 : 165-184 (1938).

An example of insightful learning may be seen in an experiment conducted by Professor Kellogg[63] and his wife on their small son Donald and a young ape Gua who was being reared with the boy in their home. In this experiment a cookie was attached to a cord suspended from the ceiling and placed approximately a meter from where a chair, which could be used to secure it, had been placed. As a first step, both subjects were given a demonstration of the correct solution to the problem. Although he failed on the first three trials, Donald was soon able to reason out (insight) the relationships and moves involved. Gua, whose efforts were even more effective, succeeded in reaching the cookie, thus solving the problem, after one trial. The boy did his best subsequent work when the chair was left in the same position continuously. Similar results were secured by Alpert[64] in a study of the learning capacity of a group of nursery school children between 19 and 49 months of age. Seventy-five per cent made a direct attack upon the problem of fitting two short sticks together in order to secure a toy placed some distance from the pen in which they were confined. Many of the children's solutions appeared to result from immediate insight into the involvements of the problem. In some cases a gradual process of reasoning or gaining insight was in evidence. It is apparent that very young children have the capacity to solve motor problems and to develop neuromuscular skills when such activities are presented in pattern form and adapted to their stage of development.

Directing Learning Through Evaluation.—*Learning goes forward with relatively greater effectiveness when the learner is provided with some criterion for indicating specifically what progress he is making.* Children are interested in evaluating their success or failure in attaining cherished objectives and are motivated by knowledge of the degree of satisfactory progress being made. The child who knows to what extent he is achieving, for example, the writing skill he has set as a goal finds his

[63] W. N. Kellogg and L. A. Kellogg, *The Ape and the Child: A Study of Environmental Influence Upon Early Behavior,* New York, McGraw-Hill Book Co., Inc., 1933, pp. 213-219.
[64] A. Alpert, *The Solving of Problem-Situations by Preschool Children,* Teachers College Contributions to Education, No. 323, Columbia Univ., 1928.

practice periods much more meaningful than is the case where the extent of progress is obscure. Evaluation methods should thus be utilized as positive forms of child guidance and should be designed to motivate children to achieve to the extent of their abilities. Many a child has been stimulated to added effort by the simple expediency of charting his progress on a line graph.

Good results have also been secured by basing teaching procedures on the testimony of test data. Such a plan enables the

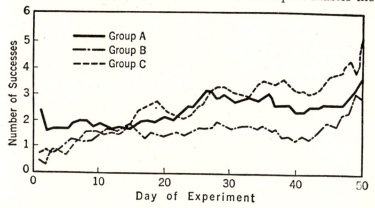

Figure 74. Learning Curves of Three Groups of Children in Tossing a Ring

Group A had no instruction, group B had some instruction, group C was given specific training.

(From F. L. Goodenough and C. R. Brian, "Certain Factors Underlying the Acquisition of Motor Skill by Preschool Children," *Journal of Experimental Psychology*, 12:134 (1929).)

teacher to direct the child's learning activities in harmony with his needs as disclosed by an objective evaluation of progress. Goodenough and Brian [65] have reported a study in which 20 preschool children were thus evaluated in their progress in tossing rings over a post under varying conditions. The first group (A) of 10 children was given no instructions but received a liberal amount of praise and encouragement. A second group (B) of 6 children was given a brief demonstration and some criticisms, but was not taught a particular procedure for

[65] Florence L. Goodenough and C. R. Brian, "Certain Factors Underlying the Acquisition of Motor Skill by Preschool Children," *Journal of Experimental Psychology*, 12:127-155 (1929).

tossing the balls. The 4 children in group C were given, in addition to a preliminary demonstration and some criticism, a definite, efficient procedure to follow and required to utilize it throughout. The superiority of the method of giving definite instructions based on an objective knowledge of progress is demonstrated by the results shown in Figure 74. As can be seen, the results were consistently in favor of group C throughout the 50-day experimental period. Outcomes such as these accentuate the importance of using evaluation techniques such as tests, ratings, observations, interviews, and teacher judgments in efforts to discover progress being made in motor or other skills. All progress might well be evaluated by teachers or parents and children working together in the interest of personally and socially desirable achievements.

Broad Integrated Development.—*Learning is facilitated when it goes forward under conditions in which the child also experiences wholesome personal and social growth.* It is an axiom of psychology that a subject learns at his maximum rate in connection with activities which afford him a means to the satisfying of personal needs. It is probably true, for example, that the typical schoolboy masters a handcraft readily and skillfully when such an activity contributes to his status and when it is taught by a teacher concerning whose solicitude and sympathy for his general welfare the boy can have no doubt. This is comparable to saying that the learner responds emotionally (affectively) as well as intellectually to the way in which a teacher deals with him in the teaching of a skill.

Many psychologists have elaborated the above concept by insisting that the "whole" child—emotional, social, moral, intellectual, etc.—reacts to an entire situation, which in his case may include arithmetic problems, the teacher's attitude and actions, the temperature of the room, the attitudes of other pupils, and the like confronting him as a total stimulus pattern. In this sense learning concerns the whole person and results in an entire reorganization of the individual's patterns of behavior. The guidance of learning is thus more effective when the child's interests and attitudes, as well as his fundamental physical, personal, and social needs are considered in determining the organization of his learning experiences.

It should also be recognized that the development of desirable motor skills may be a significant factor in the child's personal and social adjustment. Other factors being equal, the child

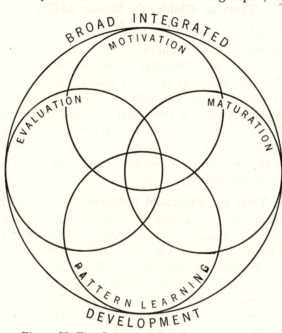

Figure 75. Five Integrated Principles of Learning
(Developed in collaboration with D. T. Graffam.)

who is skillful in a game or athletic activity is more likely than others to make social contacts, to have good times with associates, and to develop attitudes of mutuality and cooperation. Research has also shown that the acquisition of motor skill tends to increase a child's self-confidence, social poise, and capacity to cope with frustrations.[66]   It can thus be said that motor skills are not only aids to the building of personal and social qualities in childhood, but that they are an indispensable part

[66] Arthur T. Jersild, "Education in Motor Activities," *Child Development and the Curriculum, Thirty-Eighth Yearbook of the National Society for the Study of Education,* Bloomington (Ill.), Public School Pub. Co., 1939, Part I.

of broad integrated development. This does not mean that a child can develop *general* motor ability, a factor which apparently does not exist; [67] it suggests, rather, that he will profit by the acquisition of one or more *specific* motor skills.

Tests of Children's Motor Ability

Since students of child development now recognize the specialized nature of motor abilities; that is, that a child may be proficient in one such skill while being unable to perform another, it is customary to speak of motor tests as measuring either composite or specific abilities. Tests of motor ability now available are for the most part designed to measure such motor skills as (1) steadiness, (2) accuracy, (3) speed, and (4) strength of voluntary movements. Tests suitable for children may also be classed as measures of (1) preschool and (2) school-age motor ability.

Motor Tests for Preschool Children.—Many of the wide variety of motor skills which the preschool child is capable of performing lend themselves to measurement by developmental scales. On such a basis successes and failures may be recorded under relatively controlled conditions, and with children of varying ages. The content of such scales is illustrated by the following items taken from a developmental schedule for infants and young children by Cunningham.[68] The complete scale includes more items at each age level.

Twelve Months Tests:
    To remove a paper cap from head.
    To tap a small bell.
    To obtain a toy from a second step.

Eighteen Months Tests:
    To get off a 10-inch stool.
    To climb three steps.
    To climb upon a low box.

[67] For references on this point see Clarence E. Ragsdale, "Motor Development of the Child," in *Child Psychology* (C. E. Skinner and P. L. Harriman, editors), New York, The Macmillan Co., 1941, pp. 103-104.
    [68] Bess V. Cunningham, "An Experiment in Measuring Gross Motor Development of Infants and Young Children," *Journal of Educational Psychology*, 18, 458-464 (1927).

Twenty-four Months Tests:
  To climb upon a chair, height 17½ inches.
  To throw a bean bag into a 12-inch hole after practice.
  To roll a bowling ball 9 feet over a small obstacle.
Thirty Months Tests:
  To throw a bean bag into a hole at 3 feet, twice with three trials.
  To walk up an 8-foot plank elevated 8 inches at the upper end.
  To roll a ball up an inclined board 3 feet 8 inches long.
Thirty-six Months Tests:
  To walk on a 4 x 4 x 4 beam without stepping off more than twice.
  To walk up steps without support.
  To jump with two feet from an 8-inch elevation.

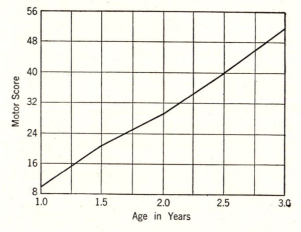

Figure 76. Motor Development in Children One to Three Years of Age

(Adapted from Bess V. Cunningham, "An Experiment in Measuring Gross Motor Development of Infants and Young Children," *Journal of Educational Psychology*, 18:458-464 (1927).)

As can be ascertained from Figure 76, motor development between the ages of twelve and thirty-six months, as measured by the Cunningham test, is very marked. Similar results are in evidence when the Gesell Developmental Schedule,[69] which has now been published in test form, the Bayley [70] scale, which measures motor control from the first month to the third year,

[69] Arnold Gesell, *Gesell Developmental Schedules*, New York, Psychological Corp., 1940.
[70] Nancy Bayley, *The Development of Motor Abilities During the First Three Years*, Monographs of the Society for Research in Child Development, Vol. 1, No. 1 (1935).

or the Wellman [71] series, in which preschool norms have been established for ascending and descending stairs, for throwing, catching, and bouncing balls, and for hopping, skipping, and walking on paths are used.

Specific preschool tests of steadiness of movement have been designed to measure such responses as making as many clicks as possible while holding a stylus in holes of various sizes in an apparatus supplied with batteries and a telegraph sounder (see Figure 77), and balancing oneself while walking on a narrow

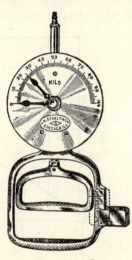

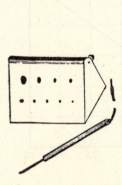

Figure 77. Steadiness Tester   Figure 78. The Hand Dynamometer
(By permission of C. H. Stoelting Co.)   (By permission of C. H. Stoelting Co.)

board. *Accuracy* of movement has been tested by the child's skill, for example, in drawing a line between two printed converging lines, or in moving a metal stylus down a narrowing path between two strips of metal, thus attempting to keep a buzzer sounding continuously.[72] Other precision tests involve tracing pencil mazes, hitting at targets, and striking crosses on paper with a pencil.

[71] C. L. McCaskill and Beth L. Wellman, "A Study of Common Motor Achievements at the Preschool Ages," *Child Development*, 9: 141-150 (1938).
[72] Beth L. Wellman, "The Development of Motor Coordination in Young Children," *Univ. of Iowa Studies in Child Welfare*, Vol. 3, No. 4 (1925).

Speed of movement has been determined by facility in such movements as placing pegs in the holes of a peg board, punching holes in paper, buttoning strips of cloth, sorting cards, and tapping with the fingers.[73] As for *strength,* it has been tested by measuring the child's hand grip, the strength of his back, his legs, and other major muscle groups. As Figure 78 suggests, hand grip may be measured by the number of kilograms (or pounds) the child is able to register with his grip on the dynamometer. Other methods may be used to measure the strength of muscles in other parts of the body.

Motor Tests for School Age Children.—Probably the best known composite motor test for children of school age is the one by Brace,[74] in which a wide range of relatively complex skills is measured in terms of point scores. The following items are characteristic of the general nature of the entire scale:

"Holding the left foot in the right hand behind the right leg, hop around on one spot in a circle three times without losing balance.

"Jump into the air and clap the feet together once and land with feet at least two inches apart.

"Fold the arms behind the back, kneel onto both knees, and get up without losing balance or moving the feet about.

"Jump into the air and make a full turn left, landing on the same spot and not losing balance, i.e., moving feet after they first hit the floor.

"Hold either foot in the opposing hand and jump through the loop thus made."

Tests of specific motor skill for older children are similar to those devised for infants and young children but involve in addition extensions to care for more complex activities. The child's rhythmic ability, for example, has been judged by having him strike two blocks, attached by an electric circuit to a

[73] Florence L. Goodenough, "A Further Study of Speed of Tapping in Early Childhood," *Journal of Applied Psychology,* 19 : 309-319 (1935).
[74] D. K. Brace, *Measuring Motor Ability,* New York, A. S. Barnes & Co., 1927 ; V. S. Vickers, L. Poyntz, and M. P. Baum, "The Brace Scale Used with Young Children," *Research Quarterly of the American Assn. for Health, Physical Education, and Recreation,* 13 : 299-308 (1942).

recording drum, together in time with music. Other tests include a paper-and-pencil form of the tapping test, more complicated mazes, throwing small rings over a peg, shooting arrows at a target, throwing beanbags through various sized holes, and even typewriting and telegraph operating.[75] The mirror-drawing test, in which the child is required to trace a star-shaped figure seen only through a mirror, is also used with school-age children. Other investigators have established norms for tapping for ages five to eleven,[76] for the dropping of marbles through holes in a box in the case of children from six to sixteen years of age,[77] and for strength of pupils in grades one to three.[78]

Growth Results Revealed by Tests.—As a scrutiny of the foregoing figures as well as other test results shows, speed, accuracy, and steadiness of voluntary movements increase rapidly throughout childhood. The gains made are, however, much greater for children around two to four years of age than for those ranging between four and six years. The six-year-old's movements are, nevertheless, twice as accurate and certainly much more differentiated than those of his three-year-old "brother." Complex skills begin to come into their own after the eighth or ninth year when the child engages more and more in such differentiated motor activities as swimming, bicycling, skating, baseball, and a variety of competitive sports. It is at this age that both boys and girls develop an appreciable share of the muscular strength which will characterize them as adults. The typical twelve-year-old possesses twice as strong a hand grip as he did at seven, a ratio which is again doubled in the case of boys by the age of seventeen. Muscles of the upper back develop even more rapidly between the ages mentioned.

[75] Arthur T. Jersild, *op. cit.*, pp. 71-76.
[76] Blake Crider, "A New Tapping Test," *Child Development,* 11 : 69-70 (1940).
[77] Joseph E. Moore, "A Test of Eye-Hand Coordination," *Journal of Applied Psychology*, 21 : 668-672 (1937).
[78] Aileen Carpenter, "Strength Testing in the First Three Grades," *Research Quarterly of the American Assn. for Health, Physical Education, and Recreation,* 13 : 328-332 (1942).

Summary and Implications

Motor development is dependent upon structural integrity, maturational processes, and, especially in the case of more complex activities, the learning factor. As the sequences for walking and for prehension illustrate, maturational development follows the two primary laws of cephalo-caudal and proximo-distal development, a fact which should be recognized by those responsible for the growing child's care. Observation has also shown that motor functions follow in the wake of structural development and that mass action precedes specialized responses of a skilled nature.

Although infants are able to move about in various ways during the early months, most children are not able to walk until approximately the fourteenth month or later. Such development may be retarded by illness, faulty nutrition, cold or slippery floors, painful accidents, unsuitable clothing, or subnormal intelligence. The more skilled performances appear during the third year and later, and may be improved by training and exercise. Motor tests have shown that speed, accuracy, and steadiness of voluntary movement, as well as strength, improve with increasing age. It is apparent, nevertheless, that motor abilities are specific rather than general; that is, that a child may be accurate without being quick, or that he may be proficient in running while being relatively unskillful in ball-throwing.

Parents and others who understand the nature of motor development will appreciate the importance of providing the child with freedom of movement, with suitable objects with which to play and explore, and with incentives to continuous action. They will also aid the child in learning to walk by providing rugs that will not slide, furniture that can be used for stable support, floors that will insure non-skid traction, and the encouragement of activities designed to promote the development of the large muscles. Such favorable opportunities will assist the child not only in developing neuromuscular skills but in adjusting to social situations and requirements. The child who possesses motor skills enjoys a distinct advantage in the social realm. Unlike the inferior child, who encounters a certain amount of ridicule, he tends to draw favorable comparisons to himself and to be wanted in group activities.

Teachers of both primary and elementary school children can aid their motor development by utilizing the principles of learning advocated by educational psychologists. These include (1) motivation through capitalization of the child's interests and needs, (2) the adjustment of motor activities to the child's physical and intellectual level, (3) the presentation of learning activities in meaningful pattern form, (4) stimulation to added achievement through periodic evaluation of the child's degree of success, and (5) accompanying motor development with a broad program of all-round personal and social growth. Although many detailed teaching techniques are implied in such a group of principles, they may be used as a frame of reference for implementing both motor and intellectual development.

QUESTIONS FOR DISCUSSION

1. What is the significance of the *cephalo-caudal* sequence in organism development for the later teaching of motor skills to children? Does this phenomenon explain why a child is able, for example, to throw things before he can walk? What other sequences of development does it explain?

2. To what extent does the structure-function principle indicate at what age one should teach a child to pull a wagon, to propel a scooter, or to play a musical instrument? On what basis would one determine when a child is "ready" for these and similar neuromuscular activities?

3. By what logic can it be argued that infant behavior develops from mass action to specialized responses in much the same manner as in the case, for example, of water lizards? What tangible evidence can be brought to bear on this question? Quote such authorities as you can find.

4. Point out the general sequences through which a child passes in learning to crawl and walk. To what degree is this development determined by maturation? By stimuli in the environment? Can these two influences be separated? If so, how?

5. What arguments can you advance against Gesell's assertion that maturation accounts for motor development more adequately than does learning? Is there anything mystic about

the belief that an inner principle determines the course of neuromuscular growth? Explain.

6. What violations in teaching, of the knowledge that gross movements precede more detailed and skilled responses, have you observed in connection with elementary schools? Show why attempts to require young children to develop detailed skills in handwriting have as a rule failed.

7. Is motivation as valuable in the teaching and learning of motor skills as in verbal fields? Justify your position with facts. Explain how a maximum of motivation may be secured in active games, motor skills, and other activities of a neuromuscular nature.

8. Show how pattern learning can be applied in the mastery of handwriting, swimming, riding a bicycle, or playing touch football. What are some of the obstacles to such a method? Find instances where this technique has been used and report the results. Indicate whether it was given a fair trial.

9. State the circumstances under which motor learning goes forward most adequately. Cite an example in which a child has learned a motor skill at a maximum rate because conditions were ideal. Show how motivation was achieved.

10. What factors other than speed, accuracy, and strength can be measured by objective tests? At what age do children begin to engage in such complex motor skills as bicycling, skating, ball playing, etc.? Can skill in these activities be measured accurately? How?

RECOMMENDED READINGS

Bayley, Nancy. *The Development of Motor Abilities During the First Three Years.* Monographs of the Society for Research in Child Development. Vol. 1, No. 1 (1935).

Bayley, Nancy, and Espenschade, Anna. "Motor Development from Birth to Maturity," in *Review of Educational Research,* Vol. 14, No. 5 (Dec., 1944), Ch. 5.

Cruze, Wendell W. *Educational Psychology.* New York: The Ronald Press Co., 1942, Chs. 5, 8.

Gates, A. I., Jersild, A. T., McConnell, T. R., and Challman, R. C. *Educational Psychology.* New York: The Macmillan Co., 1942, Chs. 3, 9, 10, 11, 12.

Gesell, Arnold, et al. *The First Five Years of Life: A Guide to the Study of the Preschool Child.* New York: Harper & Bros., 1940.

Goodenough, Florence L. *Developmental Psychology.* New York: D. Appleton-Century Co., Inc., 1945.

Jersild, Arthur T. *Music, Thirty-eighth Yearbook, National Society for the Study of Education.* Bloomington (Ill.) : Public School Pub. Co., 1939, Part I, Ch. 6.

McCloy, C. H. *Tests and Measurements in Health and Physical Education.* New York: F. S. Crofts & Co., 1939.

McGraw, Myrtle B. *Growth: A Study of Johnny and Jimmy.* New York: D. Appleton-Century Co., Inc., 1935.

Merry, F. K., and Merry, R. V. *From Infancy to Adolescence.* New York: Harper & Bros., 1940, Chs. 3, 6, 9.

Nagge, Joseph W. *Psychology of the Child.* New York: The Ronald Press Co., 1942, Chs. 3, 7.

Shirley, Mary M. *The First Two Years.* Vol. I: *Postural and Locomotor Development.* Minneapolis: Univ. of Minnesota Press, 1931.

Stoddard, George D., and Wellman, Beth L. *Child Psychology.* New York: The Macmillan Co., 1934, Ch. 3.

CHAPTER 11

LANGUAGE: ITS ORIGIN AND DEVELOPMENT

VOCAL LANGUAGE IS THE VEHICLE by means of which man communicates his ideas, his wishes, and his attitudes to other individuals. The capacity to exchange words and other symbols of ideas and feelings obviously serves to satisfy a variety of human needs. It is through this avenue that children secure not only information but a great deal of experience. Language is a means of both personal expression and social communication. It is, indeed, one of the principal factors in affecting personality development and social growth.

The ability to use words; that is, to communicate verbally, is dependent for its development upon both mental and physical growth. A child cannot use word symbols—and words are symbols of experiences—until he has reached a stage of experiential maturation which makes possible such an intellectual activity. Neither can he speak intelligibly until his vocal organs and related structures are sufficiently mature to permit of such intricate responses. Many animals, especially those of a higher infrahuman variety, possess elaborate physical equipment for vocalization, yet man alone has the capacity to use his structural potentialities in the form of fluent and meaningful speech.

How Language Is Learned

There has been considerable speculation concerning the origin of language responses in man, a problem which seems imbedded in the hazy history of the distant past. Some have supposed that vocal language developed as an improvement over sign language and that both of these forms of communication progressed with the development of man's nervous system. Others have thought that speech sounds grew out of single cries of pain and laughter associated with experiences involving danger, pleasure, and other affective states. It has also been suggested that speech developed out of a natural harmony between sound and sense as illustrated in such words, for example, as "bang," "thud," and "clang." This theory has been extended to include words derived from sounds occurring during strenuous physical exercise.

Many psychologists do not, however, place credence in these theories of the origin of language. They are much more concerned with the questions of how language is learned by children and what factors affect language development. Speech is considered a normal response to impinging language stimuli and is regarded as being made possible by the presence in the human organism of appropriate neurological, muscular, and other physical structures. Language is a form of behavior and is a natural function of the normal child when he has reached the necessary stages of experiential and structural maturation.

Mass Action to Differentiated Sounds.—The earlier belief that children's verbal language activities were instinctive in nature is no longer held by most students of the subject. It is recognized that linguistic skills are learned responses made possible by the child's capacity for modification of behavior and by his structural equipment for effecting vocalizations. The development of speech in children is in large measure a function of the integrated action of such physiological mechanisms as the vocal cords of the larynx, the oral and nasal cavities, the tongue, the lips, and the teeth. These and the more gross structures of the body (lungs, diaphragm, windpipe, etc.) operate together to make possible the flow of speech induced in the developing child by his own undifferentiated vocalizations, as well as by the speech patterns of others.

Observing parents will have noted that the child comprehends spoken language months before he can speak, also that he conveys meanings by means of both sign language and various sounds or cries. The baby may exhibit considerable animation at hearing such words as "daddy" or "kitten," and may respond with rapt attention to the sound of his name. He is also able to communicate his desires to his parents by means of gestures, grimaces, and various approach or withdrawal movements.

The earliest vocalizations of the child are spontaneous in character and undifferentiated as to sound. These mass-action vocal responses, which occur in forms apparently determined by laryngeal development, soon tend, however, to become differentiated and to have a more specific reference to feelings of cold, hunger, pain, and dampness, as well as to states of bodily well-being and organic tonicity. Such vocalizations include sounds of vowel origin similar to ă and ä (sometimes hä or ah), and later to vowel-consonant combinations comparable to mă and gä. More involved vowel sounds such as ŭv and pŭp often appear in subsequent development. It is out of these random (but physically caused) cries, grunts, cooings, and "babbling" expressions of organic satisfaction that the child's language skills evolve.

Some have thought that the young child gets his start in linguistic development through *imitation* of the words spoken to him by members of his family. As a matter of fact, he can imitate only the sounds which are in his vocal repertoire at the time. Only at a later stage of linguistic development, when much more vocal control is at his command, can the child reproduce words addressed to him by an adult. As many a parent will testify, efforts at inducing a baby to imitate sounds which are beyond its level of maturity (too differentiated) are fruitless. Imitation in the language responses of children less than one year of age is undoubtedly rare.

Learning the Names of Objects.—The processes by which the immature child comes to name objects; that is, to associate them with the appropriate words, has been described by Allport [1] as follows:

When the infant vocalizes, for example, the meaningless sound "da," he simultaneously reacts to it as an auditory stimulus. When he has heard himself say "da" a number of times,

[1] Floyd H. Allport, *Social Psychology*, Boston, Houghton Mifflin Co., 1924, Ch. 8. See also E. B. Holt, *Animal Drive and the Learning Process*, New York, Henry Holt & Co., Inc., 1931, Chs. 7, 13.

the child learns to connect the sound produced with the motor act of vocalizing. Experience has revealed that young children tend to repeat such "hearsay" (see Figure 79) reactions over and over. When once under way, this circuitous response provides its own stimulation. As Allport[2] brings out, the inability of deaf children to learn to talk in a normal manner is probably due to the absence of such preliminary experience.

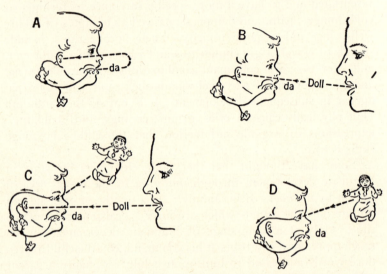

Figure 79. The Development of Language Responses in the Infant
(From F. H. Allport, *Social Psychology*, Boston, Houghton Mifflin Co., 1924, p. 184.)

When the child has come to say "da" or "da-da" consistently, an adult can condition him to say "da" whenever he (the adult) says a meaningful word, such as "doll," which closely resembles it. The child thus learns to say "da" as a response to a stimulus, not by imitating his teacher, but because his teacher imitated his undifferentiated vocalizing. The developing child is never able to imitate meaningful word sounds which he has not previously made in his spontaneous language responses.

As depicted in Figure 79, C and D, the child who has learned to say "da" can readily be taught to associate the word with

[2] Floyd H. Allport, *op. cit.*, pp. 185-186.

a doll by having the latter presented simultaneously with the vocal expression "doll." When this criterion for the establishment of the conditioned response has been met the learner soon comes to name the doll-object (as "da," because he cannot yet pronounce "doll") when it is brought to his attention. It is thus evident that the names and meanings of words are learned by hearing them in connection with the objects or events for which they are symbolic representations. The child learns what "mama," "daddy," and "kitty," mean by associating them with the sight or sound of the objects for which they stand. It may, however, be some time before he is able to pronounce the words in question adequately.

The child's acquisition of language skills illustrates well the general laws of development. As in the instance of motor development, he progresses from vague, undifferentiated verbal responses to those of a more particularized and specific nature. Before he can pronounce "kitty" he may say "kicky" or "ticky," and previous to the ability to say "car" he may respond with "tar" or "taie." Furthermore, the name "kitty" at first bears such a broad generalized meaning to the young child that he responds with it at the sight of dogs, lambs, squirrels, and any other relatively small furry animals. The word "daddy" is also often directed toward objects (men) other than the specific one to which it belongs, sometimes to the discomfiture of the mother.

With further experience and development, differentiation in the use of words is rapidly achieved. The child soon learns to pronounce his words with surprising accuracy. He will continue, however, to make errors in grammatical usage, in the finer shades of meaning, and when he reaches the writing stage, in the spelling of words. Object naming itself soon progresses to the use of short sentences in place of single words. Instead of merely saying "wagon," the developing child may respond with "Give me the wagon," or "Where is the wagon?" With added experience in the use of words, he will react with such possessives as "mine," "mamma's," and "baby's," and such questions as "Who is it?" and "What is it?"

The Role of Language in Thinking.—There has been some controversy over the question of whether language and thought activities are ultimately identical; that is, whether thought processes can proceed without the use of subvocal (inner) words. The fact that children, and some adults, talk aloud as they think, and that thought must be expressed to others in the form of words, have been brought forward as evidence for the position that thought is essentially subvocal speech. This point of view involves certain academic arguments, but has been promoted by a number of psychologists, notably J. B. Watson, the father of behaviorism. It has been supported by the researches of Jacobsen,[3] who found that adults do not experience ideas or other thought processes when their vocal cords are thoroughly relaxed.

The view has suffered, on the other hand, from experimental findings that tongue movements are not always in evidence when thought is in process, and that the larynx is inactive during whispering, an activity which appears to involve the presence of thought.[4] Köhler's [5] researches on the learning process in apes indicated as well that infrahuman animals apparently perform feats requiring thought processes of varying degrees of complexity without being able to use words in the human sense of such vocalization. Judging from these and other findings, it is likely that thought does not necessarily involve language processes, implicit or otherwise, in the sense of requiring the use of word symbols. Language may make possible the enrichment and extension of thought, but is probably not synonymous with it.

The developing child early learns that he must frequently suppress his inclinations to say things "right out loud." As he grows older he is required to refrain from speaking when others are conversing and to be more quiet in the presence of his elders. He may even be laughed at when he is talking to himself. Such pressures cause the child gradually to substitute subvocal

---

[3] Edmund Jacobson, *Progressive Relaxation*, Chicago, Univ. of Chicago Press, 1938, Ch. 10.
[4] A. M. Thorson, "The Relation of Tongue Movements to Internal Speech," *Journal of Experimental Psychology*, 8 : 1-32 (1925).
[5] Wolfgang Köhler, *The Mentality of Apes*, New York, Harcourt, Brace & Co., 1927.

responses (thoughts) for his apparently unwelcomed overt speech activities. If whispering or talking in a low voice are also frowned upon, the child is practically required to short-circuit his verbal activities in favor of thinking.

To the extent that it explains the development of the young child's ability to think and to deal with abstract concepts, this theory of the role of language in forwarding the thought processes suggests how he gradually becomes capable of dealing symbolically with his material environment. Thinking is apparently neither a so-called instinct nor the result of an alleged inner unfolding of intelligence; it is rather a product of experience, in part at least, with words and the objective realities for which words stand. Symbolic thinking makes possible much economy of random behavior and many fundamental modes of adjustment.

The Function of Language in Childhood.—One might be led to believe that young children employ language activities chiefly to communicate with adults and with other children, or to promote social play. According to several investigations in which units of children's language—sentences and short groups of sentences—were analyzed for their content reference, such is not primarily the case. The speech activities of children are for the most part egocentric; they talk about themselves and to themselves much more than is the case with normal adults. Young children have a decided tendency to engage in monologues when they are apparently playing. And since they are primarily concerned with their own thoughts and interests, children's speech is characteristically self-assertive.

As suggested in the discussion of personality dynamics (Chapter 5), children are sensitive to recognition of their personal worth and to their importance in the scheme of things. It is thus not surprising that researches should disclose the egocentric nature of much of young children's responses, linguistic or otherwise. Actually much of their language is calculated to express self-assertion, to command, to dominate, and to attract attention to self-display. Young children have not yet learned the advantages of social cooperation and of mutuality in the solution of their problems.

A study [6] in which the conversation of 27 kindergarten children was recorded for three fifteen-minute periods involving outdoor play, a classroom period, and a luncheon conversation is illustrative of the nature of their spontaneous remarks. As

TABLE 23. CLASSIFICATION OF 3,125 REMARKS MADE BY 27 KINDERGARTEN CHILDREN

Classification	Number	Per Cent
I. Self-assertion	1,275	40.8
II. Self-depreciation	8	.25
III. Evidences of social consciousness	116	3.7
IV. Verbalized perceptions	259	8.3
V. Linguistic experimentation	188	6.0
VI. Dramatic play	148	4.7
VII. Questions	311	9.95
VIII. Rational thought	193	6.2
IX. Statements of fact	500	16.0
X. Answers of "yes" and "no"	127	4.1
Total	3,125	100.0

(Condensed from H. Rugg, L. Krueger, and A. Sondergaard, Studies in Child Personality, I: "A Study of the Language of Kindergarten Children," *Journal of Educational Psychology*, 20: 9 (1929).)

can be noted from Table 23, of the 3,125 remarks made, nearly one-half were classed as "self-assertive." Very few conversations gave evidence of social consciousness. In fact, only one remark in more than every 25 indicated any interest in other children. Only eight remarks, or one in every 400, showed a tendency toward self-depreciation. These data are suggestive of the nature of child personality.

Piaget,[7] a pioneer investigator in the field of children's language, found their responses to be characteristically egocentric (38 per cent) and attributed that fact to the absence of true social maturity in children before approximately ages seven or

[6] H. Rugg, L. Krueger, and A. Sondergaard, Studies in Child Personality, I: "A Study of the Language of Kindergarten Children," *Journal of Educational Psychology*, 20: 1-18 (1929).
[7] Jean Piaget, *The Language and Thought of the Child*, New York, Harcourt Brace & Co., 1926.

eight. Piaget stated that groups of young children approximately ages seven or eight were inclined to play with dolls and talk at the same time, without paying much attention to each other. He also noted that mimicry and gestures were used in the children's play about as frequently as were words.

An investigation by McCarthy [8] suggested, somewhat to the contrary, that children's speech is much less egocentric than Piaget and others have supposed. She made the significant observation that a child's language responses are to a considerable extent determined by the types of situations in which he is called upon to respond. Egocentric language appeared more frequently in play situations with other children than it did, for example, in conversations with adults. McCarthy's findings thus differ from Piaget's, probably because of differing criteria for judging children's language responses and because of the variable effects on children of different types of social situations. It is generally recognized that children are originally characteristically egocentric, but that they become more socialized as they achieve greater maturity. Those who fail to develop in this manner may later be marked by infantilisms in speech, and frequently in behavior.

Speech as an Avenue to Socialization.—Socialized speech represents a relatively mature stage of language development, and is usually indicative of a growing social consciousness. However, socialized language, which tends to increase noticeably after the seventh or eighth year, is an implement for the development of further socialization, as well as being a sign of social growth. It is through communication with others that the growing child learns his first lessons in cooperation and acquires the sense of belongingness with individuals outside of the family group so essential to personal and social adjustment.

The earlier stages of socialized speech are characterized by considerable self-assertion and evidences of egocentricism. The child is, nevertheless, on his way toward maturity in both language and behavior when he asks and answers questions. de-

---

[8] Dorothea A. McCarthy, "A Comparison of Children's Language in Different Situations and in Relation to Personality Traits," *Pedagogical Seminary and Journal of Genetic Psychology*, 36 : 583-591 (1929).

fends a given course of action, agrees to do things, argues over suggestions, tells other children what to do or what not to do, and endeavors to understand the motives of those who speak to him. These and similar activities are more socialized than the monologues, the repetitions of words (echolalia), the talking to one's self during group play, and the dual monologues of earlier egocentric language responses in which the child almost completely disregards an audience and feels that he has a hearer when he talks to himself.

In an effort to classify the general types of socialized speech responses of children in the earlier stages of such development, Piaget [9] has listed seven. The categories are presented in the full realization that a child's language is determined to a considerable extent by the specific influences which play upon him in any given situation. The types of socialized speech responses include: (1) *adapted information,* in which the child solicits and makes responses to his audience, adapts to its points of view, and makes remarks which are associated with the situation at hand; (2) *criticism,* which includes remarks about the behavior of others and complaints about frustrating experiences; (3) *emotionally toned responses,* in which the child exhibits considerable stress in making requests, threats, and commands; (4) *questions,* in which responses are solicited from an audience; (5) *answers,* in which the child responds to queries from an audience; (6) *social phrases,* a classification which includes such good-manner responses as "please," "thank you," "goodbye," and "excuse me"; and (7) *dramatic imitation,* in which the child mimics animals or adults who make sounds intended to imitate those of dogs, cats, cows, trains, automobiles, and the like.

It has been observed that, in general, talkative babies become talkative children, and that speech tendencies influence the child's personality development during the first years.[10] This is no doubt true but, as Shirley's declaration that the child's manner of expressing himself is compatible with his other personality traits suggests, *both* his speech patterns and

9 Jean Piaget, *op. cit.*
10 Mary M. Shirley, *The First Two Years,* Vol. III: *Personality Manifestations,* Minneapolis, Univ. of Minnesota Press, 1933, pp. 154-155.

his other personality qualities are probably the result of the type of parental handling he has experienced. Willingness to converse with people on a socialized basis may aid in further personality development, but such a tendency is itself an aspect of good personality that must have been brought about by constructive early home conditions.

The same may be said of children who stutter, who, according to a study by Johnson,[11] are frequently nervously unstable, self-conscious, and generally depressed. Their speech defect no doubt engendered feelings of inadequacy, yet the stuttering symptoms were themselves probably caused by the same early environmental influences which occasioned the nervous instability as such. Such a speech handicap retards the development of the socialization process, but is itself often an expression of the failure of parents and others to provide the child with the dynamic satisfactions which lead naturally to satisfactory emotional development.

The Genetic Development of Language

The language development of children has been studied by more or less unorganized observational methods since at least the latter part of the eighteenth century. The technique used has usually been that of systematic note taking by a parent or relative of the spontaneous language expressions of one or more children. A number of compilations of the words used by a child over a period of from a few months to around three years have been published.[12] Although these observations are usually made under conditions too variable to permit the making of accurate comparisons, they have been found useful as points of departure for the development of more scientific observational techniques.

More recent studies of development in facility with spoken language have been made under conditions designed to insure a maximum uniformity of experimental control, and opportu-

---

[11] W. Johnson, "The Influence of Stuttering on the Personality," *Univ. of Iowa Studies in Child Welfare*, Vol. 5, No. 5 (1932).

[12] See the discussion of baby biographies in Chapter 1 of this volume.

nity for the verification by others of the results obtained.[13] Psychologists have, for example, recorded and examined the spontaneous conversations of young children during specified periods of playtime. They have also made careful analyses of the free conversations of preschool children in their home environments. Although it is by no means easy to secure representative samplings of children's total language equipment, an excellent beginning in this direction has been made.

Children's Pre-verbal Language Behavior.—Children very early come to make non-verbal signs and gestures which serve as important means of communication with adults. It is through such primitive language behavior that they elicit satisfying responses and desired rewards from those whom they are in a position to influence. The child is thus able to carry on a kind of sign language with his parents before he can control them through articulate verbalizations. He may, for example, cry for his food when hungry, reach up his arms when he wants to be picked up, shake his head when a nap is suggested, smile when he hears his puppy scratching on the door, and move about excitedly when he sees his mother approaching. These and similar conditioned responses are the precursors of more adaptive reactions of a verbal variety.

It is in these early pre-verbal responses that students of child development discover the beginnings of intelligent behavior. It is in such essentially adaptive responses that the young child displays his potential capacity for solving problematic situations, for exerting a measure of control over his elders, and for adjusting to the material requirements of his environment. The ability to effect pre-language adaptive reactions suggests as well the probability that children entertain ideas—that is, that they think—about objects not present to their senses, and about ways of securing desired results. In short, the child's gestures and movements probably come to mean something to him in the adjustment sense.

[13] John E. Anderson, "The Development of Spoken Language," in *Child Development and the Curriculum, Thirty-Eighth Yearbook, National Society for the Study of Education*, Bloomington (Ill.), Public School Pub. Co., 1939, Part I, Ch. 10. See also Dorothea A. McCarthy, "Language Development," in *Handbook of Child Psychology* (edited by Carl Murchison), Worcester, Clark Univ. Press, 1933, Ch. 8.

Undifferentiated vocalizations are also important means of communication with adults, at least as signals of the child's state of bodily well-being. Just as certain cries are indicative of the presence of pain, so sounds indicating joy may mean a condition of organism well-being or a pleasant anticipation (nursing, bathing, etc.). Although it is doubtful whether babies utilize such means of communication in a conscious effort to influence their elders, they are among the spontaneous sounds out of which articulate speech responses will in time (usually) differentiate.

An experiment by Hunter [14] with his thirteen-months-old daughter, who was obviously not yet able to utilize adequate spoken language, is suggestive of the hypothesis that young children entertain ideas, or at least that they act upon past impressions, during their pre-verbal days. Subsequently to handing the child a favorite toy, the experimenter took it from her and placed it in one of a group of boxes before which she had been seated. As soon as it was evident that the child had seen in which box the toy was placed, she was thoroughly distracted by a previously planned play activity. Upon being later placed in a position facing the boxes, she was given the opportunity of reaching in the appropriate compartment for her previously abandoned toy. In most of 284 trials, which occupied a three-month period and in which the delay span was extended from 10 to 24 seconds, this child responded by hunting for the toy as soon as she was placed in a position facing the stimulus object. Similar results were obtained by Allen [15] in an investigation utilizing a group of year-old infants.

The conclusion has been drawn from these and similar experiments that young children are able to appropriate *ideas* in responding to problematic situations previous to the time when adequate speech reactions are available. Whether such ideas are based upon neural processes, kinesthetic "sets," or a form of bodily conditioning is not as yet certain. It is clear, however, that children of the age discussed are sufficiently capable of

[14] Walter S. Hunter, "The Delayed Reaction in a Child," *Psychological Review,* 24 : 74-87 (1917).

[15] C. N. Allen, "Individual Differences in Delayed Reaction of Infants," *Archives of Psychology,* No. 127 (1931).

utilizing non-verbal *symbolic* responses to make associations with situations which are retained throughout appreciable periods of distraction. Spoken language is thus apparently not wholly essential to ideational behavior in human beings.

The Form of Developing Speech Reactions.—Although children exhibit marked individual differences in language development, such progress is characterized by certain broad sequences that may be said to be common to all. These sequences may be classified as: (1) the period of infant vocalization and babblings, (2) the period of initial word using, (3) the development of word meaning, (4) development of the ability to express thought units, and (5) the period of mastering the more mature speech forms. The first three of these sequences, together with a consideration of sex differences in linguistic development, will occupy the attention of the present section.

INFANT VOCALIZATIONS AND BABBLINGS. The first sound made by the newborn infant, the birth cry, is purely mechanical in nature and has no known emotional or intellectual meaning.[16] It does, however, mark the beginning of oral speech. Later sounds made by the neonate and the infant during the first weeks of postnatal life are but vocal responses to sensations of pain, hunger, cold, dampness, and other bodily discomforts. Although at least one investigator [17] differs, it is commonly believed that such physiological stimuli produce vocalizations differing in intensity alone, and not in quality of sound. It is claimed, however, that these rudimentary utterances resemble the vowel and consonant sounds out of which later word responses develop.

Newborn infants are incapable of producing all of the vocal sounds necessary for adequate speech, and it is a matter of some uncertainty in what order their speech sounds develop. According to some investigators,[18] the vowels, especially *a* and *u,* are spoken first. The first consonants to appear are the so-called

[16] J. C. Fenton, *A Practical Psychology of Babyhood,* Boston, Houghton Mifflin Co., 1925, p. 6.
[17] C. H. Bean, "An Unusual Opportunity to Investigate the Psychology of Language," *Journal of Genetic Psychology,* 40 : 181-203 (1932).
[18] See Mary M. Shirley, *The First Two Years,* Vol. II : *Intellectual Development,* Minneapolis, Univ. of Minnesota Press, 1933, pp. 48-54. Also Dorothea A. McCarthy, *op. cit.*

labials (produced by using the teeth), and in *t* and *d*. The gut-
turals (made by the throat), particularly *k* and *g,* are produced
early in the child's career, and are followed by the sibilants or *s*
and *z* sounds. Although there is some disagreement, it is believed that *f, v, r,* and *l* are among the last sounds to appear. All
of these sounds are first made as undifferentiated responses to

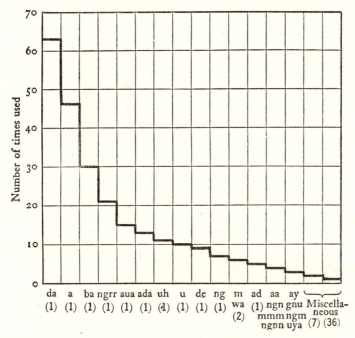

Figure 80. The 64 Different Sounds Distinguished in the Vocalizations of a
Six-Months-Old Child for a 24-Hour Period

(From Arnold Gesell, *Mental Growth of the Preschool Child,* New York, The Macmillan
Co., 1925, p. 216.)

physiological stimuli, and are not an organized part of the
child's meaningful speech responses until several years have
passed. "Baby talk," in which the *r* and *i* sounds are still unsuccessfully managed, often persists until the fifth or sixth
year.

The maturing of language behavior, both pre-verbal and
linguistic, has been studied by a number of students of the sub-

TABLE 24. THE MATURING OF VOCAL BEHAVIOR

Behavior Items	Weeks of Age														
	4	6	8	12	16	20	24	28	32	36	40	44	48	52	56
1. Face brightens	40	68													
2. Chuckles	0	0	36	42	24										
3. Smiles	22	65	96	100	100										
4. Laughs	0	0	7	31	88										
5. No vocalization heard	45	31	21	15	28										
6. Vocalizes small throaty noises	84	72	3	4	4										
7. Vocalizes ah-uh-eh	40	96	82	96	67										
8. Coos	0	3	42	88	76										
9. Blows bubbles	0	0	3	42	44										
10. Gurgles	0	0	10	42	56										
11. Vocalizes da					0	7	7	18	59	64	63	62	69	67	59
12. Vocalizes ma or mu					5	11	26	43	47	51	60	52	60	64	64
13. Two syl., 2nd rep. first, ma-ma, ba-ba, etc.					14	11	7	25	66	70	80	83	86	79	91
14. Makes "d" sound					0	7	22	21	66	64	69	62	88	67	73
15. Makes "m" sound					5	11	26	43	47	58	63	55	60	64	64
16. Makes "e" sound (at end of word)					0	4	7	7	16	12	14	35	46	48	64
17. Makes "b" sound					9	4	15	14	22	24	32	41	32	57	64
18. Says no "word"					100	100	100	93	88	79	66	31	23	12	5
19. Says one "word" or more							0	7	12	21	34	69	77	88	95
20. Says two "words" or more							0	4	0	3	3	28	34	67	86
21. Says three "words" or more											0	10	26	40	68
22. Says four "words" or more											0	7	9	26	36

The apparent break in the table at sixteen weeks is occasioned by the decision of the investigators to abandon the study of non-language responses in favor of those of a linguistic nature. (From Arnold Gesell and H. Thompson, *Infant Behavior: Its Genesis and Growth*, New York, McGraw-Hill Book Co., Inc., 1934, p. 249.)

ject, but is perhaps best illustrated in the researches of Gesell [19] and his associates (see Table 24). The table, which includes the so-called babbling stage of development (approximately ages six to ten months), in which the child repeats sounds as the result of hearing himself say them (circular reflex), portrays the genetic development of language behavior from the fourth to the fifty-sixth week in terms of the *percentages* of children manifesting the various responses. It will be noted, for example, that whereas no infants gurgled at the age of six weeks, 56 per cent did so at sixteen weeks. Similarly, although 100 per cent spoke no words at twenty-four weeks, only 5 per cent were unable to do so at fifty-six weeks.

THE WORD-USING PERIOD. As indicated in a previous section of this chapter, the child learns to use words by repeating sounds which he hears others make, but which were originally in the repertoire of his own undifferentiated vocalizations. As one volume [20] on the subject states it, "This imitation of the sounds (words) made by others is a forerunner of connecting them with specific situations and objects. Constant repetition, plus selection of sounds approved by people in his environment, leads him (the child) to the place where he substitutes the spoken word for a specific situation or object, thus completing the transition to *real* speech." The child may, for example, connect the word "bang" with the throwing of an object to the floor and with hearing the noise produced, if someone uses the word as he enacts this usually gleeful episode. The same type of process may lead him to connect the word "mama" with his mother, "woof-woof" with his dog, "baby" with himself, etc.

The one-word stage of language development, which the majority of children reach between fifteen and eighteen months, is greatly accelerated by the coaching of individuals who are willing to give the child names of objects that have significance for him and that he can pronounce. Before the child realizes the usefulness of names or senses that everything and everyone has a name, he is interested in forming the sounds coupled with

---

[19] Arnold Gesell and H. Thompson, *Infant Behavior: Its Genesis and Growth*, New York, McGraw-Hill Book Co., Inc., 1934.

[20] Frieda K. Merry and Ralph V. Merry, *From Infancy to Adolescence*, New York, Harper & Bros., 1940, p. 79.

them. As he comes to comprehend the presence of names and the fact that everything has such a label he passes through what his elders call the "naming" stage. The developing child thus begins to organize his behavior around the objects for which he knows the names. His ability to use words now enables him to secure many satisfactions which were formerly out of his reach or which he did not know existed. This is especially true when the child has reached the stage where he can convey a complete idea (called *expletive* sense), a "one-word-sentence," with a single name. At this point "Dolly!" may actually mean, "Give me the dolly" or "Look at the dolly."

The child's mastery of words and their more simple meanings enables him to make more and more complex adjustments to his environment. A summary of the adaptive functions of such word learning by Waring [21] is indicative of its usefulness :

> "1. The language labels may serve as means for the recall of these and similar experiences.
> 2. They may serve as means for securing the repetition of the experience.
> 3. They may serve as stimuli for such behavior as they have been associated with.
> 4. They may serve as centers about which the child organizes his experiences until they gradually form generalized concepts which he can use as criteria for evaluating possible ways of behaving and for deciding what to do and how to do and act."

In view of the usefulness of words in effecting adjustments, it behooves parents and others who are vested with comparable responsibilities to assist the child in organizing his experiences around words which may serve as stimuli for desirable behavior. Words should be associated with the kind of behavior adults wish the child to learn.

THE DEVELOPMENT OF WORD MEANINGS. Words are becoming meaningful to the child when he connects such words as

21 Ethel B. Waring, *The Relation Between Early Language Habits and Early Habits of Conduct Control*, Teachers College Contributions to Education No. 260, Columbia Univ., 1927, p. 5.

"daddy," "kitty," and "choo-choo" with his father, his cat, and a railroad train, respectively. It is not long, however, until he progresses from one-word sentences to the use of such two-word sentences as "doggie bad," "baby sleep," or "dolly gone." The fact that these expressions stand for more complete sentences suggests the degree of capacity to discriminate among meanings characteristic of children ranging in age from approximately 18 months to two years or more.

The child's qualitative use of words also shows marked development with increasing age. Because of his experiences with them, the child comes to know the meaning of events, objects, and to some extent the behavior of people. Objects take on more and more meaning as he manipulates them through feeling, pulling, striking, lifting, throwing, dropping, rolling, and in some instances smelling, tasting, and hearing. As he learns the words for objects and their manipulation, the alert child senses their meaning for activity as it affects him. The typical four- or five-year-old can usually define such words as "chair," "shoe," "table," "horse," and "car" in terms of their use. He is likely, for example, to define chair as "A chair is to sit on" and car as "A car is to ride in." Such words have meaning for him in terms of possibilities for action.

Development in capacity to comprehend the meaning of words is perhaps most adequately portrayed in the requirements of the Stanford Revision of the Simon-Binet mental scale by Terman and Merrill.[22] At five years the typical child can define "ball," "bat," and "stove" in terms of use, the usual response to ball being "to play with." At seven he is able to state the similarities between such words as "wood" and "coal" or "iron" and "silver." A typical answer to the first is that "wood and coal both burn." At the eighth year the child is usually able to state both similarities and differences between such words as "baseball" and "orange" and "ocean" and "river." An adequate answer to the first of these may read "Both are round and baseball is a game and orange is a fruit." The typical eleven-year-old is able to define such abstract words as "connection,"

[22] Lewis M. Terman and Maud A. Merrill, *Measuring Intelligence*, Boston, Houghton Mifflin Co., 1937, Part II.

"conquer," and "revenge." Responses to the first word have included "The relation between things," and "If somebody had a broken rope they'd tie the rope together, connect it." As these progressive requirements and responses indicate, the developing child shows increasing ability to understand the likenesses and differences among words and to define them in abstract terms.

A warning designed to aid growing children in distinguishing between general terms and more specific words has been given by Morgan [23] in this connection. To quote him, "When they first experience a situation the generalized name for that object or event should be given, and the specific ones applied later on. An illustration will show the mistake that may be made here. A child's first experience with a book happened to be with a Bible. As he touched it an adult said, 'Bible.' The next book he came in contact with was a novel but he called it a Bible. In other words, Bible is a specific type of book. When he first experienced book it should have been called 'book.' Later he could have been taught to discriminate among varieties of books and to apply their respective names." Such a procedure would prevent the naive child from calling his mother's fur a cat, from naming a woman in a fur coat a bear, and from calling strange men "daddy."

SEX AND SOCIAL DIFFERENCES IN DEVELOPMENT. It is well known that the female child excels her male "brother" in rate of physiological development. It is not so widely known that she is similarly accelerated in linguistic development. For reasons that are not clear to students of the subject, baby girls vocalize more frequently than male infants even during neonate days.[24] It has been found as well that, in general, girls speak more plainly than boys at all ages between eighteen and fifty-four months.[25] Girls also not only use longer sentences than boys, they progress along the usual sequences of language development more rapidly than do the latter. The extent and nature of sex differences in language ability, between the ages

[23] J. J. B. Morgan, *Child Psychology*, New York, Farrar & Rinehart, Inc., 1942, p. 311.

[24] M. C. Gatewood and A. P. Weiss, "Race and Sex Differences in Newborn Infants," *Journal of Genetic Psychology*, 38 : 31-49 (1930).

[25] Dorothea A. McCarthy, *The Language Development of the Preschool Child*, Minneapolis, Univ. of Minnesota Press, 1930.

of five and ten years, have been studied by Davis [26] and are set forth in Table 25. Here again girls are found to be generally superior to boys, a phenomenon which appears even in the linguistic development of prematurely born infants.[27]

TABLE 25. SUMMARY OF SEX DIFFERENCES IN CHILDREN'S LINGUISTIC SKILL

Measure	Boys	Girls
Percentage having perfect articulation at 5½ years...	56	73
Percentage having perfect articulation at 9½ years...	87	95
Substitutions of *d* for *th*.............................	429	214
Substitutions of *w* for *r*..............................	81	32
Substitutions of *t, th* for *s*..........................	3	78
Mean number of words per remark, both upper and lower social classes...............................	5.13	5.35
Percentage of single-word expressions...............	18.0	19.6
Percentage of answers..............................	20.9	28.0
Percentage of questions.............................	10.3	8.4
Percentage of emotionally toned remarks.............	2.9	4.1
Percentage of elaborated sentences..................	5.8	6.7
Mean number of infinitives per 1,000 words..........	9.1	10.5
Mean number of auxiliary verbs per 1,000 words.....	59	62
Mean number of errors per 1,000 words..............	28	25
Mean number of different words....................	102	107
Pronoun index	0.41	0.42
Percentage of conjunctions	2.8	3.6
Incidence of slang per 1,000 words.................	9	6

(Adapted from E. A. Davis, *The Development of Linguistic Skill in Twins, Singletons with Siblings, and Only Children from Ages Five to Ten Years*, Minneapolis, Univ. of Minnesota Press, 1937, p. 133.)

A variety of researches testify to the fact that children of superior socio-economic status tend to be precocious in linguistic development. Such homes apparently provide a higher type of stimulation to language progress than do those of a more economically modest variety. A study by Smith,[28] in which children of contrasting social status were matched with respect

[26] Edith A. Davis, *The Development of Linguistic Skill in Twins, Singletons with Siblings, and Only Children From Ages Five to Ten Years*, Minneapolis, Univ. of Minnesota Press, 1937.

[27] J. H. Hess, G. J. Mohr, and P. F. Bartelme, *The Physical and Mental Growth of Prematurely Born Children*, Chicago, Univ. of Chicago Press, 1934.

[28] Medorah E. Smith, "An Investigation of the Development of the Sentence and the Extent of Vocabulary in Young Children," *Univ. of Iowa Studies in Child Welfare*, Vol. 3, No. 5 (1926).

to sex, chronological age, and mental ability, showed that those of higher social status also excelled in knowledge of words. Although little difference was found in the length of sentences used, the socially superior group was accelerated six months in vocabulary development. A similar relationship between language development and socio-economic status has been reported by Young [29] in a matched group study of the language responses of 74 children ranging in age from thirty to sixty-five months.

In her previously mentioned investigation of language development, McCarthy [30] found certain differences between two

TABLE 26. DIFFERENCES BETWEEN THE MEAN LENGTHS OF LANGUAGE RESPONSES IN THE UPPER AND LOWER OCCUPATIONAL GROUPS

| Chronological Ages of Children (Months) | Mean for Occupational Groups | | Diff. | Diff. |
	Upper Half	Lower Half		SD diff.
18..................	1.61	1.33	.28	1.11
24 and 30...........	3.01	2.34	.67	2.51
36 and 42...........	5.38	3.28	2.10	10.55
48 and 54...........	4.84	4.20	.64	5.66

(Adapted from Dorothea A. McCarthy, *The Language Development of the Preschool Child*, Minneapolis, Univ. of Minnesota Press. 1930, p. 58.)

contrasted groups of eighteen- to fifty-four-months-old children selected on the basis of the occupational status of their parents. As Table 26 reveals, the children of the upper occupational group excelled their less favored classmates in mean length of language responses (also all aspects of sentence construction) in all of the age categories investigated. These and similar studies make it clear that children in the upper social and economic brackets have the advantage so far as language development is concerned. This advantage is maintained even when mental ages are held constant for the upper and lower socio-economic groups.

[29] Florence M. Young, *An Analysis of Certain Variables in a Developmental Study of Language*, Genetic Psychology Monographs, Vol. 23, No. 1 (1941), pp. 3-141.
[30] Dorothea A. McCarthy, *op. cit.*

Growth of the Child's Vocabulary.—A number of studies concerning the vocabulary development of children have been made in both Europe and America. Some of these were carried on in connection with baby biographies, others have utilized more quantitative research techniques. A common method has been that of noting all the words used spontaneously by children of different ages. In the case of older children, it has been customary to count all the words used during a given period of time—for example, thirty minutes—and to analyze the results for frequency of word usage. Vocabulary tests have been worked out for children and have provided much valuable information regarding development in facility with words.

One of the most revealing experimental investigations of vocabulary growth published is that by Smith,[31] in which the average size of vocabularies of children from one to six years of age was ascertained. After constructing a list of 203 words in common use among children by the method of selecting every twentieth word from the Thorndike list of the 10,000 most commonly used words in the English language and checking these against published children's vocabularies, this investigator established word norms (averages) for children of the ages indicated. The 203 words were presented to 273 children in connection with objects, pictures, or certain standardized descriptive situations. The results of the study, which may be seen in Table 27, have proved to be reliable in relation to previously published vocabularies, to baby biography studies, to the Descoeudres test, and to the vocabulary sections of the Stanford-Binet scale.

As Smith's data show, once speech activity is begun, the average child shows rapid progress. From the ability at age one of using 3 words, he develops to the extent that he can use 896 words at three and 2,562 at age six. From this point, size of vocabulary continues to develop at a rate commensurate with the growing child's home environment, educational opportunities, and desire to improve to approximately 15,000 words at the time of graduation from high school. According to the norms of the original Stanford-Binet mental scale, vocabulary

---

[31] Medorah E. Smith, *op. cit.*

TABLE 27. AVERAGE SIZE OF VOCABULARIES OF 273 CHILDREN * FROM
EIGHT MONTHS TO SIX YEARS OF AGE

| Age Groups | | Number of | Vocabulary | |
Years	Months	Children	Number of Words	Gain
..	— 8	13	0	..
..	— 10	17	1	1
1	— 0	52	3	2
1	— 3	19	19	16
1	— 6	14	22	3
1	— 9	14	118	96
2	— 0	25	272	154
2	— 6	14	446	174
3	— 0	20	896	450
3	— 6	26	1,222	326
4	— 0	26	1,540	318
4	— 6	32	1,870	330
5	— 0	20	2,072	202
5	— 6	27	2,289	217
6	— 0	9	2,562	273

* Forty-three children were tested more than once, some three or four times.
(From Medorah E. Smith, "An Investigation of the Development of the Sentence and
Extent of Vocabulary in Young Children," *Univ. of Iowa Studies in Child Welfare*,
Vol. 3, No. 5 (1926), p. 54.)

size increases until intellectual maturity has been reached at the
following rate: eight years, 3,600 words; ten years, 5,400
words; twelve years, 7,200 words; fourteen years, 9,000 words;
sixteen years (average adult), 11,700 words; and eighteen
years (superior adult), 13,500 words.[32]

Investigations pertaining to the most frequently used words
in childhood include a survey of those used by kindergarten
children,[33] a study of those most familiar to children in
France,[34] and a compilation of those used most often by the
subjects of Smith's [35] investigation. In the French study the
words familiar to children were ascertained by asking them to
write as many words as they could think of during a fifteen-

[32] Lewis M. Terman, *The Measurement of Intelligence*, Boston, Houghton
Mifflin Co., 1916, p. 226.
[33] Madeline D. Horn, "The Thousand and Three Words Most Frequently
Used by Kindergarten Children," *Childhood Education*, 3 : 118-122 (1926).
[34] Daniel A. Prescott, "Le Vocabulaire des Enfants des Ecoles Primaires
de Genève," *Archives de Psychologie*, 21 : 225-261 (1929).
[35] Medorah E. Smith, *op. cit.*

minute period. The results disclosed the fact that, since the total number of different words given by seven-year-olds was 793 and that for thirteen-year-olds 3,222, the number of words a child actually uses is relatively small as compared to the number with which he is familiar. An extensive record (124 one-hour observations of word usage) of the words used by children ages two to six in Smith's study revealed the 24 words shown in Table 28, as being the most commonly spoken.

TABLE 28. WORDS MOST COMMONLY USED BY PRESCHOOL CHILDREN DURING SPONTANEOUS PLAY

Word	Frequency	Word	Frequency
I	2,543	my	569
is	1,611	want	542
it	1,041	go	518
you	955	have	481
that	790	me	469
do	787	see	459
a (or an)	748	on	442
this	712	oh	429
not (n't)	674	there	428
the	664	get	422
here	632	can	401
to (inf.)	627	got	398

(From Medorah E. Smith, "An Investigation of the Development of the Sentence and the Extent of Vocabulary in Young Children," *Univ. of Iowa Studies in Child Welfare*, Vol. 3, No. 5 (1926), p. 26.)

Factors Influencing Vocabulary Extension.—Smith's conclusion that social status is not an important factor in the determination of size of vocabulary has been challenged by other investigators. She found that 22 pairs of young children, matched as to mental and chronological age, from the supposedly socially superior University School (Iowa) and the less favored Day School differed little in vocabulary size. Although she apparently did not control the factor of intelligence adequately, Descoeudres [36] found children in the higher social brackets to be greatly superior in vocabulary ability. A check on Smith's re-

[36] Alice Descoeudres, *Le Development de L'enfant de Deux à Sept Ans*, Paris. Delachaux et Niestle (no date).

sults, in which 31 orphanage children were matched with 31 children of similar mental age and I.Q. from Smith's original study, also demonstrated the verbal superiority of children from superior homes. In fact, the orphanage children were inferior to the Iowa University group at every mental age studied.[37] It has been assumed from these data that Smith's two groups were probably not markedly different in social composition, or that the children involved were not representative of their social status as described by the investigator. Research in general thus suggests that, no matter how intelligent he may appear to be, a child is dependent for vocabulary development upon an intellectually stimulating environment.

The thesis that appropriate training influences the size of a child's vocabulary has been subjected to investigation in a study by Strayer,[38] in which identical twins were used as subjects. When she had reached the age of eighty-four weeks, one of the twins was given intensive vocabulary training for a period of five weeks. The other twin was given an identical course of training for a period of four weeks, but beginning at the age of eighty-nine weeks. Controlled observations were made and recorded for each twin on a 24-hour program for an experimental period of 63 days. The results made it evident that systematic intellectual stimulation of the kind provided is effective in increasing children's vocabularies. The investigator brought out the to-be-expected point, however, that vocabulary training entered upon with the maturational advantage of five weeks (second twin) resulted in a more comprehensive and meaningful type of response.

It can thus be concluded that vocabulary development is stimulated by educational opportunities at any age subsequent to the onset of capacity to verbalize words. The child who is given opportunities for self-expression and who is provided with experiences suitable to the development of language facility, is in a favorable position to learn the meaning of words

37 H. M. Williams and M. L. McFarland, "A Revision of the Smith Vocabulary Test for Preschool Children," *Univ. of Iowa Studies in Child Welfare*, Vol. 13, No. 2 (1937).
38 Lois C. Strayer, *Language and Growth: The Relative Efficacy of Early and Deferred Vocabulary Training, Studied by the Method of Co-Twin Control*, Genetic Psychology Monographs, Vol. 8, No. 3 (1930), pp. 209-319.

and to speak with clarity of thought.[39] It is through frequent conversations, repetitions of stories, educational games, listening to other children's experiences, and socialized activities that children make constructive contacts with language and learn to express themselves verbally. Development at higher linguistic levels continues as the growing child becomes more mature mentally, makes increasingly broader language contacts, masters the linguistic requirements of his school, and becomes progressively more active in making social adaptations.[40]

Parts of Speech Used by Children.—The young child expresses most of his verbal ideas through the use of nouns, or words used as though they were nouns. The child of approximately two years utilizes this form of speech in registering protests, in asking questions, in making requests, and in naming objects or people. From 50 to 60 per cent of his spoken words are used as nouns in these and similar ways. If the child says "car," he may mean "give me the car," "isn't the car nice," or "don't take the car." If he says "bow-wow," the child may refer to a pet dog, to the sounds made by dogs, or to being protected from a furry animal. It is thus difficult to analyze and classify the parts of speech used by young children.

It is not long, however, until there is a decrease in the relative number of nouns and pseudo-nouns used and an increase in the number of verbs, pronouns, adjectives, adverbs, or other less simple forms of speech. As an analysis of children's conversations has shown, their words not only become more involved grammatically, they also evolve from the more vivid egoistic, commanding, and requesting variety to the less colorful verbalizations characteristic of adults.[41] As children gain in the command of language they gradually abandon the more concrete nouns in favor of pronouns, and give up their one-word sentences for those involving not only verbs and adjectives but prepositions, conjunctions, and interjections.

[39] Walter W. Parker, "Language and Thinking," *School and Society,* 52: 232-234 (1940).
[40] Noel B. Cuff, "Vocabulary Tests," *Journal of Educational Psychology,* 21: 212-220 (1930).
[41] Margaret M. Nice, "An Analysis of the Conversation of Children and Adults," *Child Development,* 3: 204-246 (1932).

A study by Nice [42] of her own four-year-old daughter's speech responses (Table 29) illustrates the early domination of nouns and the extent to which other parts of speech are utilized at that age. This investigator ascertained, however, that although a child's vocabulary characteristically contains more nouns than verbs or other parts of speech, verbs usually predominate in frequency of use in the child's everyday speech. There is evidence that action words are most extensively used by young children and that those next in frequency have reference to the self or to personal associates (pronouns).

TABLE 29. PARTS OF SPEECH OF DIFFERENT WORDS EMPLOYED IN ALL-DAY CONVERSATIONS

	Number	Per Cent	Per Cent in Whole Vocabulary
Nouns	302	41.4	52.2
Verbs	192	27.6	23.2
Adjectives	90	12.4	11.2
Adverbs	69	9.5	7.6
Pronouns	32	4.3	2.9
Prepositions	18	2.5	1.6
Interjections	14	1.9	0.4
Conjunctions	3	0.4	0.9
Total	720		100.0

(From Margaret M. Nice, "Concerning All-Day Conversations," *Pedagogical Seminary,* 27:170 (1920).)

McCarthy's [43] more elaborate research, to which reference has previously been made, has substantiated the above findings. As can be seen from her data (Table 30), the developing child tends to use verbs most frequently, with pronouns and nouns following in frequency of occurrence, in that order. It thus appears that whereas nouns predominate in the vocabularies of young children, pronouns and verbs come to do so with added maturity and a more extensive general vocabulary.

[42] Margaret M. Nice, "Concerning All-Day Conversation," *Pedagogical Seminary,* 27 : 166-177 (1920).
[43] Dorothea A. McCarthy, *Language Development of the Pre-school Child,* Minneapolis, Univ. of Minnesota Press, 1930.

TABLE 30. AVERAGE PERCENTAGE FREQUENCIES FOR PARTS OF SPEECH
OCCURRING IN THE CONVERSATIONS OF CHILDREN

Age in Months	Verbs	Pronouns	Nouns	Adj.	Adv.	Prep.	Conj.	Interj.	Misc.
18	14	10	50	10	8	..	1	8	..
24	21	15	39	10	7	4	1	2	2
30	23	19	26	14	7	5	2	3	2
36	23	19	23	16	7	7	2	2	1
42	26	20	19	16	8	6	2	2	1
48	26	22	20	15	6	7	4	1	1
54	25	21	19	15	7	7	4	1	1

(Adapted from Dorothea A. McCarthy, *The Language Development of the Preschool Child*, Minneapolis, Univ. of Minnesota Press, 1930, Ch. 6.)

The Child's Sentence Development.—With growth in size of vocabulary and with mounting insight into the meaning of words, comes the ability to combine the latter into increasingly complex sentences. The exact nature of this increase is difficult to measure, but has been studied to some extent by analyzing both the verbal and written language expressions of children, as well as the number and length of their clauses. An analysis by La Brant [44] of the length and number of clauses in the written compositions of 986 public school pupils in grades four to twelve (ages nine to sixteen years), showed that increase in both the length of clauses and in the number of subordinate clauses used is a function of general language maturity. In contrast to other investigators,[45] La Brant concluded that increase in the use of complex sentences (subordinate clauses) is more nearly an accompaniment of chronological age than it is of mental age.

Rate of development in ability to use compound and complex sentences has been ascertained for a sampling of highly selected children (average I.Q. 136) by Fisher.[46] According to her findings, one of the 72 children included in the study used a compound sentence at twenty-four months and all were able

[44] Lou L. La Brant, *A Study of Certain Language Developments in Children in Grades Four to Twelve, Inclusive*, Genetic Psychology Monographs, Vol. 14, No. 5 (1933), pp. 387-491.
[45] H. M. Williams and M. F. Little, "An Analytical Scale of Language Achievement," *Univ. of Iowa Studies in Child Welfare*, Vol. 13, No. 2 (1937).
[46] Mary S. Fisher, "Language Patterns of Pre-school Children," *Journal of Experimental Education*, 1: 70-85 (1932-33).

to so respond at the age of thirty-four months. The first complex sentence was expressed by a twenty-seven-months-old child, but all were able to use such sentences by the thirty-second month. Although they did not always use their more mature patterns of speech, the children in this group had acquired the sentence ability characteristic of adults by their fourth year.

In her study of sentence development in young children, Smith [47] found that the number of words per sentence increased from 1.7 at two years to 3.3 at three years and 4.6 at five years. Although a wide range of individual differences was found, each child developed steadily in length of sentences used, in the complexity of his sentence structure, and in the number of words needed for the adequate expression of ideas.

Perhaps the most satisfactory summary of sequences in the development of sentence length and structure is that by Nice,[48] in which the following four stages of sentence formation were outlined:

1. The *single word* stage, which commences at approximately the beginning of the second year and lasts from four to twelve months.

2. The *two-word* sentence stage, which appears by approximately the middle of the second year and which extends to around twenty-seven months. This period is marked by a preponderance of nouns and a concomitant lack of verbs, articles, prepositions, and conjunctions.

3. The *short sentence* stage (three to four words), which begins around the twenty-eighth month and lasts until approximately the fourth year. During this period verbs are not inflected and prepositions, conjunctions, auxiliary verbs, articles, and pronouns are often omitted.

4. The *complete sentence* stage, from around the fourth year on, in which six to eight words characterized by increased complexity and definitions are used. Pronouns, articles, prepositions, and conjunctions now come into use.

47 Medorah E. Smith, "An Investigation of the Development of the Sentence and the Extent of Vocabulary in Young Children," *Univ. of Iowa Studies in Child Welfare*, Vol. 3, No. 5 (1926).
48 Margaret M. Nice, "Length of Sentences as a Criterion of a Child's Progress in Speech," *Journal of Educational Psychology*, 16: 370-379 (1925).

The testimony of the studies reviewed would appear to be that sentence development is from single "naming" words to increasingly more complex combinations of words in which articles, auxiliary and copulative verbs, prepositions, and con-junctions play an increasingly prominent and clarifying role. More mature development brings in its wake ability to use independent and subordinate clauses in more complex and meaningful ways.

How the Child Learns to Read.—Most children have made considerable progress toward learning to read before beginning the formal study of this basic skill. By the time he enters the first grade in school the typical child has developed a speaking vocabulary of around 2,500 words. He can also use sentences averaging approximately five or six words in length. If he has been reared in a reasonably stimulating environment, he has also encountered many experiences calculated to enable him to understand the word symbols which he will be called upon to read. In fact, the average first-grader recognizes some printed words and can give their meaning. He may also be able to give the names of a number of letters of the alphabet upon seeing them in visual form.

A modern method of teaching the child the meaning of a word symbol is to present it to him in connection with its pic-torial equivalent. When the learner sees a picture of the object in question, hears the associated spoken word, and sees the appropriate printed word, the last named soon becomes mean-ingful to him as a symbol of the object. It is thus logical for a child who has seen a picture of a dog (which he recognizes), and who has seen the word for dog in close association with it, to respond later with the spoken word "dog" upon seeing the printed word for dog. This is especially true when his teacher makes the relationship clear by speaking the appropriate word in several similar contexts.

It was formerly thought that a child learned to read most rapidly by mastering the names of the letters of the alphabet and subsequently spelling out simple words. It is now believed that such an atomistic method actually hinders progress in reading by failing to give the child the advantage of learning words, phrases, or short sentences as meaningful units. Just as the development of motor abilities progresses from gross, undifferentiated responses to later more detailed skills, so learning to read is a matter of progressing from undifferentiated verbal units, such as words, phrases, or sentences, to the details of spelling and word construction. Only after the learner has responded to a word-symbol situation as a meaningful whole can he identify and understand the involvements of otherwise meaningless parts of the total experience.

The developing child learns, for example, what the printed symbol "brown" means after first having comprehended the meaning of the complete sentence, "This is a brown bear." The word "brown" derives its meaning from its place in the larger more meaningful unit (sentence). As one pair of authors [49] nave said, the child may not have a name for the sentence as such, but he understands it as a thought unit. Similarly, the learner comes to comprehend the functions of single letters or parts of a word. The letters *b, r, o, w, n* become meaningful as related aspects of the total word "brown." Even similar looking characters, such as *p* and *q, b* and *d,* and *w* and *m,* take on appropriate meaning when they are presented as elements of whole but contrasted words. Such development is aided if the child is encouraged to begin writing words and phrases as wholes as he learns to read them orally.

THE PROBLEM OF READING READINESS. With the onset of interest in the measurement of eye movements in reading, it came to be believed that reading skill could be improved by emphasis upon regularity in eye fixations and by the control of the return sweep in going from line to line of the printed page. It was thought that these and other mechanics of the reading process lay at the foundation of both rate and comprehension in reading.[50] However, now that students of the subject have recognized the fact that unsatisfactory eye movements are *symptoms* and not *causes* of reading disability, new emphasis

[49] R. H. Wheeler and F. T. Perkins, *Principles of Mental Development,* New York, T. Y. Crowell Co., 1932, pp. 451-452.
[50] Guy T. Buswell, *Fundamental Reading Habits: A Study of Their Development,* Univ. of Chicago Supplementary Educational Monographs, No. 21, 1922.

has been placed on the importance of children's interests [51] and upon the adjustment of reading materials to their maturation (intellectual) level.

Another recent stress is that on techniques for the development of reading readiness in preschool children.[52] It is felt that children have been required to attempt the mastery of symbolic materials before they were intellectually or experientially ready for such an abstract task. Factors that contribute to such reading readiness are said to include: (1) non-defective mentality, (2) good physical condition, (3) a home in which English is spoken, (4) adequate cultural experiences, (5) home and community experiences which include field trips, excursions, pictures, and educational games, (6) sufficient social experience, (7) emotional stability, (8) preschool language experience, (9) reading experiences with play activities, blocks, and maps, and (10) if possible, attendance at kindergarten. Absence of these background factors, particularly that of lack of interest or incentive, which is sometimes caused by indifferent or oversolicitous parental handling, is often at the base of reading disability.

Factors Affecting Language Development

There are a number of factors, both physiological and psychological, which militate against the development of language skills. These include: (1) insufficient mentality or intellectual experience, (2) sensory defects and other physical limitations, (3) poor speech environment and low socio-economic home conditions, (4) emotional maladjustments conducive to stuttering and comparable speech disorders, and (5) such handicaps as bilingualism, lack of companions, and limited opportunity for hearing other people speak. Unless the various conditions requisite to the development of speech abilities are available to the child, the mere fact that he is in an environment where speech activities may be heard is no guarantee that

---

[51] Paul A. Witty and David Kopel, *Reading and the Educative Process,* Boston, Ginn & Co., 1939, Ch. 2.

[52] Nila B. Smith, "Techniques for Determining and Developing Reading Readiness," in *Teacher's Guide for the First Year,* New York, Silver, Burdett & Co., 1936, Ch. 23.

he will acquire the necessary verbal skills. It is thus essential that the retarding effects of the above-mentioned factors be understood.

Intelligence and Beginning Language.—A close relationship has been found between intelligence, as measured at a later date by tests, and the age at which a child begins to talk intelligibly. Children of superior intelligence usually talk earlier than do their associates of average mental ability. Children of subnormal mentality are, on the other hand, much slower than the average in developing linguistic skill. The average gifted child begins to talk during his eleventh month, the average normal (intellectually) child during his fifteenth month, and the average feebleminded child at approximately his thirty-eighth month.[53] There are also wide individual differences in time of beginning language among members of each of these three groups. However, as has been previously mentioned, children who are slow in learning to talk are not necessarily subnormal mentally.

It is well to realize, also, that some children who appear to be feebleminded may merely be retarded because of lack of opportunity to hear and respond to a normal amount of speech activities. Such children frequently learn to speak normally at a later age when stimulated to do so by a more dynamic environment in general and by adequate companions in particular.[54] Two investigators [55] have even reported the development of techniques for teaching special cases of delayed speaking how to manipulate their mouth and throat muscles in ways calculated to hasten the acquisition of normal speech abilities. No mental retardation has been found in the case of most of these children.

[53] Lewis M. Terman *et al., Genetic Studies of Genius,* Vol. I: *Mental and Physical Traits of a Thousand Gifted Children,* Stanford University, Stanford Univ. Press, 1925, p. 187. Also, Cyrus D. Mead, *The Relation of General Intelligence to Certain Mental and Physical Traits,* Teachers College Contributions to Education, No. 76, Columbia Univ., 1916, p. 117.
[54] Isaac A. Abt, H. M. Adler, and Phyllis F. Bartelme, The Relationship Between the Onset of Speech and Intelligence, *Journal of the American Medical Assn.,* 93: 1351-1355 (1929).
[55] S. M. Stinchfield and E. H. Young, *Children with Delayed or Defective Speech,* Stanford University, Stanford Univ. Press, 1938.

The question has frequently been raised whether linguistic development is a function of native intelligence or whether superior scores made on intelligence tests are the result of previous language development. It has been shown, for instance, that a child can raise his intelligence quotient by improving his reading skill. This question is, however, an unsettled one, especially since some children do and others do not make about the same scores in the language and non-language sections of intelligence tests. There is evidence (see Chapter 3) that intellectual level as determined by verbal intelligence test score is contingent upon the possession of language skills.[56]

Physical Condition and Language Ability.—Unfortunately, an appreciable fraction of the child population suffers from sensory or motor impairments. Those related to speech development are for the most part of an auditory, vocal, or motor nature. Cases of total deafness in young children are undoubtedly rare, yet a substantial number suffer from hearing loss of greater or lesser degree. Such children usually exhibit marked language retardation. They may, however, avoid detection in infancy by displaying the usual tendency to babble frequently.[57] These children are often quick to compensate for such a defect in later years, and may carry the handicap for a considerable period of time without realizing that they are different from other children or that they should enjoy better hearing. Even parents are misled by the partially deaf child's ability to compensate through extra alertness in the use of his other senses. A child who makes no progress toward learning to talk by the age of eighteen or twenty months should be examined for hearing impairment by a competent physician or other adequate source.

Disorders of articulation are sometimes traceable to abnormalities of the speech organs or their associated structures. Malformed jaws, defective palate, irregular teeth, abnormal tongue, and harelip are associated in some cases with failure to develop satisfactorily with respect to language abilities. It

[56] Esther Grace Nolan, "Reading Difficulty Versus Low Mentality," *California Journal of Secondary Education,* 17 : 34-39 (1942).
[57] William Stern, *Psychology of Early Childhood,* New York, Henry Holt & Co., Inc., 1930, p. 143.

is possible, as well, that lesions of the nervous system are causal factors in the failure of speech skills to develop. According to one clinician,[58] structural impairments account for approximately 10 per cent of early speech disorders. It is nevertheless believed by many that most faulty speech articulation in children is brought about by factors other than structural abnormalities.

There is some evidence that children's vocal activities may be temporarily held in abeyance while locomotor skills are being established. Shirley [59] found, for example, that children tend to vocalize less than usual while learning to reach for objects during approximately the fourteenth to twenty-third weeks, while learning to sit alone around the thirty-first week (average), and when beginning to creep at about the thirty-third to thirty-fourth week. In this study, speech activities increased rapidly after the ability to walk had been well established. These trends have not, however, been confirmed by certain other studies [60] in which the amount of vocalization was found to be somewhat proportional to degree of locomotor skill.

Home Conditions and Language Development.—The child's home environment is very influential in determining his language development. The socio-economic status of a child's family is closely related to his vocabulary and other speech progress. As McCarthy [61] has stated, "Children of the upper occupational groups are markedly superior to those of the lower occupational groups in all of the items of the construction [sentence] analysis." She goes on to say that with respect to structurally incomplete vocal responses "in the higher ages, this type of response is approximately 20 per cent greater among the children of lower occupational groups, indicating a less mature stage of linguistic development among them."

[58] C. M. Louttit, *Clinical Psychology*, New York, Harper & Bros., 1936, p. 432.

[59] Mary M. Shirley, *The First Two Years*, Vol. II: *Intellectual Development*, Minneapolis, Univ. of Minnesota Press, 1933, pp. 69-71.

[60] See, for example, Florence L. Goodenough, "Inter-relationships in the Behavior of Young Children," *Child Development*, 1: 29-47 (1930). Also Beth L. Wellman *et al.*, "Speech Sounds of Young Children," *Univ. of Iowa Studies in Child Welfare*, Vol. 5, No. 2 (1931).

[61] Dorothea A. McCarthy, *Language Development of the Preschool Child*, Minneapolis, Univ. of Minnesota Press, 1930, p. 110.

These and other linguistic differences are evident even when the factors of age and intelligence are held constant. It is not surprising that homes which provide superior intellectual stimulation and more adequate examples of language usage should bring about precocious linguistic development in children.

It has been claimed that bilingualism, or early contact with more than one language, may retard the child's linguistic development. The evidence on this point is, nevertheless, somewhat conflicting. It may be that it makes a difference whether the child encounters two languages from the start or whether he is called upon to learn a second language after reaching school age. A study by Smith [62] suggested that, in the case of a small number of young children, those who had just begun to talk but who were changed to an environment where their words no longer elicited the intended reactions from people, tended to give up efforts at talking for a time. Another investigation by the same author [63] disclosed that a bilingual environment does not delay the first use of words but that it may cause retardation in later linguistic development. That bilingualism in the home does not necessarily seriously affect a child's mental development or ability to master his school work has been shown in an extensive study by Arsenian.[64] This investigation involved a comparative study of the achievements of monoglot and bilingual children of American-born and foreign-born Italian, Jewish, and mixed parentage, ages nine to fourteen years, and matched as to race, sex, age, and socio-economic status. Children from foreign language backgrounds do, however, sometimes experience sufficient teasing and ostracism because of language and other differences to bring about serious emotional disturbances.

Little information is available concerning the effect on a child's language development of the age of his companions. It has been assumed that children who associate a great deal with

[62] Medorah E. Smith, "A Study of Five Bilingual Children from the Same Family," *Child Development*, 2: 184-187 (1931).

[63] Medorah E. Smith, "A Study of the Speech of Eight Bilingual Children of the Same Family," *Child Development*, 6: 19-25 (1935).

[64] S. Arsenian, *Bilingualism and Mental Development*, Teachers College Contributions to Education, No. 712, Columbia Univ., 1937.

adults will be precocious in this respect. Day [65] has shown that twins, who are frequently thrown together more than they are with older associates, tend to be retarded in all aspects of language development and that such retardation increases with age from two to five years. This situation is attributed to the twin's negligible need for language contacts with children or others older than himself and to the ease with which he can communicate with his co-twin without learning the intricacies of increasingly more complicated language forms.

It has been claimed that this explanation accounts for the alleged slowness of the Dionne quintuplets in learning to speak fluently—they had mainly each other with whom to communicate and their childish sign language was to a great extent sufficient for such purposes. Such an explanation tends to obviate the assumption that children who are slow in language development are necessarily below average intellectually.

Speech Defects and Their Correction.—Unfortunately, the course of language development does not always proceed without disturbances. Speech disorders of varying degrees of seriousness occasionally arise to deter the child's linguistic growth. These have been classified by Travis,[66] an authority in speech pathology, as (1) disorders of rhythm in verbal expression, (2) disorders of articulation and vocalization, and (3) disorders of symbolic formulation and expression. To these categories have been added (1) disorders of speech resulting from paralyses, (2) nasal speech, (3) speech disorders accompanying endocrine dysfunctioning, and (4) disorders caused by deafness and hearing defects.[67] In view of the specialized nature of speech pathology, the present treatment must of necessity be confined to problems associated with disorders of articulation and of rhythm, especially stuttering (the involuntary repetition of sounds and words).

[65] Ella J. Day, The Development of Language in Twins: I, "A Comparison of Twins and Single Children," *Child Development*, 3 : 179-199 (1932).
[66] Lee Edward Travis, "Speech Pathology," in *Handbook of Child Psychology* (edited by Carl Murchison), Worcester, Clark Univ. Press, 1933, Ch. 16.
[67] M. F. Palmer and C. D. Osborn, "One Thousand Consecutive Cases of Speech Defects," *Transactions of the Kansas Academy of Science*, 41 : 263-266 (1938).

Differing criteria for judging speech deficiencies have resulted in diverse estimates concerning the probable number of children who are thus afflicted. It is believed that at least 1 per cent of American school children stutter, and that probably 15 to 20 per cent of the entire population do so at some period in their lives. In Indiana the incidence of speech defects has been reported as 3.7 per cent.[68] A survey by Wallin [69] of a large school system revealed that 2.8 per cent of the pupils were suffering from speech disorders, and that of this group 26.9 per cent were stutterers, 57.1 per cent lispers, and the remaining 16 per cent miscellaneous in nature. This investigator also noted that the proportion of children who stutter shows an increase between grades one to eight. If some children "outgrow" stuttering, as is popularly supposed, they do so before the termination of the preschool age.

DISORDERS OF ARTICULATION AND VOCALIZATION. Poor articulation in childhood, of which "baby talk" is an example, is often caused by the failure of parents and others to provide the proper models of complete speech forms. This and other examples of incomplete verbal learning may be due in part to hearing disorders, to short auditory memory span, to mental deficiency, or to faulty home training. It is possible, further, that disorders of the central nervous system and defects of the palate, mouth, teeth, and other speech organs may contribute to inadequacies of verbalization.

Articulatory disorders, particularly lisping, decrease as the children concerned make progress through the grades. This fact is probably due to the favorable influence of the school environment on children who have learned to lisp in their homes and who previously have experienced little or no encouragement to overcome such a habit. Added maturity of the speech organs and their accessory mechanics may also have contributed to such an outcome. At any rate, correction of faulty articulation is not as difficult to effect as is improvement in the case of disorders of rhythm.

[68] C. M. Louttit and E. C. Halls, "Survey of Speech Defects Among Public School Children of Indiana," *Journal of Speech Disorders*, 1 : 73-80 (1936).
[69] J. E. W. Wallin, *Clinical and Abnormal Psychology*, Boston, Houghton Mifflin Co., 1927, pp. 454-455, 464-466.

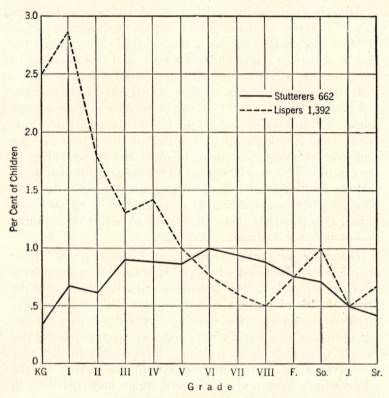

Figure 81. Grade Distribution of Stuttering and Lisping in School
(From J. E. W. Wallin, *Clinical and Abnormal Psychology,* Boston, Houghton Mifflin
Co., 1927, p. 466.)

DISORDERS OF RHYTHM—STUTTERING AND STAMMERING.
Stuttering, as most cases of rhythmic inadequacy are called, has
its origin for the most part in early childhood. The fact that
its greatest frequency is found between the ages of two and four
suggests its close association with the young child's striving for
satisfaction of his dynamic needs. According to Brooks,[70] 85
per cent of stuttering cases develop before the age of eight.
This writer also asserts that stutterers are on the average retarded in school approximately one year, probably because of

[70] Fowler D. Brooks, *Child Psychology,* Boston, Houghton Mifflin Co., 1937,
p. 198.

difficulties in their oral class work.   Practically all investigators have found stuttering to be more widespread among boys than among girls (approximately 20 males to 1 female).

Investigators are not agreed as to the probable causes of stuttering and stammering.   Some [71] feel that organic anomalies, such as defects of the speech organs, chemical imbalance, nutritional deficiency, or disturbances of the speech center—preferred hand relationship in the brain (cortical dominance)—are to a great extent responsible for such disorders.   There is, nevertheless, a strong tendency, even on the part of former exponents of organic etiology, to ascribe stuttering and stammering to disturbances in the psychological life of the child.   On this basis these speech disorders are viewed as symptoms of emotional maladjustment and deep-lying psychological tensions which hark back to frustrating childhood experiences.[72]

As the present author [73] has brought out elsewhere, stuttering (or stammering) may be regarded as a nervous manifestation, and frequently represents a maladjustment of the *entire personality*.   The child stutters with his whole body and not with part of it, such, for example, as the speech organs.   The stutterer may be veritably honeycombed with emotional conflicts, prejudices, feelings of inferiority, and fear of people or social situations.   His speech spasms which, incidentally, do not always appear under secure and serene conditions, are symptoms of his tensions of insecurity or inadequacy.   It could thus be reasoned that the stutterer's symptoms cannot be expected to disappear until his underlying emotional stresses are relieved and his entire personality virtually reorganized.   Methods for such reconstruction are varied but include the removal of organic defects and difficulties when present, as well as physical and psychological relaxation.[74]   To quote one writer,[75] "Ex-

[71] See Lee Edward Travis, *Speech Pathology*, New York, D. Appleton-Century Co., Inc., 1931. Also R. West, "Is Stuttering Abnormal?" *Journal of Abnormal and Social Psychology*, 31 : 76-86, 1936.

[72] LaVange Hunt Richardson, *The Personality of Stutterers*, Psychological Monographs, Vol. 56, No. 7 (1944), pp. 1-41. See also J. M. Fletcher, *The Problem of Stuttering*, New York, Longmans, Green & Co., 1928.

[73] Louis P. Thorpe, "Psychological Mechanisms of Stammering," *Journal of General Psychology*, 19 : 97-109 (1938).

[74] Edmund Jacobson, *Progressive Relaxation*, Chicago, Univ. of Chicago Press, 1938.

[75] Joseph W. Nagge, *Psychology of the Child*, New York, The Ronald Press Co., 1942, p. 309.

ercises in breathing control, . . . teaching the subject to be calm, reducing anxiety and fear to a minimum, and the removal of irritating factors in the social and family life of the stutterer are also important steps in therapy. The stutterer is a problem child, and each problem child is an individual case which requires particular study to uncover the etiology of the psychological basis of his difficulties." Negative practice,[76] free association, oral suggestion,[77] reevaluation of his values and goals by the individual, and the development of intelligent insight into emotional mechanisms involved are also useful methods in the case of adults.

HAND PREFERENCE AND STUTTERING. As was discussed at more length in Chapter 10, there is a widespread belief, evidently based on the cortical-dominance theory, that change of a child's handedness from left to right is likely to cause stuttering. Evidence on this point is inconclusive but leans toward the conclusion that change of handedness as such does not necessarily cause a speech disorder. Although it is true that a fairly high proportion of children who have been required to change hands are stutterers,[78] a great many are not.[79]

The conclusion can be drawn from these data that it is possible to change a child's handedness in such an efficient and unemotional manner that no unfavorable speech reactions develop. It is probably only when a child is made to feel inferior and abnormal that such a change brings about emotional stresses leading to speech anomalies.

Summary and Implications

The beginnings of speech date from the spontaneous vocalizations of the neonate. From these sounds issue the undifferentiated babblings of the infant of from five to ten months of

[76] Knight Dunlap, *Habits: Their Making and Unmaking,* New York, Liveright Pub. Corp., 1932. See also, by the same author, "Stammering: Its Nature, Etiology, and Therapy," *Journal of Comparative Psychology,* 37 : 187-202 (1944).

[77] Louis P. Thorpe, *Personality and Life,* New York, Longmans, Green & Co., 1941, pp. 195-197.

[78] S. T. Orton and Lee Edward Travis, Studies in Stuttering, IV: "Studies of Action Currents in Stutterers," *Archives of Neurology and Psychiatry,* 21 : 61-68 (1929).

[79] Beaufort S. Parson, *Lefthandedness,* New York, The Macmillan Co., 1924.

age. Words, though crudely enunciated at first, gain meaning by being associated with objects or people. The child subsequently passes from the stage of verbalization in which one word conveys the meaning of a sentence to that in which nouns and verbs are combined, and finally to the point where he can exemplify the various forms of speech used in everyday conversations.

The child's language development is made possible by the operation of the inseparable factors of maturation and learning. Speech is a function of certain organs and their accessory mechanisms, but is dependent as well upon the presence in the child's environment of stimulating language patterns and experiences. The development of linguistic skills illustrates the principles of learning by way of which all abilities not dependent alone on bodily structure come into existence. Such learning is a continuous process of development from cruder, more general types of verbal reactions to those characterized by differentiation and varying degrees of specificity.

Handicaps to satisfactory linguistic development include imperfect hearing, defective speech organs, birth injuries, subnormal intelligence, serious illness, a non-stimulating environment, and perhaps to some extent bilingual home. Twins, whose language activities are confined largely to each other, and children whose parents or nurses speak to them but little are also handicapped in speech development. Sensitive children, whose verbal attempts are characterized by hesitation, may be blocked in their progress by ridicule or sarcasm. The child who is nagged and otherwise placed under a cloud of insecurity may also develop tensions leading to stuttering. Some children are deprived of the incentive to talk by the overattentiveness of parents who anticipate and care for their every need. Others are pressed beyond their ability by overanxious parents and may become so discouraged as to decline to attempt further language development for a time.

Conditions conducive to language growth include encouraging the child to secure objects and responses from people through appropriate verbalization, giving approval in voice and in manner to correct word usages, creating conditions conducive to congenial conversations, rewarding verbal efforts by giving legitimate satisfactions, being consistent in the use of words so as not to confuse the child, and as far as possible using correct English in all contacts with the child.

Words, and language in general, not only enable the developing child to converse and to enjoy social play, they may also serve the function of relieving his emotional tensions. Slang words, the connotations of which may seem meaningless, often provide a sense of relief that obviates the necessity of engaging in antisocial behavior. The small boy who exclaims "dog-gone-it" signifies by the pitch and intonation of his voice that he is relieving an emotional tension. Although swear words are undesirable and should not be encouraged by giving the child extra attention (even though disparaging) when he utters them, the use of emphatic language for the expression of ideas or for the reduction of stresses may well be encouraged.

QUESTIONS FOR DISCUSSION

1. By what process, other than that explained in this chapter, could a child learn the names of objects and people? What is the objection to the view that children learn differentiated sounds through imitation of the language of their elders?

2. Why is it so easy to believe that, even in childhood, words (language) are essential to thinking? What evidence can be advanced against this view? Is an answer to this question essential in the education of children in language or thinking? Explain.

3. How can language teachers support the claim that speech is the chief avenue to socialization? Can young children be made thoroughly social through the avenue of language alone? What other factors, if any, need to be taken into account here?

4. What are the principal factors productive of vocabulary development in early childhood? What is the relationship between socio-economic status and such development? Could children be stimulated to more rapid progress in the use of words? Would such an endeavor be profitable?

5. Would it be possible to accelerate the language development of children if more adequate sentence structure and accurate grammatical constructions were used by their elders? Do chil-

dren learn language skills by rule or principally through responding to the usages of people with whom they associate?

6. Are children who fail to read at the usual age for such development necessarily subnormal mentally? Do such children have
unusual nervous systems or inadequate brain structure? Is it
true that failure to read may indicate emotional blocking or an
infantile attitude? Explain this point.

7. What bearing might a child's physical condition have on language development? What are the involvements here of hearing defects? Explain how malformations of the mouth and
associated structures could cause retardation in linguistic activities.

8. Why are home conditions so influential in language growth?
Is it true that children from the higher occupational groups
are superior to those in the lower occupational brackets in
sentence structure, extent of vocabulary, and other language
skills? What is your analysis of this situation?

9. How do you account for the fact that most speech disorders are
apparently caused, not by structural defects, but by emotional
disturbances? What evidence is there for the assertion that
stuttering, for example, represents a maladjustment of the
entire personality?

10. What is the present attitude toward belief that defects of the
speech organs, chemical imbalance, nutritional deficiency, and
disturbances of cortical dominance are primary causes of stuttering? What is the evidence for change of handedness as
a cause of speech disorders?

Recommended Readings

Anderson, John E. "The Development of Spoken Language," in *Child De-
velopment and the Curriculum, Thirty-Eighth Yearbook of the National
Society for the Study of Education.* Bloomington (Ill.) : Public School
Pub. Co., 1939, Part I, Ch. 10.

Boynton, Paul L. *Psychology of Child Development.* Minneapolis: Educational Publishers, 1938, Ch. 8.

Gesell, Arnold, and Thompson, H. *Infant Behavior: Its Genesis and Growth.*
New York: McGraw-Hill Book Co., Inc., 1934.

Hurlock, Elizabeth B. *Child Development.* New York: McGraw-Hill Book
Co., Inc., 1942, Ch. 7.

Jersild, Arthur T. *Child Psychology.* New York: Prentice-Hall, Inc., 1940,
Ch. 5.

McCarthy, Dorothea A. *The Language Development of the Preschool Child.*
Minneapolis: Univ. of Minnesota Press, 1930.

Merry, Frieda K., and Merry, Ralph V. *From Infancy to Adolescence.*
New York: Harper & Bros., 1940, Ch. 4.

Piaget, Jean. *The Language and Thought of the Child.* New York: Harcourt, Brace & Co., 1926.

Smith, Medorah E. "An Investigation of the Development of the Sentence and the Extent of Vocabulary in Young Children." *Univ. of Iowa Studies in Child Welfare,* Vol. 3, No. 5 (1926).

Stoddard, George D., and Wellman, Beth L. *Child Psychology.* New York: The Macmillan Co., 1934, Ch. 6.

Travis, Lee Edward. "Speech Pathology," in *Handbook of Child Psychology.* (Edited by Carl Murchison.) Worcester: Clark Univ. Press, 1933, Ch. 16.

Witty, Paul A., and Kopel, David. *Reading and the Educative Process.* Boston: Ginn & Co., 1939.

Chemical imbalance

CHAPTER 12

HOW THE CHILD'S UNDERSTANDING DEVELOPS

THE DEVELOPMENT OF LINGUISTIC ABILITY and growth in capacity for deriving meaning from experience are related aspects of a single process. As the child comes to associate words with objects and events, and learns to verbalize about his experiences, he may be regarded as growing in understanding—in facility for judging the adjustment value of ideas, attitudes, and acts. The growing child does not develop a general capacity for abstracting meaning from all experiences, he comes rather to respond in characteristic overt or verbal ways to given stimulating situations.

As indicated in Chapter 11, the developing boy or girl learns the meaning of words by associating them with objects or experiences. The word "mother" means no more than any other combination of sounds to the young child until it is repeatedly applied to the individual whom more mature individuals recognize as one of his parents. The child has grown in understanding when his behavior is influenced by the mere mention of his mother's name, or perhaps on being told that his mother is coming soon. Many a small child has smiled or moved excitedly in his crib upon hearing such an announcement. Mention of the word "mother" comes to evoke ideas of feeding, bathing, stories, punishment, or other anticipated experiences. Understanding is expressed through the medium of language, but develops, as the following discussion will show, in the wake of experience and favorable educational opportunities.

The Individual Nature of Meaning

Since meanings result from individual experience, there is no basis for maintaining that a given stimulus should affect two or more children similarly. A dog may mean a potential

515

playmate to one boy and a fearsome animal who is likely to bite to another. This may be true whether the dog is seen or merely referred to. Children should be taught not to be too sure of their own interpretations of experiences and to be tolerant of the viewpoints advanced by others. The individual nature of experience creates many diversities of meaning which must be reconciled if children are to understand the reactions of others to their own interpretations.

The Effect of Variations in Sensory Acuity.—It was at one time believed that practically all individuals are born with keener acuity in some sensory organs than in others. Many were of the opinion that certain children learned best through the medium of the eyes, that others could best be reached by way of the ears, and that still others were more sensitive to stimuli coming through tactual or possibly other channels. Evidence has shown, however, that children who were alleged to be, for example, "eye-minded" or "ear-minded" were simply responding in ways that were made more or less habitual by the methods used in educating them. It is now apparent that an individual may be acute in all sensory fields, and that the sensory organ which will receive major attention is to a considerable extent determined by the types of experiences previously encountered.

Sensory defects or deficiencies may, however, require a child to gain his understanding of the world about him through such channels as are adequate to receive the appropriate stimuli. A child suffering from marked hearing loss will as far as possible compensate by interpreting his experiences through visual and other routes. The same may be said with respect to other sensory defects. The receiving of information and the gaining of meanings are dependent upon the status of the various sense organs. Interpretations of experience are thus influenced in part by the state of affairs obtaining in a child's sensory equipment.

Individuals with sensory deficiencies are not always as handicapped, so far as the gaining of meaning from experience is concerned, as many have supposed. Both visual and auditory loss may in some cases be compensated for in part by mechanical aids. In the case of hearing deficiency, it is possible to communicate with others through the medium of lip reading. Even more important is the fact that one's critical observations of natural phenomena and of cause and effect relationships are gained by way, not of the unassisted senses, but of the more meticulous methods of science. Experimental and quantitative techniques, not casual sensory impressions, are the modern avenues to rich meaning and understanding. The dictum that "seeing (or hearing) is believing" is no longer accepted by informed individuals. Children should thus neither be urged nor expected to place complete reliance upon the loose testimony of their senses. They should use their sensory capacities to the full, however, in their efforts to draw dependable and meaningful conclusions from their experiences.

The Individual Nature of Experience.—No two children encounter precisely the same situations and no two thus possess a similar background for the interpretation of words and experiences. As was shown in a previous chapter, this fact holds even in the case of such closely related individuals as identical twins. Each will elicit a somewhat different attitude from the parents and each will experience a unique constellation of constantly shifting situations. One twin may read books that are uninteresting to the other and may be quarreling with a playmate while his brother is cooperating happily with friends. It is therefore not surprising that each child should interpret words and new experiences in terms of a pattern of meaning that is strictly his own.

So far as the gaining of meaning from the printed page is concerned, *"Words mean only what they represent in our experience. Poverty of ideas is therefore associated with meagerness of contact with the world of things and persons."* [1] As Horn [2] has put it, "the sentence 'He lost his way in a blizzard,'

---

[1] Arthur I. Gates, Arthur T. Jersild, T. R. McConnell, and Robert C. Challman, *Educational Psychology,* New York, The Macmillan Co., 1942, p. 429. By permission.

[2] Ernest Horn, *Methods of Instruction in the Social Studies,* New York, Chas. Scribner's Sons, 1937, pp. 177-178. See also Paul McKee, "Improving Our Instructional Talking," *Bulletin of the Ernest Horn Elementary School,* Vol. 1, No. 1 (1942).

must of necessity have limited meaning for one who has spent his whole life in Florida." This author also points out that an elementary school pupil who had lived thus far on a treeless plain would get little meaning from the statement that "On the seaward side of the mountains of Australia are dense hardwood forests. Among the most valuable trees are the eucalyptus, sometimes known as gum trees." To such a child this declaration would abound with vagueness and uncertainty. Only when the words in a book stand for ideas he has previously encountered in personal experiences can a child gain meaning from them. Teachers should thus not assume that children understand everything they say in their "instructional talking."

That children vary in the simple judgments they can render is illustrated by their responses to mental test items. Four-year-old children of comparable I.Q. differ in ability to select the longer of two lines and to recognize the difference between a circle and a square. The ability to cope with either of these problems is in part contingent upon a background of concrete experience with the lines and figures concerned. Many an otherwise intelligent child has been unable to tie a bow knot (Stanford-Binet scale) because his parents failed to provide him with the incentive or the opportunity to develop such a skill. Furthermore, children from such mild climates as, for example, Southern California, have usually not had sufficient experience with coal to state its relationship to wood or other fuels. Even the words in an examination mean somewhat different things to different children.

The Emotional Involvements of Experience.—It is said that all experiences have their affective or feeling aspect. Both children and adults tend to develop emotional attitudes in connection with specific life situations which vitally affect their behavior in a more or less generalized way, and which influence the meanings which they attach to experiences. One boy who had been humiliated by a teacher in front of his classmates developed a general dislike for teachers which carried over into high school and which caused him to regard all instructors as his natural enemies. Such an attitude toward the role of the teacher is a far cry from the meaning associated with the word by a pupil who has experienced little but helpfulness from teachers.

The child who enjoys happy experiences in connection with religious teachings in early life will be likely to develop a benevolent attitude toward religion in general. To him institutional religion may stand for something constructive and vital, a cause to be cherished and preserved. The child who, on the contrary, encountered little but restraint and denial of childish joys in connection with religious practice, will in all likelihood come to regard the religious life as one of unnecessary frustration and unwarranted taboos. In short, attitudes regarding religion are derived from the affective side of the individual's childhood experiences in connection with it. And so it is with political parties, social groups, economic questions, the rules of warfare, and the like—an individual's attitudes toward them frequently are influenced by the emotional experiences encountered in relation to them during the formative years.

The Personal Nature of Interpretations.—Individuals differ in outlook because they have been conditioned by different patterns of experience. If every member of a given group of children of similar endowment had experienced precisely the same sequence of home, school, and other situations, both affectively and intellectually, and had made the same contacts with the world at large, it is likely that they would resemble one another in outlook much more closely than is usually the case. Such children's interpretations of experiences would no doubt be relatively similar. It is, of course, patent that no such identity of experience can possibly occur in a world of constantly shifting stimuli. It is therefore to be expected that each child will interpret experiences in terms of his particular intellectual and affective outlook, and in relation to the fulfillment of his dynamic physical and psychological needs.

The child develops a personal attitude toward people on the basis of their treatment of him, and judges new acquaintances in terms of their general resemblance to persons whom he has learned to like or dislike. A given child may appear to another child of the opposite sex as a desirable playmate, but may affect still another child as an individual to be distrusted and shunned. Popular music may be a source of pleasure to one youth and an expression of depravity of musical taste to another. One adult may display an emotional preference for antique furniture whereas another may greatly prefer modern furniture. Two individuals, both of whom witnessed the same automobile accident, may make conflicting courtroom reports regarding the disposition of the blame involved.

A child's meanings must necessarily be developed in terms of the circumstances of his environment. When placed in a limiting environment, the child develops meanings and interpretations that are out of harmony with the realities of the external world. When confined to an intellectually barren environment, he fails to develop familiarity with concepts that are essential to mental development. Dogmatic interpretations are as a rule the result of prolonged indoctrination or of insufficient contact with the realities of life. All interpretations of experience, especially those made in childhood, are thus of a personal nature, and are likely to remain more or less subjective until subjected (if ever) to the rigors of scientific verification.

The Development of Children's Concepts

A concept stands for a large number or *class* of objects which have certain characteristics in common, or which are marked by similar relationships with other objects. The mention of a given concept will usually suggest the features possessed in common by the objects or relationships involved. The concept "horse," for example, refers to a certain group of animals possessing four legs, a mane, a tail, hoofs, and other characteristic features. Such a concept can be limited to animals of this class having very similar features but, like many flexible concepts, is often expanded to include such related class objects as mules, donkeys, and zebras.

Children's Early Conceptual Ideas.—The child's original concepts are gross and undifferentiated. It is only with growth and experience that he comes to comprehend the more differentiated meanings involved in most concepts. The young child who has recently learned to apply the name "kitty" to either a live kitten or a picture of a cat, will usually proceed to say "nice kitty" when confronted by a dog, when shown a picture of a lamb, upon seeing a squirrel in the yard, or even when playing with the fur collar on his mother's coat. It takes time and teaching to enable the growing child to differentiate among similar animals and to say "kitty" only when the class object possesses certain distinctive features peculiar to the cat family. The ability to make such increasingly refined and discriminatory responses is regarded as the basis of man's intellectual mastery of his world. The grasp of meanings is fundamental to the child's adequate adjustment—physical or psychological.

As barren environment studies (Chapter 3) have shown, development of the ability to make finer and more correct discriminations among concepts is to a considerable extent a function of the richness of a child's intellectual experiences. Observations have shown that under reasonably normal circumstances the young child's conceptual ideas develop rapidly during the early years. His understanding of cats, dogs, and other familiar animals expands until he can identify and name many varieties of cats or dogs, etc. His comprehension of the various meanings of such a word, for example, as "fruit" may expand to include apples, oranges, grapes, etc., "fruit juice," the "fruits of knowledge," "fruit of the family tree," and artificial fruit as ornamentation. One eight-year-old boy became so interested in butterflies that he learned to distinguish several species and to name a number of specific butterflies within each classification. The fact that the young child distinguishes between familiar and unfamiliar objects, people, and toys indicates that he begins to comprehend meanings even before he is able to express them verbally.

The child's capacity for grasping concepts not only develops from a vague discernment of total situations to an increasingly refined comprehension of likenesses and differences among the details involved, it evolves from the more concrete level to one dealing with abstractions and verbal symbols. To put it in

Curti's [3] language, "This discriminating ability must, at the very first, function on a sensorimotor level, but when the child learns to apply names to the different parts (or learns other symbolic responses), the foundation is laid for thinking about them. Soon in the absence of the object the name of the object, merely thought of, will arouse symbolic responses standing for its various features. Thus the word 'dog' may elicit the thought four-footed, barking, and the like, according to the richness of the child's experience with dogs." When he is able to deal with class objects on a *verbal* basis, the child is utilizing *abstract* concepts.

The adequate handling of abstract ideas and concepts, particularly those of an involved nature (mathematical, philosophical, scientific, etc.), is made possible only by maturity and experience, and therefore develops slowly in childhood. It is not until their later childhood years that most mentally normal children acquire the ability to use symbolic responses standing for the common elements of class objects and to differentiate between these and elements that are unlike.

Conceptual Development and Children's Drawings. Hurlock and Thomson [4] have shown that young children perceive the general rather than the specific features in their drawings as well as in their reactions to concrete objects. In the investigation in question, children ranging from ages four and one-half to eight and one-half years were asked to draw eight commonplace objects; namely, a man, a girl, a horse, a dog, a tree, an automobile, a flower, and a boat, without restriction and in any way they wished. No effort was made to circumscribe the children's spontaneous drawing methods. The stated purpose was to ascertain what meanings the various objects had for the children. It was found that with increase in age there was a decided tendency for the subjects to respond to the more specific elements in the drawings and to be more accurate in the presentation of details. One six-year-old boy included the

[3] Margaret W. Curti, *Child Psychology*, New York, Longmans, Green & Co., 1938, pp. 300-301. See also Livingston Welch and Louis Long, "Comparison of the Reasoning Ability of Two Age Groups," *Journal of Genetic Psychology*, 62: 63-76 (1943).

[4] Elizabeth B. Hurlock and J. L. Thomson, "Children's Drawings: An Experimental Study of Perception," *Child Development*, 5: 127-138 (1934).

ground, the wheels, the body, a top, a driver, and the steering wheel in his drawing of an automobile, but failed to be concerned about springs or a drive shaft. The children tended at all ages, however, to draw objects as complete units, in most instances with some background material.

Griffiths' [5] investigation of the drawings of a group of English and Australian children (mental ages from three to six and one-half years) is indicative of the sequences of conceptual development in pictorial productions. The findings showed that young children progress by steps from an original scribbling stage, through one characterized by the combining of lines and simple geometric figures, into another of placing various figures in juxtaposition, and finally to a stage of development in which a series of pictures carrying a common theme is often produced.

In her extensive study of children's drawings, Goodenough [6] found that most children show considerable consistency in their comprehension of the form of parts of the human body. Their portrayals of anatomic structures reveal fairly adequate conceptions of the human physique. Goodenough reports further that unselected children tend to use very similar devices for depicting movement, perspective, and the like in their drawings. This investigator believes that the concepts portrayed in pictorial creations develop in an orderly sequence in children. Her studies further corroborate the belief that children reflect their conception of the material world in their drawings and that their pictorial productions indicate their notion of the relative significance of objects present in their environment.

The fact that children interpret objects or pictures on their face value as they appear to them was demonstrated in a research by Shaffer [7] in which children's ability to interpret cartoons as used in the social studies was investigated. Seventeen cartoons taken from an experimental course in history,

---

[5] R. Griffiths, *A Study of Imagination in Young Children,* London, Keagan Paul, 1935.

[6] Florence L. Goodenough, "Children's Drawings," in *Handbook of Child Psychology* (edited by Carl Murchison), Worcester, Clark Univ. Press, 1933, Ch. 14.

[7] Laurance F. Shaffer, *Children's Interpretations of Cartoons,* New York, Teachers College, Columbia Univ., 1930.

geography, and civics for grades seven to nine were presented to a group of children in all grades from the fourth to the twelfth, with a view to noting the responses as associated with age. Here, too, meanings tended to evolve with maturity and education from general titles or descriptions to concrete interpretations, and finally, with the older children, to abstract interpretations and meanings. The more subtle and less apparent meanings were lost on the younger children but caught the attention of many of the older pupils. Some of these were, however, incorrectly interpreted.

CONCEPTUAL DEVELOPMENT AND CHILDREN'S QUESTIONS. Considerable insight into children's ideational development can be gained from a scrutiny of their typical questions at given levels of maturity. From his earliest years, the child is sufficiently curious to ask a great many questions concerning the objects and events about him. Some of these questions are undoubtedly designed to gain attention and establish social contacts, but the majority are believed to be expressions of genuine curiosity through which the child adds to his store of information and checks the validity of his previous interpretations. The extent to which he will continue such verbal exploration appears to be contingent upon the success a child achieves in satisfying his needs by this method. According to Hurlock,[8] the questioning age begins at about the third year and reaches its climax at approximately six years.

A number of studies of language development have shown the extent to which questions occupy the child's attention. An early biography by Boyd[9] of his young daughter's remarks disclosed that of 1,250 noted, 21.6 per cent were in question form. A somewhat similar ratio was found earlier by Brandenburg,[10] who reported 18 per cent questions at thirty-eight months and 20 per cent at fifty-two months in the case of his own child's conversations. Rugg et al.,[11] found that at the kindergarten

[8] Elizabeth B. Hurlock, *Child Development*, New York, McGraw-Hill Book Co., Inc., 1942, p. 289.
[9] W. Boyd, "Development of Sentence Structure in Childhood," *British Journal of Psychology*, 17: 181-191 (1926).
[10] G. C. Brandenburg, "The Language of a Three-Year-Old Child," *Pedagogical Seminary*, 22: 89-120 (1915).
[11] H. Rugg, L. Krueger, and A. Sondergaard, "A Study of the Language of Kindergarten Children," *Journal of Educational Psychology*, 20: 1-18 (1929).

level approximately one-tenth of children's remarks are in the form of questions. Judging from Fisher's [12] data, nursery school children's questions rise from a proportion of 2 per cent at eighteen to twenty-four months to 15 per cent at three years. It should be noted, however, that all these data were secured from children studied in the company of parents and adults, not from situations in which children conversed spontaneously with one another.

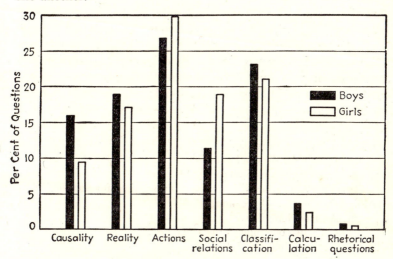

Figure 82. Percentage Distribution Among the Functional Categories of Questions Asked by Boys and Girls

(From E. A. Davis, "The Form and Function of Children's Questions," *Child Development,* 3:67 (1932).)

Probably the most extensive study of children's questions in relation to conceptual maturity is the one by Davis [13] in which mothers were asked to record the questions raised (also the circumstances involved) by a sampling of 73 children ranging from three to twelve years of age. Of the 3,650 questions asked, 87.8 per cent appeared to arise from immediate situations, 10.8 per cent from remembered or remote events, and

[12] Mary S. Fisher, *Language Patterns of Preschool Children,* Child Development Monographs, No. 15 (1934).

[13] E. A. Davis, "The Form and Function of Children's Questions," *Child Development,* 3 : 57-74 (1932). See also George L. Fahey, "The Questioning Activity of Children," *Journal of Genetic Psychology,* 60 : 337-357 (1942).

1.4 from sources that could not be accounted for. The data showed that boys ask questions at a more rapid rate than do girls, also that they ask more questions relating to causal explanations than is the case with girls. As Figure 82 shows, girls are more inclined to ask questions relating to social situations.

However, although it has been found that ordinary situations often stimulate children to ask a series of logically related questions, it has been doubted whether their spontaneous questions are reliable measures of either interest or ability to think critically.

Typical of the conceptual nature of children's questions are the following, as quoted by Jersild [14] from a report of the queries of a four-and-one-half-year-old:

CHILD: What time is it?
MOTHER: 6:30.
CHILD: What means that?
MOTHER: What do you mean?
CHILD: What means 6:30?
MOTHER: Well, when it's evening it means time for you to think of bed and time for me to get dinner.
CHILD: How long is 6:30?
MOTHER: Just one minute, then it is 6:31.
CHILD: Is a minute big?
MOTHER: No, very short.
CHILD: Just a little bit like this? (*Demonstrates with finger and thumb and a tiny pinch.*)
MOTHER: I'll show you with my watch.
CHILD: (*Watches watch for a minute or two, then speaks.*) Do you like me, mummy? (*Dismissed subject of time.*)

Information Possessed by Children.—Psychologists have not found it possible to ascertain the increasing store of information acquired by children as they grow older and respond to the educational opportunities afforded them. Studies dealing with information possessed by children have not as yet made available a standard inventory for the determination of norms

14 Arthur T. Jersild, *Child Psychology*, New York, Prentice-Hall, Inc., 1940, pp. 343-344.

at given ages. It may be that such an inventory is impossible of realization with children experiencing such diverse backgrounds as American elementary school pupils. It was found, however, in one study [15] that only a fifth of a group of city children ranging in age from eight to twelve years knew that animals other than cows and goats produced milk for their young. There are, nevertheless, some investigations which have been concerned with the subject of children's information. A sampling of these will be reviewed.

GENERAL INFORMATION. A study by Probst [16] of the general information possessed by children, aged five years and four months to six years, who were about to enroll in the first grade in the city of Minneapolis is suggestive. The showing made by the 100 children in the categories represented in the test makes it evident that many youngsters of this age are naive about not only the nature of natural phenomena but about items of general information as well. "Clang" associations, such as "carpenters fix carpet sweepers," "energine is put in the radiators of cars," and "butter is made by butterflies," were common among young children. A sex difference was indicated by the fact that the average boy knew the answers to ten more items than was the case with the average girl. Although in many instances the percentage of correct answers was the same for all occupational groups, children from the higher social brackets made better average scores than did those from the more lowly occupational callings.

A unique feature of this study was the failure of all but one child to name one of the candidates for the presidency in connection with the political campaign which was in progress at the time. It appears that such political contests have almost no significance for five-year-olds. Mention of the names of the candidates merely caused the children to associate them with names of neighbors which they resembled. Some of the children also tended to answer certain questions in terms of asso-

[15] Arthur I. Gates, Arthur T. Jersild, T. R. McConnell, and Robert C. Challman, *Educational Psychology*, New York, The Macmillan Co., 1942, p. 202.
[16] C. A. Probst, "A General Information Test for Kindergarten Children," *Child Development*, 2 : 81-95 (1931).

TABLE 31. PERCENTAGE OF CHILDREN IN GREATER NEW YORK CHOOSING THE CORRECT ALTERNATIVE ANSWER OR SUPPLYING THE CORRECT ANSWER TO VARIOUS ITEMS OF AN INFORMATION TEST

Test Item	Percentage of Children Giving Correct Answer				
	Aged 8	Aged 9	Aged 10	Aged 11	Aged 12[a]
The sun rises in the: (a) east; (b) north; (c) west; (d) south..............	54	51	63	66	71
The moon sets in the: (a) east; (b) north; (c) west; (d) south..............	29	40	35	50	49
Up the Hudson River is: (a) east; (b) north; (c) west; (d) south.........	29	50	59	54	65
To the Rocky Mountains is: (a) east; (b) north; (c) west; (d) south......	10	34	53	59	70
A boy walks a mile in about: (a) 1 hour; (b) 2 hours; (c) 25 minutes; (d) 5 minutes.....................	27	44	58	52	47
A soldier can march in day about: (a) 5 miles; (b) 100 miles; (c) 200 miles; (d) 30 miles.................	42	53	60	64	52
A ton of coal would: (a) fill this classroom; (b) almost fill this classroom; (c) not nearly fill this classroom....	22	36	55	54	61
Which is bigger, a corn plant or a wheat plant?.....................	54	58	66	77	77
Which is bigger, a tiger or a cow?......	67	72	73	78	79
Which is bigger a duck or a goose?.....	92	84	91	89	79
Which of the following is known as: (a) a President; (b) an actor; (c) prizefighter; (d) a Senator:					
Copeland?.........................	8	10	25	29	40
Wagner?...........................	8	18	25	32	37
Coolidge?..........................	37	38	46	54	58
Hoover?...........................	45	66	76	84	95
Roosevelt?.........................	93	97	96	99	100
Jack Dempsey?.....................	62	65	82	82	86
Joe Louis?.........................	79	92	96	98	95
Clark Gable?.......................	87	96	98	98	100
From what animal do we get:					
Caviar?...........................	6	7	9	9	6
Venison?..........................	14	18	19	31	—
Mutton?...........................	6	12	30	45	39
Bacon?............................	41	51	67	63	65
Beef?.............................	48	48	62	74	78
Pork?.............................	32	65	84	92	91
Does a mother ...... have milk for her baby?[b]					
Elephant?.........................	18	16	23	18	20
Wolf?.............................	19	19	28	32	20
Goat?.............................	69	81	90	91	93

[a] The twelve-year-olds were not as representative as the younger children, since they included no pupil above the sixth grade.
[b] Introductory item: A mother cow has milk for her baby, but a mother hen does not. Does a mother ...... have milk for her baby?

TABLE 31. (*Continued*)

Test Item	Percentage of Children Giving Correct Answer				
	Aged 8	Aged 9	Aged 10	Aged 11	Aged 12[a]
Do the following grow: (*a*) on vines, (*b*) in the ground; (*c*) on trees; (*d*) on bushes:					
Peanuts?............................	20	39	29	36	33
Watermelons?......................	10	17	45	48	45
Carrots?...........................	65	80	73	91	93
Oranges?..........................	87	86	95	91	91
Apples?...........................	98	96	99	99	98
Potatoes?.........................	78	90	92	95	98
Which of the following comes from: (*a*) an animal; (*b*) a mine; (*c*) a plant, (*d*) the air:					
Linen?............................	29	50	69	68	83
Salt?.............................	30	44	74	82	85
Sugar?............................	44	58	75	82	80
Cotton?...........................	42	75	87	90	92
Leather?..........................	63	68	82	92	80
Coal?.............................	64	82	94	96	92
Wool?.............................	89	93	95	93	94
Meat?.............................	92	100	91	99	100

(From Arthur T. Jersild, *Child Psychology*, New York, Prentice-Hall, Inc., 1940, pp. 353-354.)

ciations among words, i.e., that "seeds" and "flowers" are manufactured in the Ford "plant."

Further data concerning the information in certain areas possessed by school children eight to twelve years of age has been presented by Jersild.[17] Answers from the older of the 500 New York City pupils concerned were received from test blanks and those from the younger children were secured from interviews. As Table 31 discloses, there was considerable lack of knowledge in some of the categories of the test. The investigator felt that even smaller percentages of children might have answered some of the items correctly if the factor of guessing could have been eliminated. Relatively few of the children recognized the names of their current state senators even when the latter had been featured prominently in the newspapers. Although some knew (had probably memorized) the direction in which such explorers as Columbus and Byrd went

[17] Arthur T. Jersild, *op. cit.*, pp. 352-356. (Adapted from an unpublished study.)

in quest of their discoveries, they appeared to have little notion of direction in relation to local geography.

Such findings may mean that many items in the information test were "over the children's heads" or possibly that the teaching methods used in the schools concerned were inadequate. Research is no doubt needed on this point. Jersild did find, however, that the brighter pupils were correct in many more instances than were those classed as dull, except in the case of such everyday matters as where peanuts grow, how far a man can walk in a day, and the like. The investigator believed that, even though he may be lacking in information on many items which adults take for granted, the average child possesses a store of information that is both meaningful and useful to him. He declared that "a failure on the part of adults to appreciate a child's viewpoint or lack of understanding can often be observed in connection with the teaching of science and the social studies in the elementary grades. In past years, many schools have placed much emphasis on . . . topics such as conservation, technological unemployment, monopoly, government control, problems of production and consumption, democratic as against other forms of government, and so forth. What often seems to happen is that these topics are treated in a manner that is just as unrealistic, from the point of view of the child's interest and understanding, as were some of the old-fashioned drills in history dates and in grammar."

SPACE PERCEPTION. The determination of direction and distance is not accomplished spontaneously by young children. To judge distance the child must compare the space to be traversed with objects or people with whose size he is familiar. The cutaneous and kinesthetic senses, as well as visual sensations, are involved in making estimates of space, direction, and distance. When the child begins to creep and crawl, these factors become more functional, and soon he makes sufficiently accurate judgments to negotiate familiar distances. Continued play with carts, wagons, tricycles, and similar equipment leads to the perception of cues which makes estimates of distances and directions even more accurate. Long distances, which the child is unable to relate to his own body, continue to baffle him for some time. School experiences with inches, feet, and measures of space and weight make their contribution to the growing child's perception of space and distance.

Experimental investigations of space perception in children are not lacking. In a comparative study of four-year-olds and adults, Updegraff [18] found little difference, so far as acuity in the visual perception of distance is concerned, between them. The children were able to distinguish which of two objects, at a distance of approximately one meter, was the farther away when they were separated by 5 centimeters. Dunford [19] attempted to ascertain the improvement with age that could be expected in accuracy of localization of cutaneous stimulation applied to the back of the hand. Children of ages three, five, seven, nine, eleven, and fifteen were blindfolded and subsequently required to point to the place on the skin being stimulated. In this instance, improvement did not follow with age or even with experience. Although all the original localizations were quite accurate, the nine-year-old group achieved the highest score. Eleven-year-olds made a poorer showing than either the three- or fifteen-year-old groups.

A similar investigation by Renshaw and associates [20] confirmed the finding that children are superior to adults in ability to localize cutaneous sensations, and attributed this fact to the former's superiority in kinesthetic-tactual coordination. It was believed that the adult had trained his visual abilities to the extent that he would excel in situations involving acute vision rather than kinesthetic sensitivity. In the case of blind subjects, the adults were consistently more accurate than children in the localization of touch stimulations.

NUMBER CONCEPTS. Children begin to verbalize numbers soon after they acquire the ability to talk. Precisely when a child can use numbers in a meaningful way is difficult to determine, but it seems certain that during the second year and

[18] Ruth Updegraff, "The Visual Perception of Distance in Young Children and Adults: A Comparative Study," *Univ. of Iowa Studies in Child Welfare,* Vol. 4, No. 4 (1930).

[19] R. E. Dunford, "The Genetic Development of Cutaneous Localization," *Journal of Genetic Psychology,* 37 : 499-513 (1930).

[20] S. Renshaw, R. J. Wherry, and L. G. Newlin, "Cutaneous Localization in Congenitally Blind vs. Seeing Children and Adults," *Journal of Genetic Psychology,* 38 : 239-248 (1930).

possibly later, they represent mere verbalizations. The evidence from baby biographies has not been sufficiently substantial to clarify this issue. There are, however, some data pertaining to the development of ability to use and understand numbers. In a study of kindergarten children (four and one-half to six years of age) Douglass [21] found that they were able to distinguish among the first few numbers. The children were asked to tell how many dots there were on a flash card shown briefly, and how many marbles the experimenter held in his hand when they, too, were glimpsed briefly. It was found that children of this age have an accurate conception of the numbers "one" and "two," a good idea of "three," a "serviceable" conception of "four," and only a vague notion of numbers from five to ten. The older children used the higher numbers with greater skill than that manifested by their juniors. The investigator concluded that number concepts develop as a function of age and educational opportunity.

The normal development of number concepts has been shown by Terman and Merrill [22] in connection with their 1937 revision of the Stanford-Binet mental scale. According to the findings, the typical five-year-old can count four blocks, beads, and pennies. By the sixth year the average child is able to count three, five, seven, and nine cubes, respectively. Wheeler and Perkins [23] have advanced a method which they believe would result in a much more adequate comprehension of number relationships on the part of elementary school pupils if intelligently utilized. Their suggestion would involve, among other procedures, a timely transition from numbers in concrete form to those of a verbal nature, and a thorough early mastery of the relationships among all of the verbal numbers from one to ten and later to the higher numbers. The fact that a child can

---

[21] H. R. Douglass, "The Development of Number Concepts in Children of Pre-School and Kindergarten Ages," *Journal of Experimental Psychology,* 8 : 443-470 (1925). Also Louis Long and Livingston Welch, "The Development of Abilities to Discriminate Numbers," *Journal of Genetic Psychology,* 59 : 377-387 (1941).

[22] Lewis M. Terman and Maud A. Merrill, *Measuring Intelligence,* Boston, Houghton Mifflin Co., 1937.

[23] R. H. Wheeler and F. T. Perkins, *Principles of Mental Development,* New York, T. Y. Crowell Co., 1932, pp. 479-490.

verbalize given numbers does not mean that he understands their numerical values.

Werner [24] has listed the phases of development in childhood of the number concept as including: (1) the level of qualitative configuration or use of such expressions as "many," "lots," and "herd"; (2) the level of concrete number-configurations, or counting; (3) the level of concrete schematic numbers, or use of the fingers in counting; and (4) the level of abstract number concepts. Young children's concepts of large numbers, particularly those over 100, are as a rule vague. They have little conception of what they mean when they use such expressions as "thousands," "millions," or "trillions." It takes experience and mathematical study to ascertain the meaning of abstract numerical concepts.

TIME PERCEPTION. The ability to perceive passage of time is not well developed in children. Even when account is taken of the nature of the activity in which the child is engaged, he has great difficulty in judging the amount of time that has elapsed. Time apparently passes very quickly for a child when he is happily engaged and slowly when he is idle or bored. The young child's lack of comprehension of the time element is thus probably the cause of much of his apparent disobedience both in meeting appointments and in his tendency to be late to school. Because certain activities are associated with them, children are usually able to tell day from night, morning from evening, Sunday from Saturday, the season of the year, and other contrasted time elements. Most four-year-olds know what day it is, but will not have a clear conception of months and seasons until a year or more later. Recognition of the year as a span of time appears to be learned last of all.

Some studies of children's sense of time have been made. The following are illustrative of their approach and findings. Elkine,[25] for example, instructed ten- to fifteen-year-old boys and girls to judge the length of the time intervals, 5, 10, 15, and 30 seconds and 1, 2, 3, and 5 minutes. Many extensive errors

[24] H. Werner, *Comparative Psychology of Mental Development* (trans. by E. B. Garside), New York, Harper & Bros., 1940, p. 298.

[25] D. Elkine, "De L'orientation de L'enfant d'age Scolaire dans les Relations Temporelles," *Journal de Psychologie,* 25: 425-429 (1928).

in judgment were found, as well as a tendency to overestimate the length of short intervals and to underestimate the span of the longer ones. The best judgments related to intervals of from 30 seconds to one minute in duration. So far as general time concepts are concerned, Pistor [26] has reported that the formal study of subjects involving much chronology does not apparently increase the efficiency of children.

Friedman [27] questioned kindergarten and primary school children about time concepts and found that, although the typical child's notion of "a short time ago" is much clearer than that of "a long time ago," it is somewhat vague to the age of about eleven or twelve. Time concepts were found to be more closely related to grade level than to intelligence quotient.

A more extensive study in this field is that by Oakden and Sturt,[28] in which an effort was made to ascertain children's (1) understanding of words and symbols pertaining to time, (2) ability to conceive of time as extending into both the past and the future, (3) knowledge of the characteristics of definite time epochs, (4) methods of thinking about historical data, and (5) sense of the importance of the time element as compared to other factors in their experience. In connection with simple time concepts it was found that four-year-old children have little understanding of the time of day or its meaning; that five-year-olds are more competent in answering questions relating to the time of day than they are in estimating the duration of time; that after the seventh year the child possesses a fairly accurate knowledge of time duration; and that by the age of eight or ten most children are able to name both the day of the month and the year in question. Ability to think of the past passes through the stages in which the past differs from the present largely in the sense of differences in practices (wearing of skins and the worship of idols), and in which it belongs in a series of successive epochs. It was found that knowledge of time evolves with development from around the age of three or

[26] F. Pistor, "How Time Concepts Are Acquired," *Educational Method*, 20: 107-112 (1940).

[27] K. C. Friedman, "Time Concepts of Elementary-school Children," *Elementary School Journal*, 44:337-342 (1944).

[28] F. C. Oakden and M. Sturt. "The Development of the Knowledge of Time in Children," *British Journal of Psychology*, 12:309-336 (1922).

four to thirteen or fourteen, with eleven as a high point in speed of advancement in all types of time concepts.

PERCEPTION OF WEIGHT. Children experience difficulty in judging weight because they do not realize that different types of materials involve distinctly different degrees of weight. Being influenced more by size than by texture or density, the naive child is likely to expect more weight in a ball of yarn than in a much smaller iron ball. Such expectations probably account for frequent failures to make appropriate neuromuscular adjustments to objects upon attempting to handle them, and possibly for some of children's accidents with household objects. It requires experience for a young child to learn that certain articles and toys are light in weight and that others are much heavier. Children of normal intelligence soon discover, however, that the weight of articles must be judged in terms of their materials as well as of their size.

Children do somewhat better when asked to judge the differences in weight between or among articles of similar size and appearance but differing in weight. According to Baldwin and Stecher's [29] findings, children from three to six years of age are able to discriminate between such weights as 3 and 24 grams, respectively. A small number can distinguish between 3 and 6, and 9 and 12 grams, respectively. Many children of these ages are able to differentiate between 3 and 6 grams even in the case of similar appearing weights. In the original Stanford revision of the Binet mental scale, it was established that the average five-year-old can tell the difference between 3 and 15 gram weights. It is believed that ability in weight perception reaches its peak of improvement at approximately the twelfth year and that little advance in such discrimination is achieved after that age.[30]

DISCRIMINATION OF SIZE AND FORM. Children begin early in life to understand both differences in the length of objects and differences in the size of boxes, toys, geometric figures, and similar familiar forms. There is evidence that such dis-

[29] B. T. Baldwin and L. I. Stecher, *The Psychology of the Preschool Child,* New York, D. Appleton-Century Co., Inc., 1924.

[30] Elizabeth B. Hurlock, *Child Development,* New York, McGraw-Hill Book Co., Inc., 1942, p. 296.

crimination is sometimes present as early as the second or third year of life. A study by Hicks and Stewart [31] of the ability of children between the ages of two and five to select the middle one of three boxes of different sizes is indicative of the course of development in this area of understanding. Although nearly all of the subjects in the two-year-old group were unable to make the distinctions desired, all of the children beyond that age were able to do so when given the benefit of practice. Extensive individual differences in ability to choose the correct box were in evidence within each age (yearly) level. Quickness of mastery of the problem involved was in general related to the child's mental age.

Thrum [32] has reported somewhat similar findings with children of the same ages. In this instance the subjects were required to select the "biggest," the "middle-sized," and the "smallest" figures among groups of circles, triangles, and other geometric figures. The children found the "biggest" figure the easiest to find, the "smallest" next easiest, and the "middle-sized" most difficult of all to choose. Discrimination of size became increasingly difficult to accomplish as the figures to be compared were reduced in size. Children below three years of age were unable to make satisfactory choices among the figures. This finding is in harmony with the norms on the Terman and Merrill [33] (Stanford-Binet) scale, which place the ability to distinguish between sticks 2 and 2½ inches in length at age three and one-half years.

When appropriate experimental methods are used, very young children are able to discriminate among a variety of geometric forms. In an experiment by Munn and Steining [34] children were required to choose the box with a certain figure

[31] J. A. Hicks and F. D. Stewart, "The Learning of Abstract Concepts of Size," *Child Development*, 1 : 195-203 (1930).
[32] M. E. Thrum. "The Development of Concepts of Magnitude," *Child Development*, 6 : 120-140 (1935). See also Louis Long, "Size Discrimination in Children," *Child Development*, 12 : 247-254 (1941).
[33] Lewis M. Terman and Maud A. Merrill, *Measuring Intelligence*, Boston, Houghton Mifflin Co., 1937.
[34] N. L. Munn and B. R. Steining, "The Relative Efficacy of Form and Background in a Child's Discrimination of Visual Patterns," *Journal of Genetic Psychology*, 39 : 73-90 (1931). See also I. Huang, "Abstraction of Form and Color in Children as a Function of the Stimulus Objects," *Journal of Genetic Psychology*, 66 : 59-62 (1945).

from among a group of such boxes containing other figures before securing a desired reward. Form perception was subsequently observed in children less than two years of age. One
child of fifteen months was successful in distinguishing between circles and squares, crosses and squares, circles and
crosses, triangles and circles, and other such figures. That the

Figure 83. Child Playing with Special Blocks Designed to Teach Discrimination of Shape

(From W. Rand, M. E. Sweeny, and E. L. Vincent, *Growth and Development of the
Young Child*, Philadelphia, W. B. Saunders Co., 1940, p. 176.)

child's ability to perceive differences in form increases with age,
at least between the ages of two and six years, was demonstrated by Baldwin and Wellman.[35] These investigators studied the subjects' ability to fit pegs correctly on a series of four
Wallin peg boards. No sex differences were found, but all of
the children improved with growth and experience.

[35] B. T. Baldwin and B. L. Wellman, "The Pegboard as a Means of Analyzing
Form Perception and Motor Control in Young Children," *Journal of Genetic Psychology*, 35 : 389-414 (1928).

The ability of children, three to six years of age, to recognize roundness, as contrasted with squareness, has been studied by Long.[36] After being trained to respond to a ball when the latter was paired with a block, the children were confronted with cylindrical, spherical, and two-dimensional figures. The responses showed that all of the subjects had developed the concept of spherical roundness, including its cylindrical and two-dimensional forms. The previously mentioned Terman-Merrill revision of the Stanford-Binet scale has also indicated the ages at which children possess such form perception. In this test two-year-olds are required to put round and square blocks into their appropriate receptacles on a form board; three-year-olds are expected to copy a circle; at four, forms must be matched; at five, the subject must copy a square; and at seven, the norm calls for the ability to copy a diamond-shaped figure.

The Immature Nature of Children's Beliefs.—Because of their immaturity, children experience considerable difficulty in grasping the meaning of much that they see and hear. It is thus to be expected that they will accept as bona fide much faulty information, and that they will engage in naive reasoning. An adult's recall of his own early erroneous impressions and childhood misinterpretations is suggestive of the handicaps under which all children operate in their efforts to secure an adequate understanding of language and the concepts of natural phenomena which it conveys. Children's misconceptions and false beliefs can therefore be classified as issuing in the main from (1) faulty information, (2) an inadequate knowledge of words, and (3) certain forms of fallacious reasoning.

Faulty Information. Children pick up erroneous information from a number of sources. Unless they have become distrustful of their associates, young children are likely to accept as true practically everything they are told unless, of course, the "facts" in question are completely out of harmony with their own experience or that of others whom they regard as authorities. Children are particularly prone to believe what

<hr>

36 L. Long, "Conceptual Relationships in Children: the Concept of Roundness." *Journal of Genetic Psychology,* 57 : 289-315 (1940).

their parents tell them and what they see in print. It is not un-common for parents to answer a child superficially without con-sidering the involvements of the questions asked, or to make up somewhat ridiculous answers to satisfy the child's curiosity. Many parents (and other adults) themselves hold highly un-sound beliefs which they pass on to their children. Children thus grow up believing erroneous and distorted ideas concern-ing the world in which they live, and particularly of the cause and effect relationships which operate in natural phenomena. In instances where these misinterpretations are not eventually corrected, the individuals concerned will lack a mastery of cer-tain common facts and principles, and are likely to fail in the solution of many everyday problems.

Illustrative of the erroneous beliefs often accepted by chil-dren, some of which frequently persist into adulthood, are the following: that a copper wire fastened about the body will pre-vent rheumatism; that the face shows how intelligent a person is; that a severe mental shock causes a person's hair to turn white overnight; that a snake never dies until after the sun goes down; that brunette girls are more dependable than blondes; that one could dig a hole all the way to China; that wrongdoing is caused by the intervention of devils; that a rabbit's foot always brings good luck; and that earthquakes are caused by the ill-will of gods. Children are also quick to adopt false notions concerning sex matters, especially when their parents fail to educate them in this respect and thus force upon them the necessity of picking up such fragments of in-formation as they can obtain from equally ignorant friends or from sexually morbid elders.

A study by Huff [37] of the weaknesses of children's (kinder-garten to high school) concepts of natural phenomena as re-lated to common objects in their environment, is suggestive of their immaturity in this area of experience. Nearly 50 per cent of the erroneous ideas pertained to such phenomena as the nature of growing wheat, the use of a hoe, the source of sugar, the characteristics of a beach, and what makes the clock go.

[37] R. L. Huff, "Percept Content of School Children's Minds," *Journal of Genetic Psychology*, 34:129-143 (1927).

Between 40 and 45 per cent of the children were ignorant about the nature of beehives, where grapes grow, the source of silk, the definition of an island, and how water gets into a faucet. Approximately 35 to 40 per cent of the subjects did not know the source of copper wire or the origin of gas in the kitchen stove. Huff believed that ignorance of these and similar phenomena is the result of an impoverished environment. This interpretation was supported by the fact that the concepts best known to most of the children were commonly met in their daily experience, and that those least known were not a part of their environment.

INADEQUATE KNOWLEDGE OF WORDS.   Because of his limited vocabulary and his consequent lack of comprehension, the child frequently mistakes the meaning of words and phrases used by those with whom he communicates.   Somewhat humorous, yet significant, illustrations of this tendency have been noted by one author [38] as follows: "A child was overheard to give this version of the oath of allegiance to the flag: 'I pledge a legion to the flag and to the Republic of Richard Sands; one notion and a vegetable with liberty and justice to all.' Another sang: 'Long train run over us (Long to reign over us)'; and another patriotically intoned: 'I love thy rots and chills (rocks and rills).' After a moment's hesitation on a line in *The Night Before Christmas,* a child came forth with: 'I rushed to the window and vomited (threw up!) the sash.'"   One child, after listening intently to a eulogy of a general seated on a horse in a public monument, shocked his father by inquiring admiringly "But who is the man sitting on the general!"   These and similar incongruities are illustrative of the young child's naivety in the understanding of concepts, and provide a basis for sympathy with his tendency to make social and other verbal blunders.

FALLACIOUS REASONING.   Erroneous reasoning in childhood may stem from a variety of causes.   In addition to (a) faulty information and (b) the misunderstanding of words, just discussed, may be added (c) vivid imagination, (d) ab-

---

[38] Arthur T. Jersild, *op. cit.,* pp. 360-361.

sence of a critical attitude, (e) wishful thinking, and (f) personal bias based on efforts to maintain one's ego status. Vivid imagination (to be discussed in more detail in a later section) may cause a child to draw conclusions that are not justified by objective facts, and to confuse actual experiences with those of a phantasy nature. The immature boy or girl may, for example, indulge in lies of which he is not aware, or imagine that he is enjoying the company of a playmate who actually does not exist (imaginary playmate).

The absence of a critical attitude, the results of which have already been presented, often causes the child to associate wrong meanings with the situations he observes and to come to conclusions which may seem to an enlightened adult entirely unwarranted. Thus he may believe that there is a pot of gold at the end of the rainbow, that a man in the moon smiles at people on this earth, that storks actually deliver babies to mothers, and that Santa Claus brings toys down through the chimney. Wishful thinking has led some children to believe, for example, that their parents (one or both) are not their own, that they are going to be given a trip to the country, that their family has inherited money, or that they will be famous when they grow up. Wishful thinking influences the thoughts of both adults and children because it helps them to atone for certain deprivations and to enjoy in thought many satisfying experiences which they are not able to achieve in reality.

The influence of personal bias, or faulty conception of the self, is illustrated in a study [39] in which a group of 423 children were asked to check the word in each pair of contrasted words that most nearly described them. The contrasts included such personality descriptions as *careful-careless, daring-ambitious, patient-impatient, generous-stingy,* and *cowardly-brave.* Of the 12,690 responses, all but 763 (6 per cent) indicated the presence of socially desirable (according to adult standards) traits. Of the undesirable traits, admission was most often made of being *proud, daring,* or *bad-tempered.* It will be noticed that these are among the least-condemned undesirable temperamental traits. Being actuated by the dynamic need for acceptance and status, the children apparently utilized the mechanism of portraying themselves as others would like them. Like adults, children tend to underestimate the extent to which they possess undesirable personality qualities.

Stimulating the Child's Understanding.—It is apparent from the above considerations and studies that children form many erroneous concepts in their efforts to comprehend the meaning of words and adapt themselves to the requirements of their material environment. Adults are prone to overestimate both children's degree of understanding regarding natural phenomena and their maturity in relation to abstract concepts. Much work needs to be done in ascertaining levels when given children are "ready" to master concepts of one variety or another. It is incumbent upon parents and teachers to utilize the best means possible for stimulating understanding, and not to expect a show of intellectual maturity from children before they have had the opportunity of gaining the abstract insights expected.

It must be recognized that a child's conceptual ideas will develop and become functional only to the extent that opportunities in his environment make possible. An adequate understanding on the part of the child of natural forces, of the psychological nature of people, of time, space, number, form, and the like, and of his own tendencies will develop with proper teaching and guided experience. The extent of the child's ultimate mastery of his material, social, and conceptual world will be contingent upon the advances that his immediate elders have made, and upon the experience of the social group of which he is an integral part. Originally immature ideas may later become comprehensive and accurate if the developing child is given opportunities to help himself in an atmosphere of stimulation and rich experience.

Characteristics of Reasoning in Childhood

Students of child development have engaged in much conjecture concerning the nature of reflective thought at various levels of maturity. To what extent and with what degree of congruity children reason have always been elusive but intriguing questions to psychologists. A scrutiny of the researches pertaining to the characteristics of reasoning in children and an analysis of their reflective thinking should thus be of value in determining the course of intellectual development.

Difficulties in Studying Children's Thinking.—Many writers have declared that young children do not reason. It is their contention that reasoning is a complex mental process which is impossible of attainment, even to a rudimentary degree, in childhood. Others have insisted that reasoning is a process of discerning relationships which begins in early childhood with simple trial and error experiences and which develops with experience and maturity through more and more intricate stages until the ability to solve abstract and mathematical problems is achieved. It is not uncommon to hear the argument advanced that children cannot reason before they are around seven years of age, and that they should thus not be expected to cope with problems involving cause and effect relationships. Opponents of this view say that young children possess the ability to reason in an elementary way and that they enjoy exercising this function, but that their elders stifle their reflective development by requiring acceptance of authoritative statements and by surrounding them with dull curricular materials in school.

Considerable evidence indicative of the ability of young children to reason and to make inferences upon the basis of the effects of past experience has been advanced by the exponents of the latter view. They remind us, for example, that under appropriate conditions children from two to four years of age can place blocks in their acceptable places in form boards, take a ring off a book, place a hat on a rack, turn a door knob, use a stick to bring an object within reach, and recover an article that has been covered by an upturned cup. Older children have been observed to hide behind doors or walls to avoid detection, unhook the latch on screen doors, "reason" that, when swallowed, an apple seed will grow in the stomach, turn out lights when it is time to go to bed, and declare that one must run if he is in danger of being late to school. Such adaptive responses and judgment formations are believed to clinch the case for the presence of reasoning ability in children. Opponents of this view are inclined, however, to reply that these and similar adaptive reactions are but simple conditionings or naive reflections devoid of any cognizance of cause and effect relationships.

Additional evidence for children's ability to reason in the form of discernment of likenesses and differences among the elements of objects is afforded by the norms of the Terman-Merrill revision of the Stanford-Binet intelligence scale. Here we find seven-year-olds capable of telling in what way wood and coal, an apple and a peach, a ship and an automobile, and iron and silver are alike. Eight-year-olds possess the ability to delineate both the similarities and differences between a baseball and an orange, an airplane and a kite, an ocean and a river, and a penny and a quarter. At age eleven the typical child can tell in what way each of the following list of three things are alike: a snake, a cow, and a sparrow; a rose, a potato, and a tree; wool, cotton, and leather; a knifeblade, a penny, and a piece of wire; a book, a teacher, and a newspaper.

The study of reflective thought in children involves difficulties in addition to those already mentioned. One of these is the practical impossibility of adults freeing themselves sufficiently from their own point of view in thinking to appreciate that of the less experienced child. The result is that adults do not understand the processes of reflective thinking as they operate in child life. It is difficult as well to secure adequate samplings of children's reasoning under conditions that will not militate against spontaneity. The research worker who relies upon conversations and questions is likely to lose the true significance of children's untrammelled ideas and concepts. It has nevertheless been possible to make some progress in this field. The work of Piaget in Switzerland, as well as that of a small group of English and American scholars, has thrown at least preliminary light on the characteristics of reasoning in children.

Egocentrism and Childhood Reasoning.—As the result of extensive studies of children's unrestrained speech, Piaget [40] has reached certain conclusions regarding its essential nature. He avoided some of the difficulties mentioned above by proceeding on the assumption that children's remarks reflect their thinking, and subsequently recording their spontaneous speech reactions when they were associating with companions. The results obtained led Piaget to believe that children's thinking is characteristically egocentric (self-centered) rather than socialized, and that it is composed largely of capricious needs and impulses designed to conform, not to reality or to other people's wishes, but to their own pleasure. It was also concluded that the child's conception of the world and of physical causation is marked by belief in animism and artificialism.

According to Piaget, egocentric thinking predominates during the initial seven or eight years of life, the first two or so of which are characterized by *autistic* tendencies, or the disposition to harbor fleeting, effortless phantasies and reveries of a pleasurable nature. Mental activity during this early period is limited by the absence of experience and materials of a content variety. The egocentric child is said to center his thinking upon himself and to regard himself as the focal point of all interest and activity. Impersonal thoughts are believed to be rare before the age of eight. The impressionable child is also sufficiently gullible to have faith in the declarations of his elders, some of whom usually indoctrinate him with beliefs difficult to shake off in later life.

Piaget [41] has also emphasized the egocentric nature of children's conversations. The child engages in pseudo-conversations ("collective monologues") by talking to himself when he is apparently addressing his remarks to another child. He asks questions, but even when answered by a playmate goes right on with his personal conversation regardless of what the other child might have said. Piaget calculated what he called the *coefficient of egocentricity* in a child's speech by ascertaining the

[40] Jean Piaget, *The Language and Thought of the Child,* New York, Harcourt, Brace & Co., 1926.
[41] Jean Piaget, *Judgment and Reasoning in the Child,* New York, Harcourt, Brace & Co., 1928.

proportion of spontaneous remarks of a self-centered variety uttered in a given length of time, and found it to be between .54 and .60 for children three to five years of age and approximately .45 for those between five and seven. It was believed that these ratios would have been higher had it been possible to measure the thoughts which the children did not express verbally.

Other investigations, which have served as checks on Piaget's work, have in some instances disclosed disagreements both as to the correctness of his analysis of children's thought processes and the age at which egocentric thinking predominates. In a study involving the verbal reactions of children to pictures and toys, but in which social responses to grown-ups were not eliminated or controlled, McCarthy [42] found a considerably smaller per cent of egocentric expressions than did Piaget. The number of responses, fifty for each child, was, however, somewhat small. Investigations by Johnson and Josey,[43] by Day,[44] and by Grigsby [45] disagree with Piaget concerning the age at which certain thought processes, particularly egocentrism, are in evidence. All of these investigators report that socialized speech appears at an earlier age and in greater proportion than Piaget's suggested ages of seven or eight. It is probable that the discrepancies involved are explicable in terms of the techniques used (spontaneous conversations versus responses to questions or pictures), differences in the thought content and customs of the countries concerned, and differences between the French and English languages as media for the expression of thought.

It is also possible that whether a child overcomes intellectual egocentricity before the age of approximately eight may be determined by the extent to which he mingles freely with other

[42] Dorothea A. McCarthy, *Language Development of the Preschool Child,* Minneapolis, Univ. of Minnesota Press, 1930.

[43] Edwin C. Johnson and Charles C. Josey, "A Note on the Development of the Thought Forms of Children as Described by Piaget," *Journal of Abnormal and Social Psychology,* 26: 338-339 (1931).

[44] Ella J. Day, The Development of Language in Twins, I: "A Comparison of Twins and Single Children," *Child Development,* 3: 179-199 (1932).

[45] Olive J. Grigsby, "An Experimental Study of the Development of Concepts of Relationship in Pre-school Children as Evidenced by Their Expressive Ability," *Journal of Experimental Education,* 1: 144-162 (1932-33).

children and with adults. As Hazlitt,[46] who has done much to check the validity of Piaget's findings, says, "The truth seems to be that the child's egocentrism is largely due to his lack of experience—his world is so often made by others to foster in him the notion that he is the center of it. His lack of experience makes him unable to see relations, and his inability to see relations makes him egocentric."

Some psychologists, Stoddard and Wellman,[47] for example, are inclined to doubt that children's speech, and consequently their thinking, is essentially egocentric. They write, "Piaget's conception of egocentric speech as lacking in social purpose might be challenged. Even though the child's talk centers largely around himself as a point of reference, it may still be primarily social. Otherwise one needs to explain why it is that the child uses conventional language at all. In fact, the evidence that twins so frequently develop a language of their own when learning to talk is an argument for the socialized aspect of all language." Anyone opposing this view might, of course, contend that speech is not necessarily an exact expression of attitudes or thought. However, since speech is the principal clue to thought content, at least in children, it is customary to accept it as the vehicle of thinking processes. Still another investigator [48] has nevertheless stated that there is no evidence to support the conclusion that autistic reasoning is a necessary phenomenon of childhood.

Regardless of one's position concerning this controversy, it would seem that Piaget has made a most useful contribution to our knowledge of the characteristics of children's thinking. Egocentrism is certainly a characteristic of childhood behavior, and it is logical to assume that thought is imbedded to a considerable extent in such an attitude.

[46] Victoria Hazlitt, "Children's Thinking," *British Journal of Psychology,* 20 : 354-361 (1929-30).

[47] George D. Stoddard and Beth L. Wellman, *Child Psychology,* New York, The Macmillan Co., 1934, pp. 94-95. See also Wayne Dennis, "Piaget's Questions Applied to a Child of Known Environment," *Pedagogical Seminary and Journal of Genetic Psychology,* 60 : 307-320 (1942).

[48] G. McHugh, "Autistic Thinking as a 'Transitory Phenomenon of Childhood,'" *Child Development,* 15 : 89-98 (1944).

Juxtaposition and Syncretism in Reasoning.—The dictionary defines *juxtaposition* as "a placing or being placed side by side." In terms of child mentality it has been used by Piaget and others to signify the child's proclivity for confusing coincidence with causation. The inexperienced child, who has not yet learned to analyze ideas and meanings, glibly assumes that ideas or events that are *found* together (are side by side) *belong* together. Juxtaposition thus indicates a failure to comprehend the relations, causal or otherwise, among objects and events that are independent of the self. Piaget found, for example, that six-year-olds were prone to say that lying is bad because "you are punished," and that "if everyone believes you, it is not a lie." The absence of logic and reasoning is also illustrated by the statement of a boy who declared that "the man fell off his bicycle because he was ill afterward," and by the story of a lad who, after being warned not to scrub his dog's teeth with his toothbrush, innocently proceeded to scrub them with his father's toothbrush.

The immature child is severely handicapped in applying general principles to specific situations or even in discerning cause and effect relationships between events and consequences. When asked why he should not wear his rubbers in the house, a child is likely to reply that his mother doesn't want him to. He may also see nothing tragic about an accident in which forty people were killed. As Piaget has shown, the child may be satisfied intellectually with the use of the word "because" without regard to what adults recognize as physical causation.

Syncretism has been referred to as "the reconciliation or union of conflicting beliefs." In the case of children's reasoning it is characterized by the reconciliation of beliefs or causal connections which intelligent adults recognize as being wholly incongruous (irreconcilable). Whereas juxtaposition in reasoning refers to the acceptance by the child (or adults) of disconnected objective factors which, although appearing together, may not actually belong together, syncretism has reference to a subjective acceptance of relationships among events that is not warranted by the facts. A child may thus declare that her father is a doctor because he has an office or because he goes to

see people often. The child regards these explanations as being
adequate; in his immature and *subjective scheme* of things they
represent good logic. The real reasons for carrying on medical
practice or her father's decision to become a doctor are "over
her head" and seem unnecessary. This type of subjective unity
is based on the child's credulous willingness to take things at
their face value and to justify whatever happens by naive reasoning in which cause and effect relationships are ignored. It is
illustrated further by the response of a three-year-old girl who,
in deciding what to do with an extra glass of milk for which
she could find no room on a tray of returned empty glasses,
poured it into one of the dirty glasses in an effort to save the
milk.

It is Piaget's [49] belief that both the superstitions and the
syncretic interpretations of proverbs noted in children are based
upon their simple, uncritical reactions to what intellectually mature adults regard as causal relationships. Children often believe, for example, that it is unlucky to break a mirror, for companions to walk on opposite sides of a tree, or to be counted as
number thirteen. Such attitudes, which often persist in behavior compelling ways into adult life, are subjectively accepted as unified patterns of syncretic belief. The same is
sometimes true of responses to proverbs—the child accepts
illogical interpretations which nevertheless harmonize with his
subjective scheme of immature belief. Piaget found much of
this type of thinking on the abstract level in his study of children's reactions to proverbs (and matched sentences) at the
Rousseau Institute in Geneva. One boy (age nine) matched
with the proverb "White dust will ne'er come out of a sack of
coal," the sentence, "People who waste their time neglect their
business," and "reasoned" that people who waste their time become black like coal and thus need to be cleaned!

Piaget has contended that it is between the ages of approximately seven and eleven or twelve that the child's thinking becomes less syncretic and increasingly more analytic. As he
gains experience and becomes more familiar with the differing

[49] Jean Piaget, *The Child's Conception of the World*, New York, Harcourt,
Brace & Co., 1929.

elements and changing aspects of situations, the growing child develops insight into the similarities and differences upon which generalizations are built, and upon the basis of which cause and effect relationships can be made. With increasing mental development he gradually comes to examine his experiences and to appreciate the point of view of others. As the child responds to the questions and attitudes of associates, he finds it increasingly difficult to justify his more simple and uncritical conclusions, and thus seeks to support his positions with observed facts and more logical arguments.

It is well to remember, however, that Piaget's conclusion that children do not exhibit genuine ability to reason analytically before the age of eleven or twelve is based on his definition of reasoning as syllogistic thinking and the capacity for setting up and examining hypotheses.[50] This advanced type of reasoning is evidently not characteristic of children much under twelve, most of whom are still in the throes of lingering egocentric attitudes. If, however, reasoning is defined in terms of verbal problem solving at a given level of development and experience, it would seem that children reason at an early age. Several investigators[51] have, in fact, shown that when confronted with problems suitable to their mental maturity level and stock of information, children exhibit relatively logical modes of reasoning. A comprehensive review of the literature on children's reasoning by Johnson[52] has shown that their methods of problem solving are very similar to those of adults, and that they think in a manner comparable to that of their more non-scientific elders.

Conclusions on Children's Reasoning.—Another postulate assumed by Piaget[53] was that, because of his limited information and experience, the child does not distinguish between ob-

50 John Dewey, *How We Think*, Boston, D. C. Heath & Co., 1933.

51 Victoria Hazlitt, *op. cit.*; T. M. Abel, "Unsynthetic Modes of Thinking Among Adults: A Discussion of Piaget's Concepts," *American Journal of Psychology*, 44 : 123-132 (1932) ; J. M. Deutsche, *The Development of Children's Concepts of Causal Relations*, Minneapolis, Univ. of Minnesota Press, 1937.

52 B. Johnson, "Development of Thought," *Child Development*, 9 : 1-8 (1938).

53 Jean Piaget, *op. cit.* See also R. W. Russell and Wayne Dennis, Studies in Animism, I: "A Standardized Procedure for the Investigation of Animism." *Journal of Genetic Psychology*, 55 : 389-400 (1939) ; and I. Huang and H. W. Lee, "Experimental Analysis of Child Animism," *Journal of Genetic Psychology*, 66 : 69-74 (1945).

jects of an animate and inanimate nature. He is said to believe, as primitive peoples are alleged to do, that all objects possess life and conscious purpose. *Animism,* as this doctrine is called, thus ascribes human characteristics to all sorts of objects, such as chairs, stones, trees, animals, vegetation, and especially to such moving objects as bicycles, automobiles, and trains. Piaget describes the various stages of development in this area, in which children are believed to move from the belief that all objects possess life to the realization that moving objects alone are so equipped, and finally to knowledge that only animals and humans, particularly the latter, are animate and conscious.

Mead,[54] who has made extensive observations of the children of savage Melanesians, has challenged Piaget's assumption of the spontaneous development of animistic thinking in children. It is her belief that, since the primitive children studied by her actually showed a disinclination rather than a tendency to endow objects with conscious intentions and human qualities, animism in Swiss children, such as Piaget studied, may be the result of education and culture of the type they experienced. As another anthropologist[55] has written, "No Manus mother would tell a child who has spent hours exploring the internal structure of a piano that the sounds were made by little fairies who stood on the wires and sang, as an English mother did."

An investigation of children's concepts of causal relationships by Deutsche[56] has contributed new data on the adequacy of their thinking. In this instance children were asked to explain what happened when a jar was placed over a candle, thus causing it to go out, when a pebble was dropped into a beaker of water, causing its level to rise, etc. They were also asked to explain such phenomena as what makes the trees grow and how clouds come to move. Although a variety of answers were

---

[54] Margaret Mead, "An Investigation of the Thought of Primitive Children with Special Reference to Animism: Preliminary Report," *The Journal of the Royal Anthropological Institute of Great Britain and Ireland,* 62: 173-190 (1932).

[55] A. Irving Hallowell, "The Child, the Savage, and Human Experience," *Proceedings of the Sixth Institute on the Exceptional Child of the Child Research Clinic of the Woods Schools,* Oct. 1939, pp. 33-34.

[56] J. M. Deutsche, *op. cit.* See also M. B. McAndrew, "An Experimental Investigation of Young Children's Ideas of Causality," *Studies in Psychology and Psychiatry, Catholic Univ. of America,* Vol. 6, No. 2 (1943).

given at all ages, most of the children, from kindergarten up, answered in terms of physical or mechanical causation, not on the basis of animism or magic. Children of various ages were able to respond in logical ways to problems of causation that were within their intellectual grasp. Deutsche believed that the adequacy of the children's answers was related to age, sex, and socio-economic status, and that they did not harmonize with Piaget's findings with Swiss children.

Present evidence points to a fundamental similarity between the reasoning processes of children and adults, especially uneducated adults. The child has less capacity for concentration and usually lacks verbal facility, but when problems are "geared" to his level of insight into the processes of natural phenomena, he apparently acquits himself as logically as do his older associates under similar circumstances. Adults, too, are naive and inconsistent when faced by problems for which they do not have adequate answers. We conclude with the words of Susan Isaacs,[57] "Taking these records as a whole, then, the first impression which the unsophisticated reader receives is that the cognitive [intellectual] behavior of little children, even in these early years, is often all very much like our own in general outline of movement. Allowing for the immense difference in knowledge and experience, they go about their business of understanding the world and what happens to them in it, very much as we do ourselves. And, contrary to some current opinions about them, they do show a lively and sustained interest in real physical events, . . ."

Imagination in Children's Thinking.—In their preschool years, particularly before the age of approximately five, children engage in a great deal of make-believe activity involving construction, picture drawing, keeping house, and similar play endeavors. A child may make a palace out of blocks, equip a play house with imaginary floor lamps, draw a picture of bomber planes in action, or become the mother of a group of dolls. Such make-believe activities enable the small boy or girl to enjoy possessions which are not forthcoming in reality, to

[57] Susan Isaacs, *Intellectual Growth in Young Children*, New York, Harcourt, Brace & Co., 1930, p. 57.

overcome limitations in skill, to adopt conditions more in harmony with desires, to manage the material environment more readily, and to enjoy better status than may actually be the case. Make-believe play thus serves many important mental functions, in addition to satisfying the child's need for a sense of mastery and competence.

THE NATURE OF IMAGINATION. Imagination in the form of phantasies and daydreams is common in the experience of children who have reached school age, particularly those who have experienced considerable loneliness and frustration. Such children—and others to a lesser extent—find imagination a convenient channel through which to escape from inferiority, rid themselves of handicaps, compensate for weaknesses, fulfill thwarted desires, and enjoy vicarious pleasures and adventures. It is through their daydreams that many children satisfy the need for ego-status, a dynamic demand which they fulfill by imagining themselves in heroic roles, as great actors or athletes, as enjoying special privileges, as possessing much desired clothes and playthings, and as being more than ordinarily popular. These and other stress-reducing phantasies differ somewhat from earlier make-believe activities in being more remote from everyday experience. Imagination may, in fact, be defined as the ideational recombination of the materials of experience in patterns that do not conform to reality.

Studies by Griffiths,[58] by Burnham,[59] and by Markey[60] have pointed out the extent to which young children engage in imaginative activities, as well as the types of make-believe situations which they utilize. From an analysis of records of a group of nursery school children's verbalizations, Burnham noted that remarks of an imaginative vein increased from 1.5 per cent at age twenty-four to twenty-nine months to 8.7 per cent at forty-two to forty-seven months. Some children made remarks dealing with imaginary topics to the extent of 26 per

[58] Ruth Griffiths, *The Study of Imagination in Early Childhood and Its Function in Mental Development*, London, Kegan Paul, 1935.
[59] M. P. Burnham, *Imaginative Behavior of Young Children as Revealed in Their Language*, Doctoral Dissertation, Teachers College, Columbia Univ., 1940, reported in Arthur T. Jersild, *Child Psychology*, New York, Prentice-Hall, Inc., 1940, p. 385.
[60] Frances V. Markey, *Imaginative Behavior in Preschool Children*, Child Development Monographs, No. 18 (1935).

cent of all remarks made. Markey, who studied preschool children's imaginative activities of both a verbal and overt nature, found that the average two-and-one-half-year-old engaged in 6½ such activities in a period of 2½ hours. Children forty months of age participated in make-believe activities to the extent of 26 during the same period of time. Make-believe activities reported include housekeeping games in which dolls are punished and icebox doors left open, ferrying passengers across rivers with blocks, stopping and starting on red and green lights, and operating radios without batteries or electricity.

Imaginary Playmates. Children over three and under approximately ten years of age frequently claim the presence of imaginary playmates. Investigations [61] of this tendency have reported from one-tenth to one-third of the children involved as having such experiences. The imaginary playmate or companion may be a supposed person, animal, or plaything whose presence seems so real as to approximate an hallucination. Belief in the reality of an imaginary playmate usually persists for some time. One small girl alarmed her mother, thus securing certain concessions, by insisting from time to time that she was playing with a cherished girl friend when no such individual was present. Such imagination is believed to be caused by loneliness or the absence of real playmates. It is not considered pathological and apparently differs only in degree from the less vivid imagery common to most individuals. Boys and girls, both bright and dull, adjusted and unadjusted, may experience the phenomenon of imaginary companions.

The Utility of Imagination. Make-believe and imagination are believed to perform several useful functions. In the case of well-adjusted children such experiences may satisfy a flair for inventiveness, provide them with opportunities to work out ideational solutions to problems, to picture objects not present to the senses, to take imaginary trips involving places of interest, and to enjoy fanciful fairy tales or myths. Play experiences with dolls, pictures, and other playthings have been

[61] M. Svendsen, "Children's Imaginary Companions," *Archives of Neurology and Psychiatry*, Vol. 32, No. 5 (1934), pp. 985-999. Also Elizabeth B. Hurlock and W. Burstein, "The Imaginary Playmate: A Questionnaire Study," *Journal of Genetic Psychology*, 41: 380-392 (1932).

used as a means of release, usually in disguised form, of pent-up stresses (play therapy), and as avenues for the expression of interests and desires which are not so readily detectable in interviews or conversations.[62] Unhappy children can utilize imagination as a mechanism of escape from frustration, loneliness, fear, and insecurity. Air-castles and forms of autistic thinking offer such relief and are beneficial if not made an end in themselves. Lonely children can atone for their plight by conjuring up imaginary friends. Fearful and otherwise insecure children can have access to the things they long for through wishful phantasy. Although children are happier when conditions enable them to adjust to real situations and people, they can gain vicarious satisfactions in the kindlier world of imagination.

Psychologists have in the main tended to emphasize the more pernicious aspects of phantasy in child life. However, some have pointed out the possibility that its negative adjustment values may be great. In a study of 81 non-psychotic children with behavior disorders, Bender and Lipkowitz [63] concluded that, even where nocturnal dreams, daydreams, illusory experiences in connection with waking and falling asleep, and auditory and visual hallucinations are in evidence, childhood phantasying is a normal process in the development of personality. The investigators believe that the more hallucinatory phantasies indicate "unsatisfactory relationships since infancy between the child and its parents, which may be further increased by greater needs in a constitutionally or organically inferior child, and finally released by a completely unsatisfactory reality. They are the child's effort to bridge the discrepancy and to experience a satisfying reality."

Summary and Implications

The young child's concepts of people, animals, and the material objects in his environment are invariably vague and general. It is only with experience that he comes to particularize

[62] See Lois B. Murphy and R. Horowitz, "Projective Methods in the Psychological Study of Children," *Journal of Experimental Education,* 7 : 133-140 (1938) ; and Lawrence K. Frank, "Projective Methods for the Study of Personality," *Journal of Psychology,* 8 : 389-413 (1939).

[63] L. Bender and H. H. Lipkowitz, "Hallucinations in Children," *American Journal of Orthopsychiatry,* 10 : 471-491 (1940).

his concepts and to interpret the meanings of situations in ways that are intelligible to his more mature elders. The information possessed by young children is relatively meager, and their beliefs, though reflective of parental teachings, are as a rule immature and naive. They have little conception of time, space, distance, weight, number, size, and form. However, with experience and instruction the child becomes increasingly more able to grapple with abstract concepts and to understand the meaning of events which take place about him. As he makes contacts with the larger world the developing child learns to comprehend the nature of physical causation and to think through the involvements of problematic situations. Inconsistency gradually gives way to the dictates of logic and, insofar as the individual has the opportunity of profiting by educational advantages, rationality supersedes credulity.

Children develop the ability very early in life to use their imagination and to engage in make-believe activities. Such phantasies apparently serve the dual purpose of enabling the child to explore and organize his world intellectually and to escape the emotional stresses of frustration. The channel of make-believe enables the child to enjoy vicariously a range of stimulating experiences which completely transcend the limitations of reality. As a retreat from defeat and futility, daydreaming may serve mental hygiene purposes. It is, of course, obvious that when made an end in itself and a continuous refuge from reality, the phantasy mechanism leads the child farther from concrete adjustment.

Parents and others can do much to develop an open-minded attitude and to point out the advantages of reasoning from cause to effect instead of in terms of wishful thinking. The child can be taught to be doubtful of superstitions and magical declarations, and to recognize the difference between actual physical phenomena and what is commonly called "bunk." The school can aid in the child's intellectual development by taking care that the problems and activities required of him are commensurate with his background of experience and ability. Teachers often take for granted a degree of maturity and understanding on the part of their pupils that does not exist, and thus present concepts and problems which cannot effectively be grasped. It is becoming an increasingly important function of the school to adapt educational materials to the maturation levels of its pupils.

Teachers can also promote the development of rational thinking in children by assisting them in increasing their fund of information, encouraging them to question rather than accept authoritative statements, enabling them to do things concretely, showing them various ways of solving problems, teaching them important generalizations that have wide transfer value, and by assigning them intriguing problems rather than arbitrary and meaningless tasks. These and similar methods of stimulating intellectual curiosity can contribute much to the child's understanding of his world.

QUESTIONS FOR DISCUSSION

1. What are the steps by which the child comes to gain meaning from his experiences? To what extent could such meanings develop if the child experienced few contacts other than those with his mother and father?

2. If children are expected to learn from "doing," what is the value of perceptual development? How far would the child get in adjusting to his environment if he had a limited stock of meanings? What dangers might he encounter under such circumstances?

3. Support the position that sensory defects do not represent as serious handicaps as was formerly supposed in the acquiring of meaning from experience. What are some of the substitute ways in which a child could acquire meaningful concepts and understandings?

4. Explain the statement "words mean only what they represent in our experience." What does this statement have to do with the individual nature of meaning? Does this indicate that children cannot profit by the experience of others? Elaborate on your answers.

5. What role can the emotions be said to play in the acquisition of meanings? Explain how experiences are interpreted in terms of their effects on a child's feelings or emotions. To

what degree do feelings outweigh reason in the determination of whom a child will and will not like? Explain.

6. How can it be said that children's conceptual development is reflected in their drawings? In their questions? Show how children project their concepts in these and other expressive activities. Suggest whether more use should be made of such avenues of expression.

7. Could appropriate teaching enable mentally normal children to master space perception, number concepts, time perception, and weight discrimination earlier than they customarily do? Suggest how this might be done. Of what value would such precocity be to the child?

8. Give examples other than those in the text of the immature nature of children's beliefs. What factors, exclusive of subnormal intelligence, could account for such naivety? Is it possible that apparently low intelligence here might be accounted for by the absence of opportunity?

9. What is meant by the expression "egocentric reasoning"? Why do investigators disagree as to when a child is egocentric in his speech? Is it possible that young children may appear to be autistic verbally when they are actually trying to be social? Explain.

10. Is the child's tendency to engage in imaginary experiences more harmful than helpful to him? What are the *pros* and *cons* of this question? What need does an imaginary playmate fill in the life of a child who has understanding parents? Elaborate.

Recommended Readings

Dewey, John. *How We Think*. Boston: D. C. Heath & Co., 1933.

Gates, Arthur I., Jersild, Arthur T., McConnell, T. R., and Challman, Robert C. *Educational Psychology*. New York: The Macmillan Co., 1942, Ch. 6.

Griffiths, Ruth. *The Study of Imagination in Early Childhood and Its Function in Mental Development*. London: Kegan Paul, 1935.

Hurlock, Elizabeth B. *Child Development*. New York: McGraw-Hill Book Co., Inc., 1942, Ch. 11.

Isaacs, Susan. *Intellectual Growth in Young Children*. New York: Harcourt, Brace & Co., 1930.

Jersild, Arthur T. *Child Psychology*. New York: Prentice-Hall, Inc., 1940, Chs. 11, 12.

Markey, Frances V. *Imaginative Behavior in Preschool Children*. Child Development Monographs, Teachers College, Columbia Univ., No. 18 (1935).

Piaget, Jean. *The Language and Thought of the Child.* New York: Harcourt, Brace & Co., 1926.

Piaget, Jean. *Judgment and Reasoning in the Child.* New York: Harcourt, Brace & Co., 1928.

Piaget, Jean. *The Child's Conception of the World.* New York: Harcourt, Brace & Co., 1929.

Salisbury, Frank S. *Human Development and Learning.* New York: McGraw-Hill Book Co., Inc., 1939, Ch. 9.

Werner, H. *Comparative Psychology of Mental Development.* (Trans. by E. B. Garside.) New York: Harper & Bros., 1940.

CHAPTER 13

THE SOCIAL EDUCATION OF THE CHILD

THE CHILD IS ORIGINALLY CONCERNED about himself. His first concepts are about his own body and his own movements. As early as the fourth or fifth month he sucks his thumb or fingers, pulls his hair, ears, and nose, and may take delight in observing his actions in a mirror. All children are deeply concerned about their own comfort and, as brought out in an earlier chapter, strive to satisfy, or get others to satisfy, their organic and psychological needs. The child is not, at birth, a social being. Education and development must thus take the direction of progressive social orientation to the end that the growing boy or girl become sociocentric rather than egocentric in outlook and behavior.

Modern society is highly organized and consequently requires a well developed social consciousness on the part of each of its members. There are today few isolated districts and few instances in which individuals can escape civic duties and social responsibilities. Twentieth-century parents and teachers are called upon as never before to guide their children in the direction of adequate social adjustment and facility in dealing harmoniously with associates. It is therefore clear that the social development of the child is a matter of considerable moment both to himself and to society.

The Function of Social Behavior

The social education of a child does not begin when he approaches adolescence or even when he enters school. By the time he reaches school age, any child has developed definite social interests and a favorable or unfavorable attitude toward those from whom he must secure many of his satisfactions. Whether or not he is able to make adequate social adjustments

will depend to a considerable extent upon the degree to which
his fundamental needs have been met in an atmosphere of security and affection. To be socially disposed a child must first
be made to feel that his elders think well of him. The emotional and social development of a child is thus contingent upon
the treatment he receives in the inner circles of his home and
later by those upon whom he is in any way dependent.

The Significance of Social Action.—The child is dependent
for his very existence upon the society into which he is born, and
eventually develops a pattern of personality that is in many
respects a product of its mores and folkways. At no time is
his social development free from the influences exerted by the
members of his family, by his associates, and by the larger
society of which he is a part. The child's great plasticity and
prolonged dependence make him a natural object of educational
efforts, and he is consequently at the mercy of a variety of
social forces. His development is molded, in part at least, by
the type of organized social life espoused by his immediate family and cultural group.

Only certain types of animals choose to live alone. Man has
discovered that he achieves his greatest satisfactions and secures himself most adequately against both the elements and
his enemies through the avenue of social living. Mankind has,
thus, reaped the benefits of sociality. He has learned to enjoy the company of his fellows and to appreciate the sense of
"belonging" that fellowship with them provides. Human beings do not thrive in isolation. As Bacon once wrote, "Whoso-
ever is delighted with solitude is either a wild beast or a God."
It is through social experience, regulated by his larger group,
that the child acquires the characteristics of civilized living.
Only the human individual acquires cultured manners and
morals, communicates by verbal language, adorns himself with
clothes, establishes governments for the protection of the common good, lives as a regular member of a family, and espouses
a religion. Unlike animals, the child is inducted into these and
other social institutions, all of which contribute to his development and to his sense of social responsibility. Acceptable social

behavior is patterned on racial experience and is the child's most direct avenue to satisfaction of his need for the approval of his fellows, a dynamic need which is itself the product of group living.

Even if he were not dependent upon his elders for physical survival, the child would still need the cultural heritage which they provide. Without human customs and practices, he would be forced to live as do the animals. He would be required to utilize cries in place of language, to go without clothing, to subsist on raw foods, to contend with wild beasts in primitive surroundings; in short, to live as a savage without benefit of human inventions and devices. The few so-called "wolf-children" who are known to have lived in some such fashion seem almost unbelievable to most humans, but their plight illustrates the condition that must of necessity obtain when no opportunity is provided for social development under civilized circumstances. Human qualities are dependent upon human associations. Social living is thus the *sine qua non* of human development, the avenue through which the child makes his contributions to his associates and receives in return a morale-building sense of personal worth.

The Nature of Social Responses.—Although he is individualistic at birth, the child is born into a social world in which his welfare is dependent upon others and in which he cannot for long remain non-social. The process by which he develops a social consciousness is apparently based, first of all, upon physiological factors and the attitudes of those who minister to his bodily needs. "When he is talked to, smiled at, fed, kept warm, petted, and cuddled he becomes sensitive to social stimulation and soon learns to detect the nature and meaning of the activities of those about him. As he grows from infancy to childhood, his interpretation of the activities of others becomes more clearly defined and differentiated. The infant does not remain passive in a world of social stimulation; he begins to make responses of his own. An examination of these early activities will show that they are made in response to stimulation involved in feeding and other types of bodily care. The beginning of social behavior, therefore, is an outgrowth of responses relating to the care and satisfaction of bodily needs." [1] As this author adds, the simple reactions which the infant originally makes to bodily satisfactions soon become socialized in the sense that they are made at the sight of the persons associated with such care.

Although meager at first, the child's social responses may, under conditions marked by proper attention, develop at a fairly rapid rate. Even the infant smiles and laughs, and seeks the company of those who contribute to his well-being. With development, the typical child comes to enjoy playing with friendly children, occasionally to offer sympathy and helpfulness to those in distress, to express loyalty to members of his group, and to seek the approval and response of an ever widening circle of acquaintances. Normally, the child's social development follows a sequence which leads eventually to social maturity.

It should not be supposed, however, that children are born with a social sense which makes it natural for them to get along well with others at increasingly higher levels of adjustment. Children must learn to make social adjustments, an ability which is aided by affectionate treatment in the home and opportunities to associate with a variety of individuals under friendly circumstances. Adequate social development requires the planning of conditions conducive to unselfish behavior on the part of the child, and social contacts with individuals who are sufficiently mature to guide behavior in desirable ways. It is apparently not possible to predict social development without taking into consideration the conditions under which the child is called upon to make his adjustments. Bühler's [2] contention that the social attitudes of infants are dependent upon a primary disposition and not upon given environmental circumstances can hardly be accepted in the light of evidence now available in this area of child development. Such a point of view infers that social growth is independent of home conditions, the presence

[1] Wendell W. Cruze, *Educational Psychology,* New York, The Ronald Press Co., 1942, p. 165.

[2] Charlotte Bühler, "The Social Behavior of Children," in *Handbook of Child Psychology* (edited by Carl Murchison), Worcester, Clark Univ. Press, 1933, Ch. 9.

of siblings, community contacts, and other such socially influential forces.

Levels of Social Development.—Social development involves increasing mutuality in relations with associates. The truly social individual is one who not only enjoys the *presence* of other persons but who prefers to *do* things with them and for them. Social behavior is thus richer in meaning than mere passive ability to get along with people with a minimum of friction—it takes the form of sincere appreciation of the needs, attitudes, interests, and worth of those with whom the child is called upon to associate. Such a social outlook usually has its genesis in early childhood. It could probably be said that social growth progresses from (1) a level on which the child is essentially egocentric socially, and in which he is characteristically self-assertive, quick to protect his own interests, and somewhat negativistic, to (2) a level on which he merely avoids injuring others, refrains from harming their property, and endeavors to avert open conflicts, to (3) a level on which he tolerates other persons' views, conforms to their wishes, becomes obedient to elders, and joins in gregarious activities, to (4) a state of development marked by mutual cooperation, consideration for the rights of others, interest in social betterment movements, social skills designed to promote harmonious relationships, and a democratic respect for individual personalities. The socially mature person understands people's basic needs and realizes that their behavior is designed to affect some form of needed adjustment. He thus deals with people and their needs instead of with so-called principles or conventions.

The Social Responses of Children

A discussion of the social responses of young children necessitates the presentation of several related aspects of social growth. These may be listed for convenience as including: (1) early social perception, (2) overt responses to social stimuli, (3) the development of social traits, and (4) the measurement of social growth. Since considerably more research material than could be presented here is available in some of these areas, an effort has been made to select that which appears to be most pertinent and useful.

The Social Perception of Infants.—Social perception connotes the ability to ascertain other people's attitudes and emotional responses from observation of their behavior and facial expressions. An individual possessing keen social perception can often make a fair estimate of the personality qualities of a new acquaintance on the basis of these and other clues (mannerisms, voice, carriage, etc.) which have become associated in his experience with such characteristics. As he develops this ability, the child becomes increasingly capable of making adequate social adjustments and of adapting his behavior to the expectations of his associates. He also learns to "size up" his parents, teachers, and friends in their varying moods, and to plan the strategy by which to get what he wants from them. Children's social errors and tactless remarks can often be ascribed to their limited experience and consequent immature social perception.

The ability to perceive the attitudes of their elders from the tone of their voices and other personal clues develops early in infants. They apparently first learn to distinguish the voices and looks of persons whom they see frequently. Later the typical child comes to differentiate among friendly, angry, and frightened voices, and to recognize the difference between animal and human vocalizations. From the ability to differentiate the human voice from other sounds at the age of one month, the average infant progresses to smiling and laughing at various people at two months, to distinguishing among familiar persons and strangers at three months, and to responding to facial expressions at six months. Karl Bühler [3] has noted, however, that the child of three months is not able to differentiate between adult expressions of friendliness and anger, and that he may smile at either of these forms of stimuli. It is not until the fifth month that the child reacts negatively to an angry expression. It is Bühler's belief that he may even then be re-

[3] Karl Bühler, *The Mental Development of the Child*, New York, Harcourt, Brace & Co., 1930, p. 160.

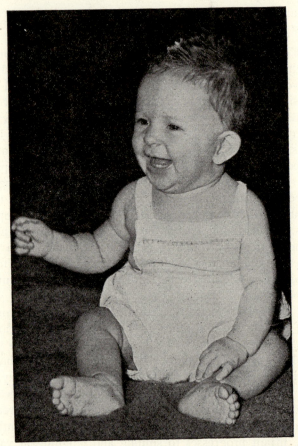

Figure 84. Social Response (smile) of a Six-Months-Old Infant

sponding to differential facial expressions without in any way understanding them. Not until the age of eight months will the average child endeavor to retreat from an angry face or hold out his arms and come toward a stranger who smiles at him.

In an experimental study of the ability of children ranging in age from three to fourteen years to interpret facial expressions, Gates [4] confronted them with photographs of an actress

[4] G. S. Gates, "An Experimental Study of the Growth of Social Perception," *Journal of Educational Psychology*, 14 : 449-461 (1923).

whose expressions were designed to exemplify joy, anger, fear, scorn, surprise, and pain. The children's responses, which were checked against those of a college class in psychology, showed that the order of difficulty of interpretation was from scorn to surprise, to fear, to anger, to pain, to laughter. Laughter was correctly identified by over 70 per cent of the kindergarten age children, but less than half were successful with pain, anger, and fear. Surprise and scorn were not understood by any of the younger children. More than half of the experimental children could identify anger at the age of seven, fear at the age of ten, and surprise at the age of eleven. It was also found that at the younger ages girls tend to be superior to boys in social perception, and that children from the higher social brackets are slightly superior to others in the same respect. It is likely that better showings than these would have been in evidence had the children been asked to identify the emotions of close acquaintances.

Early Overt Social Responses.—Social behavior is said to begin when the infant makes different responses to persons than he does to inanimate objects. The course of such development through the first two years has been delineated by several investigators. Gesell and Thompson,[5] for example, have observed the percentage of children (in their group) exhibiting certain social responses at successive ages. As Table 32 reveals, children differ markedly in time of appearance of the social behavior items listed. Some know their mother at four weeks whereas others are delayed in such response until the twelfth or sixteenth week. Certain children manage to attract attention at thirty-two weeks, while others are unable to do so until the fifty-second week. Playing peek-a-boo apparently follows an uneven course, so far as percentages of children accomplishing it is concerned. These investigators also found that the infant tends to be more alert when smiling at the eighth week, and that well-defined social excitement of a pleasurable variety is in evidence by the end of the third month.

---

[5] Arnold Gesell and H. Thompson, *Infant Behavior: Its Genesis and Growth,* New York, McGraw-Hill Book Co., Inc., 1934.

TABLE 32. TEMPORAL ORDER OF APPEARANCE OF SOCIAL BEHAVIOR ITEMS IN BABIES

Behavior Items	Babies' Ages in Weeks														
	4	6	8	12	16	20	24	28	32	36	40	44	48	52	56
	Percentage of Babies Showing Response at Given Age														
Responds to smiling and talking	8	62	63	—	—										
Visually pursues moving person	12	69	74	—	—										
Knows mother	3	21	39	81	92										
Sobers at strangers	0	3	4	35	56										
Turns head on sound of voice	0	3	26	42	50	100									
Accepts strangers	100	100	100	100	80	61	52	59	41	39	39	26	18	18	14
Withdraws from strangers				0	19	8	24	16	47	42	19	48	44	30	9
Adjusts to words					0	8	12	16	47	68	75	94	82	89	73
Responds to "bye-bye"					0	3	3	3	13	35	53	65	38	59	27
Adjusts to commands					0	0	0	3	22	23	31	55	56	73	50
Responds to inhibitory words					0	0	0	8	25	23	28	45	44	52	23
Responds to "So big"					0	0	0	0	6	7	8	8	18	34	—
Elicits attention					0	0		0	9	16	14	26	27	53	50
Plays pat-a-cake							3	6	19	23	25	42	27	50	9
Plays peek-a-boo						6	6	0	9	13	11	13	9	25	9

(From Arnold Gesell and H. Thompson, *Infant Behavior: Its Genesis and Growth*, New York, McGraw-Hill Book Co., Inc., 1934, p. 258.)

Studies of children's first social responses to adults have also been made by Bridges,[6] C. Bühler,[7] Shirley,[8] Washburn,[9] and others. Recognizing that the infant's first social contacts are usually with adults, these investigators have endeavored to ascertain the characteristic forms of social behavior that may be expected to appear in a typical infant. According to Bühler's [10] observations, such development proceeds as presented in Table 33. From this and other such lists it is possible to secure a fair

TABLE 33. RESPONSES OF INFANTS TO ADULTS, OBSERVED IN 60 PER CENT OR MORE OF THE CASES

	Age in Months
Returns glance of adult with smiling	1 to 2
Is quieted by touching	1 to 2
Cries when adult who was attending him leaves	2 to 3
Smiles back at adult	2 to 3
Disturbed when approached	2 to 3
Returns approaching glance with "lalling"	3 to 4
Displeasure when loses glance of adult	3 to 4
Quieted by caressing	4 to 5
Disturbed by the sight of people	4 to 5
Striving for attention by "lalling"	7 to 8
Stretches out hands toward adults	7 to 8
Cries when adult stops talking	7 to 8
Strives for attention by movements	8 to 9
Pulls on the clothes of adult	9 to 10
Offers adult an object	9 to 10
Imitates movements of adult with a plaything	9 to 10
Organized play activity	10 to 11

(From Charlotte Bühler, *Proceedings and Papers of the Ninth International Congress of Psychology*, 1929, pp. 99-102.)

idea of the young child's social development in relation to adults. The infant will respond to the human voice by the first month

[6] K. M. B. Bridges, "A Study of Social Development in Early Infancy," *Child Development*, 4 : 36-49 (1933).

[7] Charlotte Bühler, *The First Year of Life,* New York, John Day Co., Inc., 1930.

[8] Mary M. Shirley, *The First Two Years,* Vol. II : *Intellectual Development,* Minneapolis, Univ. of Minnesota Press, 1933.

[9] Ruth W. Washburn, "A Scheme for Grading the Reactions of Children in a New Social Situation," *Journal of Genetic Psychology,* 40 : 84-99 (1932).

[10] Charlotte Bühler, *Proceedings and Papers of the Ninth International Congress of Psychology,* 1929, pp. 99-102. For a summary of investigations of social growth in childhood see Ruth E. Arrington, "Time Sampling in Studies of Social Behavior," *Psychological Bulletin,* 40 : 81-124 (1943).

and will often stop crying at his mother's approach, and smile in response to social stimulation during the second month. By the third month the average infant may be diverted from crying by his mother's voice or by a rattle. He may also learn that crying brings attention and thus begin to dominate his elders. In the fourth month the developing child will make anticipatory movements to being picked up and will readily show delight at being otherwise attended to. The fifth or sixth month usually brings the ability to distinguish between scolding and expressions of approval. During the eighth month the infant may endeavor to repeat words spoken by others, and by the twelfth month responds to minor commands.

The responses of young children to other children have been observed by Bridges [11] and by Bühler.[12] The latter investigator has listed these as shown in Table 34. In general, it can be said

TABLE 34. RESPONSES OF INFANTS TO OTHER INFANTS, OBSERVED IN 60 PER CENT OR MORE OF THE CASES

	Age in Months
Observes other child	4 to 5
Smiles at other child	4 to 5
Cries if other child receives attention	8 to 9
Offers toy to other child	8 to 9
"Lalls" to other child	8 to 9
Imitates movements of another child	9 to 10
Opposes toy being taken away	9 to 10
Organized play activity	10 to 11
Strives for attention by means of "lalling"	10 to 11
Ill-humor if another child moves away	10 to 11
Setting aside toy and turning toward another child	11 to 12

(From Charlotte Bühler, *op. cit.*)

that the child is usually four or five months of age before he notices other children or shows an interest in their cries. Such contacts as he may initiate before the ninth or tenth month include smiling, grasping the other child's clothing or playthings, and possibly offering him a toy. It is not until the

11 K. M. B. Bridges, *op. cit.*
12 Charlotte Bühler, *op. cit.*

tenth or twelfth month that signs of cooperation and the social use of materials begin to appear. Fighting and crying when a toy is taken away may also characterize this age. A study [13] in which pairs of similar aged children were placed together for short periods of time corroborated previous findings that little social interchange occurs between infants before the ninth month. Between the ages of nine and fourteen months the children continued to give more attention to play materials than to one another. Following this age social responses came more into evidence until by the age of twenty-five months responses of a friendly and cooperative nature predominated over those of a more negative (pushing, fighting, hitting, etc.) variety. Preferences for individual children had also developed by this age.

The second year of a child's life brings in its wake increased interest in social responses. Play materials become less intriguing than playmates. By about the middle of this year fighting over toys tends to be replaced by cooperation in their use. Although much of the two-year-old child's play is of a parallel nature—close proximity but little social interchange—he soon comes to prefer play with other children. By the end of the second year most children have learned to cooperate in the use of playthings, to adjust their activities in harmony with those of playmates, and to enjoy simple games. As Bridges' [14] researches have revealed, children of this age can on occasions cooperate in group play and in following instructions given by their supervisors.

THE SOCIAL BEHAVIOR OF PRESCHOOL CHILDREN. As the child outgrows infancy and enters the preschool years his social outlook develops in keeping with other forms of progress. He now engages more frequently in group projects with his playmates, and may exhibit both aggressive and sympathetic behavior in connection with them. As Murphy's [15] study of sym-

---

[13] M. Maudry and M. Nekula, "Social Relations Between Children of the Same Age During the First Two Years of Life," *Journal of Genetic Psychology*, 54: 193-215 (1939).

[14] K. M. B. Bridges, *Social and Emotional Development of the Pre-school Child*, London, Kegan Paul, 1931.

[15] Lois B. Murphy, *Social Behavior and Child Personality*, New York, Columbia Univ. Press, 1937.

pathy behavior has shown, children develop individual personality patterns in these and other respects. Some children tend, for example, to be sympathetic without being aggressive, whereas others become predominantly aggressive.

Social conflicts varying from mild verbal duels and physical interference to quarrels and vigorous fighting are also in evidence among preschool children. Such conflicts vary with play

Figure 85. Helping

The older sister holds the tricycle while the younger climbs to the seat, then pulls the tricycle forward.
(From Margaret B. McFarland, *Relationships Between Young Sisters as Revealed in Their Overt Responses,* New York, Teachers College, Columbia Univ., 1938, p. 146.)

facilities, being greatest where play space is restricted. In a study of such conflicts, Jersild and Markey [16] found the greatest amount of quarreling and aggressive behavior in a nursery school located on the roof of a building where play facilities were limited. The least amount of social conflict was in evidence in a school possessing a large outdoor playground. The investigators classed the factors precipitating conflicts into (1) overt or verbal aggressions against another's material posses-

[16] Arthur T. Jersild and Frances V. Markey, *Conflicts Between Preschool Children,* Child Development Monographs, No. 21 (1935).

sions, space, or play activities and (2) aggressions against the person of another, and noted that the first named occurred twice as frequently as the latter. Arbitrary attempts to settle conflicts were found to be ineffective, since the removal of adult imposed restraints resulted in the greatest increase in friction in the case of children who had been most persistently and deliberately interfered with.

The social interactions of young sisters ranging in age from approximately one to six years has been investigated by Mc-

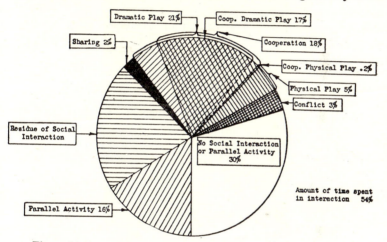

Figure 86. Social Interchange of Young Sisters—Ruth and Marie
(Based upon percentages of the total amount of observed time)
(From Margaret B. McFarland, *op. cit.*, p. 183.)

Farland.[17] This author found in substance that, although the sisters participated in considerable social interchange and behaved sympathetically toward each other more frequently than do unrelated children, signals of distress aroused a helpful response in only a small proportion of instances. Older sisters displayed affectionate responses to younger sisters three times as frequently as was the case the other way around. In general, the responses of the sisters depended upon their physical condition, the presence of other children and adults, the kind of

[17] Margaret B. McFarland, *Relationships Between Young Sisters as Revealed in Their Overt Responses,* New York, Teachers College, Columbia Univ., 1938.

material with which they were playing, and the attitude held by one child toward the other.

APPRAISALS OF SOCIAL DEVELOPMENT. Research relating to the social development of preschool children has been facilitated by the use of social behavior rating scales which, although not qualifying as accurate quantitative measuring devices, have been useful in charting social growth. Such a catalog of social behavior traits has been devised and utilized in the study of children by Berne.[18] A sampling of the thirty items (with definitions) of the scale, which were secured from daily observations over a period of three months of preschool children ranging in age from fifteen months to fifty-nine months, includes the following:

1. Obeys: Is submissive to authority; submissive to restraint or command.
2. Seeks approbation: Desires commendation, notice, sanction.
3. Interested in the group: Has attention engaged by the group.
4. Depends on adult: Depends on adult to provide activities for him; is unable to provide own activity.
5. Affectionate: Loves; has tenderness, fondness.
6. Cooperates: Works or plays with others; works or plays jointly.
7. Respects others' property rights: Respects another child's right to a possession.
8. Participates: Contributes to the social development of the room; participates and is responsible for social organization, i.e., the making or carrying out of rules.
9. Sympathizes: Is affected by emotion another feels: e.g., feels sad with another child; attempts to cheer him; feels glad with another; laughs with him, etc.
10. Understands own property rights: Knows his right to a possession he has brought to school, or his right to play with something in his possession when another child wants it.

[18] Esther V. C. Berne, "An Experimental Investigation of Social Behavior Patterns in Young Children," *Univ. of Iowa Studies in Child Welfare*, Vol. 4, No. 3 (1930).

11. Sociable: Is companionable, conversable, communicative; is fond of mingling or talking with others.
12. Kind: Is disposed to do good and confer happiness; is benevolent, well-disposed.

A rating of 82 preschool children by fifteen experienced observers with this scale resulted in a coefficient of agreement of .74, and the determination of statistically significant differences among children in some of the age groups. Three- and four-year-old children excelled the two-year-olds in sociability, rivalry, understanding of own property rights, jealousy, responsibility for self, responsibility for others, social conformance, and criticism. Cooperation was more noticeable among the four-year-olds than in the case of two- and three-year-old children. As might be expected, girls exceeded boys in maternal attitude. Berne reports that a number of experimentally induced social responses (obedience, cooperation, etc.) correlated fairly highly with the ratings.

A social development scale resembling somewhat the one by Berne has been devised and used as a research method for the study of children's social behavior by Bridges.[19] The scale is designed for the rating of children two to five years of age, and consists of two sections dealing with relations with other children and with adults, respectively. The content of the scale is indicated by the following thirty items touching relations with other children.

The child has or has not:
1. Played with another child.
2. Spoke to another child.
3. Occasionally made social contact by touching or pushing a child.
4. Imitated other children's actions.
5. Imitated children's words.
6. Imitated children's laughter.
*7. Often spoken to other children.
*8. Originated new play activity with another child.
*9. Joined group of children in play.
*10. Sought another child's approval.
*11. Asked another child for help.

19 K. M. B. Bridges, *op. cit.*

*12. Always given up toys at fair request.
 13. Usually waited turn.
 14. Tried to defend own right to materials or place.
*15. Pointed to others' errors.
*16. Tried to help others.
*17. Stopped work to aid another child.
*18. Comforted another in distress.

The child has not or has:

 19. Turned away to avoid another child's friendly advances.
*20. Usually stayed out of group marching or games.
*21. Claimed others' toys.
*22. Interfered with others' work.
 23. Destroyed others' work.
*24. Created disorder in group or led others into mischief.
*25. Frequently pulled or pushed others.
 26. Frequently complained of others to adult for own gain.
 27. Harassed new child by scoffing or shunning.
 28. Hit or pinched others for fun several times.
 29. Bitten or spit at others for fun.
 30. Teased in other ways causing irritation or discomfort.

✳ Items marked with an asterisk are those which proved to be most significant.

Judging from Bridges' scale, as the child matures during the preschool years he develops more socially desirable patterns of behavior in relations with his playmates. It can be seen that these include playing with another child, speaking to other children, giving up toys when requested, waiting his own turn, trying to help others, and comforting another in distress. Development in the avoidance of negative responses includes not claiming others' toys, not interfering with another's work, not hitting or pushing others, not tattling on others, and not causing others unnecessary discomfort. The child does not make continual improvement along these lines but, if properly guided, comes gradually to adopt and continue approved social responses. Several studies [20] have shown that social development is facilitated by attendance at nursery school. Such experience makes

20 See, for example, Helena Malley, "Growth in Social Behavior and Mental Activity after Six Months in Nursery School," Child Development, 6: 303-309 (1935). Also Arthur T. Jersild and Mary D. Fite, The Influence of Nursery School Experience on Children's Social Adjustments, Child Development Monographs, No. 25 (1939).

children more sociable as measured by the number of constructive social contacts which they make. This growth is no doubt due to the social environment and competent social guidance provided by the school.

The Development of Social Traits.—The infant is potentially capable of a wide variety of feelings and actions in relation to people, some of which are positive and desirable, others negative and antisocial. Under certain conditions he may be stimulated to smile, coo, cuddle, and pat another with his hands, whereas other situations may bring about crying, hitting, pushing, and biting. Whether these and similar tendencies are implicit in the child's constitution is a moot question but nevertheless a doubtful one. An infant may be born with physical weaknesses and glandular imbalance (often of a congenital nature), and thus possibly be disposed toward negative behavior, but it is not widely believed that specific forms of social action are germinally inherited. It is more likely that social traits or attitudes are developed as a function of types of social experience encountered, especially as these influence the child's fundamental need for acceptance and a sense of having status.

SYMPATHY. The development of a social trait (the nature of which will be discussed in a later chapter) is well illustrated in the area of sympathetic behavior. It is believed that the foundations of sympathetic action are laid in early home life in instances where the young child is well cared for physically and made to feel secure in the affection of his parents. Such a sympathetic family background is apparently conducive to the expression of helpful feelings toward another individual who may be hurt or otherwise in distress.

Experience with pain and being hurt is probably also basic to the development of sympathetic tendencies. Such sensitiveness may in some instances have an organic basis, but it is also explicable in terms of both the behavior of elders and the conditioning process. If the grown-ups around him are gentle and helpful to those in need, the child is likely to introject their behavior patterns, and to become conditioned, for example, to smile when others smile, to pick up articles dropped by others, and to comfort another child who is crying. Unsympathetic adult actions may, by the same token, stifle the beginnings of sympathetic behavior in any child.

In her exploratory study of the roots of sympathy, Murphy [21] found many instances of sympathetic behavior in children of preschool age. Two groups of New York City nursery school pupils were studied over a period of two years on the basis of observations of (1) play-situation behavior, (2) teacher ratings of specific reactions involving sympathy, and (3) experiments designed to elicit sympathetic responses without the child's knowledge of their presence. Expressions of sympathy, which were measured quantitatively in terms of the number made and received in a given period of time, included attempts to remove causes of distress, comforting another child, protecting a distressed person, punishing the apparent cause of the distress, warning another child, asking questions about the cause of the difficulty, suggesting a solution, telling another person about a child's distress, and such less affective reactions as crying or whimpering, frowning with apparent concern, shaking the head, exhibiting an anxious expression, and compression of the lips.

Although marked individual differences in sympathetic behavior were in evidence, Murphy noted that, in general, two- and three-year-old children did not tend to respond sympathetically to black and blue wounds, swellings, lumps, and other minor flesh disturbances which adults recognize as symptoms of discomfort or illness. The children also failed to be concerned about the account of Red Ridinghood being eaten by the wolf, pictures of accidents, funerals, being crippled, or carrying crutches. Children of this age have apparently not developed the discrimination and analytical ability requisite to the recognition of such signs of distress. Three-year-old children did, however, respond generally to such distress signals as bandages, blindness, injuries treated with iodine, red swellings, scars, and scratches. They also appeared sympathetic in situations involving deprivation of toys, food, or of the mother, and to those in which a child was caught in a play-pen or fallen

21 Lois B. Murphy, *op. cit.*

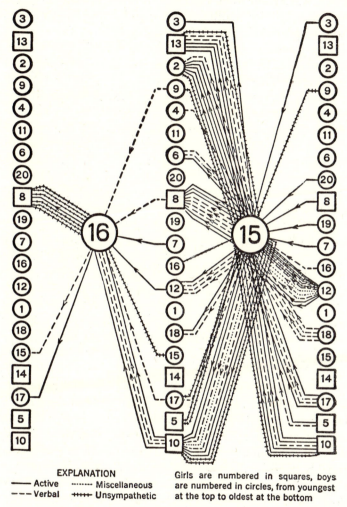

Figure 87. Diagram of Inter-Individual Social Roles in the Group

Reinhardt (16), 48 months, and Patrick (15), 50 Months. Reinhardt's few contacts included a majority of unsympathetic ones ; Patrick is more happily placed in his group and is both recipient and giver of many responses.

(From Lois B. Murphy, *Social Behavior and Child Personality*, New York, Columbia Univ. Press, 1937, p. 139.) Used by permission.

bicycle, was unable to play because of having to stay in bed, was being attacked by another child, was unable to complete an activity undertaken, was injured by a fall, or was crying. A child of this age may, thus, recognize bandages or a flow of blood as signs of distress but be unable to comprehend the import of a swelling.

Murphy endeavored, among other factors, to determine the degree of stability exhibited by her nursery children in the trait of sympathy, and found that, in the main, they responded specifically to distress situations in terms of their import for their own well-being. All correlations between scores made on the playground and those achieved in experimental situations (such, for example, as coming to the rescue of a child who is caught in a play-pen, helping a child who has fallen off a wooden block and is crying, or deciding what to do about a fish that is in danger of being taken out of water) were found to be low. Correlations between teachers' ratings and observed scores were considerably higher. These findings are in essential harmony with McFarland's [22] previously mentioned study of sister pairs in which a child's sympathy behavior depended not so much upon the degree of distress shown by a sister as upon the import of such distress for the child's own safety. A child would, for instance, sympathize with a sister when her difficulty had been caused by someone else, but would fail to display such an attitude when she herself was the instigator of the sister's distress. Murphy's data also showed that, in addition to varying with situations and the child's degree of understanding and background of experience, sympathy behavior may change markedly with time and with changes in attitude. Probably because of an ambivalent social order, in which competition and cooperation are encouraged simultaneously, the development of sympathetic behavior is accompanied by growth in aggressiveness.

COMPETITIVENESS OR AGGRESSION. The behavior of infants during the first few weeks of life is neither competitive nor cooperative. Offspring of this tender age do not comprehend what it means to excel and do not exhibit signs of want-

22 Margaret B. McFarland, *op. cit.*

ing to do or have things that are bigger or better than those of competitors. It is not long, however, until the developing youngster begins to take things from other infants and to exhibit jealousy of one who may be a rival for the affection of his

Figure 88. A Typical Instance of Quarreling in Childhood
(From Lois H. Meek, *Your Child's Development and Guidance Told in Pictures*, Philadelphia, J. B. Lippincott Co., 1940, p. 116.)

parents. With further development may come competition in matters of accomplishment and possession. It is not uncommon to hear two- or three-year-olds insist that "I am bigger," "I am older," or that "My dolly is better." Aggressiveness appears to develop with age in the typical American culture.

Bühler [23] has reported a study of infant competitiveness in which babies were placed in pairs in a crib and in which one of each pair was presented with a toy designed to arouse whatever rivalry could be elicited. Children less than six months of age seemed satisfied to be thus neglected, and merely looked wonderingly when the toys they were given were taken by another child. Although their reactions varied considerably, by the second half-year many of the infants were aggressive in grabbing other's toys or militantly resisted the taking of their own toys. Even at this age some of the children seemed more competitive and sensitive to aggression than others.

A research by Leuba [24] resulted in the finding that in certain play activities children do not exhibit much rivalry concerning accomplishments until after the third year. In this instance children two to six years of age were given the opportunity of playing with a peg board singly and later in pairs in an experimental playroom. According to the conversation and behavior records secured, the two-year-old children displayed little competition, being content to play without showing much interest in the presence of another child. The three-year-olds were only slightly competitive but exhibited more interest in what the other child was doing. Both the idea of excelling and the desire to excel appeared in most of the children between the ages of four and six years.

A somewhat more specific study, conducted by Greenberg [25] at the Psychological Institute of Vienna, was concerned with the competitive behavior of 65 children aged two to seven years as exhibited in experimental play situations. The investigator's technique was to permit pairs of children to play for a time with new building blocks at a table and then to ask of one who had completed something, the question "Which is prettier?" The children were subsequently told to build another structure and to see who could construct the "prettier" or the "bigger." Even this deliberate stimulation did not bring out competi-

23 Charlotte Bühler, "Die Ersten Sozialen Werhaltungs Weisen des Kindes," Quellen und Stud. Zur Jugendkunde, No. 5 (Jena), 1927.
24 C. Leuba, "An Experimental Study of Rivalry in Young Children," Journal of Comparative Psychology, 16 : 367-378 (1933).
25 Pearl J. Greenberg, "Competition in Children: An Experimental Study," American Journal of Psychology, 44 : 221-248 (1932).

tiveness in the two- and three-year-old children, many of whom went on playing with the blocks unmindful of what the other child was doing. These children were evidently too immature to understand the competitive nature of either the situation or the questions asked. Children over four years of age showed an increasing tendency to make favorable remarks about their own accomplishments, and to manifest an interest in the quality of their competitor's products. Greenberg noted that at the older ages, not only competitive remarks, but outright grabbing, hiding of other children's blocks, and quarreling were in evidence. The degree of competitiveness varied greatly, however, from child to child. Some competed but did no grabbing or remarking about quality; others merely played and stated upon request which structures they thought were bigger or prettier. The evidence did not appear to support the postulation of universal competitiveness in young children.

THE ETIOLOGY OF COMPETITIVENESS.   When competitiveness is present in a child who is sufficiently mature to comprehend and experience the stresses of unfavorable comparison, it is believed that his aggressiveness is a product of social situations. A summary of the studies on competition [26] does not lead to the conclusion that it is a native factor in man. Available data suggest, rather, that competitiveness in children represents a more or less specific disposition to behave in ways stimulated by the exigencies of situations. The situations in which a given child will compete vary in terms of their import for his security with those who mean something to him, and on the basis of the extent to which he is deprived of possessions which he prizes. A child may be highly competitive over one issue (such as keeping possession of a doll) and not over another (such as playing with marbles). A child may also exhibit pleasure when a friendly playmate surpasses his achievements in house building with blocks, but become quite aggressive when superseded in the same way by an unfriendly rival.

---

[26] Gardner Murphy, L. B. Murphy, and T. M. Newcomb, *Experimental Social Psychology*, New York, Harper & Bros., 1937, Ch. 8.

A child may under certain circumstances be very cooperative in a competitive situation. As one student of the subject has written, "Under the spur of competition with a visitor or camp-mate, the child may discover that he can put on his shoes in half the time it used to take, stub his toe without crying, jump into the water without cringing, endure a slight without running to mother to complain, exhibit a modicum of sportsmanship, or do homely chores without feeling abused. In such behavior there are many of the elements that are involved in competition, namely, recognizing a level of achievement as exhibited by another and striving to close the gap between this standard and one's accustomed performance, or to surpass the standard." [27]

Anthropologists who have made comparative studies of the aggressiveness of American and European versus more primitive peoples' children are, at least in some instances, of the belief that competitiveness is closely related to the particular culture pattern in which the child develops. Mead,[28] for example, has reported that certain tribes in New Guinea are so gentle and tolerant as to be strikingly non-competitive. Their children develop without a strong desire to excel and are said to be relatively free from either aggressive tendencies or feelings of inferiority. The same is apparently true of certain groups of American Indians and their children. It is thus possible that the relative competitiveness of children reared in Western cultures may be a product of adult influences and the many aggressive social attitudes and customs inherent in their family mores.

Experimental investigations by Jack [29] and by Page,[30] in which children who were backward in aggressiveness were taught to be sufficiently skillful to compete in making designs with blocks and assembling puzzles, indicated that four-year-

[27] Arthur T. Jersild, *Child Psychology,* New York, Prentice-Hall, Inc., 1940, p. 197.

[28] Margaret Mead *et al., Cooperation and Competition Among Primitive Peoples,* New York, McGraw-Hill Book Co., Inc., 1937. See also Ruth Benedict, *Patterns of Culture,* Boston, Houghton Mifflin Co., 1934.

[29] Lois M. Jack, "An Experimental Study of Ascendent Behavior in Preschool Children," *Univ. of Iowa Studies in Child Welfare,* Vol. 9, No. 3 (1934).

[30] Marjorie L. Page, "The Modification of Ascendent Behavior in Preschool Children," *Univ. of Iowa Studies in Child Welfare,* Vol. 12, No. 3 (1936).

old nursery school children can be trained to become more competitive. These and other investigators [31] have concluded that many social phases of personality formerly thought to be implicit in the child's inherited constitution are apparently the fruits of his experience and cultural surroundings. The trait of competitiveness is apparently more modifiable than was formerly thought.

The specificity of response and apparent social genesis obtaining in the case of competitiveness (aggression) probably functions as well in other social trait areas. *Negativism* (stubbornness), with its resistance to adult authority, is in evidence at about the eighteenth month and is believed to reach a peak at about the third year. *Quarreling,* with its grabbing and destruction of toys, crying and screaming, and actual hitting or pushing, is often in the picture before the child has learned to cooperate and when his activities are interfered with by other children. *Bullying,* which is characterized by pinching, poking, pulling hair, kicking, sticking pins into others, etc., is exhibited more by older and larger children than by those whose physical size and immaturity make such antics difficult or unproductive of results. *Jealousy,* as exemplified by children whose security is threatened by the arrival of a new baby or who feel that other children are surpassing them in attainment, may appear very early in life and is present at all ages in instances where the individual feels that his status is usurped by another. In well-regulated homes these attitudes decline, however, in favor of increasing *cooperation* by the fourth or fifth year. This is especially true where the child has opportunities to play with other children.

Social Development in Older Children.—When the developing child reaches school age new and more formidable experiences involving closer adult supervision are encountered. From this point on the problems of belonging and maintaining status become more complicated. As one group of authors [32]

---

[31] Mary D. Fite, *Aggressive Behavior in Young Children and Children's Attitudes toward Aggression,* Genetic Psychology Monographs, Vol. 22, No. 2 (1940), pp. 151-319 ; G. E. Chittenden, *An Experimental Study in Measuring and Modifying Assertive Behavior in Young Children,* Monographs of the Society for Research in Child Development, Vol. 7, No. 1 (1942).

[32] Gardner Murphy, L. B. Murphy, and T. M. Newcomb, *op. cit.,* p. 652.

say, "Entrance into the conventional first grade marks a sharp break in the actual structure of the child's experience. For the first time, in the case of many children, they are expected to conform to a group pattern imposed by an adult who is in charge of too many children to be constantly aware of each child as an individual." While the teacher is endeavoring thus to conventionalize the child, the child may in many cases be trying out the teacher in the sense of hoping to gain favors which are not in the unacceptable (to him) pattern of behavior. This problem, as well as those concerned with the acquiring of a wider circle of friends from whom he can secure approval, occupy much of the child's attention during the elementary school years.

CONFLICTS AMONG OLDER CHILDREN. The amount of conflict with other children engaged in by a given child is commensurate with the extent of his social activities. Such conflict is not, however, indicative of failure to make friends with associates. A research by Green [33] has shown that quarrels are frequently most common among children who are close companions. Indeed, this investigator has commented that "quarreling is a part of friendly, social intercourse at these ages," and that fighting among mutual friends is also more or less common in the case of children of school age. Such aggressive activity may be carried on on a sporting basis (boxing, wrestling, etc.) or it may be an outlet for a self-assertive attitude based on feelings of inadequacy. Some students of child development believe that a moderate amount of fighting assists the child in determining his status with his companions, and that he should not be denied reasonable expression of this attacking form of social development.

Because of the supervision usually exercised in the case of school children's activities, both in and out of the buildings, they are likely to experience fewer altercations than do youngsters of preschool age. Hostility is often in the form of criticisms, making faces, and imitating other children in ways calculated to be irritating. Such teasing and non-overt bullying

[33] E. H. Green, "Friendships and Quarrels Among Preschool Children," *Child Development*, 4: 237-252 (1933).

are no doubt often expressions of maladjustment or failure to gain acceptance through social cooperation.[34] Children may also express their animosity as a group by ignoring a child who has so far refused to cooperate as to be completely outside the pale of their good graces. One study [35] has suggested that conflictful behavior among school children may also be accentuated by excessive adult restraints.

Social conflicts occurring under unsupervised conditions are difficult to observe with accuracy and have thus not been studied with the precision accorded many other phases of child psychology. Investigators (and parents) have noted, nevertheless, that groups of children frequently adopt codes of combat to be used whenever the obstreperous behavior of their temporary enemies calls for fighting. They may throw "clods" or snowballs, threaten to tell a father or mother, sic a dog on an opponent, tattle to the teacher, laugh at another's clothing or physique, or start an out-and-out fist fight. Such conflictful behavior is greatly influenced by the kind of leadership enjoyed by the group and by the code of fighting adopted. Children from the better homes as a rule abide by such sporting codes as picking on someone their own size, warning an "enemy" before striking, and refraining from using dangerous weapons such as stones, sticks, or clubs.

COMPETITION AND COOPERATION. In spite of their interest in group activities, children of elementary school age will as a rule exert themselves more when working for individual honors than when doing something for a group. Although the incentives elicited by various projects differ, Maller [36] found that most children are powerfully motivated by the desire to make a showing for themselves. However, as Hurlock [37] has noted, when rivalry between groups is concerned many children

[34] Ernest G. Osborne, *Camping and Guidance,* New York, Association Press, 1937.

[35] Kurt Lewin, R. Lippitt, and R. White, "Patterns of Aggressive Behavior in Experimentally Created 'Social Climates,'" *Journal of Social Psychology,* 10 : 271-299 (1939).

[36] J. B. Maller, *Cooperation and Competition: An Experimental Study in Motivation,* Teachers College Contributions to Education, No. 384, Columbia Univ., 1929.

[37] Elizabeth B. Hurlock, "The Use of Group Rivalry as an Incentive," *Journal of Abnormal and Social Psychology,* 22 : 278-290 (1927).

will exert themselves as much for "their side" as they will for individual recognition. As many a teacher has discovered, relatively uninteresting school work may be attacked with zest when competition with a rival group is involved. The relative strength of individual versus group rivalry probably varies with individuals, with the nature of the incentive involved, and with the extent to which the child is permitted to work with a group of his own choosing.

To date it has not been possible to test the competitiveness and willingness to cooperate in natural social situations of school children with any degree of accuracy. Such a project would necessitate the measurement of behavior under circumstances where spontaneous cooperation in the form of assistance to friends, the acceptance of mutually beneficial tasks, or the recognition of common needs could be regarded as the natural function of a given situation. It may be that direct observation of this kind would disclose a more decided tendency toward mutuality of behavior than is evident in more limited social situations of an experimental nature. As the matter now stands, it appears that in school children competitive tendencies are stronger than those of a cooperative type. However, children of this age are far from having outgrown the egocentrism associated with immaturity. Whether or not the potentialities for cooperative behavior are as strong as those for competition and aggression, it apparently takes time and intelligently directed social education to bring about a truly sociocentric attitude in children in which personal approval is sought through social channels.

Children's Gang Interests and Activities.—When children reach the age of eight or ten they as a rule develop a more definite sense of group unity. This is the age at which children tend to lose interest in play around the home or with one or two companions. Even family gatherings and adult outings begin to lose their luster. The child is now typically interested in group games and other activities involving association with a number of friends who have common proclivities. The growing boy or girl has now acquired the type of social consciousness known as the "gang age," in which common activities and group loyalty transcend the former subservience to home controls. Thrasher,[38] the author of an extensive study of Chicago childhood gangs, defines the gang as "an interstitial group originally formed spontaneously and then integrated through conflict. It is characterized by the following types of behavior: meeting face to face, milling movement through space as a unit, conflict and planning. The result of this collective behavior is the development of tradition, unreflected internal structure, esprit de corps, solidarity, morale, group awareness and attachment to a local territory."

Gang activities, which were formerly thought to stem from an alleged instinct of gregariousness, are now believed to represent an effort on the part of maturing children to form a society commensurate with their interests and designed to meet their personal and social needs. Gang activities are not, as some have supposed, necessarily antisocial; they are, rather, expressions of cooperative group interests for which adult society has usually made no provision and which children can carry on without the usual adult supervision. To belong to a gang and to be free from restraint for a time contributes both to a child's sense of personal worth and to his need for some autonomy in the regulation of his affairs. It is in his gang, says Thrasher,[39] that a boy acquires a personality (sociologically speaking), and learns to play a social part with reference to all other members of the group. To quote, "In the developing gang he fits into his niche like a block in a puzzlebox; he is formed by the discipline the gang imposes upon him. He cannot be studied intelligently nor understood apart from this social role."

The chief characteristics of gang life are highly social in nature. They include an interest in active, competitive games and sports, a sense of belonging or pride in being accepted as a member, group loyalty as expressed in cooperation with members and an inclination to disdain those who do not belong, a reluctance to mingle with members of the opposite sex, a tendency to adopt picturesque names, and a well-nigh universal

[38] F. M. Thrasher, *The Gang*, Chicago, Univ. of Chicago Press, 1927, p. 57. See also P. H. Furfey, *The Gang Age*, New York, The Macmillan Co., 1926.
[39] F. M. Thrasher, *op. cit.*, p. 329.

proclivity for secrecy concerning gang rules and rituals. As Brown [40] has said, "The group organization itself, rather than the activity, now becomes the motivation. The members may develop a ritual varying in form merely from that of 'running the gauntlet' while each strikes the new member with an improvised paddle, to an elaborate ceremonial with grip, password, and a rather tortuous ordeal. They give a name, often ingenious and descriptive, to this organization: 'The Ravens', 'Pike Streeters', 'The Dirty Dozen', . . . 'The Tigers', and 'Pirates'. Not infrequently they develop an artificial language, have a distinctive mark of clothing, and develop rules for self-government."

Gang headquarters will often be found in a barn, a garage, an old shed, an improvised tree-house, or possibly in a vacant lot. In the case of girls, headquarters are more likely to be in a member's room at home, in a corner drug store, or in some secluded spot in the school. The criterion for location is usually a minimum of likelihood of interference from adults and opportunity for a maximum of secrecy. Decorations may include anything from school pennants and magazine pictures to photographs of movie stars or prizefighters. Such rendezvous are not infrequently furnished with a radio or an old victrola, and may in some instances be equipped with improvised lockers in which members' treasures can be safely hid from prying eyes.

Gang activities are to a considerable extent products of the culture patterns of communities, and may thus be either socially desirable or antisocial in nature. Children who have been reared in an atmosphere of security and affection and who have thus experienced at least a minimum fulfillment of their dynamic needs, will usually tend to engage in socially acceptable gang endeavors. Rejected, neglected, and overaccepted children are likely to engage in antisocial or personally harmful behavior designed to relieve their stresses of inferiority and to create a sense of self-importance. Such gangs not only engage in frequent conflicts with rival organizations, they may align themselves against the law and other agencies of society.

[40] Francis J. Brown, *The Sociology of Childhood*, New York, Prentice-Hall, Inc., 1939, p. 163.

Acceptable gang activities include active sports, exploring the countryside, collecting stamps or other articles, playing card games, organizing socials in the form of picnics, hikes, or parties, reading fiction or adventure, constructing radios or other mechanical devices, and preparing dramatic productions. Undesirable group activities may involve fighting, gambling, stealing, drinking, smoking, annoying unliked people, and various acts of vandalism. A mob spirit may also be engendered under the influence of which boys may participate in unlawful acts which they would not perpetrate singly, but which they feel obligated to carry out when loyalty to the gang is involved. As studies by Hartshorne and May [41] have shown, when under the pressure of maintaining the approval of a group, boys or girls will temporarily abandon their most firmly established codes of behavior.

The Measurement of Social Growth.—Efforts have been made for some time to measure objectively the degree of social maturity attained at a given chronological age level. There has been too great a tendency to assume that a child's social growth will follow closely upon his mental development and that high or low mental test scores are indicative of social development status.

As the studies presented in this chapter have pointed out, many forces of a non-intellectual nature combine to influence a child's outlook and social behavior. The measurement of social development has thus necessitated the construction of scales designed to ascertain growth in social adaptation *per se,* without regard to the subject's mental status, personality adjustment as such, or degree of social success.

An early social development scale designed for children who can read (ages eight to eighteen) is that by Furfey,[42] in which 196 pairs of items representing differential degrees of "developmental age" are presented. One item in each of the pairs indicates a higher level of social maturity than the other. When taking the test, the child is instructed to choose alternatives from

[41] Hugh Hartshorne and Mark A. May, *Studies in the Organization of Character,* New York, The Macmillan Co., 1930, Ch. 12.

[42] P. H. Furfey, "A Revised Scale for Measuring Developmental Age in Boys," *Child Development,* 2: 102-114 (1931).

among such comparative questions as "Would you rather be a cowboy or a banker?" "Would you rather spin tops or take pictures?" and "Would you rather have a wallet or a toy auto?" Raw scores based on the total number of mature responses made may be converted into "developmental age" terms by recourse to the table of norms provided. A coefficient of reliability of .91 indicates that the scale is quite highly consistent.

A more recent social growth scale,[43] in which separate norms for boys and girls aged five to seventeen were determined, showed that social development scores for girls are more advanced than those for boys at all ages, and that the most marked variability in social-sex development in both sexes occurs between the ages of ten and fourteen. The author of these findings has reported further that, as far as social-sex relationships are concerned, "There is at first an undifferentiated social relationship with the opposite sex until about the age of eight years, then a rising preference for children of the same sex, until puberty, when hetero-sexual feelings begin gradually to develop."

Probably the best-known social growth scale, and one which measures social competence from infancy to maturity, is the Vineland Social Maturity Scale by Doll.[44] The Vineland Scale is a standardized instrument patterned after the Stanford-Binet mental scale (except that the responses are not given by the child) in which detailed performances for each age are given in such a way as to show progressive capacity on the part of the child to look after himself and to accept responsibilities leading to ultimate social maturity. The 117 items of the scale are arranged in order of difficulty and are grouped by year norms. They thus represent progressive development in what Doll calls self-help, self-direction, occupation, communication, locomotion, and socialization. Information concerning the social development of a given child, which is to be supplied by indi-

[43] Elise H. Campbell, *The Social-sex Development of Children,* Genetic Psychology Monographs, Vol. 21, No. 4 (1939), pp. 461-552.
[44] E. A. Doll, "A Genetic Scale of Social Maturity," *American Journal of Orthopsychiatry,* 5 : 180-188 (1935). See also, by the same author, "The Vineland Social Maturity Scale," *Training School Bulletin,* No. 3, 1936.

viduals who have observed him over a period of time (from infancy if possible), is used to supplement, rather than substitute for, mental test scores. High reliability, based on repeated examinations with different examiners, and adequate validity, as determined by comparisons with the estimates of individuals familiar with the examinee, have been reported. It is not clear, however, whether the environmental factor was given adequate attention in the establishment of norms.

The author [45] of the Vineland Social Maturity Scale has concluded from experience with its use that "the child is personally dependent in his social activities during the first decade of life. In the second decade of life he moves rapidly toward self-assertion and independent action. In the third decade of life he becomes socially self-sufficient within the limits of group relationships and, through marriage or otherwise, ultimately assumes responsibility for others." Thus is the personal responsibility and social competence of the child appraised in normative terms.

The following sample items from the scale are indicative of its nature:

Year O-I

*C 1. "Crows"; laughs.

SHG 2. Balances head.

SHG 3. Grasps objects within reach.

S 4. Reaches for familiar persons.

Year III-IV

L 45. Walks downstairs one step per tread.

S 46. Plays cooperatively at kindergarten level.

SHD 47. Buttons coat or dress.

O 48. Helps at little household tasks.

* The categorical designations given the various items are indicated by letters as follows:

SHG = self-help general
SHE = self-help eating
SHD = self-help dressing
SD = self-direction

O = occupation
C = communication
L = locomotion
S = socialization

[45] E. A. Doll, "Social Maturation," *Proceedings of the Fifth Institute on the Exceptional Child of the Child Research Clinic of the Woods Schools*, 1938, pp. 31-36.

Year VI-VII

SHE 62. Uses table knife for   SHD 64. Bathes self assisted.
      spreading.
C 63. Uses pencil for writing.   SHD 65. Goes to bed unassisted.

Year X-XI

C 78. Writes occasional short   O 80. Does small remunera-
      letters.   tive work.
C 79. Makes telephone calls.   C 81. Answers ads; purchases
                                         by mail.

Years XV-XVIII

C 90. Communicates by letter.   L 92. Goes to nearby places
                                         alone.
C 91. Follows current events.   SD 93. Goes out unsupervised
                                         in daytime.

The social quotient (S.Q.) yielded by the Vineland scale can be used to determine the probable social competence of children of given intellectual levels. Recognition of the fact that a child's sense of social responsibility is not necessarily commensurate with his intellectual status may aid in guiding him to a better adjustment. Such knowledge can be used to arrange conditions conducive to the child's further social growth. Social participation suitable to his age, intellectual status, and home conditions is essential to the development of competence in the child whose S.Q. is below the norm for his age.

Structures in Social Development

The study of children's friendships has contributed notably to an understanding of their social development. Inquiries in this area of child psychology have tended to take the directions of determining (1) factors associated with the making of friendships, and (2) the nature of group patterns of friendship (social structure). These aspects of social development will be treated briefly in the order given.

Factors Determining Friendships.—Many complex factors apparently combine to determine what friendships will develop among children of any age. To ferret out these constellations of factors in any given case would be well-nigh impossible. A good beginning has, however, been made in this direction. At the preschool level Challman [46] has reported that boy playmates resemble each other most in chronological age, sociability, and physical activity. In the case of girls, the highest resemblances relate to social participation, sociality, and chronological age. At this level intellectual status, personality qualities, and physical characteristics did not seem important in the formation of friendships, at least as determined by the number of times one child was observed to play with another. Green [47] found that children two and three years of age tend constantly to add to the number of their friends (playmates), but that three- to five-year-olds are more concerned with cementing a few attachments.

At the elementary school level (grades three to eight) Seagoe [48] noted that children who live near each other, who attend the same school and class, and who are comparable in mental ability tend to select each other as friends. In fact, 75 per cent of Seagoe's friend-pairs were from the same grade or room in school. The homes of close friends were, on the average, approximately one-fourth as far apart as those of unselected children. This investigator also found a marked relationship between friends of athletic ability, courtesy, cleanliness, and personality traits. A study by Pintner and associates,[49] of fifth and eighth grade pupils, has suggested, however, that mental age and chronological age are more influential in the determination of friendships than personality qualities. Again, friend-pairs tended in general to possess similar characteristics.

An investigation by Hardy [50] of the factors making for being liked, in the case of several hundred third to seventh grade children, led to some significant contrasts. A comparison

[46] Robert C. Challman, "Factors Influencing Friendships Among Preschool Children," *Child Development*, 3 : 146-158 (1932).

[47] E. H. Green, "Friendships and Quarrels Among Preschool Children," *Child Development*, 4 : 237-252 (1933).

[48] M. V. Seagoe, "Factors Influencing the Selection of Associates," *Journal of Educational Research*, 27 : 32-40 (1933-34).

[49] Rudolph Pintner, G. Forlano, and H. Freedman, "Personality and Attitudinal Similarity Among Classroom Friends," *Journal of Applied Psychology*, 21 : 48-65 (1937).

[50] M. C. Hardy, "Social Recognition at the Elementary School Age," *Journal of Social Psychology*, 8 : 365-384 (1937).

of the characteristics of 38 pupils who were often mentioned as being well liked and 54 children who were seldom or never mentioned as being desirable disclosed the following differentials: The best-liked children were superior to their unpopular associates in classroom behavior, in dealing amicably with their playmates, in scholastic ratings, in playground activities, and in neuromuscular skills (throwing, running, catching, etc.). The more popular children were also rated as being better looking, healthier, and more active in remunerative endeavors than was the case with the least liked group. No doubt other more intangible factors contributed to the superior rating accorded the best liked children.

Factors making for the formation of friendships have also been studied at the junior and senior high school level. Jenkins,[51] for example, found that children of this age tend to form friendships with individuals of their own age, interests, and intelligence. The socio-economic status of parents was also found to be an important criterion in the selection of friends. Approximately one-fourth of Jenkin's children picked friends from their own neighborhood. Wellman's [52] study of similar aged boys and girls showed that the latter chose friends who resembled them in scholarship more than in other characteristics, but that boy friend-pairs tended to be more alike in height, chronological age, and intellectual status than in scholarship. In the case of twelve- to seventeen-year-old boys studied in summer camp situations, Partridge [53] noted that "best friends" were similar in chronological age, but that they tended to be even more alike in mental age. Evidently early adolescent children show a preference for companions whose chronological age, interests, and abilities are similar to theirs. Since they are to share his leisure time, the child of this age desires his companions to be sociable, athletic, acceptable in appearance, and his equal intellectually.

[51] G. G. Jenkins, "Factors Involved in Children's Friendships," *Journal of Educational Psychology*, 22: 440-448 (1931).
[52] Beth Wellman, "The School Child's Choice of Companions," *Journal of Educational Research*, 14: 126-132 (1926).
[53] E. D. Partridge, "A Study of Friendships Among Adolescent Boys," *Journal of Genetic Psychology*, 43: 472-477 (1933).

Group Patterns of Friendship.—A recent and promising approach to the study of social development is that of determining patterns of friendship within a group of children. Such an analysis of social structure, developed by Moreno [54] in 1934, is based on the hypothesis that the individual child can be understood only in terms of his relationships with the group of which he is a member, and that such a group can, in turn, be understood only in the light of the characteristics of the individual children comprising it. The so-called science of *sociometry* has thus been developed to measure the interpersonal relationships and the attractions and repulsions which characterize a given group of children. Such a technique is calculated to acquaint teachers with spheres of influence and social interplay operating in their classrooms, with individual children's reputations among their associates, and with factors determinative of social prestige, social aspiration, and patterns of friendship.

Social patterns drawn from classroom analyses have disclosed the presence in groups of children of: (1) *isolates*—individuals whom no one apparently wishes to number among his friends; (2) *mutual pairs*—pairs of individuals who choose each other as preferred friends; (3) *chains*—instances in which child A is friendly with child B, B is friendly with child C, and C is friendly with child D, and so on, with various of these children having friends outside of the chain; (4) *triangles*—a situation in which child A is friendly with child B, B is friendly with child C, and C is friendly with child A; and (5) *stars*—instances in which a number of children prefer a given popular child as their friend.

It has also been found that influences which children have upon each other tend to accentuate, not remove, their previously developed personality deviations. As McKinnon's [55] investigation of nursery school children who had been placed in groups conforming to their dominant behavior characteristics (conformity, invasiveness, caution, and withdrawal, respec-

[54] J. L. Moreno, *Who Shall Survive? A New Approach to the Problem of Human Interrelations,* Washington, D. C., Nervous and Mental Disease Pub. Co., 1934.

[55] Kathern M. McKinnon, *Consistency and Change in Behavior Manifestations,* Child Development Monographs, No. 30 (1942).

tively) for a period of five to six years showed, the main direction of change is toward conformity. Behavioral structures
of an undesirable kind, i.e., invasion and taking things, tended
to become less conspicuous with age because of the child's peers'
unwillingness to tolerate such actions, and because of increased
resourcefulness and ability to acquiesce in group requirements.
Withdrawing behavior appeared to be least amenable to change.

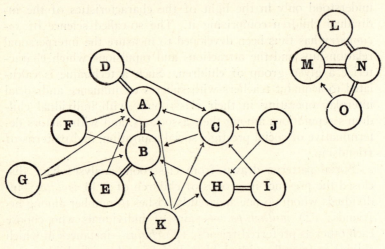

Figure 89. Friendship Structure of Girls in Classroom A
(From Merle H. Elliott, "Patterns of Friendship in the Classroom," *Progressive Education,* 18:385 (1941).)

ANALYSIS OF SOCIAL STRUCTURE. Several studies have
been made of classroom social patterns by the structural analysis method, some of which are of a statistical nature. In a non-
statistical study of Oakland (Calif.) public school children,
Elliott [56] asked them to write the names of not more than five
and preferably two or three (not including parents or teachers)
of their best friends. One of the analyses of this inquiry is
graphically represented in Figure 89, in which each circle represents an individual child, each double line a mutually recognized
friendship, and each arrow a child named as a friend by a child
who was not named in return.

[56] Merle H. Elliott, "Patterns of Friendship in the Classroom," *Progressive Education,* 18: 383-390 (1941).

Elliott discusses the implications of the figure as follows: "The girls in this room fall into two distinct cliques. Lois (L), Mary (M), and Nancy (N) are close friends. Olive (O), who is associated with this group only through Nancy, claimed Mary as a friend but is not recognized as such. One suspects that Olive is not too secure in this relationship since any temporary quarrel with Nancy may leave her on the outside. This little group of four girls is interesting in that it is so isolated from the rest of the class. These girls do not claim friendships with any girls outside the group nor are they mentioned by any of the other girls. From the latter fact it appears that they are not particularly envied or admired. The rest of the girls are dominated by Alice (A) and Barbara (B). These two girls are greatly admired by both the boys and the girls. Alice is mentioned by six boys and Barbara by five boys. (Those mentioned by the other sex are not shown in the figure.) Each of this pair, in addition to their mutual friendship, has another recognized friend. Barbara's friend, Elizabeth (E), wishes to be a friend of Alice. The rest of the girls seem to form an admiring circle around Alice and Barbara. Carol (C) could probably be a leader of these other girls if she (and they) were not so occupied with Alice and Barbara. Helen (H) and Isuko (I) have formed an alliance. The other three girls, Joan (J), Katherine (K), and Gladys (G), are definitely isolated, not being mentioned by any members of the class as best friends."

In a statistical study by Belden,[57] of classroom social structure, groups of children were asked, "Who is your best friend?" "Who do you like to work with?" and "Who, among your companions, would you like to be like?" The groups were subsequently examined in terms of their status in school achievement, intelligence, and personality adjustment as measured by standard tests. A summary of the findings disclosed that: (1) both boys and girls tend to mention as "best friends" children who are like themselves in chronological age, mental age, and school achievement. Both sexes also tend to choose friends who are slightly superior to them in personality adjustment; (2) the child, who, in relation to his fellows, is too old or too young, too bright or too dull mentally (in sigma distance from the mean), who achieves too well or too poorly, or who is

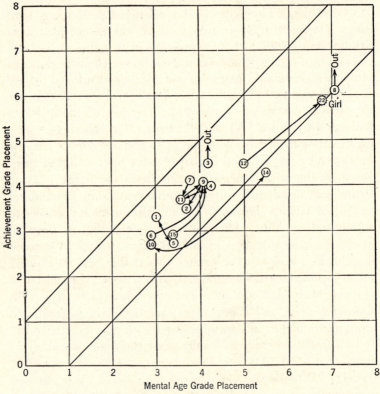

Figure 90. The Social Structure of a Fourth Grade Class of Boys

(From Daniel S. Belden, *A Study of the Nature of Social Structure,* unpub. ms., Division of Research and Guidance, Los Angeles County Schools, 1942, p. 5.)

too well or too poorly adjusted, tends to be an isolate; (3) the child who is mentally superior, but whose achievement is inferior to the chooser tends to be rejected, as does the child who is mentally inferior but whose achievement is superior to the chooser; and (4) children usually follow the socially accepted practice of avoiding as possible friends children who are decidedly either their superior or inferior in mental ability. To do otherwise would mean risking being rated publicly as inferior, either by contrast or in terms of the companion chosen. Social structure tends to be founded on equalities. In this instance, birds of a feather apparently *do* flock together.

An analysis of the group of fourth grade boys depicted in Figure 90 suggests, according to Belden, the following facts: Boy number 14, who is working significantly below his mental age position, is attracted to (and responded to by) boy number 10, the dullest child of the group. This mutual response, which spans a mental age gap of 2.5 grade placement points, is not unreasonable in terms of comparative achievements but is "brittle"—more than one sigma distance—with respect to mental age. Boy number 9 is the "star" of the group. His teacher described him as a "natural leader" around whom admirers tend to flock as a clique. Boy number 8 is superior to all the others in achievement, but chose his friends from among individuals outside the group. So far as this class is concerned, he is an isolate. No one chose him as a friend. Boy number 12 selected a girl as his best friend but was not mentioned by her. This is unusual, since few boys admit having girls as friends before adolescence. Boy number 3 also failed to receive mention by any members of the class, but mentioned having a friend outside the group.

In another sociometric study,[58] a group of fifth and sixth grade public school children were asked to express their preferences for associates in school situations. Children whose weighted acceptability scores were in the lowest quartile were subsequently studied clinically and found to group themselves in the following three categories: (1) *recessive* children, or those with no determinable expressive interests; (2) *socially uninterested* children, or those who are usually shy, passive (in school), and unliked by others; and (3) *socially ineffective* children, or those who are frequently noisy, rebellious, boastful, but still unliked by others.

---

[58] M. L. Northway, "Outsiders; a Study of the Personality Patterns of Children Least Acceptable to Their Age Mates," *Sociometry*, 7: 10-25 (1944).

UTILIZING THE RESULTS OF ANALYSES.   Results similar to those already presented were secured by Stoke [59] in a research utilizing the "Guess Who" technique. A group of children was given a list of short descriptions which might fit several persons and were asked to guess who each one was. It was possible to discern from the results secured how the children regarded each other in relation to a variety of traits. Stoke concluded that, while this type of procedure needs to be supplemented by other data, it provides many clues for remedial treatment and for the social education of children.

This view is concurred in by Elliott,[60] who suggests the following procedures in the case of isolated or other children not adequately assimilated by the group: (1) *providing opportunity for the development of friendly relations* through changes in seating, giving children opportunities to become better acquainted, putting potential friendship combinations together in working groups, and giving retiring children responsibilities for the welfare of new pupils; (2) *improving children's social skills* through instruction in courtesy and manners, the development of morale building athletic abilities, teaching children the advantages of neatness and cleanliness, and through showing children the outcomes of improved treatment of associates; and (3) *building a sense of accomplishment or competency* through appointing children to positions of responsibility, i.e., monitor or member of traffic squad, in which they can succeed, assisting them in mastering their lessons, and through praising children for performing small tasks about the school.

Factors Influencing Social Growth.—Until comparatively recent times students of child development have tended to neglect the influence on social growth of both physical factors and social structures operating in the child's environment. A number of these pioneer students proceeded on the assumption that native endowment and the process of maturation determine development, and that the behavior of normal children will proceed principally as a function of their chronological age. These

---

[59] Stuart M. Stokes, *The Social Analysis of the Classroom* (unpub. ms.), Division on Child Development and Teacher Personnel, Commission on Teacher Education, American Council on Education, 1940.
[60] Merle H. Elliott, *op. cit.,* pp. 388-390.

investigators consequently gave little attention to the conditions under which their subjects were studied or to the types of social background in which they had lived. Such a procedure is tantamount to ignoring the extent to which given social responses may have been conditioned by learning. As previous discussions have suggested, it is difficult to demonstrate that social reactions emerge "naturally," regardless of specific conditionings.

INNATE PRIMARY FACTORS. Typical of the viewpoint expressed above is the assumption by Bühler [61] that since infants exhibit marked individual differences in social behavior in the second half-year of life, these differences must be innately determined. Bühler came to this conclusion after noting that infants could be classified into three types: (1) the *socially blind* type, which pays no attention to other children and which plays without regard to other individuals or their movements; (2) the *socially dependent* type, which is markedly influenced by the presence and activities of others and which has a consuming interest in other children; and (3) the *socially independent* type, which, although aware of the presence and responses of others, is not influenced to any extent by them. The fact that social patterns approximating these descriptions have emerged from a variety of home conditions has led to the conclusion that they represent primary dispositions. The more modern interpretation of this situation is that these distinctions represent only general tendencies of an unstable nature and that they are subject to many inconsistencies. They are believed to represent the beginnings of social behavior which can be more or less readily modified by the type of treatment administered.

An investigation suggestive of spontaneous social development with a minimum of social stimulation is that by Dennis [62] in which a pair of twins were kept in a very restricted social environment until the age of seven months. Although no one smiled at, fondled, cuddled, or played with these infants, they

[61] Charlotte Bühler, "The Social Behavior of Children," in *Handbook of Child Psychology* (edited by Carl Murchison), Worcester, Clark Univ. Press, 1933, Ch. 9.

[62] Wayne Dennis, *Infant Development Under Conditions of Restricted Practice and of Minimum Social Stimulation,* Genetic Psychology Monographs, Vol. 23, No. 1 (1941), pp. 143-189.

began to smile and laugh upon reaching the age when children usually respond in these ways. Dennis believes that "if the well-being of the infant is assured, his behavioral development will take its normal course," but recognized that learning plays

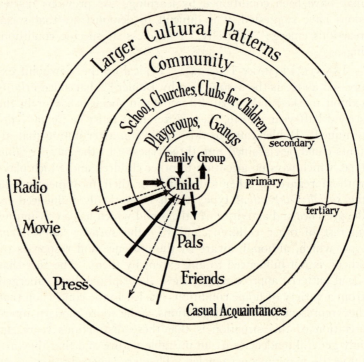

Figure 91. The Widening of the Child's Experience and the Resulting Interaction

The thickness of the arrows represents the probable relative importance of the interaction between the child and the various individuals and groups.
(From Francis J. Brown, *The Sociology of Childhood*, New York, Prentice-Hall, Inc., 1939, p. 45.)

an important part in development and that "maturation in and of itself seldom produces new developmental items."

A list of other previously mentioned investigators who have emphasized the alleged dominant role in social development played by innate factors includes: Piaget, whose studies of childhood thinking largely omitted reference to social factors:

Gesell, whose elaborate studies of maturational development have emphasized biological growth almost to the exclusion of cultural backgrounds; McGraw, whose twin studies led her to conclude that learning is relatively impotent as compared to the maturational factor; and Bayley and Shirley, whose findings, that crying in babies is fairly constant in amount during the first year and that talkative babies tend to become talkative children, caused them also to assume that innate factors are largely responsible for the social sequence through which every normal child must presumably pass.

SOCIOLOGICAL FACTORS.   In contrast to the above approach is the belief of a growing body of research workers and others that social factors and structures are more influential in the determination of child development than had formerly been supposed.[63] Realizing that social responses cannot spring forth fully developed apart from patterns of environmental influence, these individuals have emphasized the need for systematic investigations of the various aspects of the child's cultural milieu. Without concluding that children are "by nature" friendly, sociable, competitive, sympathetic, aggressive, and the like, they propose to study the effects on the child's social outlook of his association with members of the family, with playground groups and gangs, with close friends, with school, church, and club companions, with the community at large, and with the press, the movie, and the radio (see Figure 91). As previously stated, parental attitudes alone may be more fateful for the child's social development than many other aspects of his environment; it is upon them that he must depend for warm, affectional relationships and other such fundamental bases of later social growth.

The trend toward a more meticulous study of cultural influences on child socialization has been summarized by Koshuk,[64] in her critical review of this movement, as tending "away from exclusive concern with such background factors as age, sex, race, and nationality; toward recognition of the

[63] Ruth P. Koshuk, *Social Influences Affecting the Behavior of Young Children,* Monographs of the Society for Research in Child Development, Vol. 6, No. 2 (1941).

[64] *Ibid.,* p. 49.

fact that behavior occurs always in a socio-cultural setting, and toward detailed analysis and classification of such settings in relation to observed behavior; toward comparative studies of personality development in different cultures; toward comprehensive, long-term studies, with the introduction of control groups; toward experiments in the modification of social behavior; and toward systematic attempts to devise indirect methods of getting at the inner, personal organization of experience and the meaning of human relationships . . ."

Koshuk adds that with this shift in direction will come better understanding of children's problems and an increased recognition of the influence of cultural structures on their social growth. Psychiatrists will be in a better position to study the nature of the forces which determine the child's behavior trends. Psychologists and sociologists will be able better to evaluate the effects on social development of various types of group mores and of parental attitudes as they affect the child's fundamental psychological needs. Cultural anthropologists will be able to trace child development within a variety of cultures and offer suggestions for the regulation of cultural factors within a given social group. The study of the social behavior of growing children is a many-sided task which requires a constant search for methods suited to the investigation of the dynamics of personality.

Educating for Social Maturity.—The young child's self-centeredness is encouraged by the attention accorded him by his family because of his helplessness. Not until he needs the cooperation of individuals beyond the circle of his family does the child begin to become altruistic in the sense of contributing to the welfare of other persons. In short, he does not develop an attitude of concern for other children's happiness until such behavior brings him greater satisfaction than he gets by neglecting them. Parents who understand this point will begin early in the teaching of social skills.

That young children are influenced by their parents' methods of dealing with this problem, and that their developing social behavior is a function of the way they are handled is attested to by the investigations of Hartshorne and May.[65] As the result of giving children numerous opportunities for sharing their possessions with other children and for assisting their classmates, these psychologists found that no children are completely self-centered or completely unselfish. The social behavior of the children studied, including an older group nine to fifteen years of age, was found to fluctuate from situation to situation and between such closely related types of helpfulness as *doing something for other children* and *giving things away to other children*. Some relationship was found between the children's altruistic behavior and the occupational status of their family, their degree of success in school, and the extent of self-centeredness displayed by their friends. Children's specific tendencies to behave magnanimously are evidently influenced by the extent to which their parents or others have made such behavior satisfying.

SIGNS OF SOCIAL IMMATURITY. It is apparent that some individuals reach chronological maturity without at the same time developing beyond the infantile or childhood stage socially. Such persons are frequently disposed to become angry when thwarted, to be self-centered in social relations, to avoid disagreeable tasks, to be chronically jealous, to throw, break, or tear things when irritated, and to cry or pout when denied favors. As the present author [66] has written elsewhere, "If we could control the environment of children in such a way that socially desirable responses would result in feelings of security and well-being, and undesirable actions would yield unpleasantness and failure, it is probable that such infantilisms as we see exhibited when adults indulge in temper tantrums or continually get their feelings hurt would not develop. As it is, many individuals, depending upon the extent of their luck in encountering a satisfactory early environment, have developed certain false values or bad emotional traits. In addition to the familiar exhibitions of emotion seen in excessive anger, resentment, hatred, suspicion, discouragement, fear, and the like,

[65] Hugh Hartshorne and M. A. May, *Studies in Service and Self-Control,* New York, The Macmillan Co., 1929.
[66] Louis P. Thorpe, *Personality and Life,* New York, Longmans, Green & Co., 1941, p. 51.

complex and sometimes disastrous false values are formed concerning which a child may become highly emotional when challenged. *Many such attitudes are carried into adult life."*

The types of individuals who are doomed to meet with considerable frustration and maladjustment because of their infantile or adolescent level of social development have been aptly described by Richmond [67] as: (1) the *dependent security-seeking* type, described as the person who expects consideration and guidance from everyone—the clinging vine or timid soul; (2) the *unstable personality,* or self-centered, bad-tempered, quarrelsome person who will not accept responsibility; (3) the *spoiled child* type who gets his feelings hurt easily and who is resentful, incredulous, or stubborn when his wishes are not met; (4) the individual with *persistent infantile habits* who indulges in lisping, baby talk, and childish mannerisms; (5) the person with a *homosexual outlook* on life who has retained an adolescent attitude toward sex; and (6) the *psychopathic* or *paranoid* individual whose self-centeredness became crystallized at the infantile level, and who is marked by a pathological sense of self-importance and an oversuspicious attitude toward those who fail to recognize his "superiority."

STEPS IN SOCIAL EDUCATION. The most promising way to educate children for social maturity would thus seem to be: (1) to provide them with a sense of personal security and status calculated to lay the groundwork for cooperation with others; (2) to set up specific social (structural) situations in which they gain personal satisfaction by cooperating with their associates; and (3) to teach them to like other children, to regard them as being worthy, and to enjoy being with them. This sequence is much more functional and effective than the older methods of eulogizing cooperative behavior and urging children to develop certain traits and manners that would supposedly make them liked. The present emphasis is upon demonstrating to children that they have better times when they are genuinely solicitous of their companions, not that they are doing other children a favor by showing a liking for them or

[67] Winifred V. Richmond, *Personality, Its Development and Hygiene,* New York, Farrar & Rinehart, Inc., 1937, Ch. 9.

that they get a maximum of notice when they favor their associates with attention. The latter type of treatment leads to egocentrism—the attitude of catering to personal comfort and aggrandizement.

The following quotation suggests the technique to be followed in promoting social growth in young children. "The aim should be to develop an ease in social relationships to supplant the self-consciousness. Social games are probably the best means to this end. In a game the child becomes engrossed in the play, forgets himself, and accepts the other children as a part of the game. In place of the attitude that many children have which might be expressed in these words: Here I am and there is that *other* child, the child should be taught to have the attitude as expressed by 'Here *we* are.' The self-conscious child has a feeling of completeness in himself and regards the entrance of another as an intrusion. The socially adjusted child sees himself as a *member* of a group, a *partner* in a game, and a *contributor* to a common purpose. When this social integration is achieved, he feels at ease." [68] We could add that the latter type child is on his way to satisfactory social development, particularly if his people teach the attitude of "here *we* are" through concrete situations in which the child finds satisfaction in the social activities undertaken. Attitudes cannot actually be taught; they must be developed through affectively satisfying experience.

Children's Interests and Socialization

A knowledge of children's interests is essential to the guidance of their social development. Interests (or their absence) are indicative of a child's degree of social adjustment, thus knowledge concerning them can be used to plan programs of improvement. A child's concern with reading, the movies, the radio, music and art, material possessions, and other more general interests has important bearings on his chances of achieving a satisfactory adaptation to the requirements of cooperative

[68] J. J. B. Morgan, *Child Psychology*, New York, Farrar & Rinehart, Inc., 1942, pp. 524-525.

action, and should thus be considered in a discussion of social development. Since the need here is for an understanding of the import for social growth of interests which research has indicated children possess, no effort will be made to discuss the more general aspects of reading, motion pictures, the radio, and other such agencies for satisfying children's needs.

Children's General Interests.—The usual technique in ascertaining children's general interests is to give them an opportunity to express spontaneous wishes. Investigators do not, as a rule, quiz children directly concerning their interests. The questions asked by Witty and Kopel [69] in their study of 900 children selected at random from a kindergarten and elementary school population (Evanston, Ill.) of 3,400 are illustrative. These children were asked, "Suppose you could have three wishes which might come true, what would be your first wish? your second wish? your third wish?" In this instance the average for each child was nearly two wishes, with approximately 840 wishes being expressed by boys and girls combined. The apparently logical assumption was made by the investigators that the wishes named were indicative of major interests.

"Most of the children's wishes related to recreational activities (tools, books, toys, pets, and so forth). For boys, wishes for wealth, travel, and proficiency in a skilled profession are listed here in decreasing order of choice. Girls rated travel above wealth, and proficiency in the arts third. These three types of wishes maintained as high rank for boys as for girls in every grade. Frequently expressed by the girls in the primary grades were wishes for clothing. Girls in other grades wished for fame, leadership, and high social position. Wishes for success or increased proficiency in school were expressed occasionally in the upper grades. Other wishes, relatively few in number, disclosed desires for more schooling, better health, increased strength, power, entertainment, friendships, freedom from present responsibilities, security, and personal or parental happiness."

[69] Paul A. Witty and David Kopel, *Reading and the Educative Process,* Boston, Ginn & Co., 1939, pp. 46-48.

TABLE 35.   PERCENTAGE DISTRIBUTION OF CHILDREN'S WISHES

Types of Wish	All Children	Age Groups				Sex Groups		School Groups		I.Q. Groups		
		5-6	7-8	9-10	11-12	Boys	Girls	Private	Public	120 and Above	100-119	80-99
1. Specific material objects and possessions	35.8	55.0	48.0	26.0	14.0	40.0	31.5	26.3	42.1	23.3	38.3	47.9
2. Money	8.5	5.0	13.0	10.0	6.0	9.0	8.0	5.6	10.4	9.3	9.7	5.2
3. Good living quarters	2.0	1.0	0.0	2.0	5.0	2.0	2.0	1.9	2.1	1.6	1.1	4.2
4. Activities, sports, diversions	7.3	6.0	3.0	12.0	8.0	7.5	7.0	8.1	6.7	11.6	5.1	5.2
5. Opportunities and accomplishments	3.5	4.0	2.0	1.0	7.0	1.5	5.5	3.1	3.8	3.9	3.4	3.1
6. To be independent, have vocation	2.5	0.0	4.0	0.0	6.0	3.0	2.0	0.6	3.8	0.0	3.4	4.2
7. To be bright, smart	0.8	0.0	0.0	2.0	1.0	1.0	0.5	1.3	0.4	1.6	0.6	1.0
8. Moral self-improvement	0.0	0.0	1.0	2.0	0.0	0.0	0.0	0.6	0.8	1.6	0.6	0.0
9. Improved personal appearance	1.0	1.0	0.0	0.0	0.0	0.0	2.0	0.0	0.0	0.0	0.6	0.0
10. Prestige, adventure	1.0	4.0	0.0	1.0	0.0	2.0	0.0	1.3	0.8	1.6	0.6	1.0
11. Supernatural power	2.0	6.0	2.0	2.0	0.0	2.0	2.0	3.1	1.3	3.9	1.1	1.0
12. Have a baby, sibling	5.0	1.0	6.0	7.0	4.0	1.0	9.0	5.6	5.8	3.9	7.4	5.2
13. To be married, have a lover	1.0	1.0	2.0	1.0	2.0	1.0	1.0	1.3	0.8	0.8	0.6	2.1
14. Parents never die, retain parents	2.8	1.0	2.0	1.0	7.0	3.0	2.5	1.9	3.3	2.3	2.9	3.1
15. Companionship, friendship, social contacts	1.8	1.0	0.0	2.0	4.0	0.5	3.0	1.9	1.7	3.9	0.6	1.0
16. Relief from irritation and discomfort	1.3	2.0	2.0	0.0	1.0	1.0	1.5	1.3	1.3	1.6	1.1	1.0
17. Specific benefits for parents and relatives	5.0	3.0	1.0	9.0	7.0	3.5	6.5	3.8	5.8	3.9	5.7	5.2
18. General, inclusive benefits for self: health, happiness, etc.	4.8	3.0	4.0	6.0	6.0	6.0	3.5	8.1	2.5	9.3	3.4	1.0
19. General, inclusive immunities, self	0.8	0.0	2.0	1.0	0.0	1.0	0.5	1.3	0.4	0.8	1.1	0.0
20. General benefits for relatives, self	3.0	0.0	2.0	2.0	8.0	3.0	3.0	4.4	2.1	2.3	2.3	5.2
21. General benefits for others, philanthropic	9.3	5.0	6.0	13.0	13.0	9.0	9.5	18.1	3.3	13.2	10.3	2.1
22. Nothing, no more	0.0	0.0	0.0	0.0	0.0	0.0	0.0	0.0	0.0	0.0	0.0	0.0
23. No response, don't know	0.8	2.0	0.0	0.0	1.0	0.5	1.0	0.6	0.8	0.0	1.2	1.0
Number of children questioned	400	100	100	100	100	200	200	160	240	129	175	96
Number of items reported	400	100	100	100	100	200	200	160	240	129	175	96

(From Arthur T. Jersild, F. V. Markey, and C. L. Jersild, *Children's Fears, Dreams, Wishes, Daydreams, Likes, Dislikes, Pleasant and Unpleasant Memories*, Child Development Monographs, No. 12, 1933, p. 23.)

Somewhat similar results were obtained by Jersild and associates [70] in a study of the wishes of 400 public and private school children in New York City. As can be seen in Table 35, the most frequently expressed wishes again relate to material objects and possessions. This category included 37 per cent of the Evanston children, and 32 and 52 per cent of the New York private and public school children, respectively. When it is realized that the socio-economic status of the New York private school and the Evanston public school children was approximately similar, the unanimity of wishes in the case of children of equal privilege is striking. It is also noticeable that children of all elementary school ages tend to mention the same types of wishes, and that the wishes of boys and girls correspond somewhat closely. Although age differences are in evidence, chronological maturity does not appear to constitute a major factor in children's wishes.

The investigators (New York study) found that "children's thoughts (at all ages) are directed toward accomplished objective facts (and toward the acquisition of objects) rather than toward the possession of powers within themselves which would enable them to win the things they desire." A more recent study by Zeligs [71] of twelve-year-old children has suggested, however, that they are more interested than formerly in social welfare, political conditions, and family welfare, with girls expressing the greater interest in the last-named factor.

The Child and His Reading.[72]—The precursors of reading interest are probably found in the young child's enjoyment of stories, nursery rhymes, and pictures. It is not uncommon for two-year-olds to peruse picture books containing large reproductions of people, animals, and material objects familiar to them. Slightly older children enjoy simple stories of animal

[70] Arthur T. Jersild, F. V. Markey, and C. L. Jersild, *Children's Fears, Dreams, Wishes, Daydreams, Likes, Dislikes, Pleasant and Unpleasant Memories,* Child Development Monographs, No. 12 (1933).

[71] R. Zeligs, "Children's Wishes," *Journal of Applied Psychology,* 26 : 231-240 (1942). See also, by the same author, "Social Factors Annoying to Children," *Journal of Applied Psychology,* 29 : 75-82 (1945).

[72] See Lewis M. Terman and M. Lima, *Children's Reading,* New York, D. Appleton-Century Co., Inc., 1931. Also W. S. Gray, *Summary of Investigations Relating to Reading,* Univ. of Chicago Supplementary Educational Monographs, No. 28 (1925).

life, of natural phenomena, and of other children, especially when these are illustrated by bright colored pictures. Children of school age who have the opportunity to do so are inclined to read factual books whose content is adapted to their level of interest and intellectual development. Whether they continue to read depends upon the availability of books, the child's state of mental health, and the stimuli supplied by associates, parents, and teachers. According to Terman and Lima's [73] data, children six to eight years of age read on the average less than one book per month, those eight to ten read 1.5 books per month, those ten to twelve read 2 books per month, children twelve to fourteen read 3 books per month, and those fourteen to sixteen read 2.5 books for the same length of time.

Elementary school children differ greatly in their interest and taste for books, but tend to enjoy zestful plots, the element of surprise, and narratives that make demands on the imagination. As they grow older, boys develop a liking for animal stories and for adventure. Girls are more inclined to prefer stories about home life, about children, and to some extent about romance. A study by Lazar [74] of children in grades four to six disclosed that they preferred reading books concerned with action, excitement, adventure, mystery, thrills, suspense, humor, child life, animal life, sports, nature, airplanes, and inventions.

Children of high school age spend considerably more time reading magazines and newspapers than they do books,[75] and a large percentage are attracted to the cheaper type magazine or tabloid newspaper. Boys manifest an increased interest in adventure, science, athletics, and inventions and, to a lesser degree, travel, biography, and history. Girls show a decided preference for adult women's magazines, especially those dealing with fictitious and sentimental matters. A graphic representation of the reading interests of approximately 5,000 high school pupils

[73] Lewis M. Terman and M. Lima, *ob. cit.*

[74] M. Lazar, *Reading Interests, Activities, and Opportunities of Bright, Average, and Dull Children,* Teachers College Contributions to Education, No. 707, Columbia Univ., 1937.

[75] M. I. Kramer, "Children's Interests in Magazines and Newspapers," *Catholic Educational Review,* 39: 284-290 (1941).

of both sexes, based on a study by Jordan,[76] may be seen in Figure 92.

Investigations have shown that reading the so-called comics is probably the most popular of all elementary school children's reading pursuits. However, relatively few of the present-day comic strips contain humorous elements; many of them are

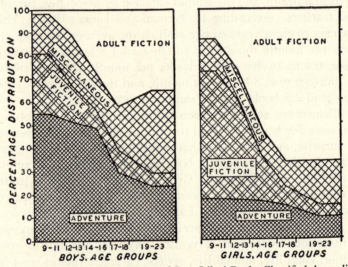

Figure 92. Percentage Distribution of Best Liked Books Classified According to Type, by Age Groups and Sex

(From F. K. Shuttleworth, *The Adolescent Period,* Monographs of the Society for Research in Child Development, Vol. 3, No. 3 (1938), based on data from A. M. Jordan, *Children's Interests in Reading,* Teachers College Contributions to Education, No. 107, Columbia Univ., 1921.)

concerned with adventure and romance. Most of them are, nevertheless, avidly perused by both adults and children. Children differ in their comic sheet preferences, but, judging from a study by Hill and Trent [77] of a group of fourth to sixth graders, the majority like strips that are mysterious, exciting, full of fighting and action, and that portray characters marked

[76] Arthur M. Jordan, *Children's Interests in Reading,* Chapel Hill (N. C.), Univ. of North Carolina Press, 1926. See also by the same author, *Children's Interests in Reading,* Teachers College Contributions to Education, No. 107, Columbia Univ., 1921.

[77] George E. Hill and M. E. Trent, "Children's Interests in Comic Strips," *Journal of Educational Research,* 34 : 30-36 (1940). Also George E. Hill, "Relation of Interests in Comic Strips to the Vocabulary of These Comics," *Journal of Educational Psychology,* 34 : 48-54 (1943).

by strength, beauty, bravery, and unlimited capacity for mastering difficulties. In the case of girls, family life and romance
also exert great appeal. Humor was relatively low in the list
of reasons for liking the comic strips. There is, however, a
slight tendency toward preference for comics with a larger proportion of slang, distorted words, and onomatopoeia (words
representing sounds).

A series of researches by Witty [78] has further substantiated
the popularity of comic pictures with elementary school pupils,
and has disclosed the fact that, judging from a sampling of
children in grades seven and eight, they read on the average
about 13 or 14 comic magazines regularly. In the case of comic
strips, 26 was the average number read, with 15 being read
regularly and 5 often. Sex differences were not pronounced
but became more noticeable in the higher grades.

Children's Motion Picture Interests.—Attendance at motion picture theaters is a favorite leisure-time activity of most
children. Although such attendance varies greatly in localities
and with different individuals, surveys have shown that the
average person attends one or more movies per week. A
study [79] conducted in Ohio indicated that 36.7 per cent of
movie-goers were minors, that 12 per cent of all admissions
were children between the ages of seven and thirteen, and that
3 per cent were children less than seven years of age. Since
they require little effort to follow and appeal to a variety of interests, motion pictures have become a powerful agency for the
dissemination of information, for the building of attitudes, and
for relief from emotional stresses.

Mitchell [80] has reported that children attend movies primarily to get "thrills." In her study boys were found to prefer
the types of thrills attendant upon western adventures, comedies, and mystery plays. Girls reacted most favorably to ro-

---

[78] Paul A. Witty, "Children's Interest in Reading the Comics," *Journal of
Experimental Education,* 10 : 100-104 (1941) ; and Paul A. Witty, E. Smith, and
A. Coomer, "Reading Comics in Grades VII and VIII," *Journal of Educational
Psychology,* 33 : 173-182 (1942).
[79] E. Dale, *Children's Attendance at Motion Pictures,* Payne Fund Studies,
New York, The Macmillan Co., 1935.
[80] Alice M. Mitchell, *Children and the Movies,* Chicago, Univ. of Chicago
Press, 1930.

mance, comedy, and "westerns." Children also like pictures which depict fighting, animal life, social situations, and thrilling stories. A study by Seagoe [81] of the movie preferences of elementary school children corroborated these findings. In this instance pupils six to nine years of age preferred active heroes and pretty heroines in comedies and cartoon pictures. Ten- to twelve-year-olds preferred adventure films to comedies. On the high school level [82] it has been found that mystery and love themes rank first and second in popularity. Westerns, war, and comedy pictures are still liked but apparently lose their appeal as children grow older. As Table 36 shows, high

TABLE 36. SEX DIFFERENCES IN MOTION PICTURE PREFERENCES

Type	Percentage of Preferences	
	Boys	Girls
Mystery	42.2	32.0
War	17.3	6.0
Comedy	11.7	8.7
Western	10.8	5.3
Melodrama	5.2	6.2
Love	4.2	29.5
Tragedy	4.6	3.2
Educational	3.5	4.2
Sex	2.08	1.1
Society	2.0	3.8

(From T. E. Sullenger, "Modern Youth and Movies," *School and Society*, 32:460 (1930).)

school boys prefer the more exciting mystery, war, comedy, and western pictures, whereas girls of this age are primarily interested in romance and love themes.

Much has been said about the probable influence of the movies on children's health, educational development, and moral behavior. Many of the indictments made have apparently been based on a mistaken notion of the relationship between *viewing* and *enacting* the various scenes and episodes involved. It was in an effort to settle this question that the Payne Foundation

[81] M. V. Seagoe, "The Child's Reactions to the Movies," *Journal of Juvenile Research*, 15: 169-180 (1931).
[82] T. E. Sullenger, "Modern Youth and Movies," *School and Society*, 32: 459-461 (1930).

supported a series of investigations [83] in a number of universities. The studies were undertaken to ascertain the effects on children—physical, educational, and moral—of viewing motion pictures.

One of the studies [84] in question showed that children are often aroused to such emotional excitement as the result of seeing certain pictures that their sleep is much more restless than usual. Many children also admitted that they were frightened by some films and that they had developed new fears. However, since in one group of 44 children who stated that they had been frightened by exciting pictures, 38 declared that they enjoyed the experience, it is considered questionable whether such emotional excitation is harmful. So far as educational progress is concerned, it was found that children learn much concerning the world about them, that they catch about three-fifths as many items of information as do adults, and that they remember as much about a picture three months after viewing it as they do after a lapse of six weeks.[85]

That children's attitudes can be modified by motion pictures has been demonstrated by a number of researches, notably that by Thurstone,[86] in which they were shown the picture entitled "Four Sons" and in which the German people were presented in a favorable light. The children's attitudes became much more friendly toward Germans as the result of viewing this film. They also became more critical of gambling after having seen "The Street of Chance," in which gambling activities were portrayed in a markedly unfavorable light.

According to some psychologists and psychiatrists who have had experience in this connection, the influence of motion pictures on delinquent conduct is relatively slight compared with the claims made by certain writers. Healy and Bronner [87] concluded from a study of 4,000 delinquency cases that only one

[83] W. W. Charters, *Motion Pictures and Youth: A Summary,* New York, The Macmillan Co., 1933, Ch. 3.

[84] Samuel Renshaw, V. L. Miller, and Dorothy P. Marquis, reported in *ibid.,* pp. 31-35.

[85] W. W. Charters, *op. cit.*

[86] L. L. Thurstone, "Influence of Motion Pictures on Children's Attitudes," *Journal of Social Psychology,* 2: 291-305 (1931).

[87] William Healy and A. F. Bronner, *Delinquents and Criminals: Their Making and Unmaking,* New York, The Macmillan Co., 1926.

per cent appeared to have been motivated in their antisocial acts by influences exerted by the motion picture. The London County Council [88] found that, in general, children ignore or are bored by questionable moral elements of motion pictures, and that in very few cases could it be concluded that children are harmed thereby. Brill,[89] a psychiatrist with experience in the correction of young criminals, has declared that he has never known of a case in which either a male or female offender committed a crime because of having seen a motion picture. It is Brill's belief that gangster pictures merely enable the potential delinquent to relieve his pent-up feelings of resentment vicariously. To quote him, "An individual who becomes a gangster as a rule does not go to the movies, or if he goes to the movies, he is not affected by them to any such extent. Every person takes from the movies what he already has." It may be, thus, that children who were already on their way to delinquency merely appear to have been influenced by motion pictures as such.

A different point of view is advanced by Blumer and Hauser,[90] who report that the movies were influential in cases of delinquency with 10 per cent of the boys and 25 per cent of the girls studied. It is their belief that the movies stimulated the youths in question, at least indirectly, to perpetrate unlawful acts through depicting criminal techniques, arousing strong sexual desires, encouraging a longing for luxury and money, and through extolling questionable modes of behavior. These investigators feel that the effects of viewing gangster type and sexually stimulating motion pictures on youthful morals is appreciable.

It may be concluded that the motion picture exerts a powerful influence in producing emotional effects, in furnishing lasting information, in shaping attitudes, and in making possible vicarious releases or "purges" from the stresses of everyday

[88] Reported in W. W. Charters, *op. cit.*

[89] A. A. Brill, "The Value of the Motion Picture in Education, with Special Reference to the Exceptional Child," *Proceedings of the Sixth Conference on Education and the Exceptional Child of the Child Research Clinic of the Woods Schools,* May 1940, pp. 15-22.

[90] H. Blumer and P. M. Hauser, *Movies, Delinquency, and Crime,* New York, The Macmillan Co., 1933.

living. The possible effects of these experiences on children's morals is at present a matter of uncertainty. Additional research is needed to clarify the specific cause and effect relationships involved in any given case in the witnessing of motion pictures.

Children's Interests in the Radio.—More popular with children than reading, phonographs, indoor games, and in many cases the cinema, is the radio. This attractive instrument has become so inexpensive that approximately two of every three homes in the United States possess one or more receiving sets. One survey [91] has shown that the average family radio is in use two and one-half hours per day. Much of this time is devoted to voluntary listening by children and youths. Due to its simplicity of operation, its wide range of programs which can be tuned in or out at will, and the appeal of its music, drama, sports and news broadcasts, religious and political talks, and comedy and mystery programs, the radio has reached an almost unprecedented pinnacle of popularity. It enables children who would otherwise be limited in their contacts to relatively small or isolated communities to become a part of the larger social world. They can now tune in to events at great distances and may, if they so desire, listen to the performances of athletes, actors, and musicians of note.

A study by Eisenberg [92] of nearly 4,000 New York City children by means of questionnaires to children and their parents, personal interviews, and compositions written by the children, has disclosed the radio preferences of boys and girls who would like to hear programs not offered at the time. Highest in the rankings were plays, mystery stories, music, stories of adventure, songs, and jokes. A relatively small per cent of the children requested programs dealing with murder, ghosts, detective stories, gangsters, tragedy, love, stories of the sea, jazz music, opera, information, and sports. Sex differences were represented by the boys' greater interest in adventure stories and plays and the girls' preferences for general music, dance music, and songs and singing.

[91] H. Cantril and G. W. Allport, *The Psychology of Radio*, New York, Harper & Bros., 1935, Ch. 5.
[92] A. L. Eisenberg, *Children and Radio Programs*, New York, Columbia Univ. Press, 1936.

In an investigation of the program preferences of nine- to eighteen-year-old urban and rural children of Washington (D. C.) and Fairfax County (Va.), marked preference was noted for comedy and variety programs and for historical or romantic drama.[93] This is somewhat of a contrast to Eisenberg's findings in the case of New York children, and suggests that radio preferences are influenced by localities and the social sanctions which obtain among them. The girls in Clark's study possessed a wide range of program interests which included drama, classical and semi-classical music, and children's programs. As can be seen from Table 37, the boys were more

TABLE 37. RELATIVE PREFERENCES FOR RADIO PROGRAMS

Program Type	Percentage of First Choice Programs for Each Program Type	
	Boys	Girls
1. Classical and semi-classical music..............	4	8
2. Religion	0	0
3. Dance, popular, and novelty type..................	15	13
4. Comedy and variety	36	25
5. Detective, crime, and mystery programs...........	13	2
6. Drama: general historical, romantic..............	14	32
7. Travel and adventure	0	0
8. Children's programs (not otherwise listed).........	8	15
9. National, public, and civic affairs.................	0	0
10. News	7	2
11. Sports	1	1
12. Adult programs (including educational, labor, agriculture)	2	2
	100	100

(From W. R. Clark, "Radio Listening Habits of Children," *Journal of Social Psychology*, 11:135 (1940).)

interested in comedy and variety, detective, crime, and mystery stories, and, to some extent, drama.

An extensive study by Jersild [94] has further clarified the question of both boys' and girls' preferences in radio listening.

93 W. R. Clark, "Radio Listening Habits of Children," *Journal of Social Psychology*, 11 : 131-149 (1940).
94 Arthur T. Jersild, *Child Psychology*, New York, Prentice-Hall, Inc., 1940, pp. 444-449.

It has also pointed out age differences in this respect. Jersild has reported that "In general, boys show a higher preference than do girls for programs involving crime and violence, but some such programs also stand high in favor with girls. Girls show a higher preference than do boys for domestic drama, 'crooners' and movie stars, and for programs in which a girl or child characters play a prominent role. Both boys and girls, however, tend to prefer a cast of characters that includes older children or adults, rather than child characters only."

There has been considerable concern on the part of some as to the effects on children's attitudes and emotions of the radio programs they hear. The children in Eisenberg's study maintained [95] that radio listening increased their vocabularies, taught them new games and stories, enlarged their knowledge of music, and provided them with information about history, geography, music, astronomy, English, health, and current events. Parents also reported that the time spent at the radio had increased the children's interest in their homes, improved their food and health habits, improved family relationships, and stressed the development of desirable character traits.

The undesirable effects of radio listening have been studied by a number of investigators. In Eisenberg's [96] report, about 10 per cent of the children attributed "acts of disobedience, stealing, setting of bad examples, mischievousness, and fears" to radio programs. Many of these children also appeared to have suffered from nightmares as the result of listening to certain types of programs. Another study,[97] embodying objective records of changes in pulse rate, blood pressure, respiration, and electrodermal responses of children listening to a variety of radio programs, made it evident that they do respond emotionally to certain of these. Emotional responses were made, however, to such a simple episode as attempting to sing a high note, as well as to such a feat of daring as stunting in an airplane. Whether such stress is harmful to the child's health or emotional stability is a matter of conjecture.

---

[95] A. L. Eisenberg, *op. cit.*, p. 144.
[96] *Ibid.*, p. 145.
[97] J. J. De Boer, "Radio and Children's Emotions," *School and Society,* 50: 369-373 (1939).

It has also been pointed out that children's love of excitement often leads them to listen to programs which their elders question, and that their preferences are very often the ones parents dislike most.[98] Other undesirable features of radio listening are said to include spending too much time unproductively, failure to participate in needed outdoor play, hearing incorrect speech, imitating flippant and affected remarks, and disturbing others who do not care to listen. In spite of these negative features, the weight of evidence appears to be overwhelmingly in favor of radio listening for children. Many of the accusations leveled against this activity are unproved, and are apparently based on *a priori* beliefs concerning the cause and effect relationships involved. The quality of children's programs appears also to be improving. With proper supervision, radio programs may contribute much to the child's understanding of the world.

Interests and Social Growth.—It is obvious that many interests lead to desirable social contacts. It has been said that, other factors being reasonably equal, the boy or girl who can play a good game of tennis (or other sport) will acquire a better personality than one who has failed to develop this or a similar interest. The point is, of course, that tennis or an equivalent activity will in most cases lead to social contacts of a zestful and cooperative nature. Children who develop active interests of this kind, and who become skillful and accommodating, usually possess feelings of success and acceptance, as well as of having made contributions to the socialization of associates. Such mutuality may be said to represent the essence of social growth. Possibilities along this line are inherent in all interests which lend themselves to group action of a socially desirable nature. Modern instructors of music, art, drama, physical education, and the like recognize the socialization values inherent in their fields. A shy, sensitive child may, for example, receive considerable social education through membership in a band, orchestra, or chorus which emphasizes social participation and engages in a variety of cooperative activities. Athletic

[98] H. P. Longstaff, "Preliminary Results of a Study of Mothers' Opinions of Children's Radio Programs," *Journal of Applied Psychology*, 20: 416-419 (1936).

activities may in the same way enable an otherwise inferior boy or girl to develop a much needed feeling of competence.

Reading, radio listening, and attendance at motion picture showings are all more or less sedentary activities, and will thus contribute to socialization only to the extent that parents and teachers adapt them to group endeavors. Schools can encourage group discussions of the materials secured through all three agencies, and can to some extent stage any one of them in a socialized setting. Parents can also arrange to make any one of the three activities a social enterprise in which members of the family cooperate and compare reactions. The vicarious and attitude-modifying benefits of reading, radio listening, and movie attendance need not be their sole contributions. They, too, can be made to aid in social development.

Fisher [99] has warned against the failure of parents and teachers to assist children in making identifications with a variety of constructive interests which will lead to social development and to ego-preserving interests in adult days. It is this psychologist's belief that too many young children lay the groundwork for later mental ill-health by making too strong emotional attachments with their parents, with material possessions, and with various egocentric values which distort their perspective, render them insensitive to more important social values, and inhibit mutuality motives which might otherwise find overt expression. There are times in every individual's life when he needs a variety of interests to which to turn for relief from sorrow, boredom, or isolation. It is in childhood that such interests are most readily developed.

Summary and Implications

The child is born into a social world in which his welfare will be contingent upon the extent to which he becomes socialized; that is, whether he deals with his companions on a basis of mutuality and cooperation. The newborn infant is concerned primarily about himself but will, in the process of growing up, become a social being. If he comes to deal with his associates

[99] V. E. Fisher, *Auto-Correctivism: The Psychology of Nervousness,* Caldwell (Idaho), The Caxton Printers, Ltd., 1937, Ch. 6.

in a manner calculated to win their esteem and approval, he will achieve the feeling of belonging which spells morale and mental health. If he fails to learn acceptable social behavior, the child is destined to some extent to become an isolate—an individual shunned by companions and consequently devoid of status. Social living is imperative in a world in which group action is the common avenue through which many individual satisfactions are achieved.

Although limited at first, the child's social responses become amplified with growth and experience. Beginning with smiling and silent laughter, the young child soon comes to seek the company of others, to play with friendly children, and to exhibit signs of sympathy and concern for the welfare of playmates. Such social development begins with self-centeredness, progresses to avoidance of injury to associates and toleration of the wishes of companions, and in the normal child ends with attitudes of concern for the rights of others. Traits of sympathy, cooperation, competitiveness, and the like develop as a function of social experience and are probably patterned after the cultural climate in which the child develops. Innate tendencies may be in the picture of social growth, but, as anthropologists have noted, social behavior is closely related to the sanctions and mores of the group in which a given child is reared. Studies of gang behavior have corroborated this point.

Recent investigations have stressed the social interrelationships existing within groups of children. Such studies have attempted to ascertain the factors making for friendships and for the choice of companions. Analyses of social structures have been made on the hypothesis that individual children can be understood only in terms of their relationships to the total group of which they are members, and that the behavior of a group is explicable only in the light of knowledge of the social tendencies of the individual children who comprise it. It has been found that child groups frequently are characterized by patterns of attraction, repulsion, and evasion that are to a considerable extent unknown to teachers and parents. Such social structures may be marked by the presence of isolates, mutual-friend pairs, friend chains, triangles, and stars—popular children whom many choose to claim as friends. The factors responsible for such configurations of social attachment are not always clear but probably include similarities of interest and ability, proximity of homes, the desire to be accepted by competent associates, and the tendency to save face by avoiding attachments with individuals who are either noticeably superior or markedly inferior to the child's conception of himself.

Children's interests represent promising avenues for the development of social attitudes. Their concern with material possessions, reading, the motion picture, the radio, and music and art have an important bearing on their chances of achieving satisfactory social adjustment. All of those interests can be tied in with social activities of a dynamic and cooperative nature. Both shy, shut-in personalities and overly aggressive children may be brought to achieve the sense of acceptance they crave through the channel of cooperative socialization with groups possessing similar interests. Homes and schools are each in a favorable position to encourage the use of reading, the radio, and other interests in socialized settings. They can also enable the child to make early identifications with interests which may serve as avenues of self-expression and socialization in mature days. Social growth is dependent upon a multiplicity of factors, many of which are apparently under the control of the social institutions in which the child develops.

QUESTIONS FOR DISCUSSION

1. What would be the probable effect on a child's personality if he were reared in isolation from other children and community associates? Has the evidence secured from studies of "wolf-children" answered this question? If not, what is your answer?
2. What is the relationship between social perception and social behavior? Is one a forerunner of the other or are they mutually independent? Can smiling in infants be considered a sign of social growth? What other infant responses might indicate social progress?

3. Trace the growth of sympathy behavior in young children as portrayed in Murphy's study, and suggest whether other social traits might be developed in the same manner. To what extent does sympathetic behavior appear to be innately or environmentally determined?

4. Is competitive behavior a universal trait in children or is it a function of certain cultures such as are found in the United States? What is the explanation of the claim that children in more primitive cultures are noticeably lacking in aggressiveness?

5. Can it be said that the advantages of pre-adolescent gang activities outweigh their disadvantages? In what way? What important need (or needs) does gang membership satisfy that might otherwise be frustrated? How can the undesirable features of gang life be controlled?

6. How valid do the measures of social growth presented in this chapter appear to be? Would you stake their findings against the judgment of experienced clinicians? In what way does the Vineland Social Maturity Scale resemble a mental test? Is its S.Q. as useful as the I.Q.?

7. What are the practical advantages to teachers and school psychologists of classroom social structure analyses? Do the disclosures of such studies indicate what should be done about isolates, stars, and cliques? Give your reactions to Elliott's proposals.

8. Contrast the sociological and innate factors which seem most influential in the social growth of young children. To what extent can parents and teachers control these forces to the child's advantage? What are the most psychologically sound steps in social education?

9. Why do children's wishes so frequently relate to material objects and possessions? What does this tendency suggest concerning their living conditions? Why do children also apparently prefer to have things given to them to developing the ability to secure them?

10. What reasons can you give for the widespread difference of opinion concerning the probable effects on character and personality of viewing motion pictures? What is the relationship between seeing or knowing about an act and actually carrying it out? Is it possible that the movie is too minor a factor to influence child behavior? Explain.

RECOMMENDED READINGS

Brown, Francis J. *The Sociology of Childhood.* New York: Prentice-Hall, Inc., 1939, Chs. 2-6.

Bühler, Charlotte. "The Social Behavior of Children," in *Handbook of Child Psychology.* (Edited by Carl Murchison.) Worcester: Clark Univ. Press, 1933, Ch. 9.

Gesell, Arnold, and Thompson, H. *Infant Behavior: Its Genesis and Growth,* New York: McGraw-Hill Book Co., Inc., 1934.

Hurlock, Elizabeth B. *Child Development.* New York: McGraw-Hill Book Co., Inc., 1942, Ch. 9.

Isaacs, Susan. *Social Development in Young Children.* London: G. Routledge & Sons, Ltd., 1933.

Jennings, Helen H. "A Sociometric Study of Emotional and Social Expansiveness," in *Child Behavior and Development.* (Edited by Roger G. Barker, *et al.*) New York: McGraw-Hill Book Co., Inc., 1943, Ch. 30.

Meek, Lois H. *Your Child's Development and Guidance Told in Pictures.* Philadelphia: J. B. Lippincott Co., 1940.

Merry, Frieda K., and Merry, Ralph V. *From Infancy to Adolescence.* New York: Harper & Bros., 1940, Chs. 9, 10, 11.

Moreno, J. L. *Who Shall Survive? A New Approach to the Problems of Human Interrelations.* Washington, D. C.: Nervous and Mental Disease Pub. Co., 1934.

Murphy, Gardner, Murphy, Lois B., and Newcomb, T. M. *Experimental Social Psychology.* New York: Harper & Bros., 1937.

Murphy, Lois B. *Social Behavior and Child Personality.* New York: Columbia Univ. Press, 1937.

Thrasher, F. M. *The Gang.* Chicago: Univ. of Chicago Press, 1927.

CHAPTER 14

SAFEGUARDING THE CHILD'S PERSONALITY

SINCE THE DEVELOPMENT OF PERSONALITY is closely associated with the process of social growth, it can be seen that much material pertaining to this important phase of child psychology has already been presented (Chapter 13). There are, however, a number of additional problems in the study of personality that demand the attention of those who propose to guide child development in this crucial area of living. It is often said of a child that he possesses "good," "bad," or "average" personality, and that he "came by" such qualities both genetically and through the process of social development. Just what is meant by the term "personality" and how it develops are important questions the answers to which are dependent upon an understanding of (1) the nature of personality, (2) the psychological organization of personality traits, (3) the origin and growth of personality qualities, and (4) the techniques of personality measurement.

Theories of the Nature of Personality

As is so often the case with psychological concepts, there is far from perfect agreement concerning the nature and organization of personality. The concept of personality has, in fact, been interpreted from a number of points of view. Some would evaluate it in terms of an individual's relations with his associates; others prefer to interpret it on the basis of the qualities possessed by a given person more or less independently of what he does in relation to people. A further view has proposed that the most significant aspects of personality are the more intangible motives and attitudes which, though hidden from consciousness, give direction and organization to behavior. Probably the most popular, albeit the most superficial, concept of personality is that which refers to an individual's dress, manners, enthusiasm, and so-called "sparkle." All of these views have import for the guidance of children; thus each will be considered in terms of the contribution that it can logically be expected to make.

Meaning of the Concept of Personality.—Few words used in modern psychology are as ambiguous as the term "personality." It apparently suggests different meanings to different investigators in both child and adult psychology. Being unable better to describe the unique individuality of a given child, psychologists and laymen alike have followed the custom of calling it his personality, with the further designation that such a personality is likable, disagreeable, strong, weak, dominant, submissive, extrovertive, introvertive, etc., as the case may be. This is, of course, a convenient way of covering up inability to describe the complicated patterns of feeling, thinking, and acting which characterize a given child. The most complicated machine yet invented is probably not as involved and difficult to understand or control as the personality of the child.

Many persons desire a standard definition of personality which will serve both to explain its nature and to render understandable its manifestations. In view of the differing conceptions of the nature of personality, such a definition is not possible of formulation. It is probably best to describe the various reaction systems, components, and attitudes which constitute what is called the personality in the broader sense of that term, and subsequently to relate them to the contrasting conceptions of personality advanced by various advocates. This we shall endeavor to do in the present discussion. The emphasis throughout will, however, be on the implications of such views for child development.

The word personality was originally derived from the Latin expression "persona," which had reference to speaking through a mask while performing on the stage. It was applied in Rome to actors and actresses who chose to cover their faces and to reveal themselves only through action and speech.

Although they did not refer specifically to personality, even the Greeks divided individuals into categories based on their temperament, special capacities, or interests. Plato, for example, classified men as being (1) intellectuals, (2) persons seeking glory and acclaim, such as soldiers and statesmen, and (3) individuals who were governed by physical appetite. Hippocrates made famous the division of personalities into the four types: (1) the *sanguine,* or quick and active person, (2) the *choleric,* or strong and easily aroused individual, (3) the *phlegmatic,* or slow and stolid type, and (4) the *melancholic,* or sad and pessimistic person. These and similar classifications have their counterpart in both pre-scientific and modern times. The scientific study of behavior is, however, of comparatively recent origin, and has led to promising concepts regarding the nature of child personality.

Some modern conceptions of personality are so broad and all-inclusive as to be virtually useless, at least as far as their implication for the guidance of children is concerned. A frequently quoted definition by Dashiell [1] is illustrative: *"A man's personality, we may conclude, is the total picture of his organized behavior, especially as it can be characterized by his fellow men in a consistent way."* Another author, Leary,[2] concurs in this omnibus type of description when he says, "Personality, in the present use of the word, must be thought of as a term indicating a synthesis, or sum total which is more than an addition; an integrated whole, a working organization. . . . Personality is the integrated sum and substance of an individual's behavior as based on inheritance [germinal] and environmental-group training." Such statements are objective and valuable in that they point out the integrated nature of the normal individual's reactions in the social realm; they are, however, too general and indefinite to qualify as working definitions of the nature and organization of personality as students of child development tend to conceive it. Perhaps least useful of all is the statement

[1] J. F. Dashiell, *Fundamentals of General Psychology,* Boston, Houghton Mifflin Co., 1937, p. 579.
[2] D. B. Leary, *Modern Psychology,* Philadelphia, J. B. Lippincott Co., 1928, pp. 184, 329.

that personality is "a descriptive term for forms or kinds of response." [3]

Attempts to define personality in terms of an aggregate of characteristics or components have also been made. In speaking of the human personality as such a totality of major components, Symonds [4] says, "Personality refers to a more complete description of the constitutional make-up including *physique, intelligence, temperament,* and *character."* This author recognizes, however, that such components should be evaluated in terms of their adequacy in insuring desirable social relationships. A somewhat more comprehensive list of categories or dimensions of personality has been presented by Katz and Schanck.[5] These components, which the authors admit are not inclusive of all that goes to make up personality, but which are regarded as operating as an integrated unit, include (1) *capacity*—the physical dimension, (2) *temperament*—the emotional dimension, (3) *traits*—the behavioral dimension, (4) *attitudes*—the subjective or verbal dimension, and (5) the *ego* or *self*—the most generalized statement of personality. An examination of the more specific items listed in connection with each of these categories in Table 38 will suggest the elaborate and interlocked nature of personality organization.

Distinction Between Personality and Character.—The terms "personality" and "character" have often been used synonymously. It seems more logical, however, to regard character as constituting one component or dimension of the total integrated personality. In this sense personality is the more inclusive term, with character being one of its aspects. Character is also usually regarded as referring to an individual's behavior as it relates to laws, social conventions, and particularly to moral considerations. In speaking of this distinction, Sandiford [6] writes, "What a man habitually did, how he responded

[3] Ross Stagner, *Psychology of Personality,* New York, McGraw-Hill Book Co., Inc., 1937, p. 5.
[4] Percival M. Symonds, *Diagnosing Personality and Conduct,* New York, D. Appleton-Century Co., Inc., 1931, pp. 560-561.
[5] D. Katz and R. L. Schanck, *Social Psychology,* New York, John Wiley & Sons, Inc., 1938, p. 417.
[6] Peter Sandiford, *Foundations of Educational Psychology,* New York, Longmans, Green & Co., 1938, p. 401.

TABLE 38. CLASSIFICATION OF TERMS DESCRIPTIVE OF PERSONALITY

I. Capacities—the physical dimension of personality:

   A. Aptitude: skills and abilities determined early in life
      1. Intelligence
      2. Special abilities

   B. Motility: simple motor characteristics
      1. Reaction time
      2. Level of activity: hyperactive-hypoactive
      3. Impulsion and inhibition

II. Temperament—the emotional dimension:

   A. Specific emotional attributes
      1. Emotional frequency and change
      2. Emotional breadth
      3. Emotional strength

   B. Temperamental types
   C. Emotional stability

III. Traits—the behavioral dimension (generalized tendencies toward action):

   A. Introversion-extroversion
   B. Ascendance-submission
   C. Persistence

IV. Attitudes—the subjective or verbal dimension:

   A. Specific interests
   B. General value attitudes
   C. Radical and reactionary attitudes

V. The ego or self—the most-generalized statement of personality:

   A. The ego as the central core of personality
   B. The level of aspiration
   C. Insight or self-objectification

(From D. Katz and R. L. Schanck, *Social Psychology*, New York, John Wiley & Sons, Inc., 1938, p. 417.)

to social situations, became the mark of his character. However, it was inevitable that these actions should be judged according to the ethical code of the time and place, hence character came to mean the moral evaluation of an individual." Character thus refers to the average moral or ethical quality of behavior as appraised by the group of which a given individual is a member.

The view that character involves conformity to conventions and moral standards has been objected to on the ground that it neglects inner forces and that it is thus too materialistic. Some students of the subject feel that, rather than being a name for the quality of overt acts, character should have reference to idealistic principles which operate to determine the direction of moral and ethical behavior. Roback,[7] who has reviewed an extensive amount of literature in this field, has declared that character is "an enduring psychophysical disposition to inhibit instinctive impulses in accordance with a regulative principle." Such a proposal infers the presence in children of good character of an inner psychic mechanism which tends to regulate behavior in accordance with guiding principles or ideals. This view has not been disproved but is out of harmony with the findings of extensive investigations,[8] some of which have shown that, in the case of children at least, behavior is determined largely by the circumstances of given stimulating situations. Children may lie or steal in one situation and refrain from doing so in another. They apparently cannot always be depended upon to be, for example, consistently generous or helpful to other children.

Differing Views of the Nature of Personality.—Since the term personality is used by philosophers, psychologists, sociologists, theologians, jurists, business men, and the general laity, it is to be expected that some of these uses will be in conflict with scientific findings. Some think of personality in terms of external appearance or manners; others feel that the word connotes deep-seated qualities which defy detection. Still others fail to recognize that inferior as well as superior qualities should enter into appraisals of personality, and that both subnormal and abnormal persons also possess personalities. Practically

[7] A. A. Roback, *The Psychology of Character*, New York, Harcourt, Brace & Co., 1927, p. 450.

[8] Hugh Hartshorne and M. A. May, *Studies in Deceit*, New York, The Macmillan Co., 1928. See also by the same authors, *Studies in Service and Self-control*, New York, The Macmillan Co., 1929.

everyone is agreed, however, that certain personality qualities are sufficiently essential to success in life to make a study of their nature and development imperative. Although numerous views of the meaning and nature of personality are extant,[9] there are at least four the pros and cons of which the student of child development should understand if he is to use intelligent methods in dealing with problems of personality development. The points of view in question have been called (1) philosophical, (2) popular, (3) biophysical, and (4) biosocial.

THE PHILOSOPHICAL VIEW OF PERSONALITY. In pre-scientific times, when psychology was a branch of philosophy, personality was commonly regarded as an inner *spiritual* entity. It was thought of as a kind of non-material central force which gave direction to behavior and which enabled man to act intelligently in a world of diverse forces and experiences. Personality was synonymous with the stream of ideas, feelings, and emotions which the individual, being self-conscious, could experience subjectively (internally). Locke[10] made personality practically the central core of man's being when he defined a person as "a thinking intelligent being, that has reason and reflection, and can consider itself as itself . . ." Such a view, which considers actions, including those concerned with facilitating social adjustments, as mere "externalizations" of the true *inner* personality, is hardly acceptable to child psychology since it is essentially philosophical (metaphysical) and practically closes the door to experimentation with the behavior of children.

There are, nevertheless, some present-day psychologists who regard personality as being too involved and elusive to be explained in behavioral terms. Melvin,[11] for example, decries attempts at defining personality in terms of external actions and declares it to be the vital center of man's existence, "which is in no sense comparable to physical substance or mechanisms." Although he recognizes that such a position is metaphysical, Mel-

---

[9] See Gordon W. Allport, *Personality, A Psychological Interpretation,* New York, Henry Holt & Co., Inc., 1937, Ch. 2.
[10] John Locke, *An Essay Concerning Human Understanding,* La Salle (Ill.), Open Court Pub. Co., Book II, Ch. 27 (1905 ed.), p. 246.
[11] A. Gordon Melvin, *Building Personality,* New York, John Day Co., Inc., 1934, p. 56.

vin believes it to be truer to the facts than views which leave out of account the more complicated factors in personality. Instead of appraising an individual by recourse to a list of traits, even though integrated, this conception of the nature of personality regards it as involving certain unknown or "*x*" factors which alone can explain the intangible qualities and characteristics possessed, for example, by statesmen, artists, teachers, poets, the common man, or even children. This interpretation also presumably makes personality a spiritual entity which is not amenable to investigation by the objective methods so essential to a study of child nature. It is thus not helpful in child psychology.

POPULAR VIEWS OF PERSONALITY. It is not uncommon to hear a given individual's personality evaluated on the basis of physical charms or grace of demeanor. Says Schwesinger,[12] "The layman is usually concerned with the externality of the person; his dress, his voice, his gestures, his manners, his motor-coordinations, his charm, his versatility—any reactions, in fact, which are socially important." This conception has been aptly called "shoe polish" personality in that it stresses the external equipment of a socially acceptable nature which an individual may be said to possess. Such a view obviously falls far short of providing insight into a given person's more significant psychological qualities. It also fails to stress the important fact that, even when desirable physical characteristics have been lost, friends of long standing appreciate each other for the deeper personality qualities which they possess. It should nevertheless be recognized that cleanliness, good grooming, polished manners, poise, and an attractive speaking voice enjoy a certain social premium. These qualities are valuable as far as they go, but are not necessarily indicative of the presence of more substantial qualities which may undergird them or atone for the lack of other desirable qualities.

Personality has also been used as a synonym for enthusiasm or drive, and for the "it" and "oomph" of motion picture advertising. These terms are, of course, decidedly indefinite, and

---

[12] Gladys C. Schwesinger, *Heredity and Environment*, New York, The Macmillan Co., 1933, p. 93. By permission.

refer, insofar as they can be understood, to the more expressive and dynamic aspects of the individual. Psychologists do not deny the existence or value of the more tangible social assets so often mentioned in popular discussions of personality, but believe that they should be more penetrating and analytical in their appraisals of personality attributes. Psychologists prefer to make a deeper study of the complex factors influencing personality development and have thus devoted themselves to a more meticulous examination of man's (and the child's) less superficial qualities, as well as his capacity for making adaptations in social situations.

THE BIOPHYSICAL CONCEPTION OF PERSONALITY. Some students of the subject feel that too much emphasis has been placed upon overt behavior as an expression of personality. It is their contention that "personality is what a man really is," [13] and that external actions merely provide clues to the reality which is within the individual when he is judged fairly. As Sandiford [14] puts it, "While it is true that personality may only become known to others through behavior, the definitions [which stress outward actions] give one the impression that personality somehow or other disappears when it is not being expressed. This is a false view. The personality, the self, the person or whatever we care to call it, is still there. When a person gives rapt attention to a performance of beautiful music there are few overt acts which give outsiders a clue to the ecstatic bubblings of the personality within, yet the personality is undoubtedly there and, . . . is known to himself." Sandiford reasons further that, regardless of the appraisals made of him by other individuals, every person has a strong or weak, social or antisocial, balanced or unbalanced, etc., personality.

G. W. Allport,[15] a leader in this field, has insisted that personality is much more than external behavior. It is his belief that if an individual's inner personality were known it would be found to present "a *solid organization* of dispositions and sentiments." Although acknowledging that it is difficult to judge what a man "really is" internally, and that his outward

---

13 Gordon W. Allport, *op. cit.,* p. 48.
14 Peter Sandiford, *op. cit.,* p. 396.
15 Gordon W. Allport, *op. cit.,* pp. 47-50.

expressions may change from hour to hour and day to day, Allport believes that personality is sufficiently stable to indicate a
"style of life" as well as distinctive *"modes of adaptation"* to
the requirements of the environment. According to this view,
personality is inwardly determined and is sufficiently constant,
though unique, to be studied and compared with other personalities. "The gay person may have his sober moments, yet the
general picture of him we carry away is one of lighthearted-
ness. This means, of course, that the average behavior remains
fairly constant with the passing of time, that the average expression of personality is a true reflection of the personality
within." [16]

In an effort more adequately to satisfy his notion of personality as man's essential inner organization, Allport [17] has
offered the following definition: "Personality is the dynamic
organization within the individual of those psychophysical systems that determine his unique adjustments to his environment." It is clear that such a statement assumes not only an
inner psychic factor in man, but an organization of active traits
or systems which lie behind and regulate outward behavior.
The stimulating effects of external conditions on children's behavior is thus neglected. It is this inadequacy of the biophysical view to explain the development of child personality
that has led to the more concrete view of personality organization which will next be presented. Children's personality patterns are distinctive, but they are apparently not characterized
by inner constancy or well developed trait systems.

THE BIOSOCIAL VIEW OF PERSONALITY.   Critics of the biophysical view of personality have been quick to point out its
relative neglect of the social factor in human relations. They
profess inability to see how an individual can be credited with
possessing personality qualities in any absolute sense apart from
the judgments of other persons. As Vernon [18] has pointed
out, an individual's personality has in a sense no meaning apart
from external social expressions and their appraisals by other

[16] Peter Sandiford, *op. cit.,* p. 399.
[17] Gordon W. Allport, *op. cit.,* p. 48.
[18] P. E. Vernon, "The Biosocial Nature of the Personality Trait," *Psychological Review,* 40 : 533-535 (1933).

persons, who in turn are influenced by their own scale of values toward various forms of behavior. This is why given forms of behavior such, for example, as correct and incorrect language, remarks of doubtful dignity, or the use of alcoholic drinks may affect different observers in markedly different ways. The same person may appear as a different personality to different people; each interprets the behavior he notes in the light of his own tastes and attitudes. Although an individual's personality expressions may be sufficiently consistent to characterize him in a general way, the relational nature of personality will prevent any two judgments of him from being identical. He could be rated as a good sport, a risque person, or a knave.

Such considerations as these have led some students of child development to adopt the *biosocial* view, or that of evaluating personality in terms of its "social stimulus value." [19] As May says, "According to the original meaning of the term, personality is that which makes one effective, or gives him influence over others. . . . It is the responses made by others to the individual as a stimulus that define his personality." This author believes that an individual's effect upon his associates is more significant than a list of his personal reaction tendencies, and that, since different people's estimates of a given person differ so noticeably, his personality qualities are not so much his "properties" as they are the impressions he makes on others.

Other definitions of personality which illustrate the relational or biosocial point of view include the following:

> ". . . the sum total of the effect made by an individual upon society." The individual is said to possess personality to the extent that he has learned "to convert his energies into habits or actions which successfully influence other people." [20]

> "Personality is the integrated totality of an individual's reactions to his social groups. . . . Sociality includes one's reactions which identify him with other persons." [21]

[19] M. A. May, "The Foundations of Personality," in *Psychology at Work* (edited by P. S. Achilles), New York, McGraw-Hill Book Co., Inc., 1932, pp. 81-85.

[20] H. C. Link, *The Return to Religion,* New York, The Macmillan Co., 1936, p. 89. By permission.

[21] E. S. Bogardus, *Sociology,* New York, The Macmillan Co., 1941, p. 15. By permission.

On this basis personality refers to the manner and effectiveness with which the individual meets his social and personal obligations and the way in which he impresses his fellows. Personality is not something that functions in a vacuum. It is something that responds so sensitively to its material and social environment that it is difficult to understand the personality of an individual without taking into account the situations in which he reacts.[22]

Allport [23] objects to the above view of personality on the ground that it deals with "external appearances" instead of with inner "psycho-physical systems." It is his belief that the biosocial conception is too narrow to include "the secret schemes, frustrations, worries, and private aspirations that never become socially effective," that it denies personality to "the solitary hermit or to Robinson Crusoe (at least before the advent of Friday)," and that it invites "a perilous distinction between 'more' and 'less' personality." To Allport "the tortured poet dwelling in attic obscurity" has as much personality as a movie queen. He also feels that it is a mistake to reason that "as we appear to others so must we be."

It is probable that the objections advanced against appraising personality in terms of social stimulus value have been based on an unnecessarily limited view of the possibilities involved. The influence that any individual exerts upon others is probably a reflection of the qualities he possesses. It is a mistake to think of biosocial personality purely in terms of so-called external appearances. The thoroughly sincere and socially competent person is usually one who has demonstrated the possession of desirable personal characteristics.[24] Inner personal adjustment and social effectiveness tend to be found together. Socially successful individuals tend also to be relatively free from "secret schemes," frustrations, nervous symptoms, feelings of guilt or inferiority, and other such efficiency-destroying handicaps. The biosocial point of view has the advantage, furthermore, of

---

[22] Robert Leeper, *Psychology of Personality and Social Adjustment,* Cornell College Book Store, 1937.
[23] Gordon W. Allport, *op. cit.,* pp. 39-43.
[24] Louis P. Thorpe, *Personality and Life,* New York, Longmans, Green & Co., 1941, pp. 134-136.

conceiving personality in terms of functional skills that can be learned, and of being objective and understandable psychologically, also, perhaps best of all, of being adaptable to *the development of concrete personality qualities in children.* When personality is defined in terms of adequate personal adjustment and of social skills which lead to further acceptance, it is well suited to a constructive program of child development.

Implications of the Biosocial View of Personality.—So far as child psychology is concerned, it is impractical to regard personality as an abstract factor or pattern of factors within the individual. The very idea of child personality requires the visualization of concrete situations involving social behavior. Many actions and attitudes observed in children could not logically be thought of as being biologically inherited or as emerging from inner guiding principles. They are apparently the products of social experience as encountered in early home life and in subsequent wider community contacts. It thus appears reasonable to conclude that personality qualities in children are to a considerable extent "home-made," and that their development can be controlled.

Such guidance can be accomplished to an extent not formerly thought possible by regarding the child as an energy system in which marked stresses arise when fundamental needs and desires are thwarted excessively. It will be recalled that children are apparently under greatest tension when their bodily needs are not met, when their need for affectionate recognition is not adequately satisfied, and when their lack of social skill in dealing with other children or adults leads to rejection. Such stresses do not arise if the child is provided with security and affection at the same time that he is taught regard for the welfare and security of others. The child who enjoys a secure start in life is on the way to adequate socialization and thus to the development of a good personality. A program characterized by balance between ego recognition and social living is apparently best calculated to safeguard the child's personality.

The advantages in the rearing of children of the biosocial view of personality have been summarized elsewhere by the present author.[25] To quote, "One reason for the widespread lack of appreciation of such important psychological bases of human relations as mutual respect and regard for the feelings of others is that so many children are reared on an individualistic program. Children so trained soon acquire the philosophy that every man should be out for what he can get, and that it should be every intelligent individual's business to get what he can before someone 'beats him to it.' This is again the 'every man for himself and the Devil take the hindmost' theory that is so damaging in human relations. That such an attitude is widespread and deeply intrenched in the outlook of a great many children cannot be gainsaid.

"It is better if boys and girls are taught that the security and happiness of each individual depends upon the actions of all. Properly guided the child can be made to realize that his acts must pass the test of fairness to others. He can be taught that the welfare of his associates, as well as his own desires, must be taken into account. With this social-pattern view of behavior as his standard and with the realization that it brings self-completeness, the growing child learns to expend his energies in social actions as well as in his own behalf. This plan reacts in everyone's favor. The child makes his contribution to the group, and experiences personal satisfaction from so doing; when associates respond with approval, the child gets his ego-recognition without having sought it [directly], and personality balance is the result."

Being concrete and tangible, such a program of personality development can be "engineered" by intelligent parents and teachers. It can be operated on the defensible assumption that social skills are definable in terms of actions and that, like other skills, they can be learned under properly motivated conditions. When undergirded by a morale emerging from having been well treated and of having been recognized as an individual of worth, such an attitude leads the child naturally to wider spheres of social living.[26] A child reared in this fashion readily learns the accepted social techniques of recognizing abilities dis-

[25] *Ibid.*, pp. 156-157.
[26] Percival M. Symonds, *The Psychology of Parent-Child Relationships,* New York, D. Appleton-Century Co., Inc., 1939, pp. 98-103.

played by others, giving associates credit for knowledge and good judgment, giving indirect compliments, showing an interest in other people's problems, emphasizing the worth of others, and making it a point to be of assistance to friends. Sincere and intelligent methods of dealing with people are easily acquired by children whose personality development was adequately guided (made satisfying) in early life.

The Psychological Nature of Personality Traits

It is a commonly accepted belief that every child is characterized by a combination of discernible personality traits which distinguish him as an individual. One child may be said to be gentle, dependable, and reticent; another is described as being honest, sympathetic, and loyal. It is thus assumed that traits exist in amount and that they involve a consistency of behavior which marks one person off from another. This is the so-called common-sense view and one that is undoubtedly widely held.

The Problem of Personality Trait Organization.—One's conception of child personality is dependent to a considerable extent upon his belief concerning the nature of personality *traits*. The problem thus arises whether traits are static, unified entities which bring about consistency in behavior, or whether they are merely names for more or less loosely organized groupings of tendencies to act in predictable ways in given situations. If one subscribes to the view that traits are fixed blocks or faculties in personality, and especially if such a view includes belief in the gene inheritance of traits, he is thereby committed to the assumption that behavior is regulated by innate and possibly predetermined factors. If, somewhat to the contrary, one accepts the position that child behavior is determined by specific stimulating situations, he takes his stand with those who believe that external conditions and not inner factors are primarily responsible for the behavior noted in children. In this sense, personality traits such as loyalty, honesty, generosity, etc., are essentially names for specific responses to social situations.

The complexity of the trait problem is further emphasized by the assertion that "traits are not units of personality, *measurable* by some fixed standard comparable to measures of height and weight. Traits are not measurable because they are not quantities." [27] It is the foregoing writer's contention that when people are said to possess, for example, "very little" tact or a "great deal" of courage, these expressions are figurative. What is apparently meant is that individuals exhibit a certain degree of *development* or expression of any given trait. Personality is primarily a *balance* or *blend* among a great many traits exhibiting varying degrees of expression; it is not a summation of traits comparable to the quantitatively determined intelligence quotient. These considerations should make it evident that the question of trait organization is, like many other problems associated with child development, marked by conflicting points of view. Some of these are apparently more useful in child psychology than others.

The Theory of "Unitary" or General Traits.—Most prominent among those who hold to the theory of generalized traits is G. W. Allport, leader of the group espousing the biophysical view of personality organization. Although recognizing that traits can be only relatively independent of one another in the integrated human personality, Allport believes that a trait may be regarded as a *"generalized* response unit that reflects personality." [28] He has more recently defined traits as "dynamic and flexible dispositions, resulting, at least in part, *from the integration of specific habits,* expressing characteristic modes of adaptation to one's surroundings." [29] This is comparable to saying that traits are dynamic factors which regulate behavior from *within* the individual, and that they account for the quality and consistency of external actions.

In describing the function of a trait, this psychologist [30] has claimed it to be "a generalized and focalized neuropsychic sys-

[27] J. H. Griffiths, *The Psychology of Human Behavior,* New York, Farrar & Rinehart, Inc., 1935, p. 466.
[28] Gordon W. Allport, "What Is a Trait of Personality," *Journal of Abnormal and Social Psychology,* 25 : 368-372 (1931).
[29] Gordon W. Allport, *Personality, A Psychological Interpretation,* New York, Henry Holt & Co., Inc., 1937, pp. 139-140.
[30] *Loc. cit.*

tem (peculiar to the individual), with the capacity to render many stimuli functionally equivalent, and to initiate and guide consistent (equivalent) forms of adaptive and expressive behavior." It is the assumption that behavior is both relatively independent of stimulating situations and determined by inner dispositions (traits) that has brought about most criticisms of the "unitary" point of view. Some psychologists consider this

Figure 93. The *Trait-Conception* of a Single Personality as a System of Focal but Interdependent Substructures, the Units Being Essentially Different in Every Personality

(From G. W. Allport, *Personality, A Psychological Interpretation,* New York, Henry Holt & Co., Inc., 1937, p. 246.)

a somewhat mystic view which fails to harmonize with the findings of research. It assumes, among other things, that trait behavior is relatively consistent regardless of external circumstances. On this basis, an individual who possessed the trait of kindness would be thoughtful of all (or nearly all) persons and animals; one who had the trait of honesty would be compelled by inner mechanisms, as it were, to be honest in all (or nearly all) situations; and the person who was unfortunate enough to be disloyal would be so in practically all instances.

That such consistency of behavior is not usually manifested, especially by children, is well known.

The Doctrine of "Specificity" of Organization.—Some psychologists believe that, instead of being fixed inner entities, personality traits are nothing more than names for *groupings of specific tendencies to act in characteristic ways.* As the Murphys [31] have written, "both the external and the internal responses of children in social situations depend so intimately upon the whole situation that it is utterly misleading to speak of traits as if they were located *in* the child. They exist only in the relation between the child and his social surroundings. . . . Even the most submissive child becomes, in a new social situation, an ascendant child." It is this and similar observations that have led many students of child development to regard trait names as convenient labels for groupings of specific actions which can only be rated in terms of the values assigned them by the individuals evaluating them. Traits are thus not so much a child's own possessions as they are action patterns in the eyes of his observers.

In harmony with this position, Curti [32] has defined traits as "more or less loosely organized systems of habits and attitudes, which have been developed in the process of adjustment to the special and varying conditions of life." Similarly, May [33] says, "My own view is that traits are only convenient names given to types or qualities of behavior which have elements in common. They are not psychological entities but rather categories for the classification of habits." This conception of trait organization is evidently based on the facts that adults may, for example, be strictly honest in business relations but be quick to deceive a train conductor who may appear to be passing them by; also that children frequently use bad language or tell lies in given situations whereas they are careful in their speech and meticulously truthful in others. Fluctuations of this kind have led

[31] Lois B. Murphy and G. Murphy, "The Influence of Social Situations upon the Behavior of Children," in *Handbook of Social Psychology* (edited by Carl Murchison), Worcester, Clark Univ. Press, 1935, p. 1093.

[32] Margaret W. Curti, *Child Psychology*, New York, Longmans, Green & Co., 1938, p. 468.

[33] Mark A. May, "Problems of Measuring Character and Personality," *Journal of Social Psychology*, 3 : 133-145 (1932).

to the realization that reactions are to a considerable extent functions of specific stimulating situations; also that they are relatively unpredictable in new situations. As one writer [34] has declared, traits (particularly moral traits) are "creations not of biology" but of "conventional ethics," and it is likely that investigators "may be attempting to measure entities that exist only in name."

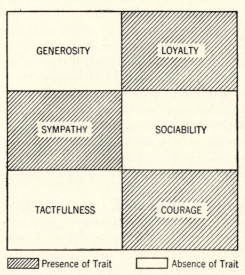

Figure 94. Traits as Unitary, Static Blocks in Personality

Evidence for the Theory of Specific Traits.—Evidence for the specificity of behavior has been strikingly apparent in investigations of such contrasted personality traits as emotional stability-neuroticism, introversion-extroversion, ascendance-submission, and the like. In a study by Allport [35] of the adjustments made by college students to a variety of specific situations involving socially dominant or submissive behavior, it was found that most of the subjects behaved neither wholly dominantly nor wholly submissively. In answering such ques-

[34] J. K. Folsom, *Social Psychology,* New York, Harper & Bros., 1931, pp. 535-538.
[35] Gordon W. Allport, "A Test for Ascendance-Submission," *Journal of Abnormal and Social Psychology,* 23 : 118-136 (1928).

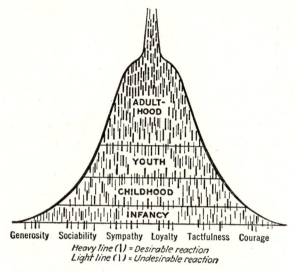

Generosity   Sociability   Sympathy   Loyalty   Tactfulness   Courage
Heavy line (|) = Desirable reaction
Light line (|) = Undesirable reaction

Figure 95. The Genetic Development of Trait Consistency

Illustrating consolidation through the increasing tendency to be influenced by guiding principles, ideals, and laws.

tions as what they would do about returning recently purchased articles which they did not wish to keep, how they would probably behave in the presence of superior business or professional associates, and whether they would seek to meet important personages at social affairs, the majority of the students indicated that their responses would fluctuate from situation to situation. As can be seen in Figure 96, the most typical response was that of being ascendant in some social situations and submissive in others. The possession by these students of consistent traits in the areas under consideration would have resulted in a bimodal (two curves) curve of distribution rather than the approximately normal curve actually secured. Most of the college students were evidently neither markedly ascendant nor markedly submissive. This finding is not unlike the results of other trait studies.

No doubt the most elaborate series of investigations of trait behavior yet undertaken, and one carried out with approximately 10,000 children and youths, was that by Hartshorne and

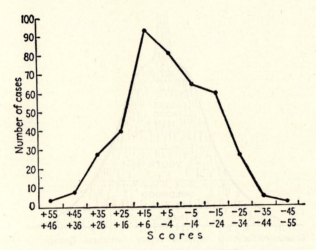

Figure 96. Distribution of Ascendance-Submission Scores of 400 College Men

Base line represents scores grouped into intervals of ten.

(From G. W. Allport, "A Test for Ascendance-Submission," *Journal of Abnormal and Social Psychology, 23*:129 (1928).)

May,[36] in which a successful effort was made to subject them to concrete test situations involving honesty, service, and self-control which they did not recognize as such. The situations utilized in the honesty field included opportunities to cheat in examinations, to keep small amounts of money (a dime, for example) found in boxes used in games, to falsify about athletic records, to peek in games involving blindfolding of the eyes, and to deceive on tests of muscular coordination. Proceeding on the assumption that the amount and character of deceptive behavior might be functions of the specific situations in which they occur, these investigators found (after five years of experimentation) that no child cheats in a wholesale way or is always honest or always dishonest. It was learned, instead, that honesty behavior fluctuates from situation to situation, and that a child who cheats on an examination may or may not, for example, keep money that he knows is not his or add more answers to a test after time is called. Honest and deceitful re-

[36] Hugh Hartshorne and M. A. May, *Studies in Deceit,* 1928; *Studies in Service and Self-control,* 1929; and *Studies in the Organization of Character,* 1930; all by The Macmillan Co., New York.

sponses were so specialized (specific) that no trait of honesty could be detected in the subjects.

These experimental data suggest that, at least in the case of children, honesty behavior is not dictated by psychological factors (traits) within the individual; it is, rather, a name for the classification of acts which have been influenced by the child's needs and the situations in which these needs had to be met. As Hartshorne and May explained their findings, deception in a child is a symptom of social friction in which a conflict between desires or needs and the prohibitions of custom is involved. When he deceives, the child is not necessarily exhibiting either a tendency in that direction or an innate disposition to be dishonest, he is merely endeavoring to solve a problem which the environment in the form of social standards has forced upon him. Before he is sufficiently mature in the sense of having developed relatively generalized attitudes toward honesty behavior (or other virtues), the child often resorts to clandestine (dishonest) ways of satisfying his desires. The investigators [37] sum up their findings by saying that honest acts are not motivated by "an inner entity operating independently of the situations in which the individuals are placed," but that they are functions of specific situations in the sense that a child "behaves similarly in different situations in proportion as these situations are alike . . . and are comprehended as opportunities for deception or honesty."

In criticizing the interpretations of the Character Inquiry by Hartshorne and May, Allport [38] points out what he believes to be inconsistencies which actually favor his belief in the unitary nature of traits, especially in older children and adults. Allport's arguments may be summarized as follows:

1. The low relationships found between test results in such a trait, for example, as honesty, mean that children "are not consistent *in the same way*, not that they are inconsistent with *themselves*. When a child seems inconsistent (steals), it is likely that

[37] Hugh Hartshorne and M. A. May, *Studies in Deceit*, New York, The Macmillan Co., 1928, p. 385. By permission.
[38] Gordon W. Allport, *Personality, A Psychological Interpretation*, New York, Henry Holt & Co., Inc., 1937, pp. 250-258.

one general trait, i.e., inferiority, has superseded the influence of another general trait, i.e., honesty.

2. The investigators made the mistake of basing their work upon *social and ethical concepts.* If they had studied natural personality qualities uncomplicated by "good" and "bad" qualities, much more consistency of behavior would have been in evidence. Moral traits tend to create the illusion of specificity, especially in children who are too young to be guided by ideals and standards.

3. The utilization of mass data for large populations of relatively

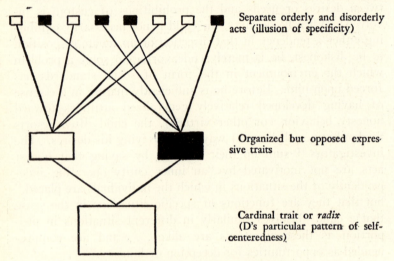

Separate orderly and disorderly acts (illusion of specificity)

Organized but opposed expressive traits

Cardinal trait or *radix* (D's particular pattern of self-centeredness)

Figure 97. An Illustration of Congruence

The unity of personality becomes apparent as more basic dynamic systems are sought.

(From G. W. Allport, *Personality, A Psychological Interpretation,* New York, Henry Holt & Co., Inc., 1937, p. 357.)

young children instead of a more intensive study of the behavior of fewer and more mature subjects was favorable to the findings secured. The method chosen, not the children's psychological nature, determined the results.

4. The findings are out of harmony with the common-sense testimony of everyday living. In spite of the specificity doctrine, we characterize our friends as being trustworthy, affable, humorous, high-strung, sociable, and the like, and feel that we can depend

upon them to continue to be so. Apparent incongruity (incongruity) of behavior is merely a case of our failure to discover the deeper units of personality organization (see Figure 97) which may involve deep-lying opposed, rather than inconsistent, traits.

Compromise View of the Nature of Traits.—Most students of child development recognize the importance of both stimulating conditions and attitudes within the individual for the determination of conduct. They differ principally as to the degree of influence that should be attributed to either of these factors. It is probably true that the influences of specific situations and of organism "sets," as the latter have resulted from the flow of experiences, enjoy a mutually interdependent relationship. From the standpoint of character traits, which involve problems similar to those encountered in personality traits (except for the moral element), Murphy et al.[39] have stated that, "It must be understood that there appears to be no 'all or none' answer to the question as to whether character (traits) is general or specific. Rather the question must be stated quantitatively: 'To what *extent* is character general; to what *extent* is it specific?' *Evidence suggests that character is predominantly specific, but to a somewhat smaller degree general.* Character is a function of two variables, of which the more important is the specific situation, but no prediction is meaningful unless the variable of existing habit organization is also given its place." If this statement were qualified by substituting the term "trait" for "character," it is probable that a tentatively adequate solution to the trait problem has been achieved.

Traits are apparently neither wholly specialized nor entirely unitary, but they no doubt tend to become generalized as the child accumulates meaningful social experience. It is probably true that a child's response in any given instance is influenced by his particular habits and attitudes, how he feels about his own status, the general social atmosphere that surrounds him, and his physical, mental, and emotional state on the occasion of the stimulation. This is practically the conclusion arrived at

[39] Gardner Murphy, Lois B. Murphy, and T. M. Newcomb, *Experimental Social Psychology,* New York, Harper & Bros., 1937, p. 604.

by Thorpe, Clark, and Tiegs [40] in their study of the reactions of several hundred school children to more than a thousand specific verbal test situations involving a variety of aspects of personal and social adjustment. It was apparent to these investigators that children of elementary school age do develop generalized tendencies to think, feel, and act with regard to situations which they face. As in the Character Inquiry,[41] this was particularly noticeable in the case of children who had reached sufficient maturity to be influenced in their behavior by social standards and generalized principles. Or, as stated by Sanford et al.,[42] in connection with an intensive study of 48 children in which extensive physical, mental, and personality measurements were employed, in the process of development social prohibitions and sanctions become integrated with the child's ego to the extent that whereas he was originally controlled by environmental pressures he is ultimately able to control himself.

The Origin and Growth of Personality Traits

The course of personality development with its accompanying social growth has been presented in a general way in preceding chapters, especially in those concerned with the influence of early home life and the process of social development. It is not the purpose here to repeat those discussions. An effort will be made, rather, to show under what conditions and by what processes personality qualities emerge in infants and children. The manner in which traits, defined either as general tendencies or as groupings of specific dispositions to behave, apparently appear will be emphasized.

How Personality Traits Emerge in Infants.—There are grounds for asserting that at birth the infant's personality is essentially "nondescript" or potential, and that it will develop with time on the basis of expansions and differentiations as de-

---

[40] Louis P. Thorpe, Willis W. Clark, and Ernest W. Tiegs, *Manual of the California Test of Personality*, Los Angeles, California Test Bureau, 1939.

[41] Hugh Hartshorne and M. A. May, *Studies in the Organization of Character*, New York, The Macmillan Co., 1930, pp. 357-359.

[42] R. Nevitt Sanford *et al.*, *Physique, Personality, and Scholarship*, Monographs of the Society for Research in Child Development, Vol. 8, No. 1 (1943), p. 639.

termined by the character of the stimulus-patterns which surround him in early life. If it can be said that the psychological life of the infant is subject to laws of development and that its growth directions are influenced by environmental pressures, it follows that personality traits are primarily products of responses to people and to cultural demands. Unless personality development is limited by metaphysical or physiological factors which are beyond control by man, the above view appears to have much to commend it. As Lerner and Murphy,[43] after an extensive investigation of young children's projective play activities, have said, "the unconscious organization of experience by the child, and his personality structure, is the result of the impact on him of all the conscious and unconscious expressions of parents' personalities, as well as their conscious attitudes toward children and their bringing-up." Whether the child will become "a genial, satisfied, constructive citizen making good use of whatever resources his world offers him; or a tense, anxious, uncertain man compulsively trying to hold on to whatever success he has gained so far" is believed to be in the main rooted in his preschool experience.

Evidence for the influence on personality traits of social factors is not hard to find. In an effort to check the frequent claim that lusty crying in newborn infants is indicative of a tempestuous temperament and that quiet behavior signifies a good disposition, Bonham and Sargeant [44] investigated the permanency of such reactions. Ratings for crying, irritability, quietness, and other traits were secured for infants a few hours of age and compared with their responses when they were eighteen to twenty-four months of age. Finding no significant relationship between the two ratings, the investigators concluded that early temperamental traits in infants are not inherent in their constitutional make-up.

Reynolds [45] studied the incidence of negativism (obstinacy)

[43] Eugene Lerner and L. B. Murphy, *Methods for the Study of Personality in Young Children*, Monographs of the Society for Research in Child Development, Vol. 6, No. 4 (1941), pp. 3-8.

[44] M. Bonham and M. K. Sargeant, *A Study of the Development of Personality Traits in Infants Eighteen to Twenty-four Months of Age*, Master of Arts Thesis, Catholic Univ. of America, 1928.

[45] N. M. Reynolds, *Negativism of Preschool Children*, Teachers College Contributions to Education, No. 299, Columbia Univ., 1928.

in young children and found that it developed among those who were consistently ignored or whose cherished forms of play and other activities were frequently denied expression. Such negativism was believed to be the result of repression or of inferiority feelings from which the children sought to escape by adopting an attitude of excessive independence. If such be the case, negativism constitutes an illustration of the genesis of a trait not present in the infant's original "nondescript" personality. The same may be true of jealousy, which Sewell [46] found to be associated frequently with the arrival in the family of a new member. When ignored or neglected in favor of a younger sibling, many children (in a sampling of 70 children) either resented the newcomer, denied any relationship to him, or actually made overt attacks upon him. In some instances the supplanted children, although formerly happily adjusted to their family, underwent observable personality changes in which shyness, timidity, daydreaming, or negativism appeared. It was found that personality changes resulting from loss of parental preferment tended to appear most noticeably between the ages of eighteen and forty-two months.

A number of investigations [47] have pointed to the probability that socio-economic status, including physical facilities, recreational equipment, intelligence of parents, and occupational rating of the father, has little bearing on a child's personality development. Emotionally maladjusted children are apparently nearly as likely to have enjoyed such a cultural background as one marked by overcrowded conditions, dilapidated furnishings, absence of books, and poverty. Judging from the above and similar findings, the primary factor in personality maladjustment is frustration or overindulgence of the child's fundamental need for parental affection and sympathetic handling. The young child's social environment registers its impact principally through the channel of parental attitudes and

[46] M. Sewell, "Some Causes of Jealousy in Young Children," *Smith College Studies in Social Work*, Vol. 1 (1930), pp. 6-22.

[47] See, for example, C. K. A. Wang, "The Significance of Early Personal History for Certain Personality Traits," *American Journal of Psychology*, 44 : 768-774 (1932). Also Kenneth V. Francis, "A Study of the Means of Influence of Socio-economic Factors upon the Personality of Children," *Journal of Juvenile Research*, 17 : 70-77 (1933).

actions. Even the infant may, if *excessively* waited on and fondled whenever he cries, come to expect such satisfactions, and to register considerable resentment when refused their fulfillment upon demand. He may also develop a condition of hypertension damaging to digestion, sleep, and ultimately to personality adjustment if treated roughly or exposed to excessive noise and confusion.

Many individuals naively conclude that temperamental or other personal tendencies which appear during the first postnatal weeks or months are necessarily biologically inherited. They apparently do not realize that parental treatment, experiences leading to conditioned responses, and in some instances organic ailments can modify personality traits to an extent not usually realized. It is probably principally in these ways that such contrasted tendencies as dominance or submission, sympathy or cruelty, cooperativeness or negativism, and emotional stability or nervousness are transmitted from parents to children. Since infantile attitudes often carry over into adult years and make their effects felt long after the causes of their appearance have been forgotten, *social* heritage is evidently a primary source of personality traits. These apparently accrue in the flexible psychological life of the infant and child as a result of the types of stimulus patterns provided by their elders.

The Process of Trait Development.—The traditional method of endeavoring to build socially desirable traits, no matter how defined, has been that of ardent verbal exhortation coupled with the laying down of rules of behavior. It has been customary to urge upon children the virtues of honesty, sympathy, generosity, obedience, etc., in glowing terms. Children have in many instances responded to such enthusiastic teachings, apparently accepting the ideals involved. However, as Charters [48] has pointed out, such resolutions are for the most part doomed to become "pleasant failures." As this writer states, in the case of children at least, such purposes will not necessarily result in desirable behavior for the reason that whereas behavior is *concrete* and *specific,* purposes are *abstract*

[48] W. W. Charters, *The Teaching of Ideals,* New York, The Macmillan Co., 1927. pp. 105-106. By permission.

and *general*. Furthermore, exhortations are not as a rule expressed at a time and place that can be associated with concrete situations in which the child's dynamic needs are involved and in which he is called upon to behave overtly.

As Charters brings out in this connection, "One does not act honestly in general; he performs a thousand specific acts of honesty. He tells the truth about the sharpened tool he ruined, about the dime he lost, or about the window that he broke in play." On this basis a child would eventually become honest (or obedient, sympathetic, tolerant, etc.) only after multiplying into the hundreds concrete acts involving honesty in which such behavior had been made both *natural* and *satisfying*. Such an approach to the development of either character or personality traits is a far cry from the older methods of wishing for them, learning to repeat rules concerning them, listening to glowing stories in which they are exemplified, or depending on the alleged regulating value of intellectual abilities.[49]

It is thus believed by many students of the subject that the stimulating situation is the fundamental unit of trait action and that it is the nucleus from which the earliest actions arise and around which consolidation of behavior must take place. Children must be taught specific trait responses, one by one at first, in these concrete situations. Only as a child grows older and acquires a large number of individual trait actions can he hope to apply rationally analyzed principles of conduct. In the meantime the appropriate specific responses must be elicited by arranging situations in which the child will more or less spontaneously do the right things (as interpreted by adults) because they are made tangibly satisfying. Desirable trait development thus involves the presence of a social environment in which intelligent supervision of a considerable share of the child's experiences is exercised.

The procedures involved in the development of the trait of sympathy have been presented by Ragsdale,[50] with the stipulation that such training includes (a) the recognition by the child of many concrete situations in which behavior exemplifying

[49] R. Nevitt Sanford *et al.*, *op. cit.*, pp. 503-506.
[50] Clarence E. Ragsdale, *Modern Psychologies and Education*, New York, The Macmillan Co., 1932, pp. 346-352.

sympathy is both desirable and appropriate and (b) specific experience in *types of action* which are recognized as embodying
sympathy. To these points could be added the fundamental
facts that, to be amenable to satisfactory development involving
social cooperation, the child should: first, have a sense of security and well-being based upon adequate acceptance by his
family; second, live in an environment in which sympathy behavior is exemplified by his elders; and third, be given the
opportunity of enjoying considerable social experience with
other children.

sympathy

Assuming that the above conditions had been met and that
a child was available for training, one might select a situation
in which another child had fallen and injured himself slightly.
The child under instruction could immediately be brought into
a position where it would be natural and satisfying to carry out
certain *specific* and *concrete* acts, such as assisting the fallen
child to his feet, fondling him, comforting him verbally, or
going for further help. Each of these acts would be appropriate under the circumstances, and each represents a concrete
enactment of sympathy behavior. The child has thus func-
tioned satisfactorily in a sympathy situation, and has had experience both in recognizing and in carrying out a *specific pattern of responses* exemplifying sympathy. He has, furthermore, been rewarded (afforded satisfaction) by the pleasure of
running to an accident, by the commendation of his older companion, and by the feeling of status which his usefulness made
possible.

A logical next step would be to multiply situations in which
the child experienced added opportunities for expressing sympathy behavior appropriate to his age and social maturity. Subsequent situations might well include those in which another
child had lost a toy, broken a doll, lost his dog, or in which a
pet animal was in distress. After adapting himself to numerous
experiences involving such behavior, the child would be on his
way to the development of the relatively consistent mode of
behavior commonly called the trait of sympathy, particularly if
a trait is defined as a grouping of related tendencies to act in
specific ways in certain situations. And so it could be for gen-

erosity, tolerance, loyalty, industry, dependability, and other such desirable traits—all are dependent for their development upon concrete responses made in a wide variety of social settings and under conditions conducive to both appropriate behavior and satisfactory rewards.

Hartshorne and May [51] have stated that, as far as moral traits are concerned, conduct can and under appropriate conditions does become more consistent as the child comes to organize his behavior in relation to principles and as social ideals are understood and accepted. Complete consistency, in the sense of always conforming to social dictates or desirable personality patterns, is apparently never reached, but may under ideal circumstances become highly developed. And, what is essential for an understanding of trait development, as principles become accepted as values and crystallize into dispositions to behave in specific ways (habits), the latter become influences for determining *the direction of behavior in new situations*. Such consolidation and consistency of response is greatly stimulated if, in the course of varied experiences, the involvements of the situations encountered by a child are explained to him. If the common elements of situations involving, for example, honesty or loyalty are pointed out, and if the possibilities of applying specific trait actions (i.e., returning money belonging to another, telling the truth about one's accomplishments, being faithful to friends) to a number of concrete situations are adequately shown, the likelihood is increased that the child will come to generalize his experiences in harmony with moral requirements and in terms of commonly accepted trait names.

Character versus Personality Development.—The assumption has been made in the above discussion that character and personality traits are sufficiently similar both in organization and amenability to modification to be developed by the method described. This may not be a valid conclusion, since it should be recognized that, whereas character development involves an

[51] Hugh Hartshorne and M. A. May, *Studies in the Organization of Character*, New York, The Macmillan Co., 1930, pp. 357-359. See also Robert S. McElhinney and Henry L. Smith, *Personality and Character Building*, Winona Lake (Ind.), Light & Life Press, 1942, Ch. 10.

acquaintance with and acceptance of moral actions and values, good personality is primarily concerned with the acquisition of acceptable *social* responses. Character education may be said to be concerned with the *rightness* or *wrongness* of behavior as determined by customs and group mores, whereas personality development envisages improvement in social dominance, social skill, emotional stability, self-confidence, self-reliance, and other such *non-moral* but socially desirable traits. Much could be said, nevertheless, for the view that the term "good personality" should be considered sufficiently inclusive to embody desirable moral behavior. It may be questioned whether the individual who disregards the rights and property of others should be regarded as possessing a desirable personality even though he is capable of mingling pleasantly with members of his group.

The concept of desirable character involves a somewhat similar dilemma. The question is often asked whether good character means mere conformance to the standards of right and wrong behavior as accepted by a social group, or whether it refers to an inner motive to live in accordance with certain idealistic values. Although these points of view are not necessarily conflicting, it is commonly felt that control through fear of the consequences of not harmonizing with moral endorsements is based upon a fundamentally self-centered "because it pays" motive. Group approval is essential to a sense of security, but genuine purpose to behave in accordance with morally sound principles is conducive to both individual and social well-being. Because of its accompanying feeling of responsibility for behavior, this type of control has been designated as *internal* regulation.[52]

Such a concept involves the danger, however, of enabling parents and teachers who desire to do so to escape responsibility for their incompetency in dealing with children's problems by claiming that the latter should "know better" when they do wrong. As the Character Inquiry and other studies [53] have

[52] A. A. Roback, *The Psychology of Character,* New York, Harcourt, Brace & Co., 1922, Chs. 25-28.
[53] V. Jones, "Children's Morals," in *Handbook of Child Psychology* (edited by Carl Murchison), Worcester, Clark Univ. Press, 1933, Ch. 11.

suggested, children probably do not possess either moral traits or an innate capacity for making moral discriminations. Investigations have shown, rather, that children develop a sense of right and wrong from parental teachings and concrete experiences. Insofar as children can be said to have attitudes toward moral behavior, these are apparently in the form of habits or dispositions to behave in specific ways that have resulted from satisfying or non-satisfying experiences.

THE DEVELOPMENT OF MORAL BEHAVIOR.   Modern child psychology does not regard the infant as being either moral or immoral.   Being devoid of all knowledge and of dispositions in this respect, the neonate is non-moral.   He is apparently possessed neither of a tendency to "sin" nor of a natural inclination to be righteous.   Neither can it be said that the young child has an inner reservoir of virtue from which honest or generous acts, for example, issue.   The child's morality can only be evaluated in terms of the quality (as determined by group regulations) of his acts as they affect the well-being of others and himself.   These will in turn be determined by the teachings he has received at the hands of his elders, by the extent to which he has been made to feel acceptable and secure, and by the degree of satisfyingness experienced in numerous concrete situations involving moral or immoral behavior as conceived by adults.

As the child learns to conform to the moral standards of his home, and to those of his school and his playmates, he comes gradually to comprehend the abstract concepts of right and wrong (as defined by his group or groups) and may develop a disposition to behave acceptably to an increasingly generalized extent.   Such development is greatly aided by the presence in the child's social environment of consistent moral standards and actions.   If such standards differ from one situation to another, the child becomes confused and, because of failure to understand why he is punished for an act at one time and rewarded for it at another, resorts to whatever evasions he can hit upon to avoid unnecessary difficulty.   As one psychologist,[54] in discussing the moral problems of an older child, has written,

---

[54] W. C. Trow, "Conflicting Codes of Morality in the Life of the Child," *Childhood Education,* 18 : 256-262 (1942).

"If a boy takes someone else's parked car and uses it for a joy ride, he is acting in rather ideal fashion in the eyes of his gang and his girl friend, . . . but this conduct is not commendable in the eyes of the school teachers or the police. . . . He discovers out of sad experiences that what his own group may reward another will punish; and his consolation lies only in the fact that what his group may punish him for may bring him a reward in another." Such conflict is also exemplified by the insistence of some parents that the child be consistently truthful to them while at the same time obeying their instructions, for example, to tell unwanted visitors who come to the door that they (the parents) are not at home.

In the case of moral traits it is essential, not only to arrange situations favorable to socially acceptable responses, but to assist the child in understanding the *reasons* for expecting certain forms of conduct. It is necessary for the child to learn why certain behavior is right, as well as that it is expected of him. If the child is eventually to be rational about his actions, he must be appraised of the principles which are expected to govern them as soon as his maturity is sufficient to permit of rational analysis. The child who is told why some acts are right and others wrong, and who is provided with satisfying situations in which to enact acceptable responses, may eventually acquire that most important of all motives—the *desire* to do what is regarded as right and to contribute to the common good in concrete ways. If given sufficient experience in guided group activities, such a child will come to realize, for example, that he must refrain from taking things belonging to others in any situation, be it candy on a neighbor's table, money in his mother's pocketbook, pencils in other children's desks, oranges on the grocery store counter, or perchance change in a public telephone booth. The morally mature child will also consider it wrong to lie about his associates, to injure those weaker than himself, to be disloyal to friends, to be a poor sport in games, and to be cruel to animals.

RELIGION AND THE CONTROL OF CONDUCT. It has been believed that the child is possessed of an instinct to worship which will ripen with his development. Such a view is subject to the weaknesses of the instinct concept in general, and is regarded by many students of child psychology as being incorrect. It has no more apparent foundation than the earlier belief that children are characterized by an inborn tendency to perpetrate evil acts. Modern observations of child development have made it increasingly apparent that parental teaching and other social influences are responsible for whatever religious proclivities and beliefs children acquire. It is thus doubtful whether children are naturally religious.

Anthropologists [55] have amassed evidence suggestive of the likelihood that religious beliefs originated in primitive man's efforts to protect himself from the ravages of disease, famine, storms, wild animals, and other destructive perils which he could not control. Having little or no knowledge of physical causation, early man apparently ascribed destructive phenomena to supernatural sources and, in an effort to safeguard himself against them, importuned the responsible gods through the medium of ceremonies and rituals. From such a naturalistic beginning religion apparently progressed to its ultimate attainment of Christian and other righteous principles of living and a sense of the sacredness of so-called "spiritual" values. Modern religion attempts to discern the most harmonious way of life and to explain man's place and destiny in the operation of the universe.

Very young children are often curious about religious questions. It is not uncommon for them to ask about God, death, heaven, and similar questions. Although these matters are remote and abstract, children become interested in them as they grow older. Stories of angels, devils, miracles, and heaven and hell are accepted without question, but may be reviewed with some scepticism in adolescent years. Children believe uncritically what they are taught by their parents and in connection with church activities, both because of their confidence in their elders and because they are not provided with alternative views of the mysteries of existence. Their religious concepts are in

[55] J. H. Breasted, *The Dawn of Conscience*, New York, Chas. Scribner's Sons, 1934.

harmony with the pictures and descriptions provided them by their parents.

As a number of investigators [56] have shown, children's ideas of God, heaven, and hell tend to be confused but concrete. One group of elementary school children regarded God as being a personal being and proceeded to appeal to him for food, toys, clothing, and the like. Heaven was thought of as a place of beauty in the ground or in the sky. It has also been regarded as a kind of Utopia in which children will be provided with candy, toys, picture books, clothes, ice-cream cones, and no school! A childish concept of God has depicted him as an old man with flowing white garments and a long beard who is ever present and who can see what everyone does. Jesus has been reputed to be a personal being who "takes you to Heaven if you're good" and "makes you well when you're sick." Jesus is also thought of by many children as a tiny baby whose mother cradled him in a barn instead of in a crib. Such ideas reflect the immature religious concepts of children, but also indicate the bizarre beliefs often taught them by their parents and teachers.

The functional value of religious belief in controlling the behavior of the child has been assumed to be extensive, and has been widely extolled by students of the subject. Whether this is so probably needs to be determined more objectively. Nevertheless, one author [57] writes, "morality . . . has always been closely related to religion. The child in the religious home and at church is impressed with the doctrine that some things must not be done because they are wrong. Sin or wrong is defined as an act against the laws of God. Morality may be given a purely secular interpretation, but it is usually supported by religious sentiments. . . . Religion exerts a powerful influence on conduct by impressing upon its adherents a

[56] See, for example, F. K. Merry and R. V. Merry, *From Infancy to Adolescence*, New York, Harper & Bros., 1940, pp. 301-303; G. Stanley Hall, "The Contents of Children's Minds on Entering School," *Pedagogical Seminary and Journal of Genetic Psychology*, 1 : 139-173 (1891) ; E. Harms, "The Development of Religious Experience in Children," *American Journal of Sociology*, 50 : 112-122 (1944).

[57] Arne S. Jensen, *Psychology of Child Behavior*, New York, Prentice-Hall, Inc., 1938, p. 409. See also Sophia L. Fahs and H. F. Sweet, *Exploring Religion with Eight Year Olds*, New York, Harper & Bros., 1930, and Meyer F. Nimkoff, *The Child*, Philadelphia, J. B. Lippincott Co., 1934, pp. 285-286.

philosophy of life. The child's ideas of a supreme power, his own relations to this higher world, are certain to dominate to a large extent his behavior. When these ideas have been thoroughly inculcated, they become a part of the inner life of the child. The force exerted by religion should come from within the child. His realization of the supreme power takes the form of membership or partnership in the invisible world. . . . From within, then, because of this attitude, comes the powerful urge to do the right and avoid the wrong."

Religious belief no doubt may provide the child with a sense of security, a guide for social living, and a motive for doing what is right, but such desirable outcomes are also contingent upon the provision in the home of sufficient affection and status to guarantee a sense of personal worth. It is doubtful whether religious teaching *per se,* relatively devoid of the morale building effects of parental example and love, can bring about desirable personal and social adjustment. If the growing child is to be impressed, for example, with the life of Jesus as a model for conduct, he must first be treated in such a way as to dispose him toward liking people and appreciating their good qualities. And, as Fahs [58] has emphasized, instead of being made acquainted with a God who presumably grants special privileges to his "chosen ones" and neglects and threatens those who do not please him, the impressionable child should be influenced to think of the Deity as a benevolent Father "who is understanding and charitable to all, even though they be what humans regard as bad."

Characteristics of a Desirable Personality.—The question is often raised as to what traits and social qualities characterize the desirable personality. Such a query is not easy to answer but can be satisfied to some extent. The present answer is not intended to depict all acceptable personal assets, including the individual's philosophy of life, his aesthetic interests, his intellectual attainments, or his personal recreational activities. The purpose here is to present the more purely social qualities and

[58] Sophia L. Fahs, "What Types of Religious Experience Are Possible and Wholesome for Exceptional Children?" *Proceedings of the Sixth Conference on Education of the Exceptional Child of the Child Research Clinic of the Woods Schools,* May, 1940, pp. 22-31.

skills possessed by the child who is regarded as being mentally healthy and who is generally well liked. Such a personality picture, which, incidentally, may be used as a pattern or criterion in the education of children, might well be so planned as to include the better elements of character and morality.

Perhaps as adequate a statement of late childhood and youthful adjusted personality as can be found is that suggested by Link [59] in the course of the development of his test of extrovertive personality. This investigator's purpose was to measure the extent to which his subjects were marked by (1) social ascendency, (2) self-determination, (3) economic self-determination, (4) adequate sex adjustment (boy-girl relationships), and (5) general extrovertive social ability. With some modifications, the findings concerning the social qualities possessed by well-adjusted, popular children and youths are somewhat as follows:

1. Children and youths who participate in wholesome physical activities, competitive or otherwise, and who consequently sleep well and regularly at night tend to have better personalities than those who live less actively. This is especially true when good health and an abundance of energy are involved.

2. Those who take part in such cooperative activities as musical organizations, dramatic presentations, and school clubs and committees are as a rule more extrovertive and socially adjusted than children who prefer to spend their spare time exclusively in the more sedentary pastimes of reading and listening to the radio. Such children enjoy being with their associates and leading an active life with them.

3. Boys and girls who are members of character building organizations such as the boy scouts, girl scouts, campfire girls, Y.M.C.A., Y.W.C.A., or who attend Sunday School or church tend to possess better personalities than those who avoid participation in these and similar enterprises. This is especially true of those who have learned to be fair and open-minded with people and who respect their beliefs and ideas.

[59] H. C. Link, "A Test of Four Personality Traits of Adolescents," *Journal of Applied Psychology*, 20: 527-534 (1936).

4. Children and youths who respect their associates and who use sincere social skills in dealing with them rate high both on personality tests and in the estimation of their friends. Such social skills include being pleasant to new acquaintances, paying intelligently worded compliments, being considerate of people's feelings, being courteous and polite, and avoiding unnecessary criticism. Children of this kind are looked upon as good sports, are quick to enter into the spirit of group gatherings, and are usually at ease socially.

5. Children who associate spontaneously with members of either sex and youths who mingle pleasantly in social affairs where both sexes are present possess better personality qualities than those who avoid or dislike members of the other sex. In the case of junior and senior high school pupils, good personality is in evidence when the boy or girl enjoys mixed parties, participates in dancing, engages in a certain amount of courting, and likes to be in the company of a boy or girl friend, as the case may be. Maladjusted youths are usually not disposed to meet and deal socially with those not of their own sex.

6. Those who are sufficiently industrious to do work of various kinds as a means of self-support and who are careful in the expenditure of money tend to possess personality qualities superior to those of children and youths who expect to be relieved of responsibilities along these lines. Typical activities include selling papers, doing chores, performing housework, selling tickets, and doing odd jobs. Children who refuse to do any of these things are as a rule somewhat cynical and lacking in social skills.

7. Children and youths who have become (to a reasonable extent) capable of subordinating immediate satisfactions in favor of more distant and worthwhile goals, and who have developed a willingness to do what is right in situations involving pleasure or pain, are as a rule socially adjusted. Such boys and girls are becoming emotionally mature, have usually formulated certain goals toward which to work, and frequently display their superior personality qualities by doing things they do not enjoy but which are expected of them, by serving on committees when the work becomes heavy, and by refraining from unnecessary escapes and rationalizations.

A group of eighty subjects from three schools was examined in an investigation [60] designed to determine the relationships between certain personality traits and social acceptance in the case of fourth grade pupils. Each child's traits were ascertained through both teacher and pupil ratings. The criteria of social acceptance utilized include: (1) choice of working companions, (2) designation of friends to receive Christmas presents, (3) election as club officers, (4) number of valentines received, (5) voting for "best citizen," and (6) listing of best friends. Socially accepted children were found to be marked by two related trait syndromes. The first of these involved desirable social aggressiveness, the children being characterized as enthusiastic, daring, and talkative. The second, called the friendly syndrome, included traits which pictured the children as being happy, friendly, and welcomed.

Studies have shown that both child and adolescent leaders as a rule possess various combinations of the physical and psychological qualities depicted above. Jack [61] found, for example, that nursery school leaders are socially ascendant, that they not only direct their companions' behavior but pursue their purposes in spite of considerable interference, and that they use bargains, threats, and reproofs in controlling the actions of associates. All of Jack's leaders seemed marked by self-confidence.

A study of Boy Scouts [62] revealed the most outstanding traits of leaders as being intelligence, dependability, appearance, and athletic ability. Physical qualities, such as adequate size and impressive voice, were also influential in determining the willingness of associates to follow the directions of scout leaders. These specifications were corroborated by an investigation [63] of the characteristics of high school student leaders, practically all of whom were found to be not only intelligent, studious, and well developed physically but *socially extrovertive* as well.

[60] M. E. Bonney, "Personality Traits of Socially Successful and Socially Unsuccessful Children," *Journal of Educational Psychology,* 34: 449-472 (1943).
[61] L. M. Jack, "An Experimental Study of Ascendent Behavior in Preschool Children," *Univ. of Iowa Studies in Child Welfare,* Vol. 9, No. 3 (1934).
[62] E. D. Partridge, *Leadership Among Adolescent Boys,* Teachers College Contributions to Education, No. 608, Columbia Univ., 1934.
[63] M. Brown, *Leadership Among High School Pupils,* Teachers College Contributions to Education, No. 559, Columbia Univ., 1933.

The general pattern of adequate personality is thus one characterized by emotional stability, social maturity, and a disposition to attack problems with confidence. The desirable pattern of child personality apparently involves a working blend of qualities that make for social acceptance and a maximum capacity for effecting intelligent adjustments to a wide variety of problems and situations. Furthermore, the specific social skills associated with such a personality are of a type that can be learned in the manner described in a previous section of this chapter. When good personality is defined in terms of social behavior it becomes concrete and teachable, and like any other set of skills, can be acquired under conditions which satisfy the child's psychological needs.

Physiological Factors Affecting Personality.—Man has for centuries been attempting to determine the personality qualities of his associates through observation of their physical features. Julius Caesar exemplified this trend when he associated his friend Cassius' "lean and hungry look" with the disposition to think too much. Present-day beliefs in this respect include the notions that a square jaw gives evidence of determination, that a receding chin indicates weak "will-power," that stout people are jolly, that thin people are quiet and introspective, that a high forehead signifies superior intelligence, that redheaded people are tempestuous, and that "blondes" are fickle and capricious. A rather extensive body of research [64] has for the most part failed to justify either these and similar beliefs or the idea that there is a clear-cut relationship, causal or otherwise, between personality traits and physical characteristics. Such popular notions are based on generalizations drawn from dramatic incidents in which such relationships were observed.

It seems more logical to reason that the possession of a good physique (male) or figure (female) provides a social advantage leading to the development of desirable personality qualities.[65] Similarly, differences in strength, beauty, and health

[64] Louis P. Thorpe, *Psychological Foundations of Personality*, New York, McGraw-Hill Book Co., Inc., 1938, pp. 478-504.
[65] P. S. de Q. Cabot, *The Relationship Between Characteristics of Personality and Physique in Adolescents*, Genetic Psychology Monographs, Vol. 20, No. 1 (1938), pp. 3-120.

may operate as significant determiners of personality characteristics. The undersized child often feels inferior and may develop attitudes conducive to antisocial forms of compensation. The oversized child has an advantage over some of his associates and may develop a tendency to bully them. In the event of adequate home training, such a child may, on the contrary, come to protect those who are less fortunate physically.

Society has adopted certain attitudes toward physical characteristics in both the male and the female that place a definite handicap on children who cannot measure up to them. The homely girl, the fat boy, the "skinny" youth, and the "runt" all feel the stigma of inferiority, and are thus likely to acquire social attitudes suggestive of their resentment. The same may be said in the case of various physical defects: defective vision, hearing handicaps, speech disorders, and certain crippled conditions increase children's feelings of inadequacy, and may lead to compensatory mechanisms in the form of daydreaming (phantasy) or overaggressive behavior. Less emphasis upon their defects by associates and more opportunity for wholesome activities in which they can excel in some way would do much to prevent the personality disorders so often resulting from a sense of physical inferiority in the children concerned.

Observation has pointed to the likelihood that health and physical energy are influential in the determination of personality development. Children who are ill or in poor health are more likely than others to give vent to outbursts of anger or to expressions of resentment. Sick children are also sometimes pampered to a degree that may interfere with their social growth. It is further true that children are likely to be more irritable when fatigued, and that they become more apathetic and inactive after a day of physical and intellectual exertion.

Boynton [66] has presented several examples which he believes illustrate the influence on personality traits of ill health. In one instance the personality of a fourteen-year-old boy, whose "atrocities" included locking friends in a bathroom for hours, destroying classmates' toys and trinkets, leaving school for no

[66] Paul L. Boynton, "Guidance—a Science or a Philosophy?" *Junior and Senior High School Clearing House*, 8: 517-520 (1934).

apparent reason, pouting for long periods, and leaving his clothes, books, and other belongings at various places indefinitely, showed great improvement as the result of a change of diet which had included foods to which he was apparently so allergic as to cause him to lose all intestinal control. It was believed that his difficulty was traceable to a peculiarity of physiological functioning. Other examples, such as Joan of Arc's lack of development of the menstrual function and Schopenhauer's dislike for women allegedly caused by a syphilitic infection, have been advanced to show the intimate relation between physiological functions and personality traits. However, in these and similar cases a variety of *social factors* undoubtedly *combined with* the physical disabilities to bring about the symptoms noted.

THE ENDOCRINE GLANDS AND PERSONALITY. Probably most dramatic of all have been the claims pertaining to the influence of glandular action upon personality development. The tendency here has been to extend known knowledge concerning the functions of the glands of internal secretion to cause and effect relationships the bases for which are speculative.

Although the entire glandular system operates in an integrated way in the maintenance of delicate chemical balances, some glands (pituitary, thymus, pineal) are primarily concerned with the regulation of physical growth, others (thyroid, parathyroid) with the stimulation of metabolism, and still others (gonads) with the development of sex characteristics. Variations in physical size, including dwarfism and giantism, with their effects on personality and social adjustment, result from imbalances in the operation of the pituitary gland. Disturbances of this, and the thymus and pineal glands, may also result in precocious sex development.

Overactivity of the thyroid gland brings about a hypertense, high-strung condition in which the child finds it very difficult to relax and rest. Hypofunctioning of this gland results, on the contrary, in a slowing down of metabolism with a corresponding apathy and sluggishness in the child's behavior. Extreme cases may eventuate in mental decline. A diseased con-

dition or removal of the gonad glands results in a marked decrease in sex interest and in the failure of secondary sex characteristics (growth of hair, change of voice, bodily development, etc.) fully to develop.

The general cause and effect relationships described represent the bulk of what is known concerning the glandular regulation of personality. Further claims that various glands and
combinations of glands determine directly the type of personality an individual will develop are too fatuous to be taken
seriously. The assertion, for example, that infancy is the
epoch of the thymus, childhood the epoch of the pineal, adolescence the epoch of the gonads, and maturity the epoch of
whatever gland or glands have survived the struggles of living
to date,[67] is not accepted by critical students of personality. As
evidence presented throughout this volume has suggested, personality qualities probably cannot be developed *independently of
social conditions.* It is unlikely, as some have supposed, that
glamour girls and career girls are motivated in their respective
areas by the dominating effects of the gonad and adrenal glands,
respectively. Actually, except in extreme cases, little is known
concerning the specific relationships that given endocrine glands
may have with specific personality traits.

A recent four-year investigation [68] of the influence of thyroid treatment upon the social behavior, school achievement,
general intelligence, and anatomic growth of elementary school
boys suffering from thyroid deficiency disclosed, however,
marked improvement in both personal and social adjustment
over the four-year period. Other findings indicated that: (1)
A large percentage of the mothers of hypothyroid children suffered from health disturbances which were directly attributable
to glandular disorders preceding the birth of the child. (2)
Symptoms of hypothyroidism did not appear in the children
until a few months after birth. (3) Retarded growth first
manifested itself in structure, later in function, and still later

---

[67] Louis Berman, *The Glands Regulating Personality*, New York, The Macmillan Co., 1921, pp. 294-296.

[68] Curtis E. Warren, *The Improvement in Social Adjustment, School Achieve-
ment, General Intelligence, and Anatomic Growth Made by Hypothyroid Boys
When Given Thyroid Therapy*, Doctoral Dissertation, The Univ. of Southern
California, 1941.

in mental development. (4) When tests of personal and social adjustment were originally applied to the group, the average ratings were either "very unsatisfactory" or "unsatisfactory." (5) In educational achievement the group at first was ten points below the norm for their age. (6) In masculinity-femininity scores the group was more feminine than the average fourteen-year-old boy, with boys making the more feminine scores having the more difficult social problems.

The investigator believed that prognoses for hypothyroid cases can be made on the basis of a medical examination and the findings of a psychiatric social worker, supplemented by the reports of a psychometrician and a visiting teacher. This is assuming, of course, that the children in question are not suffering from emotional problems that are relatively independent of glandular deficiency. A non-controlled program of endocrine therapy may include the essentials of a mental hygiene program.

Endocrinologists [69] have also demonstrated that, although deviations from normal behavior among children are associated with endocrine imbalances more often than chance would permit, such association is not necessarily causal. Many behavior maladjustments occur without benefit of glandular disorders. Both endocrine dysfunctions and personality deviations occur frequently and may often be associated by chance. Furthermore, there is evidence that glands are themselves subject to the influence of both physiological factors and external agents of a tension arousing nature. The following excerpt [70] is suggestive: "The attitude of conservative medicine toward thyroid overactivity is different from what it used to be. Years ago the thyroid was accused of causing a great majority of nervous instabilities. Now we are asking ourselves what stirs up the thyroid to misbehavior and we are finding that emotional instabilities of constitutional nature very often precede thyroid upsets."

[69] A. W. Rowe, "A Possible Endocrine Factor in the Behavior Problems of the Young," *American Journal of Orthopsychiatry,* I: 451-475 (1931). Also D. J. Ingle, "Endocrine Function and Personality," *Psychological Review,* 42: 466-479 (1935).

[70] E. L. Richards, *Behavior Aspects of Child Conduct,* New York, The Macmillan Co., 1932, pp. 144-145. By permission.

THE INFLUENCE OF DRUGS, TOXINS, AND INFECTIONS. Other physiological agents which exert marked influences on personality include drugs, toxins, and bacterial infections. The individual suffering from alcoholic intoxication may weep, laugh boisterously, stagger through the streets, or writhe in the grip of delirium tremens. The user of marihuana or opium will exhibit the particular anomalies of behavior which these drugs bring about. The sufferer from *paresis*, or syphilis of the brain, may become slovenly and indifferent as the result of this type of infection. Well-adjusted, dependable children have in many cases become serious problems after *encephalitis* (sleeping sickness), another brain infection, has run its course.[71] Tubercular patients also manifest certain personality symptoms (conflict between ambition and inertia) which seem characteristically associated with this type of physical disorder.[72]

The more common diseases such as scarlet fever and diphtheria may also leave their mark in the form of a more irascible disposition with its tendency toward anger reactions.[73] Even the content of urine and saliva correlate to some extent with personality ratings of good-naturedness, leadership, perseverance, aggressiveness, and excitability.[74] However, none of these relationships are fixed, and personality disorders growing out of the various physical disturbances are as a rule but amplifications of trends that were visible before the physical disorders set in.

Implications for Home and School.—In summarizing the implications of what is known concerning the development of character and personality traits, we can perhaps do no better than present the conclusions reached by Hartshorne and May [75] in connection with their extensive inquiry of the nature

[71] E. D. Bond and K. E. Appel, *The Treatment of Behavior Disorders Following Encephalitis: An Experiment in Re-education,* New York, The Commonwealth Fund, 1931.

[72] A. M. Muhl, "Fundamental Personality Trends in Tuberculosis Women," *Psychoanalytic Review,* 18 : 380-430 (1923).

[73] G. M. Stratton, "Emotion and the Incidence of Disease," *Journal of Abnormal and Social Psychology,* 21 : 19-23 (1926).

[74] G. J. Rich, "A Biochemical Approach to the Study of Personality," *Journal of Abnormal and Social Psychology,* 23 : 158-175 (1928).

[75] Hugh Hartshorne and M. A. May, *Studies in Deceit,* New York, The Macmillan Co., 1928, pp. 412-414.

of traits. Although their studies were concerned principally with the traits of honesty, service, and self-control, their findings are apparently applicable to a wide variety of character and personality qualities.

1. Children are not honest, sympathetic, loyal, cooperative (or their opposites), and the like by "nature." Deception is merely a form of adjustment utilized by the child when his environment thwarts the realization of his desires. Socially disapproved ways of resolving conflicts will be continued if the child finds them to be consistently successful. Socially approved methods of effecting adjustments are just as readily adopted if they prove to be rewarding. Both home and school need to create an abundance of concrete situations in which acceptable moral-social behavior is made natural and consistently satisfying.

2. The mere urging of desirable behavior by parents and teachers, even though emotionalized, has little or no relation to the control of conduct. The teaching of ideals of conduct is neither undesirable nor unnecessary, but current methods of inculcating ideals have apparently been ineffective and may have done harm. There is some evidence that physical punishment as a method of impressing the child with standards of conduct engenders socially undesirable rather than acceptable personality traits.[76]

3. An effort should be made to clarify for the child the essential difference between desirable and undesirable modes of social interaction in such a way that he may clearly evaluate the probable consequences of either approach for his own welfare as well as that of his associates. It is also necessary to point out to children *specific* desirable types of conduct which carry with them rewards in the form of social approval and personal satisfaction. *Concrete experience* in social situations which contribute to the security of associates is imperative to personality development.

4. Since many forms of undesirable behavior are associated with handicaps in social background, home conditions, personal limitations, and the like, there is need for understanding the circumstances

[76] Robert G. Bernreuter, "Progressive Education as it Relates to the Personality of the Exceptional Child," *Proceedings of the Fourth Conference on Education and the Exceptional Child of the Child Research Clinic of the Woods Schools,* May 1938, pp. 56-60.

under which particular exhibitions of condemned behavior took place before judging the blameworthiness of the child. There is no reason for believing that antisocial children would not respond in socialized ways with an equal degree of satisfaction if conditions were such as to make the latter reactions concretely rewarding. Both parents and teachers should thus be certain that they do not commit offenses (disrespect, injustice, untrustworthiness) in the eyes of their children that are conducive to antisocial conduct. Instead of attempting to teach honesty, loyalty, generosity, extroversion, etc., as expressions of inner traits, both home and school should provide numerous opportunities for the satisfying enactment of such forms of conduct as are conducive to the common welfare.

The Scientific Measurement of Personality

Objective tests of personality have been developed in an effort to identify and diagnose important factors in personal and social adjustment which were formerly regarded as being intangibles. The factors in question have defied appraisal through the avenue of ordinary intelligence and achievement tests. It has been recognized, however, that if those vested with the task of guiding children could secure tangible evidences of their characteristic modes of adjustment in a variety of situations which vitally affect them as individuals or as members of a group, they could use such information in aiding children in achieving better personal and social adjustment.

Tests (also called measures, inventories, and scales) of personality are designed to ascertain the ways in which an individual makes his necessary interpersonal adjustments and to what degree he is characterized by mental health. They are also intended to identify and evaluate the individual child's complex patterns of feeling, thinking, and acting in relation to social situations. Personality measures are not "tests" in the sense of measuring a child's capacity for solving increasingly difficult problems; they are, rather, inventories for ascertaining the extent of the child's adjustment to the requirements of his nature and of group living.

Non-scientific Methods of Evaluating Personality.[77]—
Prior to the scientific era it was common practice to judge an
individual's character and personality traits on the basis of his
physical characteristics or supposed relationship to the stars.
Such systems, which include physiognomy, phrenology, chirognomy, and astrology, have survived in the beliefs of the uninformed to this day. Although preoccupation with these pseudo-
systems has no doubt led some persons to make desirable social
contacts, it has also made possible considerable exploitation of
the public by charlatans.

Physiognomy, which has to do with the discovery of personality traits from outward appearances, especially from facial
features, has been practiced since ancient times. It proceeds
on the assumption that inner traits, moral and otherwise, are
betrayed by the contour of eyes, ears, lips, chin, brow, and nose,
and by such additional features as curved shoulders, a short
neck, a protruding pouch, long arms, and manner of walking.
It is difficult to see, however, how complex psychological traits
could be associated with gross anatomy or the details of physical constitution. If such relationships exist, they have not
been demonstrated scientifically.

Much the same can be said for *phrenology,* the doctrine that
personality qualities can be ascertained from protrusions of the
skull, which structure is in turn presumably influenced by the
localizations within cerebral regions of specific mental and
temperamental faculties. Gall (and Spurzheim) came to the
conclusion from studying the skulls of men who were known to
possess certain personality characteristics that such traits as
vice, generosity, honesty, love of mate, etc., have each their
pigeonhole in the brain surface. Such a *post hoc ergo propter
hoc* type of reasoning neglects the principles of causation, stimulus-response, and dynamic personality needs. Furthermore,
protrusions of the cranium do not correspond to either protrusions or depressions of the brain. Gall's search for units of personality and character was undoubtedly a sincere one, but

---

[77] For a more complete discussion of this topic see Louis P. Thorpe, *Psychological Foundations of Personality,* New York, McGraw-Hill Book Co., Inc., 1938,
pp. 455-478.

modern investigations have discredited the assumptions made by him and his followers.

Graphology, a system which proposes to judge personality qualities from samples of handwriting, has been utilized by both scientists and charlatans. The latter group has claimed to detect the presence of such traits or abilities as moodiness, affection, pessimism and gloom, secretiveness, pride, dependability, and mechanical ability from characteristics of an individual's handwriting. Researches have shown that such assertions are usually not warranted by the facts. Nevertheless, ever since Binet's day scientists have been endeavoring to utilize handwriting as a clue to abilities and personality qualities. Both early and recent researches show that there are possibilities beyond the limits of chance for such determination.[78] This is more than can be said for *chirognomy,* which claims the ability to ascertain a definite relationship between personality traits and shape of the hand. Research has made it clear that no correspondence exists here.

Astrology, one of the oldest of the pseudo personality-reading systems, is based upon the belief that stars and their courses influence human destiny and personality. Given the year, day, and hour of birth, the astrologer claims to be able to divulge an individual's character, personality, and various abilities. Scientists believe that, although heavenly bodies may influence human beings in indirect ways, it is naive to assume that they prognosticate personality or intellectual development. Like the previously mentioned systems, astrology has not produced evidence favorable to its postulates.

Each of the above approaches (with the possible exception of graphology) is founded on unscientific bases and inclined to draw conclusions from loose analogies and wishful thinking.

The most modern, but still uncertain, statement of a physical-temperamental relationship is the one by Sheldon,[79] which grew

---

[78] Thea S. Lewinson and Joseph Zubin, *Handwriting Analysis: A Series of Scales for Evaluating the Dynamic Aspects of Handwriting,* New York, King's Crown Press, 1942.

[79] W. H. Sheldon *et al., The Varieties of Human Physique,* New York, Harper & Bros., 1940, pp. 236-238. See also, by the same authors, *The Varieties of Temperament: A Psychology of Constitutional Differences,* New York, Harper & Bros., 1942.

out of observations of a large number of male college freshmen. According to this investigator, rotund, stocky men possess a temperament (called *vicerotonic*) marked by love for
comfortable surroundings, gratifying food, social ease, and the
ability to make others feel at home. Thin men with relatively
long limbs are said to be inhibited and introverted (shut in),
given to allergies, skin trouble, and fatigue, and to be sensitive
to noise and crowds (*cerebrotonic*). Intermediate, or symmetrically formed individuals are designated as being creative, ener-
getic, immune to fatigue, interested in activities, and men of
action (*somatotonic*). Sheldon acknowledges the existence of
many exceptions (average correlation .81) to this "rule," as
well as of varying combinations of body-type-temperamental-
characteristic. It is thus to be doubted whether he has established the relationships claimed. In fact, a study of such relationships employing data from 176 boys led another investigator [80] to conclude that they are no greater than chance expec-
tancy. Sheldon's improved procedure yielded the same paucity
of relationships to physique found in earlier researches.

Problems in the Measurement of Personality.—Many
problems confront the test maker who wishes to apply quantitative methods to the measurement of personal attributes and
social adaptability. Some psychologists have, in fact, doubted
whether science will ever be able to chart an accurate picture of,
and measure quantitatively, the intricacies of the human personality. The various aspects of personality are so elaborately interlocked that some have questioned whether they will ever lend
themselves to measurement by the same mathematical methods
used in the development of mental tests. The principal problems
encountered have been concerned with (1) the non-quantitative
nature of personality, (2) difficulties in sampling methods, (3)
the establishment of test reliability, and (4) the determination
of test validity.

The Non-quantitative Nature of Personality.
Psychologists have become so accustomed to dealing with intelligence as an accumulation of abilities ranging from zero (no

[80] D. W. Fiske, "A Study of Relationships to Somatotype," *Journal of Applied Psychology*, 28 : 504-519 (1944).

ability) up through increasing brackets of brightness to gifted status, that some have been inclined to approach the measurement of personality in the same manner. It is doubtful, however, whether personality status can be ascertained in such an additive way. Personality is a functional integration among many specific traits and tendencies to behave; it cannot be regarded as an accumulation of them. Any other view of personality organization disregards its unity and the integrated nature of its behavioral manifestations.

The difficulty of measuring personality traits will be evident when it is realized that traits are not absolute uni-dimensional entities. Test makers must thus think of such personality traits, for example, as self-control, cooperation, or loyalty in terms of *a certain degree of expression or development,* not as absolutes the possession of which is desirable in any amount. Personality trait inventories have often neglected the fact that when a given trait is present in either too excessive or too limited degree, it ceases to exist as such and merges into a related and often undesirable trait. Excessive "leadership" may, as a case in point, become "tyranny." "Dignity" may merge into "snobbishness" at one pole, and become clownishness at the other. A pattern, not amount, seems to be the desired criterion here.

DIFFICULTIES IN SAMPLING METHODS. In spite of the weaknesses inherent in the trait concept, attempts have been made to measure the extent to which children are introvertive or extrovertive, dominant or submissive, aggressive or apathetic, social or unsocial, and the like. The assumptions underlying such measurement are that uni-dimensional (single) personality traits exist, that representative responses indicative of their character can be elicited, and that such responses are amenable to measurement by quantitative methods. Research workers have, nevertheless, found high correlations between the scores of supposedly unlike traits.[81]

If research had revealed the presence in children of consistent and mutually exclusive personality traits, the problem of

[81] I. Lorge, Personality Traits by Fiat, I: "The Analysis of the Total Trait Scores and Keys of the Bernreuter Personality Inventory," *Journal of Educational Psychology,* 26 : 273-278 (1935).

measurement would be a relatively simple matter. On such a basis the entire personality of a given child could be charted by stimulating him to reveal one or two specific expressions of each of his complete repertoire of traits. Once a trait had been postulated, a reliable measure of one or more of its expressions would be sufficient to establish its existence. However, as previously reported investigations have shown, child behavior is relatively specific, being a function of concrete stimulating situations as well as of previously developed tendencies of a specific nature. It is thus not surprising that recent attempts have been made to measure the extent to which children are socially and emotionally *adjusted,* without regard to their status so far as the possession of traits is concerned.

RELIABILITY. If testing instruments are to be useful, the responses which they elicit must be consistent, i.e., they must secure comparable results when repeated after a lapse of time. In the case of personality tests it is not, however, feasible to compute reliability coefficients on the basis of repeated administrations of the same or duplicate test forms. Knowledge, understanding, and skill once attained remain relatively stable for a time and tests designed to reveal their presence will usually yield similar results on different occasions. Since personality factors, such as feelings, attitudes, prejudices, and modes of behavior, are more rapidly modified in accordance with fluctuations in experience, a repetition of the same or a comparable test would result in the measurement of personality *change* rather than in the determination of test reliability. It is for this reason that personality test coefficients of reliability are often obtained by the split-half or odd-even (items in the test) methods. On this basis the two sets of scores secured from a single administration of the test are correlated with one another and corrected with the Spearman-Brown formula. When such a coefficient is high (.90 or above) the test is said to possess high reliability.

VALIDITY. A personality test is regarded as being valid when it measures those aspects of personality or adjustment *which it purports to measure.* Validity, which is both essential and difficult to obtain, is theoretically dependent upon the availability of criteria against which to correlate test scores. In the case of personality qualities or adjustments, much use has been made of the judgment of individuals who are intimately acquainted with the subjects being tested. However, the unreliability of such judgments has usually been such as to render them well-nigh useless. As one psychologist has written, "Sometimes the judge's opinion may be poor, sometimes the individual may not reveal himself as he is, and traits which he possesses may go unrecognized, or may be clouded over by comparative factors, such as good social presence, high intelligence, and so on, which dazzle the observer to the point of befogging the presence of the trait sought." [82] Carefully constructed personality tests are thus likely to be more valid than the criteria against which they are checked.

It is because of these difficulties that test makers have for the most part turned to the practice of validating personality test items on the basis of their diagnostic value in discriminating between *contrasted groups* of children possessing the qualities being measured to the highest and lowest degrees. Less distinctly deviate subjects may be classified by this method in terms of their reactions to questions which have turned out to be consistent in diagnosing extreme cases. This is the technique used by Woodworth when he endeavored to differentiate between soldiers (World War I) with psychoneurotic tendencies and those who were sufficiently normal to perform military functions adequately. [83]

More recent techniques [84] of personality test validation have included: (1) use of the bi-serial coefficient of correlation in test item analysis and in the determination of internal consistency, (2) efforts to disguise (rationalize for the examinee) test items which might otherwise appear disparaging if answered correctly, (3) the adjustment of test items to the examinee's reading level as determined by standard word lists, (4) the in-

[82] Gladys C. Schwesinger, *Heredity and Environment,* New York, The Macmillan Co., 1933, p. 109. By permission.

[83] R. S. Woodworth, *The Personal Data Sheet,* Chicago, C. H. Stoelting Co. (no date).

[84] Ernest W. Tiegs, Willis W. Clark, and Louis P. Thorpe, "The California Test of Personality," *Journal of Educational Research,* 35 : 102-108 (1941).

clusion of teacher and pupil judgments in the final selection of test items, and, perhaps most important of all, (5) the original careful selection by experienced workers of the test items. It is by these and similar means that test makers hope to cope with the pitfalls attendant upon the establishment of reliability and validity in personality testing instruments.

Rating Methods of Measuring Personality.—Instruments designed for the measurement of personality qualities or adjustment have tended to fall into four categories: (1) *rating scales,* or paper-and-pencil devices for rating individuals on a continuous scale (continuum) of personal characteristics; (2) *personality tests* (inventories), or standardized instruments on which the subject checks his personal reactions to a wide variety of specific questions; (3) *projection methods,* in which the individual's inner personality organization as a whole as well as his phantasy life are assumed from his interpretations of pictures, ink-blots, clouds, or word lists; and (4) *direct measurement of overt behavior,* in which the subject's actions are observed in situations involving desirable and undesirable behavior and which are below the threshold of recognition (for him).

Although they are actually only blanks for recording judgments, rating scales have proved useful in the evaluation of the social behavior of children. Both self-ratings, or instances in which the child checks his own behavior, and other-person evaluations, in which acquaintances who know him well rate his behavior, have been used in the study of personality development. However, since they call for judgments of behavior without providing the necessary specific information, such scales require the pooled estimates of several competent raters.

Some rating scales have overcome the vagueness of such designations as *very poor, poor, average, good,* and *excellent* by providing a series of descriptive statements ranging from the least to the most desirable behavior. Such statements are of considerable assistance in making estimates of the status of the child being rated. An example of this technique may be

TABLE 39. ILLUSTRATIVE ITEMS FROM JÖEL'S BEHAVIOR MATURITY
RATING SCALE

Scoring Weight	
	8. *How does he face his difficulties?* (for example, when crossed)
7	1. Calmly, peacefully settles difficulty without appeal to adult (or older brother, etc.).
5	2. Makes a fuss, but settles difficulties without appeal to adult.
5	3. Attempts to settle difficulty, but also appeals to adult.
4	4. Does not attempt to settle difficulty; appeals to adult for help.
4	5. Tantrum.
	9. *For how long can he be absorbed in an activity?*
8	1. Returns to an unfinished activity of the previous day, continues and develops it.
7	2. Pursues an activity until it is finished and is not disturbed by other attractions, but does not return to it from one day to the next.
5	3. Stays with one activity until something more interesting comes up (goes from one constructive activity to another).
3	4. Often interrupts a constructive activity without taking up another one.
3	5. Shifts aimlessly about.

seen in the Jöel [85] rating scale for preschool children, which
consists of a series of twenty significant personality characteristics of children of this age. Illustrative items of the scale,
shown in Table 39, indicate the nature of *graphic* personality
descriptions. A more recent Behavior Maturity Blank by the
same author, [86] designed for junior and senior high school
youths, rates the social and emotional maturity or "grown-up-
ness" of the candidate. The following samples from this blank
are indicative of its general nature:

2. If something goes wrong, do you relieve your feelings by
   swearing?

5. Do you interrupt others while they are talking?

9. If you have spilled something, do you take care of the mess
   immediately?

15. Do you make promises and then find it impossible to keep
    them?

[85] Walther Jöel, " 'Behavior Maturity' of Children of Nursery School Age,"
Child Development, 7 : 189-199 (1936).
[86] Walther Jöel, *Behavior Maturity Blank*, Los Angeles, The Gutenberg Press,
1939.

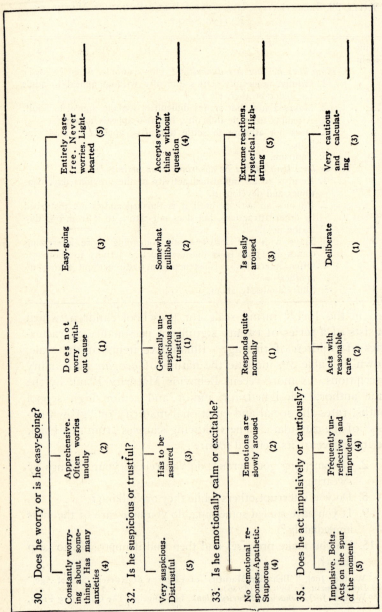

30. Does he worry or is he easy-going?

| Constantly worrying about something. Has many anxieties (4) | Apprehensive. Often worries unduly (2) | Does not worry without cause (1) | Easy-going (3) | Entirely carefree. Never worries. Lighthearted (5) |

32. Is he suspicious or trustful?

| Very suspicious. Distrustful (5) | Has to be assured (3) | Generally unsuspicious and trustful (1) | Somewhat gullible (2) | Accepts everything without question (4) |

33. Is he emotionally calm or excitable?

| No emotional responses. Apathetic. Stuporous (4) | Emotions are slowly aroused (2) | Responds quite normally (1) | Is easily aroused (3) | Extreme reactions. Hysterical. Highstrung (5) |

35. Does he act impulsively or cautiously?

| Impulsive. Bolts. Acts on the spur of the moment (5) | Frequently unreflective and imprudent (4) | Acts with reasonable care (2) | Deliberate (1) | Very cautious and calculating (3) |

Figure 98. Illustrative Items from the Haggerty-Olson-Wickman *Behavior Rating Schedule*

One of the best known rating scales for children is the Behavior Rating Schedule,[87] a section of which is shown in Figure 98. Also known as a *graphic* rating scale, this instrument embodies such refinements as are possible of attainment in this type of personality evaluation instrument. A brief description at each of the five points along the rating line is provided for convenience in making more exact estimates of the personality qualities in question. Such a procedure, when combined with the utilization of enough judges to insure reasonable accuracy and the services of those who are sufficiently acquainted with the subjects to make possible judgments of the personality traits possessed by them, has been found useful in the case of traits for which no objective measuring instruments are at present available.

Measurement Through the Use of Inventories.—Practically all of the early inventories were designed to measure an individual's status with respect to one personality trait or one aspect of adjustment (single dimensional). Among the most popular personality dimensions selected for such measurement were neurotic tendency, dominance-submission, introversion-extroversion, and emotional maturity. These and other traits were approached from the standpoint of a continuum which extended from one extreme, such as out-and-out extroversion, to the other, in this case, pronounced introversion. The first personality inventory on record, Woodworth's Personal Data Sheet,[88] was intended, as previously mentioned, to detect neurotic symptoms in soldiers drafted for service in World War I. Woodworth obtained his questions from a study of soldiers who were experiencing difficulty in making satisfactory adjustments to military conditions. The questions asked included the following: "Have you ever lost your memory for a time?" "Did you ever run away from home?" and "Did you ever have the habit of stuttering?" A revision of this inventory (Woodworth-Mathews) has been made to be used with school children.

---

[87] M. E. Haggerty, W. C. Olson, and E. K. Wickman, *Behavior Rating Schedules*, Yonkers, World Book Co., 1930.
[88] R. S. Woodworth, *op. cit.*

Following the appearance of Woodworth's inventory, the Thurstones [89] developed a similar instrument, called the Personality Schedule, which was apparently successful in differentiating neurotic college freshmen from normal students of the same age. The Thurstones' questions included such items as, "Do you get stage fright?" "Do you worry too long over humiliating experiences?" and "Do you consider yourself a rather nervous person?" The authors reported satisfactory internal consistency and a reliability coefficient of .95 for this inventory. Similar results were claimed by the Allport brothers [90] for their Test of Ascendance-Submission, which purports to measure social dominance or submission.

MULTI-DIMENSIONAL OR COMPOSITE TESTS. Personality tests or inventories of more recent origin have usually been designed to measure a number of traits or dimensions of adjustment. They have thus been designated as "broad-coverage" or "multi-dimensional" tests. Prominent among those standardized for use with children are the following:

The Rogers Adjustment Inventory,[91] one of the first composite personality tests designed for use with elementary school children (ages 9-13), is adapted to measuring a child's (1) personal inferiority, (2) social maladjustment, (3) family relationships, (4) daydreaming tendency, and (5) general adjustment. Although not as objective and reliable as some later tests, this inventory has served to locate significant maladjustment trends in children. It was standardized on 100 normal subjects and subsequently used to diagnose the responses of 50 problem children. The form of the inventory is based upon the interview method of questioning the subject concerning his wishes, his activities, and his relations with his parents.

The Aspects of Personality Inventory by Pintner et al.[92] is an eight-page questionnaire designed to measure the child's

[89] L. L. Thurstone and T. G. Thurstone, "A Neurotic Inventory (Personality Schedule)," Journal of Social Psychology, 1 : 3-30 (1930).

[90] Gordon W. Allport and Floyd H. Allport, A—S Reaction Study, New York, Houghton Mifflin Co., 1928.

[91] C. R. Rogers, Measuring Personality Adjustment in Children Nine to Thirteen Years of Age, Teachers College Contributions to Education, No. 458, Columbia Univ., 1931.

[92] Rudolph Pintner et al., Aspects of Personality Inventory, Yonkers, World Book Co., 1937.

status relative to *ascendant-submissive* behavior (the A-S test), *extrovert-introvert* behavior (the E-I test), and *emotional stability* (the E test). The three sections, which contain 35 test items each, have been standardized for elementary school children, and are based on the "same-different" type of response. A high score is considered indicative of ascendance in Section I, of extroversion in Section II, and of emotional adjustment in Section III. Low inter-correlations, ranging from —.22 to .29, among the sections indicate a tendency for ascendance to correlate slightly but positively with extroversion, for extroversion

Feelings of inferiority	Social adjustment	Family adjustment	Day-dreaming Boys	Girls	Total adjustment
0	0				8
	2				13
3	4				18
6 PREFERRED	6 ZONE	1	0	0	23
9	8	4	1	1	28
12	10	7	2	3	33
15 AVERAGE	12 ZONE	10	3 5		38
	14				43
18	16	13	4	7	48
21	18	16	5	9	53
24	20	19	6	11	58
27 CRITICAL	22 ZONE	22	7	13	63
30	24	25	8	15	68

Figure 99. Tables of Norms for the Rogers Inventory Arranged So as to Present a Child's Personality Profile

to correlate similarly with emotional stability, but for emotional stability to correlate with submissiveness rather than with dominance. Very little relationship was found between mental or chronological age and scores on the inventory.

The Case Inventory by Maller [93] is a battery of four tests and has been standardized on normal elementary school children. It is intended to measure status as to both personality adjustment and character. The letters CASE represent, respectively, (1) Controlled association for the measurement of emotionalized response patterns, (2) Adjustment (personal and social), (3) Self-scoring test for the measurement of honesty, and (4) Ethical judgment (regarding moral conflicts and ethical stand-

[93] J. B. Maller, *The Case Inventory*, New York, Bureau of Publications. Teachers College, Columbia Univ., 1935.

ards). Typical test items include, "This person is very impatient; can't await his turn," "This person quarrels over games; thinks only of self," and "This person is courteous; thoughtful of the welfare of others." Responses are made on the basis of "same-different" status. Reliability coefficients for the four sections vary from .90 to .96. The reliability of the test as a whole is .93. Since this test measures a somewhat unusual combination of factors in personality and character, it is of doubtful usefulness in measurement programs. It might, however, be of some value in the study of problem children where both ethical standards and a limited number of personality factors are involved.

The California Test of Personality [94] is designed to detect evidences of personal and social maladjustment, and has been developed in five series—primary, elementary, intermediate, secondary, and adult—ranging from kindergarten to maturity. It is thus suitable for children of all ages. This test measures the child's status in twelve areas relating to (1) *self-adjustment* (how he feels about himself) and (2) *social adjustment* (how he gets along with others), which include (a) self-reliance, sense of personal worth, sense of personal freedom, feeling of belonging, freedom from withdrawing tendencies, freedom from nervous symptoms, and (b) social standards, social skills, freedom from antisocial tendencies, family relations, school relations, and community relations. A reliability of .92 is reported for this test, the norms of which are based upon a study of over 1,000 adjustment situations which confront children at home, at school, and in a variety of other environmental circumstances. The inclusion of a profile (see Figure 100) makes it possible for teachers and counselors to see wherein a child deviates from the majority of pupils and thus to detect areas of maladjustment in which he may need remedial treatment.

The Mental Health Analysis [95] has been developed to ascertain the extent to which the child is marked by certain mental health *liabilities* and *assets*. The liabilities in question, which

[94] Louis P. Thorpe, Willis W. Clark, and Ernest W. Tiegs, *California Test of Personality*, Los Angeles, California Test Bureau, 1939-40.
[95] Louis P. Thorpe and Willis W. Clark, *Mental Health Analysis*, Los Angeles, California Test Bureau, 1946.

it is believed should as far as possible be minimized or corrected, include (1) behavioral immaturity (infantilisms), (2) emotional instability (neuroticism), (3) feelings of inadequacy (insecurity), (4) physical defects (effects on morale), and (5) nervous manifestations (functional disorders). The assets referred to, which might well be sought when not sufficiently pres-

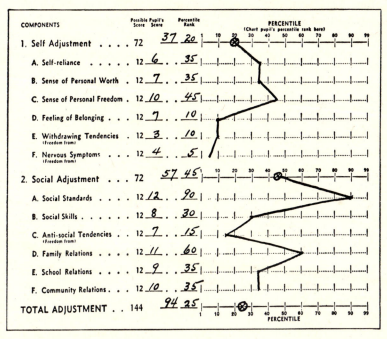

Figure 100. Personality Profile, California Test of Personality, Elementary Series

(Used by permission of the California Test Bureau, Los Angeles.)

ent, are listed as (1) close personal relationships (friendships, etc.), (2) interpersonal skills (getting along with people), (3) social participation (group activities), (4) satisfying work and recreation (school, play, etc.), and (5) outlook and goals (philosophy of life). It is the belief of the authors that such a canvass of mental health factors will assist clinicians, teachers, and others in ascertaining the unfulfilled needs of children.

The test was standardized on a representative group of public school children at the various age levels and is available in elementary, intermediate, secondary, and adult series. A reliability figure of .93 has been secured for the test as a whole. A graphic profile is included for the use of those desiring this feature.

Other personality trait or adjustment tests of recent origin which have been found useful in educational and clinical fields, but which are designed for high school and college youths, include: An Inventory of Factors S T D C R (factors in introversion-extroversion),[96] Inventory of Activities and Interests,[97] Every-day Life (self-reliance),[98] The Personality Inventory,[99] The Adjustment Inventory,[100] Temperament Analysis,[101] and Minnesota Personality Scale.[102]

Projection Methods in Personality Analysis.—Some students of child development, particularly clinicians, have felt that objective personality inventories should be supplemented by another type—the projection test—suitable for probing the substrata or unconscious life of the subject. It is believed that such "depth" analysis may in many instances reveal the general phantasy life and inner personality organization of the child without his realizing that he has projected himself thus intimately. Older techniques for securing such projections were appropriate principally for adults and included the psychiatric interview, free association (psychoanalysis), dream analysis, hypnosis, and automatic writing. Newer methods usable with children include, among others, (1) ink-blot tests, (2) picture projections (called thematic apperception tests), (3) word association tests, (4) free painting, (5) voice analysis, and (6) play therapy. Each of these approaches to an analysis of the

96 J. P. Guilford, *An Inventory of Factors S T D C R,* Beverly Hills (Calif.), Sheridan Supply Co., 1940.

97 Henry C. Link *et al., Inventory of Activities and Interests,* New York, The Psychological Corp., 1936.

98 Leland H. Stott, *Every-day Life,* Beverly Hills (Calif.), Sheridan Supply Co., 1941.

99 R. G. Bernreuter, *The Personality Inventory,* Stanford University, Stanford Univ. Press, 1931.

100 H. M. Bell, *The Adjustment Inventory,* Stanford University, Stanford Univ. Press, 1934.

101 Roswell H. Johnson, *Temperament Analysis,* Los Angeles, California Test Bureau, 1941.

102 John G. Darley and Walter J. McNamara, *Minnesota Personality Scale.* New York, The Psychological Corp., 1941.

child's inner personality organization will be briefly presented below.

THE RORSCHACH METHOD. The *ink-blot* test is based on its author's, Hermann Rorschach, belief that general personality trends can be ascertained from a subject's interpretations of what he sees in the blots.[103] Each individual reacts differently

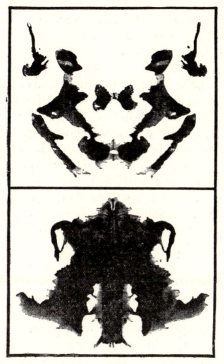

Figure 101. Sample Ink Blots from the Rorschach Test

to the ten blots (given in a certain order), but it is believed that in each instance the subject portrays (projects) a "total action" picture of his personality without realizing that he is revealing his own inner organization, introvertive-extrovertive trends, or emotional instability when these or other factors are

[103] For an extended presentation of the Rorschach method see Bruno Klopfer and D. M. Kelley, *The Rorschach Technique,* Yonkers, World Book Co., 1942. Also Marguerite R. Hertz, "Rorschach: Twenty Years After," *Psychological Bulletin,* 39: 529-572 (1942).

involved. No matter what his interpretations—whether he sees a bat, a gorilla, waiters bowing to each other, a girl riding on a horse, Santa Claus with a Christmas tree under his arm, or a man's face in the shadows—the subject is presumably exposing his intimate phantasy life and general personality trends. Experienced clinicians have found that, whereas some ink-blot interpretations indicate a tendency to be a "conformist," others point to emotional tensions, repressions, and unfulfilled needs.

Rorschach workers feel that blot interpretations reveal the individual's psychological structure as a whole, including dynamically related emotions, attitudes, and mental "sets." They also contend that considerable experience and exchange of ideas has enabled them to interpret subjective responses in such a way as to harmonize with other clinical evidence (validity). That the method can be successful with children has been attested to by a number of psychologists,[104] some of whom have established norms for as early as the preschool level.[105] However, the fact that it has not been thoroughly validated scientifically is both the unique (in the sense of having avoided an atomistic interpretation) and weak feature of the Rorschach test.

PICTURE ANALYSIS TESTS. The picture interpretation test, called by Murray [106] the *thematic apperception* method because the one giving the test can often perceive a theme or trend running through the interpretations of the various pictures shown the subject, is also based on the assumption that the individual portrays his personality in his responses. However, in the case of the pictures, some of which are apparently commonplace and others of which present dramatic situations, the subject is led to identify himself with the leading character and thus to project his own phantasies, wishes, conflicts, inade-

[104] R. Horowitz and L. B. Murphy, "Projection Methods in the Psychological Study of Children," *Journal of Experimental Education*, 7:133-140 (1938).

[105] Bruno Klopfer, "Personality Diagnosis in Early Childhood: The Application of the Rorschach Method at the Preschool Level," *Eastern Psychological Association*, Apr. 1939.

[106] Henry A. Murray, *Explorations in Personality*, New York, Oxford Univ. Press, 1938, pp. 123-124, 182. See also R. Temple and E. W. Amen, *A Study of Anxiety Reactions in Young Children by Means of a Projective Technique*, Genetic Psychology Monographs, Vol. 30 (1944), pp. 61-113.

quacies, and suppressed desires. Such an exposure of the subject's "dynamisms" is obviously helpful to the analyst. Probably the greatest weakness of Murray's system is his vague and unsupported assumption that each child (and adult) is characterized by a group of internal needs similar in nature to McDougall's now outmoded propensities (Chapter 5).

WORD ASSOCIATION TESTS. *Word association* tests have been developed to secure an individual's reactions to words that may have acquired an emotional charge in the course of his experience. Hesitations and types of affective responses to particular words in such lists are noted and interpreted in the light of the subject's other personality traits. The two word lists, one for clinical use and the other for laboratory experimentation, developed by Wilson [107] as an improvement over earlier lists by Jung and by Kent-Rosanoff, are probably the best available in this field. Such lists are designed to yield scores for the commonality or uniqueness of association processes among both children and adults.

ART ANALYSIS METHODS. Knowing that children enjoy dabbling in mud, clay, paint, and other pliable materials, psychologists have sought to find symptoms of emotional stress in their creations along these lines. Observations have indicated that children apparently find satisfying emotional outlets in free play experiences with paint. It is believed that such releases serve as "safety valves" in the case of children beset with repressions and frustrations. They are also said occasionally to reveal incipient disturbances of a serious nature in time to alleviate them. According to researchers [108] who have examined paintings produced by normal children, many six- to ten-year-olds unconsciously use art as an emotional purge, revealing their hatred of parents or siblings by putting them on paper, showing their envy of those who overshadow them, or otherwise indicating conflicts and repressions. There is little doubt

[107] Donald P. Wilson, *An Extension and Evaluation of Association Word Lists,* Doctoral Dissertation, The Univ. of Southern California, 1943.
[108] R. H. Alschuler and L. A. Hattwick, "Easel Painting as an Index of Personality in Preschool Children," *American Journal of Orthopsychiatry,* 13: 616-626 (1943). Also J. R. McIntosh and R. W. Pickford, "Some Clinical and Artistic Aspects of a Child's Drawings," *British Journal of Medical Psychology,* 19: 342-362 (1943).

that art activities in the form of drawing, finger painting, clay manipulation, etc., provide a certain catharsis as well as pointing to maladjustments. Williams[109] has, in fact, reported that drawings made by children working alone in a room devoid of pictures often reveal conflicts and desires not elicited by other methods.

Figure 102. Phantasy Painting of a Cruelly Treated Boy Who Sought Freedom From Domination Apparently in Self-Defense

(Courtesy of Pasadena, Calif., City Schools.)

VOICE ANALYSIS. The analysis through high fidelity records of the human voice made by judges who did not know the individuals in question (called "blind" analysis) has resulted in some striking correspondences with other evidences of their personality qualities.[110] One high school boy's voice record yielded interpretations closely resembling those secured from

[109] J. N. Williams, "Interpretation of Drawings Made by Maladjusted Children," *Virginia Medical Monthly*, 67 : 533-538 (1940). Also L. Bender and J. Rapaport, "Animal Drawings of Children," *American Journal of Orthopsychiatry*, 14 : 521-527 (1944).

[110] Paul J. Moses, "The Study of Personality from Records of the Voice," *Journal of Consulting Psychology*, 6 : 257-261 (1942).

Rorschach test results by a different clinician.[111] The vocal variables utilized were, however, much more elaborate than is usually the case, including, among others, symmetry of phonetic units, vocal range, basic pitch (last syllable in a declarative sentence), major or minor key, stress and emphasis, pathos, speed, pauses, monotony, quality or timbre, and nasal resonance. Such a promising approach to personality analysis will no doubt be attempted on a larger scale in the future.

PLAY THERAPY has been mentioned previously (Chapter 5), but should serve as a fitting close to this brief canvass of the more recent "depth-analysis" or projection techniques of personality appraisal. To recapitulate, the free play method is being utilized when the child is given toys or puppets upon whom to project his hidden conflicts or desires when these are sufficiently intense to call for release. Dolls representing members of the family have in some instances called forth such discernible emotional responses as spanking, burying, crushing, drowning, and talking back to various of them.[112] Levy [113] has reported that even children of the Quekchi Indians in Guatemala and of the Pilaga Indians in the Argentine show hostility and rivalry when permitted to play with dolls representing a mother or competing siblings. It is probable that children in all cultures feel the impact of rivalries and loss of preferment, and that they get a certain amount of release from projecting their stresses onto representations of those who appear to be undermining them.

Amster [114] has categorized the values of play therapy as including: (1) a diagnostic understanding of the child, (2) the establishment of a working relationship, (3) breaking through a child's defenses against anxiety, (4) enabling a child to verbalize certain conscious material and associated feelings, (5) helping a child act out unconscious material and relieve the ac-

111 Harold E. Jones, The Adolescent Growth Study, VI: "The Analysis of Voice Records," *Journal of Consulting Psychology,* 6 : 255-256 (1942).
112 Dorothy W. Baruch, "Aggression During Doll Play in a Preschool," *American Journal of Orthopsychiatry,* 11 : 252-260 (1941).
113 David M. Levy, "Sibling Rivalry Studies in Children of Primitive Groups," *American Journal of Orthopsychiatry,* 9 : 205-214 (1939).
114 F. Amster, "Differential Use of Play in Treatment of Young Children," *American Journal of Orthopsychiatry,* 13 : 62-69 (1943).

companying tension, and (6) developing a child's play interests with a view to their being carried over into his later life.

The Direct Measurement of Overt Responses.—Conduct tests such as those utilized in the Character Inquiry by Hartshorne and May might well be discussed here, but were probably sufficiently elaborated upon in a previous section. When considered in the light of circumstances in which a child is stimulated to behave, they, too, offer clues to the organization of the child's inner personality pattern. An analytical study of the specific overt responses of children in a variety of concrete situations would no doubt reveal important data concerning their state of mental health.

The increased use of both objective and projective measuring techniques in the personality field is apparently based upon a desire of educators, psychologists, psychiatrists, and pediatricians to assist children and others in making better personal and social adjustments. As the difficulties involved in personality test construction and in the making of interpretations are more adequately overcome, and as more valid and comprehensive instruments are developed, investigators interested in child development will be in a position better to detect and correct incipient personality disorders.

Summary and Implications

Personality has been defined as the integrated functioning of all of the individual's traits and reaction tendencies as these are viewed by society. However, since such a broad conception makes personality practically synonymous with "human behavior," efforts have been made to delimit its meaning and to systematize the descriptions of its structure. Of the resulting views, four—(1) philosophical, (2) popular, (3) biophysical, and (4) biosocial—have import for an understanding of the child. Because of its practical implications, the biosocial point of view, with its doctrine of the specialized nature of action traits, has been widely used in child development programs.

The scientific study of personality is still in its early stages. The nature of trait organization and the way in which traits are integrated in functioning patterns are questions yet unanswered in any final way. Researches have shown that some aspects of personality are more stable and unitary than others. There is widespread recognition that many personality qualities are socially derived; that is, that they have evolved out of social experience in harmony with the dynamic nature of the child. If defined as groupings of dispositions to behave in characteristic ways in certain situations, traits are apparently developed through a continuum of concrete experiences in which specific patterns of adjustment were satisfying to the child.

Although it has not yet been possible to measure all aspects of a child's personality, a number of practical methods for ascertaining his degree of personal and social adjustment have been developed. Rating scales, inventories, and conduct tests, as well as projection techniques for determining inner personality organization and phantasy life, have been developed to a degree that makes possible the detection and correction of many incipient emotional conflicts.

The importance for success in life of good personality qualities can hardly be overestimated. If society as a whole is to be improved, it seems imperative that children be reared in ways which will tend to insure adequate mental health plus a degree of socialization commensurate with the processes of democratic living. Neither society nor the individual can survive in a culture which neglects the harmonious development of good personality in its oncoming generations.

QUESTIONS FOR DISCUSSION

1. Discuss the common assumption that because some personality traits appear in the first weeks of life they are biologically inherited. Can you show that such traits might have been acquired? Try to do so.
2. To what extent do you think personality characteristics appearing in the early undifferentiated behavior of the infant can be further developed or obliterated by parents? How would one

control stubbornness (negativism) or the more desirable quality of cooperation? Explain in detail.

3. Are the exponents of specific versus unitary traits necessarily in direct opposition to each other? Show how differences in age and maturity of children and youths might account for the seeming conflict of views. Reconcile them if you can.

4. Why do you suppose some psychologists are so opposed to the doctrine of specificity of behavior? Could it be because the ultimate consolidation of character and personality traits would be difficult to achieve by such a view? Elaborate on this idea or offer a better one.

5. What is meant by the *relative* or biosocial nature of personality traits? Why can a given child's personality qualities never be evaluated on a strictly absolute basis? What are the implications for character education or ethical behavior of this view of traits?

6. Is it true that the presence in a child of certain desirable personality qualities implied a corresponding weakness in others? Is such a proposal in harmony with the findings of research? What are its implications for development?

7. Describe how you would develop the trait of hospitality in a given child if provided with the opportunity. To what extent would the specificity of behavior from situation to situation be an asset or a handicap? Elaborate.

8. Why is it that frequent scoldings, exhortations, and admonitions are used by so many parents and teachers as almost the sole avenues to character and personality development on the part of children? What relation, if any, is there between listening to these precepts and developing specific dispositions to behave in characteristic ways?

9. What reason can you give for the tendency of some writers to regard "personality" and "character" as being synonymous concepts? From the standpoint of a careful analysis, what is the real difference? Would the same technique be used to develop both personality and character?

10. Show how the home, the school, the church, and other social institutions might unite their forces in an intelligent effort to guarantee the personality integrity of developing children and youths. Is it conceivable that such a program could prevent the appearance of neurotic disorders?

RECOMMENDED READINGS

Allport, Gordon W. *Personality, A Psychological Interpretation.* New York: Henry Holt & Co., Inc., 1937.

Charters, W. W. *The Teaching of Ideals.* New York: The Macmillan Co., 1927, Chs. 1-6.

Griffiths, J. H. *The Psychology of Human Behavior.* New York: Farrar & Rinehart, Inc., 1935, Ch. 15.

Hartshorne, Hugh, and May, M. A. *Studies in Deceit,* 1928; *Studies in Service and Self-control,* 1929; *Studies in the Organization of Character,* 1930. New York: The Macmillan Co. (especially summaries and conclusions).

Murphy, Lois B. "Childhood Experience in Relation to Personality Development," in *Personality and the Behavior Disorders.* (Edited by J. McV. Hunt.) New York: The Ronald Press Co., 1944, Vol. II, Ch. 21.

Plant, J. S. *Personality and the Cultural Pattern.* New York: The Commonwealth Fund, 1937.

Richmond, Winifred V. *Personality: Its Development and Hygiene.* New York: Farrar & Rinehart, Inc., 1937, Chs. 3, 5.

Sandiford, Peter. *Foundations of Educational Psychology.* New York: Longmans, Green & Co., 1938, Ch. 6.

Symonds, Percival M. *Diagnosing Personality and Conduct.* New York: D. Appleton-Century Co., Inc., 1931.

Thorpe, Louis P. *Psychological Foundations of Personality.* New York: McGraw-Hill Book Co., Inc., 1938, Chs. 1, 7, 10, 11.

Thorpe, Louis P. *Personality and Life,* New York: Longmans, Green & Co., 1941, Chs. 1, 6, 7.

Tiegs, Ernest W., and Katz, Barney. *Mental Hygiene in Education.* New York: The Ronald Press Co., 1941, Ch. 13.

CHAPTER 15

MENTAL HYGIENE OF THE CHILD

CHILDREN ARE OFTEN SPOKEN OF as possessing "good" personalities or as being "well-adjusted." Such expressions are usually taken to mean that the children in question are able to make relatively harmonious adjustments to the many personal and social requirements of daily living. They are the mentally healthy children who conduct their affairs acceptably, integrate conflicting tendencies into socially acceptable patterns of response, and otherwise get along with a minimum of friction, fear, or stress.

Some children are, on the contrary, said to be "queer," "maladjusted," "neurotic," or even "pre-psychotic." These terms designate individuals who are not successful in adjusting themselves to the expectations of their more normal associates. Such children display tendencies and engage in acts that are regarded as deviations from expected patterns of behavior. Psychologically, they are described as suffering from *personality disturbances*. They are the deviates or emotionally unhealthy members of the child population.

However, freedom from personal conflict is not the criterion of normality. Everyone is confronted by a continuous series of conflicting demands which must be harmonized in favor of socially desirable living.[1] Children are called upon to decide, for instance, between the joys of playing hooky and the probable wrath of a parent, between stealing much needed money and the likelihood of severe punishment, between lying about an unseen act and making a frank admission, or between slighting lessons and the probability of rewards for good marks. The psychologically normal child is the one who has learned to resolve conflicts in ways calculated to solve the problems involved

[1] For a discussion of conflicts see Mandel Sherman, *Mental Conflicts and Personality*, New York, Longmans, Green & Co., 1938.

without at the same time endangering his security or violating his sense of what is right. Conflict is universal, and the idea of normality versus abnormality can only have reference to the manner, socially and morally speaking, in which a given child solves his constantly recurring problems.

Causes of Deviate Behavior in Children

Society's treatment of children suffering from personality disorders does not present a reassuring story. Being replete with belief in animism and superstition, as well as examples of cruelty, it has not contributed a very savory page to the history of the evolution of modern civilization.

Pre-scientific Views of Behavior Causation.—In early days persons marked by what is now recognized as neurotic, psychotic, or even eccentric behavior were thought to be possessed of devils or to be endowed by spirits with more than earthly powers. Such individuals were creatures to be feared or worshiped. Joan of Arc, for instance, was regarded by her people as being possessed of supernatural abilities. Her enemies believed her to be in league with the Devil. The Puritan fathers, even, believed that evil spirits were responsible for personality disorders.

The attitude of medieval, and sometimes modern, groups toward psychological disorders is exemplified in their treatment of so-called "witches." These unfortunate individuals, whom we now realize were suffering from personality aberrations, were believed to be in league with evil spirits and thus likely to bring calamity by inciting the ill will of the more benign gods. For their "sins" these deviates were frequently stoned, burned, or otherwise liquidated. So it came about that, owing to a gullible but nevertheless ardent belief in causation through the intervention of spirits, deranged persons were frequently tortured, derided, and imprisoned in filthy, vermin-infested dungeons. Negativistic or antisocial behavior in children was thought to be an expression of inborn evil nature and was consequently ruthlessly attacked by both parents and church bodies.

The Modern View of Behavior Disorders.—The present-day conception of the etiology of deviate behavior is, we are happy to note, far different from the above. For animism and its mystic background there has been substituted the scientific principle of *natural causation* as it operates in both organic and psychological fields. Instead of blaming maladjusted children for their unfortunate condition, we endeavor to see in their behavior the inevitable operations of cause and effect, and to offer them such assistance and opportunity for making readjustments as facilities permit. Many persons have been too prone uncritically to assign the causes of personality disturbance to heredity (so often used as a compensation for lack of knowledge), and to such factors as ill health, body build, glandular disorders, and instinctive tendencies. Some of these factors, particularly ill health and endocrine disorders, might in some cases be effects of psychological disturbances rather than causes thereof.

Physiological disorders may in some cases be responsible for abnormalities of behavior. It is, however, sometimes a question whether a personality disorder is organic in origin or whether the difficulty may be found in the emotional life of the afflicted individual. According to present knowledge, behavior deviations may spring from either or both of these sources. A report [2] recently published in France supports the view that childhood maladjustments may emanate from environmental factors, constitutional factors, or a combination of these. The environmental factors noted include: (1) inferior moral environment, (2) mentally unbalanced parent or parents, (3) pedagogical inadequacy of parents, (4) broken homes, and (5) lack of parental care and training.

Many students of child development, while not inclined to neglect the possible physiological bases for either mental disorders or abnormalities of behavior, stress the importance of social forces in the determination of child behavior. White,[3]

---

[2] M. Francois, "Les Enfants Inadaptes" (Maladjusted Children), *Année Psychologie,* 39 : 33-88 (1940).

[3] W. A. White, *The Mental Hygiene of Childhood,* Boston, Little, Brown & Co., 1919, pp. viii-ix. See also by the same author, *Twentieth Century Psychiatry,* New York, W. W. Norton & Co., Inc., 1937.

a psychiatrist, declared a number of years ago that, "It is true that many students of heredity believe that all sorts of mental qualities may be traced directly from the ancestors. Those physicians, however, who deal with the problems of mental illness see, on the contrary, these peculiarities passed on because, as a part of the child's environment, they are impressed upon it during its development period. This view has been emphasized because it has been found possible to modify so many personal mental traits. Heredity as an explanation is therefore looked upon somewhat askance because it serves to block efforts at improvement. If a certain trait is hereditary, why, that's the end of it. There is nothing to be done. So frequently, however, something can be done that this explanation is being more and more put aside as inadequate."

In an effort to summarize the general causes of maladjustment in children, Jordan [4] lists the following:

A. Thwarting of Impulses and Desires
  1. Hostility, ridicule, or indifference, real or imagined, of adults or associates, leading to a feeling of inferiority.
  2. Feeling of guilt because of sex delinquency.
  3. Organ inferiority: a facial scar, enuresis, etc., leading to feelings of guilt or shame.
  4. Too much coddling by fond parents leading to prevention of participation in community affairs.
  5. Failure in school with its attendant ridicule from other children.

B. Undue Emotional Stimulation
  1. Unnerving shocks leading to fear and extreme excitement.
  2. The presence of nervous parents or relatives.
  3. Continued overexcitement; e.g., daily attendance at movies.
  4. Too intense urging by parents to attainments beyond reach by legitimate means.

---

[4] Arthur M. Jordan, *Educational Psychology,* New York, Henry Holt & Co., Inc., 1942, pp. 403-405.

C. Bad Home Conditions
    1. Parental disagreements.
    2. Lack of affection on the part of parents.
    3. Parental separation when child is strongly attached to each.
    4. Feelings of insecurity from family financial worries.
    5. Unfavorable comparisons with other members of the family.
    6. Inability to rise to family's level of aspiration.

It seems evident from this and similar lists [5] that children's behavior and degree of personal and social adjustment are to a considerable degree determined by conditions obtaining in the social environment in which they are reared. Parental and community attitudes are potent factors in the shaping of the child's personality and mental health.

The Thwarting of Basic Needs and Maladjustment.—The more fundamental human needs—the needs which apparently furnish the motivation for children's behavior—have already been presented (Chapter 5). The point was made there that the child is called upon to adjust to many people upon whom he is dependent for the fulfillment of these needs. The needs in question may be summarized as: (1) *physiological,* such as food, water, sleep, rest, and bodily comfort and gratification; (2) *self* (ego), or the need for recognition, approval, response, self-realization, and a sense of belonging; and (3) *social* (mutuality), such as opportunities for developing social skills, for cooperating with associates, and for being an essential member of a group.

The crucial nature of these needs in the life of a child has been informally but graphically set forth by Travis and Baruch [6] in the following words: "We (including children) need, first, the sort of satisfaction that builds a feeling of security within us. Without a sense of security we have no safety, we have no anchorage, we have no peace. The kinds

    5 Ralph M. Stogdell, "Survey of Experiments of Children's Attitudes Toward Parents: 1894-1936," *Pedagogical Seminary and Journal of Genetic Psychology,* 51: 293-303 (1937).
    6 Lee Edward Travis and Dorothy W. Baruch, *Personal Problems of Everyday Life,* New York, D. Appleton-Century Co., Inc., 1941, pp. 64-65.

of satisfaction which bring security make us feel warm and loved. They make us feel comfortable. They afford us a kind of inner protection. They give us, too, the courage to come to grips with life's issues. They give us a fundamental abiding strength—a creative force which cannot exist in the presence of inner cringing. Affection and response from others brings to us satisfactions that make for security. A feeling that we have a place in the world—that we belong—helps similarly in the building of security."

Since the child's presence in a social field creates these indispensable needs, they automatically become goals toward which behavior is directed. As Gestalt psychologists put it, needs become goal activities or *tensions demanding resolution,* not only because they act as urges but also because of the "pull" of psychological and physical forces toward a satisfactory "closure." [7] On this basis, the child is more or less continually in a state of tension or imbalance which demands resolution (satisfaction) in the form of fulfillment of his basic needs. It means also that personality disturbances are likely to appear when these dynamic demands are *excessively* thwarted, or in cases where the child has not developed the social skills or cooperative techniques requisite to social acceptance. It should not be concluded, however, that occasional mild frustrations are likely to endanger the integrity of a child's personality. When fortified by a basic sense of security, most children can adjust to a remarkable amount of frustration.

Personality adjustment apparently depends upon a *balanced* satisfaction of needs. As the present author [8] has brought out more fully elsewhere, excessive fulfillment of any legitimate need is as likely to result in personality disorder as is its undue thwarting. Patterns of experience leading to a sense of security will, of course, vary greatly in detail from child to child. But so long as conditions of family and community life continue to be excessively frustrating, it is logical to expect the usual crop of unhappy children, maladjusted personalities,

[7] G. W. Hartman, *Gestalt Psychology,* New York, The Ronald Press Co., 1935, pp. 202-209.
[8] Louis P. Thorpe, "Understanding Child Nature," *Education,* 56 : 466-469 (1936).

juvenile delinquents, and criminals. It is probably the excessive thwarting of fundamental childhood needs that brings about the appearance of many of these symptoms of stress.

It should be evident that the existence of physiological and psychological needs involves the possibility of serious consequences. Conflicts and frustrations are children's common lot, inescapable features of the society in which they live; but when endured too often or too long, they become the *verae causae* of personality maladjustments. Just as the physical organism disintegrates under conditions of continual deprivation and neglect, so the morale of a child breaks when he is constantly confronted

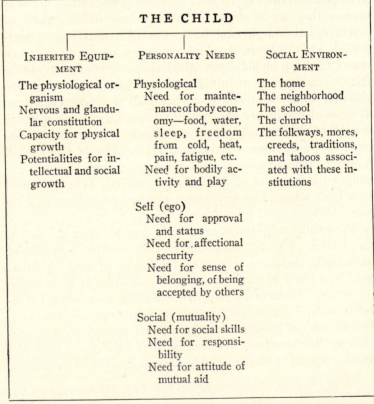

THE CHILD

Inherited Equipment	Personality Needs	Social Environment
The physiological organism	Physiological	The home
Nervous and glandular constitution	Need for maintenance of body economy—food, water, sleep, freedom from cold, heat, pain, fatigue, etc.	The neighborhood
Capacity for physical growth	Need for bodily activity and play	The school
Potentialities for intellectual and social growth		The church
		The folkways, mores, creeds, traditions, and taboos associated with these institutions
	Self (ego)	
	Need for approval and status	
	Need for affectional security	
	Need for sense of belonging, of being accepted by others	
	Social (mutuality)	
	Need for social skills	
	Need for responsibility	
	Need for attitude of mutual aid	

Figure 103. Dynamic Factors Affecting Personality Development

with hostility and insecurity. It can scarcely be denied that hearty approval and acceptance, on the one hand, and overt social scorn, on the other, are two of the most influential forces for determining the behavior of children.

In summing up the implications of the existence of fundamental needs in the child, it can be said that if the urge to satisfy them were more easily and generally fulfilled there would be much less need for courts, prisons, and corrective institutions in general. The incidence of delinquency, neurotic disorders, and widespread unhappiness is evidence that fundamental psychological requirements are by no means always satisfied, and that many children are forced into the position of relieving their stresses of insecurity in retreating or anti-social ways. Unhappy home conditions, social conventions and taboos, and numerous obstacles in the environment stand in the way of ready fulfillment of legitimate desires. It is thus to be expected that maladjustments will develop, especially in the case of children whose experience is marked by a considerable lack of security. Children differ greatly in capacity to tolerate thwarting. Whereas some are disturbed by slight deprivations, others appear relatively unmoved by greater adversities. All are, however, subject to the needs of the human species, and the demands which they make.

Examples of Reaction to Frustration.—Possibilities of personality disturbance, as caused by the frustration of dynamic needs, are illustrated by the diagrammatic chart shown in Figure 104. Crane's [9] explanation of the processes involved runs as follows: "The 'Personality' encounters a 'Situation' such as the winning of a sweetheart, and goes through a period of attempted adjustment, ending possibly in success and marriage. On the other hand, if failure results, the Personality is still maladjusted, as represented by the circle and rectangle in juxtaposition. The Personality may be able to effect a successful compromise so that the emotional tension is reduced through sublimation, as in the case of the disappointed girl who

---

[9] G. W. Crane, *Psychology Applied*, Chicago, Northwestern Univ. Press, 1944, pp. 515-517.

goes into a convent, or becomes a settlement worker or mis-
sionary.

"Again, the Situation may be too powerful for the Personality, in which case the Personality may crack. For instance,
one of the writer's former students who had been a boyhood
sweetheart and classmate of a girl who lived a few houses down
the street, learned the week before their graduation from high
school that she had betrothed herself to another senior and was
to be married shortly. The disappointed youth fled the situation immediately after commencement by entraining for California, where he remained so alcoholized for three months that
he did not know when the date arrived for the marriage. The
reverse of this response may take place where the disappointed
person breaks the Situation by murdering his rival or even his
sweetheart." Crane continues to describe how the young man
mentioned finally managed to effect a "Constructive Compromise," thus further illustrating the possible sequences in the
chart.

A study of Figure 104 will show not only how major frustrations may result in success or failure, how broken personalities may sometimes become reconstructed through intelligent
compromise, but also what unfortunate forms of both personality disorder and antisocial behavior may follow failure to
adjust to difficult and thwarting situations.

A classical example of personality maladjustment with later
reconstruction to approximately normal status is afforded by
the case of Mildred, one of the three problem children so graphically portrayed in the book *Three Problem Children*.[10] Mildred
had become morbid and inattentive in school because of inability
to master her lessons, and because she was rejected by the majority of her classmates. Even her younger sister taunted her
because of her involuntary bed-wetting (enuresis). When a
thorough study of the circumstances surrounding her home and
school life led to better home treatment, freedom from her sister's scorn (through sleeping in separate rooms), and remedial
procedures in connection with her school work, Mildred im-

10 Mary B. Sayles, *Three Problem Children*, New York, The Commonwealth
Fund, 1925.

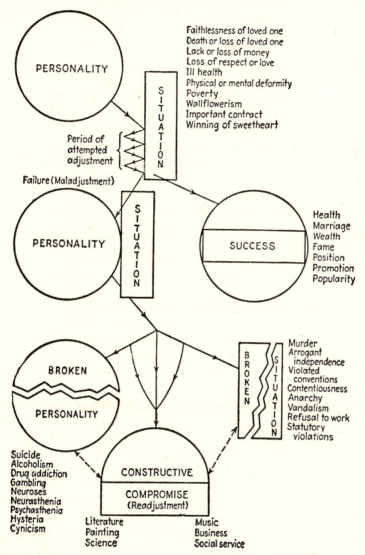

Faithlessness of loved one
Death or loss of loved one
Lack or loss of money
Loss of respect or love
Ill health
Physical or mental deformity
Poverty
Wallflowerism
Important contract
Winning of sweetheart

PERSONALITY

SITUATION

Period of attempted adjustment

Failure (Maladjustment)

PERSONALITY

SITUATION

SUCCESS

Health
Marriage
Wealth
Fame
Position
Promotion
Popularity

BROKEN

PERSONALITY

BROKEN SITUATION

Murder
Arrogant independence
Violated conventions
Contentiousness
Anarchy
Vandalism
Refusal to work
Statutory violations

Suicide
Alcoholism
Drug addiction
Gambling
Neuroses
Neurasthenia
Psychasthenia
Hysteria
Cynicism

CONSTRUCTIVE

COMPROMISE
(Readjustment)

Literature
Painting
Science

Music
Business
Social service

Figure 104. A Diagnostic Chart Showing the Various Types of Adjustments
Possible When Emotional Conflicts Are Encountered

(Adapted by G. W. Crane, *Psychology Applied*, Northwestern Univ. Press, 1941, p. 516.
from K. A. Menninger, *The Human Mind*, New York, Alfred A. Knopf, 1930, p. 26.)
Reproduced by permission of Alfred A. Knopf, Inc.

proved both in morale and in the mastery of her lessons. With an increased sense of adequacy and more friendly treatment from teachers and playmates, this child was restored to practically normal personality status.

Conflicts do not necessarily result in personality disturbances. Only those associated with continual failure or prolonged frustration of strong incentives are likely to cause undesirable emotional upheavals. Life presents one problem after another, the complexities of which are commensurate with the elaborateness of the social structure in which the child lives. It is necessary for him constantly to react to opposing desires and to work out solutions for conflicts that will ultimately be beneficial individually and socially. Those who are fortunate enough to experience such a happy outcome can agree with the writer [11] who has said, "Life is one grand, glorious struggle, which every normal individual enjoys as long as the struggle does not result in the capitulation of his ego."

Dynamisms in Adjustment to Frustration

Deviate Behavior as an Effort at Adjustment.—In considering the implications of the topic "dynamisms of adjustment," we shall accept the commonly held assumption that dynamisms are characteristic and usually indirect ways in which thwarted individuals seek to satisfy their desires and to maintain their sense of personal worth. As Tiegs and Katz[12] have written, "Mental mechanisms (dynamisms) are the devices or methods which individuals use in attempting to maintain their self-respect or prestige when they meet obstacles which they cannot overcome." Since children encounter frequent thwartings, as well as numerous threats to their sense of self-esteem, dynamisms designed to effect needed adjustments are an essential requirement. Moreover, since everyone endeavors to satisfy his fundamental needs, dynamisms should not be thought of as symptoms of personality disorder except in the extreme forms usually associated with psychological abnormality. Adjustive

11 J. J. B. Morgan, *The Psychology of the Unadjusted School Child,* New York, The Macmillan Co., 1936, p. 31. By permission.

12 Ernest W. Tiegs and Barney Katz, *Mental Hygiene in Education,* New York, The Ronald Press Co., 1941, p. 42.

processes of the kind being described are common to both normal and abnormal persons, the latter displaying them in more extensive and intensified form.

If the actions of human beings were guided by the dictates of reason the problem of making adequate psychological adjustments would be a relatively simple one. On such a basis a normal and intelligent individual who had a clear perspective of the involvements of a situation would profit thereby and make the appropriate responses. His intellect would mediate between his desires and external obstacles to their fulfillment. However, that neither children nor adults follow such a course is a fact known to all observing persons. The ability to deal with frustrating situations intelligently and without bias represents a degree of personal and social maturity seldom reached by man. Actually, most human behavior would appear to be motivated by efforts to satisfy the demands of fundamental needs.[13]

ORIGIN AND CLASSIFICATION OF THE DYNAMISMS. It is noteworthy that the dynamisms [14] under consideration, now included in practically all psychology texts, are primarily psychoanalytic concepts. They are the adjustment processes which supposedly mediate between the demands of the *id* and the permissions of the *ego;* they are the *unconscious* means by which the ego maintains its prestige in the face of illicit desires and deviations in conduct.[15] Although modern child psychology attacks adjustment problems from as objective a point of view as possible, it is indebted to psychoanalysis for not only some of its terminology, but for many practical mental hygiene suggestions.

In classifying dynamisms from the mental hygiene point of view, it has become customary to categorize them in terms of

---

[13] Louis P. Thorpe, *Personality and Life,* New York, Longmans, Green & Co., 1941, Ch. 2.

[14] Dynamisms are frequently referred to as "adjustment mechanisms" or as "mental mechanisms." However, as Healy and his associates have pointed out, whereas the term "dynamism" refers to a *driving force,* "mechanism" has reference to the structure of a machine, i.e., train, automobile, or the human body. The adjustment processes designated as dynamisms are apparently dynamic factors *actuating* behavior. Thus the use of the term dynamism. (William Healy, A. F. Bronner, and A. M. Bowers, *The Structure and Meaning of Psychoanalysis,* New York, Alfred A. Knopf, 1930.)

[15] Sigmund Freud, *General Introduction to Psychoanalysis,* New York, Liveright Pub. Corp., 1920.

their social acceptability and the characteristics of the responses they represent. Thus Shaffer [16] suggests: (1) adjustment by defense (compensation, rationalization), (2) adjustment by withdrawing (negativism, phantasy, retrogression), (3) adjustments involving fear and repression (phobias, repression), (4) adjustment by ailments (hysteria and other forms of psychoneurosis), and (5) persistent nonadjustive reactions (anxiety, worry, "nervousness"). Seashore and Katz [17] have classified the dynamisms (as mental mechanisms) on the basis of their social acceptability, i.e., whether they make for harmonious, inadequate, or poor social adjustment. This plan embodies the grouping of important dynamisms as follows:

1. Socially approved—compensation, rationalization, and substituted activities.
2. Socially tolerated—identification, projection, egocentrism.
3. Socially criticized—sympathism, regression, dissociation.
4. Socially disapproved—repression, negativism, phantasy (daydreaming).

These authors have endeavored to assist teachers in the evaluation of childhood dynamisms by suggesting criteria for determining their personal and social implications. The criteria include:

1. Progress toward original goal—To what extent does the dynamism aid the child in attaining his original goal or an adequate substitute?
2. Prestige or social status—To what extent does the dynamism enable the child to maintain his status with his group?
3. Social significance—To what extent does the dynamism aid the child in maintaining satisfactory school, home, work, and community relationships?
4. Ability to adjust—To what extent does the dynamism aid the child in developing more skill and ability to meet future problems?

[16] Laurance F. Shaffer, *The Psychology of Adjustment,* Boston, Houghton Mifflin Co., 1936, pp. 143-145.
[17] Robert H. Seashore and Barney Katz, "An Operational Definition and Classification of Mental Mechanisms," *Psychological Record,* 1: 3-24 (1937).

Although this formulation of dynamisms is limited by the possibility that in some instances their social acceptability may be determined by their degree and intensity of manifestation rather than by their form, it has proved useful in providing in-

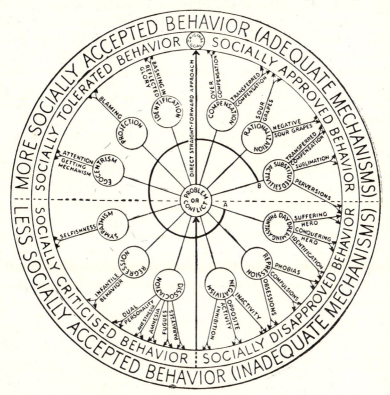

Figure 105. Behavior Mechanism Chart

(From Robert H. Seashore and Barney Katz, "An Operational Definition and Classification of Mental Mechanisms," *Psychological Record*, 1:3-24 (1937).)

sight into a wide range of commonly observed adjustment processes in children (see Figure 105).

The discussion of dynamisms selected for this book will be concerned with those apparently involved in (1) forgetting reality, (2) distorting reality, (3) atoning for reality, (4) retreating from reality, (5) attacking reality, and (6) facing reality.   These and lesser dynamisms reveal many of the child's emotional stresses and can thus be utilized to a considerable extent in the diagnosis of maladjustments.

Forgetting Reality—the Phantasy Dynamism.—One of the most satisfying forms of substitute satisfaction available to the frustrated child is that of phantasy or daydreaming. Here the defeated child may find a happy retreat from his feelings of inadequacy and insecurity. Having been thwarted in his efforts to secure ego-satisfaction in the realm of reality, he finds relief from his stresses in the domain of fancy. In his reveries he easily gains the greatly desired social approval, warm friends, and achievements so consistently denied him in the harsh world of realities.

Conquering Hero.   A common variety of the soothing phantasy dynamism is the "conquering hero" or "phantasy of grandeur" type. As these titles suggest, this adjustment process enables the child or youth to regard himself as a great hero in battle, on the football field, in a storm at sea, or perhaps as being an eminent actor, inventor, surgeon, or fighter. Illustrative of this dynamism is the case in which a greatly discouraged (through failure) schoolboy imagined himself to be the heroic conqueror of a band of wild Indians. Though wounded and deprived of his courageous comrades he held off the relentless redskins until reinforcements arrived—all in the delightful realm of phantasy. To make the story complete, the first to offer praise and adoration was his now-repentant teacher who had so harshly relegated him to the ranks of the stupid.[18]

Suffering Hero.   The reverse of the conquering hero form of daydreaming is that in which the distressed child imagines himself to be the victim of a tragic episode—the "suffering hero" type. Here the child touches the heart strings of his allegedly harsh parents or companions by imagining himself a runaway or, even better, the victim of wild beasts, of bandits, or of the crushing wheels of a railroad train. Many a child has secretly enjoyed contemplating the remorse and grief of those

[18] R. H. Wheeler, *The Science of Psychology,* New York, T. Y. Crowell Co., 1940, p. 107.

responsible, because of their cruelty, for the sorry plight in which he thus found himself.

Such are the flights of imagination of unhappy children who, because of failure to secure needed satisfactions through social channels, resort to the soothing domain of unreality where acceptance and love may be had for the asking. However, it should be clear that, when indulged in moderately to ease the pain of occasional thwartings, this dynamism is harmless. Indeed, it may even be considered helpful. Daydreaming is a universal adjustment process by means of which all of us satisfy our need for maintaining a sense of personal importance. It may also contribute to the planning of future accomplishments.

Danger arises, so far as the child's mental health is concerned, when the phantasy dynamism is used as a continual substitute for concrete accomplishments and for efforts to meet the practical requirements of everyday living. The child who constantly resorts to the gentle retreat of a make-believe world sets up a vicious circle which has no end. Finding reality increasingly defeating and the dream world correspondingly more satisfying, he loses his sense of distinction between the two. It is thus evident that, beginning with the mild daydreams of wishful thinking, a child might under harsh circumstances gradually become more and more introspective, fanciful, and sensitive, and might even reach the state of emotional apathy and exclusion of reality called schizophrenia (dementia praecox), perhaps with the delusions of grandeur and persecution characteristic of the paranoiac form of that psychosis.[19]

IDENTIFICATION. A form of phantasy in which children afflicted with feelings of insecurity and inadequacy often find relief is the dynamism of *identification,* a process by which the individual assumes the role of a person of superior attainment. Thus, the boy of meager accomplishments or inferior physical equipment may imagine himself to be Buffalo Bill, Red Grange, or perhaps Clark Gable. By identifying himself with these characters, he vicariously fights Indians, thwarts train robberies, wins football games, or enjoys the luxuries and adulation at-

---

[19] E. S. Conklin, *Principles of Abnormal Psychology,* New York, Henry Holt & Co., Inc., 1935, Ch. 9.

tendant upon being a movie star. Likewise, a lonely girl might through identification experience the lofty sentiments of Florence Nightingale or the thrills of a favorite movie queen.

When indulged in moderately, this dynamism is obviously normal and may, in the case of not too thoroughly defeated children, prove stimulating. As one writer [20] reasons, it permits a child to feel some of the importance he ascribes to his superiors. Identification should not, however, become a substitute for reality or for social action. Mental ill-health is in evidence when the majority of adjustments are made in fancy only and to the exclusion of genuine achievements. Such a dynamism becomes a symptom of deep frustration when a child uses it as an habitual retreat from the practical requirements of life. The following warning is thus apropos here: "The passage from a condition such as we have just mentioned (examples of identification) to a condition in which the insane individual identifies herself as in one case with the Empress Louisa, wears yachting clothes, and lives the part, and believes that she is the real Empress, is not as abrupt as we had formerly believed." [21]

Distorting Reality—the Dynamism of Rationalization.—

The word "rationalization" has various meanings, but as used in discussions of mental hygiene has reference to the tendency to give plausible reasons for inconsistent or undesirable behavior. It is one of the most common and convenient "defense" dynamisms in the child's repertoire of stress-reducing devices. Since they are expected to conform to social customs and certain standards of behavior, frequent failures to do so must be "explained" by children in ways adequate to safeguard their standing in the eyes of their elders. They are thus motivated to offer alibis when caught in acts suggestive of stupidity or wrong motives. The child who is poor in his school work may justify himself by insisting that his teachers are unfair. The boy who is reprimanded for defiance may declare that he is meting out their just deserts to his tormentors.

[20] R. H. Wheeler, *op. cit.,* p. 192.
[21] Arthur M. Jordan, *Educational Psychology,* New York, Henry Holt & Co., Inc., 1942, p. 420.

The rationalizing child protects himself from the necessity of acknowledging the *true* reasons for his acts by offering what appear to be *plausible* reasons. Since this blame-escaping process is motivated by a deeper desire for social approval, it is often so subtle as to escape recognition by its own author. It also tends to make him blind to any evidence damaging to his excuses. Since he has an ego to maintain, the rationalizing child endeavors to conform to its demands.

PROJECTION. A popular form of rationalization is implicit in the dynamism of "projection." [22] Projection has been termed "the tendency to put the blame for one's conduct on circumstances that are beyond one's control." [23] This ego-saving process is explanatory of the child's penchant for blaming others or obstacles in the environment for his shortcomings. Thus the tardy child blames a late breakfast or a faulty alarm clock, the failing pupil lays his difficulties at the door of a too-hard examination, and the small boy accuses the other small boy of having started a fight.

These are "buck-passing" dynamisms which illustrate the universal tendency of children to relieve their stresses of inadequacy by blaming incidental causes rather than their own inefficiency. Children must "save face" before their parents and teachers, thus their ardent efforts to avoid admission of faults.

SOUR GRAPES. Another form of rationalization is the *sour grapes* dynamism of fox-fable fame. Just as the fox is said to have saved his pride by declaring that the unattainable grapes were sour and thus undesirable, children ease their disappointment upon failing to achieve desired goals by insinuating that they are better off as it is, or that such success might not have been to their advantage. The unsuccessful boy insists that he is not disturbed at failing to master his piano lessons because such a skill is a sign of femininity. Economically underprivileged girls may disparage the possession of a bicycle by inferring that such a "contraption" is intended for boys. Likewise scho-

---

[22] Some students of the subject have contended that projection is not strictly a form of rationalization and that it should be regarded as a process of shifting responses from one person or situation to another. Nail biting may, for example, represent the shifting of a child's frustrated aggression tendencies.

[23] Caroline B. Zachry, *Personality Adjustments of School Children*, New York, Chas. Scribner's Sons, 1929, p. 175.

lastically weak pupils may defend themselves by declaring that only sissies are scholars.

These and similar responses are rationalizations, tension-resolving processes invented by unsuccessful individuals seeking' substitute satisfaction for thwarted desires. That their ego-preserving function is not always apparent to their authors seems certain, but this does not alter the fact that they are primarily defense dynamisms.

SWEET LEMON. Much the same may be said of the *sweet lemon* or *Pollyanna* dynamism, by which the individual is motivated, when a calamity befalls him, to insist that it might have been worse—indeed, that it was probably good for him. A child may have a ne'er-do-well father but insist that he is grand (in terms of other qualities) nevertheless. The budding musician may have an inferior musical instrument, but is none-the-less proud and defensive of it. The boy who is unfortunate enough to come into possession of a faulty bicycle may maintain that it is the best make of bicycle on the market. Thus do children find a pleasant escape from reality by inventing excuses for their lack of judgment or of desirable possessions.

Although rationalization in all its forms is indicative of efforts to distort reality, it does relieve the individual of unnecessary embarrassments and assists in the preservation of his prestige. It is a normal dynamism engaged in by practically everyone, especially children and adolescents who are hard pressed to maintain the approval of their elders. In its milder manifestations, rationalization is not considered a disorder of personality, but when the individual is so seriously defeated that he becomes convinced of the soundness of his "reasoning" and actually deceives himself, he is drifting into the throes of the false beliefs (distortions of reality) called *delusions*. It is herein that the danger of excessive rationalization lies.[24]

Atoning for Reality—the Dynamism of Compensation.[25]— Essential to an understanding of personality dynamics are the processes of *compensation,* a group of dynamisms by means of

[24] E. S. Conklin, *op. cit.*, pp. 179-180.

[25] Rather than being a dynamism as such, compensation may be regarded as a method of adjustment utilizing a variety of dynamisms. A few of these are described here.

which children endeavor to atone for feelings of inferiority.[26] As the process goes, every child, being motivated by a competitive society, develops at some points the feeling that he is inferior in relation to certain other children. This feeling may be based on either real or imagined inadequacies of a physical, mental, social, or economic nature, but in any case it results in intolerable tensions which seek an avenue of escape. Being unable to stand the strain of the unfavorable comparisons which his inferiority brings about, the child is driven to utilize a dynamism that will hide his defects from himself and others.

Thus may occur the appearance of compensatory behavior—the effort to atone for personal deficiencies by winning esteem and recognition through the development of personal qualities or skills along lines where success is possible. The child with a frail physique may endeavor to become a good student, all the while disparaging athletic games as the pastime of the scholastically incompetent; the unattractive girl may cultivate a winsome disposition to atone for her lack of good looks; the unpopular boy develops grand airs and a tough demeanor as compensations for feelings of inferiority and cowardice; and the musically ambitious miss with a monotonous singing voice strives to become a skilled pianist. "The child covers up or disguises, by exaggerating a desirable tendency or trait, his feelings of inferiority, sometimes in a socially acceptable manner, and sometimes in a socially disapproved one (delinquency)." [27]

Compensation may take the direction of supreme efforts to excel along a given line in spite of handicaps. Demosthenes, the orator, is said to have overcome a serious case of stuttering in his youth, and all have heard of Theodore Roosevelt, Sr.'s valiant fight against early ill health. Both Beethoven and Edison excelled in fields ordinarily requiring acute auditory sensitivity, in spite of deafness. Cases of failure to compensate in such spectacular ways probably greatly outnumber these examples, but the latter illustrate the dynamisms by means of

---

[26] Alfred Adler, *Problems of Neurosis*, Cosmopolitan Book Corp. (New York, Farrar & Rinehart, Inc.), 1930, pp. 44-47. See also E. S. Robinson, "A Concept of Compensation and Its Psychological Setting," *Journal of Abnormal and Social Psychology*, 17: 383-394 (1923).

[27] Ernest W. Tiegs and Barney Katz, *Mental Hygiene in Education*, New York, The Ronald Press Co., 1941, p. 342.

which the ego-status and emotional equilibrium of the personality are maintained.

OVERCOMPENSATION. As its title suggests, this dynamism involves overdoing in an effort to attain a desirable goal. The child overcompensates when, in order to hide an inferiority complex, he goes to extremes of effort or explanation.[28] As an example, one girl endeavored to become a social leader by giving all too-frequent parties. This process is further illustrated by the compensation of Napoleon who, as a lad in a French military school, was ridiculed by his classmates for his small stature and Corsican origin. Napoleon's bitterness led him to overcompensate to the extent of forcing the majority of European countries to recognize his superiority. Children may be said to overcompensate when, for example, they cling doggedly to a musical instrument which they cannot master or insist that they like arithmetic when they are failing in it.

COMPENSATORY IDENTIFICATION. When an individual feels that he has not attained sufficient distinction through his own efforts, he may manage to become a member of some supposedly exclusive firm, club, fraternity, school, or other desirable organization. He can then bask in the reflected glory of "his" or "our" institution. Thus the girl speaks of "our" club, the elementary pupil infers the superiority of "his" school, and the small boy brags about "my" family. In each instance, the compensating individual has inflated his ego by identifying himself with a supposedly superior organization. The same is true of those who boast of having illustrious relatives and acquaintances.

MALINGERING. This is a type of compensatory dynamism in which the subject may attempt to escape the odium of inadequacy through feigning illness or physical disability. As one writer [29] has defined it, malingering is a process of creating infirmities which can be used as plausible excuses for failure. The elementary school girl who feigns a headache can often induce her parents to excuse her from attending school, and the boy

---

[28] *Ibid.*, p. 45.
[29] M. M. Gill, "Malingering," *Bulletin of the Menninger Clinic*, 5 : 157-160 (1941).

who simulates a stomach-ache may sometimes succeed in evading distasteful chores. Practically everyone has seen instances in which small children have pretended to be tired or ill in order to be carried to bed or relieved of a promised punishment.

REGRESSION. When an individual has been so frustrated in his efforts to make satisfactory progress that he retreats to a more childish level of living where fewer demands are made upon him, he is said to be employing the *regression* dynamism. To quote one authority: [30] "Regression implies a form of behavior less mature than that which is expected of the person. By means of regression the individual is able to evade his problems by symbolic retreat into a situation with which he was able to deal previously." Patients suffering from dementia praecox (insanity) are sometimes characterized by this backward-turning dynamism. Spectacular cases have been reported in which mature individuals returned to the activities and baby talk of infancy.[31] In its mild aspects regression is illustrated by the helplessness sometimes displayed by neglected children, the tendency of others to engage in infantile forms of recreation or imaginary ills, and the contentment with which some lean on the protection afforded by religion.[32] Regression has been styled the "Old Oaken Bucket delusion" because of its suggestion of the superior joys of childhood days.

Of the dynamisms which are not socially undesirable, compensation may be one of the most constructive. It frequently leads to notable achievements as well as to stimulating feelings of personal worth. In fact, properly directed, compensation is a preferred form of treatment for attitudes of inadequacy in children. However, when carried to excess in the form of criticism of others, malingering, antisocial behavior, and regression, this type of dynamism is suggestive of deep maladjustment. Some of its victims ultimately are numbered among the completely deranged.

[30] Mandel Sherman, *Basic Problems of Behavior,* New York, Longmans, Green & Co., 1941, p. 376.
[31] William McDougall, "Four Cases of 'Regression' in Soldiers," *Journal of Abnormal and Social Psychology,* 15 : 136-156 (1920).
[32] F. L. Wells, "Mental Regression; Its Conceptions and Types," *Psychiatric Bulletin,* 9 : 445-492 (1916).

Retreating from Reality—Functional Dissociation.—In the dynamism of functional dissociation, which is also classified as a form of *hysteria,* may be witnessed some of the most amazing escapes from conflict known to the science of psychology. It is the dynamism in which the emotionally tense organism resorts, without foreknowledge on the part of the individual, to physical symptoms which automatically preclude the need for further conflict or action. This process is illustrated by unstable children who become so agitated over a coming examination that, while on the way to school, they are overtaken by vomiting spells, or other stomach disorder, thus necessitating a return home for the rest of the day.

Assuming that the child's fears were the true cause of the emotional tension, we have here a case of hysteria or functional dissociation in which part of the organism developed a disability which very conveniently relieved the child of the necessity of going through with a dreaded performance. According to clinical findings, this type of escape dynamism occurs without insight on the part of the subject. Such a retreat from intense conflict or fear is especially spectacular because of the appearance of physical disability in the form of fainting spells, muscle tremors, temporary headaches, and vomiting of emotional origin without benefit of any known underlying organic disorder.[33] It is thus apparent that as a result of intense conflict an individual's *physical functions* may become seriously impaired.

War Neurosis. Conflicts of the kind described were much in evidence during both World War I and World War II when certain emotionally unstable soldiers, some of whom were believed to have been maladjusted since childhood, were torn between conflicting desires to appear courageous in the eyes of their fellows and irrepressible longings to get home to their families and safety. Many suffered from hysterical symptoms in which the outstanding feature was anesthesia (loss of feeling) for certain motor and sensory functions. Hysterical paralysis (usually of one or more limbs), as well as functional blindness and defects of hearing, were frequently in evidence. Some cases might appear to be quite deaf, baffling every effort to detect ma-

[33] E. S. Conklin, *op. cit.,* Ch. 6.

lingering, and yet be disturbed at night by the cries of birds or the sighing of the winds. Others developed anxiety states, neurasthenia, or effort syndromes (heart palpitations, etc.). These are the famous cases of war neurosis (functional dissociation) known to most people erroneously as "shell shock." [34] Many of the symptoms, including paralysis and blindness, disappeared when the necessity of engaging in combat or the termination of the war removed the cause of the conflict. However, these dynamisms indicate the tragic extent to which conflict-torn organisms sometimes go in quest of peace (reduction of stress) without loss of ego-status.

Reports and studies [35] concerning the impact of World War II on the mental health of children have been numerous, but have for the most part been lacking in controls and consequently in scientific value. General trends appear to indicate, however, that in the case of the rank and file of children they have reacted to the stresses of raids, bombings, evacuation, and deprivations with a remarkable amount of adaptability and emotional control. A relatively small proportion have exhibited nervous or other personality disorders. The stabilizing factors here have been physical well-being, close family ties, emotional stability on the part of parents, and previous personal adjustment. Children displaying the greatest tensions have been those who were already maladjusted, who were separated from their parents, or who were more or less continually subjected to parental or teacher expressions of anxiety.

Investigations of problem children have shown that those who displayed anxiety symptoms in the early days of the war had practically all manifested previous anxiety reactions. Their insecurity appeared to stem from unsatisfactory relations with one or both parents. In the case of very young children, the symptoms exhibited were referable to their parents' anxiety rather than to the war as such. Spontaneous defense dynam-

[34] W. S. Taylor, "A Hypnoanalytic Study of Two Cases of War Neurosis," *Journal of Abnormal and Social Psychology,* 16 : 344-355 (1921-22) ; Robert P. Knight, "The Treatment of the Psychoneuroses of War," *Bulletin of the Menninger Clinic,* 7 : 148-155 (1943).

[35] H. Zorbaugh (Editor), "Children at War," *Journal of Educational Sociology,* 16 : 193-248 (1942) ; A. T. Jersild and M. F. Meigs, "Children and War," *Psychological Bulletin,* 40 : 541-573 (1943) ; L. M. Kostenbader, "Does War Frighten Children?" *Nation's Schools,* 34 : 30-31 (1944).

isms were in evidence in connection with expressions of insecurity.

Psychologists have recommended that in time of war or other major emergency parents and teachers take into account the probable effects of such traumatic conditions on children's emotional status. School programs designed to contribute to a war effort are believed to be conducive to the allaying of anxiety. Older children should be informed concerning the causes and involvements of war, as well as the reasons for the family and political disruptions experienced.

DUAL PERSONALITY. Even more astounding is the form of dissociation known as dual personality.[36] Like other forms of personality disorder it develops gradually, moving by imperceptible degrees from mild to serious stages of expression. Practically all persons are many-sided creatures of mood and differing social-behavior patterns, for they are obliged, for example, to act differently at a public gathering than at home, and to deport themselves in harmony with a variety of professional or vocational requirements. However, these fluctuations in behavior do not disturb the integrity of the personality; there is no break-up of personality integration, only a temporary domination of behavior by one pattern within the whole.

In the case of severe conflicts and fears, which usually have their origin in childhood, these tendencies toward differentiation among patterns of action may become sufficiently intensified to bring about hysterical symptoms such as anesthesias, obsessions, amnesias, somnambulisms, paralyses, and mutism. These symptoms are sometimes interpreted by their victims as indications of organic disease or as forerunners of insanity. Actually, they are amplifications of earlier tendencies. They are forms of hysteria induced by excessive conflict, and are said to be carried on by the unconscious mind without being wished or consciously induced. Their function as dynamisms is apparently to solve some problem with which their neurotic victim is struggling. They are also said to be *displacements* of repressed wishes; that

[36] For a more extensive treatise see Morton Prince, *The Dissociation of Personality*, New York, Longmans, Green & Co., 1906. Also, by the same author, *The Unconscious*, New York, The Macmillan Co., 1921, Chs. 18-20.

is, symbolic of some unfulfilled longings. In their milder form they may take the direction of broken friendships, quarrels, leaving jobs, etc.

However, in the case of some conflicts, repressed elements or organized systems which are opposed to the established personality develop into a secondary personality, thus producing the phenomenon known as "alternating" or "dual personality" so dramatically exemplified in Stevenson's hypothetical case, Dr. Jekyll and Mr. Hyde. Some psychologists refer to a dual personality as " a double mind working to contrary purposes." Individuals possessing dual personalities are regarded as suffering from disintegration of the original personality, and are considered abnormal. Repressed elements, viewed by the original personality as being opposed to it, are believed to have become sufficiently organized to form a rival personality. The dual individual may fluctuate from one of his personalities to the other without either (each of which is "insulated") recognizing the nature of its rival.

Contrary to popular belief, there are few known cases of genuine dual or multiple personality. The most famous of these include Miss Beauchamp, whom Dr. Morton Prince found to have apparently five competing personalities, Patience Worth, who was an untutored housewife in one personality and a gifted writer in the other, Felida X and Leonie B., reported by William James, and Mr. Hanna, who developed a new personality after losing his original identity through amnesia.[37] Most so-called dual personalities are merely fluctuating patterns within a general flexible total integration. Dual personalities have important implications for child psychology because of the fact that so many of them are believed to have their origin in the conflicts and frustrations of childhood.

Attacking Reality—the Defiance Dynamism.—The fact that every child encounters obstacles, conflicts, and a variety of frustrations has already been stressed. It remains to be mentioned that these stress-producing experiences often result in an attitude of defiance leading to delinquency and crime. In this

[37] For references to these cases see W. S. Taylor, *Readings in Abnormal Psychology and Mental Hygiene*, New York, D. Appleton-Century Co., Inc., 1926.

sense defiance becomes a dynamism designed to satisfy some real or imagined need in the life of the offender. It leads, in fact, to forms of conduct seemingly adjustive to the individual concerned. Unhappy home life, resentment over mistreatment, inability to succeed in school, unsympathetic discipline, and non-understanding attitudes on the part of teachers are among the factors which produce emotional tensions and which may serve as precipitating causes of antisocial behavior.

Investigations have failed to reveal a so-called delinquent or criminal type. A delinquent child is ordinarily a youngster with conduct problems who did not receive proper guidance and discipline from parents and teachers. The typical criminal is usually a former juvenile delinquent who has become confirmed in wrongdoing. The majority of crimes are committed by youths between seventeen and twenty-five years of age.

Since certain acts, such as stealing, forging checks, destroying property, and injuring others, are prohibited by law, a boy or girl who perpetrates one or more of these particular types of misbehavior and is hailed into court automatically (legally) becomes a delinquent. Offenders who are not caught may be equally defiant and blameworthy but are not classed as delinquents. A study by Freeman,[38] employing the California Test of Personality, has confirmed the findings of several previous investigations that so-called juvenile delinquents are, in the main, as well adjusted personally as the average individual of their age. Delinquents have apparently encountered more conflicts with environmental obstacles than most children. Metfessel[39] has made this point clearer by suggesting that if the word "criminal" is used to refer to an individual who has at some time performed an act that the law would class as a crime, then nearly all adults would qualify as criminals. Similarly, if a delinquent is one who has been in an organism-environment relationship called "delinquent" when apprehended, then most children and youths would qualify as delinquents.

38 Max J. Freeman, "Changing Concepts of Crime," *Journal of Criminal Psychopathology*, 4 : 290-305 (1942). See also W. L. Hellman, *Personality Study of Institutionalized Delinquent Boys*, Master's Thesis, The Univ. of Southern California, 1940.

39 Milton Metfessel, "Concepts of Motivation, Restraint, and Traits, in the Study of Crime," *Journal of General Psychology*, 23 : 415-430 (1940).

It is normal for children to seek new experience and adventure, and to be interested in gang activities. It is thus essential that parents, teachers, and social agencies provide legitimate facilities for the expression of these urges. A child's violation of the law frequently indicates that such facilities have not been provided and that parents and others, rather than the child, should be considered delinquent.[40]

Prominent among forms of conduct regarded as delinquencies are lying and stealing. Since most children probably lie to avoid punishment, to hide feelings of inferiority, to escape guilt, or to enhance their prestige, this dynamism must be considered to be normal. Lying, particularly of the variety calculated to maintain ego-status, is often associated with the phantasy dynamism in early childhood and should perhaps be considered as a fictional invention of the imagination rather than as falsification involving morals. Stealing is usually more complicated in origin and should not be thought of as being singly caused.

From the standpoint of the dynamics of adjustment, the following three principal types of motivation for lying and stealing have been suggested: [41] (1) lying and stealing to be on a par with playmates and to have what they have, (2) lying and stealing to gain attention, and (3) lying and stealing as emotional outlets for conflicts and other adjustment difficulties. All three of these motives, particularly the first and second, may be considered as defensive adjustments or defiance dynamisms.[42]

---

[40] That delinquents can be readjusted has been shown by a number of investigations. See, for example, William Healy et al., Reconstructing Behavior in Youth, New York, Alfred A. Knopf, 1929.

[41] Mandel Sherman, Mental Hygiene and Education, New York, Longmans, Green & Co., 1934, pp. 286-288.

[42] Other classifications of children's lies have been proposed. Burt, for example, believes the following list of types to be useful: (1) the playful lie—the purely imaginative tale of the young child, (2) the confusional lie—reporting inaccurately events which are not thoroughly remembered or with which one is not well acquainted, (3) the vain lie—attention-getting lies in which the narrator is usually in the center of things, (4) the malevolent (revengeful) lie—the making of false accusations incited by hate to obtain revenge, (5) the excusive lie—prevarication given in self-defense to avoid unpleasant consequences, (6) the selfish lie —deceiving others in order to obtain what one wants, and (7) the loyal (protective) lie, the so-called "white lie" given to protect another. (Cyril Burt, The Young Delinquent, New York, D. Appleton-Century Co., Inc., 1925, pp. 361-366.)

As an instance of using stealing as an adjustment dynamism, Shaffer [43] tells of a fourteen-year-old boy "who had developed a reputation for toughness and a tendency to consort with a rowdy gang with whom he participated in some street brawls and several small burglaries. This youth was found to be compensating for a fear that he would become a 'sissy.' His widowed mother had tried to keep him under close supervision, with the result that he was ridiculed as a mama's boy. He reacted to the opposite extreme in the form of an aggressive attitude that led to delinquency."

Healy and Bronner [44] have reported that 91 per cent of the delinquents examined by them gave evidence of being (or having been) unhappy, discontented, or emotionally disturbed. They classified the maladjustments by types as follows:

1. Feeling keenly either *rejected, deprived, insecure, not understood* in affectional relationships, unloved, or that love has been withdrawn.

2. Deep feeling of being *thwarted* other than affectionally: either (a) in normal impulses or desires for self-expression or other self-satisfactions, (b) in unusual desires because earlier spoiled, or (c) in adolescent urges and desires—even when (as in five cases) desire for emancipation had been blocked only by the individual's counteractive pleasure in remaining childishly attached.

3. Feeling strongly either real or fancied *inadequacies or inferiorities* in home life, in school, or in relation to companionship or to sports.

4. Intense feelings of *discomfort about family disharmonies,* parental misconduct, the conditions of family life, or parental errors in management and discipline.

5. Bitter feelings of *jealousy* toward one or more siblings, or feelings of being markedly discriminated against because another in the family circle more favored.

6. Feelings of confused unhappiness due to some deep-seated, often repressed, *internal mental conflict*—expressed in vari-

[43] Laurance F. Shaffer, *The Psychology of Adjustment,* Boston, Houghton Mifflin Co., 1936, p. 167.
[44] William Healy and Augusta F. Bronner, *New Light on Delinquency and Its Treatment,* New Haven, Yale Univ. Press, 1936, pp. 128-129.

ous kinds of delinquent acts which often are seemingly unreasonable.

7. Conscious or unconscious *sense of guilt* about earlier delinquencies or about behavior which technically was not delinquency; the guilt sense directly or indirectly activating delinquency through the individual's feelings of the need of punishment (in nearly every instance this overlaps with the last category).

Although these writers did not endeavor to show that the emotional disturbances listed were in all cases the causes of delinquency, their evidence revealed the widespread presence among delinquent youths of such stresses. They made it clear as well that the majority of the cases were characterized by friction with society (conduct problems), only a small minority being afflicted with inner conflicts (personality disorders) of a kind likely to lead to psychotic conditions.

Facing Reality—the Mutuality Adjustment.—The most satisfactory way to deal with a conflict or emotional difficulty is to face it squarely and endeavor to solve it in a way conducive to both social harmony (satisfactory to others) and personal well-being. Evasion does not augur well for ultimate adjustment, since compromise is fraught with many disadvantages and the excessive utilization of dynamisms may lead to greater chances of losing in the struggle for personal integrity. The discussion of adjustment processes has attested to the truthfulness of this statement. Thus the most constructive method of adjustment is an understanding attack on the causes of difficulty. Instead of depending upon phantasy, distortion, or retreat for his successes, the child should be enabled to achieve them through mutual activity and recognition; and in place of rationalizing his shortcomings, he should be led to see them as challenges to greater effort in behalf of cherished goals. By facing reality on a cooperative basis with his associates, the child may maintain his own self-respect and win that of others. In the case of young children the mutuality approach to personality adjustment is, of course, best guaranteed by first extending to them an affectionate security conducive to the development of a favorable attitude toward people in general, and subsequently through the teaching of social skills.

Many forms of direct attack on problems are, however, futile or destructive. Outbursts of temper, flagrant disobedience, and overt attacks on enemies are positive responses but, being disruptive of social harmony, are not conducive to adjustment. Actions of this kind, when supported by strong emotional upheavals, are subversive of social adjustment, and usually leave matters worse than before. Nevertheless, when actuated by desirable motives and intelligently pursued, the attacking method is superior to the compromises of retreat from reality.

In an extensive investigation of the attitudes taken by teachers toward children's behavior, Wickman [45] found that the more extrovertive reactions, such as whispering, defiance, moving about, showing too much interest in members of the opposite sex, destroying school property, and violating certain standards of truthfulness, which clinicians regard as attempts at attacking reality, were frowned upon by the majority of classroom teachers because of being disturbing to good order and to the dignity of the school; also that withdrawing tendencies, such as unsocialness, suspicion, depression, sensitiveness, and dreaminess, which clinicians regard as symptoms of acute introversion or regression, were rated by teachers as being harmless and even desirable forms of adjustment to school life.

The teachers in question made the natural mistake, owing no doubt to practical schoolroom considerations, of evaluating children's behavior in terms of good order and recognition of authority, whereas the clinicians were apparently thinking in terms of the effects of such behavior on personality integrity *in the long run*. Teachers must maintain reasonable order, but from the mental hygiene point of view obviously make a mistake in favoring withdrawing behavior, no matter how helpful it may be to good order on the part of shy, sensitive pupils.

---

[45] E. K. Wickman, *Children's Behavior and Teachers' Attitudes*, New York, The Commonwealth Fund, 1928, Chs. 5-9. Although several more recent studies have suggested that teachers are coming to understand the import of retreating behavior (forgetting reality) for children's ultimate adjustment, a relatively current investigation indicates that many of them still evaluate behavior in terms of immediate social disturbances and consequences. (C. E. Thompson, "The Attitudes of Various Groups Toward Behavior Problems of Children," *Journal of Abnormal and Social Psychology*, 35: 120-125 (1940).)

They are also in error to the extent that they contribute to open conflict in the case of the better adjusted youngsters who respond in more disturbing extrovertive ways. An intelligent reversal of these procedures would be desirable so far as the mental health of children is concerned. Appropriate handling of the types of child behavior mentioned would place the school in a position better to accomplish its mission as an educator of men and women characterized by socially adjusted personalities.

Understanding the Problem Child

Modern Interpretation of the "Problem Child."—Insomuch as behavior problems arise largely from unsatisfactory environmental conditions (from the standpoint of the thwarting of needs) it has become popular to speak of "children with problems" rather than of "problem children." Be that as it may, excessive frustration is almost certain to bring about symptoms of stress in children whose lot has been thus unfortunate. However, children's problems may be classed in two interlocked categories, i.e., (1) conflicts or complexes *within the self,* and (2) conflicts with people or *with the regulations of society.* As in the case of some of Wickman's subjects, a child may be repressed and sensitive and yet be well adjusted to his school in the sense of getting his lessons and conforming to the teacher's disciplinary requirements. Another pupil may violate the school's standards of decorum and thus be considered a problem even though his personal outlook is marked by good morale and a sense of well-being. Such a child is a problem only in the sense of being so regarded by a given teacher. From a mental hygiene standpoint, or even in the eyes of other teachers who prefer this particular type of youngster, he is not a problem child. Such a status is *relative* to a given teacher's or parent's standards of behavior or preference for temperament in children.

In discussing the causes of conflicts with society, Pressey and Robinson [46] include: (1) the hazards of making adjust-

---

[46] S. L. Pressey and F. P. Robinson, *Psychology and the New Education,* New York, Harper & Bros., 1944, pp. 169-172.

ments to a new neighborhood or school, with its attendant anxiety and misgivings, (2) school failures, with their thwarting of the strong craving for recognition of merited success, and (3) social conflicts in connection with home, school, community, and church, with their frequent aftermath of inferiority, frustration, and despair. Continued failure in any of these areas is almost certain to lead to undesirable "defense" dynamisms.

As an example of social conflict, which turned out to be remedial under satisfactory conditions, Bassett [47] gives the following: "In a sandy, hot, little village where green things grew only after the expenditure of much backbreaking effort, the citizens had been repeatedly infuriated by the wanton destruction of their hard-won flowerbeds by groups of adolescent boys. In desperation, they hailed the miscreants to the juvenile court where a number of them were about to be herded off to the state industrial school, when one citizen, slightly skeptical of the curative value of such a procedure, offered to take responsibility for the boys were they paroled to him. After this request was granted, he secured the use of vacant lots and straightway organized neighborhood groups into garden clubs. Soon the energies of these misguided children were being even more enthusiastically expressed in growing flowers and vegetables than they had been in the earlier destruction and the children gained new knowledge, joy in constructive effort, and a firsthand appreciation of what a flowerbed meant in the expenditure of effort."

A psychologist,[48] who states that problem behavior is often indicative of personal conflicts which may originally have been brought about by stringent social taboos, lists the incentives to such behavior as including (1) fear, (2) reaction against deprivations, (3) gratification of secret longings, (4) desire for freedom, (5) direct breaking out of repressed impulses, and (6) disguise for worse offense. Most of these factors are suggestive of excessive and unnecessary interference with dominant incentives to personal autonomy and status. It is highly

[47] Clara Bassett, *The School and Mental Health*, New York, The Commonwealth Fund, 1931, p. 12.
[48] J. J. B. Morgan, *Keeping A Sound Mind*, New York, The Macmillan Co., 1934, pp. 308-318.

probable that recognition of the fundamental needs of the child would obviate the appearance of the undesirable forms of behavior listed.

To illustrate how deprivation may lead to delinquent acts, via inner resentment, the same writer [49] gives this case: "A boy of fourteen who had never been previously involved in any misdemeanor was caught stealing a car. It seems that the engine of this car was running as the boy walked past and he could not resist the temptation to get in and drive away. Of course he was quickly apprehended and scolded severely by his parents. Upon their intervention the police dismissed him. In a few months, to the surprise of his parents, he was involved in another automobile theft. This time he and several of his comrades worked together, took a car, changed the license plates and other identifying information, kept it hidden in a deserted garage, and took turns driving it.

"This boy had what his parents described as a mania for driving cars. They had absolutely forbidden him to drive until he was sixteen and they could not understand why he had this craze to drive. A little investigation disclosed that this boy's urge to drive was largely the result of the categorical refusal of his parents when he asked to drive. Their flat denial made driving seem a very real pleasure to him; he spent hours in imagining he was driving, got road maps and planned long trips he would take, hung around garages and watched the mechanics work with cars, all of which whetted his appetite. It seemed to him an eternity to wait until he was old enough. Driving became a sort of compulsion which he could not resist. Here it seems fairly obvious that this boy's intense longing was at least partly the product of the restraining methods used by the parents."

Symptoms of Impending Maladjustment.—There are a number of physical signs, social attitudes, and deviations in behavior on the part of children which, when unduly continued, constitute danger signals of possibly deep-lying personality maladjustments. Parents and teachers need to take cognizance of these indicators with a view to relieving the stresses involved

[49] *Ibid.,* pp. 310-311. By permission.

before the difficulties become more deeply intrenched. Some of the symptoms of impending (or already present) maladjustment which can readily be detected by teachers and parents, as well as by clinicians (psychologists), are presented here with brief comments. These and similar tendencies might well serve as "weather vanes" to observing guardians of children.

PHYSICAL SIGNS OF MALADJUSTMENT. Impending maladjustments are not always detectable from general behavior, but there are certain physical signs which, judging from clinical experience, may be regarded as indicators of conflict, frustration, or other form of emotional stress. A list of such indicators would include: (1) twitching and fidgeting, (2) continual "drumming" with feet or fingers, (3) constantly "making faces," (4) stuttering and queer breathing, (5) biting fingernails, (6) other nervous mannerisms, (7) lying awake at night, (8) tossing and turning each night, (9) dreaming often, (10) having nightmares, (11) walking or talking in sleep, and (12) frequent vomiting.[50] The presence of these and other expressions of nervousness should be investigated by those interested in the prevention of more serious maladjustments. To mental hygienists such symptoms suggest the necessity of immediate action with such prophylactic measures as are appropriate under the circumstances.

THE TENDENCY TO EXCESSIVE DAYDREAMING. It is very well for an adjusted individual occasionally to reflect on his problems and plans for the future; such a practice is obviously stimulating. However, when a child carries his daydreaming to extremes or uses it as a substitute for action, it is reasonably certain that he is unhappy, that he is struggling with hidden conflicts, or that he is securing certain satisfactions, by way of the phantasy dynamism, that he has been denied in real life. On such a basis the child experiences feelings of success and status without actually accomplishing anything and may come to expect others to assume responsibilities for him. Chronic daydreaming also weakens the child's confidence for undertaking real life tasks.

[50] Arthur M. Jordan, *Educational Psychology,* New York, Henry Holt & Co., Inc., 1942, pp. 427-428.

If the sensitive, discouraged child can be enabled to secure greater joys in connection with people and concrete activities than he finds in his daydreams, he will prefer the former. Chronic daydreaming is a form of escape from reality which may lead gradually to an almost complete loss of interest in life. In its ultimate form such a disorder is known as *schizophrenia,* a psychosis (insanity) marked by extreme emotional apathy and marked indifference toward people.

THE DISPOSITION TO HATE PEOPLE. Hate is a defensive reaction to real or imagined wrongs. Children hate people who mistreat them or otherwise compromise their security. Although hate is usually a specific response to an equally specific person or situation, it may under some circumstances spread to a variety of situations. One incorrigible boy, for example, told of the development of a hatred for all school teachers after having been hit on the head with a book before the class by his sixth grade teacher. The extent to which negativistic, criminalistic, or psychotic behavior may develop as a result of feelings of revenge and hatred is disquieting to those concerned with the mental health of children. Hate is one of the principal requisites for the development of delusions of persecution. It goes without saying, thus, that everyone concerned with the care of children should be deeply interested in removing the causes of hate—an attitude which sometimes leads to symptoms of insanity.

CONSTANT FEELINGS OF INFERIORITY. Many children are obsessed with the belief that they are incapable of accomplishing ordinary tasks in a satisfactory way. Such feelings are based on a deep-seated sense of inadequacy or fear. The victim of this complex avoids responsibilities because he believes he is incapable of meeting them. This condition is often a matter of attitude rather than of fact. One junior high school girl of the author's acquaintance previously lived in continual fear that her every move was an inferior one. She felt incapable of deciding what courses to take in school, whether to keep her present music teacher or seek a better one, what classmates to seek as friends, and even whether her intelligence was normal (after making a high I.Q. score).

Feelings of inferiority and inadequacy may permeate the child's personality to the extent of affecting his behavior in a wide variety of activities. It is extremely difficult to convince some young sufferers from the so-called "inferiority complex" that they have any prospects of succeeding in future endeavors, and this in the face of positive evidence of even superior capacity for so doing. The distressing feature of such a condition is that it frequently leads to compensatory actions which further limit the child's chances of making satisfactory social adjustments. The inferior child may manifest such miscarriages of adjustment as being spiteful, worrying unduly, showing excessive embarrassment, becoming highly sensitive, casting aspersions on the accomplishments of others, talking and blustering loudly, pouting, showing extreme timidity, stuttering, and even attempting suicide.[51] It is small wonder that mental hygienists look upon excessive feelings of inferiority as symptoms of impending grave maladjustment.

THE TENDENCY TOWARD REGRESSION. The well-adjusted child usually endeavors to get ahead; he lives in anticipation of future joys; he has little concern with the days he has left behind. The backward-looking dynamism is the way of unsuccessful persons whose principal achievements are in the past. Unfortunately, some children, because of inability to cope with hardships, attempt to regress to an earlier and more protected level of living in which they have previously experienced success. From the standpoint of mental health, such a tendency should be checked by the provision of such gratifying activities, such interesting outlets, and such enduring satisfactions as will ensure forward striving.

Many cases of pathological regression have been reported, and in each instance they have been extremely difficult to correct. The stress of more or less continual insecurity or failure is conducive to the giving up of the struggle for advancement. This is especially true in the case of children *whose early home life was characterized by rejection or neglect.* Some have sought

[51] *Ibid.,* pp. 428-429.

shelter in the gentle retreat of the phantasy world, while others have returned to less frustrating levels of adjustment.[52] The tendency to be satisfied with mediocre accomplishments or to regress is a significant danger signal and merits the serious attention of the mental hygienist, be he psychologist, parent, or teacher.

OTHER SYMPTOMS OF MALADJUSTMENT. Children not infrequently live in such an atmosphere of ridicule and hostility that they experience little realization of their need for recognition and status. Being rebuffed and criticized for so many of their actions, they naturally turn to such modes of escape and evasion as are available to them.

Some try to justify themselves by becoming "pathological liars," and adopt the crude method in their behavior of letting the end justify the means. Others become morbidly cruel, chronically suspicious, addicted to temper tantrums, or given to malingering. The more defiant children may resort to truancy, stealing, sex vagaries, or running away from home. Research has revealed the more detailed characteristics of several of these "types" of children. Riemer,[53] for example, found that runaway children are markedly antagonistic, impulsive, distrustful, and, paradoxically, sometimes sheepishly docile one moment and negativistic the next. This investigator regards running away as a defensive attitude for a "begging" type of personality.

Benjamin[54] has reported, from a study of 207 negativistic children, that the symptoms most often found are feeding difficulties, vomiting, sleeplessness, speech difficulties, breath holding spells, enuresis, and encopresis. Most of these symptoms are said to be related to the child's inability to adapt himself to the life of the community.

Investigations of Children's Behavior Problems.—That the symptoms of maladjustment presented in the foregoing

[52] F. L. Wells, *op. cit.*
[53] M. D. Riemer, "Runaway Children," *American Journal of Orthopsychiatry,* 10 : 522-527 (1940).
[54] E. Benjamin, "The Period of Resistance in Early Childhood, Its Significance for the Development of the Problem Child," *American Journal of Diseases of Children,* 63 : 1019-1079 (1942).

paragraphs are common among "problem" children has been attested to by a number of researches. Ackerson,[55] who has made a study of the behavior problems of 5,000 children referred to the psychological clinic of the Illinois Institute for

TABLE 40. THE MOST FREQUENTLY APPEARING BEHAVIOR DIFFICULTIES AND REASONS FOR REFERENCE TO CLINIC

	Noted in Following Per Cent of Cases
1. "Nervousness," restlessness, irritable temperament	41
2. Disobedience, incorrigibility, stubbornness, contrariness, defiant attitude	40
3. Retardation in school	37
4. Question of feeblemindedness or inadequate intelligence (not a staff notation)	31
5. Temper display, "tantrums," irritable temperament	31
6. Dull, slow manner, listlessness, lack of initiative or ambition	30
7. Stealing	26
8. Immature, childish manner or judgment, impaired judgment	25
9. Fighting, quarrelsomeness, violence, threatening violence	25
10. Enuresis or bed-wetting (beyond third birthday)	25
11. Lying, marked untruthfulness	24
12. Advice re placement, commitment, or institutionalization	24
13. Poor work in school	23
14. "Crying spells," crying easily	22
15. Truancy from school	19
16. Masturbation	19
17. Truancy from home	18
18. Sensitiveness or worrisomeness (general), sensitiveness or worry over some specific fact or episode	18
19. Bashfulness, shyness	17

(Adapted from Luton Ackerson, *Children's Behavior Problems*, Chicago, Univ. of Chicago Press, 1931, pp. 57-68, by Joseph W. Nagge, *Psychology of the Child*, New York, The Ronald Press Co., 1942, p. 463.)

Juvenile Research, lists the behavior most commonly manifested by problem children (in order of frequency) as shown in Table 40. As the data show, the behavior of such children tends to be marked by nervousness, incorrigibility, and defiance. In this

[55] Luton Ackerson, *Children's Behavior Problems*, Chicago, Univ. of Chicago Press, 1931, pp. 102-103. See also, by the same author, *Children's Behavior Problems*, Vol. II: *Relative Importance and Relations Among Traits*, Chicago, Univ. of Chicago Press, 1942.

instance the children also displayed a high incidence of inferior intellectual development, poor physical condition, retardation in school, and lack of initiative. As has been the case in other studies, it was found that boys show a greater average number of both conduct and personality problems than do girls. The number of personality and behavior problems ranged from none in some instances to 99 in two of the children (ages one to eighteen years).

A questionnaire study [56] of the outstanding problems experienced by parents (277 homes) in the management of their children made it evident that problems vary somewhat with the age of the child. Those most frequently observed between the ages of three and five were thumb-sucking, bed-wetting, attention-seeking, temper-tantrums, and dawdling. From ages five to seven, whining, dawdling, and disobedience were most frequently mentioned. In the seven to eleven year age range, willfulness, irritability, and quick discouragement were predominant in number of occurrences. From ages eleven to eighteen the most frequent problems were avoidance of responsibility, shyness, easy discouragement, selfishness, and satisfaction with mediocre performances.

"Problem" Parents and Maladjusted Teachers.—As previously mentioned (Chapter 6), any discussion of the welfare of children must consider the influence exerted by the family. The emotional attitude of the parents, especially of the mother, toward a child, and the extent to which they are in a position to offer it affectional security have everything to do with its state of mental health. It thus seems appropriate to emphasize again the importance of adequate parental handling. In his volume dealing with problem children, Rogers [57] writes, "evidence points to the primary place of the mother in the home, since the child's standards show a closer association with the mother's ideas than with any other source. Several investigators have shown the close relationship between the wholesomeness of parental discipline and the behavior difficul-

[56] A. Long, "Parents' Reports of Undesirable Behavior in Children," *Child Development*, 12: 43-62 (1941).
[57] Carl R. Rogers, *The Clinical Treatment of the Problem Child*, Boston, Houghton Mifflin Co., 1939, p. 9.

ties of the child. Unwise or unwholesome discipline, even though crudely judged and measured, correlates very significantly with delinquent behavior."

It is therefore not surprising that problem (maladjusted) parents encounter serious difficulties with children. Many parents give expression to their emotional stresses of insecurity or inadequacy at the expense of their children, thus making the home a breeding ground for further distortions of personality. A study [58] of the home environments of a group of problem children aged eight to fourteen years is illustrative. Approximately one-half of the homes were marked by neurotic behavior on the part of parents. In addition to quarreling violently, these mothers and fathers severely criticized their children's teachers and refused to cooperate with school authorities. They not only complained about the school, but denounced the city in which they were living, derided their employers, and disparaged their own occupations. Their attitude toward their children was also a critical one. A similar situation was found [59] in connection with case studies of a group of unloved children. It was shown that nervous parents bring about resentful, nervous behavior in their children by not wanting them and by not loving them.

Some of the principal parental attitudes leading to behavior problems in children have been listed as:

1. *Rejection*—The child is made to feel unwanted or despised because he interferes with parental welfare, is not attractive, or does not come up to parental expectations in other ways.

2. *Unfavorable comparisons*—Continuous unfavorable comparisons between siblings or other children in regard to abilities, capabilities, attractiveness, and the like.

3. *Teasing*—Teasing the child by jeering remarks, undesirable nicknames, or taunting or railing comments.

4. *Disapproval*—Evidences of disapproval by scolding, nagging, scorn, disgust, ridicule, and similar measures.

[58] E. R. Lotz, "Emotional Status of the Parents of Problem and Psychopathic Children," *School and Society,* 42 : 239-240 (1935).
[59] J. M. Hill, "Unwanted—Unloved Children: A Study of Nervous Parent-Child Relationship," *Diseases of the Nervous System,* 2 : 135-139 (1941).

5. *Punishment*—Constant deprivation of privileges, corporal punishment, and pitiless persecution by threats of bodily harm.

6. *Oversolicitude*—Overattention, overprotection, and pampering without offering opportunities for the child to make decisions or assume responsibilities.[60]

As an example of the outcome of defective parental handling, the authors of the above list present the following:

"Frank D. was a junior in college when he sought psychological guidance. He was aware of pronounced feelings of inferiority. He claimed that he had always had feelings of inferiority, inadequacy, and incompetence. He asserted that never in his life had he received encouragement or compliments for any achievement. He was an only child but had many relatives. He was frequently criticized by his mother, and his weak points were constantly compared with the strong points of his cousins. Whether or not this was meant to stimulate him to attain greater success Frank did not know. He was made to feel that the other children were more dependable, got better grades, and were more grown up. As he matured he avoided doing anything in which he had to compete directly with any of his relatives. In high school he found these feelings of inferiority, inadequacy, and incompetency permeating all of his relationships with other students. In college he avoids participating in any school activity, never volunteers to recite in class, and makes no effort to make friends." [61]

An investigation by Stott,[62] utilizing a "family adjustment" score and a standardized test of personality, suggested that "many instances of parental failure—instances where the child of 'good' parents with fine attitudes and the noblest of attitudes does not turn out well—are chargeable to the parents' failure to distinguish between their *own* purposes and desires, and the peculiar individual needs of the child. The 'black sheep' of the 'good family' is often the result of parental failure, either to

---

[60] Ernest W. Tiegs and Barney Katz, *op. cit.*, pp. 343-344.
[61] *Ibid.*, p. 344.
[62] Leland H. Stott, "Parent-Adolescent Adjustment, Its Measurement and Significance," *Character and Personality,* 10 : 140-150 (1941).

see that particular individual problem or to cope successfully with it." As may be seen from the correlations in Table 41,

TABLE 41. CORRELATIONS BETWEEN THE "FAMILY-LIFE" VARIABLE AND SCORES ON THE CALIFORNIA TEST OF PERSONALITY

California Test Score	r	σ_r
Total adjustment	+ .62	.030
I. Self-adjustment	+ .50	.034
a. Self-reliance	+ .27	.045
b. Sense of personal worth	+ .32	.042
c. Sense of personal freedom	+ .55	.033
d. Feeling of belonging	+ .44	.037
e. Freedom from withdrawing tendencies	+ .46	.038
f. Freedom from nervous symptoms	+ .33	.042
II. Social adjustment	+ .62	.030
a. Social standards	+ .27	.045
b. Social skills	+ .42	.038
c. Freedom from antisocial tendencies	+ .44	.037
d. Family relations	+ .65	.028
e. School relations	+ .43	.037
f. Community relations	+ .36	.040

(From Leland H. Stott, "Parent-Adolescent Adjustment, Its Measurement and Significance," *Character and Personality*, 10:146 (1941).)

children who find it difficult to make personal and social adjustments tend to be the very ones whose relations with their parents are not satisfactory.

Stott's study emphasizes the importance of the *individual* parent-child relationship. Since every child occupies a unique role in the family constellation, slight early differences in temperament between parent and child may become intensified to the point of constituting serious mental health problems. The same home might thus provide an excellent emotional environment for one child but an exceedingly stressful one for another.

It appears that parents who hope to promote satisfactory development in their children must first become well-adjusted themselves. Marital compatibility and personal emotional well-being on the part of parents apparently enables child adjustment to follow largely as a matter of course.[63]

[63] Dorothy W. Baruch, "Contrasts in Marital Relationships Inpinging on Child Adjustment: Two Cases," *Journal of Genetic Psychology*, 53: 159-171 (1938).

EXAMPLES OF TEACHER INADEQUACIES. From the mental hygiene point of view, teacher inadequacies tend to classify themselves into (1) failure to be interested in or to recognize symptoms of emotional maladjustment in children, and (2) personal maladjustments which lead to conflict and the amplification of problem behavior in children. Each of these deficiencies will be discussed briefly.

Although childhood is the "golden age" of preventive hygiene, it is frequently during school days that incipient neurotic trends become sufficiently pronounced to attract attention. Serious personality maladjustments occur literally by the thousand under the very eyes of teachers. Many of these well-meaning individuals, who have been called the "architects of the wholesome personality development of the Nation's children," are apparently unable to detect the early symptoms of either neurotic disorders or what in legal terms is called "insanity." "It is the rare teacher, who knows, for example, that the little girl whose feelings are constantly being hurt by the suspicion that her companions have talked about her is exhibiting a symptom which is identical in kind with those that accompany certain forms of *dementia praecox.* . . . Only the exceptional teacher sees the fundamental relationship between introvertive daydreaming, which is pathological, and creative imagination, which is a work of genius, and thus is able to avoid the one and afford life-giving expression to the other." [64]

Some teachers apparently do not comprehend the nature of the underlying causes of children's behavior. Being concerned with symptoms, discipline, and, above all, meticulous good order, they perhaps "fail to see the trees for the forest," i.e., symptoms, as overt acts, blind them to the existence of deeper running conflicts and maladjustments. Thus, instead of dealing intelligently with emotional dynamisms of evasion, retreat, and antisocial compensation, they are likely to attack such *expressions* of maladjustment as lying, stealing, truancy, cruelty, destroying property, etc., from the moral point of view. More attention to the underlying causes of the child's difficulty

[64] J. M. Fletcher, *Psychology in Education.* New York, Doubleday, Doran & Co., 1934, pp. 266-267. Also Leo Kanner, "The Role of the School in the Treatment of Rejected Children," *The Nervous Child,* 3 : 236-248 (1944).

would often reveal that his lot has been a hard one, worthy of the teacher's sympathy, and that his misbehavior is symptomatic of underlying frustrations or conflict—the child's misguided call for help.

Concerning the fact that cases ultimately diagnosed as true paranoia (a severe psychosis characterized by conceit in the form of delusions of grandeur and by systematic delusions of persecution) sometimes show good school records in spite of exhibiting considerable conceit and egotism, and a markedly suspicious attitude, one writer [65] comments, "now the fact that a child during his school days may manifest symptoms that are the same fundamentally as those which make up this inescapable psychosis, without having such symptoms recognized until it has become too late to do anything about it, is an interesting commentary on our educational philosophy. What, pray, is a good school record?"

If teachers are to accept the challenge implied here it is evident that, in addition to being well informed, they must themselves be relatively free from personality maladjustments. As conditions now stand, many teachers are afflicted with chronic disorders of personality which bid fair to result in the development of emotional disturbances in the very children whom they are expected to educate for successful social living. Maladjusted teachers not only fail to do constructive academic work with boys and girls, but they stimulate, from virgin soil as it were, the development of actual delinquencies and warped personalities.[66]

As to the incidence of mental disorders among teachers, Fenton [67] reports from a study of 241 teachers that 77.6 per cent were considered to be in reasonably good mental health and at least fairly well adjusted so far as teaching was concerned. They got along well with their colleagues, did their work effectively, and met their community obligations satisfactorily. Of the total group, 22.5 per cent were found by their principal or superintendent (also the investigator) to be malad-

[65] *Ibid.*, p. 267.
[66] J. E. W. Wallin, *Personality Maladjustments and Mental Hygiene,* New York, McGraw-Hill Book Co., 1935, pp. 100-107.
[67] Norman Fenton, *Mental Hygiene in School Practice,* Stanford University, Stanford Univ. Press, 1943, pp. 288-290.

justed and to be in need of assistance along mental health lines. Their disorders included psychoneurotic and lesser personality deviations of a kind that interfered with teaching efficiency. However, not all of the latter group were seriously handicapped in their classroom work. Only 15.4 per cent of the total group were considered to be definitely inadequate in their professional activities because of maladjustments.

As an example of teacher inadequacy, the same author [68] tells of a second grade teacher who, presumably as the result of having been pampered excessively by an overdevoted mother, was jealous of other teachers and critical of her principal for alleged favoritism. She made very few friends and dominated her pupils to the extent of refusing to permit them to whisper, move their chairs, or engage in activities in which they could make things of interest to themselves but which might result in an untidy looking room. It was only after a stormy scene with the principal that she was led to change her tactics sufficiently to retain her position. Even the most conservative parents had complained of her austere methods. It is not difficult to imagine the influence such a teacher would have on the personalities of children passing through her grade.

Wallin [69] writes of a teacher who, owing to the cruelty and persecution of one of her own early teachers, developed an inferiority attitude sufficiently severe to keep her in a permanent state of timidity even after she had abundant evidence of possessing excellent ability. Even after becoming a teacher, she apparently could not overcome the feeling that her supposed ability was spurious, and that she was in reality "putting it over" on everyone who knew her.

Preston [70] has cited the cases of 100 children who often complained of functional (no discoverable physical basis) stomach-aches, headaches, dizziness, heart flutter, and a score of other ailments, and who were found to be waging a losing battle with some fear, worry, or other adversity encountered in school or at home. The children reported that some of their

[68] Ibid., pp. 298-301.
[69] J. E. W. Wallin, op. cit., p. 104.
[70] Mary I. Preston, "Physical Complaints Without Organic Basis," Journal of Pediatrics, 17: 279-304 (1940).

teachers were cross or impatient with them; that other teachers made "cutting remarks"; and that some accused them of being lazy, stupid, or dumb. In some cases classmates scorned or ridiculed them. Certain of them were also subjected to disapprobation, nagging, or punishment at home. Being unable to overcome these adversities, the children were believed to have "conjured up" (unconsciously) the personal ailments mentioned as dynamisms of escape. The investigator believed that many of the children needed the "manufactured" illness to banish thoughts of frightening experiences, to relieve them from school responsibilities, and to secure more attention, sympathy, and love.

In a study of 100 women teachers attending a university summer session, Peck [71] found (through personality tests and biographical data) 33 per cent to be emotionally maladjusted, with 12 per cent of these in definite need of psychiatric advice. Nineteen per cent of the teachers appeared to be well adjusted, with 48 per cent being "average." Of the one-third who were to some extent maladjusted, many were shy and nervous and felt that they deserved a better lot in life. Twenty-five per cent were often in a state of excitement, were easily upset, did not plan their work ahead, disliked responsibility, had frequent indigestion, feared insanity, and wrestled with a conflict between sex and morality. One-fifth reported frequent low spirits, and one-sixth admitted that they lost their tempers easily. Teachers whose personal records showed that they were *unhappy in childhood or adolescence* reported more symptoms of maladjustment than those who indicated that their early years were happy ones.

An investigation designed to secure information concerning a group of 700 teachers (New York City) who had become so maladjusted that it was necessary to place them in hospitals for mental patients has been reported by Mason.[72] The age at which the teacher group entered the hospitals is somewhat younger than that for the average patient in New York State.

---

[71] Leigh Peck, "Study of the Adjustment Difficulties of a Group of Women Teachers," *Journal of Educational Psychology*, 27 : 401-416 (1936).
[72] Frances V. Mason, "A Study of Seven Hundred Maladjusted School Teachers," *Mental Hygiene*, 15 : 576-599 (1931).

Whereas 52.5 per cent of the institutionalized population in New York State had entered a hospital before that age, 67.8 per cent of the teachers entered before the age of forty-five. Of the psychotic disorders, dementia praecox (schizophrenia) came first (37.38 per cent), manic-depressive psychosis second (23.86 per cent), and paranoia third (6.13 per cent). A significant fact brought out by the study was the small number of cases in which the mental disorder appeared attributable to difficulties encountered in the school situation.

The attitudes manifested by these teachers while they were still in the schoolroom included (in rank order): (a) for men —introversion, ambition, hyperactivity, efficiency, neuroticism, quiet and retiring disposition, anxiety, irritability, selfishness, and eccentricity; (b) for women—ambition, hyperactivity, efficiency, quiet and retiring disposition, irritability, introversion, neuroticism, anxiety, selfishness, and eccentricity.

It was recognized that while the school can hardly be held accountable to any appreciable extent for the mental breakdown of teachers, the effect upon children and adolescents of being under the supervision of a teacher undergoing the severe stress incidental to the onset of any form of insanity must be decidedly detrimental.

There is no place in vital education for the fussy, worried teacher; the jealous, domineering teacher; the teacher who looks on every erring child as a lost soul; the teacher who is hopelessly shocked at every mention of sex; the depressed, fearful, harassed teacher; and the teacher who regards her pupils as her natural enemies.[73] Children need enthusiastic teachers who themselves enjoy sufficient friends, relaxing recreations, and varied interests to insure wholesome personality and balance of views.

Whether teachers realize it or not, the personality qualities of their pupils are to a considerable extent influenced by them. To the young child the teacher's size, maturity, newness, and authority vest her with an influence which is far greater than commonly supposed. He will not only vie with other children for her approval, but will be sensitive to her attitude in a multi-

[73] Clara Bassett, *op. cit.*, p. 47.

tude of school situations. A smile of approval or a few words
of commendation may provide the child with a feeling of adequacy which he very much desires. By the same token, ridicule,
unfavorable criticism, or sarcasm may lead to a sense of inferiority or lack of status that persists for years. Thus mental-
hygiene practice, especially from the early detection and prevention angle, lies directly within the range of the teacher's
duties.

Nervous Habits and Their Treatment.—Children frequently exhibit nervous symptoms of a physical nature, the roots
of which apparently extend back to early childhood or infancy.
Included among these are thumb-sucking, nail-biting, tics, and
enuresis.

THUMB-SUCKING. Although some psychologists do not class
thumb-sucking as a nervous symptom, it is unquestionably one
of the most common physical habits indulged in by young children. Parents and teachers alike have frequently been baffled
in their attempts to cope with it and have usually attained little
success. Most children and infants enjoy sucking. The structural mechanisms for this activity are well developed at birth,
with the result that sucking is easily stimulated. Most infants
will suck not only the thumb, but fingers, fist, toys, or other
articles that lend themselves to this response. According to
Kanner,[74] babies have been born sucking their thumbs. Levy [75]
believes this phenomenon to be the result of accidental contact
of the thumb with the mouth, the satisfying sensations of which
led the fetus to continue sucking the thumb. Usually, however,
this tendency is not in evidence until a few days or weeks after
birth.

A frequent cause of thumb-sucking is believed to be an unsatisfied desire to suck that persists after feeding. This desire
may be due to discontinuing the infant's feeding before he is
satisfied, whether by breast or by bottle. Some students of the

74 Leo Kanner, *Child Psychiatry,* Springfield (Ill.), Chas. C. Thomas, 1937,
p. 331.
75 David M. Levy, "Finger-Sucking and Accessory Movement in Early Infancy. An Etiologic Study," *American Journal of Psychiatry,* 7 : 881-918 (1928).

subject [76] believe that the child's penchant for sucking, aside from the act of food-getting, is fundamental in that it satisfies his need for a feeling of closeness and of "belonging." Nutritional factors may also be responsible for excessive thumb-sucking.[77] Insufficient feeding results in restlessness and a tendency to seek satisfaction by continuing sucking movements through inserting the thumb in the mouth. Since this process is entirely normal, occasional thumb-sucking on the part of the child should be no cause for concern unless it persists after the age of approximately two-and-a-half or three.

Most chronic thumb-suckers have probably become so because of the emotional behavior displayed by their parents, many of whom try to solve the problem by scolding and spanking the child. The habit thus becomes the basis of an attention-getting technique, i.e., the child discovers that the most effective method of getting recognition is through sucking his thumb. Finding it easy to become the center of things he may make little effort to gain attention by more socially approved methods. The thumb-sucking habit may also result in feelings of inferiority. When ridiculed by members of the family or by other children, the thumb-sucking child may become very sensitive, with the result that his fear of criticism causes him to withdraw from social contacts.

As previously mentioned, continued thumb-sucking may cause malformations of the jaw and malalignment of the teeth.[78] However, this condition does not occur as frequently as has often been claimed. Malformations are rare if the habit is corrected before the age of six or seven, prior to second dentition (permanent teeth).[79] Whatever malocclusion occurs tends to correct itself before that time. The major handicaps resulting from thumb-sucking are apparently primarily psychological.

A number of methods of treatment for thumb-sucking have been suggested. The child should be actively engaged with

[76] Lee Edward Travis and Dorothy W. Baruch, *Personal Problems of Every-day Life*, New York, D. Appleton-Century Co., Inc., 1941, pp. 180-181.

[77] C. M. Louttit, *Clinical Psychology*, New York, Harper & Bros., 1936, p. 333.

[78] Samuel J. Lewis, "Thumb-Sucking: Cause of Malocclusion in Deciduous Teeth," *Journal of the American Dental Assn.*, 17: 1060-1073 (1930).

[79] Samuel J. Lewis, "Effect of Thumb- and Finger-Sucking on the Primary Dental Arches," *Child Development*, 8: 93-98 (1937).

plenty of opportunities for playing with toys, swings, pets, and playmates. It is often the child who has become disinterested because of having to play by himself who resorts to thumb-sucking. Adequate treatment may necessitate a change of environment involving new playmates. In addition to such a program, the child should be given adequate rest after meals, with manipulative toys of a simple nature to occupy his hands. Such a practice tends to eliminate any emotional tension and to keep the child's hands too busy to be employed in thumb-sucking.

When the child is sucking his thumb it is best to make no comments. It is preferable to give him some toy or article in the preferred hand or to initiate some interesting activity. Both parents and teachers should recognize that patience is essential in the modification of nervous habits and that, if success is to be achieved, the cooperation of the subject must be secured.

NAIL-BITING. Although as prevalent as thumb-sucking, nail-biting appears at a later age and is carried over much more frequently into adolescence and adulthood. In a study of over 3,000 school children, Wechsler [80] found this habit to be present by the age of four and to be in evidence in 44 per cent of the school population at age thirteen. Because of its high incidence in adults, both parents and teachers have tended to minimize the seriousness of nail-biting.

According to Kanner,[81] nail-biting is primarily an expression of tenseness. Nail-biting children are usually sensitive, irritable, hyperactive, and excitable, presumably as the result of thwarting or failure and negative disciplinary measures in the home or school. A child who lives in fear of corporal punishment usually exhibits this or some other emotionally toned form of behavior. It is thus believed that nail-biting serves as a tension discharging process for the children concerned. In this respect it differs from thumb-sucking, which is in many instances a leisurely habit. As in the case of thumb-sucking, the attitude of parents (and teachers) will for the most part determine the extent or severity of the symptom.

80 D. Wechsler, "The Incidence and Significance of Fingernail Biting in Children," *Psychoanalytic Review*, 18 : 201-209 (1931).
81 Leo Kanner, *op. cit.*, pp. 335-338.

One of the advantages to the child of nail-biting is its effectiveness as an attention-getting technique. Parents frequently scold or yell at the child, thus confirming his feeling that he can become the center of attention with but little effort. If, however, he is continually scolded, threatened, and punished in some way, the child may develop deep-seated feelings of personal inadequacy. Such an attitude will in turn cause him to avoid social activities and the development of social skills.

The first step in the treatment of nail-biting is to discover and, when possible, remove the causes of the underlying emotional tension. The mere provision of affectional security (or promotion of successful achievement) will in some instances cause the habit to disappear. Both parents and teachers can aid the child in overcoming this nervous symptom by making him feel acceptable and competent. Sufficient opportunities should be provided for physical relaxation, since such a condition is conducive to the elimination of tension. Scoldings, threats, or punishments are never successful in the treatment of nail-biting; they produce additional tensions and thus reinforce the habit.

Like verbal punishment, mechanical devices and the application of bad tasting substances, such as quinine or iodine, have been of little avail in the treatment of nail-biting. Such methods not only fail to get at the cause of emotional tensions, but produce further stresses leading to reinforcement of the nail-biting habit. To be preferred, for older children and adults, is Dunlap's [82] *negative practice* method, in which the subject is taught to devote a certain amount of effort to deliberate (voluntary) practice in nail-biting. Such a practice tends both to reduce emotional stress and to gain control over the nail-biting habit. However, its use requires a desire on the part of the subject to improve and willingness to exclude other considerations while deliberately biting the nails. It is also essential that it be accompanied by therapeutic procedures designed to alleviate the causes of the child's condition.

Tics. A tic is a twitching or spasmodic movement of a localized group of muscles. Such twitchings are more or less

---

[82] Knight Dunlap, *Habits: Their Making and Unmaking*, New York, Liveright Pub. Corp., 1933, Chs. 11, 12.

rhythmic, and on the surface appear to bear no significant relationship to the individual's personal problems. Wrinkling of the nose, twitching of the mouth, blinking of the eyes, puckering of the lips, and grimaces of various types are the most common tics among children. Other twitchings include shrugging the shoulders, jerking the head, jerking the arms, twisting the neck, and clearing the throat. Tics occur most frequently in children between the ages of six to fourteen who also tend to manifest symptoms of sensitiveness, restlessness, and self-consciousness.[83]

Although tics may be of either organic or psychological origin, there is considerable agreement that in the majority of cases their etiology is psychological, i.e., that they grow out of emotional conflicts.[84] Those developing on an organic basis are usually due to an irritating condition. Children with defective eyesight (conjunctivitis), for example, may resort to more or less regular blinking to get relief from the physical irritation entailed.[85] Such rhythmic behavior readily develops into a habit and may persist long after the physical condition has been satisfactorily remedied.

Tics of psychological origin are apparently symptoms of emotional conflict. Like physical symptoms, tics are purposeful in nature; they in some way serve to relieve an unpleasant emotional condition in the child. It is presumed that the facial twitchings or other such hysterical symptoms offer a certain emotional release with a minimum of harm to the child at the time.

Some psychologists [86] take the psychoanalytic point of view that a tic is symbolic of a repressed desire, that it represents the displacement of some unrecognized urge. The child's facial twitchings may thus be calculated to hurt someone; that is, to create discomfort or embarrassment for a disliked father or mother. In an older subject such a tic might serve as a dis-

---

[83] Leo Kanner, *op. cit.*, pp. 329-331.

[84] J. E. W. Wallin, *Clinical and Abnormal Psychology,* Boston, Houghton Mifflin Co., 1927, pp. 529-530.

[85] C. M. Louttit, *op. cit.*, pp. 336-337.

[86] Lee Edward Travis and Dorothy W. Baruch, *op. cit.*, Ch. 5. See also M. H. Mahler, "Tics and Impulsions in Children: a Study of Motility," *Psychoanalytic Quarterly,* 13: 430-444 (1944).

placement for a socially taboo and thoroughly repressed sexual urge. In this sense these symptoms (blinking, twitching, etc.) serve as outlets for repressed emotional tensions. The same may be said of nail-biting and enuresis, both of which are believed by psychoanalysts to be symptoms of repression.

In addition to serving as emotional releases, tics, like nail-biting and thumb-sucking, may become attention-getting devices. Children prefer disparagement to being more or less completely ignored. Tics may, however, lead to feelings of inferiority and inadequacy because of derisive remarks from other children and members of the famly. If the child feels that there is something wrong with him and that he is undesirably different from other children, his conflicts may become sufficiently intense to exaggerate the tic. Since tics are frequently annoying to others they may cause the child to lose friends and thus to experience more difficulty in making social adjustments.

As in the case of other nervous symptoms, the treatment of tics must begin with a disclosure of the emotional conflicts involved. Not until their basic causes have been detected and removed can any success in the correction of tics be expected. Unfavorable comparisons, rejection, sibling rivalries, and other home and family relationships are frequently the focal point of the difficulty. Failures and unfavorable school relationships may also be responsible for severe emotional stresses. Reduction in the child's emotional tension can be brought about by modifying these relationships in favor of more ego-satisfying experiences.

The previously mentioned negative practice technique developed by Dunlap [87] has in some cases proved successful with tics. According to this theory, the actual practice of periodic facial twitching, blinking of the eyes, or other rhythmic movements under conditions appropriate to the destruction of the habit aids in gaining voluntary control over the tic and in gradually eliminating it. Most tics are, however, too complicated in origin and effect to permit of treatment by parents or teachers. Such disorders should be referred to recognized psychologists or psychiatrists who are specialists in psychotherapy.

[87] Knight Dunlap, *op. cit.*

ENURESIS. Enuresis has reference to inability to inhibit urination at an age when the child should possess such control. The ability to retain urine in the bladder is usually lacking in the child until around two to two and one-half years of age. It has been estimated that from 10 to 35 per cent of the child population is enuretic. The incidence of nocturnal enuresis in male children at the Vineland Training School has been reported to be about 10 per cent.[88] Such a situation causes much inconvenience and embarrassment to parents, teachers, and others. In view of the fact that enuresis is apparently associated primarily with emotional instability, it also suggests the extent of nervousness among children.

Specialists have found that for the majority of cases no physical basis for enuresis can be ascertained. Some cases can be traced to the after-effects of certain childhood diseases, but for the most part enuresis appears to be a functional disorder which is best treated by psychological methods. This assumption has been strengthened by the finding of a high incidence of voluntary bed-wetting in children after emotional excitement. It has also been noted that enuresis tends to be associated with nail-biting, speech disorders, temper tantrums, and antisocial (stealing) tendencies.[89]

An example of nocturnal enuresis is afforded by the case of a seven-year-old boy of normal intelligence and good health whose bed-wetting was associated with a recurrent nightmare involving friction with an older brother. It was ascertained that considerable rivalry existed between the brothers in their relations with their parents. The younger child had developed a strong mother-fixation and it was believed that the enuresis was, at least in part, a regressive symptom of an urge to return to a state of infancy in which a major share of the mother's attention might be secured.[90]

[88] M. N. Partridge, "A Study of Nocturnal Enuresis in Boys," *Journal of Delinquency,* 11 : 296-308 (1927).
[89] J. J. Michaels and S. E. Goodman, "Incidence and Intercorrelations of Enuresis and other Neuropathic Traits in So-Called Normal Children," *American Journal of Orthopsychiatry,* 4 : 76-106 (1934) ; J. J. Michaels, "The Relationship of Antisocial Traits to the Electroencephalogram in Children with Behavior Disorders," *Psychosomatic Medicine,* 7 : 41-44 (1945).
[90] L. Pátzaj-Liebermann, "Enuresis Nocturna," *Zeitschrift für Kinderpsychiatrie,* 10 : 161-167 (1944).

A number of types of treatment for enuresis have been suggested. Improvement in enuretic condition has followed the
administration of a variety of prescribed drugs. The finding
that the mere injection of water, which the patient supposes to
be medicine, sometimes leads to apparent cures, indicates that
suggestion must be a prominent factor in such improvement.[91]

Psychologists and pediatricians advocate the avoidance of
all emotional excitement in relation to enuresis by making the
child feel that it is his problem and by discussing it objectively
with him. The child is brought to see that he is doing no one
but himself a favor by keeping dry and that he can succeed in
so doing if he has the desire. The procedure is carried out in a
matter-of-fact attitude, with the child keeping a record of his
successes and reviewing them with his "counselor." No disappointment is expressed when occasional lapses occur. With
such a positive approach replacing criticism, psychotherapeutic
methods can be used with children as young as two and one-half
years of age.[92]

As one writer [93] has stated the problem, "Enuresis, thumb-
sucking, and nail-biting are related behaviors, since a psychologically inadequate suppression of the symptoms of one of these
may lead only to a breaking out of some other manifestation of
the unsatisfied motivating forces which are causing the disturbance. The aim of adequate treatment should be directed,
not at the relief of symptoms alone, but at the redirection of
the motivating forces seeking expression. This involves the
reeducation of the total personality."

A Constructive Mental Hygiene Program

Foundation of the Adjustment Program.—It is well to remember that in both physical and psychological respects nature's
phenomena appear to operate on the basis of inexorable laws.
Whether one has reference to "physical," "intellectual," "emotional," or "moral" matters, all proceed in a cause and effect

[91] A. Friedell, "A Reversal of the Concentration of the Urine in Children
Having Enuresis," *American Journal of Diseases of Children,* 33 : 717-721 (1927).
[92] J. L. Despert, "Urinary Control and Enuresis," *Psychosomatic Medicine,*
6 : 294-307 (1944).
[93] Joseph W. Nagge, *Psychology of the Child.* New York, The Ronald Press
Co., 1942, p. 479.

manner implicit in the natural order of things. There is apparently no chaos, no magic, no irregularity in the never-ending sequence of events. It is a profound mystery how life arises and how the intricate operations of nature function as they do, but through it all can be seen the principle of causation, at least in broad outline.

In applying this important principle to mental-hygiene problems Bassett,[94] a psychologist, has written, "The teacher [and, we would add, others] must keep in mind the fact that the difficult personality traits of behavior of the child are not due to any mysterious dispensation, but are the logical outcome of the life experiences of the individual and can be traced with fair clearness back through the years to their causes. The child's difficulties do not suddenly and perversely happen out of a clear sky. They usually have a long, intricate history extending into the past, in which the careful observer may discern the sequences of cause and effect. Thus, the path of understanding will require a greater expenditure of time and effort in patient inquiry than does the method of trial and punishment, but the constructive results flowing from the former method are incalculably greater."

Controlling the Child's Environment.—From what has been said one can appreciate the importance of a suitable and intelligently controlled environment for the rearing of children. In addition to providing affectional security, parents need to provide their children with enough of the material good things of life to obviate the necessity of their indulging excessively in wishful daydreaming. They can also teach children such social skills as will enable them to develop friendships and enjoy the respect of those who mean something to their welfare. It is apparently a fundamental principle that well-nourished, conflict-free, and socialized children do not develop either neurotic symptoms or delinquent tendencies. They are not stimulated to do so; causation does not operate in such fashion.

In instances where undesirable behavior has already come into the picture, parents and others can attempt to ferret out

94 Clara Bassett, *op. cit.*, p. 11.

the motives back of overt acts and endeavor to supply the child with more desirable outlets for his needs. This is the important principle of *substitution* which, in intelligent homes and schools, is superseding the older method of thwarting the child's needs. Since so many wholesome substitute activities are available in the realms of play, recreation, athletics, music, art, work, reading, scout organizations, and the like, such a method offers great possibilities.

The environment can also be controlled so as to enable the child to develop the important habit of succeeding. Successful accomplishment is an effective factor for the development of a confident outlook on life. Merited success usually brings in its wake praise, favorable recognition, friends, rewards, and other forms of satisfaction. Success can be assured if adults see to it that the child, especially the timid boy or girl, is given tasks which, although sufficiently difficult to demand effort, are possible of attainment. Successes can then be pyramided until self-confidence has been attained. Appropriate activities can be selected from any promising sphere—scholarship, sports, mechanics, music, art, or social leadership. To profit by the mental health-giving effects of successful effort, every child should become skillful in some activity, be it only playing a harmonica or monitoring a small hallway. The morale-building effect of any merited success is apparently practically the same.

The properly controlled environment will also provide avenues to invigorating play and recreation, the child's outlet for social tendencies and activity needs. Joyous play provides relaxation and a morale that are ideally calculated to aid in the development of a well-adjusted personality. The medievals, being in the grip of the morbid doctrine of moral depravity, believed that play was of the devil; but today no one but an eccentric would hold such a view. Play not only offers physical and social activity, but provides the child with an opportunity to enjoy legitimate freedom of action.

Most important of all, the environment, in the form of an adequate home, provides the child with the fulfillment of his most fundamental psychological need—*affectional security.* Here he may be accorded the feeling of belonging, of being wanted, of being an individual in his own right. Only under such circumstances can the child develop confidence, optimism, cooperation, and other qualities leading to social adjustment. The home is the citadel of personality building; thus parents should possess an understanding of child nature, of the dynamisms of behavior, and of the consequences of inadequate fulfillment of basic needs.

It was considerations such as these that led to the formulation of the justly famous Children's Charter [95] of the White House Conference. This document, which is essentially a mental-hygiene program, might well be reproduced in this connection, but we must content ourselves with the presentation of but a few of its proposals. The following are typical of the complete Charter:

1. For every child spiritual and moral training to help him to stand firm under pressure of life.
2. For every child understanding and guarding of his personality as his most precious right.
3. For every child a home and that love and security which a home provides; and for that child who must receive foster care, the nearest substitute for his own home.
7. For every child a dwelling place safe, sanitary, and wholesome, with reasonable provisions for privacy; free from conditions which tend to thwart his development; and a home environment harmonious and enriching.
9. For every child a community which recognizes and plans for his needs, protects him from physical dangers, moral hazards, and disease; provides him with safe and wholesome places for play and recreation; and makes provision for his cultural and social needs.

Such is the controlled environment—it is one designed to ensure sound mental health and social development through the avenues of balanced fulfillment of fundamental needs, sympathetic though firm control, and the utilization of psychologically sound guidance procedures.

[95] White House Conference on Child Health and Protection, *Dependent and Neglected Children*, New York, D. Appleton-Century Co., Inc., 1933.

The School Program and Mental Health.—The very foundation of the nursery school-kindergarten program is its concern for mental and physical health. Here well-supervised but spontaneous play and constructive social activities initiate the young child into happy group experiences. The pliable child is stimulated to develop desirable social traits, gradually to overcome infantile egocentrism, and to experience emotionally stable living.

Such a program is often continued in the elementary school, but here certain additional and more specific features of school organization may be said to enter the mental hygiene picture. These may be classified as (1) *general* organization for the promoting of mental health, and (2) *specific* organization for dealing with mental hygiene problems.

GENERAL ORGANIZATION FOR MENTAL HEALTH. The principal features of the modern school program which may be said to lend themselves to the promotion of pupil mental health include:

1. *A psychologically sound philosophy.* Such a philosophy should reflect a spirit of democracy, an atmosphere of legitimate freedom, initiative, and shared activity, and an educational program in which pupils and teachers live happily together while engaged in academically, culturally, and socially useful endeavors. The teacher in such a school will center her attention on the child and his development to the end that the basic demands of his nature are met in an atmosphere of cooperation and security.

2. *Attention to physical health and growth.* The adequate school will give periodical health examinations, encourage teachers to watch for symptoms of health disability, where possible provide the services of medical and dental specialists, protect the child against communicable diseases, and promote health instruction and practices.

3. *A comprehensive program of activities.* From the mental hygiene point of view, pupil activities should include types of play and recreation, as well as scholastic endeavors, that lend themselves to joyous social participation and the development of social skills. Such activities should lead naturally to habits of self-control, self-

direction, responsibility, resourcefulness, and respect for the rights and property of others.

4. *Effective methods of study and work.* The mental health of the child is enhanced by training in effective methods of work. Both the sense of self-confidence which such achievement engenders and the recognition from others which it affords are conducive to feelings of personal well-being. Every child should experience the satisfaction and sense of competence that the mastery of work and study responsibilities provides.

5. *The adjustment of tasks to maturity levels.* Nothing but grief can come from the setting of arbitrary scholastic standards for all children in a grade or group to master. Under such conditions the more capable pupils will exert half-hearted efforts while the intellectually handicapped experience the sting of failure. Either outcome militates against the mental health of the children concerned.

SPECIAL ORGANIZATION FOR MENTAL HEALTH.[96] What might be called a special organization for dealing with the mental hygiene problems of the school may well include: (1) the tying in of school practices with the mental hygiene program, and (2) provisions for the services of trained psychological, psychiatric, social, and medical personnel.

1. Examples of the first category may be listed as (a) the utilization for mental hygiene ends of pupil record folders, (b) using report cards for mental health purposes, (c) evaluating the teacher's work in terms of her personal and social equipment for the promotion of pupil mental health, (d) offering in-service mental hygiene instruction to all teachers, (e) selecting new teachers on the basis of education and fitness for mental hygiene work with children, and (f) educating teachers in guidance and counseling techniques.

2. As far as their budgets and comprehensiveness of educational planning will permit, schools interested in the mental hygiene point of view will include on their staff (a) one or more teachers competent to consult with other teachers regarding pupil maladjust-

---

[96] Cf. Charles R. Foster, *Mental Hygiene in New Jersey Schools,* School of Education, Rutgers Univ., 1939, Ch. 2.

ments, (b) a child guidance committee composed of members of the school staff and, when expedient, qualified persons in the community, (c) a nurse, who might also serve as attendance officer, (d) a visiting teacher competent to secure appropriate information about problem pupils from homes and communities, (e) a psychologist (full-time or provided by city or county school office) qualified to carry on diagnostic testing services and clinical procedures with maladjusted pupils, and, when possible, (f) the services of a medical doctor, a dentist, and a psychiatrist. The latter specialist would be called upon to assist in the care and disposition of difficult cases involving organic disorders and pre-psychotic symptoms.

Where available child guidance clinics should be utilized in the adjustment of cases involving behavior problems, speech disorders, spastic conditions, hysterical symptoms, and other maladjustments. Clinics can also assist in publishing the results of research, in the education of parents and teachers, and in the coordination of medical, psychological, and psychiatric services.[97]

A Mental Hygiene Program for Children.—Mental hygiene principles for children must rest, at least for the present, on the findings of empirical experience and clinical practice. However, a wealth of practical material of tested value is available from these sources and from the literature on child development. The list of principles presented here may be thought of as a resumé of the suggestions advanced in the previous sections of this chapter.

1. *Care of the child's physical health.* The desirability of good physical health has already been mentioned, but no mental hygiene program would be adequate without its inclusion. Poor physical condition tends to reduce the joy of living, to produce worry and irritability, and to make social adjustments more difficult. Children with sound bodies, who have been taught desirable health habits, possess a favorable basis for the maintenance of mental health.

2. *Adequate play and recreational activities.* The fact that children enjoy play indicates that it contributes to a sense of well-being and emotional adjustment. The further fact that properly super-

[97] G. S. Stevenson, *Child Guidance Clinics,* New York, The Commonwealth Fund, 1934.

vised play and recreation may lead to the development of social cooperation and recognition of the rules of fair play and mutuality is suggestive of its great value in the promotion of personality and social growth.

3. *Development of social interdependence.* Although the child is originally dependent upon his parents for a sense of acceptance, he must later win such recognition through his own efforts. It is thus imperative that he learn to respect the views and rights of his playmates and others. He will eventually need to curtail his immediate wishes in favor of those expressed by his associates, and to be sufficiently skillful socially to respect the interests of those whose acceptance he seeks.

4. *A balanced program of work and responsibility.* If the child is to gain favorable recognition as he develops, he must be taught to accept responsibilities and to carry them out. When organized around meaningful tasks, work provides a certain zest and sense of self-esteem even to a child. Simple duties in connection with the care of clothing, toys, and the home provide children with the opportunity of becoming self-reliant and dependable.

5. *Opportunity to develop basic skills.* The child who possesses the essential scholastic and motor skills is in a favorable position adequately to meet the demands of the home, the school, and the playground. Since everyone admires skill, such equipment obviously leads to favorable notice and enhanced opportunities for making new friendships. Useful knowledge may also aid in the development of self-confidence by virtue of the greater effectiveness in social relations which it makes possible.

6. *Presentation of a wholesome attitude toward sex.* Sex is honorable and children should be taught to respect it. Upon parents rests the responsibility of giving their children instruction suited to their age and development. Sex information should be given when the child's curiosity is evident and in proportion to his capacity for comprehending it. Children should be told the truth, not falsehoods, about sex.

7. *A consistent and reasonable program of discipline.* Punishment should be administered for the benefit of the offending child, not as an emotional release for the individual doing the punishing. The test of its adequacy should be whether the punishment results

in improved personal and social adjustment on the part of the recipient. Too much discipline (control) may be more harmful than too little. Intelligent discipline has come to mean psychologically sound efforts to guide a child's conduct in harmony with social standards and his emotional nature.

8. *The presence of adults in whom the child can confide.* Ideally, every child should be able to count his parents as confidants. They should be in a position to listen sympathetically to his problems and his misgivings. However, since such a situation by no means always obtains, it is essential that the child find some other trustworthy and acceptable adult with whom he can talk over his difficulties. Children are so constituted that vocal expression of their emotional tensions does them good. Such releases are essential to the maintenance of mental health.

Summary and Implications

The pre-scientific views that misbehavior and abnormal conduct are motivated by an evil nature and the intervention of animate spirits, respectively, have given way to a realization that socially maladjustive actions are frequently the result of frustration of fundamental organic and psychological needs. It is also believed that so-called deviate behavior performs the function for the individual concerned of arresting some threat to his ego-integrity. Frustrated individuals would apparently rather develop face-saving ailments than acknowledge inadequacy or incompetency.

In harmony with these findings, it has been noted that children will resort to phantasy, rationalization, and compensation dynamisms in their efforts to avert admissions of inferiority, weakness, or incompetence. The defiance dynamism is the outlet utilized by those who have become antagonized by rejection, neglect, or other threat to their integrity and sense of personal worth. Functional dissociation—the development of ailments —is utilized as an avenue of retreat from the defeats of reality by those faced with conflicts for which there are apparently no other solutions. The mutuality approach to social adjustment is obviously to be preferred to all others, but requires a basically friendly attitude toward people. Such a disposition is most readily acquired by children fortunate enough to have experienced a psychologically sound early home life.

Problem children are the products of problem parents, maladjusted teachers, and other inadequate adults. Physical disabilities add their contribution to the toll of maladjustment. But frustrations, disappointments, and defeats are to a great extent responsible for the emotional and nervous symptoms so prevalent among children and youths. Thumb-sucking, nail-biting, enuresis, tics, and similar symptoms are apparently expressions, symbolic or otherwise, of unsatisfied desires, thwarted needs, and other dynamic forces.

An adequate mental hygiene program for children will include intelligent control of home, school, and community conditions. It will be concerned with the child's physical health, his personal integrity, his social adjustment, and the development of such skills and abilities as life will demand of him. The problem of mental hygiene is that of guaranteeing an integration of self-adjustment and social development. To accomplish such a desirable outcome it is necessary to realize that the child is a feeling and thinking organism, that childhood is the period of growth and development, and that the character of the adjustments made by the child will be determined largely by the social forces playing upon him.

Questions for Discussion

1. Elaborate upon the relationship that obtains between "fundamental needs" of the child and the phenomenon of "adjustment dynamisms." Does this prove that the child is a mechanical organism or does it argue for the presence of a need for adjustment? Defend your view.

2. Show how a childhood "inferiority complex" may become either an asset or a liability in the development of personality. How can the natural tendency to compensate for a feeling of inadequacy be capitalized on in this process? Give an example.

3. In the face of the fact that a moderate use of psychological escape and defense dynamisms is considered normal and

natural, why do some psychologists warn us concerning them? Is it true that the behavior patterns of an outright neurotic child differ from those of a normal child only in degree? Discuss this question.

4. Refute the criticism that the idea of personality disorders being caused by excessive thwarting of basic needs is too mechanistic to apply to children. How does the phenomenon of "conflicts with self" tie up with the principle of "fundamental life needs"? How may such conflicts be avoided?

5. Trace one or more general psychological cause and effect relationships as they develop in inner personal conflicts. To what extent can such conflicts be alleviated by environmental conditions? Defend the idea that parents can prevent the appearance of emotional conflicts in their children.

6. Do you believe that understanding parents who are willing to provide wholesome home conditions can prevent excessive "escape" behavior on the part of their children? If so, explain in detail how this would be done. Remember that personal conflicts can easily arise in children of well-to-do parents.

7. With life presenting as many conflicts as it does, how can one justify the contention that the avenue to personality adjustment lies in facing and attacking reality? What desirable personality qualities do children develop when they "face the music"? What are the implications for adjustment of the "retreating dynamism?"

8. In fairness to psychoanalysis, how would you meet the objection that both its theory and practice are too unscientific to be useful with children? Show how psychoanalytic workers have contributed to an understanding of the personality development of children.

9. Is there any evidence supporting the accusation that some teachers not only neglect children who are suffering from personality disorders but that they actually contribute to their further emotional disturbance? Under what conditions would such a situation be likely to develop? How can it be prevented?

10. In what respects are mental hygiene principles similar to those which have proved successful in physical hygiene? Can such principles be used successfully in readjusting maladjusted children or are they restricted to preventive work only? Give examples.

Recommended Readings

Allen, Frederick H. *Psychotherapy With Children.* New York: W. W. Norton & Co., Inc., 1942.

Bakwin, Ruth M., and Bakwin, Harry. *Psychologic Care During Infancy and Childhood.* New York: D. Appleton-Century Co., Inc., 1942.

Crow, Lester D., and Crow, Alice C. *Mental Hygiene in School and Home Life.* New York: McGraw-Hill Book Co., Inc., 1942.

Fenton, Norman. *Mental Hygiene in School Practice.* Stanford University: Stanford Univ. Press, 1943.

Kanner, Leo. *Child Psychiatry.* Springfield (Ill.): Chas. C. Thomas, 1937.

Kanner, Leo. "Behavior Disorders in Childhood," in *Personality and the Behavior Disorders.* (Edited by J. McV. Hunt.) New York: The Ronald Press Co., 1944, Vol. II, Ch. 25.

Klein, D. B. *Mental Hygiene: The Psychology of Personal Adjustment.* New York: Henry Holt & Co., Inc., 1944.

Rivlin, H. N. *Educating for Adjustment.* New York: D. Appleton-Century Co., Inc., 1936.

Rogers, Carl R. *The Clinical Treatment of the Problem Child.* Boston: Houghton Mifflin Co., 1939.

Sherman, Mandel. *Basic Problems of Behavior.* New York: Longmans, Green & Co., 1941.

Tiegs, Ernest W., and Katz, Barney. *Mental Hygiene in Education.* New York: The Ronald Press Co., 1941.

Travis, Lee Edward, and Baruch, Dorothy W. *Personal Problems of Everyday Life.* New York: D. Appleton-Century Co., Inc., 1941.

Witty, Paul A., and Skinner, C. E. (Editors). *Mental Hygiene in Modern Education.* New York: Farrar & Rinehart, Inc., 1939.

AUTHOR INDEX

Abel, T. M., 550
Abernethy, M. E., 341
Abt, I. A., 502
Ackerson, L., 329, 738
Adler, A., 196, 197, 240, 719
Adler, H. M., 502
Aldrich, C. A., 140, 252
Allen, C. N., 481
Allen, F. H., 766
Allen, M. F., 282
Allen, S., 189
Allport, F. H., 471, 472, 686
Allport, G. W., 409, 619, 634, 636, 637, 639, 643, 644, 646, 649, 650, 686, 699
Almack, J. C., 313
Alpert, A., 456
Alschuler, R. H., 693
Amatruda, C. S., 26, 179, 365
Amen, E. W., 388, 692
Ames, L. B., 432
Amster, F., 695
Anderson, J. E., 39, 259, 269, 480, 513
Appel, K. E., 673
Appleton, L. E., 201
Arey, L. B., 69
Arrington, R. E., 569
Arsenian, S., 505
Arthur, G., 335

Bakwin, H. B., 766
Bakwin, R. M., 766
Baldwin, B. T., 98, 282, 326, 535, 537
Ball, E. S., 232
Bard, P., 375
Barker, R. G., 408
Barrett, H. E., 118
Bartelme, P. F., 489, 502
Baruch, D. W., 231, 695, 704, 742, 749, 752, 766
Bassett, C., 211, 213, 233, 732, 747, 756
Baum, M. P., 463
Bayer, L. M., 291
Bayley, N., 286, 287, 323, 324, 349, 365, 387, 427, 431, 461, 467
Baylor, E. M. H., 216
Bean, C. H., 482

Belden, D. S., 599, 600
Bell, H. M., 690
Bender, L., 555, 694
Benedict, R., 584
Benjamin, E., 737
Bergum, M., 227
Berman, L., 671
Berne, E. V. C., 574
Bernreuter, R. G., 674, 690
Bienstock, S. F., 445
Binet, A., 317
Blanchard, P., 231, 259
Blanton, M. G., 140
Blatz, W. E., 85, 91
Blumer, H., 618
Bogardus, E. S., 638
Boll, E. S., 232
Bond, E. D., 673
Bonham, M., 653
Bonney, M. E., 667
Bonstelle, J., 16
Book, W. F., 98
Bossard, J. H. S., 232
Bott, H., 202
Bowers, A. M., 711
Boyd, W., 524
Boynton, B., 289
Boynton, P. L., 39, 252, 279, 280, 281, 286, 287, 288, 301, 313, 339, 365, 368, 444, 513, 669
Brace, D. K., 463
Brandenburg, G. C., 524
Breasted, J. H., 662
Breckenridge, M. E., 313
Breeze, K. W., 427
Brian, C. R., 457
Bridges, C. B., 46, 51
Bridges, K. M. B., 35, 39, 383, 386, 569, 570, 571, 575
Briggs, T. H., 368
Brill, A. A., 618
Brill, A. C., 259
Bronner, A. F., 216, 617, 711, 728
Brooks, F. D., 131, 365, 508
Brown, F. J., 5, 39, 590, 604, 627
Brown, M., 667
Bryan, E. S., 140

767

SUBJECT INDEX

Abnormal behavior, as an effort at adjustment, 710-711
Acquired characteristics, and heredity, 72-73
Adaptability, development of, 163-165
Adjustment program, foundation of, 755-756
Adrenalin, role of, 377
Adult adjustment, meaning of infancy for, 33
Aggression, in children, 580-585
Aims of child study, 6-7
Art analysis tests, 693-694
Aspect of Personality Inventory, 686-687
Astrology, as method of evaluation, 677
Auditory acuity, of the infant, 139-141

Babinski (plantar) reflex, nature of, 150-151
Barren environment studies, contrasting interpretations of, 103-104
evidence from, 99-101
influence noted, 101-103
Behavior causation, pre-scientific views of, 701
Behavior disorders, modern view of, 702-704
Behavior problems, investigations of, 737-739
Beliefs, immature nature of children's, 538-542
Biophysical view of personality, 636-637
Biosocial view of personality, 637-640
implications of for personality, 640-642
Birth, degree of maturity at, 136
Blending, phenomenon of, 58-59
Body structures, data on growth of, 279-286
growth rates of, 286-292
Body types, and personality, 677-678
Brain experimentation, evidence from, 82-83

California Test of Personality, 688
Case Inventory, 687-688
Cell relationships, in-utero, 64-65
Character, as distinguished from personality, 631-633
Character development vs. personality development, 658-661
Chicago investigation (foster-home placement), evidence from, 105-107
Childhood, the new significance of, 6
Children, as miniature adults, 9-10
reasons for present interest in, 4-6
traditional ways of dealing with, 3-4
Chromosomes, as bearers of heredity, 45-46
Compensation, dynamism of, 718-720
Compensatory identification, dynamism of, 720
Competition, in children, 587-588
Competitiveness, development of, 580-583
etiology of, 583-585
Conceptual ideas, and children's drawings, 522-524
and children's questions, 524-526
children's early, 520-522
Conditioned response, applications of to children, 405-407
definition of, 395
early experiments on with children, 396-399
Pavlov's study of in dogs, 395-396
recent American experiments on, 400-402
Russian investigations of with children, 398-399
Watson's investigations of, 402-404
Conduct, control through religion, 661-664
Conflicts, among older children, 586-587
Congenital inheritance, factors in, 71-72
Conquering hero, dynamism of, 714

Alma Plew